MISSISSIPPI

The WPA Guide to the Magnolia State

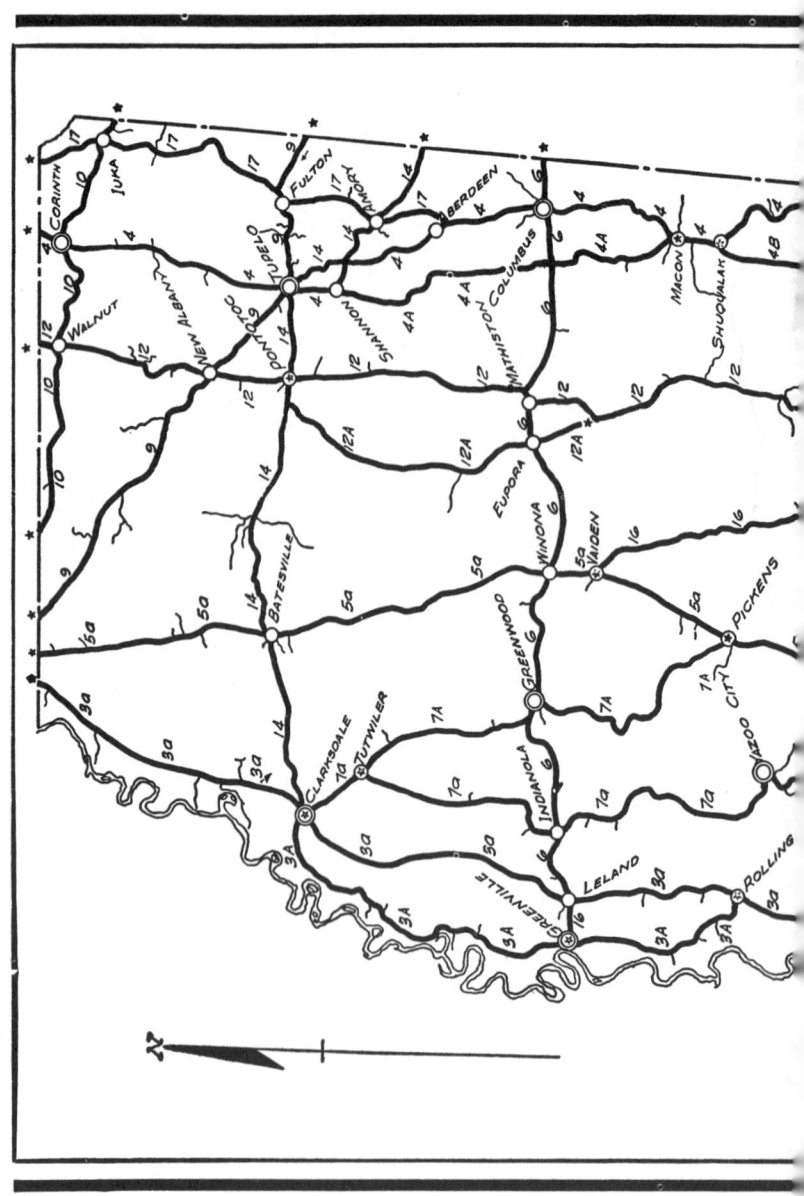

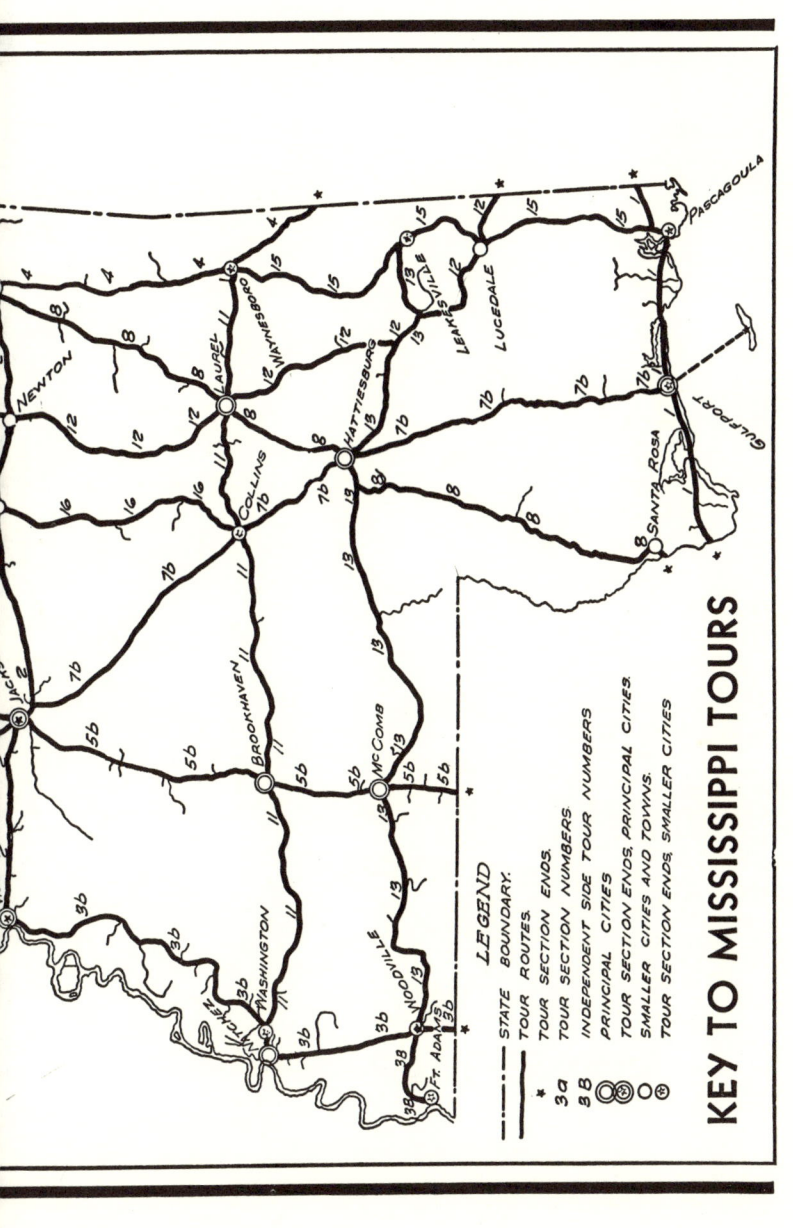

MISSISSIPPI

The WPA Guide to the Magnolia State

Compiled and written by the Federal Writers' Project
of the Works Progress Administration

With an introduction by Robert S. McElvaine

University Press of Mississippi
Jackson

www.upress.state.ms.us

The University Press of Mississippi is a member
of the Association of American University Presses.

Introduction copyright © 1988 by University Press of Mississippi
All rights reserved
Manufactured in the United States of America

Published in 1938 by Viking Press
Published in 1988 and 2009 by University Press of Mississippi

∞
Library of Congress Cataloging-in-Publication Data

Federal Writers' Project of the Works Progress Administration (Miss.)
  Mississippi : the WPA guide to the Magnolia state / compiled and written by the Federal Writers' Project of the Works Progress Administration ; with an introduction by Robert S. McElvaine.
    p. cm.
  Originally published: New York : Viking Press, 1938.
  Includes bibliographical references and index.
  ISBN 978-1-60473-292-4 (pbk. : alk. paper) 1. Mississippi.
2. Mississippi—Guidebooks. I. Title.
F341.F45 2009
976.2—dc22   2009013405

British Library Cataloging-in-Publication Data available

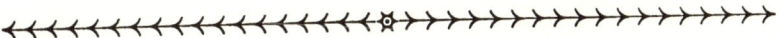

Introduction
by Robert S. McElvaine

THIS REMARKABLE VOLUME is part of a series of state guides created by the Federal Writers Project of the Works Progress Administration during the Great Depression of the 1930s. The FWP was a subdivision of one of the New Deal's most innovative programs. When the WPA was launched in 1935, it was intended to serve several purposes. One objective was simply to provide small payments to the unemployed in order to help their families survive. Another was to produce "useful" public projects that were not likely to be undertaken by private enterprise. A third goal was to try to preserve the skills and self-respect of Depression victims by replacing the demoralizing and stigmatizing practice of making direct relief payments with that of paying people for meaningful work. Harry Hopkins, the WPA administrator, believed in trying to give people work suited for their training and talents. He saw no point in putting a fine artist to work digging ditches.

Hopkins and his supporters also had other reasons for pushing special programs for unemployed artists and professionals. They saw in these programs an opportunity to develop a genuine American culture, distinct from the imitations of European culture that had long characterized "high culture" in the United States. The *Zeitgeist* of the Depression era was democratic, egalitarian, and proudly American. Out of these ingredients Hopkins and his assistants fashioned a group of work relief projects for the arts.

The WPA arts projects were included in what was known collectively as Federal One: The Federal Writers' Project, the Federal Theatre Project, the Federal Art Project, and the Federal Music Project. They represented a daring venture into public patronage of the arts. This was a decided departure from the usual American practice, which had been to allow virtually no role for any level of government in supporting artistic undertakings. Two very different dangers threatened the effort from the outset: the lack of support from a public that had difficulty seeing writing or painting as "work" that ought to be financed by relief appropriations and the possibility that federal funding might undermine the independence and creativity of the artists. Although the lack of strong public support eventually did the WPA arts projects in, the threat of bureaucratic interference never seriously materialized.

The Federal Writers Project included individuals of widely varied degrees of ability. Many teachers, librarians, and professionals who were neither manual laborers nor writers were judged by WPA officials to be sufficiently close in occupation to writing to be

INTRODUCTION

assigned to the FWP. But if many "writers" who worked on the FWP served more to advance the ideal of democratic participation than to improve the Project's final products, other writers of enormous talent, such as Richard Wright, John Cheever, Ralph Ellison, Saul Bellow, and Margaret Walker, also found employment with the Project.

The FWP produced many projects of lasting value. Perhaps the most significant was the collection of narratives from some 2,000 former slaves. The FWP's interest in "American stuff" and its commitment to the egalitarianism of the age led it also to collect and write down oral life histories from many "ordinary" people from varying backgrounds. The organization made particular efforts to collect folklore from all parts of America.

The mid-thirties celebration of all things American was the source of the idea for the FWP's largest project: the writing of "guides" for each of the states, as well as the leading American territories and many cities. The present volume is a reissue of one of those state guides, originally published in 1938.

We tend to think today of state guide books in terms of those put out by automobile clubs or travel agencies. Such catalogs—for that is what most of them amount to—are usually updated annually. How, then, can it make sense to reissue, without alteration, a state guide book published exactly a half century ago?

The reader will not need to venture very far into the pages that follow to find an answer. Part of it lies in the fact that this book contains as much history as it does information for tourists. But history texts are also updated regularly and any school district still using history books that are ten—let alone fifty—years old is rightly considered to be placing its students at a serious disadvantage by depriving them of proper educational materials.

Such apparent drawbacks have not deterred the successful republication of several other WPA state guides in recent years. The basic reason that these volumes stand up so well fifty years after their creation is that their authors sought to delve into the essence of the areas about which they were writing. *Mississippi: The WPA Guide to the Magnolia State* captures important parts of the state's heritage in a way that has never been duplicated. It tells us about numerous interesting spots in Mississippi that can still be found and observed with pleasure. More important, though, is the guide's analysis of the history and folkways of Mississippians, black and white, *circa* 1937. Much of the book amounts to an exercise in what might be termed introspective anthropology. Certain practices have not changed much in a half century, but in many respects Mississippi in the age of Roosevelt was a strikingly different place from what it is today.

To read this book is to go back in time. For some older readers, it will be an experience that brings back many memories, most of them fond. Younger readers in Mississippi can discover here a large portion of their heritage. Many of the folkways and practices described here have come close to receding into history. Very little cotton is picked by hand anymore. Home canning is not yet a lost art, but it is not the major part of rural life that it still was in the thirties. Other practices will strike some modern Mississippians as quaint, but the present-day reader will find the folkways of an almost entirely rural state a half century ago unfailingly interesting.

The volume's multiple authors—who remain anonymous—were Mississippians who were part of their time and place, but who made serious efforts to transcend their situation. They write with an understanding of and a fondness for their subject matter, but they seem to find some of the practices of their fellow residents amusing. The writers sometimes display a paternal attitude towards the citizenry of their home state.

In this fascinating book we enter a time when all the main routes were blue highways—and there weren't very many of them. The state was engaged in a major program of highway building, but there were no undifferentiated Interstate highways on which travellers could bypass the locales that gave the state its character. Today the tourist often has difficulty knowing what state he is in. Such plainly was not the case when this *Guide* was written. The unique flavor of Mississippi in a bygone age is evident throughout the book. We see a time before the dominance of the electronic media, when political speeches and religious meetings were major social events and the chief forms of entertainment. Such happenings still serve these purposes for some Mississippians today, of course, but to a vastly lesser degree than they did in the thirties.

Mississippi in the Depression years was an extremely poor state. It still is, in many ways, of course, but one is struck by how much poorer most people were then. Yet few of them seemed to realize it. Poverty was so widespread that most people seemed to accept it as an inevitable part of life. But we should remember that poverty as we view what might otherwise seem a rather idyllic life. The farther removed yesterday becomes, the more of a glow it tends to take on.

We find here a time when white Mississippians had absolute faith in the Democratic party. The Party of the Fathers was, for all practical purposes, the only party in the state. The reason, of course unstated in the pages that follow, was that the one-party system served the goal of maintaining white supremacy.

The treatment of race is among the most interesting aspects of the book. In this, as in so much else, the *Guide* is a product of its time and place. As one would anticipate, the authors reflect the viewpoints of a half century ago. They do not seem to be particularly unfriendly in their attitudes toward nonwhites. Rather, they simply assume white superiority as a given and proceed from there. Native Americans plainly do not count. Mississippi's history is said to have begun in 1528, when the Spanish began to explore the region. The people who occupied the area for several millennia before the arrival of Europeans were just not considered to be part of history.

It is revealing that although the customs and beliefs of Indians as described here often look silly, they are similar in many respects to the folkways identified as typifying Mississippians.

On the whole, the book treats blacks in a more kindly manner than one might expect from a study undertaken well before the advent of the civil rights movement. There is no question, though, about from whose perspective the writing is being done. It will be noticed that the section on "White Folkways" is written in the first person plural, while that on "Negro Folkways" is written in the third person plural. The attitude toward blacks is one that assumes that they "know their place," that that place is far below the one enjoyed by whites, and that blacks are content in their place. Blacks are stereotyped as "a genial mass." "The Mississippi folk Negro," we read, "seems carefree and shrewd and does not bother himself with the problems the white man has to solve." He is said to leave "the so-called Negro Question . . . for the white man to cope with."

All of this is viewed with apparent satisfaction. The racial system is portrayed as working well; whites are portrayed as generous and blacks are said to share in all good things and have their needs met. One does not get the impression that the writers were consciously painting a deceptive portrait. Their racial assumptions were such that they seem to have believed that the system was best and that blacks were pleased with it.

There is, on the other hand, a frank realization that blacks had a culture that they kept their own, one that whites did not understand—and were not intended to understand. It is clear that this culture contains African survivals in its religious practices and folk beliefs. When temporarily freed of the need for working for "the man," blacks entered an independent culture from which whites were excluded: "The Negro . . . simply cannot see a white person on Saturday unless that person owes him something."

Perhaps the greatest irony in the Mississippi Guide is its contention that "instead of expressing himself creatively, the Negro has been placed in the position of being an almost inexhaustible reservoir of material for the creative efforts of others." We are told that the black's "emotions and inherent sense of rhythm found expression in song, the only external expression, other than the handicrafts, that could surmount his paucity of tools." This was written at a time when a black man from Mississippi, Richard Wright, was working on his masterpiece *Native Son*—while employed by the very same Federal Writers' Project that was contending that blacks' creative achievements were confined to song and handicrafts.

One of the attractions of the Mississippi Guide for readers today is that it was written at a time of hope for the state—a time when change, at least of a certain sort and degree, had become acceptable. This provides a connection between that time and this, reaching over the intervening half century. The changes that were attempted in Mississippi in the thirties were stimulated in part by New Deal programs emanating from Washington.

Even more, though, they were the result of a realization on the part of people within the state that the old economic system was no longer viable.

In economic terms, Mississippi remained in the 1930s a colonial region. Its economy centered on extractive, resource-destroying activities: principally cotton and timber. Prior to the thirties there was little attempt at either soil conservation or reforestation. Efforts in these directions were undertaken in the Depression years, as was a more ambitious program of economic diversification inaugurated in 1936. Governor Hugh Lawson White's plan to "Balance Agriculture With Industry" (BAWI) included special tax breaks and factory construction supported by public funds to lure industrial enterprises into the state.

The degree to which the attempt to change Mississippi's economy a half century ago succeeded—and the degree to which it failed—can serve as useful lessons to Mississippians as they again seek to modernize the state in the late eighties and nineties. The BAWI program succeeded in bringing some industries into the state. Some diversification resulted. The basic problem, though, was that the attempt to alter the economy in the thirties was made without a corresponding attempt to reform the social system. The only sort of change that was acceptable fifty years ago was that which posed no threat to white supremacy. Most meaningful changes were opposed for fear that they might lead to *the* change: a rearrangement in race relations. This meant, among other things, that there was no attempt to upgrade or equalize education. As an old saying pointed out, in order to hold the black man down in the ditch, it was necessary for the white man to stay there with him. Under these circumstances, the only inducement Mississippi could offer industries was a cheap, docile, poorly educated, nonunion labor force. Naturally the sort of industries that were attracted by this resource were not the more advanced or the better-paying companies.

It never made any sense for a state mired at the bottom of the national economy to oppose change, but that is just what most white Mississippians did from the antebellum period until quite recently. We are now in a time, however, in which drastic changes in race relations have been underway for a quarter century. More fundamental economic and social changes are now possible because they have ceased to be the threat to "things as they are" that they used to be.

This introduction can deal with only a small portion of what is contained in the Mississippi Guide. Anyone interested in any aspect of the Magnolia State will find many small but fascinating items on the pages that follow. Many Mississippians have long treasured their copies of the original edition of the *Guide*. Now a new generation can learn why. The republication of this volume is long overdue.

Robert S. McElvaine
Millsaps College

Foreword

HERE is a book which takes us vividly into the South in the first period of its greatness and brings us by natural steps up to the contemporary scene where a new South is in the making. To the visitor Mississippi offers modern methods of agriculture in the northern Delta region, a playground on the Gulf Coast, and some of the finest examples of old plantation architecture in Natchez and its other historic towns. This Guide, with its charm, its occasional irony, and its comprehensiveness, could have been written only from self-knowledge and from a knowledge of modern America. It is the modest yet proud statement of their accomplishments by the people of this Gulf State.

This volume is one of the American Guide Series, which, when complete, will cover the forty-eight States and several hundred communities, as well as Alaska, Puerto Rico, and Hawaii. With each new volume that leaves the press a new trait is added to the portrait of America today.

Administrator

Preface

MISSISSIPPI: *A Guide to the Magnolia State*, goes beyond the limits of a conventional guidebook, first, in its attempt to picture and explain contemporary Mississippi by presenting its people, culture, physiography, politics, folkways, economics, and industry in relation to the historical past; and, second, in its narrative detailed description of points of interest. The extensive research involved in preparing the present volume brought out the fact that Mississippi's development holds incidents, hitherto untold, as dramatic and colorful as those of many an imaginative story. Though primarily a guidebook, it will serve also as a springboard from which those interested in research may plunge into the almost undisturbed waters of Mississippiana.

Main emphasis has been placed upon the typical and average people of the State, rather than the exceptional elements. Thus, the two essays on folkways deal almost wholly with the Mississippi farmer—the whites of the Central and Tennessee Hills, the Negroes of the Delta. It is this great agricultural majority, comprising more than four-fifths of the State's population, that has had no place in portrayals of Mississippi life by William Faulkner at one extreme and by Stark Young at the other.

Difficulties encountered were many; first-hand information, often by word of mouth, required checking, and source material was not always reliable. Preparation of tours, at a time when the State is engaged in an extensive road-building program, necessitated frequent alterations. Occasional inaccuracies, it is hoped, will be reported and corrected in subsequent editions.

For valuable assistance in preparing the book, grateful acknowledgment is due a number of persons and organizations. Particularly helpful have been the officials of the State governmental departments, city chambers of commerce, the State University and State College, Mississippi State College for Women, and members of the American Institute of Architects. Among the individuals whose aid should receive appreciative mention are Miss Bessie Cary Lemly, Harris Dickson, Dr. William Clifford Morse, Moreau B. Chambers, and Beverly Martin. A special word of thanks is due Thomas Garner James, who gave valuable information and advice in connection with the section whose title is *The State in the Making*.

ERI DOUGLASS, *State Director*
GENE HOLCOMB, *State Editor*

WORKS PROGRESS ADMINISTRATION

Harry L. Hopkins, *Administrator*
Ellen S. Woodward, *Assistant Administrator*
Henry G. Alsberg, *Director of Federal Writers' Project*

Contents

INTRODUCTION, By Robert S. McElvaine	vii
FOREWORD, By Harry L. Hopkins, Administrator	xiii
PREFACE, By the State Director and State Editor	xv
LIST OF ILLUSTRATIONS	xxi
LIST OF MAPS	xxv
NOTATIONS ON THE USE OF THE BOOK	xxvii
GENERAL INFORMATION	xxix
CALENDAR OF EVENTS	xxxiii

I. Mississippi: The General Background

MISSISSIPPI PAST AND PRESENT

What Is Mississippi?	3
White Folkways	8
Negro Folkways	22

BEFORE THE WHITE MAN CAME

Natural Setting	31
Archeology and Indians	45

THE STATE IN THE MAKING

An Outline of Four Centuries	60
Transportation	79
Agriculture	92
Industry and Commerce	106
Religion	112
Education	118
The Press	128

THE CREATIVE EFFORT

Arts and Letters	134
Architecture	142
Music	157

II. Main Street and Courthouse Square

(CITY AND TOWN DESCRIPTIONS AND CITY TOURS)

Biloxi	165
Columbus	179
Greenwood	189
Gulfport	194
Holly Springs	200
Jackson	208
Laurel	222
Meridian	227
Natchez	233
Oxford	254
Tupelo	261
Vicksburg	266

III. Tours

TOUR 1	(Mobile, Ala.)–Biloxi–Gulfport–(New Orleans, La.). [U.S. 90]	285
1A	Gulfport to Ship Island	303
2	(Livingston, Ala.)–Meridian–Jackson–Vicksburg–(Monroe, La.). [U.S. 80]	304
3	(Memphis, Tenn.)–Clarksdale–Vicksburg–Natchez–(Baton Rouge, La.). [U.S. 61]	
	Section a. Tennessee Line to Vicksburg	315
	Section b. Vicksburg to Louisiana Line	324
3A	Clarksdale–Greenville–Rolling Fork. [STATE 1]	346
3B	Woodville–Fort Adams, Fort Adams Road	358
4	(Jackson, Tenn.)–Corinth–Tupelo–Columbus–Meridian–Waynesboro–(Mobile, Ala.). [U.S. 45]	361
4A	Shannon–West Point–Macon. [STATE 23, STATE 25]	373
4B	Shuqualak–Meridian. [STATE 39]	377

CONTENTS

5 (Memphis, Tenn.)–Grenada–Jackson–Brookhaven–
McComb–(New Orleans, La.). [U.S. 51]
   Section a. Tennessee Line to Jackson   380
   Section b. Jackson to Louisiana Line   391
6 (Tuscaloosa, Ala.)–Columbus–Winona–Greenwood–
Greenville–(Lake Village, Ark.). [U.S. 82]   397
7 Clarksdale–Indianola–Yazoo City–Jackson–
Hattiesburg–Gulfport. [U.S. 49, U.S. 49W]
   Section a. Clarksdale to Jackson   406
   Section b. Jackson to Gulfport   414
7A Tutwiler–Greenwood–Lexington–
Pickens. [U.S. 49E, STATE 12]   420
8 (Livingston, Ala.)–Meridian–Laurel–Hattiesburg–
Picayune–Santa Rosa–(New Orleans, La.). [U.S. 11]   423
9 (Hamilton, Ala.)–Tupelo–New Albany–
Holly Springs–(Memphis, Tenn.). [U.S. 78]   434
10 (Florence, Ala.)–Iuka–Corinth–Walnut–
Slayden–(Memphis, Tenn.). [U.S. 72]   441
11 Waynesboro–Laurel–Brookhaven–
Washington–(Ferraday, La.). [U.S. 84]   447
12 (Bolivar, Tenn.)–Pontotoc–Bay Springs–Laurel–
Lucedale–(Mobile, Ala.). [STATE 15]   456
12A Springville–Calhoun City–Ackerman. [STATE 9]   471
13 Junction with STATE 63–Hattiesburg–Columbia–
McComb–Woodville. [STATE 24]   475
14 (Winfield, Ala.)–Amory–Tupelo–Oxford–
Clarksdale. [STATE 6]   484
15 Waynesboro–Leakesville–Lucedale–
Moss Point. [STATE 63]   490
16 Vaiden–Kosciusko–Carthage–Raleigh–
Junction with U.S. 84. [STATE 35]   493
17 (Pickwick, Tenn.)–Iuka–Fulton–Amory–
Junction with U.S. 45. [STATE 25]   500

CHRONOLOGY   509
BIBLIOGRAPHY   523
INDEX   531

Illustrations

MISSISSIPPI RIVER FROM NATCHEZ BLUFFS *Photograph by Earl M. Norman*	PAGE 4–5
GATHERING FOR A POLITICAL RALLY *Photograph by Eudora Welty*	9
A COUNTRY CHURCH *Photograph by W. Lincoln Highton*	12
SHANTYBOAT LIFE *Photograph by Eudora Welty*	16
MAMMY GLASPER *Photograph by Willa Johnson*	23
HOLT COLLIER *Photograph by Willa Johnson*	25
MAGNOLIA GRANDIFLORA: THE STATE FLOWER *Photograph by E. E. Johnson*	32
YUCCA PLANT, OR "SPANISH BAYONET" *Photograph by W. Lincoln Highton*	41
PORTER'S FLEET PASSING THE CONFEDERATE BATTERIES AT VICKSBURG *Photograph from Brady Print Collection, Library of Congress*	72
TOWBOAT ON THE MISSISSIPPI *Photograph by Colquitt Clark*	80
IN THE 1830'S *Photograph from Illinois Central Railroad*	86
IN THE 1930'S *Photograph from Gulf, Mobile, and Northern Railroad*	87
COTTON BOLL *Photograph by Willa Johnson*	93
EN ROUTE TO COTTON HOUSE *Photograph from Mississippi Agricultural Extension Service*	102
LYCEUM BUILDING, "OLE MISS," UNIVERSITY OF MISSISSIPPI, OXFORD *Photograph by J. R. Cofield*	126
A "DOG-TROT" CABIN *Photograph by Gene Holcomb*	143
McGAHEY HOUSE, A BLACK PRAIRIE HOME, COLUMBUS *Photograph by E. E. Johnson*	145
DUNLEITH, NATCHEZ *Photograph by Mary Ethel Dismukes*	147
THE BRIARS, NATCHEZ *Photograph by Earl M. Norman*	148

ILLUSTRATIONS

MELROSE, NEAR NATCHEZ	150
Photograph by R. I. Bostwick	
STAIRWAY AT COTTAGE GARDEN, NATCHEZ	154
Photograph by Earl M. Norman	
OYSTER FLEET, BILOXI	167
Photograph by Anthony V. Ragusin	
BENACHI AVENUE, BILOXI	171
Photograph by W. A. Russell	
LIGHTHOUSE, BILOXI	174
Photograph by Gene Holcomb	
A SOUTHERN PLANTER HOME, BILOXI	177
Photograph from Pictorial Archives of Early American Architecture Library of Congress	
CLOCK TOWER, MISSISSIPPI STATE COLLEGE FOR WOMEN, COLUMBUS	183
Photograph by O. N. Pruitt	
WOODWARD HOUSE, COLUMBUS	188
Photograph by O. N. Pruitt	
LOADING BALES OF COTTON, GULFPORT	195
Photograph by Ed Lipscomb	
MUNICIPAL GARDEN AND CIVIC CENTER, JACKSON	210
Photograph by H. R. Hiatt	
NEW CAPITOL, JACKSON	212
Photograph by H. R. Hiatt	
OLD CAPITOL, JACKSON	215
Photograph by H. R. Hiatt	
MANSHIP HOME, JACKSON	219
Photograph by Gene Holcomb	
GOVERNOR'S MANSION, JACKSON	221
Photograph by H. R. Hiatt	
PULPWOOD READY FOR PROCESSING, LAUREL	224
Photograph by W. Lincoln Highton	
ART MUSEUM AND LIBRARY, LAUREL	226
Photograph by W. Lincoln Highton	
TEXTILE MILL, MERIDIAN	229
Photograph by James A. Butters	
CONTI HOUSE, NATCHEZ	242
Photograph by Mary Ethel Dismukes	
CONNELLY'S TAVERN, NATCHEZ	245
Photograph by Earl M. Norman	
ARLINGTON, NATCHEZ	251
Photograph by Earl M. Norman	

ILLUSTRATIONS

HOME OF WILLIAM FAULKNER, OXFORD *Photograph by Willa Johnson*	257
MISSISSIPPI MONUMENT, VICKSBURG NATIONAL MILITARY PARK *Photograph from National Park Service*	270
WARREN COUNTY COURTHOUSE, VICKSBURG *Photograph by James A. Butters*	274
MCNUTT HOME, VICKSBURG *Photograph by James A. Butters*	278
BOAT BUILDING, PASCAGOULA *Photograph by Anthony V. Ragusin*	288
OLD SPANISH FORT, PASCAGOULA *Photograph from Mississippi Advertising Commission*	289
BEAUVOIR, HOME OF JEFFERSON DAVIS, NEAR BILOXI *Photograph by W. Lincoln Highton*	293
PIRATE'S HOUSE, WAVELAND *Photograph from Pictorial Archives of Early American Architecture Library of Congress*	301
HIGHWAY THROUGH LOESS BLUFFS TO VICKSBURG *Photograph by W. A. Russell*	314
RUINS OF WINDSOR, NEAR PORT GIBSON *Photograph by Earl M. Norman*	329
THE BURR OAKS, JEFFERSON COLLEGE CAMPUS, WASHINGTON *Photograph by Earl M. Norman*	334
D'EVEREUX, NEAR NATCHEZ *Photograph by Earl M. Norman*	337
LINDEN, NEAR NATCHEZ *Photograph by Earl M. Norman*	339
TAKING COTTON TO THE GIN *Photograph from Rose Seed Company, Clarksdale*	347
MOONLIGHT ON LAKE WASHINGTON, ELKLAND *Photograph by Willa Johnson*	355
TAKING THE QUEEN BEE *Photograph by Ed Lipscomb*	376
THE COUNTY AGENT VISITS *Photograph from U. S. Department of Agriculture*	387
TOMBIGBEE RIVER BRIDGE, COLUMBUS *Photograph by O. N. Pruitt*	398
TWIN TOWERS, MISSISSIPPI STATE COLLEGE, STARKVILLE *Photograph by J. M. Pruitt*	399
MALMAISON, NORTH CARROLLTON *Photograph from National Park Service*	404

ILLUSTRATIONS

Cultivating a Field of Young Cotton	411
Photograph from Case Tractor Company	
Longleaf Pines	415
Photograph by W. Lincoln Highton	
Second-Growth Pines	424
Photograph by W. Lincoln Highton	
Gathering Pecans	430
Photograph by Gene Holcomb	
A Cabin in the Cotton	445
Photograph by W. Lincoln Highton	
A One-Mule-Power Cane Press	449
Photograph by Eudora Welty	
Covered Graves in a Country Churchyard	451
Photograph by W. Lincoln Highton	
A Hardwood Sawmill	457
Photograph by W. Lincoln Highton	
Choctaw Handicraft, Indian Agency, Philadelphia	465
Photograph by Willa Johnson	
"Mississippi Choctaw"	466
Photograph by A. C. Hector	
A Young Choctaw	467
Photograph by A. C. Hector	
Building a Terrace to Control Erosion	489
Photograph from U. S. Department of Agriculture	
Longleaf Pine Tapped for Turpentine	491
Photograph by W. Lincoln Highton	
The Carder	501
Photograph by Mary Ethel Dismukes	
Boy, Broom, and Butterbeans	504
Photograph by W. Lincoln Highton	

Maps

MISSISSIPPI (Large Map of State)	Back Pocket
KEY TO MISSISSIPPI TOURS	Front End Page
GEOLOGICAL FORMATIONS, MINERAL DEPOSITS, AND TIMBER RESOURCES	Page 36
RECREATION AREAS	44
THE INDIANS IN MISSISSIPPI	48
TERRITORIAL ACQUISITIONS: 1801–1832	62
MISSISSIPPI IN 1817	68
COUNTIES OF MISSISSIPPI	78
TRANSPORTATION	83
AGRICULTURAL RESOURCES	97
BILOXI	Reverse Side, State Map
COLUMBUS	Page 180–1
HOLLY SPRINGS	202
JACKSON	Reverse Side, State Map
NATCHEZ	Page 234–5
VICKSBURG	268
THE VICKSBURG CAMPAIGN	273
VICKSBURG NATIONAL MILITARY PARK	276

Notations on the Use of the Book

General Information contains practical information on the State as a whole. Specific information is given at the beginning of each city and tour description.

The Essay Section is designed to give a reasonably comprehensive survey of the State in its various aspects. Limitations of space forbid detailed treatments, but many persons, places, and events mentioned in the essays are discussed at some length in the city and tour descriptions. A classified bibliography is included in the book.

Cities and Towns. Twelve cities are given separate treatment in the section *Main Street and Courthouse Square.* Each of these cities represents some phase of the cultural, economic, historical, or political life of the State, or some one of its geographic divisions. At the end of each description is a list of the important nearby points of interest with cross-references to the tours on which these places are described.

Maps are provided for six of the cities. Points of interest are numbered in the descriptions to correspond with numbers on the maps. Conditions of admission vary from time to time; those given in this book are for February 1938. "*(Open)*" means "open at all reasonable hours, free of charge."

Tours. Each tour is a description of towns and points of interest along a highway bearing a single Federal or State number. Cross-references are given for descriptions of cities in *Main Street and Courthouse Square.* For convenience in identifying inter-State routes, the names of the nearest out-of-State cities of importance are placed within parentheses in the tour headings.

Included in the main route description are the descriptions of minor routes branching from the main route; these are printed in smaller type.

All main route descriptions are written North to South and East to West but can be followed quite as easily in the reverse directions. The names of railroads paralleling highways are noted in the tour headings; thus railroad travelers can use the route descriptions quite as easily as can motorists.

Mileages are cumulative, beginning at the northernmost or easternmost points on the main highways. Where long routes have been divided into sections, mileages have been started afresh at the beginning of each section. Mileages on side routes are counted from the junctions with the main routes. All mileages are necessarily relative; minor reroutings of roads and individual driving habits—such as manner of rounding curves and of passing other cars—will produce variations between the listed mileages and those shown on speedometers.

Mississippi is engaged (1938) in an extensive program of highway development, which involves some highway rerouting in order to eliminate curves and to take advantage of better subsoil for roadbeds. For this reason some of the tour routings and mileages of February 1938 will be inaccurate within a year; if difficulty is experienced in finding points of interest, travelers should make inquiries locally.

Those who have already selected the routes they wish to follow should consult the tour key-map and the tour table of contents to find the descriptions they want; those who want to find the descriptions of, or routes leading to, specific towns and points of interest should consult the index.

General Information

Railroads: Illinois Central System (Illinois Central, Gulf & Ship Island, Yazoo & Mississippi Valley); Southern Railway System (New Orleans & Northeastern, Southern, Alabama & Great Southern); Mobile & Ohio; Gulf, Mobile & Northern; St. Louis-San Francisco (Frisco); Mississippi Central; Columbus & Greenville. Lines of the IC System run N. and S., E. and W. The GM&N and the M&O run N. and S. The Southern System runs diagonally across the State from Alabama to Louisiana. Other lines form connections with the trunk lines.

Highways: Network of paved roads and many roads in process of paving. No border inspection.

Bus Lines: Tri-State Transit; Teche-Greyhound and affiliated lines; Magnolia; Dixie Coaches; Oliver Coach Lines; Delta Transportation Co.; Varnado; White Eagle; Bracy; Dunlap; Dixie Greyhound; Gulf Transport Co.

Waterways: Inland Waterways Corporation; Mississippi Valley Barge Lines; New Orleans & Vicksburg Packet Co.; Valley Line. Steam ferry service at Dundee, Friar Point, Greenville, Vicksburg, and Natchez. Port of Gulfport on the Gulf of Mexico.

Airlines: Chicago & Southern (New Orleans to Chicago) stops at Jackson. Delta Line (Charleston to Dallas) stops at Jackson and Meridian.

Traffic Regulations: No parking on bridges or roadways; speed limit on highways 50 m.p.h., 10 m.p.h. when passing schools and churches, in cities 20-30 m.p.h. No racing or shooting on highways, no sirens, cutouts must be muffled within certain limits. School busses not to be passed when halted.

Accommodations: In cities most hostelries built or renovated since 1928, ample facilities. Jackson crowded during conventions and State Fair Week in October, Natchez during spring Pilgrimage, and Gulf Coast during winter and summer seasons. In the rural sections tourist camps, new for the most part since new concrete highways have been constructed, are at strategic points near towns. Camping facilities in national forests and State parks.

Climate and Equipment: In summer, which comes early and lingers late, light clothing is necessary, though nights in Delta and Coastal Plain will be cool in early summer and latter part of August. Topcoat usually sufficient in winter, with coatless Christmas not uncommon. For the hiker, hunter, swimmer, or picknicker, equipment may be obtained near most recreational centers.

Fish and Game Laws: Game fish, bass, trout, crappie, pike, and sunfish may be taken at any season. Limit of 25 of any species per day; bass not under 10 in.; sunfish not under 5 in. Illegal to sell game fish or to take by explosives, chemicals, or to handgrab. Non-resident annual license, $5.25; 10-day license, $1.50; 3-day license, $1.25; obtained at sheriff's office or from State game wardens.

Hunting Regulations: Open season for squirrels, Oct. 1 to Dec. 31; opossum, Oct. 1 to Jan. 31; rabbits (gun) Nov. 20 to Jan. 31, without gun, all year; fox, open year round, may be taken with hounds only. Deer, closed in most counties, limited in others (obtain bulletin from State commission); bear, closed; quail, Dec. 10 to Feb. 22; turkey, April 1 to April 20, closed in northern Supreme Court district; ducks, geese, and brant, Nov. 27 to Dec. 26; rails (except coot), Sept. 1 to Nov. 30; woodcock, Dec. 1 to Dec. 31; coot and snipe, Nov. 27 to Dec. 26; doves, Sept. 15 to Oct. 1 and Nov. 20 to Jan. 15. No open season on wood-duck, bufflehead duck, ruddy duck, snow geese, and swan. *Licenses:* Non-resident $25.25 (State), $10.25 (county). Federal "duck stamp" for taking migratory waterfowl, $1. License issued by county wardens and sheriffs. Duck stamps at post office. *Limits:* Bag limit: Quail, 12; ducks, 10 in aggregate of all kinds; geese and brant, 5 in aggregate; rails, 15 in aggregate; woodcock, 4; coot, 25; snipe, 15; doves, 15; squirrels, 8; rabbits, 10. One deer (buck) and one turkey (gobbler) per season. *General Laws:* Unlawful to procure license under assumed name, false address, or to lend, transfer, or borrow and use license. Tags and badges must be displayed conspicuously on clothing.

Recreational Areas: Leaf River Forest, off US 49 near Brooklyn; Biloxi Forest, SE. of Saucier on US 49; Chickasawhay Forest, local road between Richton and Waynesboro; Homochitto Forest, off US 84 on Forest Service road near Meadville; Bienville Forest, 18 m. SW. of the town of Forest, State 35; Holly Springs Forest; Delta Purchase Unit, between Rolling Fork and Yazoo City.

State Parks: LeRoy Percy State Park, 4 m. W. of Hollandale, US 61; Tombigbee Park, 7½ m. E. of Tupelo, US 78; Clarkco Park, near Quitman in Clarke County; Legion State Park, ½ m. E. of Louisville, State 15; Tishomingo Park, 3 m. SE. of Tishomingo, 2 m. off State 25 on local road; Holmes County Park, 3 m. S. of Durant, US 51; Spring Lake Park, 7 m. S. of Holly Springs, State 7; Roosevelt Park, 3 m. SW. of Morton, US 80; Percy Quin Park, near McComb. State parks cover a total of 8,565 acres.

Precautions for Tourist: Avoid *unmarked springs.* Mosquitoes in Coastal Meadow and in Delta regions, except in municipalities; campers should take netting. *Poisonous Plants, Reptiles, Dangerous Animals, Insects:* Rattlesnakes, moccasins, coral snakes. Poisonous plants include the ivies and other vines. Berries should not be eaten unless true identity is known. Mosquitoes, black widow spiders generally distributed. Few bear, wildcats, bobcats in dense canebrakes in south and west Mississippi. Alligators in few Delta lakes and in swamplands of south Mississippi.

General Tourist Service: Traffic regulations bulletin from State highway department information service; general laws from Secretary of State, information service; fish and game laws from game and fish commission; chambers of commerce and hotels furnish general information; Mississippi Advertising Commission, Jackson.

Calendar of Events
("nfd" means no fixed date)

Jan.	nfd	Gulf Coast	Opening of winter tourist season
	nfd	Statewide	Field trials
Feb.	2nd wk. prior Lent	Biloxi	Mardi Gras
	nfd	Biloxi	Golf Tournaments
	nfd	Gulfport	Annual Fox Hunters' Meet
	nfd	Holly Springs	U. S. Field Trials
March	nfd	Biloxi	Golf tournaments
	nfd	Jackson	Southern intercollegiate basketball tournaments
	nfd	Brooklyn	S. Miss. Gun & Dog Club field trials
	nfd	Gulf Coast	Azalea Trail and Spring Festival
	nfd	Vicksburg	Historical Tours
	nfd	Holly Springs	Garden Pilgrimage
	nfd	Natchez	Pilgrimage to old estates
April	1st wk.	Natchez	Pilgrimage to old estates
	nfd	Laurel	Garden Club Festival
	nfd	Pearl River Co.	Tung tree trail tours
	26	Statewide	Memorial Services (Confederate)
May	8	Statewide	Emancipation Day (Negro)
	1st Sat. & Sun.	Eggville	Sacred Harp Singing
	2nd & 3rd Suns.	Dennis	Foot Washing Services
June	1st wk.	Hattiesburg	S. Miss. Singing Convention
	2nd wk.	Jackson	Miss. Championship Tennis tourney
	nfd	Gulf Coast	Opening of summer tourist season
	nfd	Allison's Wells	Bridge Tournament
	nfd	Wiggins	Pickle Festival
	nfd	Gulfport	Southern Marble Tournament
July	10 days preceding the 4th	Biloxi	Summer Sports Carnival
	4	Biloxi	Regatta
	nfd	Gulfport	Gulfport Yacht Club Regatta

	nfd	Gulfport	Mackerel Rodeo
	nfd	Lake	Patrons' Union
	nfd	Philadelphia	Neshoba County Fair
	nfd	Pass Christian	Tarpon Rodeo
	nfd	Mound Bayou	Founders' Day
Aug.	Sun. preceding the 15th	Biloxi	Blessing of Shrimp Fleet
	Last Sun.	Gulfside	Negro Song Fest
	nfd	Jackson	Water Pageant
	nfd	Water Valley	Watermelon Festival
Sept.	nfd	Clarksdale	Delta Staple Cotton Festival
	nfd	Utica Institute	Negro Farmers' Conference
Oct.	2nd wk.	Jackson	Miss. State Fair
	nfd	Tupelo	Northeast Miss.–Ala. Fair
	nfd	Jackson	Horse Show
	1st wk.	Meridian	Miss. Fair and Dairy Show
	14-15	Meridian	Pilgrimage to Sam Dale's Grave
	nfd	Rosedale	Rose Show
Nov.	nfd	Statewide	Fall flower shows
Dec.	wk. preceding Christmas	Hattiesburg	Handel's "Messiah" (oratorio)

There are numerous local events that will be found under individual city treatments.

PART I
The General Background

Mississippi Past and Present

What Is Mississippi?

WERE a person to ask, "What is Mississippi?" he undoubtedly would be told, "It is a farming State where nearly everyone who may vote votes the Democratic ticket," or "It is a place where half the population is Negro and the remainder is Anglo-Saxon," or, more vaguely, "That is where everybody grows cotton on land which only a few of them own." And these answers, in themselves, would be correct, though their connotations would be wrong. For while the white people of Mississippi are mostly Democrats, Anglo-Saxons, and farmers, they are not one big family of Democratic and Anglo-Saxon farmers. Rather, Mississippi is a large community of people whose culture is made different by the very land that affords them a common bond. The people of the Black Prairie Belt, for instance, are as different culturally from the people of the Piney Woods as are the Deltans from the people of the Tennessee River Hills. Yet for the most part they all farm for a living, vote the Democratic ticket, and trace their ancestry back to the British Isles.

For this reason, to see Mississippi as it really is, one must understand it as composed of eight distinct geographical units, each with its own sectional background, and each but a part of the whole. To do this gives a perspective which resolves the seeming paradox presented by the writings of Mississippi's two best known interpreters, Stark Young and William Faulkner. Each author simply pictures the section that has conditioned him, and nothing more.

The most clearly defined of the eight sections are the Delta and the Coast. David Cohn has said that the Delta "begins in the lobby of the Peabody Hotel at Memphis and ends on Catfish Row in Vicksburg," and this is possibly more exact than to say that it is a leaf-shaped plain lying in the northwestern part of the State, with its greatest length 200 miles and its greatest width 85 miles. For the native Mississippian long has accepted as fact that the Delta is more than a distinct geographical unit—it is also a way of life. The word "Delta" connotes for him persons charmingly lacking in provincialism, rather than wide flat fields

MISSISSIPPI RIVER

steaming with fertility and squat plantation towns that are all alike. Settled on land as unstable as it is productive, and eternally concerned with two variables and one constant, the planter here has evolved an active yet irresponsible way of life. The variable factors are high water and the price of cotton; the constant is the Negro. In character with all people who are possessed of broad acres and easy labor, the Delta is politically conservative and economically diverse.

Antithetic to the Delta's hectic activity and periodic tension is the lazy halcyon atmosphere of the Coast. Here, where the soil is too sandy to lend itself to intensive agriculture, worry and tautness are vanquished

FROM NATCHEZ BLUFFS

by a conspiracy of summer breezes, winter greenery, blue waters, and foreign gayety. Since the War between the States, the ingenious natives have lent their talents to the conspiracy, and today the Coast is recognized first and last as a pleasure resort.

Between the Delta and the Coast are three other sections. The loamy brown hills that stretch southward from Vicksburg through Natchez to Woodville are, next to the Coast, the oldest settled portion of the State. Here, in the "Natchez District," rich bluffs and bottomlands once produced crops of virgin luxuriance; and these crops, product of slave and earth, once enabled men and women to build a civilization that could not be disregarded. It is this former plantation civilization, with its ease and plenty, its white-columned mansions, formal manners, and gracious kindly people, that Stark Young has depicted. And it is here that the somewhat faded tapestry of landed culture, classic manors, bric-a-brac, and leisured ladies and gentlemen remains to charm and fascinate, like pages in a storybook.

Not so sharply defined topographically, but easily distinguishable as an economic unit, is the trucking, fruit growing, and nut growing area lying east of the bluffs, where the tomato and cabbage industries at Crystal Springs and Hazelhurst are tangible proofs of this section's use of soil too thin for cotton. This section is each year the scene of a dramatic battle with the elements, a race for the profits to be gained from reaching eastern markets ahead of the Texas truck farmers. In years when the prize is won, this trucking section is the wealthiest in the State. Yet, in contrast to most Mississippians, the people here have excellent memories; they remember the years when the prize was lost, and are careful in their economy.

Again not so sharply defined geographically, and gradually becoming less defined economically, are the Piney Woods, lying east of the trucking section and north of the Coast. This is a rather haphazard and irregular triangle, whose scenery of stumps, "ghost" lumber towns, and hastily reforested areas tells its saga. Strong men and women have been reared here, but the earth has been neither fecund enough to facilitate their getting away from it nor sterile enough to drive them away. Until lumbering built a few fair-sized towns out of the wilderness, it was a pioneer country; and now that the forests have been ravished, and the cheaply built mill houses are rotting, as the unused mill machinery rusts about them, it is pioneer country once more. Like all pioneers, the Piney Woods people are economically poor, politically unpredictable, and in a constant state of economic transition. Evidences of recent change are the new textile mills at Hattiesburg, Laurel, and Picayune, the new tung tree orchards to the south, and the De Soto National Forest in the center of the area.

The five sections so far described compose the southern and western portions of the State. In the extreme northeastern corner, between the Tombigbee and Tennessee Rivers, is the wedge-shaped group of uplands known locally as the Tennessee Hills. Here, living in as "old English" a style as their upland cousins of the Georgia and Carolina Piedmont, is a group of hill-born and hill-bred farmers who are fiercely independent, and who insistently retain the early Anglo-Saxon and Scotch-Irish characteristics that their great-grandparents brought to the section. Housed in compact "dog-trot" homes perched on steep hillsides, these people, like those of the Piney Woods, have always been the yeomen—the non-slave owners—of the State, possessed of an inherited distrust of the planter and of the aristocratic system that great plantations breed. This attitude is important because these hillfolk, when joined with those of the Piney Woods, determine the political fortunes of the State.

Just west of the Tennessee Hills is the Black Prairie, a comparatively treeless and rolling plateau that was once a small replica of the Natchez District and is now spotted with silos and cheese factories, cotton mills, dairy barns, and condenseries. The Prairie has never had to bother with the Piney Woods' problem of clearing timber and stumps from the fields; neither has it had to contend with the hill country's nemesis of erosion nor the Delta's problem of drainage. Because of these natural advantages, it not only won cultural distinction before the War between the States, but since the war it has kept approximately a generation ahead of the rest of the State. The Prairie farmer, like all good farmers, loves his land, but he is not afraid of the machine. Meat packing plants, garment factories, dairy products enterprises, and the Tennessee Valley Authority came first to the Prairie.

West of the Prairie and east of the Delta is the low-hill, small-farming section known as the Central Hills, the largest section of the State. This broken series of clay hills evidences more clearly than any other region the misfortunes that descended on Mississippi after the War between the States. When the war completely upset the economy upon which ante-bellum prosperity had been based, it not only destroyed surplus capital but also fixed on the State the share-cropping and credit system—the enemy of diversification and the chain that binds the tenant to the merchant-banker and to poverty. The merchant-banker has continuously demanded that cotton, and cotton alone, be grown to repay his financial advances. Yet, repeated sowing of this basic crop on clay hillsides caused sheet erosion. Great red gullies have consumed the fertility of the land, until today an occasional ante-bellum mansion teetering crazily on the edge of a 50-foot precipice offers mute evidence of the decay Faulkner has seen fit to depict in his novels. Lacking the virility of new blood and the impetus of new industry, portions of the Central Hills have degenerated. Cotton here no longer has the kingly power to pull white-columned mansions out of the earth, for the earth has too often felt the plow.

These eight family-like sections grouped together form the great neighborhood called Mississippi, a neighborhood where the birthright of knowing the drive of the plow in a puissant earth binds the sections more closely than geographical boundaries, a neighborhood of earth-rooted individuals who know and understand one another, and who collectively face an industrial revolution with hoes grasped tightly in their clay-stained hands.

White Folkways

A farmer people with a mental background of furrowed hot fields and a hope for rain, we Mississippi white folk are both dependent on and modified by the sporadic blessings of forces that we cannot control. Like the well water we drink, we are bosomed by the earth that conditions us. We think as our land thinks, and those who understand our simple psychology and accept our way as being complete rather than clever find us tolerant but not susceptible, easy to amuse but hard to convince. Our faith is in God, next year's crop, and the Democratic Party.

This leads, not to gaunt hookworm-infested character, but to independence and paradox. Dependent on the land, we have a basic quality of mind that is as obstinate as the mules we plow, yet our notions take tall erratic flights and are as unpredictable as the ways of a spring-born calf. Born with an inherent regard for the Constitution, we prefer our own interpretations to those of others. Fervent prohibitionists, our preference is for "ho'-made corn." We read the cotton quotations as a daily ritual, but the small cryptic figures we read have little to do with when we sell. That, like the choice of candidate for our vote, depends on the notions we take. One year in five is for us a "good year," but our business is done and our households are run on the simple acceptance that next year will be "good." This adjective is not a judgment by moral scales, but by cotton scales, and it does not imply we merely have raised a lot of cotton, but that while doing so, Texas cotton either has been rained-under or burnt-out, thus making prices high. If we should swap a good library for a second-rate stump speech and not ask for boot, it would be thoroughly in tune with our hearts. For deep within each of us lies politics. It is our football, baseball, and tennis rolled into one. We enjoy it; we will hitch up and drive

GATHERING FOR A POLITICAL RALLY

for miles in order to hear and applaud the vitriolic phrases of a candidate we have already reckoned we'll vote against. Popular belief to the contrary, our greatest fear is not the boll weevil but Republican tariffs. Our greatest worry is the weather. To paraphrase—as the weather goes, so goes Mississippi's year.

For us calendars are bits of advertisements that the storekeeper mails out about the time taxes are due. They are usually of oblong dimensions, with brightly colored Biblical pictures at the top and small neat pads of black numerals at the bottom. They are pretty and tasteful and fit to tack up in our bedrooms; but, beyond that and the fact that our very hopeful imaginations may see in the receipt of one an indication of extended credit, they have little to do with our year. For, eating hog jowls and black-eyed peas on New Year's Day notwithstanding, our year neither begins with the first day of January nor ends with the last night of December. Our year begins with planting-time and ends with the gathering-in. Between these two extremes comes the hoeing-and-chopping season and a spell of laying-by. In all, this covers a period of about seven months—from March, when the snowy white blooms of the cottonwood tree tell us not only to put our cottonseed in the ground, but, more happily, to resume our charging at the store, until sometime in September, when we pick, gin, and bale the soft white bolls we have raised, and are told in a way less subtle than by the receipt of a calendar to stop our charging at the store. Yet it is enough. It is a "year," and for us complete. Come the tenth of the month following, and we will have weighed it, tagged it, and laid it quietly aside as having been simply "good" or "bad."

The remaining months, those falling in autumn and winter, have for us a peculiar nature. Like "Dog Days" and "Indian Summer," they are intangible spells, the lapse between an ending and beginning. We think of them as a stretch of daylights and darks, marred perhaps by the hibernating habit of our credit, but otherwise nice. We ingeniously while them away by selling our cotton, paying a small amount on our charge account, a smaller one on our mortgage; by attending barbecues, neighborhood parties, protracted meetings, and county fairs. If we are young but of likely age, we ignore the charge account and forget the mortgage in order to build a house and get married.

Should our convictions prove false, however, and the year isn't one which warrants the epitaph "good," then these months aren't even a nice run of daylights and darks. They are a complete lapse of time. We hunt and fish and, sometimes, chop the wood while our wives milk the cows and gather eggs. But mostly, we just piddle about, studying the wind and sky and earth—watching for signs that bewilder our agricultural colleges but prove the grace which nourishes our faith in next year's crop.

These signs are physical but not scientific. They have to do with the soil and the elements, and they tell us not only when to plant, but also how our planting will probably turn out. Most of them are superstitions, but they work.

The first and basic sign is the "twelve-day idea." This, in reality, is a series of signs, a sort of preview of the coming year, and is based on the idea that each of the first 12 days of January represents and holds the chief characteristic of the correspondingly numbered month. Carried to its logical conclusion, it becomes rather complicated, something one should grow up with to understand fully. For instance: If the second day of January is cloudless but cold, we note the fact, and, turning to the second month, February, we mark it "Dry and Cold." Then, by some strange, hybrid faculty born of experience and deduction, we know a late spring will follow—so we curb our spirits and refuse early planting. In like manner, if the fifth day of January is rainy, we expect a rainy May, and visions of more grass than corn in June sets us to sharpening our hoes. Other and more simple signs of what we are about to receive are: Moonlight during Christmas means light crops; darkness, heavy crops. If the wind is from the south on the 22nd day of March, the year will be dry. Each day it thunders in February should be carefully marked on the calendar so that the garden may be covered up on the corresponding days in April, for it will surely frost those days. If there are three frosts, rain will follow. But, happily, winter is over when the fig tree leafs; we may get ourselves ready to plant.

Early vegetables—cabbage plants, greens, spinach, and onion sets—go into the ground during the freak spell called "January Thaw." This is a short stretch of mild, warm days when ant larvae move up near the soil's surface to tell us the earth is good and just moist enough. For the next planting Saint Valentine's Day is preferred, but, since it is potatoes, a root vegetable, we are to plant, we who are wise will wait until the moon is right—leaf vegetables do better when planted in the light of the moon, root vegetables when planted in the dark phase. Good Friday is a holy day and will bring good fortune to beans and early vegetables if they are planted before the night sets in. For the planting of our staple crop there is but one sign we can trust, "Plant cotton when the cottonwood blooms."

Such signs, plus the nationally known Ground-hog Day, pertain to the seasons, to planting, and to the months in general. They tell us, for instance, that May will be a rainy month, but not the days it will rain. Yet, once the newly planted seeds have transformed themselves into young and tender shoots, it is imperative that we know the specific days. We cannot stop the rain, prevent the frost, or end the too-dry spell, but, once forewarned of their immediate approach, we *can* prepare to a degree our fields, our gardens, our piles of fertilizer, our stacks of hay, and thus be able to drop the self-explanatory phrase "bad year" into our creditor's lap without a quirk of conscience. So we need and have a few very specific signs— quick, flashing bits of handwriting on the earth and in the sky:

If the sun sets behind a bank of clouds on Sunday, it will rain before Wednesday; if it sets in the same obscurity on Wednesday, rain will fall before Sunday. In either case, one does well to have his fertilizer stacked before quitting for the night. A red sunset, like a rainbow in the morning, brings wind rather than rain, while a rainbow in the late afternoon or a streaked sunset brings fair and dry weather respectively. When smoke hangs flat and the swallows fly low, it is about to cloud up; so just before rainfall we stop off our plowing and leave the field. This is not to escape getting wet, but to lessen the danger of being struck by the lightning that will be drawn by the eyes of our horse or mule. If smoke and birds fly high,

A COUNTRY CHURCH

however, or if the lightning shifts to the south, we may go ahead with our plowing; fair weather is in the offing. A halo around the sun brings an immediate change of weather, and one should remember that a morning shower, like an old person's dance, never lasts long. Three months after the first strident laugh of the katydid, frost will fall, and we may call our hogs in to fatten. Winter isn't yet at hand—a long spell of lazy warm weather called Indian Summer will follow the frost—but a cold snap is in the making, and *that* will bring hog-killing time. Curing hams, making sausages, grinding hogshead cheese; eating backbone and spare-ribs and chit'lings!

Hogs we can raise ourselves, so hog meat, in one form or another, is our staple dish. We eat it fresh in winter, cured in spring, and salted in summer; we use the fat as a base for cooking vegetables. These vegetables are chiefly turnip greens, collards, cabbages, beans, and peas. In the fall and winter the weekday meal is cooked on a large, black, wood-burning kitchen stove and served hot twice a day. In farming time, when everyone is either too hurried or too tired to have a conscious sense of taste, it is cooked in the gray obscurity of early morning and placed in deep, wide "warmers" attached to the stove. At dinner (noon) and supper it is served and eaten cold.

On Sunday, however, or when company comes, the meal becomes a feast. The housewife, forewarned of approaching company by the crowing of a rooster in the yard, makes lavish preparation—she "puts the big pot in the little pot and fries the skillet." In addition to baked ham and fried ham, there is chicken with the meaty joints fried and the lean joints made palatable by thick strips of juicy white dumplings, three or four kinds of vegetables, biscuits, corn bread, several varieties of cake, and a pie or two. These are all placed on the table at one time, with the meat dishes at the end. The housewife "won't sit just yet," but the family and company will. They sit down together, eagerly, expectantly awaiting the saying of the blessing. While the dishes are passed from one person to another, with each helping himself, the housewife hovers near, watching, ready to replenish a platter by a hurried trip to the kitchen. If one should be accidentally slighted, it is said that his nose has been bridged. The person taking the last biscuit is obligated to kiss the cook. If the hostess is the sort to insist on one's eating heartily, she will make a good stepmother.

The house may be a two-room frame cabin, but most probably an increase in family size will have caused it to be expanded into a four- or five-room construction with a porch across front and rear, a chimney on each side, and the dog-trot enclosed. It sits facing the road from the edge of a field that stretches and rolls until the lineated shade of a dark, warm forest joins it abruptly to the sky. To the rear and to one side is the garden. If the children are home, the front yard, creeping unsodded from beneath the porch, is naked and clean. If the children are grown and have moved to places of their own, verbena, old maids, phlox, and four-o'clocks, crowd each other for space. This is due more to a taste for cleanliness than for beauty. Our housewives haven't the time to be always sweeping the yard, so they just plant flowers and "let 'em have it." If the house is in the Delta, and is not the house of a planter, it will not have a yard at all; cotton will grow to within a few feet of porch and eaves.

The wife is the key to the house. Her domestic life gravitates between the bedroom, the kitchen, the chicken-yard, and sometimes the field. She bears the children with the aid of a midwife and nurses them herself. She readies-up the house, cooks the family meals, and gathers the eggs. In addition she knows and administers the folksy remedies that have been in the family for generations.

Some of the remedies were taken originally from the Indian, some were contributed by the Negro, but the majority of them have the earthy taste of old England, Ireland, and Scotland. For instance:

A ball of camphor gum tied about the neck and resting on the chest will cure neuralgia. To ease a sick head, drink a cup of hot catnip tea; to check nausea or constant vomiting, beat peach-tree leaves, cover with water, then drink slowly. A piece of horse-radish well chewed is good for hoarseness; and a small bag of tea placed on the eye will cure a cold. To stop the flow of blood, saturate the wound with turpentine and castor oil. When cows feed on fresh grass in May, their butter is good for chapped hands. Since rheumatism includes every misery from a crick in the neck to a strained knee, a preventive is better than a cure; so carry an Irish potato in a pocket or a buckeye near the chest and never be troubled with it in any form.

The housewife is not too busy, however, to accompany the family to town on Saturday, and there walk about, looking at the show windows and greeting friends; or to prepare a shoe box of food to be auctioned to the highest bidder at the box supper given at the church to raise money for a new piano; or to run up to a neighbor's house, where a group of women-folks are "quilting a piece for Sara Adams," who is to be married just as soon as crops are gathered and John has the time to 'tend to such a thing. She does all of these things, then joins the family in its simple but intensely homey socials. And, come a Saturday, she will prepare and give a "to-do" of her own—one at the house and for all the family together.

The "to-do" will probably be a neighborhood party—an ingathering of families from down the road, from over the bottom, from just across the field a piece. It is purely social, with no labor, no "pounding presents" attached. Death and distance are the party's only limitations. At dark the families, from Grandpa down, begin to arrive on trucks, in wagons, in cars, horseback, and on foot. Two hours after dark, 50 or more men, women, young folks, and children are mingling in and about the house. Warm cordiality and equal acceptance set the tone. The old folks gravitate to the porch and to the yard, talking crops and politics, or snitching a wink or two of sleep. The children play in the hallway, or if they are "poor-mouthers," worry their mothers until sleep gets the best of them. Then they are deposited on pallets strewn over the floor of a reserved back room.

The young folks move restlessly in and out of the "front room," which contains a piano or a foot-pumped organ, the storekeeper's calendar, and the biggest feather bed and prettiest hand-tufted bedspread in the house. Here we are direct and natural in our association, with none of the legendary timidity in our manner. We sit on the bed, on the cane-bottom chairs, in the windows. One or two of the boys will have had a snort or two of corn, and our antics increase with the stuffiness of the room. Courting couples wander outside under the trees, up and down the road, or just sit alone somewhere, content to be together and to listen to dismembered phrases that escape from mingled conversation and drift independently out to them: "I'm not even about to do it . . . ," ". . . he plenty lit a shuck . . . ," "out yonder, I'd say . . . ," ". . . it's the pure D truth . . . ," ". . . I ain't studyin' you . . . ," '. . . slow poke . . ."—distinctly folksy phrases that are never burdened with the letter "r."

Music is continual. A third of the persons present are natural musicians and have brought their instruments: French harp, Jew's harp, fiddle, saxophone, guitar, accordion. Many of the girls have had piano at the consolidated school. They play popular pieces and well-loved hymns and folk ballads which tell a legend and end with a moral—"The Blue Eyed Boy" "who has broken every vow"; "That Waxford Girl," who was "an expert girl with dark and rolling eyes"; "Kinnie Wagner," who shot the sheriff, kissed the prettiest girl in town, and left "to live a life of sin." Those who do not play either sing or don't sing as the notion strikes them.

The water bucket, sitting on a back-porch shelf with its bright metal dipper beside it, is popular and the boys take turns at the nearby well bringing up bucketfuls fresh from the earth. Fried chicken, boiled ham, banana cake, and "ho'-made" pickles are waiting in the kitchen. Shortly after midnight the guests begin to leave, going by families according to the distance they have to travel and their mode of getting there. By three o'clock they are gone.

There was a time in the past when our social life was tied up with work, such as house-raising, logrolling, and hog-killing. But today we have more time and economy, and our socials move on larger planes. We hold county fairs and attend barbecues, all-day singings, and religious services. These are, in turn, manifestations of the soil, of politics, of re-

SHANTYBOAT LIFE

ligion; and, being for us dramatically personal, each one is knit closely with the other.

Many of our counties own commodious, centrally located, fenced-in spaces called fair grounds where yearly exhibitions are held. These grounds are lined with exhibition booths, livestock barns, a grandstand, a race track with an athletic field in the center, and a roomy administration building. The annual exhibition is, ostensibly, a competition for prizes in turnips, pumpkins, heifers, cakes, hogs, and other rural pulchritude, but, actually, it is our Victorian excuse for importing a street carnival. The carnival, loudly ballyhooed with bright but startling pictures, offers a midway with rides as ingeniously contrived as they are various in form: free vaudeville acts, side shows, fireworks, and other pulse-throbbing activities that cause a momentary forgetfulness of furrowed hot fields. Other counties extend the scope beyond their geographical boundaries and hold straight-out carnivals, with the section's money-crop—cotton, watermelons, strawberries—reigning as king. Yet the motive is always the same; a crop has been made, and in one grand outburst our pent-up emotions splash the countryside.

Such self-expression sometimes takes unique form. In Neshoba County, the custom of permitting anyone who has a predilection for hearing the sound of his own voice to attend the fair and make a speech has metamorphosed the fair into a political jamboree. Here our candidates for political office toss their hats into the ring. From especially built platforms they loudly point with pride and view with alarm. They are for the land, the farmer, and lower taxes. Emphatically, they are against whoever is in office. Crowded below them, we listen and heckle and cheer and drink soda pop. The candidate tells us we are the "backbone of the State," and we know that it is true, not because we are possessed of certain endowed virtues, but because we are a majority and have the vote.

But politics is too dear to the hearts of all of us to be localized. Once a campaign for election is launched, it becomes the recreation of all the counties, towns, communities, clubs, and individuals within the State. It is a summer pageant of speakings in a setting of open-air barbecues. A barbecue with speaking will be announced to take place at a certain locality, on a certain day; and though scarcely 20 families comprise the neighborhood, when the time arrives, hundreds, even thousands will be gathered for the occasion. The speaking continues through the day, the principal or "main speaker" alone talking four hours or more. Because we stand on our land and will brook no foolishness concerning it, his speech will have to do with personalities, not platforms; and we will score him, not on his intelligence, but on his ability to string invective adjectives without a break. A candidate once called his opponent "a willful, obstinate, unsavory, obnoxious, pusillanimous, pestilential, pernicious, and perversable liar" without pausing for breath, and even his enemies removed their hats.

As we listen to a speaker, we crowd about a narrow table of incredible length and select a piece of brown, damp meat. The meat is juicy, with a pungent, peppery odor, and eats well with a slice of thick white bread. With these clutched, one in one hand and one in the other, we join a group of friends to munch, talk, and listen. Nearby, more barbecue is being prepared in ancient style. A trench, two, four, or six feet in length, has been dug and a slow-burning oak or hickory fire started on its bottom. Suspended over but held close to the smoldering flame on slender saplings are carcasses of lamb and goat. About these stand a few women and an old man, the women to look and give advice, the man to baste with rich red seasoning by means of swabs attached to long, lean sticks. The odor from the peppery, hot sauce, and the woody smoke from charred coals permeate the grounds and whet our appetites. Leaving our friends and momentarily forgetting the speaker, we ease back to the table for more.

These barbecues with speakings make the line between our social activities and our politics a thin one, but even it is more discernible than the one separating our social from our religious activities. For, with us, these last two blend at the edges, with one passing smoothly, almost unnoticeably, into the other. It is transition through a common denominator, and the common denominator is song.

Through the long Central Hills, in the black northeast Prairie, in the Piney Woods, the Tennessee Hills, and, lately, in the newly developed "white spots" of the Delta, we sing—not as individuals but as communities, counties, and districts. And we do not sing a mere song or two; we bring our lunch and pallets for our babies and sing all day.

The feat is not a simple one. The *Sacred Harp's* 500 pages contain no newfangled song with a harmony that can be faked. It holds to the ancient "shape-notes," the "fa, sol, la" songs brought down from Elizabethan England and written in four parts, on separate staffs, with each part carrying to a degree a melodic pattern of its own. This is complex; it calls for technique and a training for tone. As any "leader" worth his salt will declare, a tone-ignorant person can ruin a singing any day.

To avoid such a calamity, each county has its "school." The school is a "leader," or singing master who goes from community to community, like an old-time Methodist circuit-rider, teaching the youngsters to "pitch," to know "tone lengths" and "tone shapes"—the circle, triangle, square, etc. During the process, he also teaches the songs adapted to each "occasion": "Invitation," ("Ye Who Are Weary"); "Glorification," ("Glory for Me!" or "We Praise Thee O God!"); and "Funerals," ("Just Beyond the River").

When a novice has learned such fundamentals, he is eligible for membership in the County Singing Convention and permitted to join in the "singings" with all the vibrant volume his lungs can muster. Perhaps he later will prove worthy of becoming a "leader" himself or, less important, a duly elected officer of the District (sectional) Singing Association, of which his county convention is a member. One never can be certain about a singer—not beyond the fact that he will be at the singing, singing lustily and religiously, like the rest of us.

The singing is at the "church-house," a small, white "shotgun" structure placed just off the road in the sun-speckled shade of a grove. It is scheduled to begin at nine sharp in the morning, but time is a negligible quantity to people who put seeds into the ground and wait for them to grow; at ten o'clock we are still arriving, in cars, in school busses, in wagons, and a few in "Hoover carts"—an ingeniously contrived two-wheel, automobile-tired lolly brought into prominence by the depression. We have on our Sunday clothes, with here and there an unobtrusive patch, but only the district's politician will wear a coat.

Inside the church, the leader faces us from the pulpit. He is a lean, Cassius-like fellow with the voice of an angel. With ancient ritual he directs us through eighteenth century singing-school procedure; he speaks of "lesson" and "class," not of song and choir.

"The lesson," he announces, "will commence on Number six-three."

We watch him peer closely at his book, and listen breathlessly as he softly sets the pitch. Then his hand sweeps to right, to center, to left, and we proclaim the tune he has pitched. We go through the tune together— soprano, alto, tenor, and bass singing the syllables, "fa, sol, la . . . ," calling to life notes that told the stern but virginal Elizabeth how the tune should go. With the tune pitched at last, the leader adjusts his glasses and looks about. "The words," he demands; and we sing the words:

"Brethren, we have met to worship and to adore the Lord, our God. . . ."

As the singing continues, leader after leader is called upon. Each is a good leader and will tolerate no dragging, yet a point of courtesy and common-sense democracy demands that when his turn is finished he must give way to another. All who can lead must have a chance to lead. A casual coming and going among the class (congregation) is evident. But it, too, is informal and does not affect the charged feeling in the little church-house. The songs are burning and familiar. They are the life we live. As the hands of our leaders wave us through the deep rhythm of the spirituals, we feel our emotions in songs. We sing to please ourselves, and the deep organic surge keeps our voices together.

At noon, however, the *Sacred Harp* is laid momentarily aside, and we go outside for dinner on the grounds. Mules, tied nearby and sensing neglect, bray long and deep. Dust, kicked up by thudding heels, rises to make breathing difficult and to intensify the heat. Yet no one notices, for baskets of food have been brought forth and their contents spread in long, shady rows beneath the trees. A stout, middle-aged lady with a hand for such things faces the milling, conversing crowd, gathers up the folds of her apron and carefully wipes her hands.

"You folks can come on now," she says. "You men folks take some of everything and eat all you want."

After a time, a leader gathers a group about him within the church. He pitches a tune and asks for the words; and "Come Ye Faithful . . ." rolls beckoning out into the grove, fetching us in. A new song is selected.

"I don't like it drug out," the leader cautions. "I like it pert, like you did before you ate."

His arm sweeps down, sweeps us back into the archaic splendor of choral music. The songs move from lesson to lesson; the leadership swings from the seasoned old fellows to the young and obviously frightened tyro. But the tune never wavers, the rhythm does not drag. All that remains is movement and sound, with the latter still unabatedly prominent. We have found a grace of heart and, for the moment, a joyous way of living.

Yet it must end. As the sun drops blood-red behind the grove, the oldest leader comes forward and pitches a tune. "The words," he demands, and in the waning light we give him the words:

"God be with you till we meet again. . . ."

This expression of emotion in song is a fitting prelude to our religion, which possesses an ethical foundation revealed in everyday living, and an emotional background brought forward at yearly "meetings." In other places these meetings are called "revivals," but we are more realistic. If we are Methodist, we refer to our meeting as the "camp-meeting," a term derived from the fact that in days not long ago the people literally camped about the meeting ground. Today this custom is rare, yet at McHenry in Stone County it survives in a camp that was constructed sometime in the early 1800's. If we are Baptist, we say "protracted meeting." In either case, we mean what the name implies, a series of religious services for a number of days. The number usually extends through ten or fourteen, with a preaching in the afternoon, supper on the ground, and another preaching at night. Each service begins with lukewarm singing, rises on the rhetorical prowess of the preacher, and ends with a zealousness that borders on the "shout." The meeting is more a dramatic display of movement and sound than a solemn, sublimated worship.

The preacher, whether our pastor or an itinerant evangelist, understands our preference for feeling rather than for knowing, and he builds his sermons on the fact. He does not preach against sin. He preaches against sins, and he names them: drinking, gambling, fornication, card-playing, dancing, and stealing. One by one he holds them up for our inspection. With charged words he sweeps us into homes these sins have visited and shows us the wreckage they have wrought. The scene fascinates with its horror; we sit tense and expectant, as if awaiting the onrush of doom. A little girl, immunized by innocence of the outside world, gets to her feet and strolls along the grassy aisle. A baby, lying on a pallet at its mother's feet, begins to fret. But we are spellbound and do not notice. Without sympathy or attention the mother takes her child into her lap and soothes it with milk from a well-filled breast.

The preacher talks on, giving us unstintingly of his best. Then, suddenly, he changes his approach. Tangibles are exchanged for things less tangible, yet, for us, more obvious. The Lord and Salvation replace hell's-fire-and-damnation. Condemnation is forsaken for hope. His voice is soft and consoling; his roots seem in the earth rather than in Heaven. He speaks of things which we who are dependent on sources beyond our control can understand. He speaks of hope and faith and things to come. The earth is not ours, and if we should doubt, we need only to look to the clean, unsodded plot flanking the church-house. Here sunlight by day and moonlight by night glide down cold white marble headstones and are absorbed in dark, oval-shaped mounds; and here we gather once a year to hold Memorial Services for our fathers, who came from over the mountains and down into the wilderness with just such a zealous preacher leading them. We came out of the land and we will return to the land, and, the preacher's voice drones on, we will be contented there. The landlord will furnish as liberally as we want, and the crops will be always good. It is a promise, as cool as rain after a long dry spell; and somehow we know that it is true. Someone, usually a man, assures us that it is true: "Amen. Amen," he says. Sometimes a woman cries out, then gets to her feet and cries out again. But before our emotions reach the breaking point, the preacher more often breaks off, disconnects the current. He announces a hymn, which we sing with more bewilderment than enthusiasm; then with a prayer he dismisses us.

It is a nerve-wracking interlude, an electrical charge in an even flow of life. But it purges our soul and refreshes our song. Somehow it gives us the thing we need. For soon taxes will be due, the landlord will have to be seen, and furnishing for another "year" will have to be arranged. In no time at all, we will be noting the first 12 days in January, marking the sort of weather the new year will bring. We will be readying ourselves for planting; and when the cycle of the crops swings in again, our simple way of living will follow closely in the rhythm of its wake.

Negro Folkways

Different from the Louisiana folk Negro in speech and from the east coast Negro in heritage, the Mississippi folk Negro stands alone, a prismatic personality. Those who know him well enough to understand something of his psychology, his character, and his needs, and like him well enough to accept his deficiencies, find him to be wise but credulous—a superstitious paradox. He seems to see all things, hear all things, believe all things. But ask him a question and he will have neither seen, heard, nor believed. He counsels with himself and walks his way alone.

When he does talk, however, the Negro achieves a natural vigor of speech that few writers obtain. With a severely limited vocabulary and an innocence of grammatical niceties, he resourcefully gathers all the color of a scene and in simple words drives home his meaning with sledge-hammer force. This was illustrated when a Governor visited the State Penitentiary at Parchman and interviewed some of the long-term convicts. His conversation with one of them, a Negro, as reported by the newspapers, ran as follows:

> Governor: "What are you here for, boy?"
> Prisoner: "I was shootin craps, cap'n, an' killed a nigger."
> Governor: "Why did you kill him?"
> Prisoner: "I made my point, suh, and he wouldn't recognize it."

The Mississippi folk Negro neither lays up monetary treasures nor invests in things of tangible value. He spends money for medical and legal advice, a virtue that undoubtedly would bring him praise but for the fact that he has never been known to take anyone's advice about anything. The remaining portion of his crop money goes to the dentist, the burial association, and to places of entertainment. In the distant future he hopes to be buried in style; for the present he may be satisfied with a gold tooth —one on a plate and in front, that he can take out, look at, then put back for others to see.

Yet, his greatest joys, getting religion and being baptized, are free. For him religion is something more than a code of conduct with doctrinal points on righteous living. Like his song, it is the released stream of his

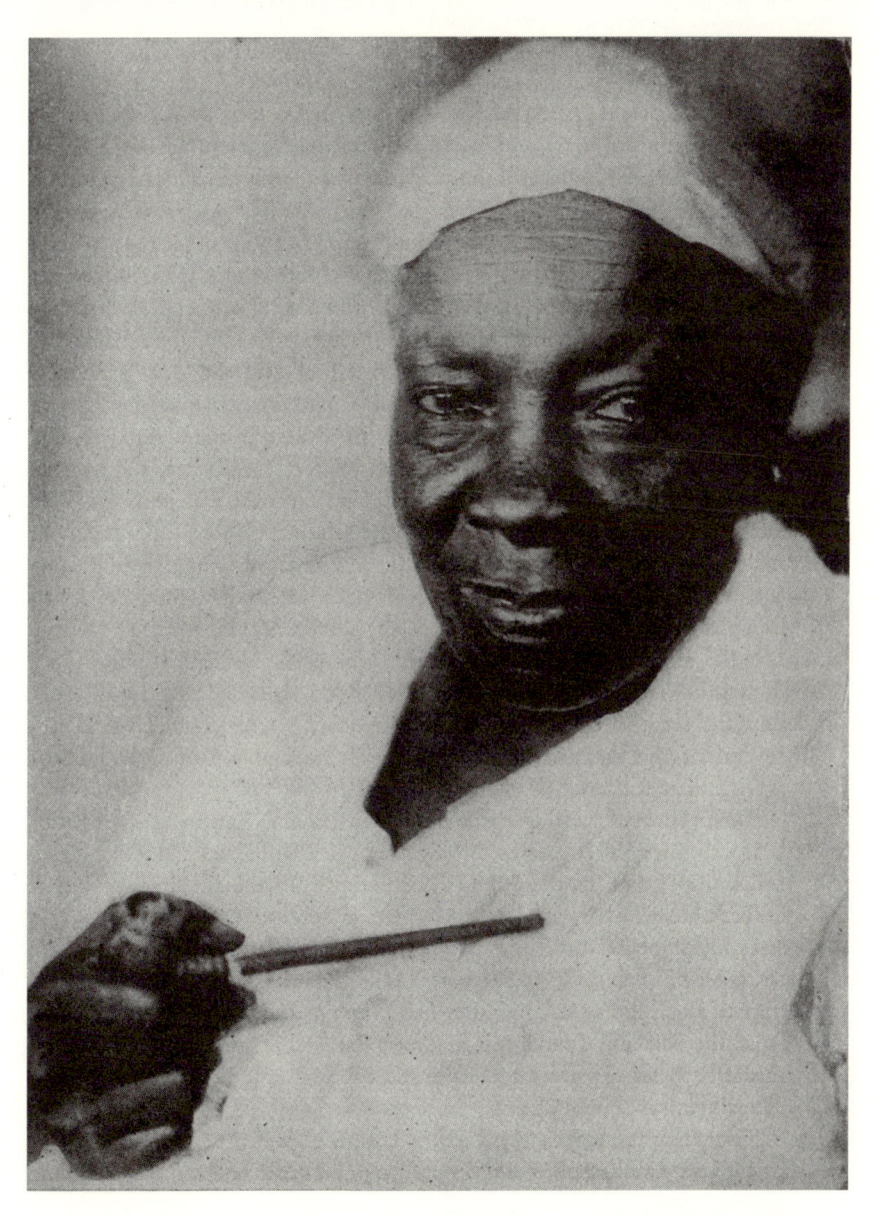

MAMMY GLASPER

pent-up emotions, the channel through which he floats to higher ground. Also, like his song, it is unconcious art, primarily sensuous and shot through with voodooism. For weeks prior to the annual "protracted meeting," he fasts and prays and works himself into a state of feeling that will make the church services highly exhilarating and weirdly African. For this reason his religious leader is more an emotional expert than a practical theologian. He moans, groans, and injects various other psychological stimuli which he does not understand himself. His manner is always unhurried and unctuously subtle, and his power among his people is absolute.

Such a leader was Cindy Mitchell, an old woman of Leflore County. So great was her hold on her followers that they said she was "sanctified" and they called her the Good Shepherd. Cindy always closed her services with a dance, during which she would sit in a corner and sing, "It ain't no sin t' dance so long as yu don't cross yo' feet!" They say, she once announced that on a certain day she would walk on the waters of the Yalobusha River. She secretly laid some planks on uprights, just below the muddy surface of the stream. But on the appointed day, her slowly moving feet discovered that the planks had been removed. Horrified at the thought of drowning, but confident of her power, she turned slowly to face the crowd. "I ain't goin' to walk," she declared. "Th' Lawd Himsef' done said, 'Don't do it, Cindy, not befo' folks that ain't got th' faith of a mustard seed.'" The charge filled the throng with religious zeal, and several of the doubtful brothers themselves became "sanctified" in the services that followed.

The protracted meeting has its "mo'nahs bench," "fasting and praying," "comin' through" experiences, meeting of "candidates," the "right of fellowship," and, as the climax, "baptizing." In the preliminary service, before the preacher takes charge, there is singing, tapping of feet, and swaying of bodies until the congregation gets happy. Then the preacher rises, slowly comes forward to the pulpit, and begins his sermon. The opened Book lies before him, but he scarcely notices it. His message comes from the soil and from the racial peculiarities of his people. When his throat becomes dry and tired from his exhortations, he sits down to rest. The singing is started again.

Since the preacher has worked his best, the singing at this time is done in earnest. The best men singers gather in a corner and the leader intones a phrase of some song. The phrase is repeated over and over with other men singers joining in. The song rises slowly and steadily, increasing in volume and tempo, until the urge of its weird harmony and spiritual uplift forces hands to clap rhythmically with the steady cadence of a drum.

Soon a woman leaps out into the aisle. She is "moved by the spirit" she cries, and slowly, rigidly, she begins "the shout," or if it is a Holiness meeting, the "Holy Dance." It is shuffling, intricate; her heels thud on

HOLT COLLIER

the floor. Other women become moved. With arms held stiff and bent at the elbow and hands hanging limp from the wrist, they slowly, jerkily, circle the church, forming a tight chain with their bodies.

"Shout the praise o' God!" someone demands, and even the sinners join in the singing. They sing lustily, with all reason subordinated to sound. The ring of shouters moves faster and faster, yet the feet keep the step; the rhythm is not broken. When the strain reaches the breaking point the leader raises his hand. The song is hushed. The circling chain halts, breaks apart. The shouters go back to their seats. They are breathing hard and are wet with sweat.

In the pause that follows, the preacher comes forward and begins to talk. Perhaps it is a continuation of his sermon; perhaps it is something entirely new. No one knows and no one cares. His voice has taken on the strange hollow quality of the hand-clapping and seems to float above his listeners. No matter what he says, someone sitting in the Amen Corner nods his head and shouts, "Amen!" This response is not a privilege, but a duty. Now and then someone jumps to his feet and "professes." He has seen the light, he shouts, and is now "turned." To distinguish him when the time comes for "experiences," a member places a piece of white cloth on his sleeve.

Near the end of the meeting the "candidates" must face the officers and members and relate their "experiences." The experience is the visionary journey he had made while on the road to salvation and must resemble the experiences of a professed member, else the candidate will not be acceptable to full membership. As these spiritual journeys are recounted, in the rich metaphor and Biblical phraseology of the "saved," the responses of the audience rise to the pitch of religious ecstasy.

The meeting ends in a great baptizing usually held early in the morning or on Sunday afternoon. Dressed in white gowns and caps, the candidates who have been accepted into membership are led out by two deacons into the water of some creek or pond, the preacher preceding them. The congregation gathers on the bank and sings, "Let's Go Down to the Jordan." The minister puts his hand on a candidate's head and says, "I baptize thee." As the new member goes quickly under the water and rises hysterically happy, everyone breaks into a shout "Praise th' Lord! Praise God!" Another sinner has been washed of his sins.

In many small Delta towns on Saturday white folks make it a habit to attend to business early and get off the streets. For "Saddy" is the Negro's day. He arrives in wagons, in trucks, in automobiles, and on foot. By noon he literally overruns the town. If he is a day laborer, he has his pay day cash to spend. If he is a farmer, he has his rations to draw. In either case, he has news to exchange and the hand of every other Negro in town to shake. He is a busy man, and one not of his race is apt to be stepped on, sat on, or have his passage along the walk blocked for hours. The Negro does not do these things intentionally, he simply cannot see a white person on Saturday unless that person owes him something.

In preparation for his day in town, his mode of dress, like a majority of his ways, is governed by the psychology of the occasion. If he is a town Negro, the thought of impressing the many country girls with his position is overwhelming, and he dons the best his wardrobe has to offer. If he is a country Negro he thinks of the talk he is to have with his furnisher and, wisely saving his best or Sunday-suit for the day its name implies, wears overalls or some other work garment. The women make efforts to improve their appearance. Some wear neat gingham or calico dresses. Others, particularly those who are unmarried, imitate the latest styles. This practice often leads to the rather ludicrous spectacle of a young and highly rouged Negro woman struggling through the crowd with the pale blue train of an evening gown trailing behind her.

The standard rations the furnishing men allow the tenant Negro are a peck of corn meal, three pounds of salt meat, two pounds of sugar, one pound of coffee, one gallon of black molasses, and one plug of either "Red Coon," "Brown Mule," "Dixie Land," or "Wild Goose" chewing tobacco. This collection is supposed to last him one week, but unless an eye is kept on him, he will eat it all before Saturday.

> "Ole Mosser give me a pound o' meat.
> I et it all on Monday;
> Den I et 'is 'lasses all de week,
> An' buttermilk for Sunday."

On the other hand, if he is working for wages and "eating himself," he can live a surprisingly long time on three soda crackers, a can of sardines, and a nickel's worth of cheese.

When ill, the rural Negro has his peculiar methods. He discards all the stored-up information he has gathered by frequent trips to the doctor. The remedies he wants come from custom, not from science. At these times he calls a powerful root doctor or hoodoo woman to diagnose his case for him. If the trouble be insanity, boils, or constipation, the verdict invariably is that a secret enemy has "fixed" him and nothing in the world but a powerful "toby" or "jack" (charm) can dispel this conjuration. The old woman provides the "toby" for a price. The materials she uses in it and the way she puts it together do not follow any ancient formula, but depend almost entirely upon some momentary whim. The lining of a chicken's gizzard, powdered blue glass, pine resin, a rooster's spur, ashes, rusty nails tied in a bracelet around the foot, asafetida and alum are considered good, but the victim's own hair baked in a cake and fed to him is best. Perhaps the "papa toby" of them all, one which is sure to possess the virtue or vice necessary to drive away the hoodoo, is the ever useful piece of red flannel thrust inside of a hollowed-out pecan hull.

Should the diagnosis show that the illness is not due to the conjuring power of an enemy, other remedies are available. Some of these nostrums came originally from the Indian, some from the folk medicine of England, and many can be traced through voodooism to Africa. For toothache, smoke and buttermilk, or a red pepper mixed with biscuit dough, are good remedies. For sore throat, a piece of string is tied about the topmost lock of the sufferer's hair. For getting rid of a sty, the patient should stand at some cross-road and recite, "Sty, Sty, come off my eye; light on the next one passing by."

Cough syrup made of mullein leaves, sugar, and vinegar is perhaps a bit more reasonable. Another cough medicine is tar and honey. Red clay, softened with vinegar, is bound over bruises to remove soreness. Poultices of elm bark are used to reduce inflammation. Sulphur and molasses and sassafras tea are standard remedies for improving and thinning the blood in the early spring.

When gelatin capsules cannot be had, "slippery elm" is used. The inner bark of the elm tree is cut into strips and soaked in water until it becomes a slippery substance. The medicine—quinine or calomel or some mixture in a "dough pill"—is rolled up in this mass and given to the patient on the theory that the medicine will not taste bad and will go down "slick." One of the oldest treatments in the Delta country for chills and fever is the administering of water in which the bark of the red oak tree has been soaked. Mutton suet and beef tallow are used for rubbing the chest and throat in case of a cold. Another treatment for colds is soaking a stocking in kerosene and sleeping with it tied around the throat.

After receiving such treatments, if the patient is sufficiently resistive, he survives. If not, he dies. Among the Negroes in Mississippi, death is generally conceded to be the work of nature, not voodooism. The figure of Death occurs frequently in their songs:

> "Oh Death he is a little man,
> And he goes from do' to do' " . . .

Should a man die suddenly, and die "hard," that is, with attendant delirium, death will be attributed to the hostility of a spirit, which may have taken him for violating any one of several taboos. An axe or a hoe may have been brought into the house and then carried out again through some door other than the one by which it entered. His clock, which has not run for some time, may have struck unexpectedly. Perhaps a rat nibbled the household linen or someone's clothes, or a star fell suddenly. It may have been that he had unwittingly cut a window in his house after it had been finished and he had lived in it, or that his rooster crowed soon after sundown. Whatever the cause, death sometimes brings a slight compensation. If someone else in the house is sick at the time, that person's health immediately improves.

The moment death comes, the mirrors and pictures in the room are carefully turned to the wall, else they will tarnish and hold a lasting picture of the corpse. The news then goes forth, "Old Tom is dead," and from miles around Negroes who never before have heard of Old Tom come together in his cabin. Old Tom is up on his dues to the lodge and to the burial association, so his funeral is a great occasion. In death Old Tom realizes his most ardent desire, that of being buried "in style"—and the survivors have a social gathering.

None of his kinsmen dares assist in the preparation of his body for burial, but it is washed and the grave clothes are put on. A coin is put on each eye and a dish of salt is placed on his chest. The salt, it is said, keeps him from "purging" (swelling), while the money closes his eyes.

Then his hair is combed out (a woman's hair is never plaited, for the devil will send his blackbirds to unplait it and they will be heard at work inside the coffin even after it has been placed in the ground), and with his feet shoeless, he lies ready for the wake. During the wake his body is never left alone, nor is the floor swept. "Neighbors," who may live miles away and have never seen him before, sit with him, and food is served and songs are sung.

If he was an unimportant Negro, the wake lasts only three days; but if he was important, as was the Reverend Frank Cook, it goes on and on. Cook, a Baptist minister, was the popular pastor of four churches: Pleasant Green Church in Natchez, St. Stephen's in Vidalia, Louisiana, a church in New Orleans, and a church in Ohio. He died in Natchez, October 22, 1922. The wake began that night and lasted until Wednesday, the 25th, when his body was taken to New Orleans where another wake was held, lasting until Saturday the 29th. On Sunday his body, having been brought to Natchez, was carried to Vidalia and placed in Young's Chapel, his mother's church, where the parson preached over him night and day until Tuesday the 31st. Nine days after his death, his family was compelled by law to bury him.

At the cemetery, the Negro in Mississippi observes various omens. If a horse neighs or lies down during the service, or if the casket slips while it is being lowered into the grave, it is a sure sign that someone present soon will follow. To leave the grave before it is filled, or to be the first to go away from the graveyard is another pointed invitation to death. At the close of the service everyone throws a handful of dirt upon the box as a tribute of respect to the dead. A person never points at the grave, for fear his finger will rot off or his mother's teeth will drop out.

In some sections of Mississippi after a funeral, all cups, pans, and buckets are emptied, food being thrown out to the west, because the spirit will remain on the premises if encouraged by free access to food and water. It is bad luck to call a coffin pretty, and if a pregnant woman looks into a grave she will never feel the baby. The dead person can rest assured that his clothes and cup and saucer will never be used by anyone else. The cups and saucers are broken and the pieces are placed on his grave together with bottles of medicine used in his last sickness, while his garments hang unused, since no one wishes to feel the ghost of the owner tugging at them.

The Mississippi folk Negro today is a genial mass of remarkable qualities. He seems carefree and shrewd and does not bother himself with the problems the white man has to solve. The tariff and currency do not interest him in the least. He has his standard, silver, and he wants no other kind. As for the so-called Negro Question—that, too, is just another problem he has left for the white man to cope with. Seated in the white man's wagon, and subtly letting the white man worry with the reins, the Negro assures himself a share of all things good. Once a landlord was asked if the Negro really had a soul. "If he hasn't," the landlord replied, "it's the first thing that a white man ever had that a Negro didn't share if he stayed with him long enough."

Before the White Man Came

Natural Setting

Geography and Topography

Taking its name from the majestic river that forms the greater portion of its western boundary, Mississippi is bounded on the north by Tennessee, on the east by Alabama, and at the northeast corner by the Tennessee River. To outline a part of the southern boundary, Louisiana extends eastward like the toe of a boot as far as the Pearl River, which flows southward to form the southern portion of the western boundary. The remainder of the southern boundary is the Mississippi Sound, a shallow body of water lying north of a chain of low, sandy keys that act as a buffer against the deeper waters of the Gulf of Mexico. The coast line, including the irregularities and the islands, is 202 miles long, but the distance between its extremities, as the crow flies, is only 88 miles.

The area between these boundaries covers 46,865 square miles, of which 503 are water surface. The extreme width is 180 miles; the extreme length is 330 miles. The State is thirty-first in size among the forty-eight, and ranks twenty-third in population. In 1930 the population was 2,009,821 of which 50.2 percent was Negro. Of the white population, 99.3 percent was native born. The Negro population is concentrated largely in cotton-growing sections—the Yazoo-Mississippi Delta and the Black Prairie.

Contrary to popular impressions about the topographical character of Mississippi, the only portions of a flat swampy nature are the Yazoo-Mississippi Delta and the river bottoms. The surface in general is hilly, reaching a maximum elevation of 780 feet in the northeast corner and slowly descending to form a panorama of rolling hills, which merge into the tidal meadows of the Gulf Coast. From a physiographic point of view, this surface is broken into ten regions that conform quite closely to the geological structure of the State.

The alluvial plain—a basin lying between the Mississippi River and the Yazoo River in the northwestern part of the State and colloquially called the Delta—is the most pronounced surface feature. Stretching north for

MAGNOLIA GRANDIFLORA: THE STATE FLOWER

approximately 200 miles from the juncture of the two rivers, and averaging about 65 miles in width, this immense area contains some of the richest land in the world. Nearly all of it is bottomland, produced and fed through countless eons by the inundations of the Mississippi River and reclaimed for usage by a system of powerful levees that hold the floods in check. The alluvial deposits have been found to be 35 feet deep in many places. Dark, mellow, sandy loam occurs near the streams, while a black sticky clay called "buckshot" obtains in the lower parts away from the drainage courses. Versatility of this "Delta" soil makes the area one of the most productive on earth.

Skirting the eastern margin of the Delta is a range of rugged precipitous hills known as the Bluff Hills, or, scientifically, the Loess Hills. All streams flow through these hills in narrow gorges whose sides in many places are vertical walls. This region of hills varies in width from five to fifteen miles and follows the eastward curve of the border of the Delta from above the Tennessee State Line southward, hugging the east bank of the Mississippi River from Vicksburg as far as the Louisiana Line. The soil of this district is brown loam underlain by a yellowish calcareous silt. This loess, peculiarly formed by mechanical action rather than by chemical disintegration, is in reality rock dust blown here after one great glacier, then another, had overridden the country north of the Ohio and Missouri Rivers. For this reason the Bluff Hills contain little or no rock, a fact which greatly amazed the early New England settlers upon their arrival in the region. The loess, varying in thickness from thirty to ninety feet, is exceedingly rich in plant food, and yet is cut so deeply by stream erosion that it is almost impossible of cultivation.

The rugged Tennessee River Hills in the northeastern part of the State have an average altitude of some 650 feet, rising to 780 feet at their highest point. The streams flow through narrow deep ravines in short swift courses to the Tennessee and Tombigbee Rivers. The hills are of pebbly, red, sandy loam, while the loam of the river bottoms is rich, black, and sandy. Toward the south and west the slopes are less precipitous and the creeks flow more slowly toward the various streams. Geologically, the ancient Paleozoic era is represented in these hills by both the Pennsylvanian and Devonian systems, and it is here that the oldest geological formations in the State are found.

Sweeping in a crescent around the western border of the Tennessee River Hills from Corinth through Macon is a low-lying belt of prairie land that is different in almost every respect from the hill country. Its surface consists of smooth, rolling, almost treeless earth covered with grass the greater part of the year. The soil is black, calcareous, clay loam, furnishing an exceedingly fertile farming district. The Black Prairie lies at a considerably lower level than do the eastern hills; the greatest altitude in the northern part is about 400 feet, and the surface slopes southward to a level of approximately 179 feet.

The wedge-shaped Pontotoc Ridge extends for about 150 miles along the western border of the Black Prairie. These hills enter the State in the northeast corner and move southward to form a point just north of Ackerman. The soil is rich sandy loam which, before erosion set in, grew a diversity of crops.

The Flatwoods, a narrow band of flat, poorly-drained land, sweeps in an open crescent around the western and southern margin of the Black Prairie and Pontotoc Ridge. The soil is uniformly gray sticky clay that retains water tenaciously. It is difficult to cultivate and generally unproductive.

The North Central Hills embrace all that portion of north central Mississippi lying between the Flatwoods on the east and the Bluffs overlooking the Delta on the west. The characteristic soil of this area is a fertile yellowish-brown loam containing much silt and clay. It varies in thickness from two to fifteen feet, is fertile and adapted to raising various crops.

Directly south of the North Central Hills is the Jackson Prairie Belt, a district of rolling land interspersed with numerous small prairies. It reaches across the State from the bluffs of the Mississippi to the Alabama State line, a narrow strip with an extreme width of 40 miles. Its black calcareous soil forms another expanse of fine fertile farmlands.

The entire southern half of Mississippi, south of the Jackson Prairie to within a few miles of the coast, is known as the longleaf pine belt or, more simply, the Piney Woods. The soil here is a red and yellow sandy loam that is fairly productive. The area at one time was covered with longleaf yellow pine, large tracts of which remain in spite of ruthless cutting.

Between the longleaf pine hills and the Gulf of Mexico is a low lying region from five to fifteen miles in width called the Coastal Plain Meadows. The surface is level and gently rolling but broken in spots by depressions. Because of the generally low altitude of this region the streams flow toward the Gulf with only moderate force and become sluggish toward the coast. The soil is gray and sandy in the higher portions, but in the low swampy meadows where water usually stands, it becomes black and peat-like.

Mississippi is drained by a multitude of rivers, picturesque in name and setting. The Pontotoc Ridge forms a divide separating the Mississippi river system from the Alabama river system to the east. The Tallahatchie,

NATURAL SETTING 35

Yalobusha, Yocona, Coldwater, Big Flower, Little Flower, and Skuna carry the waters of the western slope through the Yazoo into the Mississippi at Vicksburg. The Tennessee and Tombigbee drain the northeastern portion of the State, the latter through Alabama into Mobile Bay, and the former by curving northward into the Ohio. In the southeast the Leaf and Chickasawhay form the Pascagoula that empties into Pascagoula Bay, while the Escatawpa flows into the bay from the east. In the southwest, the Big Black and the Homochitto run into the Mississippi. In the south and central part, the Pearl, with its tributaries the Yokahockany, the Strong, and the Bogue Chitto, empties into the Gulf.

Climate

Mississippi enjoys a relatively agreeable climate. The average mean temperature over a 48-year period has been 64.6 degrees. This varies in summer and winter respectively between 81 and 48 degrees. The average frost-free season is approximately 250 days in southern Mississippi, over 200 days in central Mississippi, and drops below 200 days only in the extreme northern part of the State. The first frost usually occurs in November, with the last occurring near the middle of March. The annual rainfall ranges between 60 inches on the Coast to 49 inches in the north, with the average annual precipitation approximately 54 inches. This rainfall is evenly distributed throughout the State and is generally lightest during the months of September, October, and November. This almost sub-tropical climate not only makes for pleasant living, but assures approximately a nine-month growing season.

Geologic History

The oldest rocks, those represented by the Canadian Shield about Hudson Bay, the Piedmont district in the East, and the Rocky Mountain district in the West, have no surface representation in Mississippi whatsoever. Much of Mississippi's ancient geologic history lies beneath younger beds of the Coastal Plain deposits, which begin with the Cretaceous of the Mesozoic, or third, geologic era. Surface rocks in the northeastern part of the State, however, do go back to the Devonian and Pennsylvanian periods of the Paleozoic, or second, geologic era, which ended nearly two hundred million years ago.

These Paleozoic sedimentary beds accumulated in the old Appalachian trough, mostly from fragmental material derived from Appalachian land,

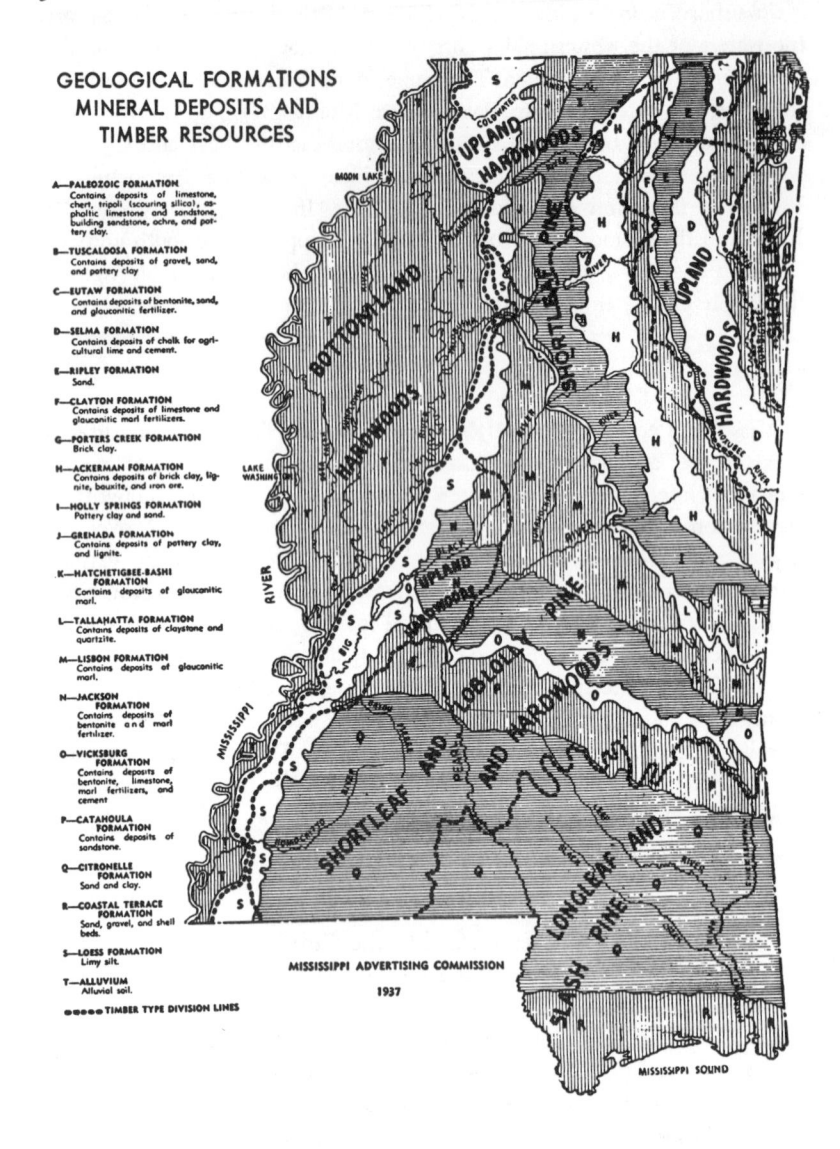

GEOLOGICAL FORMATIONS MINERAL DEPOSITS AND TIMBER RESOURCES

A—PALEOZOIC FORMATION
  Contains deposits of limestone, chert, tripoli (scouring silica), asphaltic limestone and sandstone, building sandstone, ochre, and pottery clay.

B—TUSCALOOSA FORMATION
  Contains deposits of gravel, sand, and pottery clay

C—EUTAW FORMATION
  Contains deposits of bentonite, sand, and glauconitic fertilizer.

D—SELMA FORMATION
  Contains deposits of chalk for agricultural lime and cement.

E—RIPLEY FORMATION
  Sand.

F—CLAYTON FORMATION
  Contains deposits of limestone and glauconitic marl fertilizers.

G—PORTERS CREEK FORMATION
  Brick clay.

H—ACKERMAN FORMATION
  Contains deposits of brick clay, lignite, bauxite, and iron ore.

I—HOLLY SPRINGS FORMATION
  Pottery clay and sand.

J—GRENADA FORMATION
  Contains deposits of pottery clay, and lignite.

K—HATCHETIGBEE-BASHI FORMATION
  Contains deposits of glauconitic marl.

L—TALLAHATTA FORMATION
  Contains deposits of claystone and quartzite.

M—LISBON FORMATION
  Contains deposits of glauconitic marl.

N—JACKSON FORMATION
  Contains deposits of bentonite and marl fertilizer.

O—VICKSBURG FORMATION
  Contains deposits of bentonite, limestone, marl fertilizers, and cement

P—CATAHOULA FORMATION
  Contains deposits of sandstone.

Q—CITRONELLE FORMATION
  Sand and clay.

R—COASTAL TERRACE FORMATION
  Sand, gravel, and shell beds.

S—LOESS FORMATION
  Limy silt.

T—ALLUVIUM
  Alluvial soil.

●●●●● TIMBER TYPE DIVISION LINES

MISSISSIPPI ADVERTISING COMMISSION
1937

the region where the Piedmont Plateau and Atlantic Coastal Plains now are. Some of the deposits were derived from the limy shells and tests of marine plants and animals.

During the first two epochs of the Devonian period practically no sediments were swept into the Mississippi part of this ancient interior sea, so that fairly pure limy material from the shells of marine animals was ground up and cemented in the form of New Scotland and Island Hill limestones. Later, the sea became muddy and sufficiently shallow to permit vegetable matter to grow and accumulate, along with the fine sediments, to form the black carbonaceous shales of the Whetstone Branch formations.

During the earliest part of the Mississippian epoch (first in the Pennsylvanian period) the condition of the sea was again such that the limy tests, or shells, of marine animals accumulated along with some fine clays to form the impure clayey Carmack and Iuka limestones. Some of the material deposited at this time became, on alteration, the flints and cherts of these limestones. Untold ages later the limy material of the surface limestones was dissolved and carried away by ground waters, thus setting free the chert detritus which forms such a conspicuous surface material today.

In the late Mississippian, the sea again transgressed the land of this region, reached its maximum extension, and then retreated. The sea worked over the weathered surface rock and deposited residual material in the form of sand and mud, which on consolidation became sandstone and shale. During the maximum extension the sea received little sediment, so that the limy tests of its dead animals were ground up by the waves and cemented into limestone. On retreating, the sea again worked over the surface materials and deposited them to form later sandstone and shales.

Although represented only beneath the surface in Mississippi, Pennsylvanian (epoch following the Mississippian) beds farther to the north, show that the Paleozoic sea withdrew from the Appalachian trough, except for brief invasions when a few thin layers of limestone accumulated. Rather, this part of the continent stood about at sea level so that swamps spread far and wide over the area. In and about these swamps vegetation grew luxuriantly and accumulated in these waters where it was compacted and preserved in the form of coal, forming the great Appalachian coal fields. Some of these plants were trees that grew to be several feet in diameter and more than 100 feet in height, but that have since declined until today they are represented by the prostrate and weakly club mosses and ground pines.

Throughout most of the Permian, latest period of the Paleozoic era, the newly accumulated sediments that had been collecting for millions of years were subjected to a side thrust from the southeast Atlantic side which slowly forced them into an enormous series of upfolds, the

Appalachian mountains stretching from Canada into Georgia, Alabama, and Mississippi.

Throughout the first of the next geologic era, the Mesozoic, no known sediments were accumulating in Mississippi. For more than a million years, it is estimated, the newly formed high Appalachian Mountains of Mississippi, as well as farther north, were being worn down by stream erosion until, in the Cretaceous period (latest of the Mesozoic era), they had been reduced to a plain upon which the earliest Cretaceous sediments were deposited. Consequently much of Mississippi's Appalachian history, like most of its Paleozoic beds, lies buried beneath Coastal Plain deposits. And consequently, too, these old rocks lie at the surface only along the valley of the Tennessee River and along the lower stretches of the tributary valleys of this river.

As the Cretaceous sea of the Mesozoic era was advancing on this old planed surface, the Tuscaloosa sands, gravels, and clays were being laid down upon it as fluvial deposits. When eventually the sea did reach Mississippi, sand, gravel, and clay deposition gave way to a calcareous sand deposition that formed the green sand marls of the Tombigbee member of the Eutaw series, as it is called in Mississippi and Alabama. Huge oyster, clam, and cephalopod shells in these sands show how thrivingly the shell fish forms grew in this sea.

Eventually the Eutaw sea became clearer and passed quietly into the Selma sea, which, besides some mud and a little sand, received the great deposits of limy material that form the Selma chalk. Like its predecessor, the Selma sea teemed with large cephalopod and oyster life. Most famous of all, perhaps, were the giant sea-lizards *(Mosossaurs)* that swam these waters, parts of whose skeletons are found in many Selma chalk exposures in the famous Black Prairie belt.

The alternately clear and muddy Selma sea gave way at length to the more turbulent Ripley sea in which clay and sand were deposited as well as limy sand or marl. The Ripley sea withdrew near the close of the Mesozoic era.

When the sea did come back in the Cenozoic, or most recent, geologic era, it was filled with modern life. In the northern part of the State the Clayton sea teemed with a large gastropod *(Turritella mortoni)* whose shell bore a spire three or four inches in height. The limy material of these and other shells accumulated by itself or mixed with sand and clay to form either limestone or marl. Later, here and farther south, nearly pure clay accumulated, probably under deltaic conditions, to form the Porters Creek clay (Grim).

Near the beginning of Cenozoic times, the marine waters of the Gulf, it seems, extended northward. Deposits indicate a series of oscillations between marine and swampy conditions. Where Jackson now is, this early sea was rich with shell fish life, for sandy material within the present city limits is filled with fossil forms of shells. Somewhat later the huge whale-like Zeuglodons, 70 to 80 feet in length, swam the borders of the waters then stretching far to the east from the site of the present bluffs of the Mississippi River. Vertebrae in the clays of this sea measure 8 to 10 inches in diameter and 14 to 16 inches in length. In the region around Vicksburg the formations are abundantly filled with marine shells.

During the Pliocene epoch (immediately preceding the Pleistocene, or glacial epoch) beds, mostly of sand and gravel, were deposited under such different environmental conditions that their origin is the subject of controversy. Gulfward, these sediments seem to have been deposited in shallow marine waters; landward, in estuaries; and still farther inland, along stream courses. Accordingly, they lap over a series of older and older beds away from the Gulf.

During Pleistocene times, when one great glacier after another overrode much of the North American Continent north of the Ohio and Missouri Rivers, very different conditions obtained in Mississippi. Along the broad flat terrace plains of the Gulf border, loam, sand, and clay were being deposited; along the successively lower and lower terraces of the stream courses, loam, clay, sand, and gravel were deposited as flood plain material while each of these terraces in turn served as the stream's flood plain. Still farther north along the east bluff of the Mississippi River, in fact forming the bluff itself, an intermediate material was being deposited by the wind. This material, picked up from the flood plain of the river, had been deposited by the flood waters issuing from the glacier itself far to the north.

In recent times, deposition within the borders of the State is confined largely to flood plains of the streams, especially that of the Mississippi River. This is the material of the so-called Mississippi Delta, which is not deltaic material at all, but rather flood plain deposits.

Except for the partly cemented limy deposits that form the Selma chalk and for the cementation of a few minor beds, practically the whole Coastal Plain beds still remain in the unconsolidated state of deposition.

Mineral Resources

The Paleozoic rocks of Tishomingo County contain sandstone suitable for building purposes; pure silica suitable for scouring material; and fragmental material that can be used as coarse aggregate in concrete. They also contain limestones useful, when crushed, for agricultural purposes. Near the State line and in Alabama they contain considerable quantities of asphaltic material.

The Mesozoic beds contain an abundance of sand and gravel suitable for concrete and for road material; high grade clays for pottery ware; green sands that are valuable as plant food; chalk that may be ground for agricultural lime and for cement purposes; and marl that forms rich soils. More recently discovered deposits are the bentonite beds—a form of volcanic dust that is valuable as a bleaching clay and for the treating of which a $350,000 plant has been erected at Jackson.

The Cenozoic (or Recent) group contains clays that will make brick for building purposes; beds of lignite that will serve as fuel when higher grade coals are exhausted, or that experimentation may show to be valuable for other purposes; beds of bauxite that will be valuable when the higher grade aluminum ores are exhausted; and beds of carbonate iron ores that are being mined for paint pigment; but above all a lens of clay in the Holly Springs sand that is utilized in excellent pottery ware.

In addition are green sands, limy marls, and limestones that make rich soils on weathering; limestones that may be used for cement purposes where the overburden is not prohibitive; and bentonitic bleaching clays that rank first in the United States; gravels that make excellent gravel roads and coarse aggregate for concrete; loess that yields an extremely rich soil; and flood plain deposits of the so-called Mississippi River Delta that constitute the rich alluvial empire of Mississippi and other States.

One of the last and one of the most important thus far of Mississippi's mineral resources is the gas produced in the Jackson Gas Field (not to mention the well-nigh exhausted Amory Gas Field) which, in 1932, 1933, and 1934, produced more than nine billion cubic feet each year; in 1935 to the value of $2,171,000.

Plant and Animal Life

In the period between March and November Mississippi's countryside is bright with flowers. Green Virginia creeper, white and yellow dwarf dandelions, black-eyed-susans with dark brown centers and dull gold petals, purple wood violets and wisteria, papaw, buckeye, cinnamon fern, and tiny pink and white Cherokee roses catch the sun from open fields or gleam in the shade of heavy forest. In fall, the dying foliage of deciduous trees on the northern hills presents what is perhaps Mississippi's most

YUCCA PLANT, OR "SPANISH BAYONET"

spectacular natural scene. In winter the brown sedge grass along the Coast and the brown cotton stalks in the Delta appear first gold then purple in the setting sun.

On the uplands, along stream bottoms and on moist slopes, heavy forests of post and white oak, hickory, honey locust, poplar, maple, sycamore, and magnolia tower above huckleberry, hazelnut, and mountain laurel. In the lowlands of the Delta, stream banks are heavy with willow, bald cypress, tupelo, black gum, and sweet gum. The Piney Woods of southern Mississippi stay green the year around with tall, long-leafed pine, while giant live oaks and gray Spanish moss keep the Gulf Coast area in almost perpetual shade.

Animals were abundant in Mississippi when white men first began to settle here. The bison, bear, wildcat, wolf, and cougar were roaming in the wilderness. Muskrat and beaver lodges were common and mink and otter were plentiful. The bison and the bear were the first to go; then the indiscriminate slaughtering of beaver and otter by trappers annihilated these fur-bearing animals. The modern hunter occasionally kills a deer or trails a fox, but even these are scarce except in some portions of the State. However, the threatened shortage of these and other animals is being remedied through the work of the Fish and Game Commission. The cotton-tail rabbit, fox and gray squirrel, raccoon and opossum are the modern sportsman's chief game.

Approximately all kinds of fresh-water fish are found in Mississippi's lakes and streams. The most important of these from the sportsman's point of view are the black bass, the speckled trout, the buffalo, carp, shovel-bill cat, channel cat and mud cat, bream, and perch. In the Gulf Coast area, where the fisherman can cast his line in a different stream each day in the year, there are in addition to the ones named the red fish, sheepshead, mullet, croaker, and drum.

It is also on the coast that birds gather in greatest number throughout the year. As far as is known no large nesting colonies of gulls, terns, or brown pelicans exist here, but these birds do rear their young close by in Louisiana and Alabama and feed commonly in the Mississippi Sound. Although more numerous during the winter, such species as the brown pelican, the black skimmer (locally known as the shearwater), the royal tern, and Caspian tern, and the laughing gull, occur in varying numbers throughout the spring and summer. The least tern, the smallest of this group, nests in small colonies on stretches of sandy beach, but departs for its winter home in Central and South America in late September, not to be seen again until the following April. The more northern gulls—the herring gull, the ring-billed gull, and Bonaparte's gull—occur in flocks of varying size during the winter months. Shore birds, represented by approximately 35 species of sandpiper and plover, are a characteristic feature of the open beaches. One of the most interesting of this group is the Cuban snowy plover, limited in its distribution to the Gulf Coast from Florida to Texas. This plover is found only on the open beaches. Its light plumage blends so perfectly with the sand that it can easily be overlooked.

Sea birds often are of more interest on the coast than the smaller land birds, but the spring and fall migrations of the latter are fascinating. Apparently little effort is involved in making the flight across the Gulf of Mexico. Such small migrants as warblers, sparrows, and thrushes go inland many miles during good weather, before taking shelter in suitable stretches of wood or underbrush. Because of this habit, many species that commonly nest farther north are almost unknown on the coast, and there are days when only the characteristic breeding birds are observed. There are intervals, however, when inclement weather makes a long flight hazardous and uncertain, and at such times stretches of woods bordering the water will teem with small birds awaiting a favorable chance to continue their journey. Observation has shown that migration in the spring is materially retarded by northwest winds, and in the fall by storms from the southeast.

In the salt marshes are found the Louisiana clapper rail and Howell's seaside sparrow (both limited in their range to a narrow stretch of the coast), the least bittern, and many species of heron. Among the latter group is the stately egret, a bird once almost exterminated by plume hunters but now regaining its former numbers through adequate protection.

The State's chief game birds, the partridge and the migratory duck, are also being restored through the protection of adequate game laws. Until recently the partridge was plentiful in the open fields in all sections of Mississippi, but the hunters have driven them to the protection of woods and thickets.

Much of the State, especially the southern half, is covered by pine timber, and here can be found such representative birds of the open woods as pine warbler, the brown-headed nuthatch, Bachman's sparrow, considered by many the finest songster in the South, and the red-cockaded woodpecker. The last is unique among the woodpeckers in that it smears the opening to its nest cavity with pitch dug from the solid wood of a living pine, frequently making the nest conspicuous for some distance.

The bottom lands and hillsides of northern and central Mississippi, where undergrowth is thick, support a distinctly larger population of birds, and without exception they are species rarely if ever found in the pine

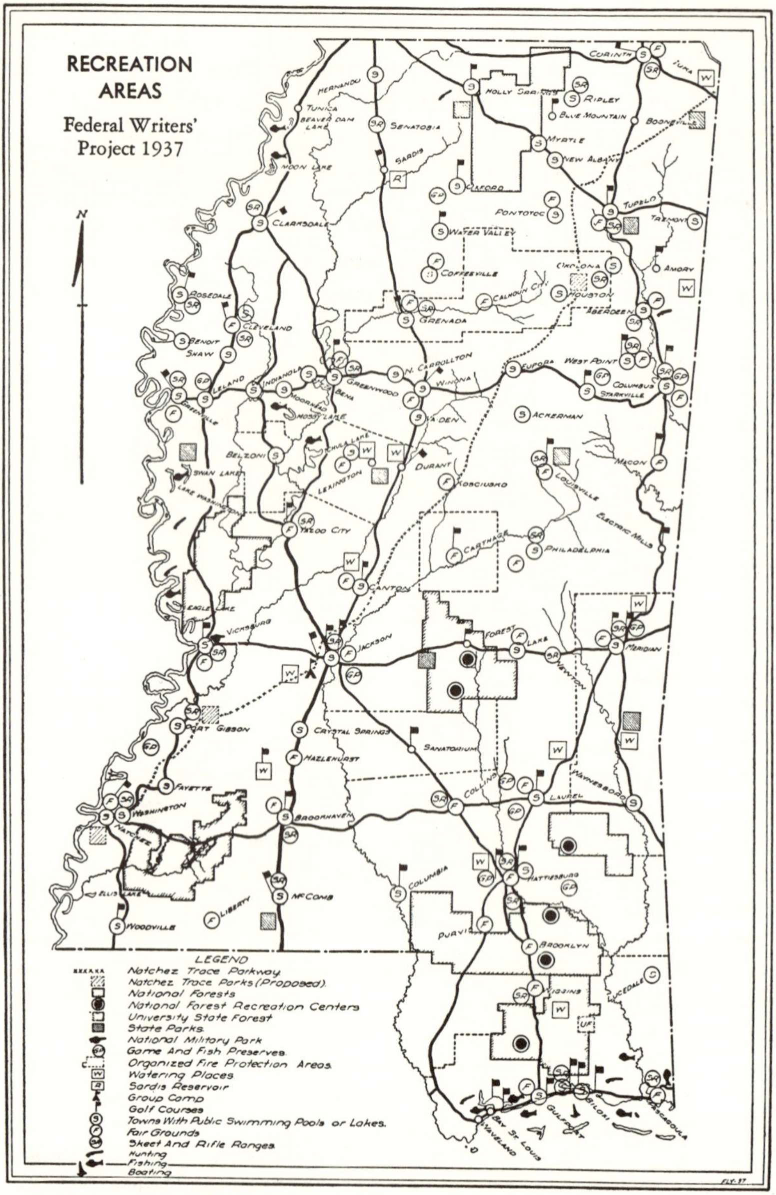
RECREATION
AREAS
Federal Writers'
Project 1937
N
Hernando
Tunica
Senatobia
Sardis
Holly Springs
Corinth
Iuka
Ripley
Blue Mountain
Booneville
Myrtle
New Albany
Oxford
Moon Lake
Clarksdale
Pontotoc
Tupelo
Tremont
Water Valley
Coffeeville
Okolona
Amory
Houston
Rosedale
Cleveland
Grenada
Aberdeen
Benoit
Shaw
West Point
Columbus
Starkville
Leland
Indianola
Greenwood
Winona
Eupora
Greenville
Moorhead
Belzoni
Durant
Ackerman
Macon
Lexington
Kosciusko
Louisville
Yazoo City
Electric Mills
Carthage
Philadelphia
Canton
Vicksburg
Jackson
Forest
Lake
Newton
Meridian
Port Gibson
Crystal Springs
Sanatorium
Hazlehurst
Fayette
Washington
Natchez
Brookhaven
Collins
Laurel
Waynesboro
Hattiesburg
McComb
Columbia
Liberty
Woodville
Purvis
Brooklyn
Wiggins
Lucedale
Gulfport
Biloxi
Pascagoula
Bay St Louis
Waveland
LEGEND
Natchez Trace Parkway
Natchez Trace Parks (Proposed)
National Forests
National Forest Recreation Centers
University State Forest
State Parks
National Military Park
Game And Fish Preserves
Organized Fire Protection Areas
Watering Places
Sardis Reservoir
Group Camp
Golf Courses
Towns With Public Swimming Pools or Lakes
Fair Grounds
Skeet And Rifle Ranges
Hunting
Fishing
Boating

woods. Here throughout the summer are some of the most vividly plumaged of the State's smaller birds—the prothonotary and hooded warblers, and the indigo bunting, as well as the drab-colored and little known Swainson's warbler. In the larger stretches of timbered swamp, wild turkeys survive in fair numbers, and rumor suggests the presence of the ivory-billed woodpecker, a bird considered almost extinct and, if present, the rarest species in the State. The slightly smaller but almost as impressive pileated woodpecker is fairly plentiful, and while wary and difficult to approach is not an uncommon sight in the hardwood timber forests.

In the Delta, the dickcissel, the painted bunting, the bronzed grackle and, rarely, the cowbird build their nests. The painted bunting, a surprising yet harmonious combination of green, blue, yellow, and red, fortunately can be seen without undue difficulty throughout the summer.

Archeology and Indians

Archeology

Though lack of evidence has made it impossible to establish a basis for a chronology of prehistoric sites, and there is no evidence that any of the Folsom people lived in Mississippi, the State is rich in aboriginal remains in the form of mounds and village sites. The mounds—a part of the mound builder complex that extended up the entire Mississippi Valley and eastward along the Ohio—are composed of earth and vary in size from scarcely perceptible swellings of the ground to great hillocks 50 to 60 feet high with crowns one-fifth of an acre in extent. Nanih Waiya, the sacred mound of the Choctaw, has a base 218 feet by 140 feet and is 22 feet in height *(see Tour 12)*. The giant, only partly artificial, Selsertown Mound is a rectangular pyramid about 600 feet long and 400 feet broad, covering nearly 6 acres of ground *(see Tour 3, Sec. b)*.

The triple demands of custom, occasion, and need dictated the Indian's purpose in building these mounds. Those situated along the Mississippi River (erected on hills and bluffs) were used for signal towers and dwelling sites. There is a theory also that the tallest of these were artificial islands upon which the Indians climbed for refuge when the Mississippi and its lower tributaries overflowed. In this same section, at Phillip in Leflore County, long irregular embankments parallel the Tallahatchie River with the ends abutting on the banks of small bayous. These earth walls, according to Dr. Calvin S. Brown (archeologist of the Mississippi State Geological Survey), probably were used for fortifications. Farther south, one-half mile from the union of Lake George and Sunflower River, in the historic country of the Yazoo, lies a great fortified village site. Surrounded by an earth wall, 25 mounds here cluster about the central or main mound, which rises 55 or 60 feet to command a view of the whole fortification. The main mound is approximately square, with a base covering one and three-fourths acres and a summit area of one-fifth of an acre. This impressive group, known as Mound Place, is a work of such magnificence that archeologists maintain it should be surveyed, mapped, and preserved for future generations.

(The above-mentioned mounds are only several of the outstanding; for additional data and locations, see *Tour 3, Tour 4, Tour 12,* and *Side Tour 3A.*)

Within recent years, Dr. Brown and Moreau Chambers (curator of State archives and State field archeologist) have done much to bring the life of the primitive Indian to light. Many implements and objects of polished stone and chipped flint have been found. Of these implements the grooved ones are called axes, and the smooth or ungrooved ones, celts. Stone hoes, spades, mortars, pestles, bowls, cups, plates, nails, troughs, and other agricultural and domestic utensils are additional evidence of the aborigines' progress. The best collections are the exhibits in the New Capitol, Jackson; the Butler collection of Yazoo County; the Chapman collection, Columbus; the Ticer and the Brown collections, Oxford; and the Barringer collection, Monroe, Louisiana.

The term discoidal stone is applied to a large variety of circular stones. Some of them are concave on both faces, some are convex, some are flat on one side, and others are variously modified. They are popularly called chunkey, or chunky, stones because of the game in which they were used by the Indians. Other artifacts of this class are canoe-shaped boatstones, spuds, heads, banner stones, and animal representations with faces and figures. These are found in the museums and private collections previously named and in the Clark collection at Clarksdale.

The pipe or calumet was of great ceremonial importance to the Indian. It was smoked at the ratification of treaties, at marriages, at declarations of war, and at other important social and political events. These pipes varied in size, shape, and workmanship, and were made of fragile clay unadorned, of pottery, of sandstone, limestone, and other stone. Among the most elaborate pipes found in Mississippi is one unearthed in Jefferson County, the bowl of which is decorated with a seated human figure 5.4 inches high. The figure is holding a pipe in his hands, his chin resting upon the bowl just below the rim. A stone pipe, remarkable in design and carving, found in Yazoo County, shows a naked savage seated with hands resting on knees and legs folded under the body. Two steatite pipes with figures carved on the stems, one from Natchez and one from Jefferson County, are now in the University of Pennsylvania collection. In the Millsaps College collection at Jackson is a more recent pipe made in the form of a tomahawk.

An abundance of shells, both marine and fresh-water, were available to the Indian of Mississippi. Along the coast and the large rivers, shell mounds or refuse heaps accumulated. Shell was a favorite material for the manufacture of beads. In the early Colonial days shell money was used in trade with the Indians; the beads were both circular and fist shaped. The circular type can be seen in the Butler collection, now in the museum at the New Capitol. In the Clark collection at Clarksdale are many of the flat type that were uncovered in a mound in Coahoma County.

The Indians used bone, tooth, stag horn, tortoise shell, and other hard animal parts in manufacturing implements and ornaments. Projectile points and piercing implements were often made of bone and stag horn and many of these have been preserved, a number of them in the collection at the Capitol.

With the possible exception of the pipes, the pottery shows the art of the Mississippi Indians at its best. The Davies collection and the State collection display the finest examples.

Indians

In 1699, when D'Iberville planted his colony on the Gulf coast and began to push slowly up the winding rivers, the territory now Mississippi was the center of an Indian population conservatively estimated at 25,000 to 30,000. Of these the three largest groups were the Chickasaw, the Natchez, and the Choctaw tribes, each a member of the great Muskhogean linguistic family, yet characteristically different. The Chickasaw, who preferred war to farming and whose territory extended northward through western Tennessee and into Kentucky, had their principal villages along

48 MISSISSIPPI: THE GENERAL BACKGROUND

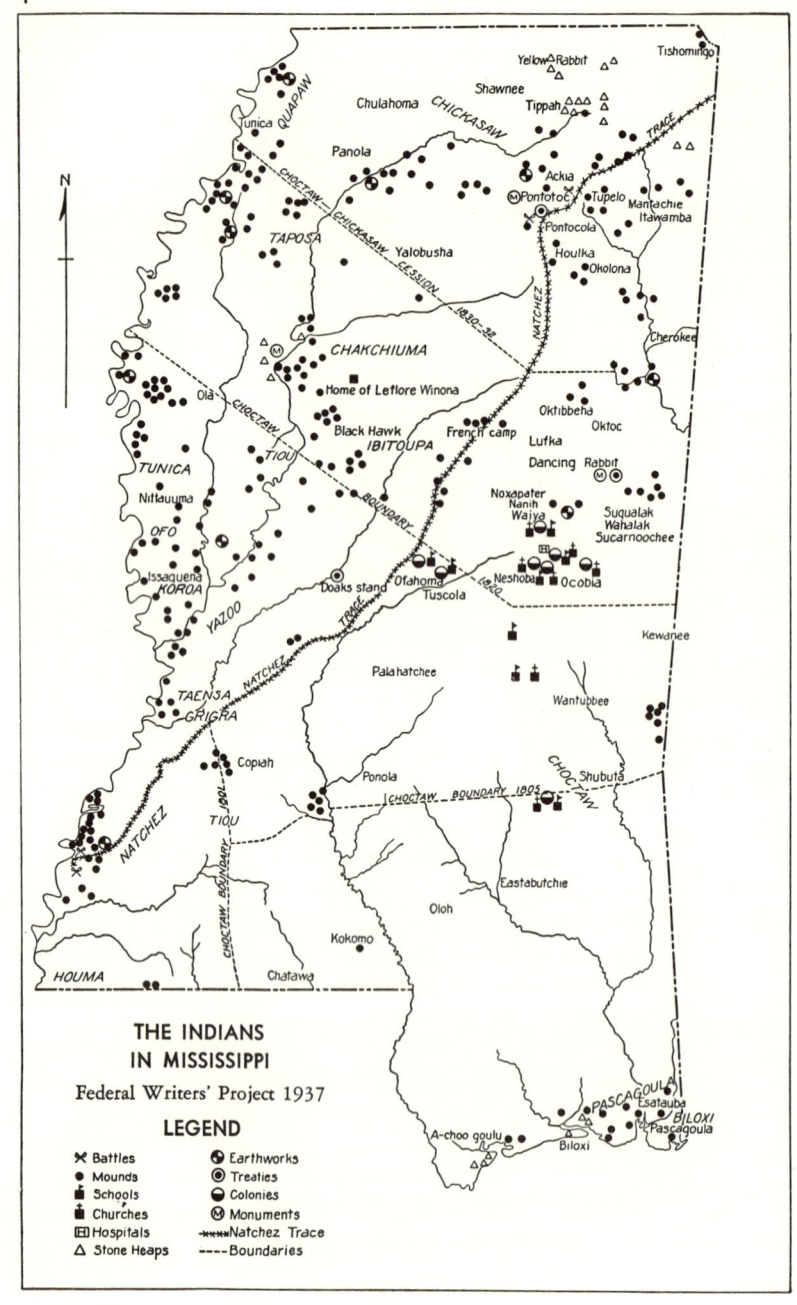

THE INDIANS
IN MISSISSIPPI
Federal Writers' Project 1937
LEGEND
✗ Battles   ⊕ Earthworks
● Mounds   ⊙ Treaties
▪ Schools   ● Colonies
▪ Churches   Ⓜ Monuments
🏥 Hospitals   ×××× Natchez Trace
△ Stone Heaps   ---- Boundaries

the Pontotoc Ridge in what are now Pontotoc, Chickasaw, and Lee Counties. The Natchez lived on the lower Mississippi in what is now Adams County, and the Choctaw, largest of all Mississippi tribes, occupied the southern half of the State, plus an adjacent part of Alabama *(see Indian Map)*. Dr. John R. Swanton, foremost authority on the southwestern Indians, says that the Choctaw seem to have enjoyed an enviable position. They loved war less than truth and truth less than oratory, and were slow in all things save horticulture and diplomacy. Like the meek, they were slowly inheriting the earth because their neighbors could not compete with them economically.

Three smaller and less important members of the Muskhogean family, the Chakchiuma, the Ibitoupa, and the Taposa, dwelt on the upper Yazoo River, unhappily between the Chickasaw and Choctaw, two traditional enemies; while the Pascagoula and the Acolopissa, both of whom are believed to have been closely related to the Choctaw, lived on the Pascagoula and Pearl Rivers respectively. On the lower Yazoo, in the west central part of the State, were the Tunica, Yazoo, Koroa, Tiou, and Grigra tribes, formerly considered a separate stock but now united by ethnologists with the Chitimacha of Grand Lake and Bayou Teche, Louisiana, and the Atakapa between Vermillion Bayou and Galveston, Texas. The great Siouan or Dakotan family, later to play an important part in the winning of the West, was represented in Mississippi by the Biloxi, a small tribe dwelling on the Gulf coast, and the Ofo, called Ofogoula or Dog People by the French, who lived to the north on the Yazoo. In 1699 the Biloxi, who called themselves Teneka Haya or First People, met Iberville and helped him establish the earliest permanent settlement of the colony of Louisiana near the city that now bears their name.

These tribes seem to have belonged to a broad-headed people of a light mahogany complexion and with black hair and eyes. The men, with perhaps the Choctaw excepted, were remarkable examples of physical perfection. Claiborne, early Mississippi historian, says of them, "They were tall, well developed, active, with classic features and intellectual expressions; they were grave, haughty, deliberate and always self-possessed." The Natchez, according to Charlevoix and Dumont, stood six feet or more in height, and Gayarre adds, "There was not a man among them who was either overloaded with flesh, or almost completely deprived of this necessary appendage to the body." The average height among the Choctaw was about five feet six inches. But, undoubtedly, the Choctaw custom of flattening their heads by securing bags of sand to the soft skulls of infant male children partly accounts for this disparity in height.

Neither the ethnologists nor the early chroniclers agree concerning the women. But considering the state of degradation in which they were kept and the hard labor to which they were subjected, it is not surprising that the Indian maidens, however small and beautifully formed, with sparkling eyes and long black hair, lost their charm while young and were deteriorated utterly by middle age.

From an economic point of view all the tribes were basically the same. All of them had once been forced by economic necessity to live along the Gulf coast, but an acquired knowledge of planting enabled many to move inland. Here they established settlements behind earth-wall fortifications or, in the bayou-ribbed western section of the State, near tall artificial mounds. In the winter they hunted; in spring and summer they planted their fields and fished. After winter hunting trips, which sometimes carried them to Ohio and the Carolinas, they returned to their settlements in the spring to plant their fields. Fish, small game animals, roots, berries, and the like served for food until the early corn was ripe; then the early corn carried them until July or August when late or flour corn was ready to eat. From then until autumn the products of the field, supplemented by small game and fish, rendered life comparatively easy. This was a season of relaxation and plenty during which most of the ceremonies took place, particularly those of a social nature, and much of the manufacturing was done; baskets, textiles, wooden and horn objects, pipes, and other articles were produced both for home consumption and trade. In late November the Indians once more scattered to hunt until planting time. On the coast the Pascagoula and Biloxi, who benefited by the spring run of fish, stopped their hunting early to establish themselves near fish weirs until planting time.

The Natchez and other tribes built compact, fort-like villages, with the huts facing a central square. In the squares of the Chakchiuma stood tall poles on which they hung scalps, beads, bones, and other articles, some of which made a queer whistling sound in the wind. This sound, their prophets said, was a voice telling them a Choctaw or Chickasaw was killing a Chakchiuma—so a party would go on the warpath, kill the first Choctaw or Chickasaw they met, and hang his scalp on the pole. They then waited for another passage of the wind.

The Chickasaw built long one-street towns that were in reality a series of distinct villages. One of these, Long Town, was composed of seven villages strung along a ridge. Red Grass was fortified with pickets, and was the scene of young D'Artaguiette's defeat when he came down from Canada to join Bienville in 1736 *(see Tour 12)*. It was also the impregnability of these unfriendly Chickasaw towns that stood between the French of Louisiana and the French of the Ohio and prevented them from uniting in a solid front against the westward-moving English settlers.

The Choctaw built their barrier towns compact like those of the lesser tribes. But their inland settlements, where they carried on their farming, resembled extensive plantations with the cabins a gunshot distance from each other.

Indian cabins were made of rough-hewn posts chinked with mud, bark, and, in the lowlands, Spanish moss. The roofs were of cypress or pine bark, or of intermingled grass and reeds. These roofs were so skilfully woven they lasted 20 years without leaking. A hole usually was left in the top of the cabin to let out the smoke (fires being built in the center of the cabins), but there were no windows and only one door, an opening about three or four feet high and two feet wide. Inside the cabins the walls were lined with cane beds that were covered with bison skins and used during the day as tables and chairs.

Land was cleared for planting by burning the underbrush and smaller growth, while the trees were girdled and left to die. For implements the Indians used a stone, a crude hoe made of a large shell or the shoulder blade of a bison, and a stick to make holes for planting the seed. The Choctaw, who took their farming seriously and who often had to supply their enemy, the Chickasaw, with corn, erected small booths near their farms and stationed young people in them to drive away the crows. But even the Choctaw were forced to labor by hand, for the Indians had no domesticated animals to toil for them.

The staple crop was corn, with beans, pumpkins, melons, and, sometimes, sunflowers planted with it. Tobacco was raised as a luxury for the men only. *Tom-ful-la (tafula)* or "big hominy" was the standard dish. Another dish, *bota kapusi* or "cold meal," was a favorite because of its sustaining qualities in times of war and famine. This parched corn flour would keep without spoiling as long as it was dry, and a man could travel a week on a quart of it. For smoking, the men mixed their tobacco weed with the dried leaf of either the aromatic sumac or the sweetgum, thus giving it a mellow, and, some chroniclers say, delightful flavor.

In prehistoric times the most important game animal was the deer, but later the bison attained greater importance. (The bison is supposed to have been driven out of Mississippi by a great drought in the early 1700's, but the Biloxi, more given to romance, declared that it was not a drought but the Most Ancient of Rabbits, who drove them angrily out of his realm.) The Choctaw considered the ribs and liver of a bear a luxury, but among the tribes in general this animal was hunted more for the seasoning quality of its fat than for its flesh. Venison and turkey meat were stewed with bear oil and served with corn cakes and a beverage of acidulate honey and water; or a slice of venison, a slice of turkey, and a slice of bear meat were placed on a stick and barbecued in a position which forced the bear fat to drip over the turkey and venison, giving them a high seasoning. Gayarré, a French historian, rapt in his appreciation of culinary art, muses over the fact that the Natchez "never could be persuaded to eat of the skilfully made dishes of the French because they were afraid of the ingredients which entered into their composition. They never ate salads or anything raw or uncooked except ripe fruits, and they never could relish wine." Their relish for brandy, however, was keen and they looked down on the French for mixing it with water. Herring and sturgeon (both now extinct on the coast), alligators, crawfish, and shellfish also were eaten.

Unindustrialized and left free to eat according to the promptings of their stomachs, the Indians had no fixed hours for meals. They ate when they pleased and never together. The only exception to this was when a feast was given. The men then ate by messes, out of a bowl set in the center of the group and with a wooden or horn spoon passed from one to the other. The women and children, sitting apart, followed the same procedure.

Deer were stalked by single hunters, and bears were sought out in their dens, driven to the open by means of fire, and killed as they tried to escape. (Aware of the need of conservation, long before the white men came the Indians established areas in which the bears were allowed to breed unmolested.) Characteristically, the Chickasaw left the small game to the boys, and even the boys would not hunt the beaver. Animals so easily killed were not worthy of a warrior, they said. Fish were caught by hooks, shot with arrows, or speared (often at night with the help of fire). In dry seasons pools left by thin, vapid streams were dragged for fish with nets, or else the fish were stupefied by means of buck-eye, devil's shoestring, or other poisonous plants.

Clothing was made principally of deer and porcupine skins and consisted of a breechcloth for the man and a short skirt for the woman. When traveling they wore moccasins and leggings for protection against briars and bushes. Skins, particularly those of the porcupine, were embroidered with considerable art, the drawings being somewhat Gothic in character, and dyed solid colors "of which they liked best the white, the yellow, the red, and the black; their taste being to use them in alternate strips." (Gayarré.) Cloaks were made of wild-goose or other bird feathers woven into patterns, or, for women particularly, of mulberry bark woven in a down-weaving loom. During very severe weather the tribes in the northern part of the State wore robes of bear or bison skins; but in summer they, like the men and women of the more southerly tribes, went half-naked and barefooted. Except when in mourning, the women quite uniformly wore their hair long, sometimes plaited but more often loose. Men's styles differed with the tribes. The Natchez, for instance, shaved their heads, friar-like, leaving a long, twisted tuft of hair to dangle from the crown down over their left shoulder. To this small feathers were attached. Ornaments were worn in profusion by both sexes and paint was a necessity. Garters, belts, and head bands were woven of bison or opossum hair and ornamented with beads. Shell, bone, and copper beads were used as ear and nose ornaments. From earliest times the Choctaw and Chickasaw made annual raids west of the Mississippi and brought back bars of silver and copper, which they fashioned into ornaments.

The Indian woman about to become a mother retired into the woods alone and in a few hours returned with her child and resumed her work. Immediately after birth the child was carried to a stream and washed, then taken to the hut and placed in a cradle. This cradle was usually two and one-half feet long, eight or nine inches wide, and six inches high. Unlike the modern cradle, its rocking motion was forward and backward like our rocking chairs. Being light, the cradle was placed on the mother's bed at night. If the child were a Choctaw boy, Adair tells us, ". . . part of the cradle where the head reposes was fashioned like a brick-mould." This was to help flatten the child's head. But whatever the tribe or sex Indian children received constant attention, being allowed to suckle as often and as long as they pleased, and having their bodies rubbed with oil each day. The oil rendered the limbs more flexible and prevented the bites of flies and mosquitoes.

With the exception of the Choctaw who feared water, the children of both sexes when three years old were taken each morning, summer and winter, to a nearby stream to bathe. At this time of life they were impressed with the inviolable rule that quarrels and fights would not be tolerated—the penalty for transgression being the shame of having to live for a certain time in utter seclusion. As no Indian, young or old, could endure humiliation, the fear of such disgrace made them so cautious of trespassing on another's rights that the few "penal laws" existing within the tribes seldom had to be enforced.

Male children were taught to hunt and to fight, female children to prepare the food, make the clothing, weave the baskets, mold the pottery, and tend the fields. The boys on reaching their twelfth year were committed to the charge of the oldest men or the Ancients of their respective families, the eldest brother of the mother being preferable among the Choctaw. Under the Ancient's tuition they learned the moral precepts that were to regulate their lives. They also learned to run, jump, wrestle, and practice with the bow. For target practice a bunch of grass about the size of the fist was attached to a stick and shot at, or small animals, such as squirrels and rabbits, were hunted. The boy who proved the most skilful marksman received the preeminent distinction of being styled "Young Warrior." The one next in skill was called "Apprentice Warrior." (It is interesting to note that, similar to a theory growing among educators today, whippings or blows of any kind never were given the Indian boy as corrective measures. Appeals to his pride or shame were resorted to.) The Ancients, whose decisions were supreme, received implicit obedience, and because of this influence the elderly male members of every family were paid the most profound respect.

This marked respect did not extend, however, to the women. "In all assemblies, either public or private, even in the privacy of the family circle, the youngest boy had precedence over the oldest woman"—a circumstance that seems to have produced a docile and timid temperament in the woman. A quarrel between husband and wife would have been regarded as scandalous.

Yet, according to our standards of morality, the unmarried women were extremely profligate. With the Choctaw again excepted, there was a looseness of relations between sexes before marriage that struck the early chroniclers as especially interesting. When a scarcity of food made it necessary for the officers and soldiers of Fort Maurepas to find quarters with the Biloxi and Pascagoula tribes, Penicaut naively remarked that it was "an arrangement which Indian maidens and French soldiers enjoyed alike." In the estimation of the Natchez this profligacy was a merit. ". . . all their women," Gayarre quotes from an unnamed source, "while single, were allowed to sell their favors; and she who acquired the wealthiest marriage portion by this traffic, was looked upon as having the most attraction, and as being far superior to all the females of her tribe." Marriage, however, transformed these professed courtesans into so many Lucretias, both husband and wife becoming patterns of fidelity.

As suggested, the standard was reversed by the Choctaw. Among Claiborne's notes is this observation: Marriage took place early; seduction before marriage rare; adultery more common; divorce frequent.

Marriages were never contracted without the consent of the older members of both families nor were the young people forced into alliances against their will. (Elopement is found in legend only and always with a tragic ending.) But there was an inviolable rule that no man could marry into his own *ikas* or clan. When these clans were established is not known, but every tribe in Mississippi was divided into from three to ten of them with regulations for their perpetuation. "The regulations by which the clans were perpetuated amongst the nations were, first, that no man could marry into his own clan; second, that every child belongs to his or her mother's clan. Among the Choctaw there are two great divisions, each of which is subdivided into four clans; and no man can marry into any of the four clans belonging to his division." (Gallatin: 1830.) The restriction among the other tribes, however, did not extend beyond the clan to which the man belonged.

A Choctaw warrior applied to the maternal uncle of the girl, and they agreed on the price which also was paid to the uncle. Then, on an appointed day, the groom appeared at a designated place to loiter until noon. At that time the bride left the lodge of her parents and, eluding her gathered friends, ran into the adjacent woods. The female friends of the groom immediately gave chase and, if she were anxious for the match, caught her easily and brought her back among the groom's friends. But the groom then would have disappeared. The bride sat down and the friends of both sides threw little presents into her lap, while female relatives tied beads in her hair. When this ceremony was over she was conducted to a hut adjoining that of her parents and here the groom sought her that night. At sunrise they were man and wife.

The Chickasaw warrior who had been accepted painted his face and went to the house of the bride's parents, where she met him at the door. Inside, among parents and relatives, the youth presented her with a piece of venison and she gave him an ear of corn. Then he repaired to her bed for the night. But the Natchez, in their Athenian-like way, had a more formal ceremony. When a marriage was to take place among them the two families met at the house of the groom and the young couple stood before the oldest man to hear the duties they were about to assume. After the vows—strangely like Christian promises—were taken, the husband escorted his wife to his bed, saying, "Here is our bed; keep it undefiled."

Polygamy was tolerated by the Choctaw and the Natchez. In each tribe, however, a marriage endured only according to the inclination of the parties concerned. Either could dissolve it at pleasure. When this occurred, as it often did, the children went with the mother, and the father no longer had control over them.

Curiously, the most powerful and populous tribe, the Choctaw, was also the most peaceful and democratic. Their chiefs attained their position through merit alone and then were hardly more than counselors. The warlike Chickasaw, who never numbered more than 5,000 warriors, were controlled by a form of military aristocracy, while the power of the Biloxi and Ofo chiefs varied, some being very feeble. The Natchez, perhaps at once the most civilized and the most barbaric tribe in the South, set up an absolute monarchy, their chief claiming descent on the female side from the sun.

The Great Sun of the Natchez, whose person was sacred and mandates absolute, lived a retired life in the "great village" on St. Catherine's Creek (Adams County). His house, the dimensions of which were all about 30 feet, stood on a mound fronting the village square. The door faced the east, so that the Great Sun might greet the first morning beams of his celestial brother with a prolonged howl and three puffs of his calumet, then wave his hand from east to west, to show the sun its daily path. The mother of the Great Sun bore the title of Woman Chief, and though she did not meddle in the government she held the power of life and death and was paid great honor. The royal family and members of the nobility were forbidden to marry among their equals, a prohibition that proved revolting to the pride of many. It was the offensiveness of this law that led a female Sun (Princess) to propose marriage through her mother to Du Pratz, a nobleman, hoping to bring about a revolution in the social system of her nation. Another female Sun was called the Proud because, rebelling against this law, she refused to sell her favors to any save the nobility.

Like the Peruvians the Natchez had two languages, one reserved for the "stinkards," or lower classes, the other for the nobles and the women. Both languages were very rich yet there was no similarity between them. The women spoke the language of the nobles with an affected pronunciation totally different from that of the men. The French, who seem to have associated more with the women than with the men, took the women's pronunciation—thus provoking the rebuke to one of them from a Sun: "Since thou hast the pretension to be a man, why dost thou lisp like a woman?"

A majority of the tribes believed in a Supreme Being or Great Spirit of the Universe but they had no particular notion of his character and, with the exception of the Natchez, no set form of worship. The Natchez, different in religion as in everything else, worshipped the sun. The sun, they believed, was a male spirit who had molded the first man. Their ideas of woman's creation were indefinite. One legend is that a short time after the first man was made, he was taken with a violent fit of sneezing and something in the shape of a woman, as big as his thumb, bolted from his nose. On falling to the ground it began to dance around and around, growing larger and larger until at last it grew into the actual size and shape of a woman. That evil spirits abounded, they were well aware. They tried to placate them by fasting and praying. When the Natchez wanted rain or fair weather, they fasted. But in either case the Great Sun abstained for nine days from meat and fish, living on nothing but a little boiled corn. During this time he also took particular care not to communicate in any way with his wives.

The temple of the great village, where the Great Sun resided, was near St. Catherine's Creek on a mound said to be eight feet high. The door of the temple, like the door of the chief's house, faced the east. In the largest room was an altar six feet long, two feet wide, and four feet high, and on it a reed basket containing the bones of the preceding Great Sun. It was here before the sacred fire that the Great Sun, who was also high priest by virtue of his kinship to the sun, officiated. Only those of royal blood, or such visitors as the Sun considered sufficiently distinguished, could enter this room. The stinkards were not permitted to enter any part of the temple. In the smaller room were sundry small objects which the Indians seem never to have explained to the white men. On the roof of the temple sat three wooden birds twice the size of a goose, with their feathers painted white and sprinkled with red. These birds faced east toward the rising sun.

Like all people who place credence in spirits the Indians were superstitious. They believed in witches and ghosts and were afraid to travel alone at night. So, quite naturally, they had, as a privileged caste, the rain maker and the medicine man. The medicine man interpreted dreams, charmed away spells, and healed the sick; the rain maker in periods of protracted drought saved the crops and the water supply by bringing rain. The method of the medicine man in curing a patient was to roll him in a blanket and, bending over him, suck the painful spot. If sucking, kneading, pounding, and growling did no good and the patient grew worse and died, the doctor declared that some malicious witch had interfered to defeat his purpose. The relatives of the dead man then would formally demand the witch be pointed out, and after several days of apparent thought the doctor would indicate some old, decrepit woman who, without formality, would be put to death.

The rainmaker enjoyed the privilege of being paid in advance. He always gave the Indians to understand that spirits did no business on credit, and, as he was never called on until the crops were burning and the supply of water was exhausted, the Indians were rarely in a position to haggle over terms. Yet if he failed—and he sometimes did—he did not attribute his failure to witchcraft as did the doctor, but said that he himself was to blame. He was *na-koo-a* (angry), he explained, and the credulous Indians then desperate, would beg to know what could be done to restore his good humor. But he, still posing as too angry to talk, would seclude himself and wait until the signs of a change in weather appeared. When the signs appeared he suddenly would come out into the village square and tell the Indians that if they doubled his fee the rain would come. They, glad to propitiate his anger, brought even more than he demanded, and soon the rain came as he had promised.

The Choctaw separated the flesh from the bones of their deceased and preserved them, at first in a mortuary, then in a mound constructed for this purpose. The Chickasaw buried their dead in the earth, often under the flooring of the lodge itself. The body of a Biloxi or Pascagoula was placed in a coffin made of reeds and left until nothing but dried bones remained; these then were transferred to a wicker coffer and put away in small temples. When a Natchez chieftain died hundreds of people were sacrificed to pay him honor, these being considered meat and victuals for the deceased.

Pitched battles between tribes were seldom fought. Warfare with them consisted mostly in ambuscades and surprises. But even so prudent a type of battle failed to ward off devastating defeats. A well-aimed blow cunningly delivered often all but annihilated a nation, at which time the nation applied through ambassadors to a neutral nation for protection. If the protection were granted, they abandoned their own territory and merged with the nation that had become a sort of foster parent to them. And this was the fate of all the Mississippi tribes but two, the Choctaw and the Chickasaw.

The most progressive of the tribes was the first to go. The French coveted Natchez lands and demanded from them the site of their principal village, White Apple. For this reason the tribe agreed upon a general massacre of the French. The butchery began in November 1729, and 250 victims fell the first day. French forces under Le Seur soon retaliated, however, and in January 1730, surprised the Natchez village, liberated the captives, losing but two of their own men. This was followed by another victory in February that scattered the Natchez tribe. Some fled westward and some were sold as slaves, the Great Sun among them, and the Natchez tribe no longer existed.

The Tunicas were defeated in 1763, and in 1817 the entire tribe emigrated to Louisiana where they intermarried with both the French and the Negro. The Yazoo, like the Natchez, were practically annihilated by the French, following an Indian massacre in 1729. The Biloxi, Pascagoula, and some of the Six Town Choctaw, who had a strong attachment for the French, followed them into Louisiana about 1764. The Chakchiuma were practically exterminated by the combined forces of Choctaw and Chickasaw tribes, who had grown weary of the former tribe's continued thieving. The few Chakchiuma who remained merged with the Chickasaw Nation in 1836.

From 1776, when English rule was challenged by the North American Colonies, the history of the Chickasaw and Choctaw tribes is one of steadily giving way before advancing white settlement and steadily increasing friction. The end was the removal of the Indians to the West between 1832 and 1834.

In 1801 treaties between the United States and the Chickasaw Nation gave the Government the right-of-way on the Natchez Trace, and in 1805 the Choctaw surrendered their south Mississippi lands. This act was the beginning of the end. A little more than a quarter of a century later neither the Chickasaw nor the Choctaw held any possessions east of the Mississippi River. The year 1820 saw the Treaty of Doak's Stand; the Treaty of Washington came in 1826; and in 1830 the Choctaw chieftains signed the Treaty of Dancing Rabbit Creek. This treaty removed all but a small portion of this nation to what is now Oklahoma. On October 20, 1832, the Treaty of Pontotoc was signed between the Chickasaw Nation and the United States. By this treaty the Chickasaw ceded all their possessions in Mississippi and east of the Mississippi River and allowed themselves to be moved to Oklahoma. It is to be noted, however, that in Oklahoma the Chickasaw and the Choctaw formed well-defined and stable governments. The descendants of the 3,000 Choctaw of pure blood who refused to leave Mississippi still till the soil of their ancestors *(see Tour 12)*.

The State in the Making

An Outline of Four Centuries

Nearly a century before the *Mayflower* anchored at Plymouth Rock in 1620, Mississippi's history began. Spanish treasure ships linking the western hemisphere to the dynastic empire of Charles V made the Caribbean and the Gulf of Mexico a Spanish Main.

In 1528 Panfilo de Narvaez, armed with a grant from Charles V, landed in Florida. Before the year was out the leader of the expedition—his ships scattered and his following reduced—vanished into a Gulf storm; there were few survivors. The expedition of Nunez Beltran Guzman two years later fared little better. Guzman failed to discover the fabulous "seven cities of Cibola," said to lie far north of Mexico City. But rumors of vast treasures and wonderful people tempted the monk, Marcos de Niza, in 1539; and Estevan, his Negro scout, actually sighted a formidable pueblo of the Zuni.

In the next year, Mendoza, Viceroy of Mexico, sent Francisco Vasquez de Coronado, with a strong force of soldiers and friendly Indians, to take possession of the northern land, and, more particularly, of its portable riches. Coronado found little he could carry away, and spent himself in searching farther to the north, or northeast—even to the valley of the Platte River—for Quivera, where he hoped to find a rich city. He found merely a pastoral Indian village. Bitterly disappointed, Coronado, in 1541, turned southward, apparently by the route that was to become the Santa Fe Trail.

Roaming in the interior at the same time, in a vain search for gold, was another Spanish expedition, headed by De Soto. In the summer of 1541 the Coronado and De Soto parties seemed to be within a few days' march of each other; and Coronado, suspecting this, sent a messenger to find De Soto. But he was unsuccessful.

De Soto comes more directly into Mississippi history. Of all the explorers of that period, he, probably, was the only one to enter the region now within the State.

AN OUTLINE OF FOUR CENTURIES 61

Hernando (Fernando) de Soto, of gentle birth but needy, had accompanied Pizarro to Peru in 1531. Together, they had plundered the rich empire of the Incas. A few years later, De Soto, now a gentleman of renown and possessed of vast wealth, appeared at the Spanish court "with the retinue of a nobleman." When he asked for permission to undertake the conquest of Florida at his own expense, King Charles V readily acquiesced, commissioning him also as Governor of Cuba, and captain-general of any provinces he might conquer.

After wandering through the wilds of what are now the States of Florida, Georgia, and Alabama, he entered Mississippi in 1540. Somewhere below the site of Memphis, Tennessee, he discovered the Mississippi River in May 1541. After veering westward, De Soto, dejected and near death, returned to the river; and upon its banks he died, May 21, 1542. His body was buried in the waters that were to give him immortality, close to the present site of Natchez.

After De Soto, the primeval country was not disturbed until the 17th century. In 1673, Father Marquette and the trader Joliet, inspired by the ambition of Louis XIV, descended the Mississippi River from the mouth of the Wisconsin River to a point below the mouth of the Arkansas River —"from the latitude of 42° to 34°" as Marquette's own narrative has it. Their voyage prepared the way for Robert Cavelier, Sieur de la Salle, who in 1682 followed the course of the Mississippi to its mouth and, in a sweeping gesture, claimed the whole valley for France. In rapid succession, Hennepin, Cadillac, and Tonti, among others, made further explorations on the river.

It was Pierre le Moyne, Sieur d'Iberville, however, who founded the first permanent white colony in the lower Mississippi Valley. Iberville, having urged upon the French court the importance of taking possession of La Salle's "Louisiana" and of finding an entrance to the Mississippi from the sea, left Brest on October 24, 1698, with a commission from Louis XIV to occupy Louisiana. Accompanying him were nearly 200 colonists, with whose aid in 1699 he established Fort de Maurepas at what is now Ocean Springs. This settlement *(see Tour 1)* was the seat of government for a territory that extended eastward to present-day Pittsburg and westward to the present Yellowstone National Park.

Before La Salle's explorations had established France's claims to the Mississippi Valley, however, this region had been included in the so-called Carolina Grant made in 1629–30 to Sir Robert Heath by King Charles I of England. In 1633 it was included in the Charles II grant to Clarendon, Carteret, and others. Eventually a London physician, Coxe, put forth pre-

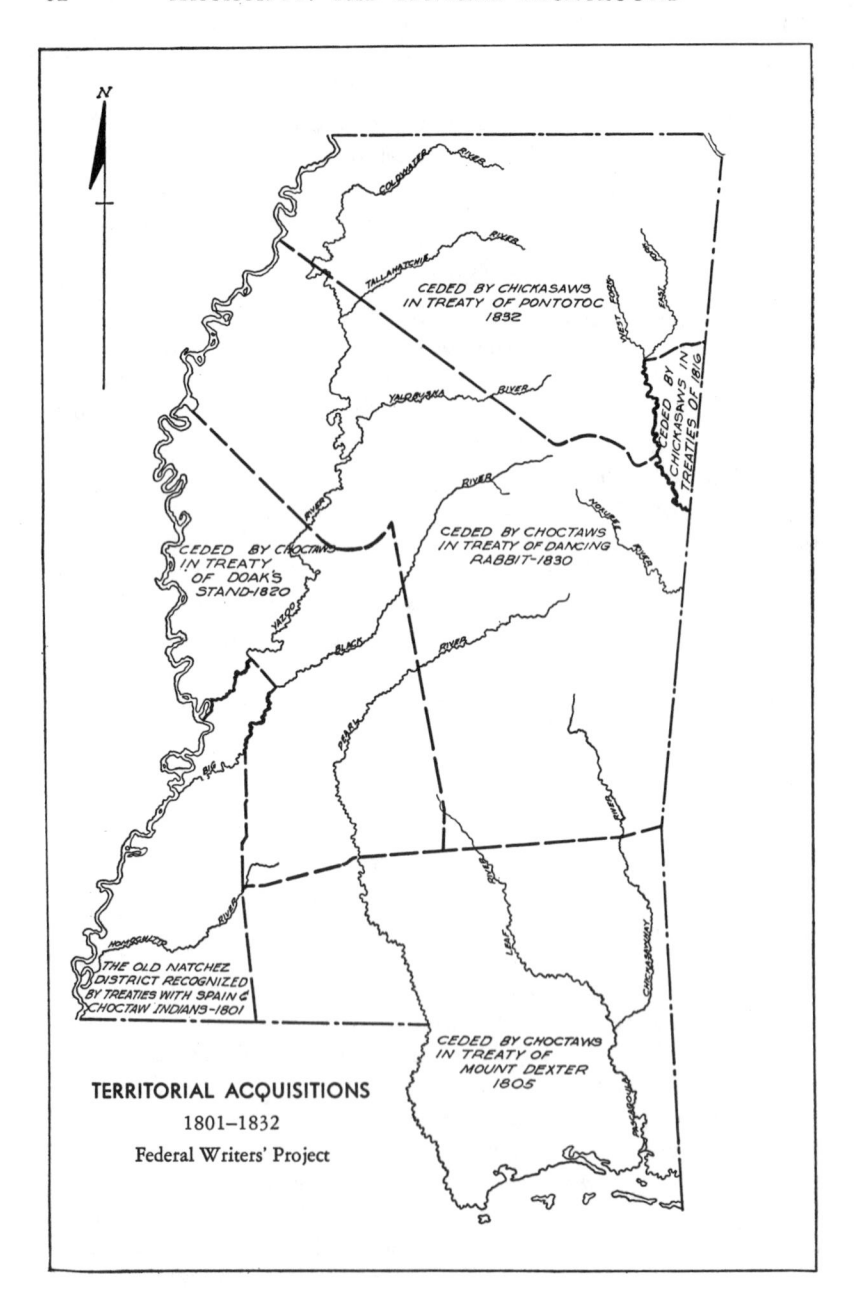

TERRITORIAL ACQUISITIONS
1801–1832
Federal Writers' Project

AN OUTLINE OF FOUR CENTURIES

tensions to the mouth of the Mississippi, which two English vessels were sent to explore. But in September 1699, Jean Baptiste Le Moyne, Sieur de Bienville, brother of Sieur d'Iberville, encountered one of these English ships about fifty miles from the mouth of the Mississippi. Assured that this was not the Mississippi but a dependency of Canada belonging to the French, the English commander left the river and the early colonization of the region to the French. The point where this encounter occurred has since been known as English Turn.

In 1702, England having declared war on France, the French King gave orders to Iberville to build a fort on the Mobile River and to remove the Fort Maurepas colony thence. Thus, in case of trouble with the English who were moving westward from the Carolinas, the French settlers would be near their Spanish friends at Fort Pensacola. The seat of government was removed eighteen leagues up the river to the new fort, named Louis de la Mobile, and the first white family arrived there in May 1702. In 1711 the settlement of Mobile was inundated, causing the removal of colonists to the present Mobile.

Biloxi, however, was not abandoned. From this settlement Iberville and Bienville penetrated the surrounding country, establishing trading posts and forts, among which was Fort Rosalie founded on the bluffs of Natchez in 1716. In 1704 twenty or more young women destined for marriage with the colonists landed at Mobile and Ship Island—Fort Maurepas' port and outer bulwark. This was the first of several shipments of "Casket Girls," French orphans and peasants who came voluntarily to the New World as prospective wives for the settlers. Each girl brought with her a small "dot" and a chest containing a trousseau provided by the government.

On September 14, 1712, Louisiana was temporarily assigned by Louis XIV to a great French merchant and financier, Anthony Crozat, Marquis de Chatel. It has been said that "Never in the history of the world was such a magnificent domain, even temporarily, placed in the sole keeping of one man." For a term of 15 years Crozat was granted a monopoly of the trade of Louisiana. To assist and abet his agents, the troops in the colony were placed at his disposal. All the shipping in the colony was his, on condition that it be replaced at the end of his term. Yet "Crozat never came to Louisiana"; and it must not be thought that Louisiana was a populous territory when turned over to Crozat. There were a few settlements on the Kaskaskia, Wabash, and Illinois Rivers, but the total number of Europeans in the whole territory was only 380.

Though Crozat was in commercial control, Bienville was Acting Governor until March 1717. Approving the site of the New Orleans as the most favorable location for a great commercial center, he agitated for the removal of the capital to that point, though other influences favored Fort Rosalie. The opinion of Bienville prevailed; the village of New Orleans was laid out in 1717 or 1718, and in 1723 the seat of government was moved to the new location.

Despairing of making his Louisiana monopoly profitable, Crozat relinquished his charter to the King in August 1717. In that same year John Law, Scotch adventurer and financier living in France, originated his famous "Mississippi Scheme" to resuscitate French finances, then at low ebb because of the wars of Louis XIV. Louisiana was believed to abound in precious metals, and Law held that by developing the province money would flow into France. In 1717 the *Compagnie des Indes Occidentales,* commonly known as the Mississippi Company, with Law as its director, was chartered and its shares were eagerly bought by the public. For the exclusive privilege of developing Louisiana, the company was obligated to introduce within 25 years 6,000 white colonists and 3,000 Negro slaves. As a result, in 1718 grants for settlement were made on the Yazoo River, on Bay St Louis, Pascagoula Bay, and at Natchez. In 1720 three hundred colonists settled at Natchez; and in the following year the same number, destined for the lands of Mme. de Chaumont, a court favorite, arrived at Pascagoula. In 1722 a company of Germans, settlers on John Law's grant on the Arkansas River, descended the river to a point near New Orleans, where they made a settlement.

In 1718 Law persuaded the Duke of Orleans, regent of France, to charter a national bank, which became the *Banque Royale,* with Law as director-general. When in 1719 the *Compagnie des Indes* absorbed the French East India Company, it marketed a large issue of shares which sold at enormous premiums. The *Banque Royale,* the National Bank, to keep pace with the astounding inflation of the company's stock, flooded the country with paper money. As the stock rose, paper currency to the face value of 2,700,000,000 livres went into circulation. But the expected flow of wealth from Louisiana into France did not materialize.

The French Government became more and more involved in the difficulties of the trading company, while Law gained increasing power over State finances. He controlled the mint, and his companies became the receivers-general of France. In March 1720 the *Compagnie des Indes* was merged with the national bank. A month later John Law, as its head, became comptroller-general of finances. Public confidence began to waver; shrewd financiers began to send their gold to Brussels and

London. A run on the bank caused the government to issue an edict deflating both bank and company stock. Law sought to stave off disaster by forbidding the export of gold and silver, and by making the hoarding of metallic currency a crime. But in July 1720, his great financial empire crumbled. The bank was compelled to stop payment, and Law fled from France. He died in Vienna in 1729.

With the collapse of the "Mississippi Bubble," followed by a devastating storm in the summer of 1723, began a series of troubles that eventually retarded the Louisiana colony. In 1726, Bienville was recalled to France and Perier, a harsh uncompromising character who lacked Bienville's tact in dealing with the Indians, became commander-general of Louisiana. The pressure of the colonists on the Natchez Indians led to the massacre of the French garrison at Fort Rosalie on November 29, 1729. In retaliation, Perier virtually exterminated the Natchez tribe. In 1732, King George II of England extended British claims westward from the Carolina Colonies to the Mississippi River, including a part of Mississippi in the proprietary charter of Georgia. With British support, the warlike Chickasaw tribe blocked French expansion into northern Mississippi; and in a series of wars against the French under the reinstated Bienville, this tribe successfully checked the rising fortunes of the colony. The repulse of the French at Ackia in 1736 was the turning point.

The intrigue of the British with the Chickasaw against the French was but one phase of the contest between France and Great Britain for sovereignty over the far-flung territory from the mouth of the St. Lawrence to the Gulf of Mexico. In 1762, foreseeing defeat in her struggle with England, France ceded to Spain, New Orleans and all of the Louisiana territory west of the Mississippi; and the following year the Treaty of Paris awarded to England all of France's territory east of the Mississippi and north of a little above Baton Rouge, Louisiana. George III thereupon supplanted Louis XV as the ruler of the valley.

The English genius for colonization, which had marked the development of the Atlantic seaboard, was demonstrated also in the settlement of the rich agricultural lands around Natchez. Fort Rosalie under Governor George Johnstone was rebuilt and renamed Panmure. Land grants to retired English army and navy officers, such as the Amos Ogden Mandamus on the Homochitto River *(see Tour 3, Sec. b)*, were the spur to a migration of Protestants, land-loving settlers who contrasted greatly with the Catholic remnants of the French period. When the Thirteen Colonies revolted on the seaboard in 1776, British West Florida (including the Natchez District) remained loyal to the Crown. Its remoteness from the center of action made it a haven for fleeing Royalists; but anxious not to be involved in the conflict, the Natchez District gave a promise of neutrality to James Willing, the representative sent by the American Continental Congress. Willing, however, quickly lost the colonists' respect by stealing sections of their lands and a shipment of supplies.

Spain, taking advantage of British preoccupation with the revolution, re-established its authority in the Gulf country in 1779. Moving up the river, Spanish troops took over Natchez in 1781. But Spanish rule in the Natchez country defeated its own end. Purposely mild to attract emigrants from the new Republic of the United States, it eventually was overthrown by the increasing pro-American sentiment. Protestantism, served by such zealous preachers as Richard Curtis, Samuel Swayze, and Adam Cloud, gained on Catholicism despite the rigid Spanish laws regarding religion.

Although British West Florida had extended north to 32° 28', by the second Treaty of Paris in 1783, England recognized United States' claims south to the 31st parallel. This Spain refused to do. For a period of years, therefore, sovereignty to the land between 31° and 32° 28' was under dispute, Spain claiming it by right of conquest and the United States by right of treaty. To complicate matters further, the State of Georgia also claimed the region by her charter of 1732, even going so far as to organize it into the County of Bourbon in 1785 and to sell it in the notorious "Yazoo Fraud" of 1795. By the treaty of Madrid in 1795 the dispute between the United States and Spain was theoretically settled in favor of the former. But the Spanish took their time in evacuating Natchez; Andrew Ellicott, a Quaker surveyor appointed to run the line of demarcation, was kept waiting a year on this account. When American troops arrived in 1798, the Spanish at last evacuated their posts, and the American flag was officially raised. By act of Congress on April 7, 1798, the Mississippi Territory was created, and the century of Old World dominance had ended. Natchez became the first Territorial capital; but on February 1, 1802, the seat of government was removed six miles east to the town of Washington.

But though the shackles of Europe had fallen from the Territory, it had still to consolidate its position. The labyrinthian complications of disputed sovereignties to the region had been but a surface sign of deeper conflicts which lay inherent in the people who composed its population. On the Gulf Coast were descendants of French settlers; around Natchez was a small but influential group of Englishmen whose allegiance to the Republic was grudging; new settlers, with antecedents in the older Colonies, were independence incarnate. These people, not yet knit into the fabric of American life and economically remote from the seaboard, were divided by old allegiances and easily swayed by the power of a personality. Their only bond was a common hatred of Spain, a hatred intensified when that country, in July 1802, forbade any land grants to American citizens, and in October of the same year closed the port of New Orleans to American goods. Neither the opening of the port in March 1803 nor the Louisiana Purchase a month later, diminished the settlers' common opposition to Spain. When crises arose, the unity of the Territory was maintained not by allegiance to the United States but by an intense distrust of foreigners that acted as a nucleus for policy formation.

Following consummation of the Louisiana Purchase in April 1803, the opening of the Mississippi River, and the cession of western lands by the State of Georgia, a land boom swept Mississippi. On March 3, 1803, Congress passed a measure providing for a survey of the Territory; the surveyor-general's office was established at Washington, Mississippi, with Isaac Briggs as the first incumbent; and, following the traditional national urge for land, people began to pour into Mississippi from the eastern areas, including New England.

An example of anti-Spanish sentiment was the response to Aaron Burr's expedition in 1806. Presented to the residents as a scheme to occupy Spanish territory and perhaps create a new state in the Southwest, Burr's plans were blocked only by the duplicity of James Wilkinson and an alignment of national politics that found President Jefferson taking the role of Burr's chief accuser. However, when Burr surrendered to Mississippi authorities in January 1807, and was awaiting trial at Washington, the Territorial capital, leaders of the community vied with one another for the honor of entertaining him as their guest.

Following the cession of Louisiana in 1803, Spain held the Baton Rouge and Manchac districts, lying between New Orleans and the Natchez district, and also the coast region, formerly under the government of Mobile. All this territory was formerly French Louisiana, and the American Government was making claims to it as a part of the French concession. The Kemper brothers, who then were living near Pinckneyville, initiated the first open and organized rebellion against Spanish authority. The Kemper movement, the plot to capture Mobile, and the operations of Aaron Burr were all connected, and all hastened the actual annexation of the territory to the United States. The Kempers raised the flag of revolu-

MISSISSIPPI IN 1817

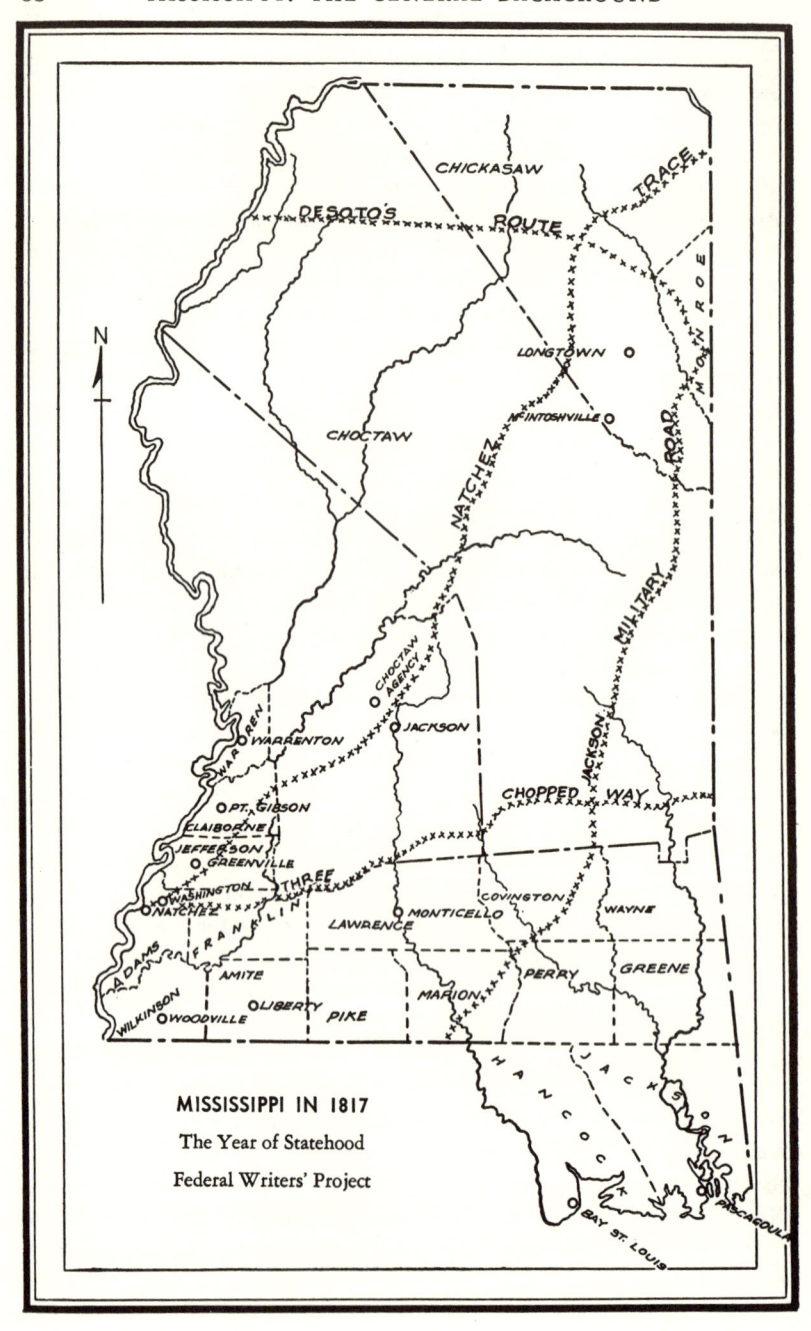

The Year of Statehood

Federal Writers' Project

AN OUTLINE OF FOUR CENTURIES 69

tion in the Baton Rouge district. The United States claimed that under the French title the Sabine River was the western boundary of its territory, and that beyond this stream began the Spanish province of Texas. The Spanish claimed a line east of the Sabine, at the Arroyo Hondo, halfway between Natchitoches and Adeas. In October 1805 small detachments of Spanish troops crossed the Sabine and occupied the Arroyo Hondo line. Under orders from Washington, American troops advanced, and the Spanish retired beyond the Sabine. But late in the summer of 1806, Spanish troops again advanced east of the Sabine. In October General Wilkinson effected a truce, and the Spanish retired beyond the Sabine "pending the negotiations between the United States and Spain." But some time passed and there was still no agreement. The continued occupation of the Baton Rouge district by Spanish authorities was becoming more and more unbearable to the American settler. Throughout much of 1809, border warfare was waged. In the summer of 1810, settlers' meetings at Baton Rouge proposed the adoption of a constitutional government. The Spanish governor sent to Pensacola for reinforcements. The American party gathered its forces and on September 23, 1810, attacked and captured the Spanish fort at St. Francisville. The town of Baton Rouge surrendered, the Spanish troops and civil authorities being allowed to retire to Pensacola.

An American convention immediately assembled, and proclaimed "the Territory of West Florida a free and independent State." A constitution was adopted and a government organized under the name of "the Free State of Florida." On October 11, 1810, the convention applied to the United States for admission as a State into the Union. On October 27, President Madison issued a proclamation empowering Governor Claiborne of the "Territory of New Orleans" to take possession of West Florida. The territory south of Mississippi Territory eastward to Perdido River had been conveyed to the United States as a part of the Louisiana Purchase. Governor Claiborne was instructed that if military forces were needed to establish his jurisdiction in that area they would be supplied. Accompanied by military, the Governor went to Baton Rouge, and by proclamation declared West Florida the "Territory of Orleans." Mobile, not included in this territory, was held by the Spanish until the War of 1812. During that war British alliance with northern Indian tribes under Tecumseh was outmaneuvered by the friendly Choctaw chieftain, Pushmataha. The Creek uprisings brought active service for the Mississippi Militia over a considerable period. The first engagement was the battle at Burnt Corn (then in Mississippi, now in Alabama) on July 17, 1813; and on August 30 a massacre at Fort Mimms shocked the country. Immediately Andrew Jackson organized a company of Tennessee volunteers to avenge the outrage and wage a campaign against the Creek Nation. Fighting with Jackson against the Creeks was the youthful Sam Houston. In 1814 a British fleet overwhelmed a small American force off Bay St. Louis in the last naval engagement of the war; but this defeat was avenged by the victory of New Orleans, in which Mississippi troops played a prominent part.

The same spirit of independence that had shaken off European claims to the territory was manifested in the quarrel between the people and their appointed Territorial governors, the conflict being especially pronounced during the Sargent administration. By 1810 the Territory was clamoring for statehood; and in 1817 the western portion was admitted to the Union by act of Congress on December 10, as the State of Mississippi.

During the Territorial period, when political unity was being achieved, a cotton boom had given the people a basis for economic unity. The high price of cotton and the low price of land drew from the older South (the Piedmont principally) the "Great Migration" that was to complete the settlement of Mississippi and annex it to the cotton kingdom.

The changes wrought by this influx of new people between 1817 and 1832 are politically enshrined in the State constitutions of these years. The first constitution was written by George Poindexter, an exceptionally brilliant lawyer who represented the Whigs of the State, and was a reflection of the conservative if not actually aristocratic character of the Natchez district planters. The convention adopting this constitution assembled July 7, 1817, at the Methodist meeting house in Washington *(see Tour 3, Sec. b)*. Cowles Mead, a Virginian who had migrated from Georgia, proposed that the new State be called Washington. His proposal received 17 votes, as against 23 for the name of Mississippi. By 1832 the State contained many small farmers, Jacksonian Democrats steeped in Jacksonian principles; and the constitution adopted in that year was in many respects the most democratic State constitution of the time. It even provided for an elective judiciary.

The feverish pressure of the immigrants who followed the westward moving cotton boom drove the Indians out of Mississippi. The treaty of Doak's Stand in 1820 opened 5,500,000 acres of Choctaw land to white settlement, and resulted in an immediate influx of population. By 1829, however, only about one-third of the tract had been sold to settlers or speculators; it was claimed that the Indians possessed the "fat of the land." As only about half the land of the State was open to white settlers, many demanded that the Indians yield all their territory and move westward. By the treaty of Dancing Rabbit Creek in 1830, the Choctaw Nation ceded to the United States "the entire country they own and possess east of the Mississippi River; and they agree to move beyond the Mississippi River as early as practicable." In 1832 the Chickasaw ceded their lands in northern Mississippi. These accessions not only rounded out the State geographically, but were evidences of the peculiar nature of the early cotton economy, which made free and easily cultivated land a prerequisite to wealth. One tangible evidence of this wealth was the opening of the State University at Oxford in 1848. Significantly, Oxford was one of the towns that sprang into being almost in the center of the newly acquired lands.

Loyal to King Cotton, Mississippians justified their expansionist sentiments by chivalric military and oratorical exploits in the struggle for Texas independence and admission to the Union. This struggle was climaxed by the War with Mexico in 1846. Robert J. Walker and Henry S. Foote, orators, John A. Quitman and Jefferson Davis, soldiers, were the leading expansionists of the period. These men more than any others kept the slave States on an equality with the North in the race for possession of a continent.

When the election of 1860 forced the issue between union and secession, economic interests molded the political alignments in Mississippi. The older and wealthy families, loath to trust their fortunes to an untried government, were for the Union, and so were the poorer people or yeomanry. The great middle class, however, was for secession. By their numbers, ability, and reckless courage, they swept the Whigs and yeomen with them into withdrawal from the Union. On January 9, 1861, they made Mississippi the second State of the Confederacy.

The fact that Jefferson Davis, a resident of Mississippi, was President of the Confederacy drew the State particularly close to the new government. Lingering doubts as to the righteousness of the southern cause were lost in the roar of cannon that followed the capture of Fort Sumter. The State threw its resources into the war magnificently; at Manassas five regiments of Mississipians participated as units of the Army of Virginia.

During the first year of war, activity in Mississippi was chiefly of a preparatory sort. But the year 1862 brought the war closer home. Union forces concentrated on two primary objectives in the State: Vicksburg and with it, control of the Mississippi River, and the isolation of Mississippi troops from arms and supplies. In April the first military invasion of the State began. After the Federal victory at Shiloh, General Halleck led 100,-000 troops against Corinth, and made northeastern Mississippi a battleground for the remainder of the year. Hard fighting took place at Corinth,

PORTER'S FLEET PASSING THE CONFEDERATE BATTERIES AT VICKSBURG

Iuka, and Holly Springs, with General Grant moving stubbornly southward toward Vicksburg. This prolonged campaign against Vicksburg and the dogged defense of the city were the most important military maneuvers in the State *(see Vicksburg, Holly Springs, Tours 2, 3, 4, and 17)*. After the fall of the city on July 4, 1863, the greater part of the Confederate field forces were transferred to other States, with only cavalry under Generals Stephen D. Lee and Nathan B. Forrest remaining to protect the people from raids and to hamper General Sherman in his march across the State. The devastation brought by this march was summed up by Sherman himself: "The wholesale destruction is terrible to contemplate."

The disruption of normal habits of life caused by the armies in Mississippi is reflected in the hurried and frequent changes of capitals during the war—from Jackson to Enterprise to Meridian, back to Jackson, back to Meridian, thence to Columbus, to Macon, and finally back again to Jackson.

In the four years of war, Mississippi contributed approximately 80,000 men to the Confederate armies, including 5 major generals and 29 brigadier generals. Of the 80,000, fewer than 20,000 were "present or accounted for" on April 2, 1865. The supplies of food and arms provided by the State cannot be estimated. It is significant that the 80,000 Mississippi enlistments were greater than the State's total number of white males between the ages of 18 and 45 cited in the 1860 census. Such an amazing contribution of a State's man-power to war has had few equals in modern times. When hostilities ceased, Mississippi was a ruin.

After the fall of the Confederacy, Governor Charles Clark called a special session of the legislature to meet in Jackson on May 18, 1865. But the legislature had no more than assembled when word came that General Osband, commander of a brigade of Negro troops, had received orders for the members' arrest. The legislature hastily adjourned. General Osband's arrest of Governor Clark on a charge of high treason ushered in the disorder of the Reconstruction Period. This period was so shameful and confused that, for Mississippians, the term "ante bellum" assumed by contrast a halcyon significance that not even the war had given it, and one that clung to it long after the term had lost meaning for the North.

Judge William L. Sharkey, an old-line Whig appointed Provisional Governor by President Johnson, called an election for a constitutional convention, the first to meet in the South under the President's reconstruction policy. The convention, meeting in August, 1865, was composed of 70 Whigs and 18 Democrats, as compared with the 84 Democrats and 25 Whigs of the Secession Convention. The Constitution of Mississippi was amended to abolish slavery. At the general election called by the convention, General Benjamin G. Humphreys, a Whig and Union man who had served in the Army of Virginia, was selected as Governor. He was inaugurated in October 1865.

A special session of the legislature held in 1866-67 refused to ratify the 13th and 14th Amendments to the United States Constitution. The National Congress retaliated in March 1867 by placing Mississippi in the Fourth Military District, under the command of Major General E. O. C. Ord, whose use of Negro troops was especially repugnant to Mississippians. In 1868, General Alva C. Gillem, commander of the military subdistrict of Mississippi, called a constitutional convention. At that time, 60,-167 Negro and 46,636 white males were registered as voters. This "Black and Tan" convention submitted a constitution to the people in June, but it was defeated and General Humphreys was returned to the Governor's chair. General Irwin McDowell (who had replaced Ord) issued a military order for the removal of Humphreys from the executive offices and mansion, and began a regime in which all civil government was ended. In 1869 all persons who had been associated with the Confederacy were disqualified as officeholders and their places filled with Negroes, "carpetbaggers," and "scalawags."

When President Grant ordered the constitution, with certain objectionable features omitted, to be resubmitted to the people in November 1869, the faction of the Republican Party headed by James L. Alcorn, a former Whig and the faction's candidate for Governor, rode into power with the ratification of the constitution. In February 1870, Mississippi was readmitted to the Union as a State.

Governor Alcorn's troubles with a legislature containing 35 Negroes were emphasized when the panic of 1873 caused further distress in the State. In the gubernatorial campaign of that year, Adelbert V. Ames, with solid Negro support, defeated Alcorn in an election that marked the climax of Negro rule. Out of 152 seats in the legislature, 64 were held by Negroes and 24 by "carpetbaggers"; the Lieutenant Governor, the Secretaries of State, Immigration, and Agriculture, and the Superintendent of Education as well as nearly all local officeholders, were Negroes. In character with any political movement that suddenly raises a submerged class to power, the Ames administration was marked by extravagance and corruption. It intensified the post-war hardships of Mississippi to an almost unbearable degree.

In the exceptionally bitter campaign of 1875, one in which acts of terrorism were committed by both parties, a coalition party of Democrats and Whigs under the leadership of L. Q. C. Lamar (then a Congressman, later a member of the Cabinet, and eventually a Justice of the United States Supreme Court), James Z. George (later Chief Justice of Mississippi and United States Senator), Edward C. Walthall (who succeeded Lamar as United States Senator, and was in turn succeeded by William V. Sullivan) and John M. Stone (later Governor), aided by Alcorn's white Republicans, defeated the Ames administration in 62 out of 74 counties. The first act of the new legislature was to investigate the State officials. The impeached Negro Superintendent of Education was first to resign. The Negro Lieutenant Governor was convicted on an impeachment charge in March 1876 and removed from office. Under fire of impeachment charges, Governor Ames resigned March 29, and was succeeded in office by the President of the Senate, John M. Stone.

The Constitution of 1890 gave white supremacy the force of legal sanction by restricting Negro suffrage under a system of apportionment of representatives in counties heavily populated by whites, and by an educational clause later used as a model in other southern States. Since 1875 only the Democratic Party has held political power in Mississippi.

For many years poignant memories of the war and Reconstruction Period influenced the political thoughts of Mississippi voters. Until 1890 they held loyally to their former Confederate leaders as post-war political captains. But with white supremacy safely entrenched by the constitution of 1890, political alignments reflected the diverse interests and sympathies of Mississippi classes. Within the party a split developed between the older, once-great leaders and the younger, newly empowered masses—a split that echoed the early nineteenth century break between Whigs and Democrats. This schism also reflected the changed economic position of the once wealthy planters. Deprived of their mainstay of Negro labor, with capital gone, and unused to farm work, many of them moved from their plantations into the county seats, where they lived precariously from rents and sales of their land.

The smaller farmer, a man schooled in hatred both of the class above him and of the Negro who threatened competition with him, took over piecemeal the former plantations. Aided by the new tool of a political election primary, the members of this group broke up the closed circle of planter leadership by elevating their "Great White Chief," James K. Vardaman, to the governorship in 1904. Since that time the small farmer class has constituted the politically potent majority of the electorate.

The legislature of 1900 provided appropriations for the building of a new State capitol. This structure was completed in 1903 at a cost of more than a million dollars, and here inaugural ceremonies for Governor Vardaman were held.

With Vardaman the old order changed. Legislation of the period of 1904–25 is indicative of a growing social consciousness. Bills were passed providing for the establishment of county agricultural high schools for whites (1908) and a State normal college (1910); for regulation of child labor (1912); for the consolidation of rural schools (1916); for the establishment of an illiteracy commission (1916), a State commission of education (1924), and a State library commission (1926). Though broadening its concepts of the highest good of the people as a whole, Mississippi remained rooted in conservatism. In 1904 the "Jim Crow" Law was passed; in 1908 the importation and sale of intoxicating liquor were prohibited; and in 1926 the teaching of evolution in State schools was forbidden.

President Wilson's declaration of war upon Germany was ratified by the State on April 6, 1917. At Payne Field, Clay County, in May 1918, one of the earliest aviation schools of the war was established, and here approximately 1,500 men received instruction during the course of the war. To Camp Shelby, established in 1917 in Forrest County, came recruits from every part of the United States; one of the chief mobilization centers for all branches of the Army, Camp Shelby at its peak of activity had 60,000 soldiers in training. At the close of the war, the records showed that Mississippi had provided approximately 66,000 men to the United States Army and Navy, and had contributed nearly $80,000,000 in Liberty Loans.

The most disastrous flood recorded in the history of the Mississippi River swept the Delta in April 1927, taking a heavy toll in lives and property. For years, since the ante-bellum settlements of the Lake Washington region and the post-war opening of the land north of this area, flood control had been first in charge of individuals, then under authority of county and district levee boards. After the 1927 flood, the National Congress accepted the problem as a matter of national concern; and on May 5, 1928, the Flood Control Act, launched in the lower house of Congress by William Whittington of Washington County, Mississippi, was passed. This act removed the burden of flood control from the people and placed it under the direction of the Corps of Engineers of the United States Army, appropriating $325,000,000 to be expended in the work. The Army engineers established a laboratory for scientific study of the Mississippi River and its currents *(see Tour 2)*, then began to heighten and strengthen levees, dig cut-offs, and build reservoirs. In 1936 an additional $272,000,000 was added to the sum remaining under the 1928 act. The success of the control measures was proved in 1937 when the great crest sent down the Mississippi by the Ohio River's history-making flood was held in bounds, leaving the Delta unharmed.

Though Mississippi is still one of the most predominantly agricultural States in the Union, there are indications that its one-sided preoccupations with cotton farming is changing. Some of the evidences of change are more than a century old; others are so recent that they have not yet been assayed. The first major break was the development of a large-scale lumber and timber-product industry in southern Mississippi's Piney Woods. Coming with the building of railroads through the forests (a project for which Captain William Hardy was largely responsible) at the turn of the century, this industry set a new pattern of livelihood. The small stock-raisers and one-horse cotton farmers became sawmill hands, and the largest yeomanry section of the State was raised to a position of economic power. But with the exhaustion of its virgin timber reserves, the Piney Woods region is faced with the problem of returning either to small-crop cotton farming or to such things as cattle and fruit raising, and the making of pulpwood products *(see INDUSTRY and COMMERCE)*.

Another break in the habitual "one-crop" way of life came with the march of the boll weevil across the State in 1909. The dismay caused by this pest prompted a movement for agricultural diversification, which was accelerated in 1931 by the crisis in cotton prices. This diversification brought the tomato and cabbage raising industry to the trucking section, and the dairying plants to the Black Prairie. Greatly reenforced by the campaign of soil conservation, this movement has resulted in many other agricultural activities to supplement cotton growing *(see AGRICULTURE)*.

After the World War, falling land values, due to low cotton prices and exhaustion of the Piney Woods timber, had a disastrous effect upon the revenues of the State. In the late 1920's and early 1930's, the budget could not be balanced. Governor Theodore G. Bilbo made several attempts to provide additional tax revenues, but a hostile legislature blocked each measure. When, in January 1932, Sennett M. Conner took office as Governor, pledged to the passage of a sales tax, the deficit amounted to $13,486,760. On May 1, the sales tax bill, providing a two percent tax on all purchases, became a law; and before the end of 1935 the deficit had been wiped out, with the State's treasury showing a cash balance of more than $1,200,000. During the first two years of operation, the tax cost the average citizen approximately ten cents a month, though it increased the State's income approximately 25 percent.

The legislature of 1932 also provided for the reduction of the property tax levy by empowering the Governor, upon recommendations of the State auditor, State treasurer, and chairman of the tax commission, to cut the levy as much as 50 percent whenever the State's financial condition justified such action. Continuing its policy of lifting the tax burden from home owners, the legislature of 1934 exempted from State taxes homesteads valued up to $1,000, and provided for personal property exemptions. In 1935 the homestead exemption was raised to $2,500. Approximately 90 percent of the State's home owners are exempt from State property taxes (1938). At the head of the State Tax Commission is Alfred H. Stone, president of the National Association of Tax Administrators.

During the last decade Mississippi has witnessed a development that may prove more potent than either lumber or the boll weevil in shifting the State's economic interests to activities other than cotton. The Tennessee Valley Authority, established by Congress in 1934, supplemented the earlier electric transmission systems in the State. These lines and the opening of a natural gas field at Jackson in 1930 provide two of the links that had been missing in the chain of industrial development. In a State that heretofore has failed to process its raw materials, the coming of low-cost power and fuel may well initiate an industrial revolution.

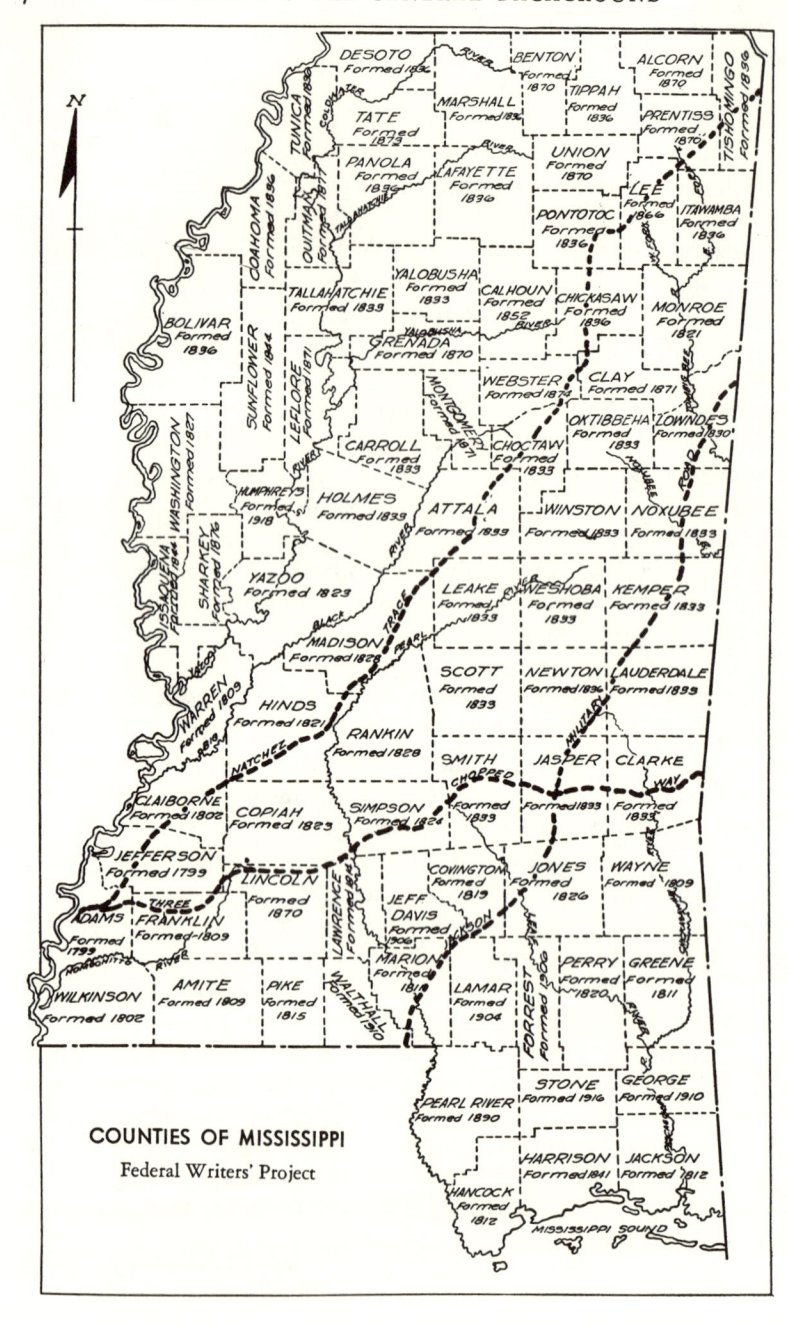

COUNTIES OF MISSISSIPPI
Federal Writers' Project

In 1936 Hugh L. White was elected Governor on a pledge "to balance agriculture with industry." Under his leadership, the legislature of that year authorized municipalities to issue bonds for the purpose of erecting plant buildings for industrial enterprises, and to exempt from ad valorem taxation for five years certain classes of industrial enterprise. Under this program, Mississippi is undergoing an industrial development that, measured by statistics, is remarkable. If these signs can be taken as auguries of the future, Mississippi's agrarian way of life may soon be fundamentally altered.

Transportation

The story of Mississippi's social and economic development can be outlined in its history of transportation.

Except for the marches of Hernando De Soto in 1540-41, travel in the exploration period was by water. Along the Coast, in the sixteenth century, *conquistadores* sailed in search of gold. In the seventeenth century, after France had won the Great Lakes and Quebec was built, French priests and *voyageurs* paddled their canoes in a great arc around the English seaboard colonies and pushed toward the center of the continent. La Salle, Tonti, and Fathers Davion and Montigny descended the Mississippi to its mouth. In 1699 D'Iberville and Bienville planted the first permanent colony at old Biloxi.

In like manner, the early settlements either hugged the coast line—Pascagoula, Pass Christian, and Bay St. Louis—or, gravitated upstream to the better land, the river banks. Natchez developed on the Mississippi River upstream from New Orleans. On the Pearl, Simon Favre made his settlement well up the river and, later, John Ford *(see Tour 13)* settled upstream from him. On the Pascagoula, the *voyageurs* who intended to farm left the lower harbor to hunters and fishermen and moved above the marsh. Of the river settlements, however, those on the Mississippi were more numerous, more important, and wealthier.

Although they were overshadowed by the Mississippi, the State's other

TOWBOAT ON THE MISSISSIPPI

streams experienced a like development. An 1825 map revealing the Natchez district well established, with an organized county government, also indicates settlements on the Pearl and the Pascagoula. From Ford's on the Pearl, the settlements moved up the valley to Columbia (second capital of the State), then to Monticello (home of two governors in the 1830's), and at last to Jackson, the State capital. Pearlington, built on hummocks of solid land where the Pearl meets the Gulf, was the trading post for cotton and lumber shipped down by flatboat. On the fan-shaped section drained by the Pascagoula tributaries were Augusta and Winchester.

The map of 1825 shows settlements along the Tombigbee River, entirely separate and over 200 miles from Natchez. The Tombigbee rises in north Mississippi, one fork in the foothills of the Tennessee and the other on the slopes east of Pontotoc Ridge. From the junction of the forks, near Amory, the river was formerly navigable to Mobile. Thus Cotton Gin Port, Plymouth, West Port, Columbus, and Aberdeen developed much as the Mississippi River settlements.

Roughly, from the 1780's to 1900, life on the Mississippi was a succession of growth, decline, and renewed growth. First was the transition from canoes to clumsy, raft-like cargo boats, overbalancing traffic upstream from New Orleans with that coming down from the Ohio. The river routes to Natchez from the eastern States were the Ohio and the Tennessee joined to the Mississippi. From Pittsburg on the Ohio and Fort Chissel at the headwaters of the Tennessee, the pioneers floated downstream toward New Orleans. After 1781, when the Spanish took over Natchez, its interests for a decade were associated with New Orleans; during the 1790's, however, the upper country became more important to its development. The Northwest Ordinance of 1787 started the great migration; and as the lands along the Ohio filled with settlers, more of them came down the Mississippi. The flatboats they used were heavy forts set on barges which carried them with their provisions and livestock.

In 1798 the force of American penetration into the Natchez district was sufficient to drive out the Spaniards. At approximately the same time, the planters shifted from tobacco to cotton. The resulting pressure of immigration and traffic was increased greatly; cotton demanded an outlet to a world market, and the Mississippi served as the connecting link from Natchez, just as it became the trade route between that city and the upper valley. The combined pressure of people and goods required the opening of the port of New Orleans, and influenced the purchase of the Louisiana Territory from France in 1803 *(see OUTLINE OF FOUR CENTURIES).*

Until 1811 keelboats and broadhorns brought the produce downstream. Then a new phase of traffic began, when the *New Orleans,* built by Fulton, became the first steamboat to navigate the river. The *New Orleans* made the trip despite the earthquakes which in places reversed the current of the Mississippi. The *Comet* and the *Vesuvius* followed, and steam domination became an actuality when Henry Shreve's *Washington,* in 1817, made the trip from New Orleans to Louisville in 25 days. The lines of the *Washington* foretold the familiar Mississippi River type of boat—double decks, with high-pressure engines raised to allow a shallow broad hull.

The introduction of steam brought to a close the career of the professional flatboatman, whose responsibility it was to get the pioneer and his family past shoal water and snags, Indians and outlaws. The dangers and the rough work of manning the sweeps demanded a rough man, one who could in a moment become "a combination of rubber ball, wildcat, and a shrieking maniac." He was a "ring-tailed roarer"; like his legendary hero, Mike Fink, he could "outrun, outhop, outjump, throw down, drag out, and lick any man in the country" *(see VICKSBURG).*

As the splendid, embellished steamer overshadowed the rough flatboat, so the gambler with ruffled shirt, gaudy vest, Paris boots, and easy manner overshadowed the flatboatman. The gamblers, unlike the pilots (who were a race apart), were part and tradition of a steamer's life. Captains were superstitious about leaving a wharf without one of them on board.

In their heyday, from 1835 to the War between the States, nearly 1,000 gamblers worked the big boats between St. Louis and New Orleans.

The commerce that made the gambler possible hints at the luxury the steamers afforded. The cotton planter, with his agent or factor in New Orleans and almost unlimited credit, had money or credit for gambling, and the steamers catered to his taste. On his frequent trips down the river to New Orleans, he was offered the best of food, a library, a bar, a newspaper printed on board, and a gaming room.

As the speed and service of the steamers improved, the river grew in importance. Grand Gulf at the mouth of the Big Black tributary, Vicksburg at the mouth of the Yazoo, and the inland shipping points, on the sluggish streams that cut the Delta's swamps and backed into the hills, were growing towns. Leota Landing brought the boats close to beautiful Lake Washington *(see Side Tour 3A)*, and from Greenville to the lake there stand ante-bellum homes marking the settlement of the oldest section of the Delta. Yazoo City and Greenwood (originally Williams' Landing) on the Yazoo, Grenada on the Yalobusha, and old Wyatt at the head of navigation on the Tallahatchie, were the far inland towns serviced by boats from the Mississippi. Across the swampy and thickly forested Delta, steamboats could at high water leave the Mississippi at Yazoo Pass and float across the submerged bottoms to the Coldwater. There they could swing down the Tallahatchie to its confluence with the Yalobusha. From that point they would follow the Yazoo past Greenwood and Yazoo City, meeting the Mississippi again at Vicksburg.

Coasting trade was a characteristic of river transportation just before the war. The fast, errand-running steamer, which could stop anywhere along the bank at any time to deliver a fan, a doll, a bottle of New Orleans bourbon, or a keg of nails, supplanted the slow "storeboat" of flatboat days, and aided greatly in making New Orleans the shopping center of the lower valley. A less obvious result of the errand-running steamer was the stifling of local trade. Only Natchez and Vicksburg were able to rise permanently above the village status, because they were convenient way stations. The other towns along the river either caved into the stream, like one-half of Grand Gulf, or were pushed inland by a changing whim of the current, like the other half of Grand Gulf; they were deserted, to rot in the sun. Riverbank dwellers who were neither planters nor customers became woodcutters to feed the smoke-belching steamers.

The rivers were the first travel routes because they were the easier paths to follow. Only a few Indian paths and buffalo trails, seldom more than a foot or two wide, were cut through the wilderness; and these had to fol-

TRANSPORTATION

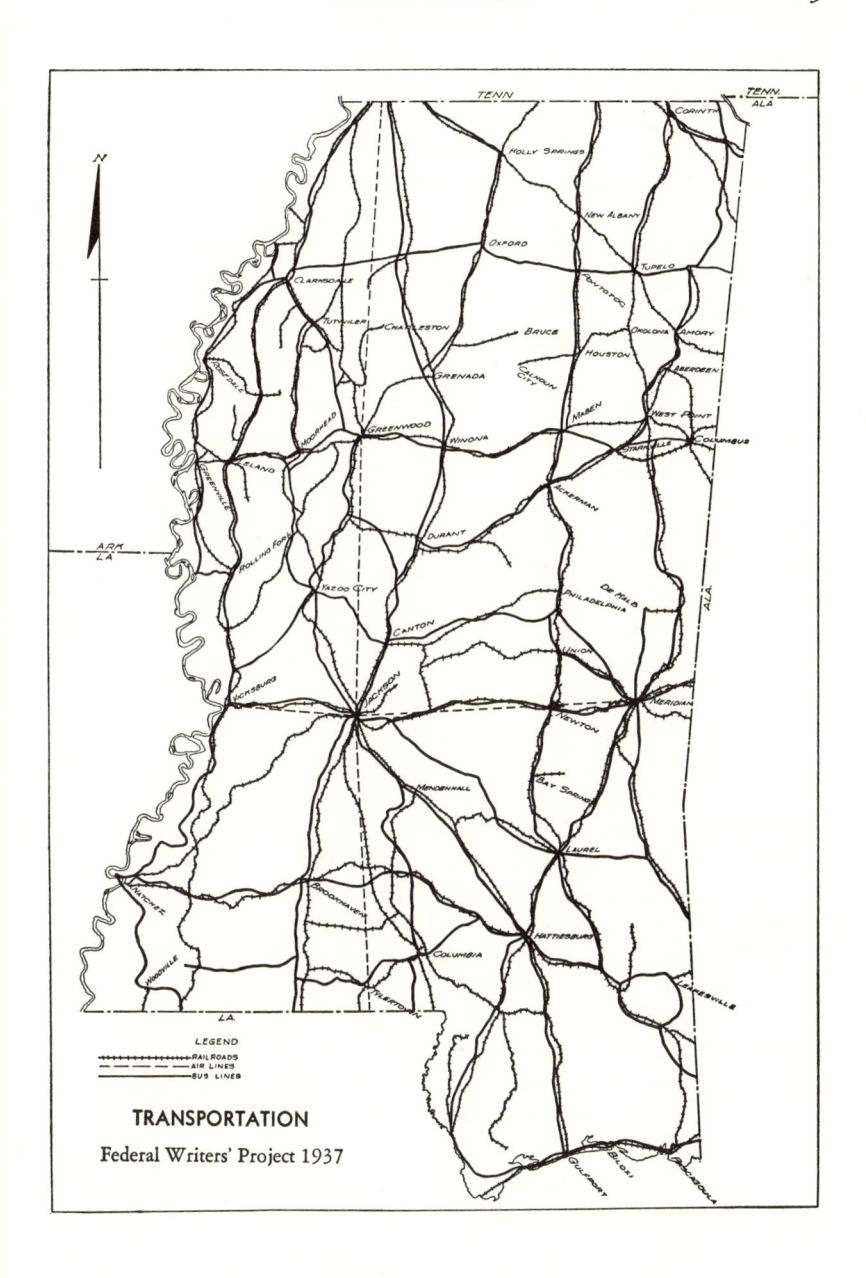

TRANSPORTATION
Federal Writers' Project 1937

low the ridges almost slavishly to escape the water-choked bogs in the stream bottoms.

At the time of the great migration of flatboats on the Mississippi, and until the use of steam, roughly the period 1800–20, the State's roads suddenly became important and were rapidly developed. Their importance lay in furnishing the only route for boatmen to return to the Ohio and Tennessee. The flatboats never came back; they could not, with their bulk, be poled against the current; and once downstream they usually were scrapped and sold as lumber. This created a demand for a road over which the boatmen could return from New Orleans to the Tennessee River. The first and most famous of these roads was the Natchez Trace, developed from an Indian trail which followed the watershed from Natchez northeastward between the Big Black and the Pearl to the foothills of the Pontotoc Ridge. There it left the divide and struck more eastwardly across the Tombigbee, meeting the Tennessee near Muscle Shoals.

The Trace ran through the wilderness and the country of the Choctaw and Chickasaw, two powerful Indian tribes. In 1801 Gen. James Wilkinson, commander at Fort Adams *(see Side Tour 3B)*, made treaties with these tribes. They granted the United States the right to lay out a wagon road "between the settlements of Mero district in . . . Tennessee, and those of Natchez in the Mississippi Territory." The work of widening the trail was done by United States soldiers. The treaties, however, permitted the Indians to retain the inns and "necessary ferries over the watercourses crossed by the said road." Described as a post road, it was placed under the direction of the Post Office Department and given an appropriation for improvement in 1806. It was to be the making of the Southwest. Mail carriers, traders, boatmen, and supercargoes from New Orleans followed it north; an increasing stream of settlers afoot and on horseback traveled on it south to the new Eldorado of the lower Mississippi Valley.

Truth and imagination are inextricably interwoven in the story of the Trace. It was for 300 miles a wilderness road, yet all who passed that way carried with them much or all of their fortune. Approaching, the horsemen bore the "stake" to set them up in the new Territory; returning, they carried the proceeds of cotton and other sales. To fasten on this stream of wealth came the outlaws who formerly infested the river: the Harpes, Mason, Hare, and the Murrell gang. Together they branded the early nineteenth century as the "outlaw years," and until 1835 they made the Trace as dark and bloody as Daniel Boone and his followers had found Kentucky.

The Harpes were the first. Shunned as abnormal by other outlaws, they became the scourge of the frontier from the Cumberland to the Mississippi. The head of "Big" Harpe, severed from his body by vigilantes, left his name upon the spot where it was fastened in a tree near the junction of the Cumberland and the Ohio.

Mason, a supercriminal, physically brave but morally weak, was the soldier turned outlaw. His robbery of Colonel Baker in 1801, his first on the Trace, gave the victim's name to Baker's Creek west of Jackson *(see Tour 2)*. Two years later Mason was tomahawked by two of his former followers, and his head, "rolled in blue clay to prevent putrefaction," was carried to Natchez for the reward. But even in death he was to end the career of "Little" Harpe, one of the two who had tomahawked him. Harpe, long in hiding after his brother's death, was recognized as he tried to claim the reward. He escaped with his companion, but was recaptured at old Greenville, on the Trace 20 miles north of Natchez, and there hanged *(see Tour 3, Sec. b)*.

Joseph Thompson Hare, the hoodlum, was among the first who shrewdly saw the possibilities of banditry on the Trace. The Trace made him rich, but moody. In its wilderness he went to pieces, saw visions, was captured, and hanged.

Murrell was the last. In him the passion of the others rose high enough to envisage empire. He was a student of crime, not a bandit. But the Trace no longer crossed a wilderness when he was caught and convicted of the crime of stealing Negroes. With him the dread of wilderness and its major outlaws ended.

But there were other roads. From Natchez they spread like rays from the sun. South to New Orleans the Trace travelers could follow two paths, besides El Camino Real (Sp., *King's Highway*), to Fort Adams: one through Woodville, the other cutting across country southeast through Liberty. Eastward from Natchez the Three-Chopped Way, so called because it was blazed with three notches cut in the trail-marking trees, ran to Fort St. Stephens on the lower Tombigbee and to Fort Stoddert in Georgia. It was the first road to bridge the eastern and western parts of the Mississippi Territory, and one of the earliest roads in the Southwest, having been opened prior to 1807. Cutting across a myriad of streams, it broke the rule of roads "riding the ridges" by having "causeways across all boggy guts and branches." From Natchez it passed through Monticello and Winchester. Later, along its side or nearby, grew Meadville, Mount Carmel, and Ellisville.

From the Natchez Trace, branch trails led to the river towns of Bruinsburg, Warrenton, and Walnut Hills (later Vicksburg). From the region

IN THE 1830'S

of what is now Pontotoc, an old Indian path led southeast past Lochinvar *(see Tour 12)* and along the divide west of Cotton Gin Port to Waverly on the Tombigbee *(see Tour 4)*. It was probably along this path that De Soto marched across the prairie.

In 1810 the United States opened a road from Cotton Gin Port to Colbert's Ferry on the Tennessee just below Muscle Shoals. This road, named Gaines' Trace for the surveyor who negotiated for it with the Indians, rivals the Natchez Trace for historical interest. From Fort St. Stephens, the Federal Government engaged in a bitter struggle for Indian trade against the Spanish posts at Mobile and Pensacola, but it was harassed by the duties and delayed shipments of supplies for which the Spanish revenue authorities at Mobile were responsible. To offset these handicaps supplies were shipped from Pittsburg down the Ohio and up the Tennessee to the shoals, across the divide to Cotton Gin Port on the Tombigbee, and down to Fort St. Stephens. The wagon road from Colbert's Ferry to Cotton Gin Port thus became an important artery of travel and trade.

Another road of importance was the old Jackson Military Road, au-

IN THE 1930'S

thorized by Congress in 1816, and completed in 1820. Andrew Jackson's troubles in his Creek campaign with the canebrakes and marshes of south Mississippi, and his fight with the British at New Orleans in 1815, were probably the compelling forces behind the road's construction. Built from Muscle Shoals for military purposes, it ran through Columbus southwest, penetrated the uninhabited Piney Woods, passed close to Columbia, and ended at Lake Pontchartrain. The road permitted a shorter route between Nashville and New Orleans than the Natchez Trace. The first telegraph line and the first stage line between these cities came into operation along this road.

Between the Natchez Trace and the Jackson Military Road about 1820 grew a well-traveled trail known as the Robinson Road, crossing the Tombigbee at Columbus, and running through Indian country past what is now Louisville to Doak's Stand, joining the Natchez Trace near the Choctaw Agency. As early as 1823 the Federal Government appropriated considerable sums to improve it, as did the Mississippi Legislature in 1824. Although its terminus was some ten miles north of the capital at Jackson, the Robinson Road was for a number of years the only direct route from Jackson to the populous settlements along the Tombigbee.

From the same Tombigbee settlements other roads were to develop. As

Memphis grew in importance, the old trail joining Cotton Gin Port to Pontotoc was made to connect with it through Lafayette Springs, across the Tallahatchie near the head of navigation, and on through Holly Springs. A trail led west from Pontotoc (probably along the divide between the Yocona and the Yalobusha) to the Delta, near what is now Charleston, and through the Delta's swamps and lakes by a marvelously circuitous route to the Mississippi in what has become Bolivar County. It was known as Indian Charlie's Trace.

These roads began as feeders to the river settlements and, in the early period of the nineteenth century, were subsidiary to river transportation. But their gradual extension was evidence of a growth away from the streams. With the first mail carried over the Natchez Trace (about 1796), the interior began to assume importance; and with the successive Indian cessions of 1820, 1830, and 1832 (themselves evidences of pressure of white population in the interior), the State was rounded out. No longer were the settlements strung solely along the streams.

The story of the railroads is similar. Constructed as feeders to the river, by the 1830's they experienced a vigorous extensive growth. Like the roads, they made possible the development of the great stretches of territory between and apart from the watercourses.

Of the plantation settlements in southwestern Mississippi in the 1830's, only Woodville lacked a creek on which cotton could be floated to the river. In 1831 the Mississippi Legislature chartered a company to build a railroad from Woodville south to the Mississippi River at St. Francisville, Louisiana. The company thus formed was the first in the State, the second in the Mississippi Valley, and the fifth in the United States *(see Tour 3, Sec. b)*. Beginning with this railroad, Mississippi became a testing ground for early American railroad experiments. The first major proposal was the "Mississippi Railroad," discussed at a meeting in Natchez in 1834. It was designed to connect Natchez with Jackson, and, eventually, to extend to the Tennessee. At approximately the same time the Vicksburg Commercial R.R. and Banking Company received a charter to build from Vicksburg to Jackson, and in 1836 the Mississippi and Alabama Company was permitted to build from Jackson east through Brandon to the Tombigbee in Alabama.

In 1837 a survey would have shown work actually under way on the Woodville and St. Francisville, Natchez-Jackson, Grand Gulf and Port Gibson, and Vicksburg and Jackson lines. Proposals were made for lines connecting New Orleans and Liberty, Grand Gulf and Jackson, Pontotoc and Aberdeen (in the Tombigbee area), Jackson and Mobile, and New

Orleans and Nashville. Only the last one of these proposed lines would have threatened competition with the river, and that, significantly, was the only one to meet serious opposition.

But though the proposed lines were, with the one exception, no more than adjuncts to transportation on the Mississippi, the State by 1837 was changing. Mississippi's first constitution that could be called "democratic" had been adopted in 1832. The internal improvement act of 1839 provided for a loan of $5,000,000 for a port on the Mississippi Sound and a railroad connecting it with Jackson. Natchez, in short, was having to fight for its position of importance.

In breaking away from the river, however, the interior settlers overreached themselves. The early 1830's were flush times—coming just as the Indian cessions opened up a vast new territory. Most of the proposed railroads, with the help of a sympathetic State administration, established their own banks. From 1836 to 1838 the number of the State's banks increased from five to 24, and the nominal capital from $12,000,000 to $62,000,000. Of the increased capitalization, however, only $19,000,000 represented tangible value. All the banks issued paper money in profusion, using the notes to finance the railroads. When Jackson's specie circular precipitated the crash in 1837, the collapse of the banks meant the end of railroad building.

The 1840's saw a continued aftermath of the speculation. In the scandal of the wrecked Union and Planters Banks, with everyone owing everyone else and no prospect of the debts being paid, and with slave owners fleeing to Texas from the debtors' law, construction work was impossible. The golden age of the steamboat, too, then in full sway on the river, was no encouragement to competitive builders.

Nevertheless, by 1850, the railroads had made the final break with the river; for that year saw the completion of the New Orleans, Jackson & Great Northern, a railroad between New Orleans and Canton which equaled that of any in the United States. This line was joined at Canton by the Mississippi Central to give a through route to Jackson, Tennessee. From Grenada another line, the Mississippi & Tennessee, extended to Memphis. A through railroad east and west, the Southern, connected Vicksburg, Jackson, and Meridian. The Mobile & Ohio, running from Mobile through Meridian and up the Black Prairie belt to Corinth, was completed in 1861. Through Corinth east and west ran the Memphis & Charleston. The only other railroads were the early river feeders which had survived the 1837 crash: the Woodville & St. Francisville (then known as the West Feliciana), and the Grand Gulf & Port Gibson. All these roads, except the two last named, had been aided in their construction by loans from the State and by land grants from the Federal Government, in return for which they contracted to carry Government mails and freight at reduced rates.

When Union armies came to Mississippi in 1862, the railroad properties were the first to be wrecked. Major battles were fought around the junctions of Corinth, Meridian, Jackson, and Vicksburg. The line from Grenada to Memphis did not carry a through train from 1862 to 1866. The Mississippi Central was torn apart and its southern partner, the New Orleans, Jackson & Great Northern, badly damaged. The Mobile & Ohio was wrecked near Meridian and almost destroyed north of Okolona as far as Corinth. None of these roads, however, was as abused as the Southern, from Vicksburg to Meridian, which bore the brunt of the campaigns against Vicksburg, and later was almost wholly destroyed by General Sherman.

Surviving the havoc that struck the railroads, the river steamboats enjoyed their final prosperity. When the *Robert E. Lee* raced the *Natchez,* with a deckhand sitting on the safety valve, it set a record that has yet to be equaled by a river boat. But coasting trade found no basis in post-war civilization, and the long-distance cargoes came to an end with the revival of railroad building in the 1880's. The showboats held on for a while, but they depended on the isolation, rather than the activity of the old river towns.

When the Reconstruction period came to an end, the railroad builders (among them many northerners) recovered their enthusiasm. Mileage increased from 1,127 in 1880 to 2,366 in 1889. In 1869 the Mobile & New Orleans (now the Louisville & Nashville) was laid along the coast where boat travel had been undisputed since 1699, and in 1883 one of the early river-feeder railroads, the Grand Gulf & Port Gibson, was torn up and abandoned. Also in 1883, R. T. Wilson was building a railroad from New Orleans to Memphis which paralleled the Mississippi.

Other important roads built in the 1880's were to connect Yazoo City with Jackson, Meridian with New Orleans (cutting across the Piney Woods), and Natchez with Jackson. Since 1885 the only major roads which have not been extensions of the lines already named, have been the Gulf & Ship Island from Jackson to Gulfport, and the Gulf, Mobile & Northern from Mobile to Laurel and up the west center of the State through Pontotoc—both of them giving outlets for the Piney Woods. The total trackage of 24 lines in the State today is 4,142 miles.

The effect of railroad building in Mississippi, as in other States, was a redistribution of population. The list of river and other settlements which missed the rights of way is a directory of ghost towns.

The development of highways in Mississippi is the story of the transition from the winding trails of the first quarter of the nineteenth century to the thoroughfares of today. The twisting wagon and ox-cart paths along the ridges were to continue in use until the coming of the automobile required new roads. The change has been made largely since 1910.

The first law authorizing the issuance of bonds for highway construction was passed in 1912, an act setting up special road districts with local service primarily in mind. The bonds were voted by local taxpayers, as liens on local property, and the road locations were selected largely to serve those who paid for them. The result was not to straighten the old roads, but in many cases to make the route even longer.

It was not until 1916 that the thoughts of the more progressive interests crystallized in the passage of the Federal Aid Road Act. In the same year the legislature formed the Mississippi Highway Department (appropriating $6,500 for maintenance for a two-year period) the chief duty of which was distribution of Federal Aid funds and supervision of the work done. In 1918 the legislature continued its appropriation and recognized the abolition of county lines in developing a State highway system. In 1919 the first set of standard bridges was worked out by the department with the aid of the Federal Bureau of Public Roads.

Although the legislature in 1920 appropriated $100,000 for the highway department and changed it from a three-member appointive board to an eight-member elective commission and in 1922 levied the first gasoline tax, no system of highways was indicated until the passage of the Stansel Act in 1930, which specified 6,000 miles of roads without, however, providing State funds for construction. Federal Aid funds, Emergency and National Recovery grants allotted to the State under the Roosevelt Administration were the only moneys available for paving.

Up to February 29, 1936, however, relief funds amounting to $6,000,000 have been put under contract for grading, draining, bridge building and grade-crossing elimination. In addition, nearly, 300 miles of roads have been relocated. In this four-year period a daily average of 4,894 people have been employed on the State's highways.

Mississippi's first planned program for highway building was drawn in January 1936, with provision for the expenditure of $42,500,000, of which $23,000,000 represented notes issued by the State, and the remainder Federal allocations. The sum was marked for a system of primary and secondary roads to touch each of the State's 82 counties.

Given priority in paving are three east-west, and three north-south routes.

The transportation picture today includes water, rail, highway, and air. The World War's congestion of freight and passenger trains compelled the return to river traffic. In 1917 the Inland Waterways Corporation was formed by the Federal Government, to operate (with a subsidy) the Federal Barge Lines. Flatboats and palatial stern wheelers on the Mississippi have given way to slow but powerful oil-burning towboats pushing half-mile-long strings of barges around the river bends, a single tow holding as much freight as several trainloads. With the Government maintaining the channel, private barge lines have followed.

The subsidies and channel upkeep provided by the Federal Government is matching the earlier grants made to the railroads. Terminal docks are located at Natchez, Vicksburg, and Greenville; the last-named is one of the largest and most modern in the South. Steam ferry service is available at Friar Point, Dundee, Greenville, Vicksburg, and Natchez. Ocean steamers dock in the deep-water harbors at Gulfport and Pascagoula.

Busses operate daily on more than 3,000 miles of road within the State, and with the completion of the new paving program further development of passenger and freight lines can be expected. Regular service is maintained by 57 motortrucking companies.

The State is now served by two air lines, one operating daily between Chicago and New Orleans, the other between Charleston, South Carolina, and Dallas, Texas. Both lines stop regularly at Jackson, and at other cities by appointment. Mississippi has 25 landing fields, 13 of them equipped for night flying.

Agriculture

Agriculture in Mississippi began to develop with the period of British rule. Previously, the French, with several large grants of land near Natchez and on the Yazoo River, had made several attempts to raise tobacco and indigo. But there is no indication that anything was exported except articles procured through trade with Indians. The landholders were, for the most

COTTON BOLL

part, men of rank in France who contented themselves with sending slaves and destitute peasants to improve their American estates. Without pride of ownership or the continued interest of their supporters to spur them, the immigrants were unable to develop the land.

The English colonists, however, settled along the rich virgin bluffs around Natchez and engaged in subsistence farming. They grew Indian corn, wheat, oats, rice, potatoes, cotton, flax, tobacco, and indigo. Tobacco and indigo were their export crops. For their own needs they also raised stock and tended orchards. They grew their own herb medicines; tanned their own leather and worked it into saddles and shoes; grew flax for thread and wove it into linen. Rice was their most important article of diet. Their cotton, the black, or naked-seed, variety, though unprolific and susceptible to rot, was distinguished by its fine soft staple. They picked the lint from the seed by hand or with small roller gins, and spun and wove it at home, using indigo and wild plants for dyes.

With the beginning of Spanish rule in West Florida, in 1781, tobacco became the staple export crop of the Natchez District. Some tobacco was under cultivation, but with the Spanish offer to buy all that could be grown (to encourage colonization) the plantings were greatly increased. The leaves were packed in hogsheads by the larger planters and in "carrets" by the smaller growers; the "carret" took shape from a pile of leaves compressed and dried under a tightly wrapped cloth, then wrapped with rope made of the inner bark of the basswood or linden tree. The barrels often were hauled to Natchez by shafts attached directly to the heads, thus functioning as both carriers and wheels. To convey the tobacco to the King's warehouses in New Orleans, several planters would unite and build a flatboat, which one of the number would accompany to deliver the tobacco and—if it passed inspection—to receive the proceeds. He returned home by land, generally on foot. The payment was made in written acknowledgment, or *bon,* which the governor or commandant at Natchez redeemed with cash. This procedure obviated the labor and risk of packing specie several hundred miles.

The certainty of this tobacco trade encouraged the planters to make large investments in slaves, but the entrance of the Kentucky product into the market, and the forced indifference of the Spanish Government as its imperial ambitions were stifled in Europe, ended the enterprise and consequently bankrupted many planters.

Until the failure of the tobacco industry, indigo had been of slight importance. Then for a brief interlude between the end of tobacco culture and the rise of cotton culture, the making of indigo dye became the colonists' most profitable pursuit. The plant, called *Indigofera tinctoria,* is said to have been introduced from India. It flourished luxuriantly, and, except for the tender care required by young plants, was cultivated with great ease.

At maturity indigo stood about three feet in height. Before going to seed, it was cut with a reap hook, tied in bundles, and thrown into steeping vats built of heavy planks above the ground. The steeping vats drained into other vats, called beaters, in which the liquid was churned. The sun supplied the heat to hasten the fermentation and decay. When the grain or coloring matter separated and settled to the bottom, it was shoveled with wooden scoops into draining boxes lined with canvas, dried in molds, cut into cubes, seasoned, and packed for shipping. The deeply colored product was the most valued, though a light blue shade called "floton" was produced in large quantities. The price for indigo in the latter part of the eighteenth century ranged from $1.50 to $2.00 a pound and the production per man amounted to about 150 pounds. The whole task of raising and processing it, however, was arduous and unpleasant work. The plant when growing was infested by swarms of grasshoppers, which sometimes killed the whole crop, and the odor arising from the putrid weed thrown from the vats was almost unbearable. The drainings into nearby streams from these refuse accumulations killed the fish, and the entire process of cultivation and manufacturing produced myriads of flies. By 1797 Whitney's gin had given new life to the cotton industry, and the enthusiasm for indigo disappeared.

All that happened in Mississippi's agricultural history before 1800, however, was but a prelude to the history of the cotton kingdom. From 1800 until well into the twentieth century, the story of Mississippi's agriculture has been the story of cotton.

Cotton culture was fixed in Mississippi as the result of three technological developments: the perfection of spinning machines in the last half of the eighteenth century; the perfection of a cotton gin which made easier the arduous process of separating cotton lint from the seed; and the improvement of species through selection and standardization.

The first recorded improvement in species was the introduction of Mexican seed cotton in 1806. One version of the story concerns a Mexican trader who was in the habit of stopping at a plantation near the town of Rodney (then called Petit Gulf). On one of his visits he brought with him a small package of cottonseed. Amazing results followed the planting of this seed, totally unlike the black type then grown in Mississippi. The yield was extraordinarily large and the bolls did not rot. The fame of the new variety, called Petit Gulf for the plantation on which it was first grown, spread immediately.

A more colorful version of the introduction is that Walter Burling of Natchez, envoy to Mexico, was secretly presented the seed—stuffed into dolls—by the Mexican viceroy, as it was then against Spanish law for the seed to be exported.

With the introduction of the Petit Gulf variety the "great cotton era" began. An indication of the way men were absorbed with the culture of this one plant is given in the fact that between 1794 (the year Whitney patented his gin) and 1804, the value of the United States cotton crop jumped from $150,000 to $8,000,000. This tremendous boom in cotton lifted Mississippians from the frontiersmen class almost overnight. Possibly never since has such a transition occurred so rapidly.

Land was plentiful, so no attempt was made at intensive culture through fertilization. Nor was the land even cleared, except for the underbrush; trees were girdled and left to rot and fall. But iron was dear, dearer than either land or slave, so plows and cultivating instruments were of the crudest types. Between 1806 and the coming of the boll weevil almost 100 years later, careful cultivation was unnecessary. Cotton grew easily and profits mounted. The high price of the staple (except for the panic years, 1837 and in the 1890's), the cheapness of land and labor, the extreme hardiness of the plant, and the ease with which it could be cultivated, all combined to establish cotton on the throne which survived even the War between the States.

The spinning mills of England not only set the market prices for cotton but also largely influenced the variety grown. Because longer fibers made possible a finer thread and cloth, a premium was placed on long staple. This caused a constant, if haphazard, experimentation to breed varieties that would combine high yields with long staple, yet be adaptable to local climate and soil. The Mexican type introduced in 1806 subsequently became the parent stock for numberless varieties and the source of much improvement through cross-breeding with the older black-seed species.

Ranking of the varieties of cotton developed before 1860 would be impossible without qualifying their merits according to local climatic and soil demands, but it is true that many, if not the majority, of the most famous varieties were bred first in Mississippi. Belle Creole, Jethro, Parker, and Petit Gulf, all Mississippi-bred stock, were as well known in the lower Mississippi Valley as the points of favorite race horses or steamboats.

The business of cotton involved many factors peculiar to itself and

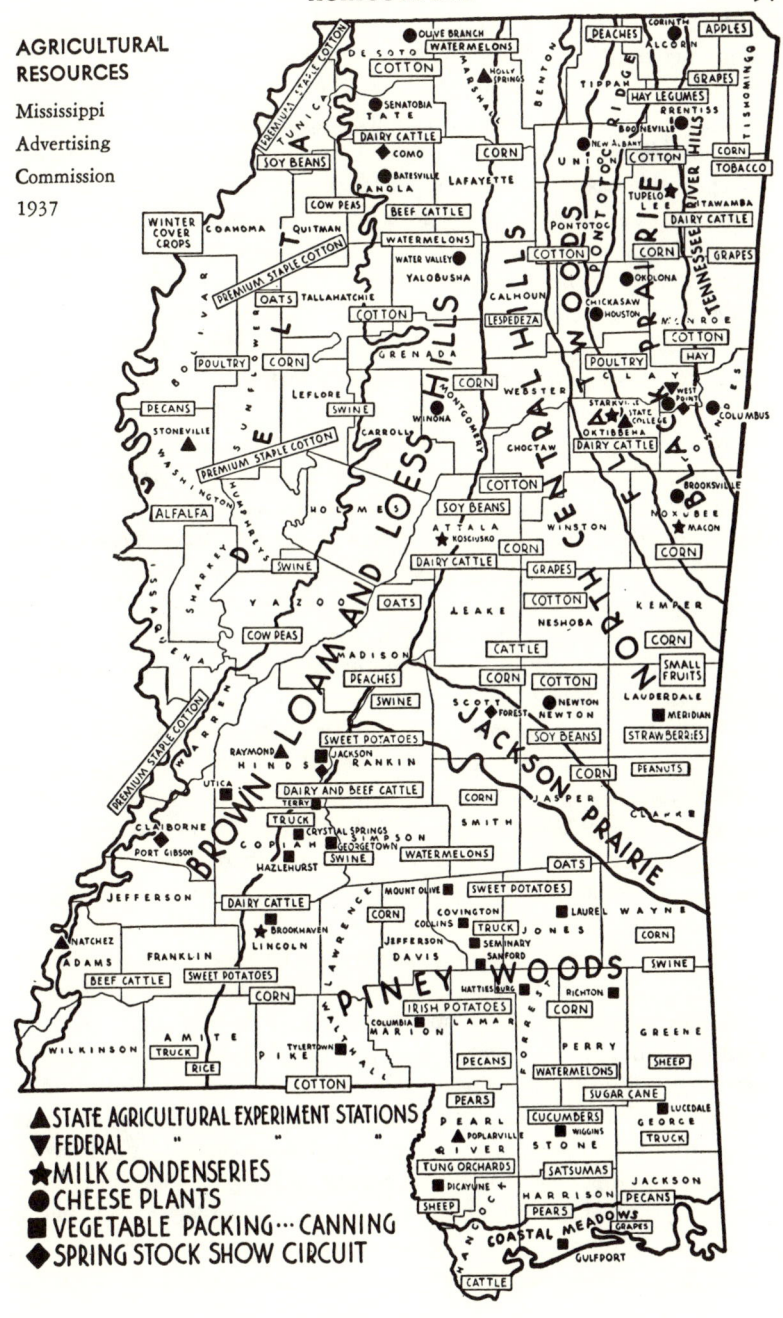

AGRICULTURE

AGRICULTURAL RESOURCES

Mississippi Advertising Commission 1937

▲ STATE AGRICULTURAL EXPERIMENT STATIONS
▼ FEDERAL " " "
★ MILK CONDENSERIES
● CHEESE PLANTS
■ VEGETABLE PACKING ⋯ CANNING
◆ SPRING STOCK SHOW CIRCUIT

wholly unlike other agricultural or mercantile enterprises. The peculiar relations between land, labor, plant investment, and financial backing, as they applied to the cotton industry, established a separate economy that has yet to be integrated properly with the general economic system. The terms of this problem are now understood though its solution rests with the future.

Good cotton land in Mississippi was, except for brief intervals, relatively cheap and plentiful. Plant investment was almost unnecessary, since the cultivation of cotton required no machinery. But financial backing was necessary because the planter usually began as a debtor. The transfer of cotton from planter to mill owner was complicated by the peculiarities of foreign exchange, sometimes delaying receipt of the proceeds of the sale as long as a year after the crop had been put in the ground. Rising with the steady hum of English mill machinery, however, the cotton market was so certain and so good before 1860 that the usual relation of planter and money lender was reversed. It was not a case of the planter pleading for money, but the lender begging that the planter accept his loans. With the exception of the panic year of 1837, it is doubtful whether a single planter between Memphis and New Orleans ever had to submit to credit restrictions.

This made labor the only factor that was at a premium in the cultivation of cotton. It was the relative pressure of labor costs that determined the current attitude toward slavery. Sentiment for slavery rose with the accession of new groups of planters to the land and fell as the new landowners improved their economic status. In the 1820's, when the cotton land around Natchez was well taken up and the planter had accumulated means to hire labor, there began a strong movement to return the slaves to Africa. But in 1830 and 1832, when new cotton lands were opened and people moved in with the debts of their first few years of operation impending, the feeling for African colonization died.

The War between the States, followed by ten years of miserable confusion, left an indelible mark upon the social and economic life of Mississippi. The work of two generations in building a civilization on cotton was destroyed. In 1875 Mississippi once more started from scratch, but this time on a different footing. Here was the landowner, with all his capital, equipment, and resources exhausted, sunk under a burden of debt; the fertile cotton land alone was his, but he had no money to pay for labor to produce the crops. No longer was the money-lender importuning him to accept loans. And here was labor, the Negro: free under the law, but unemployed and unorganized to produce on his own; destitute, and often starving. One thing the landowner—former master—and the jobless ex-slave held in common; that was the knowledge of how to cultivate and handle cotton. And the world price of cotton was high.

All these circumstances led naturally to an arrangement whereby the labor undertook to work the land for the privilege of living on it and sharing in its product, while the landowner supervised the labor and marketed the cotton. This marked the beginning of a modern form of economic slavery, the tenant-credit system.

With the planter and the laborer under the yoke of the tenant-credit system, the merchant entered the cotton business in the guise of banker, and his store replaced the plantation as the center of post-war economy. He advanced credit on future cotton—the only asset of either landlord or tenant; lending on risky security, his interest rate was high. Unlike the ante-bellum money-lender, the merchant was in a position to dictate to the planter. His dictation, naturally, was to grow cotton. So, with post-war cotton prices and the demands of the merchant-creditor looming before him, the dazed and penniless planter abandoned diversification for the one-crop system. Hastened destruction of his land, through soil erosion, was a natural consequence *(see Tour 5, Sec. a)*.

The geography of cotton culture before the war saw first southwestern Mississippi marked off and tilled, then the Pearl and the Tombigbee River Valleys. As long as farming was confined to the fairly level second bottom lands of these valleys, erosion was not a serious problem. However, after the land boom of the 1830's, and with railroads to help solve the problem of transportation, new cotton farmers moved into the hills and basins of northern and central Mississippi, and erosion was aggravated to an extent which few economic historians have realized *(see HOLLY SPRINGS)*. Thus the first State geologist, Eugene Hilgard, writing of the country around Oxford in the 1850's, noticed that: "Even the present generation is rife with complaints about the exhaustion of the soils—in a region which, thirty years ago, had but just received the first scratch of the plowshare. In some parts of the State, the deserted homesteads and fields of broomsedge, lone groves of peach and China trees by the roadside, amid a young growth of forest trees, might well remind the traveller of the descriptions given of the aspect of Europe after the Thirty Years' War." Another 75 years saw the full extent of this soil tragedy.

Later, hill-country plantations washed into gullies and forced the opening of the last section in the State to cotton. This was the swampy flood plain, colloquially called the Delta, which, except for the Lake Washington district, had not been settled because of its almost annual submersion and the constant menace of malaria. But despite yellow fever, malaria, high water, lack of capital, and the inertia bred by the hot Mississippi sun, post-war planters contrived to move from the eroded hills to the steaming, rich bottom lands.

In the Delta, a land as fertile as the valley of the Nile, two problems had to be solved: first, the clearing and draining of the land; and second, the protection of the plantation against overflows. Indeed, had it not been for the heavy burdens of flood control and drainage, Delta planters of the 1890's might again have reached the heights attained by the ante-bellum Natchez planters. Clearing the land was a Herculean task lightened somewhat by the building of railroads in the middle of the 1880's.

With the land cleared, the cotton planters' fight was not against overflow alone. The need of improvement in variety was still insistent. Cotton breeding toward long-staple varieties continued after the war, with John Griffin, of Greenville, a half-century ahead of geneticists in proving the soundness of the back-cross method. The Griffin variety, the result of selective breeding from 1857 until the end of the century, combined the hardiness of the green-seed upland plant with the long staple of sea-island cotton.

But, unhappily, the long staple was a late-maturing variety. The length of the staple required a proportionately long maturation period, and this meant a correspondingly long period for the ravages of the boll weevil. When the insect entered Mississippi, disaster resulted to the varieties of cotton which had been developed by 1909.

The crisis brought by the weevil made marked changes in the farming of certain Mississippi areas. The narrow section that extends south of Jackson, between the Piney Woods and Natchez Bluffs, abandoned cotton as a major crop and turned to truck farming. The more progressive of the farmers in 1876 had realized the suitability of this section's thin topsoil for raising vegetables, and in that year shipped a carload of tomatoes to the northern market. Thus the disaster that struck a majority of Mississipi's farms caused one small section to break from the non-rotating, cash-crop system and turn to diversification. Today, the vegetables—beans, tomatoes and cabbage especially—from this section compete successfully with those from the trucking area of Texas, and when the market is favorable the farmers of this section are the most prosperous in the State.

The Prairie section of the State was too fertile to abandon cotton but efforts were made to supplement it with legumes and other cover crops. Planting in summer and winter, the farmers here annually harvest four cuttings of alfalfa hay of one ton each per acre. As a result, the dairy produce industry has increased until the Prairie is the State's leading section in condenseries, creameries, and cheese plants. These plants give the farmer a biweekly cash market for his farm byproducts, but they have not weaned him from his first love, cotton.

The truck-farming and the Prairie sections include only 12 or so of Mississippi's 82 counties. The remainder of the State stuck to cotton and prepared to fight the boll weevil. The campaign against the weevil meant the end of unscientific, slipshod cotton farming. The objective of breeders was to combine an early-maturing plant with a long staple, and the task called for expert breeding knowledge. It is a tribute to Mississippians that they have developed several acceptable varieties, including the Delfos, Missdel, Stoneville, and Delta and Pine Land.

In the cotton crisis since the World War the weevil has been only one of the disturbing factors. The social and economic plight of the increasing number of tenant farmers and the aggravated problem of soil erosion have assumed proportions that engage the attention and resources of the National Government.

By converting the fever-infested swamps of the Delta into productive fertile fields, a few of the planters escaped the curse of erosion. But neither they nor the majority who remained to farm the eroding hillsides could free themselves from the tenant-credit system, with its imposition of the one-crop method of farming. As a result of this system approximately five-sixths of the State's agricultural lands are reclassed as "doubtful," and a steadily increasing number of its people are hopelessly sinking into debt. According to the 1930 census 47 out of every 100 persons in Mississippi were tenants. This proportion exceeded by 25 percent that of any other State and amounted to five times that of the average for the United States. Only Texas, in the *total number* of its tenant population, exceeded Mississippi. Significantly, Texas is also the only State that produces more cotton.

In 1880, only five years after the Reconstruction period had ended, the ratio of owners to tenants on Mississippi farms was approximately six to four. By 1920 the ratio had shifted to something like three to seven. In 1930 the census recorded 312,663 farms in the State, and of these 225,617, or more than seven in ten, were operated by tenants. In ten of the most densely populated cotton counties, about 94 percent of the farm population were tenants.

Bad crop years and low prices, a combination that few individual landowners can master, concentrated, through the channels of unpaid mortgages and loans, great tracts of land under the control of corporations—banks, insurance companies, and mercantile houses. In other instances, individual

EN ROUTE TO COTTON HOUSE

owners sought additional capital by forming companies and selling stock to urban capitalists. This brought to the plantations involved the absentee landlord system. Many of the absentee landlords live within the State, but a majority of the corporations are either out-of-State or foreign concerns.

To operate their holdings these absentee landlords employ managers, often the former owner of the property. The managers, to encourage high production yields at low production costs, receive part of their pay in bonuses or commissions on profits made. Like the tenant, they share with the owners a part of the risk of each crop.

Panther Burn, a 12,411-acre plantation in Sharkey County owned by McGee & Co., Leland, is typical of the plantations owned by Mississippi companies. On the plantation approximately 2,000 Negro tenants live in tree-shaded, four-room, frame houses. For their use there are a brick church, a school, and two stores. The houses, scattered over the plantation, are not provided with modern conveniences or sanitation *(see Tour 3, Sec. a)*.

The Delta and Pine Land Co. plantation near Scott is owned by a syndicate of British mill owners and has total assets of approximately $5,000,000. Embracing 38,000 acres, the plantation is divided into 11 units, each under a unit manager and the whole under a general manager. The labor is performed by about 3,300 Negro sharecroppers, representing 1,000 families. In 1936 approximately 11,700 acres were planted in cotton; on these were averaged 638 pounds of premium grade lint cotton per acre—15,000 bales in all—for which was received a maximum price of 13.25 cents per pound. (The average United States cotton farmer raised 187 pounds per acre and received an average of about 11.9 cents per pound.) These croppers also raised 950 pounds of cottonseed per acre, getting $40 a ton for it against a United States average of 600 pounds per acre at $32 per ton. The plantation's gross earnings, exclusive of the sharecroppers' share, were $879,000. After deducting gross expenses, taxes, bond interests, and bonuses, the net earnings were $153,000. Under the Agricultural Adjustment Administration the plantation received $68,000 from the Government; the plantation paid the Government $105,000 income taxes. For their share the tenant families received an average of $525 ($205 in credit during season and $320 in cash at end of season). When neither production nor price is as good as that of 1936 and the tenant is left with a deficit, the Delta and Pine Land management, like a majority of Mississippi plantation managements, writes it off and clears the debt *(see Tour 3, Sec. a)*.

The problem of tenancy is neither confined to the Delta nor is it restricted to the Negro. The number of white families who were unable to find a secure place in the expanding culture and were consequently forced to accept the system has increased steadily. In 1900 only 21.9 percent of the tenant farms were operated by white men, whereas by 1930 this figure had risen to 29 percent. In this same generation in which the number of white tenant farmers *increased,* the number of Negro tenant farmers decreased by 5.6 percent. During the five depression years after 1930, the number of Negro tenants decreased so greatly that it more than offset the increase among white tenants, allowing for the first time a decrease in tenancy as a whole. Thus, with the trend of tenancy increasing among white people and decreasing among the Negroes, the problems of agricultural Mississippi are found to be fundamentally economic, without respect to race.

These 225,617 Mississippi tenant families, both white and Negro, are divided into three classes: first, *Renters,* who hire land for a fixed amount to be paid either in crop values or in cash; second, *Share-tenants,* who furnish their own equipment and work animals, and agree to pay a fixed percent of the cash crop (cotton) as rental; and, third, *Sharecroppers,* who pay a larger percent of the crop, and in turn are furnished the land, implements, animals, fertilizer, house, fuel, and food. The first group, few in number, are removed from the cast of subservient tenancy by their relative independence. The second and third groups are the dependent workers. The share-tenants, supplying much of their equipment, pay the landowner one-fourth or one-third of the crop. The sharecroppers, supplying almost nothing but their labor, usually pay one-half of the crop. Both groups, however, must pay out of their own share for all that is supplied them in the way of seed, fertilizer, and food. Of these two groups, approximately 60 percent were croppers, or specifically, 135,293 of the 225,617 tenant families, in 1930, were in the lowest category of dependence.

From the beginning of the development of cotton, labor costs have been more subject to control than the costs of land, equipment, seed, taxes, and interest. That this traditional cheap labor is now provided by the tenants is proved by their standards of living. Submerged by practically every other force in the economy of cotton, they are reduced to the level of bare existence. The size of the tenant family bears no relevancy to the shelter provided; it is up to them to crowd somehow into the traditional three- or four-room house on the tenancy. And though land is both productive and abundant, their diet is probably the meagerest and least balanced among any large group in America. Food crops mature during the same season as cotton, making it virtually impossible under the one cash-crop system to raise subsistence crops. Indeed, the growing of household produce is not encouraged by landlords, whose viewpoint must reflect the wishes of financial backers. The final decision in the matter, as on the question of acreage to be planted or the amount of fertilizer to be used (theoretically the prerogative of the landowner), also rests with the men who advance money for the crop. Obviously, the diet of the tenants is largely limited to dried and canned goods from commissaries and local stores. This food and other necessities, obtained on credit during the crop season, is called "furnishings." It must be paid for out of the tenant's share of the crop at harvest time.

From this interdependence of tenant and landowner, our stock of folklore has been enriched by tales of unreliability and shiftlessness on the part of the tenants, and of fancy prices at the commissary, exorbitant interest, and careless accounts on the part of the landlords. But the case against the tenant-credit system cannot be rested on the improvidence of the tenants any more than it can be vindicated by the personal indictment of landlords. Under the drive of the merchant-bankers, the landlords could hardly act otherwise. The tenants are under a similar compulsion. That bad economic and social habits have developed on the part of both is evidence of a pernicious system.

These social and economic problems of the submerged portion of our agricultural population accompany another major factor. That is the depletion of soil fertility. For 139 years, from the time Whitney invented his gin until the establishment of the Agricultural Adjustment Administration in 1933, cotton held a monopoly on the land. Mississippi has never produced a surplus of human and livestock food, and it rarely produced even a sufficiency. This continual planting of one land-deteriorating crop lasted until the eroded and exhausted lands became barren or were washed from under the plow. To meet the situation, the Federal Government provided a system of bounties for sustaining the farmer if he should abandon his single cash-crop plan and try to restore the fertility of his land with legumes and cover crops that would bring no immediate cash. Conservation units, with headquarters at Meridian, were established to check erosion in the various soil areas of the State. These units have demonstrated erosion control and the refertilization of the land by cropping systems, terracing, proper land usage, and reforestation.

The work of soil conservation is still in the experimental stage, and the Agricultural Adjustment Administration is no more. But the Agricultural Census of 1935 shows results *(see Agricultural Map)*. From being just a cotton grower the average Mississippi farmer has added to his skills the practices of animal husbandry, food and feed production, home gardening, horticulture, and silviculture. He increased his food and feed crop acreage —in corn and hay particularly—by 63 percent, pasture acreage 27 percent, number of cattle 66 percent, and number of swine 26 percent. He *decreased* his cotton acreage by 36 percent. In 1936, on the reduced acreage, he produced 1,910,661 bales of cotton—the third largest crop in Mississippi's history. In addition he received more than $10,600,000 from the Government for his efforts.

These three years, which have seen the one-crop method of farming uprooted, have given to Mississippi agriculture added wealth and security in the form of cash, improved land, and better diets. But whether or not the farmer has been sufficiently braced to resist the traditional "cash crop" after governmental bounties are withdrawn is problematical. He will still have to finance his operations, and his only source for doing this is still the familiar product of war and reconstruction. The merchant-banker remains.

Industry and Commerce

Until 1920 Mississippi's industrial development was due more to sporadic reactions of an agricultural people against low-price years than to any systematic foresight. When the price of cotton was low the Mississippian talked and dreamed of basing his livelihood on something less erratic; but, when prices rose, if there had been any industrial beginning made it was forgotten in the rush to market. The result was continued dependence on cotton, only slightly relieved by the income from the State's sole industry —lumber. In the 1920's, however, a few public leaders took cognizance of this precarious position. After making an inventory of the State's resources and potentialities and considering trends outside Mississippi, they evolved a plan for industrial advancement. And, in 1936, an industrial act passed by the Mississippi legislature more or less officially opened for development one of industry's last frontiers.

The State's editors and writers referred to this act as a declaration of independence, since it was Mississippi's first determined break from reliance on cotton. To the average citizen it meant the end of blind loyalty and destruction of the illusion that cotton still possessed royal power. In reality, the act was a recognition of the fact that soil erosion, timber exploitation, and continued loss of world markets had almost entirely removed the traditional sources of income—cotton and lumber—and that, without stabilized industries to counterbalance the losses, Mississippi's economic system had broken down.

Mississippi had reached the peak of the ante-bellum speculative era in 1840. Then the Natchez district was enjoying the cultural advantages of a second generation of wealth; the Piney Woods had been settled since the 1820's; and the Central Hills were being developed by men made reckless by the fact that they had much to gain and little to lose. A State bank at Jackson, the capital, was helping to finance planters by means of a $5,250,000 bond issue, raised in the interests of cotton but not incident to industrial development. There were few industries; such as there were fell into the category either of "home manufactories"—tanneries, charcoal kilns, grist mills (or cotton processing plants), gins and cottonseed mills. These latter, few in number, were mostly in the Natchez district and had been established by planters for the purpose of facilitating the handling of cotton rather than as an approach to industrial development.

The charcoal kilns were operated by men of the non-slaveholding class who lived among the pines of south Mississippi. Small individual operators were scattered throughout the Piney Woods section. They used the crudest and cheapest methods and, as little capital was involved, the individual output was small. Conical mounds covered with pine needles and earth and left open at the top were used as kilns. Each kiln could contain enough pine slabs or blocks to make several hundred pounds of charcoal. New Orleans was the chief market for the product; though Mobile and the towns along the Coast used it for cooking and heating purposes, and here also the masters of sailing vessels purchased a supply.

A Mississippian, John Ross, in 1801 made the first written suggestion that valuable oil could be pressed from the cottonseed, but it was not until 1834, at Natchez, that the first mill was erected. Just north of Natchez at Washington, Eleazer Carver had begun in 1807 the manufacture of cotton gins. Still, when Mississippi reached its first "industrial peak" in 1840, the number of persons engaged in manufacture was only 5,060. Two years later the State repudiated its banking bonds and, by 1850, the number of industrial employees had slumped to 3,154. Before there could be any recovery, the War between the States began, and for the following four years even cotton was forgotten.

The war and resulting industrial stagnation affected Mississippi grievously. So great was the depression in all industry that Governor Alcorn estimated a 62 percent loss in home manufactures between 1860 and 1870. To encourage development, money invested in manufactures was exempted from taxation. Probably as a result of this exemption the Mississippi Cotton Mills, the largest textile mill in the State, was established at Wesson in 1871, and soon had 30,000 spindles in operation, consuming 10,000 bales of cotton annually.

The depressed price of cotton in the late 1870's brought to the people generally their first realization that agriculture in the State should be supplemented by industry. When, in the 1880's, the price continued to hover around seven and eight cents a pound, the State adopted a definite program for industrial development. In 1882 Governor Robert Lowry told the legislature that "the president or manager of a successful factory among us, ought to be more highly appreciated and honored by us than any public functionary in the land. Whatever legislation can be accomplished in his behalf shall have my cordial approval and support." As a result the legislature passed "an act to encourage the establishment of factories in this State and to exempt them from taxation." The period of exemption was to extend ten years beyond the time the factory was completed and in operation. To help carry out the purposes of the act a Commission of Immigration was appointed, and a *Handbook of Facts for Immigrants* was prepared for distribution in Northern and Eastern manufacturing centers.

The handbook, timed to take advantage of the southward trend of textile industries, stated that Mississippi offered abundant water power, cheap fuel, and inexpensive labor. Mills operating at Columbus, Wesson, Enterprise, Natchez, Corinth, "and other points" were listed as having operated at a profit. Unfortunately, however, the statement concerning water power and cheap fuel was erroneous; Mississippi had no coal supplies or fall lines, and no power lines had yet been strung. Hence, during the period from 1880–1890 the State's population increased many times faster than the number of manufacturing plants.

But, though the attempt to establish manufacturing plants failed because of the lack of natural and artificial power, industry in another form began. The lumber industry, developed in southern Mississippi, was destined to become for a generation the only rival of cotton in the State's economic system.

With the exhaustion of the timber supply in Michigan and the Great Lakes region the lumber industry, seeking new forests to conquer, moved southward. Prior to this, Mississippi's lumber industry had been confined to a few small units that operated along the banks of the Pearl and Pascagoula Rivers. But these operations, like those of the charcoal industry, had no great amount of capital behind them. The output scarcely did more than suggest to out-of-State capitalists the potential wealth of Mississippi's pine forests.

The rise of the lumber industry began in earnest along the Illinois Central R.R., which cut through the southwestern section of the pine zone. Here, west of the Pearl River, the Enochs Lumber Company purchased at a small price great tracts of virgin timber and built a mill at Fernwood, near McComb. From the mill, log roads penetrated the forest for miles in each direction. The White Lumber Company, another pioneer concern, established a mill at Columbia, and, operating westward toward Liberty, built the Liberty-White R.R. as a branch from the Illinois Central line. But even these first large mills did little more than scratch the surface; the greater forests lay east of Pearl River.

In 1881 the Southern R.R. pushed northeastward from New Orleans into Mississippi, across Pearl River and through the Piney Woods, penetrating the heart of almost untouched forests. With the laying of this trackage, large lumbering interests gradually acquired extensive holdings east of the Pearl River. Mills sprang up all along the line; Hattiesburg, Laurel, and other towns were founded. Then, in 1902, the Gulf & Ship Island R.R. was built, cutting from the north downward through the heart of the forests and ending at Gulfport, the new deep water port. With the harbor as an outlet and the two trunk lines connected with small log roads, the Piney Woods entered a period of lumbering that is equalled in Mississippi history only by the early flush times of cotton speculation. In 1900 this industry had 844 establishments employing 9,676 persons; in 1925 it reached the maximum production of 3,127,678,000 feet, with an employment by 917 establishments of 39,075 persons. This number represented more than two-thirds of all labor employed in industry.

In the late 1920's, however, the lumber industry began to decline. The larger mills, having cut practically all accessible timber, began to move their machinery from the State, leaving the clean-up operations to small concerns. In 1931 there were only 468 establishments left, with a decline in employment to 12,388 persons. In 1933 only 792,031,000 feet were cut. The Piney Woods inhabitant whose grandfather was a small cattle raiser, and whose father had been a small time sheepman, was no longer a sawmill hand.

Paralleling the decline of the lumber industry, other factors were at work forcing a change in the State's economy. Soil erosion had eaten the vitality from great tracts of land, making it impossible to raise more than a mere subsistence on the cotton farms. Foreign competition had gradually narrowed the cotton market until either the price of cotton had to be "pegged" by the Government or the farmer took a loss on what he had raised. With enforced control of acreage and the increasing use of farm machinery had come a large displacement of former cotton hands and tenants. The number of unemployed cotton workers and unemployed sawmill laborers forced recognition of the fact that, with lumbering as the sole industry and cotton as the one cash crop, Mississippi could no longer maintain a standard of living anywhere nearly commensurate with its possibilities. The State had to reorganize its economic system or else remain, paradoxically, well-endowed as compared with the other States with the prerequisites for a high standard of living, but ranking near the bottom in actual wealth and income.

Much was done during the 1930's to close this gap between potentialities and accomplishments, but agricultural diversification, reforestation, and the establishment of new industries take time and effort. The dairy cattle industry is directly dependent on the development of creameries, cheese plants, and condenseries which, in turn, require capital and experience in the dairy products business if they are to compete in national markets. Profits from poultry and swine are conditional upon the improvement of flocks and herds, possible only with capital and expert animal husbandry. Production crops, other than cotton, are hampered by lack of marketing facilities, but the building of cold storage plants, the development of effective marketing associations, the employment of skilled technique in growing perishable and specialty crops—all these take capital. Unfortunately, the State's wealth had eroded with its lands.

While Mississippians were posing this problem of need for but dearth of capital, industry in the Nation as a whole had been on the move. The cost factors of production and distribution that formerly had kept industry tied to certain key sections were being altered by the extension of power transmission systems and natural gas lines. The tendency was toward decentralization with an increasing emphasis on regional marketing. Considering the possibilities of high speed, low cost transportation in relation to the increasingly larger share played by taxation and labor in manufacturing, industrialists in the North and in the East glanced southward for an answer to their growing restlessness.

Certain technological advance also warranted major shifts in particular types of industry. New processes in the manufacture of paper make slash pine available as raw material for Kraft and even newsprint papers. Processing plants can be brought directly to the farm, where modern diversified agriculture provides various raw materials, some of them new to industry: the soybean, the sweet potato, wood pulp, and tung oil for use respectively in the making of plastics, starch, synthetic fibres, and paint and varnish.

The 1925–30 crisis in Mississippi's economic life coincided with this increasing change in the distribution of the Nation's industries. Linking the two in a new State economy was accomplished by the opening of natural gas fields near Jackson and the development of high transmission electric power systems. Rates were offered through two privately owned companies and the Tennessee Valley Authority that were as low as, if not lower than, those in any other part of the country. These new sources of fuel and power, and the unusually even distribution of the population, made Mississippi attractive to industries seeking decentralization.

From 1931 to 1936 new incorporated capital in the State averaged over $400,000,000 a year, approximately 27 times greater than the annual average for the five-year period 1921–1926. Between the Federal business census of 1933 and that of 1935, the number of industrial establishments increased by 390. In the average percentage of increases in these same years (figured by the number of manufacturing establishments, number of wage earners, amount of wages paid, and value of manufactured products) Mississippi was second in the United States. The value of manufactured products in Mississippi was 67.6% higher in 1935 than in 1933; the number of industrial workers increased 32.8%; the amount of wages 46.6%; and the volume of retail sales 27%.

During 1936 heavy construction in Mississippi increased 333% as compared with the national average increase of 71%; commercial car sales increased 69% while the national average was 25%; and farm income 24% as compared with the national average of 13%.

At Laurel a company manufacturing synthetic wall board realized the possibility of developing timber products plants other than sawmills. The first paper mill in the South to make bleached Kraft paper from pine was built on the Coast; and to demonstrate proper methods in raising pine trees, a slash pine nursery was established at Brooklyn. A new processing plant at Jackson to develop the bentonite deposits of Smith County is perhaps a beginning in exploiting the State's virtually untapped mineral supply.

With the virgin pines lost to southern Mississippi, the lower section of the Piney Woods has turned to raising tung nuts; and here one of the largest tung-nut crushing mills has been established *(see Tour 8)*. This industry, as well as the long established turpentine and resin industry in this section, finds an excellent market among paint and varnish manufacturers.

In the Prairie and Central Hills, more than 300 milk-utilizing plants and the mid-South's largest poultry packing plant have been built to offer a home market for the farmer's products. Over the State a score or more new garment factories have been opened, mostly branch plants of national concerns, planned to use the surplus rural labor made available by decreased farm operations *(see* TUPELO, MERIDIAN; *Tours 4, 5 and 12).*

As an added incentive to out-of-State capital and experienced management, the legislature passed the Industrial Act in 1936. This act, aimed to help "balance agriculture with industry," recognized the State's limited capital and authorized the municipalities to issue bonds for the purpose of erecting plants for industrial enterprises, and exempted from ad valorem taxation for five years certain classes of industries. An Industrial Commission was formed, charged with the responsibility of examining both the industries and the communities that expected to take advantage of the new act. An advertising fund was granted and an advertising commission created.

Thus Mississippi, for the first time in its history, has a planned program for industrial development. Under the "balance agriculture with industry" plan, Mississippi communities can offer land and factory buildings, together with tax exemption for a period of five years, in return for the ability and business experience of the incoming industrialists.

Religion

Unlike the older Atlantic States, Mississippi was not opened to settlement by Europeans seeking economic and religious freedom. It was opened by agents of his Christian Majesty, the King of France, seeking new sources of revenue and by Roman Catholic priests seeking converts. The Cross traveled with the Fleur de Lis; and when La Salle came down the Mississippi to plant the King's banner in the Lower Valley, Father Zenobius Membre was with him to officiate at the celebration of mass. This

RELIGION

first mass was said near Fort Adams in 1682. In the 17 years that followed, the religious order tightened its hold. St. Valier, Roman Catholic Bishop of Quebec, acting on orders from Rome, sent Fathers Montigny, St. Cosme, and Davion into the territory to establish missions. Fathers Montigny and St. Cosme settled among the Natchez tribe, while Father Davion established himself on the lower Yazoo River among the Tunica. When d'Iberville's colony pushed in from Ship Island to the mainland in 1699 and established Fort Maurepas, the first permanent white settlement in the Mississippi Valley, Father Davion was able to leave his work in charge of Indian converts and pay the settlement a visit. This first colony was the nucleus for other settlements in the region; and each band of explorers, soldiers, and settlers that went out from it was accompanied by a priest. Father Richard celebrated mass at the establishing of Krebs Fort *(see Tour 1)*, and Father Senat was burned by the Chickasaw after D'Artaguiette's defeat south of Pontotoc *(see Tour 12)*.

For nearly a century the territory remained almost entirely Catholic. But as a result of intrigue and of the Seven Year's War, ending in 1763, France lost her New World possessions, and Mississippi, as a British possession, came to be dominated by Anglo-Saxons. These new settlers from the eastern States were of Tory caste, accustomed to a certain amount of ease, culture, and gracious living; and though they were politically conservative, they believed emphatically in the separation of Church and State. With the same determination that left their mark on the State's agriculture, they drove the wedge of Protestantism into the almost solidly Catholic society.

In 1779, however, British rule gave way to Spanish rule, and once more Roman Catholicism became the official religion of the territory. Spain had two objectives in the lower Mississippi Valley: to develop the territory and to keep it Roman Catholic. By lenient civil laws the first was magnificently accomplished. But, ironically, the means to this accomplishment defeated the second purpose. For the lenient laws that aided so greatly in the development of the territory also drew more and more Anglo-Saxon Protestants from the older States; and these Protestants, finding a common cause in their opposition to Spain's rigid religious laws, united in a conspiracy of sorts against the government. Prohibited from organizing churches of their own, they held secret meetings in their homes and in the sylvan gloom of moss-draped forests. Under such militant preachers as Richard Curtis, Tobias Gibson, and Adam Cloud (Baptist, Methodist, and Episcopalian, respectively) Mississippi once more made the transition from Roman Catholicism to Protestantism. The first Baptist church in Mississippi was organized in 1791; and when the territory was annexed to the

United States in 1798, not only had this church superseded the authority of the Roman Catholic Church, but the framework of other sects had been laid. The first Methodist church was organized in the town of Washington in 1799. The first Presbyterian church, after some previous preaching in Jefferson County, was organized in 1804. In 1798 Samuel Swayze, a Congregationalist minister from New Jersey, built the first Protestant Church edifice in the State *(see Tour 3, Sec. b)*.

The admission of Mississippi into the Union in 1817 was the beginning of the so-called "great migration" from the older States. Second sons of aristocratic Tidewater families, coolly determined Scotch-Irish farmers, restless adventurers, and dissatisfied backwoodsmen poured down from the mountains into the newly acquired lands. And with this sweep of settlers into the State, religious doctrines, like political philosophies and styles of architecture, were transplanted from one section of the country to the other. The Episcopal Church flourished first along the Mississippi River, where rich bottomlands drew wealthy planters and slave owners. Later this sect, which generally identified itself with the settlers who held to the Tory ideology in the civilization they were shaping, moved northward into the upper river country and into the Lake Washington and Lake Lee regions of the Delta. In the Lake Washington area, Bishop Otey built St. John's Episcopal Church near Glen Allan in 1844 *(see Side Tour 3A)*, and with this as a focal point the doctrine of Episcopal faith spread throughout the lower portion of the Delta.

After organizing their first church in 1804, the Presbyterians in Mississippi were reenforced by Scotch-Irish families who migrated from the Carolinas to settle in the Natchez district. So quickly did they grow in numbers that the Mississippi Presbytery, under the jurisdiction of the Presbytery of Kentucky, was formed in 1816. Thirteen years later this sect founded Oakland College *(see Tour 3, Sec. b)*, thus leading the other denominations in inaugurating religious education in Mississippi. Growing out of its efforts to Christianize the Chickasaw Indians, the Cumberland Presbyterian Church of Tennessee gained a foothold in northern Mississippi as early as 1820. When the Chickasaw ceded their lands to the United States in 1832, the Scotch Covenanters were among the first to settle here.

The Missionary Baptist Church, so called to distinguish it from the Primitive Baptist, had a particularly strong appeal among the independent farmers who settled in the Piney Woods of southern Mississippi. They also established missions among the Indians of northern Mississippi, and, like the Presbyterians, after the cession of Indian lands to the Government, they had a foothold in this section. The Primitive Baptist churches were

RELIGION 115

established by settlers who kept close to the elemental in their way of life. This denomination was strongest along the Tennessee River.

In number of members, the Methodist Church came next to the Baptist. Spreading from their first church organization at Washington in 1799, and given great impetus by the eccentric evangelist, Lorenzo Dow, who established a church at Kingston in 1803 *(see Tour 3, Sec. b)* and then conducted a series of "camp meetings" in the territory, the Methodists distributed their churches throughout the State.

In the years between the end of Spanish rule and 1837, the Roman Catholics in Mississippi had become almost destitute of spiritual attention. The number of priests had slowly decreased until in 1837 there were only two. In that year, however, Pope Gregory XVI established a new diocese to embrace the entire State, and made Natchez its cathedral city. New priests were sent from Europe to administer to the Irish Catholics at Paulding and Bassfield, and to Catholic families along the Coast. On the Coast, the work of this denomination among the Negroes has been outstanding; at Bay St. Louis is the first seminary in America to train Negro boys for the priesthood. Other schools for Negroes were established at Biloxi and Jackson. The Natchez Diocese, since erection, has founded 24 schools and two orphanages.

The first Christian (sometimes called Campbellite) church was established in 1838 near Jackson. Several years later this denomination founded Newton College, near Woodville, an institution that had a large enrollment until the outbreak of the War between the States. The last denomination to organize a church in Mississippi's ante-bellum period was the Lutheran. This sect was introduced into the State by settlers from South Carolina, who settled near Sallis in 1840 and, in 1846, established here the New Hope Congregation Church.

These early churches fitted neatly into the early Mississippian's way of life. Not only did they give him an opportunity for formal worship but they offered him a means for emotional expression. The evangelistic spirit of these churches was a part of the so-called "southern temperament." They were also a part of the frontiersman's life, and as such were administered by men who were themselves pioneers. These divines, circuit riders, missionaries, itinerant evangelists, and camp-meeting crusaders understood the art of living life "in the raw." As A. P. Hudson points out in his *Humor of the Old Deep South,* they also were men with a considerable native sense of humor, otherwise they would have gone the way of Mr. Davidson in *Rain.* The famous Lorenzo Dow, who sat on the steps of his cabin in a canebrake watching his "star set in the west," and who once thought "it was a gone case" with him when Indians grabbed his bridle reins somewhere on the old Natchez Trace, is typical. Dow, a New Englander by birth, ranged up and down the Atlantic seaboard in a determined effort to convert to Protestantism all the inhabitants of that vast region. His activity in Mississippi centered about the Natchez country, where, undaunted by rebuffs, he made up in zeal and resourcefulness what he lacked in education. Speaking on the subject "Judgment Day" at one of his "revivals," and wishing to give effectiveness to the sermon, he arranged with a little Negro boy to climb to the top of a tall pine tree and at a specified point in the sermon to blow vociferously on a horn. His plans went off without a hitch and the audience was frightened even beyond his expectations. But, recovering and seeing through his hoax, the audience became indignant and prepared to break up the meeting. Dow, however, was ready for them. Impressively continuing his sermon, he said, "And now, Brethren, if a little Negro boy blowing on a tin horn in the top of a pine tree can make you feel so, how will you feel when the last day really comes?" And there was the Reverend Mr. Foster, who once hid in the mud of a bog, "playing mud turtle so well that [he] even fooled the Indians."

When slavery became a national issue, Mississippi Protestant churches, like those of other southern States, endeavored to reconcile slavery with Christianity. Both Methodist and Baptist denominations split with their national organizations in the 1840's, and formed organizations of their own. But notwithstanding this split, by 1860 these two denominations were the acknowledged religious leaders in the State. Unlike their closest rival, the Presbyterian, they appealed not to the Tory element but to the large class of small independent farmers.

After the War between the States, Mississippi's religious life was affected by three distinct influences: the organization of Negro churches, the spread of church-supported schools and colleges, and the rise of towns in social and economic importance. These influences were direct results of the breakdown of the plantation system. Previously, Negroes had been forbidden by law to organize churches of their own; instead, they had worshipped from especially constructed balconies in the churches of their masters or (presumably) they had not worshipped at all. With freedom, however, they were permitted to worship when and how they pleased. One of their first acts was to organize churches of their own. These churches were at first under the supervision of white churches, but later they were organized into independent units, such as the African Methodist Episcopal Conference and the Colored Baptist Association. In the Negro as in the white churches, the Methodist and Baptist denominations attracted the greatest number of members. Similar in dogma and concept to white religious organizations, the Negro sects have retained an emotional quality in their services peculiarly their own.

Reconstruction transferred social and economic power from the farms to the towns. The store usurped the prestige of the plantation; and with the growth of towns in population and importance, membership in urban churches increased. After the 1870's the church treasuries began to fill so rapidly that the denominations were able to execute many of the social reforms they had advocated. Missionaries, of the type once sent by the older States to establish and maintain churches in Mississippi, now were sent by Mississippi churches to perform a similar heroic task in foreign lands. Before 1865 an occasional church-supported school had been founded in Mississippi, but most of these were in fact preparatory academies; Mississippians to be educated in the professions went out of the State to school. After 1865, however, when few of the "upper class" had the means to send their children East and when the "common man" had risen to a status of comparative economic security, the church stepped into the field of education. Between 1865 and 1891, the State's religious denominations founded 123 educational institutions. Though some of these institutions held college rating, the majority were planned simply to fill the need of a public school system. When such a system was inaugurated by the State, a majority of the denominational schools disappeared.

One other effect of the rise of towns on religion in Mississippi was the comparatively large influx of Jewish people. Woodville, Meridian, Greenville, Vicksburg, Jackson, and Natchez acquired well-defined Jewish populations. The State's first synagogue was founded at Woodville in 1866.

Today, the Protestant church is perhaps the greatest social force in Mississippi life. Public spirited, though deep rooted in conservatism, the minister is often a greater force in molding public opinion in a community than is the editor of the local newspaper. Controversial subjects such as political philosophies, prohibition, child labor, wage-labor laws, and the Ku Klux Klan often are aired in the pulpits. Like his predecessors, the circuit rider and the itinerant evangelist of frontier days, the minister is versatile; he can enliven any occasion with an exhortation or an anecdote, and he is at home on public platforms and at barbecues. The congregations as a whole share his orthodoxy. They support his suggested enterprises, share his conservative social theories, and enjoy the zest of denominational competition. Occasionally, church bodies meet in assembly to draft resolutions on matters of general moral concern. Occasionally, they focus their denunciations upon local evils of social, economic, and industrial life. It is significant, however, that such resolutions have lost much of the force that they once exerted.

Individualism in urban churches has been somewhat sacrificed to organization. Taking their cue from the efficiency of modern business concerns, the churches maintain building committees, finance committees, and recreational committees. Church buildings, equipped with recreation rooms, dining rooms, and kitchens are indicative of their efforts to regain the place in the community's social life that they unwittingly let slip to the schools.

Rural churches, though greatly drained by the urban churches' absorption of their vitality in the form of members, wealth, and ministerial material, have retained much of their warmth and simplicity. Throughout rural Mississippi many sects still hold all-day singings, box suppers, and "protracted meetings." They also continue to practice "churching," or striking the name of an erring member from the rolls. Here the church is still the center of community life. And here, too, modern skepticism is lacking. Belief in God is accepted with the same unquestioning faith as are the revolutions of the sun and the cycle of the crops.

Education

The first attempts to establish schools before Territorial days were made shortly after 1772 by the English Protestant settlers—the Congregationalists and Baptists near Natchez and the Methodists of Vicksburg and vicinity. These attempts were crushed temporarily by the authorities of the second Spanish period (1779–98). Of necessity and desire the planters hired private tutors for their children or sent them to Eastern or European colleges.

The first act of incorporation for any purpose passed by the Territorial legislature was that of May 13, 1802, establishing Jefferson College. This college, still in operation as Jefferson Military Academy, at Washington six miles from Natchez, began active work in 1811. Supported at first by private donations, the proceeds of a lottery, and student fees,

EDUCATION 119

it later received land-grant assistance. One year before the incorporation of Jefferson College, the Reverend David Ker, a Scotchman, opened at Natchez the first public school for girls. Eight academies were incorporated in the Mississippi Territory, six of which were within the present limits of the State of Mississippi.

Of the pioneer academies established in the new State the earliest of note was the Elizabeth Female Academy near Washington *(see Tour 3, Sec. b)*. The school opened in November 1818, was granted its charter February 1819, and operated under the auspices of the Methodist Church until it finally closed about 1843. Edward Mayes, in *History of Education in Mississippi*, says it achieved "the dignity of a college in fact, although not in name." If this statement is true, it was the first chartered college in the United States to confer degrees upon women.

Hampstead Academy (shown in some records Hamstead), incorporated in 1826 after the middle section of Choctaw lands had been opened to settlement, was established at Mount Salus, now Clinton. Begun as a private venture and for a while under the control of the Clinton Presbytery, in 1850 it was taken over by the Baptist Church under the name of Mississippi College. It is now (1937) one of Mississippi's leading liberal arts colleges.

A third pioneer school of note was Oakland College near Rodney Landing, begun in 1830 as a Presbyterian institution to educate a native ministry in the Southwest. In 1871 it was purchased by the State and dedicated to the higher education of Negro men. In 1878 it was reorganized as the Alcorn Agricultural and Mechanical College, the only State-owned institution of higher education for Negroes in Mississippi. The Agricultural Land Scrip Fund, established by an act of Congress in 1862, made possible this reorganization. In 1902 the college was made coeducational (1936–37 enrollment, 434).

Many of the best schools and colleges in the State either were established under the direction of the Protestant churches or have received aid from them. Prior to the War between the States, 158 special charters were granted by the legislature to institutions of learning, and during the period from the close of the war until 1891 there were 123 more. Fourteen of these were organized by the Baptist Church within a period of ten years. These numbers do not include the institutions under the general laws of the State, nor those content to operate without charters. They were called by all names—academies, high schools, colleges, universities; but nearly all claimed to give sound instruction in the classics, higher mathematics, philosophy, the natural sciences, and modern languages.

Although many of these schools were really of little better than high school standing and lasted only a short time, they served well a State with a small and greatly scattered population. Especially popular were the female colleges where, in the absence of public schools in their communities, the daughters of the planters could board. From the early Protestant church schools have developed many of the leading present-day schools and colleges. The first Roman Catholic schools were in connection with the Indian missions. There are now (1937) parochial schools and private academies in many of the cities, ten of approved high school rank.

Acts of Congress of 1803 and 1805 reserved for school purposes the sixteenth section of each township in Mississippi. Under these acts there should be now a vast amount of income available for educational purposes, but by mismanagement, sale, leasing for 99 years at small rates, or out-and-out loss, the greater part of the fund has been dissipated, and most of the sixteenth section schools remain a myth. One notable exception is Franklin Academy, established at Columbus in 1821, which, although a part of the city school system, still benefits from its sixteenth section income. It has been in operation continuously since its beginning, and was by 24 years the first free school established in the State.

Although since 1803 schools in the State were established or aided by sixteenth sections donated by Congress, and, since 1821, to a small extent by the Literary Fund established in that year by the legislature, no serious consideration seems to have been given to a general system of common schools until 1843. In that year it was made a campaign issue by A. G. Brown, candidate for the office of Governor. In 1846 Brown, as Governor, succeeded in securing the passage of an act to establish a general system of schools. But the schools that grew out of this act had no uniformity since they differed as the counties differed in wealth and efficiency of management. Not until 1870 was a uniform system of public education organized in Mississippi. Each county in the State and each city of 5,000 population (later including those of 1,000) was made a district in which free public schools were to be maintained for at least four months of the year under the supervision of a board of school directors. Under this system there existed in each county many one- or two-teacher schools.

Before the War between the States there were no public schools for Negroes. According to Garner in his *Reconstruction in Mississippi:*

> With the occupation of the state by the Federal Armies, the work of teaching the Negroes began. The first schools established for this purpose were at Corinth shortly after the occupation of that territory by the Union troops in 1862. The American Missionary Association, the Freedman's Aid Society, and

EDUCATION 121

the Society of Friends had established schools about Vicksburg before the close of the war. Upon the organization of the Freedman's Bureau, a more systematized and comprehensive plan of Negro education was undertaken. Joseph Warren, chaplain of a Negro regiment, was appointed superintendent of freedmen's schools for the state at large. These schools were under military supervision, and benevolent associations supplied them with books and, in many cases, furnished clothing to the students.

In 1865 there were 30 Negro schools; by 1869 there were 81 with 105 teachers, 40 of whom were Negroes.

During the period of reconstruction an elaborate and expensive system of education, to include both white and Negro children, was formulated after the plans of the eastern States. State normal schools for Negroes were established at Holly Springs and at Tougaloo, near Jackson, and were liberally supported by the legislature. (These have been discontinued since 1903, leaving no State-owned schools for the training of Negro teachers.) To the impoverished taxpayers, this reconstruction legislation was a great burden. Yet, as Garner continues, "when the reconstructionists surrendered the government to the democracy, in 1876, the public school system which they had fathered had become firmly established, its efficiency increased, and its administration made somewhat less expensive than at first." The Democrats made provisions for continuing the system and guaranteed an annual five-month term instead of the former one of four months.

Until 1885 all the public schools manifested a low degree of vitality. Free education for white and Negro alike was openly combated because of the excessive taxation imposed upon the war-impoverished people, but the retrenchments made by the legislature of 1886 made the issue a little more popular. The 15 years preceding 1900 brought a gradual growth and improvement in the State school system.

The period from 1900 to 1930 was one of decided progress. A bill passed in 1910, providing for the consolidation of rural schools with transportation at public expense, brought about a vast improvement in educational advantages for the children scattered on farms and in small villages. Before that date the cities and towns had the only public high schools in the State. In that year began the development of county agricultural high schools. In the following decade 50 such schools were organized, so distributed as to cover almost the entire State. In the rural areas they brought a deeper interest in education and a demand that high school facilities be within the reach of every girl and boy in Mississippi. The outcome has been that many of the consolidated schools have become of accredited high school standing, and the majority of the rural children can live at home and yet have facilities equal to those offered the children in the State's most progressive cities and towns. With the accrediting of these consolidated schools many of the agricultural high schools have been absorbed into the county program of education.

The report of August 1937 shows a total of 20 agricultural high schools for white children, all approved by the State Accrediting Commission and 7 of the group accredited by the Southern Association of Colleges and Secondary Schools. Ten of these are separate schools while 10 are connected with State-supported junior colleges. There are three agricultural high schools for Negroes, one approved and two on probation. The number of consolidated schools of high school rank for white children is approximately 850, all with free transportation; for Negro children there are 40, half of which have free transportation. Of the 510 approved four-year high schools for white children, 77 are accredited by the Southern Association. There are 54 approved high schools for Negroes, two of which are accredited by the Southern Association: the high school departments of Southern Christian Institute and Tougaloo College.

Since the passage, in 1917, of the Federal Vocational Education Act, commonly referred to as the Smith-Hughes Act after its co-authors, 593 departments of vocational training have been established in Mississippi schools. Under this act funds are available to any public school approved by the State Board of Education and willing to match Smith-Hughes funds. During the term 1936–37 the following number of high schools received vocational aid: agricultural, 172 white, 87 Negro; home economics, 197 white, 37 Negro; industrial and trade, 85 white, 15 Negro.

In response to the need for an extended secondary school program, the present 11 State-supported junior colleges were established between the years 1922 and 1929. Their 1936–37 enrollment was 3,243. They are fairly evenly distributed over the State, are coeducational, have nominal fees, and all but one have agricultural high school departments. There are eight other white junior colleges in the State, five of which are church-supported schools for girls. Hillman College in Clinton, Mississippi Synodical College in Holly Springs, and All Saints College in Vicksburg are under the respective jurisdiction of the Baptist, Presbyterian, and Episcopal Churches. Whitworth College, Brookhaven, and Grenada College, Grenada, are Methodist schools. The combined enrollment of these church schools for 1936–37 was 571. There are three privately controlled white schools of junior college rank. Clark Memorial College, Newton, and Wood Junior College, Mathiston, are coeducational, with respective enrollments of 81 and 125. Gulf Park College,

EDUCATION

Gulfport, is a private school for girls, with an enrollment of 254 (1937). There are three accredited Negro schools of junior college rank: Mary Holmes Seminary, West Point, Okolona Industrial School, Okolona, and Southern Christian Institute, Edwards. These are under the respective jurisdictions of the Northern Presbyterian, Episcopal, and Christian Churches.

Special schools have been provided for special groups. In 1847, the Institute for the Blind and, in 1854, the Institute for the Deaf and Dumb were established at Jackson. The Industrial and Training School, for "the care and training of children under 18 years of age, found to be destitute, abandoned, or delinquent," was established in 1916 at Columbia. This was followed in 1920 by the School for the Feeble Minded, at Ellisville. Negroes are admitted to the Institute for the Deaf and Dumb and the School for the Feeble Minded. These four schools are State-supported.

The first attempts to educate the Indians were made by missionaries, incidental to their efforts to Christianize them. The Elliot Mission, established in 1818 in what is now Grenada County, and the Mayhew Mission, an outgrowth of this some 70 miles east, continued until the Indian removal (1830), at which time many of the teachers and priests followed their charges to their new homes in the West. Prior to the War between the States and through the Reconstruction Period no effort was made toward the education or training of those Indians who remained in Mississippi. An act was passed in 1882 that provided schools for the Indian children in the eastern part of the State where the number warranted a school. Indian education was taken over from the State by the U. S. Government in 1918 through its Indian agency at Philadelphia, Mississippi. Of the seven day-schools under Government sponsorship, the one at Tucker is typical *(see Tour 12)*.

There are about 150 full-blooded Chinese children of school age in the Delta, where live most of the Chinese in the State. Since these children are prohibited by law from attending the white public schools, they, for the most part, are taught privately in small groups, each family paying a part of the cost, or are sent out of the State, even to China, for their education. In a few of the towns where there are only one or two children they are given special permission to attend the local schools; in many places they attend the Negro schools. All children of mixed Chinese and Negro blood must attend the Negro schools. The only public school for the Chinese is at Greenville, a one-room frame structure where about 25 children are taught by an American teacher who belongs to the regular city school faculty. The work in this school extends through the eighth grade. In 1937 the Chinese Mission school, with an enrollment of about 35, was opened at Cleveland under the sponsorship of the Baptist Church. Full-blooded Chinese from all parts of the Delta attend. There are boarding facilities for those from a distance. The curriculum is that of other public schools supplemented by courses in Chinese language and literature.

The educational advantages of the Negroes have not kept pace with those of the white children. Of the 3,753 public Negro schools, only 2,313 are in publicly owned buildings. While many of these are modern and adequately equipped, the 1,440 other Negro schools in the State are in churches, lodge buildings, garages, tenant houses, old stores, and similar buildings. The greatest stimulus toward the betterment of this condition has been the Julius Rosenwald Fund, of which, since 1919, half a million dollars have been spent in building and equipping Negro schoolhouses in Mississippi. Since 1932 funds have not been available for building purposes but may be secured by school libraries for the purchase of books. Many of the Negro schools in the rural sections are still one- and two-teacher schools, often poorly equipped. The school term for rural schools for Negroes averages five months; that in the city schools for Negroes varies from eight to nine months. The salaries for teachers in the Negro rural schools vary from $18.00 to $50.00 per month, with an average of $25.00. In the Negro city schools the average salary is about $35.00.

Each county Negro school has its separate Negro board of directors. In each city school system there is one board, composed of white men and women, over all schools for both white and Negro alike. The city superintendent of schools, in every case a white man, is also superintendent of the city Negro schools. In many of these schools work of a relatively high standard is done, especially in the vocational courses.

Since 60 percent of all Negroes in public schools are in the first three grades and only about five percent of the public high school enrollment are Negroes, many schools of high school rank or above have been organized under private management or under the jurisdiction of some church. Besides the church schools already named, there are four others which are supported by Negro churches: Mississippi Industrial College, Holly Springs, Natchez College, Natchez, Saints Industrial Institute, Lexington, and Campbell College, Jackson. These are under the respective jurisdictions of the Methodist, Baptist, Sanctified, and African Methodist Churches.

The three independently controlled Negro schools—Utica Institute, Prentiss Normal and Industrial Institute, and Piney Woods School, founded in 1903, 1907 and 1910 respectively—are supported by voluntary contributions and money earned by their traveling groups of singers. All three are boarding schools of accredited high school rank. The Piney Woods School, with the best industrial plant, not only has more singers on tour than any other Negro school—as many as 14 quartets have been on tour at one time—but is the only school with a department for the blind. Prentiss Industrial Institute is the only Negro school in the State founded and headed by native Mississippi Negroes. Utica Institute is outstanding for its singing of Negro spirituals, and its quintet has the distinction of having sung in Europe. Perhaps the school's most interesting accomplishment is its promulgation of the annual Negro Farmers' Conference, the object of which is to encourage Negro farmers to become landowners.

There are three senior colleges for Negroes in addition to the State-owned Alcorn Agricultural and Mechanical College. Tougaloo College, at Tougaloo, seven miles north of Jackson, was founded in 1869 by the American Missionary Association of the Congregational Church. It is the only senior college for Negroes in Mississippi approved by the Southern Association. Its students have contributed to an anthology called *The Brown Thrush*, the first intercollegiate anthology compiled by Negro students. Among these contributors is Jonathan Brooks, whose poetry has appeared in national periodicals. In its music department more attention is paid to the classics than to spirituals. It is one of the few colleges in the State offering pipe organ instruction. Rust College, Holly Springs, organized in 1870 and supported by the Northern Methodist Church, is noted for its music, especially its traveling groups of singers who supplement the school funds by their concerts. Jackson College, organized at Natchez in 1877 under the auspices of the Baptist Church, was moved to Jackson in 1884. Besides courses in the liberal arts it offers teacher training and music. As in all the Negro colleges of the State, singing plays a large part in its activities.

Five of the ten senior colleges for white students in Mississippi are State-supported; five are church schools. The oldest of the former group is the University of Mississippi, Oxford (1936-37 enrollment, 1,361). Edward Mayes, in *History of Education in Mississippi*, says:

> The university . . . was, in fact, founded by the Congress of the United States, by the acts of March 3, 1815, and February 20, 1819. The former act, that which provided for the survey of the boundary line fixed by the treaty with the Creek Indians, donated 36 sections of the public lands for the use of a seminary

LYCEUM BUILDING, "OLE MISS," STATE UNIVERSITY, OXFORD

of learning in the (then) Mississippi Territory. When the State was organized in 1817, all of the Creek lands were left within the Alabama Territory, and the fact led to the act of 1819. By this act a similar quantity of land in lieu of the Creek lands was granted and the title vested in the State, in trust, for the support of a seminary of learning therein.

A vast amount of these lands was sold or leased and the money invested in stock of the Planters Bank. Since 1880 the State has paid to the university, biennially, a sum approximating $65,000, which represents interest

EDUCATION 127

at six percent on this money lost in the failure of the bank in 1840. The same year (1840) the legislature voted to use the remaining income from seminary lands for the establishment of the university. Its charter was granted in 1844; in 1846, William Nicholl, an Englishman, was elected supervising architect for the proposed buildings, the first of which was the Lyceum, now used for administrative purposes and classrooms; the university was opened in the fall of 1848. Exercises were suspended from 1861 until late 1865 because of the War between the States. The property, though occupied sometimes by the Confederates, sometimes by the Federals, was preserved intact. Begun as a liberal arts college, with a law department added in 1885, it now offers the usual university courses.

Mississippi State College, Starkville (1936–37 enrollment, 1,933), owes its origin to the Agricultural Land Scrip Fund established by an act of Congress in 1862. It was chartered as Mississippi Agricultural and Mechanical College in 1878 and shared this fund equally with Alcorn Agricultural and Mechanical College for Negroes. Begun purely as an agricultural and mechanical college in response to the request of the farmers of the State for scientific training for their sons, the college expanded later. Courses in the liberal arts, schools of science, education, business, aviation, and pre-medicine, a graduate school, and an agricultural extension department were added. In 1930 the institution was made coeducational; in 1932 its name was changed.

Mississippi State College for Women, Columbus (1936–37 enrollment, 952), opened in 1885 as the Mississippi Industrial Institute and College, the first State-supported institution for the higher education of women in the United States. Incorporated in 1884, it was the successor to the Columbus Female Institute begun in 1848. Although emphasis was placed on the industrial courses, music and fine arts were included in its first curriculum. It offers courses in the liberal arts, secretarial training, library science, dramatics, music and art, and has unusually good departments of physical education and teacher training.

Mississippi State Teachers College, Hattiesburg (1936–37 enrollment, 859), was incorporated as the Mississippi Normal College by legislative act of 1910, and opened two years later. In 1922 the legislature authorized the granting of the degree of Bachelor of Science, and in 1934, the degree of Bachelor of Music. The name was changed in 1924. Delta State Teachers College, Cleveland (1936–37 enrollment, 367), was established by legislative act of 1924, and opened the following year. It now confers the degree of Bachelor of Science in Education, and has added courses in music and art. Its choral work is not surpassed in the State.

Of the church-supported senior colleges, the oldest is Mississippi College (1936–37 enrollment, 395), a liberal arts college for men. Women are admitted to the junior and senior classes by special arrangement. (This college was among the pioneer academies.) Millsaps College, Jackson (1936–37 enrollment, 415), established in 1892 under the auspices of the Methodist Episcopal Church, South, is a coeducational liberal arts college with emphasis upon training for the Methodist ministry. An endowment of $50,000 was donated by Major R. W. Millsaps with the provision that the Church raise an equal sum.

Blue Mountain College, Blue Mountain (1936–37 enrollment, 301), established in 1873 by General M. P. Lowrey as a private school for girls, is the oldest senior college for women in the State. In 1920 the Mississippi Baptist Convention assumed control of the school. Especial emphasis is placed on the departments of speech arts, fine arts, and music. Belhaven College, Jackson (1936–37 enrollment, 257), established as a private school for girls in 1894, came under the control of the Mississippi Presbytery in 1911. Its art and music departments are outstanding. Mississippi Woman's College, Hattiesburg (1936–37 enrollment, 176), under the management of the Baptist Church, was established in 1911 on a site presented to the Baptist Convention by W.S.F. Tatum. Since 1926 it has been an accredited senior college with an excellent music department.

The Press

In the late summer of 1798, Winthrop Sargent arrived in the 82-year-old town of Natchez to assume the duties of Governor of the newly created Mississippi Territory. A few days later he summed up one of the Territory's greatest difficulties in a letter to the Secretary of State. "We have no printing offices in this country [and] we are remote from all others," he wrote. "A small traveling press, sufficient for half a sheet of post paper, which would give four pages, would be a blessing to the people of the territory, and I would myself contrive to manage it." The reason for this lack of printing facilities, the Governor might have added, was that this eastern portion of the lower Mississippi Valley had been under Spanish rule for the previous 20 years, and only one printing press had been allowed in all the valley. That one was at New Orleans and was for government use only. Not even handbills could be posted in the Natchez District without official permission.

In compliance with the Governor's request, Lieutenant Andrew Marschalk was ordered to pack the little hand-press with which he had been experimenting while on duty at Walnut Hills (Vicksburg), and to proceed to Natchez. There Marschalk set up his press, put aside the poems he had been printing, and began the more practical work of publishing the laws of the Mississippi Territory. This piece of work gave him considerable prestige. Apparently it also injected printer's ink into his blood, for in 1802 he resigned from the Army, founded a newspaper, and began what was to become the more exciting career of journalism. Before he died in 1837 he had fought several duels, been fined for contempt of court (which he "fully intended to contempt"), and served as Mississippi's first public printer. He is remembered as "the father of journalism in Mississippi."

The paternity of Mississippi's press, however, falls to Marschalk because of the importance of his paper rather than for its priority. Before the first issue of his *Mississippi Herald*, on July 26, 1802, two other publications, the *Mississippi Gazette* in August 1800, and the *Intelligencer* in 1801, had appeared. Moreover, the *Gazette*, published by Benjamin Stokes on the little press bought from Marschalk, was a success. But the *Herald* soon eclipsed these two papers both in power and in circulation. By its editorial policy it struck the tone of Mississippi journalism for three-quarters of the century to come. Marschalk subordinated news stories to editorials, then highly seasoned his editorials with personal abuse. His paper became a rabid political sheet; and this was the character of the newspapers that followed.

In 1808 Mississippi had four newspapers, all in Natchez. But soon thereafter Marschalk moved to the town of Washington to establish the Washington *Republican*, and in 1812 the Woodville *Republican* was founded. This latter paper is the oldest in the State among those still published. In its files are details of the Napoleonic Wars, national political campaigns, and slavery laws. Except for the year 1831, however, the files offer little local news. In that year an anonymous citizen wrote to the paper, pointing out the advantages offered the country by the new means of transportation "called railroads." The letter, signed "Publius," was printed by the *Republican*, and followed by an editorial. The results were a meeting of Woodville citizens, the appointment of a committee, and the construction of a railroad. This railroad was the Woodville & West Feliciana, fifth railroad to be chartered in the United States *(see Tour 3, Sec. b)*.

With Natchez, Woodville, and Washington editors paving the way, and with a great influx of people into the State from the Carolinas, Virginia, Georgia, Kentucky, and Tennessee, other newspapers were born. Like the seat of government, they began gradually to shift from the river country towards the interior. When the government at last found a permanent location and Jackson became the political storm center of the State, two new but important papers were founded here. These were the *Pearl River Gazette* and the *State Register,* both established in 1823.

These early Mississippi newspapers vied with one another for the lucrative printing contracts awarded by the State, as almost the only means of financial survival. In January 1820, Richard C. Langdon, of the *Mississippi Republican,* was given the contract, with Marschalk's old title of public printer. But in February he was called before the State House of Representatives, charged with contempt in publishing "two pieces highly inflammatory on the members thereof, and calculated to disturb the coolness and deliberation of this body." Langdon was defended by Jefferson Davis' brother, Joseph, but he was dismissed from his office by a vote of 17 to 10.

Advertising agencies were unknown in these early days; if an editor desired out-of-town advertisements, he had to secure the business himself. Advertising space, commonly used to promote snuff, beverages, tobacco, and patent medicines, was generally sold at a price of $30 a year for a "square." At the end of the first year the advertiser often forgot to pay for the renewal of his announcement; yet, like his free subscription to the paper, it would continue indefinitely. As the number of squares sold by the paper increased, the size of the paper became larger. A few journals grew so large and bulky that their square-filled sheets could hardly be handled conveniently. These papers were referred to by their less fortunate rivals as "our bed quilt contemporaries."

Mississippians have ever been fond of politics, and in the fever of the so-called "flush times" of the 1830's their appetite for it seemed insatiable. Every citizen carried a political theory in his pocket, exhibiting it on every occasion. The professions of law and politics were one, not two. This fitted neatly into the individualistic policies of opinionated editors. Almost every paper, with the exception of the well-edited literary weekly, *Ariel,* was a political organ. One-third of each issue was devoted to the virtues of its editor's political views; much of the remaining two-thirds consisted of invective against the vices of the opposition.

The *Natchez,* edited by James H. Cook, was a power in the Whig Party. Opposing it was the *Statesman,* vociferously pro-Democratic and edited by such men as J. F. H. Claiborne and Robert J. Walker. The Polk-Clay Presidential campaign of 1844 brought forth almost as large a crop of newspapers as had the campaign of Andrew Jackson. Typical of these was *Harry of the West,* established in Grenada by J. J. Choate in 1844, but sold in 1846 and renamed after its title no longer represented the uppermost question of the day. During this period Alexander McClung, "the Black Knight of the South," established the *True Issue,* one of the most ably edited newspapers in the Southwest. McClung's editorials on the National Bank issue and the tariff were justly famous; Seargent S. Prentiss is said to have used numerous extracts from them in his political campaigns. But by December 17, 1844, the *Mississippi Democrat* of Carrollton *(see Tour 6)* was speaking of the "carriage already built and sent to bring the Whig president-elect to Washington." With Polk elected, a great many of the papers, exhausted by their prodigious efforts, collapsed.

The trenchant editorials plus the keen rivalry natural to extremely partisan papers made it necessary for the editors to be expert pugilists and duelists as well as journalists. An editor made no assertion that he could not defend with fists or firearms. In Vicksburg the *Whig,* a daily paper published from 1840 to 1860, and the *Tri-Weekly Sentinel,* owned by W. W. Green and James Hagen, had a particularly bloody history. On one occasion Hagen engaged McCardle, then editor of the *Whig,* in a duel. McCardle was wounded, but recovered and lived to see Hagen shot down in a street fight by Daniel Adams, a Jackson citizen whom Hagen had offended in an editorial. The four editors who succeeded Hagen on the *Sentinel* also met violent deaths. The paper discontinued publication in 1857.

The sentiment for secession united the newspapers of the State in common denunciation of the Unionists. But the war that shortly followed dealt them a staggering blow. Machinery and paper were almost impossible to obtain, and the able-bodied printers left their presses to shoulder rifles. The calamity was climaxed when Federal troops, marching through the State, destroyed both presses and type. Sometimes the type was dumped into a river or a well; in the case of the Jackson *Mississippian* it was strewn through the streets. But a few papers still managed to survive. The *Evening Citizen,* the first afternoon paper to be published in Vicksburg, continued operation not only through the first years of war but throughout the siege. Its final edition, issued July 4, 1863, was printed on wallpaper because the supply of news-print was entirely exhausted. As this last issue went to press, the victorious Federal Army marched into the city, and one blue-clad trooper entered the plant and added the item: "Vicksburg has this day surrendered to General Grant."

With the coming of peace, many new papers were founded and a few of the old revived. In the latter group was the *Eastern Clarion,* established at Paulding in the 1830's, then moved to Meridian, and again at the close of the war to Jackson. Here it became the *Clarion* and later the *Daily Clarion-Ledger,* one of Mississippi's largest present-day newspapers. These older papers, of which the *Clarion* was typical, were defiant of the reconstruction policy and suffered tremendously because of their views. The new papers, usually managed by northerners recently moved into the State, supported the Government's policy and grew rich from State printing contracts. Practically all national advertising went to the Republican press. The *Pilot,* published by Kimball, Raymond & Company of Jackson, was perhaps the most powerful in the newer group. On one occasion an irate Democrat, A. J. Frantz, went to Jackson intending to avenge his party by killing the paper's editor. The editor, however, discreetly hid himself, and the spectators who had gathered to see the fight were disappointed. They branded the Republican editor as a coward, and hoisting Frantz to their shoulders they proclaimed him the "first man to win a victory over the Yankees since the war." The bloodless outcome of this event, however, was not typical, and a score or more of editors were killed in Vicksburg during the Reconstruction Period.

In 1866 the older newspaper publishers organized a press association as a retaliative measure. Republicans were barred from it, and until the withdrawal of Federal troops it remained the "Democratic Press Association of Mississippi." After the troops withdrew, Republican papers disappeared entirely, and the Democratic papers turned their editorials from abuse of northerners to work for State reform. Public opinion shaped by the papers caused a committee to be appointed in 1881 to investigate charges of brutality to convicts leased by the State as laborers to private enterprises. This investigation led to changes in the penal system adopted by the Constitutional Convention of 1890. Other causes espoused by the newspapers of the post-Reconstruction Period were the fight against mob legislation and the advocacy of local option in liquor traffic.

At the turn of the century, the weekly papers reigned supreme. There was at least one to every county, and they were judged entirely by the quality of their editorials. At the end of 1910, however, the dailies began to enjoy the advantages of national press services and by enlarged circulation to encroach upon the weeklies. Mississippi journalism subsequently underwent a change. For the first time in the State's newspaper history, opinion began to be subordinated to news.

If Marschalk, "the father of Mississippi journalism," were able to enumerate his posterity today he would find himself blessed with 130 publications, 20 of which are dailies and the remainder weeklies. The dailies, he would discover, have exchanged vitriolic editorials and frontpage advertisements of "Pure Old Brandy" for "spot news" dispatches and syndicated columns of contemporary eastern papers. The dailies have replaced their outmoded machinery with linotypes and rotary presses, and have become members of one or more of the large press services. The weeklies have been arbitrarily assigned the task of printing local news and guiding the people in trade and politics. In a way, they have become virtual chambers of commerce for the smaller towns. They help to develop local industry by publicity and stock-selling campaigns, and to promote community spirit. Yet their intimate contact with the town's life and their provincial enthusiasm have retained for them an importance that cannot be over-emphasized. Organs of the village citizens and county farmers, the weeklies represent the bulk of Mississippi's population. They fight their subscribers' political battles, mold opinions into well-defined issues, and at the same time keep alive an interest in the social doings of Mr. and Mrs. Jones.

The Creative Effort

Arts and Letters

Since a people's artistic expression, and what they choose from the art of others, is determined largely by their way of life, it is best for understanding to look first at the Mississippian, then at his creative efforts. A brief survey of his traditions and environment will reveal the Mississippian's capacity for enjoyment, his humors, and his philosophy; and it is these, going beyond externals, that strike the notes of his character as it is revealed in the records he has left.

Of the two million individuals who are now Mississippians, slightly more than half are Negroes. The remainder, to an extent greater than in any other State, are native-born descendants of English, Scotch, and Irish stock. The minority peoples—French, Spanish, and Indian—did not infuse their blood in any appreciable quantity, neither did they leave any indelible impression on Mississippi tradition, custom, or temperament. With the possible exception of southwest Mississippi's architectural tradition, established by the Spanish from the West Indies, there is little Indian, French, or Spanish art influence evident in the present culture. French settlement along the coast left traces of the mother tongue and established the Catholic religion, but this influence is slight compared with the British and Negro heritage of the State as a whole.

The Negro, bringing with him to Mississippi remnants of his African tribal culture, was placed in the position of a slave performing the heavy manual labor on which a civilization rested. Generally he dwelt apart from white associations, lived in the field and in segregated cabins. He received no schooling in languages or indigenous art forms. If he showed originality, he sometimes was allowed to express himself in wood and iron working—carving stair rails, cabinets, and mantels for his white master's home—but, generally, as long as he performed his menial task of cultivating the fields he was left to his own devices. The simpler beliefs of Protestant Christianity were taught him and were learned readily by him; but these were assimilated in his own way. Hence his emotions and inherent sense of rhythm found expression in song, the only external expression, other than the handicrafts, that could surmount his paucity of tools.

This handicap, twisted by changing circumstances into almost completely economic form, has lingered with the Negro. Since emancipation, the Negro has been too occupied with economic problems and too busy assimilating the culture of the society about him to have the time for creative expression. That he is still deeply imaginative is evidenced by his song, anecdotes, and cabin gardens. But even these, like his religion, emotions, and physical appearance, have become subjects for the white artist. Instead of expressing himself creatively, the Negro has been placed in the position of being an almost inexhaustible reservoir of material for the creative efforts of others. The young Syrian sculptor, Leon Koury of Greenville, first won recognition for his modeling of a Negro's head, and has since devoted much of his time to portraiture of Negro subjects. The painter, John McCrady, has found his best material in the Negro. His painting, *Swing Low, Sweet Chariot,* recognized as his greatest work to date, interprets the Negro's idea of death and ascension to heaven.

The culture of white Mississippians has been more complex, composed of Scotch, Irish, and English influences, with the last predominating. There has always been a close relationship between the Englishman's life and his creative efforts. This makes it possible, to a degree, to explain the white Mississippian's external expressions in connection with his more or less material existence. His financial status, the amount of leisure he has had, and his purpose in life have greatly influenced his creative efforts, if not his temperament.

There were three migrations of English, Scotch, and Irish stock to Mississippi. The first was the migration of Tory families to the Natchez country during and immediately following the American Revolution. The second was the migration from the Piedmont of the Carolinas and Virginia into the Mississippi hills and Piney Woods regions immediately after the War of 1812. The third was the "flush times" migration that brought settlers from all classes of the older South, and even from the East and North, into Indian lands opened by the treaty of 1832.

These three groups, though all of one racial stock, came with different backgrounds and purposes. The Tories were comparatively wealthy and by habit were accustomed to a certain amount of ease and gracious living. Their ideal was the English country squire. They placed emphasis on permanency, family background, and conservatism in arts and politics. They built homes that would endure, filled the homes with accepted *objets d'art,* planted formal gardens, and wherever possible preserved in detail the code they had brought with them. Fortunately for their continued peace of mind the cotton culture supported them in their accepted way of life. It gave them money to spend and a plantation to rule. It enabled them to buy Negro slaves, hire private tutors for their children, buy harps and pianos for their music rooms, and engage itinerant painters to do the family portraits. Unfortunately, it shielded them from emotional crises and left them contented to express themselves as patrons of art and literature rather than as painters and writers.

The hill people were in many ways quite different from the Tory group. They did not come to Mississippi to reestablish an empire. Instead, they came from King's Mountain to escape a world that was too much for them. Preferring the alternative of independent isolation, they purposely forsook hope of wealth and leisure to hide themselves in the hilly retreats of northeastern Mississippi or in the great stretches of the Piney Woods. Here, scattered on small farms with their trading centers hardly more than crossroad stores, these people retained with remarkable purity their traditions. Folk songs and stories were their literature, and because they had no financial means with which to supply their domestic needs, their artistic urge found expression in such utilitarian handicrafts as quilt-making and woodwork.

The people who came to Mississippi on the crest of the "flush times" had purposes more nearly like what are considered "American" today. They moved to Mississippi in order "to get ahead." They meant to begin a tradition, not to continue one. Temperamentally, they were not contemplative or contented men; rather they were men of action, fired by hope of gain and believing that all things were within their grasp. This belief in progress held in temporary abeyance their desire for leisure.

But if they had some of the so-called failings attributed to Americans, they also had, to an exceptional degree, American strength. They were plungers, men with initiative, pioneers, fighters. They cared little for tradition but demanded that each man prove his worth. They acknowledged no upper class and were more willing to trust their own opinions than accept the standards of others. To them external expression was utilitarian even more than it was to the Piney Woods farmer, for it was propaganda, a means to an end. They had no wish to seek an escape. Even life's amenities, it would seem from the houses they built, were sought not so much for their intrinsic value as for the fact that the amenities would be tangible proof that they had "arrived."

Of the three groups, Tory, yeoman, and speculator, placed temporarily on Mississippi's frontier stage of civilization, the yeoman remained on the frontier, while the other two groups rose for a brief period, then were plunged into the frontier once more by the devastations of the War between the States. Even in the twentieth century the Mississippi environment is, by and large, agrarian in character. It is here that the Industrial Revolution is said to be finding its last frontier. This agrarian character of the State and the people illustrates itself in Mississippi's literature.

The chief characteristic of the ante-bellum literati was their manner of taking literature in their stride. It was for them but one facet of exceedingly busy lives; and as such it held the positivism of the frontier rather than the somewhat negative protest and escape elements of more settled contemporary New England. Their literature, taken with light good-humor, was divided into five classes: lyrics dashed off by hearty, well-read men; travel books and journals that shrewdly caught the significant details of the country; reminiscences and lusty anecdotes, whose humor was akin to the spaciousness of a frontier; the oratory of men of action; and the histories and diaries of men stirred enough to feel that their own and their contemporaries' debates needed preservation.

Lyric poetry was too delicate a medium to receive more than a passing glance, and this from the Tory element alone. Unfortunately, the Tory poets were neither strong enough nor good enough to create a literature of their own. In the same manner as that in which other members of their class became patrons rather than producers of art, the poetically inclined preferred losing themselves in the lyrical expressions of classic Greece and Rome, and of Elizabethan England.

It was in tale-telling and oratory that the Mississippian's interest in literature was centered. Even semi-historical and social analyses were tied together by stories. For instance, the first book of the type of humor that later reached its peak in Mark Twain was written by A. B. Longstreet, a Georgian who came to Mississippi in 1848 to assume the chancellorship of the new State university. In his *Georgia Scenes* Longstreet set the pattern later followed by Joseph G. Baldwin's *Flush Times of Alabama and Mississippi,* Joseph B. Cobb's *Mississippi Scenes,* Henry Clay Lewis's *The Swamp Doctor's Adventures in the Southwest,* and T. W. Caskey's *Seventy Years in Dixie.* These books are histories and social analyses that find common ground in their vast anecdotal humor. They are as full of stories as a local politician's campaign speech or a country minister's sermon.

Unfortunately, the greatest stories of the ante-bellum period have been preserved only by word of mouth. A few, however, found their way into the magazine, *The Spirit of the Times,* and have since been seined out for the contemporary reader in Arthur Palmer Hudson's *Humor of the Old Deep South.* Yet as excellent as some of these stories are, they are insignificant compared to those that never have been put on paper.

The stories always were tied to known persons or events. In place of being "Pat" and "Mike" the characters were Cousin Ephie or "Old Man" McWillie, and were about the bear fight last spring in that canebrake just south of Sandy Hill. They were intended for a close-knit audience who could appreciate, because they knew, all the humor inherent in the personalities and occasions exaggerated by the stories. These tales were later penalized because of their dated and localized character, but they nevertheless had, for their time, the unmistakable stamp of living literature.

It has been said that the Mississippian would much prefer "hearing a book" to reading it. They always have preferred speaking to writing. In oratory, "the literature of action," Mississippi has the sustained excellence that began with Pushmataha (the Choctaw chieftain who matched words with the great Tecumseh and won), and continued through a century to another chieftain, James K. Vardaman, the "Great White Chief" of the so-called common man. Orators ranged from the great Whig, George Poindexter, to Mississippi's first great political ranter, Franklin Plummer. With these came a score or more of matchless orators, men who made themselves and their audiences drunk with the wine of eloquence. Perhaps no other State has sent as many able and fluent speakers to the National Congress. The dynamic force of Robert J. Walker, the sonorous apostrophes of Seargent S. Prentiss, Henry S. Foote, Albert G. Brown, and Jefferson Davis, the quiet, human dignity of L. Q. C. Lamar, Edward Cary Walthall, James Z. George, and John Sharp Williams, as well as the barbed humor of "Private John Allen," have distinguished the Congresses of which they were members. The most polished orator of them all, Alexander K. McClung, never reached Congress; and two others, James L. Alcorn and William L. Sharkey, elected to the United States Senate, were refused seats because of reconstruction policies.

The reason for this superlative oratory is contained in the training and background of the orators. The conflicting legal claims to land during the "flush times" attracted to the State some of the Nation's ablest lawyers. They had their fortunes to make, everything to gain and nothing to lose. They were schooled in and anxious for debates; forcible in argument; reckless and brilliant. For them it was but a short and natural step from swaying juries in courtroom battles over the ownership of land to swaying constituents in contests for office. For the lawyer, oratory was the escalator that could lift a political candidate to higher ground.

The orator was necessarily dramatist, philosopher, author, and speaker rolled into one. Yet the greatest of the speeches, as the greatest of the anecdotes, have never been reduced to writing. Nor can they be. The speaker was in rapport with an audience whose emotional response, denied outlet in other forms of art, lifted him to constantly greater heights. A frenzied enthusiasm, partaking of mob spirit, rose in a continuous interplay of complementing appreciation between orator and listeners. There has seldom been such an example of the moving power of speech.

Yet some of the force of the ante-bellum debates can be gained from the accounts of participants in the contests who, retiring from the actual field of battle, carried on the fight in their memoirs. Examples are the journal of Andrew Ellicott, the memoirs of General James Wilkinson, and the histories of J. F. H. Claiborne, Mississippi's Herodotus.

Ante-bellum Mississippiana is seldom prosaic. A part of its vividness is due to the contagion of the material. The travel books, first written by visitors, are absorbing narratives of life in a strange country. The *Travels* of William Bartram; the notebooks of John Pope, Fortescue Cuming, Christian Schultz, and Francis Baily; descriptions, ornithological and otherwise, of Alexander Wilson and John James Audubon; the journal of Lorenzo Dow; the autobiography of Gideon Lincecum; the retrospect of Miss Harriet Martineau; and the journeys of Frederick Law Olmsted are fascinating accounts of early days on the great river and in the heart of the cotton kingdom.

Consequently, when native Mississippians turned to chronicling the events of their State's history or to describing the life they saw about them, they did not need to pad their stories to make them dramatic. John W. Monette's masterful *History of the Discovery and Settlement of the Mississippi Valley* was among the first accounts of the early eighteenth century colonization of the lower valley by the French. Standard source books for the early nineteenth century drama of cotton culture are Joseph Holt Ingraham's *The Southwest by a Yankee,* W. H. Sparks' *The Memories of Fifty Years;* and Reuben Davis' *Recollections of Mississippi and Mississippians,* which gives clear brief summaries of outstanding Mississippi personalities.

Henry Stuart Foote's *Bench and Bar of the South and Southwest,* an informal legal history, written by one of the greatest criminal lawyers in the State, is indispensable in a reconstruction of the life and spirit of the time.

Even the most scholarly historians, inclined to a stately rotund style, often relieved their pedantic conclusions by flashes of bright humor or lapses into violent personal opinion that made them almost poetic. The zestful *joie de vivre* of the chroniclers can not escape notice.

The almost complete absence of introspective literature shows the influence of an extremely hearty and gregarious life. Miss Sherwood Bonner of Holly Springs, looking at Mississippians in retrospect, told her friend, Mr. Henry Wadsworth Longfellow, that "they had the immense dignity of those who live in inherited homes, with the simplicity of manner that comes of an assured social position. They were handsome, healthy, full of physical force as all people must be who ride horseback and do not lie awake at night to wonder why they were born." Her description gives an excellent basis for understanding the literature they produced. Instead of distilling their experiences into a more individualized art, Mississippians have been ballad-makers.

The War between the States, in place of making an essential break in their literary tradition, only gave fresh incidents from which tale-tellers could fashion their anecdotes. There is no Mississippian of the present generation who has not been reared on stories of the fighting. And there are few Mississippians who, having heard the tales, have not wondered how it was possible that the Confederacy lost.

However, after 1865, unless the world-troubled souls could express themselves in speech, they were hard put to it to make a living at literature. Hence, Mississippi since the War between the States has had her share of *émigré* writers. Miss Bonner herself was one of these, though she regretted the necessity of leaving what she always considered her home. Mississippiana continued to be her special province, and *Suwanee River Tales* is an interesting revelation of where her heart lay.

In the same period with Miss Bonner was Irwin Russell, the genius whose work was cut short by his death in New Orleans in 1879—when he was but 26 years old. As the first Southern writer to master Negro dialect in verse, Russell has won national recognition with his long poem "Christmas Night in the Quarters." His influence has endured in the work of Joel Chandler Harris, and in a more subtle way in all present-day Mississippi literature. He was the first Mississippi writer of rank to keep his art free from propaganda. He labored for no cause in his portrayal of Mississippi Negro life. He sang instead of sermonizing; and the charm and catholicity of art is patent in all that he has done.

Russell, as an individual artist, is one of a handful of Mississippi writers who have been able to break with the powerful tradition of raconteur prose and unspeculative verse. S. Newton Berryhill, the "backwoods poet," introduced unusual themes into his verse, but even such a poem as "My Castle" is marred by his weakness for rhyme.

Among contemporaries, Stark Young, William Faulkner, and William Alexander Percy stand out. But, for the average Mississippian, Harris Dickson's *Old Reliable Tales, The Story of King Cotton,* and his tales of the Mississippi are more satisfying than the highly subjective work of Young and Faulkner. In the same way, the poems of David Guyton or such a good rouser as Walter N. Malone's "Opportunity" are more widely read than the poetry of Percy.

In Young and Faulkner, Mississippi can boast of outstanding exponents of both the romantic and realistic schools of regional literature. Born near each other, reared in the same town (though at slightly different periods), these two artists have drawn accurate pictures of Southern life: one, the most charming; the other, the most revolting. It is again an indication of the wide field covered by Mississippi material that these two men can both work in it without contradiction.

Young's novels are less novels than descriptive essays of Mississippi life hung on the convenient framework of the McGehee family and its "cudns" (cousins). He has not stuck exclusively to the ante-bellum period; both *River House* and *The Torches Flare* are as modern in time and as penetrating in analysis as his essays in defense of agrarianism. Because Mr. Young has taken his stand on the near perfection of life as expressed in the ante-bellum period, *Heaven Trees* and *So Red the Rose* are more representative of his work than the two novels first named.

It is unfortunate that hill-born William Faulkner is most widely known for a novel, *Sanctuary.* Even though it is a part of the "Jefferson" set, *Sanctuary* is different from such books as *The Sound and the Fury, As I Lay Dying, Light in August,* and *Absalom, Absalom.* An aviator himself, Faulkner occasionally deserts "Jefferson" in his short stories and in such a novel as *Pylon,* but this desertion can itself be traced to his boyhood and to watching the flight of eagles from an Oxford hill. There is little of the *émigré* about Faulkner even though his most enthusiastic audience may be international. When the "Jefferson" saga is completed—and if the short stories of the "Snopeses" are ever fused in a novel—America may see its finest bit of regional interpretation.

There is much about William Alexander Percy that is in the best Mississippi literary tradition. He is a lawyer, and literature is an absorbing but not a paying interest with him. Almost his whole work is lyric poetry; and he finds his métier in the fifteenth instead of in the present century. No typical Mississippi singer, however, could have produced such thoughtful work as Percy's *Sappho in Levkas* and *Enzio's Kingdom*. Nor in their best nostalgic moments could the traditional Mississippi lyricists have written so fine a piece as Percy's "Home" which, in its implications, is as persuasive an interpretation of the Delta as any of Stark Young's pronouncements.

Young, Faulkner, and Percy have won an established audience. A younger group, now fighting for recognition, is obviously more difficult to appraise: Robert Rylee, David Cohn, and James Street. Street is a newspaperman and was brought up hearing priceless old Mississippi stories; his *Look Away* is the result. Cohn seems to be in the tradition of the Mississippi analyzers and debaters. His *God Shakes Creation* is a fine piece of analysis of Mississippi Delta society. His *Picking America's Pockets* does the same thing in writing that Mississippi's cotton statesmen have done in speeches in the halls of Congress. Robert Rylee has shown exceptional promise in his *Deep Dark River* and *St. George of Weldon*. *Deep Dark River's* "Mose Southwick" is a Negro character worthy of a permanent place in Southern literature. In *St. George of Weldon* Mr. Rylee limns the man overlooked in the contemporary labelling of all Mississippians as either planters or tenants. He finds in the Delta—of all places—a bourgeois family; and his description of this family may influence a literature which, for the sake of truth, needs to put less emphasis on the two poles of society.

Architecture

Just as transportation lines form the skeleton of the social organism, so architecture reveals its character. In Mississippi's homes the student may recreate the pattern of the State's everyday existence; and enough remains of its early architecture to evoke a period of romance that has had few equals. French *voyageur,* English Tory, Spanish Don, and South-

A "DOG-TROT" CABIN

ern planter have crossed the great stage of the State, and each has left the color of his drama in his architecture.

The French were the first to settle. On the Coast, a locale rich in lore, their impress remains in the thick squat masonry and solid shipshape timbers of the old fort on Krebs Lake at Pascagoula, built by Sieur Joseph de la Point in 1718, before the founding of New Orleans.

Following the French, in 1763 Great Britain took over the empire west of the Alleghanies; into the Natchez region English colonists pushed even while the Atlantic seaboard was cutting its bonds with the mother country. No structure like the Krebs Fort remains as a monument to English settlement. Instead, the English built log cabins and rough-hewn blockhouses indistinguishable in type from those in the eastern half of the Continent.

But if the English left little that was distinctive, the dandified ideas of the Spanish, brought in with the last score years of the eighteenth century, made a profound impression. Swinging up from the Coast as far as the Natchez bluffs, the Dons left as distinct and as civilized an architecture as could be wrung from the wilderness. It is recognizable in the pleasantly-canted roof, the strong concentration of ornament, and the flair for flamboyant, if rare, color of the type known as "Spanish Provincial."

At the close of the eighteenth century Virginia and Carolina emigrants pushed into the region about and to the south of Natchez. The effect of this mixture of Old World and New was a fusion of significance. The grand staircases, spacious rooms, and haughty colonnades of the newcomers combined admirably with the delicate spindling work and fluid lines of their predecessors to produce homes in the "Grand Manner."

The Americans who came after the Spanish, settled themselves on the Natchez bluffs and, separated by wooded ravines, built homes of a type close to the Grand Manner yet distinctively rural. They made use of the same motives, but their adaptation of it was rangy, more open. Fronted by long single or double recessed galleries, the roof forming a transverse ridge, the homes were one-story, story-and-a-half, or two-story; and their simple, unflaunted dignity marked them for what their name implies, the "Southern Planter."

At a later date the Mississippi "hill-billy" made his home north and east of the Natchez country. One to every ridge, the houses were of logs (later clapboarded) with a wide wind-swept hall, known as the "dog-trot," running through the center, and with the cook house in the rear. As the people became wealthier and more prosperous, they closed in the center hall, often decoratively, and added long front porches. The dog-trot houses were so natural and traditional to these pioneers who had migrated from Tennessee, the Piedmont of Georgia, and the Carolinas, they constitute a contribution to American architectural types. A log cabin was an indivisible unit; in order to expand, another had to be built. That the hill-billy should lay his two cabins parallel and roof the open space between to make a hallway was natural. To keep the cook shack separate was dictated by fire hazard and the desire to keep the heat from the living room—time and saving steps for his wife were no part of the frontiersman's considerations. To sheathe the logs with clapboards was the first evidence of the end of the frontier. To wall in the dog-trot and add a porch was the last.

North of the hill-billy country, in the Central Hills and especially in the Black Prairie region during the "flush times" of the 1830's, a Greek Revival type of home was introduced, known locally as the "Black Belt" from the geographic region that produced it. The Black Belt home, contrasted with the house of the Grand Manner type, placed emphasis on sheer refinement of ornament and attenuation of proportions—a trait

McGAHEY HOUSE, A BLACK PRAIRIE HOME, COLUMBUS

apparently common to all architectural cycles toward their wane. The Shields home at Macon best expresses the characteristics of this form, though many examples may be found between Macon and Aberdeen, and, less concentrated, in the Northern Hills. The Georgia emigrants who built this type were evidently remembering their native models.

A number of ante-bellum homes were "imported," a term derived from having either the builder or the architect from England, France, Scotland, or Germany. Lochinvar at Pontotoc is typical, but the best examples are in Madison County, around Canton. The Delta, too, has many imported homes in this sense of the term, distinguishable by rubbed brick forms and asymmetrical planning, considered a sin in earlier times. The Delta, last settled, was peopled by luxury-loving Kentuckians and Carolinians who built from designs more often seen in the Ohio Valley.

The character, tastes, and economy of early Mississippians left their effect also upon church architecture. Along the Coast, in the Natchez district, and, following the flush times of the 1830's, in Holly Springs, Oxford, and Columbus, the wealthy planter and professional class built many churches with slave labor. Constructed usually of home-burned brick, the churches were, as a rule, Gothic Revival in design, with tall spires and stained glass windows. St. Mary's Cathedral, Natchez, completed in

1851, the Christian Church, Columbus, and the Episcopal Church, Holly Springs, built in 1858, are examples. The windows often were imported and unmatched. Interiors expressed good taste and a touch of luxury in open beams, delicate hand-carved decorations, and solid comfortable pews. More often than not a gallery extended across the front of the auditorium for the use of slaves who were prevented by law from having a church of their own.

But as the dog-trot type of house of the Piney Woods and Central Hills differed from the planter's mansions so did the plain and straightforward churches of these sections differ from those of the older and wealthier districts. These churches were, and to a large extent are, of a type colloquially called "shotgun." Comparatively small, oblong or box-like shells, they had frame side walls and V-shaped, split-shingle roofs. Without porches or an approach of any kind other than simple wood steps, they had single entrances front and rear. Windows were of plain unstained glass. The interiors offered the plainness of open rafters, unpainted walls and floors, and pine pews—the latter as stern and temperate as the people who worshipped in them. Hundreds of these churches dot the rural sections today, but the Toxish Baptist Church is a good example of their simple box-like construction.

What is more important to the layman than architectural types, however, is the life that determined them. This story must, of course, remain conjectural, but nothing could be more intriguing than to speculate upon its varied development. An examination of the timbers in the attic of the fort at Pascagoula reveals them to be so remarkably like the ribs of a ship that it is not farfetched to ascribe them to French ship carpenters. Indeed, the crews of the vessels loading on the Coast were the only artisans, their passengers being unskilled, or else preoccupied in a fruitless search for wealth. A building with walls as thick as the fort was needed for protection from Indians, not from the elements. Oyster shells, limitless in number, and the misty swaying drapery of Spanish moss were obvious and happy materials. The moss made an ideal binding element for the cement, such masonry improving with age and becoming rock-like with the passage of centuries. The life that could be wrung from the sterile sand of the Coast was as plain and as austere as the fort's outline. The lot of the French colonists was, if romantic, not luxurious. This much the fort makes plain.

As intimated, Spanish influence was strong in southwest Mississippi architecture. The Spaniard, though a pioneer, did not abandon his traditions. His was the first in Mississippi to warrant the name of a civilized

DUNLEITH, NATCHEZ

society. Before him, the path along the river was nameless; after him, it had become *El Camino Real*—The King's Highway—and the change was indicative of what he brought. His materials were the same the French and English had access to—logs from the forest or timber from dismantled flatboats—but in his particular use of them he displayed a Castilian taste that is expressed in works of art such as Ellicott's Inn at Natchez. Balance, refinement, and grace are revealed in the slope of the roofs, and in the toothpick colonnettes and ironwork of the slender galleries.

The Castilian's taste lingered after him. The styles of three nationalities—the Georgian style, traveling southwest with the planter, and the Creole mixture of French and Spanish coming up from New Orleans—met at Natchez. The search for a type or fusion of types that would be best adapted to the region led for a time into several blind alleys. The Regency, an in-between style that originated in England under George, Prince of Wales (1810–20), left Vancourt and the back portion of Hope Villa among its few examples. More significant was the Greek Revival. Started in England at the end of the eighteenth century, this style, now closely associated with ante-bellum plantation architecture, was

THE BRIARS, NATCHEZ

spontaneously accepted in this country by the Southerner because of his wealth, his wide travel, and his classic, country-gentleman tastes. The revival in the South was a facile thing. The Mississippian created his own architecture; his slave labor was unskilled, his models no more than pictures or memories; his real pattern was the Spanish. The result was the fusion of styles found at Natchez, predominantly Georgian in character, with columns and pediments relieved by the sloping roofs and galleries that broke across the classic fronts. In Concord, the former home of the Spanish governors at Natchez, which burned in 1901, this fusion probably reached its finest expression. The great columns that gave distinction to the building sprang from the earth itself. The lower story was extended to the face of the upper verandah, whose slender balustrade and smaller piazza posts were deeply recessed under the eaves of the light roof. The effect was Spanish West Indian as much as Greek. Though Dunleith at Natchez is the best remaining example of the adaptation of the classic order to planter comfort, Arlington and Auburn are better compositions and are truer to Natchez in their grandiose conception.

The Southern Planter type of home, while not as impressive as that of the Grand Manner, was more representative. Its use of the classic formula was as easy and as unconventional as the planter's life. The gallery was the prominent feature, as well it might have been when most of the owner's life was spent either on horseback or on his porch. Though the proportions were generous, they did not overawe. The stranger stopping by must have felt he was not so much "calling" as "visiting." In the Natchez area the best remaining Planter example is The Briars. On the Coast the best example is Beauvoir. Beauvoir shows the West Indian influence in the balanced arrangement of the pavilions at each side of, and entirely separate from, the big house. Also West Indian was the custom of devoting the ground floor to the service quarters and using the breezy main or second floor, reached by a number of exterior stairways, as the center of domestic life.

The materials for construction and the kind of workman available resulted in a crudity of detail in contrast to the conception of the exterior design. Though there were notable exceptions in the interiors of some of the Grand Manner homes at Natchez—the spiral stairway at Auburn, for instance—the detail that could not be imported was often unfinished. The scattered faced brick found in the homes may have come as ballast in the one-sided export cotton trade; but where wealth was not sufficient to import brick, the builders fired their own. Around Liberty, axe and adze marks on foundation timbers and sills hewn from the forest are visible in many sturdy homes. Beams were fastened with wooden pegs or with home-forged, wrought-iron nails. Heart yellow pine, though stout, was not easily worked—another reason for the lack of finish in the interiors.

The Black Prairie and the Central Hills show the Georgian free from Spanish influences. The slender proportions characteristic of these homes may be explained partly by the fact that they were frame, not brick; the builders saw no necessity for having too thick a column as support for the light roof. The homes were two-story; the planter wanted his second story to be as much shaded as the lower story; yet to have a thirty-foot column with the Grecian-prescribed three-foot diameter would have been an absurdity. The result was the beautifully slender column which distinguishes the Black Belt portico. This break from Grecian simplicity was carried further in the ornament, especially in the bric-a-brac that later was strung between the columns just under the roof line. This was feminine, the planter evidently considering a woman's taste important, and the architects have concurred in his judgment.

Adding to the undeniable charm of many of the Delta ante-bellum homes were the piers on which they rested, dictated by the necessity of letting the periodic flood run free beneath their floors. The first of these homes on stilts were unsightly, but for a people to whom beauty was

MELROSE, NEAR NATCHEZ

a necessity, there soon evolved such combinations as Longwood and Swiftwater.

To look upon all ante-bellum homes in Mississippi, therefore, as alike in a type loosely called Southern Colonial, is to destroy half the charm. The nuances—reactions to sectional and climatic restrictions, inherited customs and variations of pioneer life—provided great individuality within the type. (At Vicksburg, for instance, homes had to be built despite the inhospitable looking bluffs. On these promontories, the houses naturally and correctly assumed features less warm, more military, more disciplined.) The crudity of interior detail, the lack of compactness, and the wasted space, as compared with the architecture of other States, mean little; the Mississippian of the period was a generous outdoor man with plenty of land and servants. The classic, white-columned house pleasingly fulfilled its function—always the chief criterion of what is good.

The architecture developed since the War between the States, however, reflects only too well Mississippi's social and economic adjustments. Out of the war and reconstruction arose a merchant-banker society that supplanted the leadership of the planter. There was a transposition of social and economic prestige from rural districts to urban centers, and with the transposition were lost the qualities that had nourished individuality in design. The urban dweller does not possess the remoteness of broad acres and wooded groves; he lives in a comparatively crowded space; his tastes are conventionalized; his land is measured in lineal feet; and his servants are paid each Saturday at noon. To fit this new locale of conveniences, customs, and tastes, the builders adopted new methods and, recently, new materials. Unfortunately, the result is often neither distinctive nor, by comparison with Natchez, especially noteworthy.

The story of the plantation's decline and continued dependence is held fast in the planter's contemporary architecture. Impoverished and faced with the immediate task of reconstruction, the landowner was left at first with little time in which to build. When he finally had gained the time, he was no longer the dictator of his tastes, for under the new system capital was not on the farm but in the towns. Within a decade rural construction reached the level of barren necessity.

The influence of urban merchant-bankers on rural building, through the power of extended credit, has reduced what was once the "big house" on the farm to a questionably comfortable frame dwelling of indefinite plan and parentage. Tenant houses, by their number, catch the eye, but they hardly warrant architectural description. They are Delta, or Piney Woods, or "southern shacks"—local color in architecture. In the Tennessee Hills, in the Central Hills, and in the Piney Woods, the poorer homes with their mud-wattle chimneys, sagging roofs, and vertical weather-boarding are as bare and stark as the poverty they represent; the bright corrugated tin roofs covering weather-beaten walls of barns represent a false economy. Many of the richer homes are uncertain in design and lacking in taste.

With the exception of Natchez, Vicksburg, Columbus, and Holly Springs, the towns, submerged both socially and economically before the war, gained from the Reconstruction Period an importance that was in direct ratio to the rural districts' decline. And, again as in the rural districts, the change developed an architecture that almost defies classification. As if hastily discarding traditional rags for costumes that better expressed their new station in life, the towns followed the North into a building boom that has lasted from the 1880's to the present (1938). Paradoxically, the late economic depression rather than the boom proved an architectural blessing.

The period between 1880 and 1914 belonged to a generation of newly empowered urban persons who expressed themselves, not in the simpler classic styles adhered to by the planter, but in elaborate display. Volume was preferred to refinement of detail; and an exterior trim of jigsaw decorations matched a gaudy interior that has come to characterize the period. (This exhibitionism sometimes resulted in houses vaguely reminiscent of the grandiose homes of the 1850's—Longwood at Natchez and the Walter place at Holly Springs). Contractors and carpenters, as much without benefit of architectural advice as had been the slaves, reproduced in their busy practice the styles made popular in the North by the boom of 1873. The Victorian Gothic, the Romanesque, and the American version of the Queen Anne were architectural types accepted as representative of wealth. In the cities these three types marked the better-class residential section. In the smaller towns, where the wealthier families usually occupied the first tree-shaded block north of the business district, the preference was for the local carpenter's version of Victorian Gothic. Such homespun variations sacrificed convenience for false splendor, and in a determination to achieve volume obliterated the lines that originally gave the design a name. The houses were of frame construction and, usually, two stories in height. With their elaborate gingerbread trimmings, bulging bay windows, and pointed turrets they remain to mark the home of the banker or merchant in a majority of Mississippi towns today. The Rowan home, with its unstudied massiveness, its twenty-three rooms, and its gingerbread exterior treatment, is an example *(see Tour 5, Sec. b)*. The elder types remain as criteria of good taste, and to these models latter-day designers return for inspiration.

The abandonment of tradition for massiveness found expression in the building of the New Capitol at Jackson in 1903. Designed by Theodore C. Link in the manner of the National Capitol and built of gray sandstone and marble, it faces the business district from ten landscaped acres *(see JACKSON)*.

The rise of the lumber industry, the establishment of railroad shops, and the building of a few cotton mills gave to the Piney Woods, to Meridian, and to Stonewall what were perhaps the first grouped, standardized houses for the working class. These houses, small frame buildings one-story high, were erected by the company and grouped close to the commissary—a barnlike frame structure raised from the ground and fronted with a narrow shed porch. Lean-to porches extend across the front and rear of the houses, and thin bisecting partitions divide the interiors into four rooms of equal size. At Quitman, once the site of the

State's largest sawmill, and D'Lo, a typical sawmill ghost town, are examples of grouped, company-owned houses.

At Laurel and at Electric Mills, however, the lumber industry placed emphasis upon housing almost from the start. Here the policy of encouraging home ownership and individuality of taste has resulted in the white millworkers' building neat cottages suited to the size and needs of their families. These low-priced cottages have enhanced in a modest way Mississippi's architectural and social scene, and have supplied an example of economical housing reform.

The World War and its aftermath of inflation brought to an end the merchant-banker era of exaggerated architectural design. Rural people, attracted by urban prosperity, migrated from farm to town, swelling the population and creating demands that the urban centers, with prewar physical equipment, were not able to meet. A decade of unrest, the 1920's brought along a fundamental alteration in Mississippi's urban architecture. A variety of types appeared. French Provincial, Dutch Colonial, and the half-timbered manor house of Elizabethan England, subject, as always, to the contractor's conception, became the popular types. These houses, the homes of business and professional families, were developed, remote from the business districts, in new residential areas called subdivisions. The Florida version of the Spanish style was adopted by a few builders on the Coast during the boom of 1925–27, but in Mississippi as a whole, this style is too conspicuously incongruous for popularity.

When the business and professional families deserted the residential area traditionally allotted to them, skilled laborers and white-collar workers moved in. Here, between the "best family" section left untouched since pre-war days and the traditional outer fringe of Negro houses, the skilled laborers and middlemen built their bungalows. These bungalows, constituting the majority of urban dwellings in Mississippi today, vary in material—wood, stucco, or brick—but they do not vary essentially in design. They are squat, low-roof houses of from four to six rooms. Sitting close to the earth, half protected by the shade of chinaberry trees, they indicate the workingman's somewhat raised standard of living; but their low ceilings, thin walls, and lack of basements show no regard either for the Mississippi climate or its traditions.

The greatest architectural change of the 1920's, however, was the advent of the skyscraper. Prior to the war the demands for office space had been comparatively light. The second and third floors of thickwalled, brick structures with cornices, built for the purpose of housing

STAIRWAY AT COTTAGE GARDEN, NATCHEZ

retail establishments on the ground floor, had been partitioned into a number of offices. But post-war prosperity and the subsequent migration to urban centers increased the need for more modern buildings. Architectural advice was sought—a procedure as new to Mississippi as were the resultant buildings—and for the first time skyscraper methods of construction were employed in commercial buildings.

At Jackson, the Tower Building (reputedly the tallest reenforced concrete building in the South: 18 stories high with a penthouse and a two-story tower) and, at Meridian, the Threefoot Building are the State's best examples of set-back design. C. H. Lindsley was architect for both buildings. Wyatt C. Hedrick, employing the same type of construction in designing the Lamar Life Insurance Building, Jackson, adorned it with Gothic motifs and a decorative treatment of the top. The thin rectangular New Merchants Bank Building, Jackson, emphasizes its 17 stories by a perpendicular treatment.

With modern designs in commercial building came also for the first time engineering methods for industrial building. The best examples of these are the buildings of the Reliance Manufacturing Company, Columbia, the Pioneer Hosiery Mill, Hattiesburg, and Meridian Garment Factory, Meridian.

In this period higher standards were gained in institutional and religious architecture. The 78 buildings of the Mississippi Insane Hospital are grouped with village-like informality on spreading, landscaped acres. The buildings, not over two stories in height, are designed in the manner of Colonial Williamsburg. The exterior walls are of red brick with white trim, and the roofs of the larger buildings are crowned with white cupolas. N. W. Overstreet and A. H. Town were the architects. At Laurel, the Presbyterian Church, designed by Rathbone DeBuys, consists of two buildings joined by a tower. The architecture of the church proper is based upon twelfth century English Gothic precedent; the other building, the church school, is Collegiate Gothic in type.

As indicated, the depression proved an architectural advantage to Mississippi. Prior to the Government's policy of extending financial aid to builders through housing agencies, a majority of Mississippi's buildings were constructed without architectural advice or planning. They were not only of indefinite design but ill-fitted to the owner's needs. But the Government, wielding the power of extended credit more intelligently than the merchant-banker, demanded that engineering principles be applied. Each applicant for a building loan was required to have the plans of his building approved by a competent staff of architects. Fortunately, the architects accepted from the beginning the hitherto ignored fact that, tradition notwithstanding, the urban Missisippian does not live out of doors; he lives and works indoors, and he has need for compactness and modern conveniences. This simple acceptance of fact is the outstanding characteristic of recent building trends.

Supervision of planning and construction brought to the State tangible evidences of two recently developed schools in architecture. The Howle home, Meridian, is typical of the school which follows traditional designs, with stress on Colonial types. The home is smaller than those of classic conception in the past, but the size does not remove the classical stamp. One story in height, with seven rooms, it is carefully detailed with a finely proportioned entrance and well-spaced windows. The exterior is of wood siding, while the interior has wood-paneled wainscoting, with wallpaper above that reproduces nicely an early pattern. The design of the R. F. Reed home, Tupelo, replaces the architectural doctrine of "balanced symmetry" with that of "utility." Built for comfortable living, it is of a flat-roof design with sun and recreational decks. The exterior walls are white reenforced concrete with steel frame and metal casement windows.

The Government, in addition to aiding in the building of dwelling houses, has placed a new Federal building, modern in design, in every town of importance, and has aided financially in the construction of municipal buildings. The Jones County jail and New Albany city hall, the latter designed as a monolithic concrete structure by E. L. Malvaney, are examples of municipal buildings, while the Meridian post office, designed by Frank Fort, is perhaps the State's outstanding Federal building. Modern in design, with fluted pilasters and no cornices, the post office building is noted for its mass and proportion rather than for its detail.

These modern buildings are both too new and too few to do more than hint that Mississippi is entering upon a new era of building that may equal if not surpass the classic period of ante-bellum days. In the meanwhile, its architecture remains a confused picture of classic mansions, vertical weatherboarded houses, tenant shacks, bungalows, voluminous gingerbread displays, and thick-walled two- and three-story commercial buildings. The integrated character of life in the ante-bellum period, reflected in an architecture of spaciousness and dignity, is lacking.

Music

If Mississippi is judged by its singing folk, rather than by the number of its symphony orchestras, truly it can be called a musical State. The Negro folk, traditionally musical, comprise more than half of Mississippi's population. The white folk, for the most part, are descendants of those early settlers who, in their westward trek, stopped in the hills of northeast Mississippi or in the Piney Woods. Living on and close to the soil, they have retained the lore, customs, and songs of their Anglo-Saxon ancestors.

The songs of the Negro fall into three groups—spirituals, work songs, and social songs. The spirituals are America's most distinctive and artistic contribution to folk music. Expressing strong emotions and simple faith, they have a beauty, power, and sincerity that are irresistible. Such songs as "Jesus the Man I'm Lookin' For," "Judgment Day is Rollin' Round," "Angels All Waitin' for Me," and "They Crucified My Lawd" show the religious fervor of the Negro spiritual. These and many others may be heard in their purest and most impressive form in the Negro churches, especially the rural ones. The white visitor who comes in a spirit of sympathetic interest is welcome, and if especially interested in folk music he will find authentic expression here. The school choruses have won international recognition for their interpretation of the spirituals *(see EDUCATION)*.

In the second group of songs are those of the levee, the railroad, the river, and the field, best of which possibly are the cotton-picking songs. The work songs are improvised, growing out of one phrase or line, with the repeated whack of the hoe or the stroke of hammer or pick setting the rhythm. An old Negro, asked to repeat a song, said, "I ain't got no reg'lar words, I jes say what my mind tells me." For this reason and because the Negro's intonations as well as the words vary with his feelings, his songs are difficult to reproduce in written form. The following improvisation heard in a cotton field near Columbia is a good example of the field song:

> *Old voice singing bass:*
> I know it was th' blood
> *High soprano in another part of field:*
> I know it was th' blood

> *Thirty or more voices together:*
> I know it was th' blood,
> I know it was th' blood,
> I know it was th' blood for me.
> Second Stanza
> *Young tenor:* One day when I was lost,
> *Young soprano:* One day when I was lost,
> *All:* One day when I was lost,
> He died upon the cross,
> I know it was th' blood for me.

Each solo singer held his last note until it was picked up by the next singer or group of singers. The workers continued for half an hour singing variations of this song as they picked the cotton.

The social songs of the Negro run the gamut of his social activities and range from the coarse song of the roustabout to the sentimental message of the lover. This group includes nursery songs, play, dance, and animal songs, as well as the "blues" and more sophisticated jazz-band and swing tunes. One of the most popular of the animal songs and one rich in personification is about "de co'tin frog:"

> De frog went a co'tin, he did ride. Uh-huh! Uh-huh!
> De frog went a co'tin, he did ride.
> Wid a sword an' a pistol by his side. Uh-huh! Uh-huh!

Contrasting with the gayety and homeliness of this song is a long line of melancholy "blues" developed from the "Memphis Blues" and the "St. Louis Blues." Because of the increasing influence of the city upon the Negro and the resulting departure from the simple life, the number of social songs has increased with a proportionate decrease in the number of spirituals and work songs. Present-day conditions are not conducive to creation of the latter—the laundry is fast supplanting the wash tub under the trees, and the modern white mother objects to having her baby sung to sleep with such a typical Negro lullaby as the following:

> Don't talk. Go to sleep!
> Eyes shet and don't you peep!
> Keep still, or he jes moans:
> "Raw Head and Bloody Bones!"

The most characteristic musical expression of Mississippi white folk is in their group singing of hymns, many of which are from the "Sacred Harp," a hymnal published in 1844. From shortly after spring planting until cotton-picking time, regular "singings" are held, reaching a height in midsummer *(see WHITE FOLKWAYS)*. Besides hymns, these folk sing the English, Scotch, and Irish ballads of their ancestors, often in modified form, and songs of American origin—cowboy and Western songs, Civil War songs, ballads of outlaws and "bad men," and those inspired by local events such as the Casey Jones tragedy. Equally as popular as the community singings are the "sociables," at which Old Fiddlers Contests are held, and singing games are played by old and young *(see Tour 17)*.

Although there is no State supervisor of music, there is music in the schools, and the larger cities have full-time supervisors of public school music. In the spring of 1926 the State High School Accrediting Commission ruled that credits be granted for high school piano and violin, and for public school music, which might include sight singing, ear training, theory of music, rhythm band, and music appreciation. Since 1935 members of high school bands and orchestras have received these credits. All licenses to teach music are issued and all credits approved by the State Board of Music Examiners, a group appointed by the State Superintendent of Education from among members of the various college faculties. Spring field meets and band contests have brought about a vast improvement in school music by provoking a greater interest in it.

The Federation of Music Clubs holds an annual contest in voice, violin, piano, organ, choral music, hymn singing, and memory. Organized in 1916, the federation has a membership approximating 3,000, with 33 senior and 70 junior groups. Scattered in towns over the State and in many of the colleges, these federated clubs serve as a great musical stimulus.

Mississippi colleges, especially those for girls, have from earliest times included music in their courses of study. Records of Elizabeth Female Academy in 1840 mention "the performance of a very fine class in music." A report on the Female Institute of Holly Springs shows "two pianos purchased in 1838," and "yearly tuition for Piano or Guitar $50, Harp $60." Old yearbooks of Hillman College, organized in 1853, give a curriculum with music included. Whitworth College, established in 1858, always has placed emphasis on music; its spring concerts once were so widely attended that special trains were run to accommodate the crowds. The burning of Amite Female Academy by the Federals caused the destruction at the same time of its 13 highly prized pianos—pianos transported with great effort and cost through the wilderness to Liberty.

In Natchez are substantial reminders that there was music of the highest type in ante-bellum Mississippi. The violin presented by Ole Bull, the famous Norwegian violinist, to his young friend, Gustave Joseph Bahin, when Bull played in Natchez in 1851, is treasured by the Bahin family. The piano played when Jenny Lind sang in Natchez the same year is at Richmond. Other famous musical instruments in Natchez are the silver-stringed Palyel-Wolfe piano at Windy Hill Manor; the century-old spinet at Arlington; the harp at Rosalie; the harpischord at Hope Farm; the piano at Longwood, which legend says was the first grand piano brought into Mississippi; the quaint square piano at Clover Nook, which was played at the Lafayette ball.

Today in the colleges for women are found most of the State's outstanding music departments. Mississippi State College for Women, organized in 1885 with music as a part of its first curriculum, has continually played an important part in the development of the higher type of music in Mississippi. It is the only college in the State with membership in the National Association of Schools of Music; its music department is the only one housed in a music hall built especially for and dedicated to this art. Here in 1904 Paderewski gave his first concert in Mississippi, and was the first artist of international fame since the War between the States to appear in concert on a Mississippi college campus. This concert was made possible by Weenonah Poindexter, the young director of the department, who signed the $1,000 contract, equal in amount to her yearly salary. An extra $1,000 from the proceeds of the concert was the beginning of a fund creating for the college an artist series which has brought to it many of the world's best musicians.

Although the University of Mississippi had no regular music department until 1930, its Glee Club has been active since 1900, and the new department gives promise of being one of major importance. State Teachers College, with an excellent music department, is best known for its Vesper Choir, which sang before the National Federation of Music Clubs in Philadelphia in 1935, and the Louisiana Federation in 1936. The Mississippi Woman's College has received special recognition for its choral and chamber music. Belhaven College, Jackson, places especial emphasis on music. Each of the above colleges confers the degree of Bachelor of Music. Delta State Teachers College and Blue Mountain College have active choral groups and offer courses in piano, voice, and violin. Mississippi State College has no music department, but has an excellent military band.

The following are among the musicians born in Mississippi who have received national recognition: Chalmers Clifton, Jackson, is State Director of New York's Federal Music Project under the Works Progress Administration, and teaches conducting at Columbia University; William Grant Still, Woodville, is best known for his Afro-American Symphony (1930), an idealization of his heritage, the spiritual, and for his Symphony in G Minor—"Song of a New Race," which was performed by the Philadelphia

Symphony Orchestra in December 1937; A. Lehman Engle, Jackson, a pianist, composer, and critic, directs the Madrigal Singers, one of the most popular of the New York WPA music groups; Walter Chapman, Clarksdale, is a pianist, composer, and teacher; Creighton Allen, Macon, is a pianist and composer. Although born in Alabama, the Negro composer, William C. Handy, nationally known as the "granddaddy of the blues," lived in Clarksdale for a number of years. He has said that his chief inspiration for the "blues" that made Beale Street famous came from his experiences in Mississippi. Mississippi's own pioneer in jazz, Bud Scott, born in Natchez, has attained more than State-wide fame. His orchestra, which may be heard at the Pilgrimage Balls, has played for three Presidents—McKinley, Theodore Roosevelt, and Taft.

No hotel or cafe in the State employs a full-time orchestra, except on the Coast during an unusually good season. The largest night clubs are along the Gulf Coast, and many of these operate only during summer tourist season. Their orchestras are imported through the American Music Association, as proprietors find that the big-name orchestras draw the crowds and local orchestras lack popular appeal. Though there is little demand for orchestral musicians, there is an active chapter of the Musicians Union, which regulates wages and insists that none but union members be employed locally. Their chief competition is from college orchestras, which, with the exception of the one from University of Mississippi, are non-union and can afford to play for lower wages than professional musicians.

The greatest single impetus toward more and better music in the State (1937) is coming from the Federal Music Project under the direction of Jerome Sage. With few unemployed symphony orchestra musicians in the State, the program is largely one of musical education. Approximately 20,000 persons are receiving musical training either in quartets, choruses, piano and violin classes, small orchestras, or listening groups. The music appreciation classes, brought to the children of the rural homes where radios have been made possible by the rural electrification program, have created a new listening group with vast musical potentialities.

PART II
Main Street and Courthouse Square

Biloxi

Railroad Stations: L. & N. Station, Reynoir and Railroad Sts., for Louisville & Nashville R.R.
Bus Station: 204 E. Beach Blvd. for Greyhound Bus Lines.
Airport: Municipal, W. Howard and Glennan Aves. No scheduled service.
Local Busses: Busses hourly to Gulfport and Pass Christian, fare 25¢. Half-hour schedule to all parts of the city, fare 5¢.
Taxis: Fare 10¢ within city.

Accommodations: Seven hotels; rooming houses; cottages; tourist cabins.

Information Service: Chamber of Commerce, Kennedy Hotel, Reynoir St.

Motion Picture Houses: One.

Swimming: Municipal pier, free; beach front, free.
Golf: Country Club, Pass Christian Rd., reasonable greens fee.
Riding: White House Stables, $1.50 per hr.; Edgewater Gulf Stables, $1.50 per hr.
Boating and Fishing: Yacht Club and hotel piers; gasoline boats chartered, $15 a day up; sailboats (skipper included) $1 per hr. up.

Annual Events: Summer Sports Carnival, 10 days preceding July 4; Regatta, July 4; Blessing of Fleet, Sunday preceding Aug. 15; Mardi Gras, for two weeks prior to Lent; golf tournaments, Feb. and March.

BILOXI * (22 alt., 14,850 pop.), the first permanent white settlement in the Mississippi Valley, holds within its narrow streets and aged, provincial houses the charm of an Old World village that has turned to fishing and the entertainment of tourists. Confined to the low ridge of a narrow, finger-like peninsula, the city stretches long and lean between the Mississippi Sound on the south and the Bay of Biloxi on the north. Howard Avenue is its backbone. Lined with one- and two-story business structures, whose stuccoed exterior walls have mellowed to a soft cream color that is in keeping with the atmosphere of the narrow street, this main artery fuses the modernity of Beach Boulevard facing the sound with the age-heavy, older section along the bay. Here, in markets and drug and department stores, the native, a fisherman or boatbuilder of proud Castilian and venturesome Gallic antecedents, meets the stranger with that subtle acceptance of fact peculiar to Old World peoples.

South of Howard Avenue and connected with it by narrow lane-like streets, where giant live-oaks arch their branches over the roadways, is the beach front. Developed primarily as a recreational center, Beach Boulevard (a part of US 90) stretches for approximately six miles between the sound, with its stepped concrete sea wall, artificial beaches, and lean, wooden piers, and a line of resort hotels, summer cottages, and amusement parks. The tone is bright—sunshine on blue-green water,

* A map of Biloxi is on the back of the State map, in pocket at end of book.

white sands, and tall green longleaf pines. The atmosphere is the gayety of people out for a holiday. Here and there among the modern cottages of frame and stucco, or bordering the wide green lawn of a hotel, which rises high above oak, pine, and camphor trees to catch the breeze that is always blowing, are planter type houses—homes left from days when ante-bellum planters came to the Coast to escape the heat and fever of their inland plantations. To the passerby these houses are often little more than glimpses of white through great boxwood hedges. Raised high off the ground, with broad wind-swept galleries and wide cool halls, they express both an appreciation of the climate and a sense of tradition. Surrounded by green lawns, solid hedges, and well-designed gardens of camellia japonicas, poinsettias, crapemyrtles, and azaleas, they give to the beach front the sense of permanence that saves it from garishness.

North of Howard Avenue the older section of the city spreads haphazardly to the shore line of the bay. This greater portion of Biloxi has remained under the influence of the natives for three centuries, and now, time-worn, graying, and slightly dingy, it holds an exotic impress that fascinates. Contrasted with the bright white and green of the beach front, its tone is the quiet serenity of sunlight and shade. Tidy, steep-roofed cottages with brick or stucco side walls aged to a deep russet or cream sit behind low picket fences in the almost eternal shade of great oak trees. Streets perpetuate their birthright in their names—Benachi, Lameuse, Cuevas, Reynoir. Many of them paved with finely crushed oyster shells, they stretch through the shade as soft and gray as the Spanish moss overhead; others are as bright and white with sunlight as patches of snow that native children read about but never see. Here, too, the force of the breeze that blows continuously against the beach front is broken, leaving the pungent odors of a well-seasoned cuisine unruffled and the dark green surface of the bay unmoved.

On the "Point" at the eastern end of Howard Avenue is a clearly defined section, strange in a State whose white population is 99 percent Anglo-Saxon. Grouped about the Wesley house, and within a stone's throw of a packing or canning plant, live the southern European peoples brought to Biloxi as laborers in the fishing industry. The cabin-like houses inhabited by these Poles, Austrians, Czechoslovakians, and Yugoslavs were built as temporary structures in 1925, but they have never been replaced or improved. Many of them rest on stilts at the water's edge. Yet the new fisherfolk, with strange customs and heavy accents, have imparted to the section a romantic atmosphere that almost hides its poverty.

Northeast, between Howard Avenue and the bay, is the Negro section. Although Biloxi has the largest foreign-born population (3.3 percent) in the State, it has the lowest percentage of urban Negro population. The majority of Biloxi's 2,445 Negroes (16.5 percent of the population), do manual labor on boats and in factories, though many find work as domestic servants and a few maintain themselves independently either by fishing or by farming small plots of truck. The

OYSTER FLEET, BILOXI

number of them who are home owners is unusually large for Mississippi. Also unusual, in the State but not for the Coast, is the fact that a majority of them are members of the Roman Catholic Church. After the War between the States the white Roman Catholics of Biloxi did good social and religious work among the Negroes of their community. For years the Negro Catholics worshipped with the whites, some even holding pews.

But in 1914 a frame structure of Gothic design, Our Mother of Sorrows Church, was built for them. Three years later the church established a school for Negro children. This school is operated independently of the Negro school maintained by the city. In 1933 a ninth grade was added to the school, and each year thereafter another grade until 1937 when the first class graduated from the 12th grade.

Biloxi, as a resort city, makes playing its business. The amusement calendar is divided by the winter and summer tourist seasons. The principal winter tourist sport is golf, with tournaments in February and March. The Biloxi Tourist Club, however, sponsors horseshoe, croquet, and roque tournaments for winter visitors, and in cooperation with the chamber of commerce promotes dances, oyster-bakes, boat trips, community sings and concerts, bridge tournaments, and picnics. The winter night club season—a changing number of establishments with changing names are scattered along the beach front—is from before Christmas to Lent.

The summer season is gayer, with swimming, boating, and racing. The Biloxi yacht race course is one of the most difficult in the South, and the annual regatta in July is rated second only to Newport in events of its kind. Each Sunday afternoon from the middle of April to Labor Day catboats and fisher-class sloops race for trophies awarded by the Biloxi Yacht Club. Each September winning skippers in the fisher-class eliminations race in the Lipton Cup series against ten other Gulf clubs. Fishing boat owners often supplement their incomes by carrying visitors to the outlying islands.

The residents, however, play almost as much as the tourists. A social study made of the fisherfolk in 1934 revealed their overwhelming preference for dancing as a recreation. Their dance halls, separate from the hotel pavilions, are numerous toward the Point. Charity dances are given occasionally for unfortunate persons or families, the use of the hall being donated by the management. Admission to these halls is usually billed: "Gentlemen 25¢, Ladies free." Free dances with free beer mark the summer political campaign. On occasions, such as a marriage ceremony, even the Slavonians forego the conservative habits that have won for them the proprietorship of a majority of the seafood packing plants. The celebration, consisting chiefly of dancing and feasting, often lasts a week. Of like expansiveness is the celebration staged when a young Slavonian achieves some success such as completing his college course or receiving a political appointment. At this time his father endeavors to have even the mayor at the celebration.

In addition to the regular mercantile and service businesses catering to the needs of both a static and transient population, Biloxi has approximately 20 canning factories for seafoods and an equal number of plants for the shipping of raw oysters. More than 2,000 boatmen are engaged in catching fish for the factories and more than 3,000 persons are employed inside. The approximately 800 boats engaged in the fishing end of the seafood industry are divided almost equally between the shrimp and oyster fleets. In many instances, however, boats are oystering at one season and shrimping at another (oyster season is from November to April; shrimp season from August 15 to June 15). The greater number of these boats are owned by individuals and are classed as "independents" to distinguish them from "factory boats."

Within this general oyster and shrimp packing industry not an inconsiderable section is devoted to the handling of fish. The fish, however, are shipped fresh since none of the canning plants is devoted to packing them. Speckled sea trout, mullet, croaker, redfish (channel bass), drum, catfish, and pompano are shipped in considerable quantities. The fishing is done by individual boats, usually around the outlying islands or in the Louisiana marshes. Most of the fish are caught by seining, but large numbers are taken at certain periods of the year by pole and line.

Like all new and expanding industries, commercial fishing in Biloxi has had its drama of conflict; and this drama has been heightened by the lawless—certainly unmoral—character of the early fishers. The Old World fishermen, starting with a single net in this land which had promised them individual fortunes, were not a folk to be squeamish about tactics. This saga of unchecked competition ended only when a few strong and ruthless men brought stability out of noisome war.

Things other than competitive strife belong to the Biloxi fishermen, however. Their saga is distinguished also by the color which the Gulf and its tree-hidden coast shed on peoples who cast their nets in its waters. In keeping with their traditions, they follow the Old World custom of blessing their fleet before it puts out for the deep-sea fishing grounds each year. In a quiet cove of the bay, beneath the white cross that commemorates the landing of the French in 1699, the fishermen anchor their boats on the Sunday preceding each August 15 and pray for a successful season. In this cathedral of nature, mass is held with all the solemn dignity and splendor of the rituals of the Roman Catholic Church. After mass, the priest steps from boat to boat, blessing the occupants. Each boat is manned by from two to five men who that day will put out to sea to work from dawn to dusk, and at night drop anchor wherever fishing is left off.

Weeks and months out among the oyster reefs and shrimp "strikes" have given them something of the romance compounded of unforgettable scenes; they have felt the quiet, thickly-moving Gulf, and have watched the horizon of long, low rollers washing at stringy islands, where dead stumps of conquered cypress mark a point that was land; they know the constant sound of wind in sails, and the taste of salt; and they have come home again to beach their schooners on bars that are white against the gray and green of moss-hung oaks.

Growing directly out of the fishing and seafood industry is the trade of shipbuilding. The Biloxi lugger (a power-propelled boat from 30 to 46 feet in length) represents the experience of generations in building boats suitable for coastal waters. Nearly all the shrimp and oyster boats operating out of Biloxi, as well as many of the luggers used in Louisiana, are Biloxi-built. Each boat averages approximately $3,000 in value. Many of the fisher-class sloops (a standard 6-meter sloop of shallow draft built for both racing and pleasure) used in the Sunday races are Biloxi-built, while the Biloxi catboat has attained more than local fame. The larger of the catboats, 21 feet long with a 10-foot beam and a sail of 30 feet at its peak, are considered the fastest boats in their class on the Coast. In addition to building, the Biloxi yards service and repair work and pleasure boats. A majority of the shipuilding factories are "backyard" factories—long open-sided sheds between the rear of a fisherman's cottage and the bay. The owner is often a skilled ship carpenter who engages in the shrimp and oyster business during part of the year and builds boats when the dull season sets in. Many of the concerns are family affairs, though the volume of production is considerable.

But perhaps all this is but the fulfillment of what the Biloxi (Ind., *first people*) knew would some day come to pass. Legendary with these Indians who once passed their time in the shade of the oaks on the shore of the bay that bears their name was the tale of white, godlike giants who, centuries before, had left their mounds as burial places on this shore and moved to the East. They were to remain in the East for a time, when they were to return to their mounds and to the shore where one had only to eat the fish and oysters and drink from Biloxi's healing springs to find contentment.

And the gods did "return," in 1682, when La Salle took possession of the Mississippi River in the name of the King of France, and 17 years later, when Pierre le Moyne, Sieur d'Iberville, dropped anchor at Ship Island *(see Side Tour 1A)* and, after a preliminary exploration of the coast, decided on the Bay of Biloxi as the place for his settlement. A boulder and a cross mark the approximate spot where the company of Frenchmen first stepped from their boats to the mainland.

From this first landing of Iberville, when Biloxi became the capital of a region including what is now Yellowstone Park, to the removal of the seat of government to New Orleans in 1723, the history of Biloxi is the history of the lower Mississippi River Valley. To Fort Maurepas, built on the eastern shore of the bay, came, in addition to the Biloxi, members of the Pascagoula, Pensacola, Chickasaw, and Choctaw tribes, rubbing their faces with white earth to honor Iberville and his brothers. Hardy *voyageurs* from Canada paddled down the Mississippi to settle in the newly opened province, bringing the strain of weathered frontier blood necessary for the founding of a permanent settlement. Chevalier Henry de Tonti and Fathers Davion and Montigny were among the more distinguished of the visitors who came from the river; and here Sauvolle, Tonti, and many knights of St. Louis lie buried where they died in the first years of the 18th century. Sauvolle, brother of Iberville, was stricken with yellow fever in August of 1701, and Tonti followed to the grave in 1704.

In 1702, because of a destructive fire, the administrative center of the colony was moved to Mobile Bay, and Dauphine Island became the harbor. In 1717, however, a typical Gulf hurricane choked the Dauphine harbor with sand, and Ship Island became again the principal anchorage

BENACHI AVENUE, BILOXI

for vessels from France. A fort was built on the island to protect the pass.

In 1719 headquarters were moved from Mobile back to Old Biloxi, and two years later across the bay to Fort Louis at New Biloxi, which remained the administrative center of the colony until Bienville procured its removal to New Orleans in 1723. But even after New Orleans had been established, ships from France continued to touch first at Ship Island.

The progress of the colony during the first score of years after 1699 was characterized by an entire neglect of agricultural pursuits, and hardships from famine and disease. The scum of France, convicts and adventurers of both sexes, was shipped as colonists, usually against their will. The occasional supplies from France, Santo Domingo, and Vera Cruz were so inadequate that the troops were quartered upon the Indian tribes. In 1718, after Crozat, the French banker, had failed in his grandiose schemes to strengthen the colony, the even more grandiose schemer, John Law, first great promoter of modern times, adopted the policy of making considerable concessions of land to wealthy and powerful personages who could introduce a specified number of settlers on the lands. Under this scheme, Negroes, Swiss, and Germans were brought to the colony; the Negroes as slaves, the Swiss and Germans as settlers. Exasperated by hunger, many of these immigrants rebelled in 1723 and attempted to reach the English settlements in the Carolinas. The hardy French Canadians survived, in many cases taking Indian wives.

France at last realized her mistake, and in order to "make a solid establishment," authorized a bishop to select the right sort of girls to become wives and establish homes. The bishop selected 80 girls who, though poor, were well reared and educated. Each was provided with a marriage outfit. They were put in charge of Sisters Gertrude, Louise, and Bergers, on board the ship *La Baline,* and landed at Ship Island, January 5, 1721. This was the third shipment of "Casket Girls." The last was sent to New Orleans, February 1728.

When the seat of government was moved to New Orleans in 1723, Biloxi slipped from the spotlight to spend a century in being shuttled back and forth like a pawn in the great chess game played by the Old World kings on the table of the New. In 1763 the Gulf Coast country, including Biloxi, was ceded to Great Britain. Sometime between 1779 and 1781 it passed under Spanish rule. In 1810 Biloxi was a passive participant in the rebellion which ousted the Spaniards; and in 1811 its first Justice of the Peace, Jacques L'Adner, took his commission from the emissary of the Government of the United States.

It was in the 1840's that Biloxi, like Pass Christian *(see Tour 1),* first became a favored summer watering place. In 1846 the editor of the Louisville (Ky.) *Journal* wrote to his wife from Biloxi a poem, entitled "To One Afar," in which was set forth the beauties of the sea breeze and bright flowers, the mocking bird's notes, the orange trees, and the blue waves of the Sound. This is among the first of the plethora of literary compliments paid to Biloxi, and foreshadowed the development of the town as a resort.

Biloxi was incorporated as a town of Hancock County February 8, 1838, and reincorporated in 1850 and 1856. After Harrison County was formed it was incorporated as a town of Harrison County in 1859, then reincorporated in 1865 and 1867. In 1896 it was incorporated as a city. Twenty-two years later (1918) it adopted the commission form of government.

The War between the States left Biloxi comparatively unharmed. Ship Island was taken, lost, and retaken by the Union forces, and the mainland was harassed by patrol boats from Fort Massachusetts, but no major engagements were fought near the town. Biloxians ran the blockade for food and supplies, giving basis for the anecdotes that preserve much of the war history of the town.

Yellow fever swept Biloxi in 1853, '78 and '97. The epidemic of 1878 claimed 600 cases and 45 deaths out of a population of 2,000. One of the victims was the son of Jefferson Davis, the President of the Confederacy.

From the 1870's through the 1890's the social life of the village was centered at the seashore camp grounds of the Mississippi Methodists, where bonfires, built in sand boxes elevated on posts, furnished the light for night services.

For many years there were no roads on the beach front, the residents using sail and rowboats for getting about; and dependence on the water early led to the boatbuilding and racing for which Biloxi is noted. Biloxi-built boats competed with boats from Pascagoula, Ocean Springs, Pass Christian, and Mississippi City, for trophies donated by the Howards (founders of the Louisiana Lottery, who made their home in Biloxi). After the war, however, the opening and paving of streets with crushed oyster shells was a major development. One erratic mayor, opposed by property owners, opened a beach road in front of their places on a day when he knew they would be in New Orleans; he also put a road through a cemetery at night, moving the graves to a new location. It is thought by some that he moved only the headstones, and that the bodies are still beneath the road.

In the 1890's the Montross Hotel (now the Riviera) on the corner of Beach and Lameuse Streets was the popular hotel. Reservations had to be made early in the season, as the people of wealth and fashion from Memphis, Chicago, Minneapolis, and other places gathered here. Accommodations, however, were poor, though full dress dinners and elegant card parties were held, enlivened by Negro cakewalks and spirituals.

This period fixed Biloxi's reputation as a resort town, and the ensuing prosperity caused Biloxians to forget that Northerners were "Yankees." The 1890's found the first winter tourists coming into this part of the Deep South.

The real growth of Biloxi after the War between the States, however, was the direct result of development of the seafood packing business. The New Orleans & Mobile Railroad (now the Louisville & Nashville), built in 1869, gave the packers a needed outlet to northern markets. Oysters first were packed in ice and shipped in the shell; later they were

LIGHTHOUSE, BILOXI

opened and shipped in tubs. The first oyster packing plant, on Back Bay at Reynoir Street, was established in 1872. The canning of shrimp was pioneered in Biloxi in 1883 by Lopez, Elmer, and Gorenflo, seniors, names still prominent in the industry. Largely because of the fresh oyster and shrimp business the population of Biloxi jumped from 954 in 1870 to 5,467 in 1900. From 1900 to 1925 the developing factories imported seasonal labor from Baltimore, the majority of which was Polish. The slums on the Point in Biloxi are the camp houses constructed for these seasonal laborers. Since 1925 Acadian French from Louisiana and former sawmill hands from the dying lumber towns of southern Mississippi have furnished the necessary labor.

Tour—20m.

E. from Main St. on Howard Ave.

1. MEMORIAL BRIDGE, E. end of Howard Ave., extending across the south end of the Bay of Biloxi in a low graceful span, connects Biloxi with Ocean Springs. Of concrete construction, it has a double-lane drive and is brilliantly lighted. A draw toward the Ocean Springs end opens for the Back Bay shrimp and oyster fleets. When the bridge was completed in 1930 at a cost of $880,000 it was said to be one of the largest World War memorials in the United States.

Retrace Howard Ave. L. on Myrtle St.; L. on 1st St.

2. UNITED STATES COAST GUARD AIR BASE, E. end of 1st St. *(open)*, is designed to become one of the key units of Coast Guard aviation in southern waters. A hangar, 160 x 100 feet, connected with a concrete apron and a wooden ramp, houses six planes, including a huge ambulance plane equipped for landing on rough seas. These planes, cooperating with the Coast Guard boats at Gulfport, aid ships in distress, rescue injured fishermen, and prevent smuggling.

Retrace 1st St.; L. on Myrtle St.; R. on Beach Blvd.

3. The CANNING AND PACKING PLANTS, Beach Blvd. (L.) between Myrtle and Cedar Sts. *(open)*, are built out over the water to facilitate the unloading of boats and the disposal of refuse. The plants employ men, women, and children to pick the shrimp, which have been packed in ice for several days to make them brittle enough to handle. The picking tables are long troughs down which the shrimp baskets are rolled. The pickers, standing on each side of the table, remove the head and scales

from the shrimp with a single dexterous twist. Buckets of alum water into which the pickers dip their hands neutralize the shrimp secretions. Payment for picking is made by weight, the wage running not quite one cent a pound. The average skilled picker earns $1.50 a day, with a few making as high as $2.50. Whistles let the pickers know when a day's supply of shrimp has been brought in, and the pickers work as long as they care to, or until the supply is exhausted. The average picking room is the scene of much conversation and occasionally a hair-pulling combat, when someone tries to edge another out of the weighing line. While the picking of shrimp is a fairly easy process requiring no tools, oyster shucking is a skilful operation, and the proficiency attained by some of the workers is amazing. Frequent shucking contests are held, with rivalry running high between contestants.

At the south end of the packing plants' piers, one of the two most prominent of the ceremonies involved in the blessing of the fleet is held. The boats blessed here, in contrast to the French-manned boats at the Iberville Cross ceremony, are manned by Slavonians. An altar is improvised on the pier, and the shrimp boats pack so closely around that the priest can step from one to another in administering his blessing.

The *WESLEY HOUSE*, NW. corner Beach Blvd. and Cedar St. *(open)*, is the two-story, cream frame community house and recreational center of the Point Cadet fishing settlement. Grouped about it are the box-like houses built prior to 1925 for housing transient Baltimore Poles during the packing season.

4. RED BRICK HOUSE WITH SLAVE QUARTERS, 947 Beach Blvd. *(private)*, is an example of ante-bellum architecture. An outside stairway and finely executed entrance doorway are architectural features of the bright red brick structure. The story is that the stairway and plain green shutters are mute traces of the result of a French tax levied on inside stairs and latticed blinds. If so, the house was built before 1763, during the period of French dominion. In the rear, the slave quarters retain their original character, with a raised hearth and Dutch oven.

5. The JOHN H. KELLER HOME, NE. corner Beach Blvd. and Bellman St. *(private)*, typifies the ante-bellum homes designed especially for this climate. Built of wide boards, painted white, its second or main floor is set high off the ground, over a dark, cool brick ground floor. A double flight of steps curves from the ground to the main floor.

6. CHURCH OF THE REDEEMER, NW. corner Beach Blvd. and Bellman St., a brown, ivy-covered, heavily buttressed structure of Gothic design, was built in 1890. The four windows placed in it are memorials to the family of Jefferson Davis. They are considered to be among the most beautiful memorial windows in the South. At the rear of the church is the old Episcopal Church that Davis attended. The pew used by the Davis family has been moved to the newer church, marked with a silver plate and draped with a Confederate flag.

In the SW. corner of the churchyard is the *RING IN THE OAK*, a curious open ring in the limb of a large live oak, perpetuating one of the most charming of the Gulf Coast Indian legends. An Indian maiden fell

A SOUTHERN PLANTER HOME, BILOXI

in love with the son of an enemy chieftain. The maiden's father, who was chief of the Biloxi tribe, refused the suit of the young brave, and pointing to the oak tree, said, "No, the young fawn can never be the light of your wigwam until a ring grows in yonder oak!" That night a terrific storm twisted the tender branches of the young oak into a distinct ring, a ring that with the years has grown firmly into the tree.

7. COMMUNITY HOUSE AND PARK, Beach Blvd. (R) between Nixon and Elmer Sts., is the center for tourist entertainment. South of Beach Boulevard and opposite Deer Island is the community house bathing pier. Between the pier and the beach drive is a children's playground. In the yard of the community house are the *IBERVILLE CANNON*, three corroded iron cannon dredged from the bottom of Back Bay and alleged to be from one of Iberville's ships.

R. from Beach Blvd. on Lameuse St.; L. on Water St.

8. The SPANISH HOUSE, 206 W. Water St. *(private)*, was built by a Spanish army captain about 1790, and is the sole relic of the period of Spanish rule in Biloxi (1780–1810). The house is severely simple, with a steep roof stepped squarely in military fashion. The original brick walls are covered with stucco and the house is divided into apartments.

9. The FRENCH HOUSE, SE. corner Water and Magnolia Sts. *(open by permission)*, is thought to have been built between 1750 and 1800. It is a tiny one-story cottage, lost in a profusion of azaleas and palms. The rambling additions are of a hybrid type of architecture, but the iron-railed porch and grille work are characteristically French.

R. from Water St. on Magnolia St.; R. on Howard Ave.; R. on Delauney St.; R. on Beach Blvd.

10. MAGNOLIA HOTEL, NW. corner Beach Blvd. and Magnolia St., was built in 1846 and is still operating. The main part, a large square broad-gabled house facing the beach, is separated from the rear portion by a long open passage and surrounded by porches with round wooden rails. This represents the type of summer hostelry inland Southerners preferred before the War between the States.

R. from Beach Blvd. on Benachi Ave.

BENACHI AVENUE, overarched with oaks, is a favorite vista for photographers, the moss-draped trees forming an archway nearly two-fifths of a mile long.

R. from Benachi Ave. on Howard Ave.; L. on Caillavet St.; R. on Division St.; L. on Oak St.; L. on E. Bay View Ave.

11. BACK BAY BOATBUILDING FACTORIES (R), E. Bay View Ave. *(open by permission)*, are unpainted frame buildings strung along the avenue. The process of boatbuilding from the initial steps to the finishing touches can be observed here.

12. BACK BAY FISHERIES (R), E. Bay View Ave., are a hodgepodge of shrimp- and oyster-packing and canning houses which extend to Iberville Bridge. The damp rank odor of fish pervades this entire section.

R. from E. Bay View Ave. on Caillavet St.

13. IBERVILLE BRIDGE, across Back Bay, is a concrete span 3,400 feet long, built in 1926 at a cost of $350,000. At the exit of the bridge (R) are visible the *IBERVILLE CROSS AND BOULDER,* commemorating the landing of Iberville. It is here that the ceremony of blessing the fleet takes place on Sunday preceding August 15.

Retrace Caillavet St.; R. on W. Bay View Ave.; R. on a narrow sandy road.

14. NAVAL RESERVE PARK was established by the Government to preserve the trees for making knees for wooden ships. Now owned by the city, the park is noteworthy for its vistas of the bay seen through moss-draped oaks. Public pier, *ZOO (open 9-5),* and picnic tables are maintained by the city.

Retrace the sandy road; R. on W. Bay View Ave.; R. on Naval Reserve Rd.; R. on Pass Christian Rd.

15. UNITED STATES VETERANS FACILITY *(open Fri. 1-5),* occupies a tract of 700 acres with frontage on Back Bay. Its buildings of whitewashed brick designed in the Colonial tradition are attractively grouped in a setting of oaks, pines, magnolias, and shrubs. The institution was opened in 1933 and is designed to accommodate 4,000 beds. The main building, five stories in height, is one of the largest single buildings in the State.

Retrace Pass Christian Rd.; R. on Porter St.

16. BILOXI LIGHTHOUSE, Porter St. and Beach Blvd. *(open),* 65 feet in height and mounted through the center by a revolving staircase and ladder, was built in 1848. Near the beginning of the War between the States, when Ship Island was taken, a Biloxi citizen climbed the tower, removed the lens and buried it. When the war was over, the

lens was dug up and returned to the tower, the nicks being the only indication of its stay underground. When Lincoln was assassinated, Biloxi demonstrated its sorrow by painting the tower of the lighthouse black. Shortly afterward, however, the Government had it painted white, its present color.

R. from Porter St. on Beach Blvd.

17. BILOXI CEMETERY, Beach Blvd. *(open)*, marks the early settlement of Biloxi. One section of the cemetery has graves so old that all inscriptions on the headstones have been effaced. Originally owned by the Fayards, the cemetery was given by them to the city, which, in turn, gave away the lots without charge. Probably unique among cemeteries of the world is the custom frequently used here of shading the graves with canopies of Spanish moss draped on bars a few feet above the headstones. On All Saints' Day decorations ranging from handsome hothouse plants to paper flowers are placed on the graves. The poor decorate the graves of their dead with shells arranged in geometric designs. The growing of flowers for All Saints' Day, and the making of paper flowers, are considerable industries on and near the Coast.

18. SEASHORE CAMP GROUNDS, Beach Blvd. (R), are the summer camping grounds for Methodists. The camp was established in 1871, with the tabernacle in the center and a semicircle of frame summer cottages. Between religious services the cottages are occupied by members of the congregation, and rented to the public between periodic camp meetings.

POINTS OF INTEREST IN ENVIRONS

Southern Memorial Park, *4.9 m.*, Beauvoir, *5.5 m.*, Edgewater Gulf Skeet Range and Golf Course, *8.5 m.*, Gulf Coast Military Academy, *8.5 m., (see Tour 1);* Harbor *(see GULFPORT);* Ship Island, *12 m. (see Side Tour 1A).*

Columbus

Railroad Stations: 6th St. and 8th Ave. S. for Mobile & Ohio R.R.; 21st St. and 2nd Ave. S. for Frisco R.R.; 13th St. and Main St. for Columbus & Greenville R.R. and Southern Ry.
Bus Station: Union Bus Station, 5th St. and 3rd Ave. S. for Tri-State Transit Co., Dixie Greyhound Lines, Dixies Coaches, and Magnolia Motor Lines.
Taxis: Intra-city 10¢ per person.

Traffic Regulations: Speed limit 30 mph. Turns in either direction at intersections except where lights direct otherwise. Limited parking.

KEY

1. Christian Church
2. Old Franklin Academy
3. Stephen D. Lee Home
4. F. M. Leigh Home
5. Alexander B. Meek Home
6. J. H. Kennebrew Home
7. J. M. Billups Home
8. Mississippi State College for Women
9. Charles McLaren Home (Humphries Home)
10. Jesse P. Woodward Home
11. Columbus Marble Plant
12. Friendship Cemetery
13. Rosedale
14. Owen's Greenhouse and Nursery

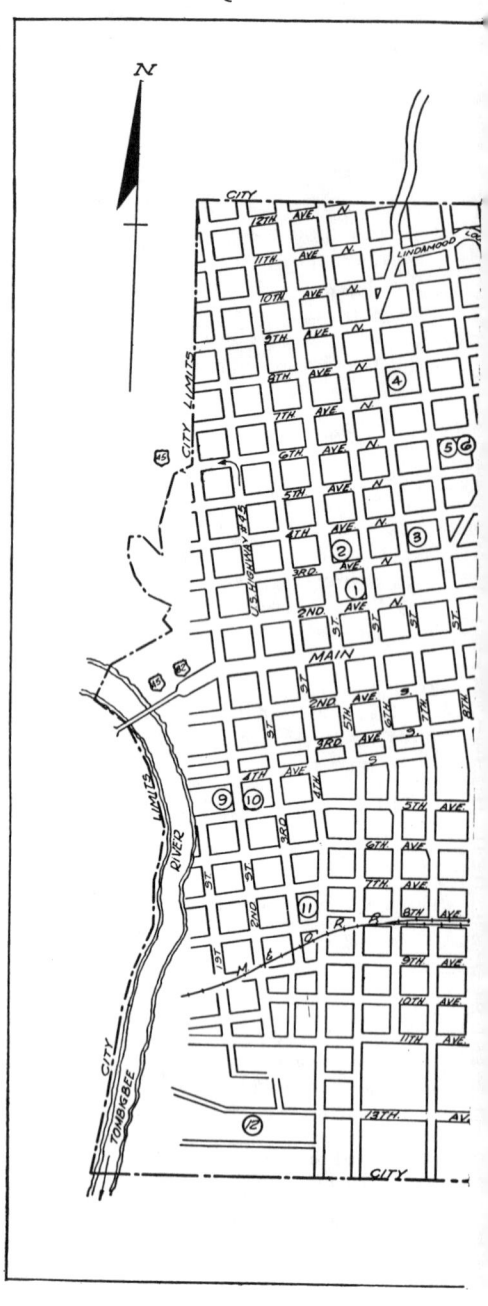

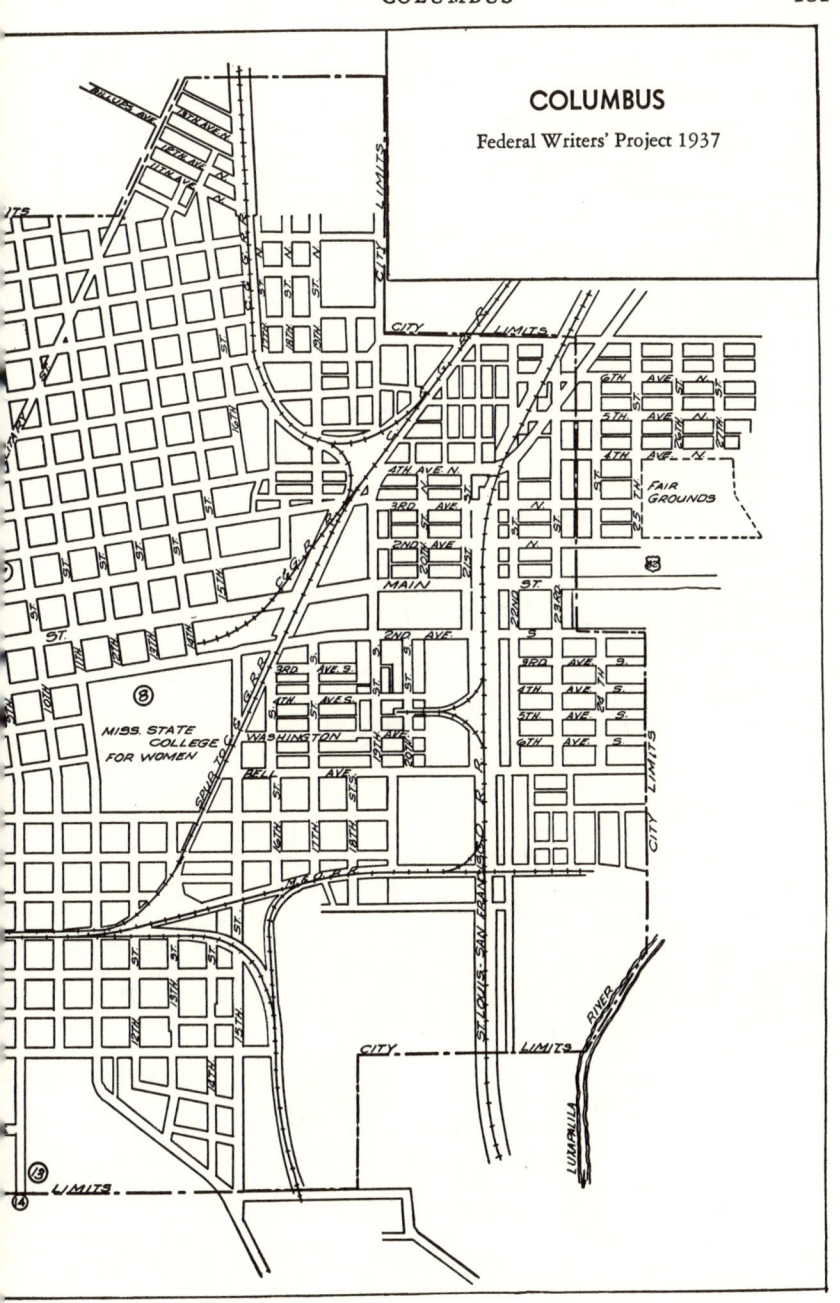

COLUMBUS

Federal Writers' Project 1937

182   MAIN STREET AND COURTHOUSE SQUARE

Accommodations: Two hotels; tourist camps.
Information Service: Chamber of Commerce, City Hall, NW. cor. Main and 6th Sts.
Motion Picture Houses: Three.
Athletics: Y.M.C.A., 6th St. and 2nd Ave. N.; Magnolia Bowl, 3rd Ave. N. bet. 5th and 6th Sts.
Swimming: Y.M.C.A.; Luxapalila Swimming Beach, 1 m. NE.
Golf: Country Club, 2 m. N. on Military Road, moderate greens fee.
Annual Events: Memorial Service, Decoration Day, April 26.

COLUMBUS (250 alt., 10,743 pop.), sprawling leisurely along the banks of Tombigbee and Luxapalila Rivers, is a city in which there is room to breathe. A comfortable old-tree shaded town, the streets are broad, the sidewalks wide, lawns are spacious, and houses are set apart in a manner characteristic of the lavish ante-bellum period in which they were built. It is the junction of the Old South with the New, with gracious lines of Georgian porticos forming a belt of mellowed beauty about a modern business district, where 20th century facades and white Doric columns stand side by side.

The same leisurely atmosphere of spaciousness is carried into "Northside," the Negro section of town. Here approximately 45 percent of Columbus's population lives in low-roofed, red frame houses that are festooned with wistaria and shaded by umbrella chinaberry trees and tall, brightly colored sunflowers. A majority of the Negro men find work with white families rather than with industries, or are delivery boys, taxi drivers, and filling station helpers. The Negro women who work are employed almost entirely as domestic servants. In their section of town they have their own stores, cafes, hotels, and recreational center.

In 1540 De Soto entered the State at a point eight miles above the present site of Columbus, and two centuries later Bienville, on his way to attack the Chickasaw Nation, passed beneath the Tombigbee bluffs; but it was not until 1817 that the white man came to the spot where the Tombigbee joins the Luxapalila and built a trading post. In that year Thomas Thomas opened a store and shortly afterward Spirus Roach built a tavern. Because Roach was gray and bent and wizened, he reminded the Indians, who came to buy his whisky, of an opossum, so they called the settlement Possum Town. In 1821, however, the Virginia and Carolina bluebloods, who had followed Thomas and Roach to grow cotton in the fertile prairie soil, expressed their distaste for Indian humor and renamed the community Columbus.

Sitting on the banks of the Tombigbee, the only artery of commerce from northeast Mississippi to the Gulf, and bordered by undulating prairies, the new trading post grew from settlement to village and from village to town, until just prior to the War between the States it was well established as a cultural center of the Black Prairie—a section referred to by slaves as "de rich folk's lan'."

From its beginning Columbus welcomed education. Situated on one of the early land grants set aside for schools, the town was a pioneer in the establishment of public institutions of learning. In 1821 Gideon

CLOCK TOWER, STATE COLLEGE FOR WOMEN, COLUMBUS

Lincecum founded Franklin Academy, the first free school in the State. In 1847 Columbus Female Institute was organized, a private academy which, 38 years later, reorganized under the name Industrial Institute and College, became the first State-supported college for women in the United States. In 1920 the name again was changed to Mississippi State

College for Women. Today the city and education are synonymous. Even the property in the downtown district comes within the 16th section belonging to the State as part of the original land grant reserved for schools. Business establishments here must lease this land from Mississippi.

However, ante-bellum Columbus was not "at home" to the more blatant aspects of progress. When the Mobile & Ohio R.R. tried to secure a right-of-way through the town, permission was refused. A railroad was unsightly, it would mar the landscape and bring undesirable people, the citizens said. And not until 1861 did they capitulate, with a few die-hards even then continuing to plant their cotton along the railroad tracks, forcing the company to erect fences to protect the rails.

During the War between the States the Confederate Government maintained a large arsenal in the town, and when Jackson fell into the hands of Federals the seat of State government was moved here immediately. The Christian church was hastily converted into a Senate chamber and the courthouse next door was prepared to receive the lower house in time for the legislative session of 1863. Politicians thronged the lobby of the Gilmer Hotel and President Davis was a guest in the Whitfield (now Billups) home. It is still told in Columbus that one night, while Davis slept, the townspeople gathered beneath a window of his room to serenade him, and that upon being awakened by the voices and the guitars, Davis, with his long night shirt trailing beneath his dressing gown, appeared on the little balcony opening off his room and delivered an address.

In the years since the War between the States three new railroads have obtained rights-of-way through the city, and, as old settlers had suspected, a new people, with an outsider's idea of progress, followed in their wake. Today the city ships cotton, hay, cattle, and hardwood lumber; it has large floral, brick, and marble industries, and is the center of a rapidly developing dairy industry.

But the aristocrats have bred their kind. The old Columbus still surrounds a 20th-century business district and sets the tempo that gives the city its tone of leisurely unconcern.

Tour—5m.

N. *from Main St. on 6th St.*

1. CHRISTIAN CHURCH, NW. corner 6th St. and 2nd Ave. N., next to the courthouse is the small Gothic Revival church that housed the refugee Legislature of 1863.

L. from 2nd Ave. N. on 5th St.

2. OLD FRANKLIN ACADEMY, NE. corner 3rd Ave. N. and 5th St., the first free school in the State, chartered in 1821, is a part of the Columbus public school system; the old academy building houses a grammar school. The three-story red brick structure with white wood trim is an example of ante-bellum Gothic Revival adapted to institutional purposes. A stone marker on the campus tells briefly the history of Franklin Academy.

R. from 5th St. on 3rd Ave. N.; L. on 7th St.

3. The STEPHEN D. LEE HOME, occupying a block on 7th St. (R) between 3rd and 4th Aves. N. *(open schooldays 9-4; Sept. to June)*, was willed to the city on the death of its owner, Stephen D. Lee, and is now a part of the Lee High School. Built in 1844 by Col. Thomas Blewett, it is a square two-story brick building, with a covered porch extending across the front. Iron grille work, said to have been cast in New Orleans and suggestive of French influence, is used for railing and columns on the porch. Iron animals on the campus formerly occupied a prominent place in the Lee garden.

Stephen D. Lee, born in Charleston, South Carolina, in 1833, was graduated from West Point in 1854 and was first lieutenant and regimental quartermaster of the 4th United States Artillery when he resigned in 1861 to join the Confederate forces. He was one of two officers sent by General Beauregard to demand the surrender of Fort Sumter, and, upon refusal, it was he who ordered the nearest battery to fire upon the fort. In the spring of 1862 he was promoted to lieutenant-colonel. After gaining distinction at Seven Pines and in the Seven Days' Battles against General McClellan's forces, he was given command of the 4th Virginia cavalry. When it became necessary to reinforce the army defending Vicksburg, he was promoted to brigadier-general and assigned to duty in the West. After the fall of Vicksburg he became lieutenant-general and was given command of the Department of Mississippi, Alabama, East Louisiana, and West Tennessee. When Hood became commander of the army of Georgia, Lee took command of Hood's corps. He saw hard fighting around Atlanta and his last campaign was in North Carolina, where he was paroled with Johnston's army. In 1865 he married Regina Harrison, of Columbus, where he made his home. He was a member of the State Senate of 1878 and a delegate to the Constitutional Convention of 1890. He was the first president of the Agricultural and Mechanical College (now Mississippi State), serving from 1880 to 1899, when he resigned to become a member of the newly created Vicksburg National Park Association. General Lee was a president of the Mississippi Historical Society, a member of the Board of Trustees of the Department of Archives and History, and the author of several papers on the War between the States. When he died in 1908, he was national commander of the United Confederate Veterans of America.

4. The F. M. LEIGH HOME, 824 N. 7th St. *(private)*, built in 1841, stands on a hill overlooking the vales and dells of the highlands. Large Doric columns support a porch that extends around two sides of

the building. Inside are antique gilded mirrors, sofas, chairs and tables of rosewood, mahogany, and cherry, and family portraits in massive frames. The flower garden at the southern end of a winding walk is landscaped with formal beds, each bordered by a low brick curb. Scattered about the yard toward the back are three outhouses and the old brick kitchen—relics of the slave era.

Retrace 7th St.; L. on 6th Ave. N.

5. The ALEXANDER B. MEEK HOME, SE. corner 6th Ave. N. and 8th St. *(private)*, was built in 1854 by William R. Cannon, who came from South Carolina to Lowndes Co. in 1830, and settled on a prairie plantation 12 miles from Columbus. Later, desiring to bring his children into town for education, he built this home. It is of the ante-bellum Classical Revival style, with the characteristic columns, entrance portico, and graceful lines. Plans were drawn for it by a Mr. Lull, who built many other Columbus houses of that period. An artist was brought from New York to paint the family portraits that remain on the walls. The library shelves were filled with books, many dating to the early 18th century. Chinaware was imported from Europe and glassware from Bohemia. When complete the house was an excellent example of the homes wealthy planters of the Black Prairie were building before the War between the States.

6. The J. H. KENNEBREW HOME, SW. corner 6th Ave. N. and 9th St. *(private)*, is designed in the Greek Revival style modeled after a Doric temple. It is simple, stately, unadorned. All the timber used in the house was cut from the forest by slaves, and only the heart of each tree was used. Each column—a single tree trunk—is hand carved.

R. from 6th Ave. N. on 9th St.

7. The J. M. BILLUPS HOME, SE. corner 9th St. and 3rd Ave. N. *(private)*, where Jefferson Davis was once a guest, built by Gov. James Whitfield about 1854 and modeled after Thomas Jefferson's "Monticello," has an octagonal hall, with doors opening on all sides. Connecting the first- and second-story halls is a broad winding stairway, the newel posts and railings made of solid Mississippi walnut. A similar stair leads from the second story to the observatory. When Major Billups purchased the home from Governor Whitfield, he had the observatory removed, and the resemblance of the home to Monticello became less apparent. All brick used in the construction of the home was made by slave labor.

L. from 9th St. on 2nd Ave. S.

8. MISSISSIPPI STATE COLLEGE FOR WOMEN, 2nd Ave. S. (R) bet. 11th and 15th Sts., holds membership in the Association of American Colleges and its graduates are eligible for full membership in the American Association of University Women.

As a pioneer in the field of education, and the first State-supported school in America to offer higher education exclusively to women, the college has many of the characteristics of the pioneer—warmth, vigor, and ruggedness—and, like all pioneers, has accumulated its traditions. There is the "wedding" of the Freshman and Junior classes, the Magnolia

Chain carried by the Seniors at commencement, and the Zouave and Singlestick drills performed on class day.

Main Dormitory, the oldest building on the campus was built in 1860, and like the Old Chapel adjoining, has ivy-covered brick walls. In the tower is the clock that has continuously marked the hours for more than half a century. The newer buildings are modern variations of Southern Colonial style, with stone Corinthian columns, broad galleries, and porticos. The last to be built (1930) is the *JOHN CLAYTON FANT LIBRARY (open weekdays 8 a.m.-9 p.m.)*, which houses 50,000 volumes, including government documents received by the library as an official depository. Here, also, is the Belle Kearney collection of curios. The college places emphasis on its Physical Education Department. It offers courses in aesthetic and acrobatic dancing. The swimming pool, occupying the lower floor of the gymnasium, is the largest indoor pool in the State.

The campus has the appearance of a well-kept Southern garden, shaded with a variety of indigenous trees, and planted in japonicas, hydrangeas, gardenias, and Japanese magnolias. A network of walks leads to a drinking fountain and sundial.

Retrace 2nd Ave. S.; L. on 2nd St.

9. The CHARLES McLAREN HOME (HUMPHRIES HOME), 514 S. 2nd St. *(private)*, built several years prior to the War between the States, is of stately proportions and exquisite detail. The lot upon which it stands occupies a block bordering the Tombigbee River. The building is of Georgian Colonial style, with massive stone Corinthian columns upholding the roof of the double porch across the front. Two lions, symbolic guards of the mansion, crouch on the cheek blocks of the steps; two greyhounds, emblems of fidelity, stretch full-length on stone slabs facing the walk.

10. The JESSE P. WOODWARD HOME, NE. corner 2nd St. and 5th Ave. S. *(private)*, is one of the State's best examples of the Southern Planter type of architecture. Built early in the 1850's by Col. W. C. Richards, the house has been restored with its original lines carefully preserved. A double flight of steps, graced by delicately wrought iron railings, dominates the entrance. The brick ground floor is occupied by study and service rooms; the family living quarters are above on the first floor. The outer walls are covered with white clapboards, and brick chimneys flank the ends. The grounds are informally landscaped with boxwood hedges and magnolias.

L. from 2nd St. on 7th Ave. S.; R. on 4th St.

11. The COLUMBUS MARBLE PLANT, 4th St. (R) between 7th and 8th Aves. S. *(open weekdays 8-4; tours)*, reputed to be the largest plant of its kind in the South, occupies a low-roofed, corrugated tin building covering an entire block. Here marble, brought from Georgia and Alabama, is cut into building blocks, slabs, and headstones.

12. FRIENDSHIP CEMETERY, long known as Odd Fellows Cemetery, 4th St. (R) facing 13th Ave. S., is situated on land purchased by the Odd Fellows in 1849 for recreational purposes. During the War between the States the 18 acres were converted into a cemetery. The first burials

WOODWARD HOUSE, COLUMBUS

were of soldiers who fell at Shiloh. Under the magnolias are the graves of about 100 Federal and 1,500 Confederate soldiers, whose names were recorded in a book since lost. Now all graves are "unknown," and so marked on the more than 1,000 headstones set up by the War Department in 1931. In one corner of the cemetery is a faded red brick vault— the grave of William Cocke, Revolutionary War veteran, legislator of Virginia, North Carolina, Tennessee and Mississippi.

Memorial Day had its origin in this cemetery on April 26, 1866. The ladies of Columbus met and marched in procession to the burial ground, where they cleared and decorated with flowers the graves of both Confederate and Union soldiers. This act inspired Francis Miles Finch's poem, "The Blue and the Gray." April 26, not the nationally recognized May 30, is still Decoration Day in Mississippi.

L. from 4th St. on 13th Ave. S.; R. on 9th St.

13. ROSEDALE, 9th St. (L) between 13th Ave. and city limits *(private)*, is the oldest brick house in Columbus. Built by Dr. Topp in 1855, it was planned by architects and decorators from New Orleans. It is a square two-story brick building surmounted by a cupola, and suggests Italian villa architecture in its general appearance. Outside walls are covered with gray stucco. A covered porch runs across the front. Full-length arched windows are used throughout. Interior walls and ceil-

ings are elaborately decorated with ornamental plaster. Holly trees in the yard were planted by Dr. Topp at the time the house was erected.

14. OWEN'S GREENHOUSE AND NURSERY, foot of 9th St., is said to be the largest of its kind in the South.

POINTS OF INTEREST IN ENVIRONS

Belmont, *9 m.*, Waverly, *7.5 m.*, Site of Old Plymouth, *9.5 m. (See Tour 4)*. Stover Apiary, *15 m. (see Side Tour 4A)*.

Greenwood

Railroad Stations: Carrollton Ave. for Yazoo & Mississippi Valley R.R.; S. end Howard St. for Columbus & Greenville R.R.
Bus Station: Union Bus Station, Weiner Hotel, 219 Carrollton Ave. for Tri-State Transit Co., Dixie Greyhound Lines.
Airport: Greenwood Airport, 2.1 m. S. off US 49E, taxi fare 50¢, time 8 min. No scheduled service.
Taxis: Fare 10¢ within city.
Accommodations: Five hotels.
Motion Picture Houses: Two.
Swimming: Country Club, Humphreys Highway; Municipal Pool, High School campus, Cotton St., nominal charge.
Golf: Country Club, Humphreys Highway, reasonable greens fee.
Tennis: Country Club, Humphreys Highway, High School campus, Cotton St.

GREENWOOD (143 alt., 11,123 pop.), the heart of what is reputed to be the greatest long staple cotton growing area in the world, is an enlarged edition of the little towns and villages that dot the Yazoo-Mississippi Delta. Completely surrounded by cotton fields, and centered about its gins, compresses and warehouses, the growing, ginning, and marketing of cotton keep up the pulse of its social and industrial life. Cotton built the gins and compresses and the pretentious mansions on the Boulevard. The fickleness of cotton crops and prices sets the standard that accustoms the city to taking its pleasures while it may.

In character with a Delta town, a river cuts the center of Greenwood. On the south bank of the green and shadowy Yazoo lies the business district; on the north bank are residences typical of Delta architecture, with tall, stilt-like foundations for protection against the constant menace of flood waters, and screened front porches against ever present mosquitoes. These homes, as well as the more pretentious mansions that line the broad street called Boulevard, represent the "good" years of the planters and merchants. Many of these homes follow the familiar colonial pattern, but interspersed with them are pastel Spanish villas and English manor houses, incongruous against the flat delta landscape. This section of Greenwood, formerly a part of the vast plantation of Sen. J. Z. George, was not opened up until 1915. Before that time a majority of the Deltans who now have residences here preferred living on their own plantations or small farms.

Surrounding the business and white residential section of Greenwood is the typically Mississippi fringe of Negro quarters. The fringe is divided into sections, each with its name and its particular group of persons. "Gritney," occupying 30 acres near the compresses, is the largest and oldest. Here the more economically well-to-do Negroes live, a majority owning their homes. "Ram-Cat Alley" furnishes Greenwood's best cooks. "G. P. Town" lies south of the railroad tracks; "Baptist Town" is to the east, where Negro Baptists live close to their church; "Buckeye Quarters," in west Greenwood, gets its name from the oil mill that employs a great many of the men as unskilled laborers; in north Greenwood, "Burkhalter's Alley" is a small but favorite district. On West Church and Williamson Streets, where approximately 20 or more houses are located in a white district, is "New Town." Negroes compose 48.4 percent of Greenwood's population. The men do menial labor at the gins, warehouses, oil mills, and other industries. During cotton chopping season and cotton picking time approximately 1,500 Negroes are transported daily from Greenwood to the outlying plantations. The women are domestic servants.

In 1834 John Williams came to the lush swamp near the confluence of the Yazoo and Yalobusha Rivers and built a river landing on 162 acres bought from the Government at $1.25 an acre. Immediately planters began to bring their cotton to his landing to be shipped down the Yazoo to New Orleans. Among their number was the Choctaw chieftain Greenwood Leflore, who brought his baled cotton here from Malmaison *(see Tour 6)* until one day Leflore discovered that Williams let his cotton lie unprotected from the weather, and the two men quarreled. In retaliation, the Indian built his own warehouse and landing at a point three miles north on the Yazoo and called it Point Leflore. But the rivalry between the landings was not as great as Leflore had expected. By 1844 Williams Landing had grown into the semblance of a village and was incorporated, ironically enough, as Greenwood, the given name of the Indian chieftain. Slowly Greenwood, with its town hall, post office, 3 saloons and 17 combination grocery stores and grog shops, absorbed the trade of Point Leflore, and with its steady flow of river trade flourished as a trading center during the ante-bellum period. Its prosperity, however, was flaunted in lavish living on outlying plantations rather than in the town itself, for at that time the planters preferred living among their fields of cotton.

The War between the States paralyzed the cotton industry. Gunboats

GREENWOOD 191

supplanted barges on the river and the railroad tracks were destroyed. Even throughout reconstruction much of the rich, black Delta lands lay fallow because there were no means of transporting such crops as were grown.

With the coming of the railroads in the 1880's, Greenwood declined as a river town but had a renascence in rails and locomotives. The Yazoo & Mississippi connected the town with the main freight line of the Illinois Central System, and the Columbus & Greenville connected it with eastern and western traffic. This gave the city, despite its inland location, another outlet to the ports of the world.

Greenwood handles more than 200,000 bales of cotton each year. Because it is a staple market, prices here are such that often cotton raised in neighboring States is brought to Greenwood for sale. In the city are 56 firms of cotton shippers, exporters, buyers, factors, and several cotton cooperative associations. The cotton is handled on the factor system, which originated after the War between the States when the planters were too poor to finance the making of a crop. The factor, a merchant-banker who advances money to the planter and takes a lien on his crop, has the cotton tagged and shipped to him in Greenwood. The theoretical advantages of this system most often pointed to are that the factor can secure cheaper storage and insurance rates and that his leased wires to New Orleans and New York give him the advantage of knowing the erratic quotas of the large export markets and thus offer the planter a better opportunity to secure a higher price for his cotton.

The activity of cotton is in two fever-pitch stages, the first, when the planter is preparing his spring planting, the second, when the crop is picked and ready for market. From December until March, Greenwood is absorbed in handling the planter's crop production loan. For whether the planter owns 200 or 2,000 acres, he has a ritual to follow before he may actually put the seeds into his ground. He must get a waiver on his mortgage and record it in the chancery clerk's office. He must make out a budget, work and rework it until it is approved by the lien holder (factor), the mortgagees, and all parties concerned. His certificates must be signed by the county agent, his abstracts must be made by reputable authorities. Repeated inspection is made of his plantation by land examiners of the various mortgages. All this activity naturally involves endless waiting on street corners and in outer offices, yet the planter takes it good-naturedly. A majority of the men with whom he does business are his friends, and conferences usually end as social occasions. When, at last, after having signed away practically every earthly possession including radio and automobile, and after specifying the exact number of acres to be planted in cotton, the amount of seed and the kind of fertilizer to be used, the number of bales of hay the mules will eat, the gallons of gas the tractor will consume, and how many pairs of shoes the children will need, the annual ordeal of the crop production loan is over. The planter will receive the money in monthly installments, duly witnessed and countersigned.

The marketing season, usually from the latter part of August through

Christmas, keeps Greenwood tensely holding its breath until the price of cotton is somewhat stabilized. For with the price, the whole economic and social life of the town is inextricably bound. Everyone from the tenant Negro to the land-owning planter feels the repercussion of a "good" or "bad" year.

Wagons and trucks piled high with cotton crowd the streets leading to the gins. At the gins they are driven on large scales that weigh the cotton before it is unloaded. The modern gin operates on the "saw" principle of the Whitney gin, but is a far cry from the original model. The whole process of ginning has been perfected to expedite labor. Suction pipes, which have the appearance of enlarged stove-pipes, draw the cotton from the wagon. An elevator system from the suction pipe to the second story of the gin transports the cotton to shoots leading to the gin saws. These saws pull the cotton apart, separating it from the seeds. The lint is removed by air blasts, going into a condenser where it receives a final beating and cleaning, and where it becomes glorified, snowy-white drifts. The final process is confining these drifts into sturdy jute bagging and binding it with metal bands. The seed is delivered by conveyor back to the planter, or, when sold directly to the ginnner, is sent to the seed house.

The baled cotton goes from the gin to the compress where Negro handlers unload and pitch it to another set of Negroes, who "bust" the bands with a band breaker and throw it into the press. The Negroes work rhythmically, singing and shouting at one another. The compress runs by steam and each time the plunger goes up with a bale the press gives a snort and lets out a puff of white vapor, making the scene noisy and exciting.

Cotton oil mills handle the cottonseed, turning it into vegetable oil, which, refined, and mixed with compound lard, is the basis for many cooking preparations. It is also used extensively in the manufacture of soap. The oil mills run continuously day and night for a period of about eight months. This continuous operation is necessary, because cotton "meat," as the seed is called, must never be allowed to cool while in the process of cooking. The meats are properly toasted; then the oil is extracted, trickling out of the press in a clear, golden stream, deliciously odorous. The hull of the seed is shaped into seed cakes, then ground into cottonseed meal, which makes fertilizer and cattle food that is valuable as a fattener and milk-producer.

POINTS OF INTEREST

1. The COURTHOUSE, squared by River Road, Cotton, Market, and Fulton Sts. with main entrance on Market St., is a large concrete structure of neo-Classic design. Rising above the principal façade is a clock tower topped with a small cupola. Below the clock is the belfry where chimes sound every quarter hour. The chimes are pitched to duplicate the tones of the Westminster chimes in London. On the hour, they peal forth the air to which has been set these words:

"Lord through this hour
Be Thou our Guide
So by Thy power
No foot shall slide."

The chimes were a gift to the County by Mrs. Lizzie George Henderson as a memorial to her husband, an early Leflore County physician, who was much respected by his neighbors and patients.

2. The TERRY HOME, 305 West Market St. *(open weekdays 9-5)*, is the oldest house in Greenwood. It was built before the War between the States. The house is occupied by Mrs. Cora Terry, granddaughter of the Choctaw chieftain, Greenwood Leflore, and is equipped with furniture and appointments from the chieftain's home, Malmaison *(see Tour 6)*. Other Leflore heirlooms here are the belt and sword presented the chieftain by President Andrew Jackson, a silver peace medal given him by Pushmataha who had received it from Thomas Jefferson, a pamphlet containing the history of the Treaty of Dancing Rabbit Creek, monogrammed china from Paris, Bohemian glass wine and brandy sets, three large volumes on Indian tribes of North America presented to Leflore by the United States Government, the red leather Leflore family Bible, a certificate of payment from the Mississippi General Land Office signed by President Martin Van Buren, and several invitations addressed to and sent from the Leflores.

3. SUPREME INSTRUMENTS CORPORATION PLANT, 414-416 Howard St. *(open weekdays 8-4; tours)*, manufactures radio testing appliances. The company has the patent on a special testing instrument and, as the only plant allowed to manufacture the instrument, has developed a world trade.

4. PLANTERS' OIL MILL GIN, East Greenwood *(not open to public)*, is one of several plants that separates cotton lint from the seed, then bales the lint.

5. FEDERAL COMPRESS AND WAREHOUSE, East Greenwood *(not open to public)*, compresses the bales of cotton delivered by the gins and stores it for shipping.

6. BUCKEYE COTTON OIL MILL, W. River Front *(not open to public)*, extracts the oil from the cottonseed, making cottonseed oil, hulls, meal, and cakes.

7. STAPLE COOPERATIVE ASSOCIATION WAREHOUSE, Market St. *(open weekdays 9-5; tours)*, grades, stores, and markets cotton for association members.

POINTS OF INTEREST IN ENVIRONS

Malmaison, *28.2 m. (see Tour 6)*; Site of Fort Pemberton, *3.2 m.*; Wreck of Star of the West, *2.4 m. (see Side Tour 7A)*.

Gulfport

Railroad Stations: Union Station, 27th Ave., for Gulf & Ship Island R.R. and Louisville & Nashville R.R.
Bus Station: 1400-24th Ave. for Tri-State, Teche-Greyhound lines.
Airport: Municipal Airport, 1 m. from City Hall, bus fare 5¢, taxi fare 10¢; time 5 min. No scheduled service.
Taxis: 10¢ upward.
City Bus: 1110-30th Ave., fare 5¢ in city limits; hourly trips to Biloxi and Pass Christian.
Traffic Regulations: Speed limit 20 mph. within business district; 30 mph. other districts. Limited parking only on certain side of designated streets. See signs.
Accommodations: Six hotels; tourist camps.
Radio Station: WGCM (1210 kc.).
Motion Picture Houses: Two.
Swimming: Municipal pier and bathing pavilion, West Beach; Markham Pool, 23rd Ave.; Small Craft Harbor.
Golf: Great Southern course, East Beach, 15 min. drive from town, or 10¢ bus fare.
Tennis: City Park, West Beach; Great Southern Hotel courts; Second St. court, 1400-2nd St.; High School campus, 20th Ave. and 15th St.
Riding: Edgewater Gulf Hotel Stables, $1.50 per hr.
Fishing: Deep-sea and fresh-water fishing boats and guides for hire at hotels.
Annual Events: Annual Fox Hunters' Meet, Feb., affiliated with Southern and National Associations; Southern Marble Tournament, June; Gulfport Yacht Club Regatta, July; Mackerel Rodeo, July; City Tennis Tournaments, July, Municipal Tennis Courts, City Park.

GULFPORT (19 alt., 12,547 pop.), fronting the Gulf of Mexico and flanked by a line of historic towns of narrow streets and old landmarks, is a planned city, with no antecedents earlier than those of the 20th century. Conceived by the Gulf & Ship Island Company as a model of unobstructed expansiveness, the old live-oaks and indigenous shrubs that characterize the Coast, were sacrificed to an atmosphere of wide, airy streets and narrow, formally planted parkways. The streets, paralleling the white concrete sea wall with arrow-like straightness, allow no informalities or small outcroppings of individuality to mar their directness. The avenues, running at right angles to the streets, are bordered by stiff, imported palms and are as orderly and patterned as an engineer's dream.

Overlooking the Gulf, the city has greater length than depth, with its length centered by its harbor and business district. Beginning at the harbor between 22nd and 31st Avenues, the business district bears the marks of two booms. The buildings of the first boom (1900-08) are of white brick, two and three stories high, with commodious, high-ceilinged interiors and dated cornices. Among them, emphasizing their

LOADING BALES OF COTTON, GULFPORT

outmoded appearance, tower apartments and hotels constructed during the boom of 1925-26. These newer buildings are of cream faced brick or stucco, with a suggestion of Spanish architecture in their pastel walls and bright tile roofs.

Extending from the business district east and west, and separated from the sea wall by narrow, neutral strips of grass and sand, is Beach Boulevard. Along this broad street overlooking the Gulf was developed a residential section during the early boom; later it was made a part of US 90, the main artery of the Coast. The houses, all on the north side facing the water, express the same spirit as the earlier business houses in that they are roomy frame structures with elaborate trimmings and many wind-swept galleries.

Northward from the boulevard is the residential section developed during the excitement of the second boom. A majority of the dwellings are compact bungalows, though a few in the subdivisions show the influence of Spanish design.

Fringing the sandy ridge further northward is the Negro section. Though there are here many aspects of the average urban Mississippi Negroes' district—three- and four-room houses, bare yards, and small garden patches—this section is above the average, with many of the homes owned by the occupants. A higher percentage of Gulfport Negroes are said to own their homes than in any other town in the State. These homes, often given undue emphasis by the drab backdrop of unkempt rental houses, are set on well-shaded and well-planted lawns. The Negroes of Gulfport comprise 25.2 percent of the population and are, for the most part, employed as stevedores or are fishermen. The stevedores receive union wages and thus are able to maintain a standard of living somewhat higher than that of the fishermen, who, equipped with nets, seines, and rowboats, usually bring into the local markets a catch sufficient only for simple needs. The Gulfport school system maintains an accredited high school for Negro children. After graduation, a fair number of the male children are sent out of the State to college. But unlike the Negroes of Natchez, only a small percentage of this educated group ever return to Gulfport as self-appointed missionaries to their race.

The beginning of Gulfport can be dated exactly at May 3, 1887. On that day a committee of the Board of Directors of the Gulf & Ship Island Company, an organization formed for the purpose of building a railroad as an outlet for the Piney Woods, and headed by Judge W. H. Hardy, accepted a civil engineer's report as to the best location for the contemplated railroad's terminal harbor on the Mississippi Coast. By 1891 the railroad was completed to Saucier, 20 miles north. Then the Union Investment Company, which held the building contract, fell into legal difficulties and Federal court proceedings brought construction to a standstill.

Immediately after this, however, Capt. J. T. Jones of New York saw the potentialities in the railroad and undertook its completion. By 1902 the entire stock of the Gulf & Ship Island R.R. had passed into his hands and within a few months the town of Gulfport became a city of 5,000 population. But the achievement found its obstacles. Yellow fever was an acute problem. Each summer brought a few cases of the plague to the Coast and with these the dreaded quarantine law. Immediately upon the development of a case all withdrawal from the city was banned; railroads were required to transfer incoming passengers, and freight and mail were fumigated before being allowed to proceed. These restrictions served to isolate Gulfport, along with other Coast towns, from the outside world during certain seasons of the year and, consequently, to check its growth. At this time all incoming vessels were inspected at the Government quarantine on Ship Island *(see Side Tour 1A)*. By 1902, however, the cause of yellow fever was at last determined and the disease brought under control. In that year the personnel of the station was withdrawn from Ship Island and the inspection service established at Gulfport, the seat of Harrison, second county in the United States to have a Board of Health.

The original plan of the Gulf & Ship Island R.R. was to extend the tracks across the 12-mile channel to Ship Island. This plan proved impracticable, and instead of carrying it out, improvements were made on the Gulfport harbor, which was opened in 1902. With its completion, the road, built through a sparsely settled section as an outlet for lumber shipments, brought a transformation to the southern part of the State. In 1911 Gulfport shipped more yellow pine than any other port in the world.

Into this ready-made city, in the pre-war boom, poured a population from many countries. A dozen languages could be heard in a morning's stroll, and court proceedings were carried on largely through interpreters. These folk were mostly seamen lured from their ships by high wages. When the lumber shipments decreased and wages became less attractive, they returned to the sea. But their comparatively short stay put a cosmopolitan mark upon the character of the town. There was no tradition by which to gauge values, and during this period Gulfport's social and political history is a story of churches and schools fighting against saloons and lawlessness. But due to a few events—the unprovoked killing of a Greek on a prominent corner, a mass Christmas night attack upon the small police force—public sentiment crystallized against the wide-open character of the town.

Shipping and lumbering brought stevedore companies and subsidiary industries, such as foundries, machine shops, ship chandlers, and building trades, to the city. But in 1906 a terrific tropical storm swept the Piney Woods and brought the shocking realization that, figuratively, the city had all its eggs in one basket. Approximately a fourth of the standing timber in south Mississippi was blown down, and by the financial repercussion every bank in Gulfport was tossed to the verge of insolvency. Recovering from the catastrophe, a move was made to develop truck gardening and to interest tourist trade.

The need for other props to the city's commercial life was made compelling by the exigencies of the World War. With lumber shipments practically at a standstill in the early years of the war, Gulfport businessmen cast about for new sources of income. The result was the sponsoring of the Mississippi Centennial Exposition in 1917, partly to celebrate the 100th anniversary of the State's admission to the Union, but more to establish the Gulf Coast as a permanent exposition site for Mississippi products and industries, with a view of developing eventually the millions of acres of idle land in the State. Before the exposition could be held, the United States entered the World War, and the buildings and grounds were taken over by the Federal Government for use as a naval training school.

In 1925 the Illinois Central System purchased the Gulf & Ship Island R.R., launching a real estate boom that continued through that year and much of 1926. With the collapse of the boom, Gulfport faced a crucial situation. The timber of the Piney Woods had been cut and never again would there be lumber shipments from Gulfport like those of the earlier period. But the years had brought a civic consciousness that united the citizens in a community drive to keep the city alive. Cotton, the State's oldest and largest industry, was sought as a new means for industrial growth; warehouses, compresses, and a yarn spinning mill—now converted into a shirt factory—were built. The climax to this development was the completion of a million-dollar pier and warehouse that gave the city shipping facilities unexcelled by any port on the Gulf.

In the fall of 1935 the Gulfport longshoremen, participating in the nation-wide strike of the International Longshoremen's Association, struck for higher wages and union recognition. Their efforts were nullified, however, through the failure of New Orleans longshoremen to make an effective tie-up with them. After a month public sentiment and the city officials turned against the strikers, as a result of which the strike failed. The longshoremen now (1938) receive union wages.

The tourist trade as a business has gained recognition in Gulfport. Recreation at a seacoast playground naturally centers on bathing, sailing, and fishing. Stretching before Gulfport and paralleling it, Cat and Ship Islands, two of a series of islands, cut off from the Gulf a wide body of tranquil water known as the Mississippi Sound. About these islands and through the Sound sweep schools of game fish—speckled sea trout, Spanish mackerel, king mackerel, bonito, cavalla, and the king of all sporting fish, the silver tarpon. Here, between May and November, is the salt water fishermen's choice. Within an hour's ride of Gulfport the freshwater fisherman can make his casts in a new stream every morning for a month, and in these streams fishing for bass, striped bass, channel bass, crappie, bream, and perch is good every day in the year.

‹‹‹‹‹‹‹‹‹‹‹‹‹‹‹‹‹‹☼›››››››››››››››››››

Tour—*1.9m.*

S. from 13th St. on 30th Ave.

1. The HARBOR AND SHIP CANAL, fronting the city between 30th and 26th Aves., is a kaleidoscopic picture of deep blue water, broken now and then by the gleam of a high-leaping mullet or trout. The voices of Negro longshoremen mingle with the rattle of winches as cotton bales are swung into the holds of cargo boats; rocking skiffs scurry from the wake of tugs laboriously docking freighters from Liverpool, Stockholm, Peiping, and Bordeaux. Here and there Negro children perch precariously on a ship's spar, each with pole and fishing line, and winging over all are great, gray pelicans and screaming white sea gulls. The ship channel is marked by beacons for its seven-mile length. At its northern end it becomes a U-shaped turning basin for large ships; its east and west sides are flanked by piers. In the northwestern corner of the U of the basin is a seafood packing plant and, adjoining it, a small municipally-owned wharf; curving southward to form the west prong of the U is the newest pier, constructed with PWA aid. This reenforced slab rests on mammoth concrete and creosoted wood pilings and covers more than five acres on the ground floor. From Bay St. Louis to Biloxi's Back Bay, this pier is visible as a long low smudge jutting seaward.

From the pier itself, southward through the channel separating Cat and Ship Islands, is a view of the squat funnels of in- and out-bound freighters.

R. from 30th Ave. on W. Beach Blvd.; R. on 31st Ave.

2. The LUTHERAN CHURCH, 31st Ave. (L) facing 13th St., formerly the first Presbyterian Church, is a small, gray, frame structure of modified Gothic architecture, built in the early 1900's. A bronze plate marks the pew in which President Woodrow Wilson sat at the time of his visit in 1913.

R. from 31st Ave. on 13th St.

3. The HARDY MONUMENT, intersection of 13th St. and 25th Ave., is a bronze bust erected to the memory of Judge W. H. Hardy, who planned the city of Gulfport. The bust is the work of Leo Tolstoy, Jr., and was cast in the Philadelphia Art Studios of Bureau Brothers. It was given to Gulfport and southern Mississippi by Lamar Hardy, lawyer of New York City and son of Captain Hardy.

R. from 13th St. on 25th Ave.; L. on E. Beach Blvd.

4. The SMALL CRAFT HARBOR, E. Beach Blvd. between 25th and 20th Aves., is a basin 1,225 feet wide, 1,500 feet long, and 10 feet deep, and is formed by the extension of 20th Ave., approximately 2,750 feet into the Gulf. The concrete extension, 40 feet wide, has a foundation of earth dredged out to form the basin and is protected on the east side by a reenforced concrete concave-type of wall that throws the waves back upon themselves. On the south end of a westward angle to the extension is a wide oblong concrete fill that serves as a protection to the basin and as a foundation for the Municipal Clubhouse and Yacht Club. Jutting into the basin from the extension are four creosoted piling docks, each 450 feet long and lined with slips for boats. On the south side of the clubhouse are the bathing pier and beach. The site was given to the city by the heirs of Captain Jones; construction was completed in 1937 with PWA aid at a cost of $350,000.

5. UNITED STATES VETERANS' FACILITY NO. 74, E. Beach Blvd. (L) between Oak St. and city limits, is one of the largest under the Veterans Administration. Situated on grounds comprising 2,000 feet of beach front, the buildings follow the governmental type of hospital structures: rectangular, two-story brick and stucco, barrack-like utility buildings. Facing the Boulevard, and more ornate than the other buildings, is the administration building of Spanish Mission architecture. The walls are sand-colored stucco on steel laths, with heavy framework construction. The health records established by Harrison County and by the naval training station, which occupied the grounds during the World War, drew the attention of Federal officials to the desirability of this section for a veterans' hospital. At the close of the war, the grounds were turned over to the Public Health Service for the establishment of a hospital. When the hospitalization of World War soldiers passed under the present board, the buildings and grounds were sold to the Government. Since then, Congress has made large appropriations for additional buildings and equipment, until the hospital has a capacity of 600 beds.

The hospital operates its own laundry, bakery, and heating plant, and receives its water supply from an artesian well.

POINTS OF INTEREST IN ENVIRONS

Paradise Point, 3.9 *m.*, St. Mark's Chapel, 3.5 *m.*, Gulf Park College, 3.2 *m.*, Gulf Coast Military Academy, 4.9 *m.* (see *Tour 1*); Ship Island, 12 *m.* (see *Side Tour 1A*).

←←←←←←←←←←←←←←←☼→→→→→→→→→→→→→→→→

Holly Springs

Railroad Stations: 959 E. Van Dorn Ave. for Illinois Central R.R.; end of E. Van Dorn Ave. for St. Louis & San Francisco (Frisco) R.R.
Bus Station: Stafford Cafe, cor. Memphis St. and Van Dorn Ave. for Dixie-Greyhound Lines, Tri-State Transit Co.
Taxis: 25¢ per person within city.
Accommodations: One hotel; tourist rooms.
Information Service: Hotel; filling stations.
Motion Picture Houses: Two.
Swimming: Experiment Station, 1 m. N. on State 7; Spring Lake State Park, 8 mi. S. on State 7.
Golf: Experiment Station, 1 m. N. on State 7.
Annual Events: Field Trials, Amateur and Professional, U. S. Field Trial Course, 10 m. SW. on Chulahoma Road, 1st wk. in February; Holly Springs Garden Pilgrimage in spring.

HOLLY SPRINGS (602 alt., 2,271 pop.), with its lovely old homes and business houses, its immense trees and boxwood hedges, gives evidence of the early culture brought to north central Mississippi by the turbulent but romantic times of the 1830's. Its heart is a courthouse square, shady, informal, with a four-faced clock in the typically Mississippi courthouse tower. Set back from the square along oak-shaded streets are homes of Georgian Colonial and Greek Revival architecture, their faded grandeur eloquent expression of a culture that sprang into being, flowered, and died with one generation.

The trading center for a wide farming district, Holly Springs is the headquarters for a soil conservation unit and the shipping point for cotton, dairying products, and clay deposits. More than one-half of the population are native born white persons while approximately 48 percent are Negroes. The latter, as proud as the white persons of their ancestral connection with the town, are almost entirely unskilled laborers or domestic servants.

Situated near the top of a ridge along which an Indian trail once led from the Mississippi River to the tribal seat of the Chickasaw Nation, Indians stopped here to drink the waters of the great spring that bubbled up in the midst of a grove of holly trees. They called the place Suavatooky or watering place, and according to legend their young chieftain Onoho with his love, a princess of a rival tribe, drowned themselves here to avoid separation. In 1832 the Chickasaw Nation ceded their lands to the United States Government, and the territory was opened to white men.

The influx of white settlers was a part of the great land and cotton fever that pulled men westward during the two decades before the war. Second sons of Tidewater families, they came with the eagerness and spirit of adventure that characterized the Forty-niners—and grew almost as wealthy planting cotton as the miners did panning gold. They bought land recklessly, worked it a year or two, then bought more. They sent to Virginia and the Carolinas for additional slaves to work the expanding and fabulously fertile tracts of land.

William Randolph, a descendant of Virginia's famed John Randolph, was not the first white man to settle at the springs, but it is he who is credited with founding the town in 1835. An indication of the settlement's feverish growth is its incorporation as a town in 1837. In 1838 the Holly Springs and Mississippi River Turnpike Company was chartered. Three years after the building of the railroad, Holly Springs was a miniature of the older Tidewater cities. Lawyers outnumbered the other professions, as squabbles over land grants raged and as the need for deeds and abstracts grew. In March 1838, one year after Holly Springs became a town, there were fourteen law offices, six doctor's offices, two banks, nine dry goods stores, five grocery stores, five churches, three hotels, and several private schools. Unlike other Mississippi towns, it scarcely knew a frontier life. In place of log cabins these second sons built mansions that rivalled one another in elaborate treatment and grand proportions. Yet these homes, while expressions of their builders, did not reveal the individuality of the homes built by the Natchez planters; instead, they re-echoed the Tidewater spirit influenced by the grandiose manner of the period in which they were built.

Although land and cotton remained the backbone of the town, whose population jumped from 1,117 in 1840 to 5,000 in 1861, other industries were established. Most notable of these was the iron foundry that furnished iron for the Mississippi Central Railroad (now a part of the Illinois Central System), for the Moresque Building in New Orleans, fences for the gardens of Holly Springs, and cannon for the Confederacy.

During the War between the States, the town suffered 61 raids, the most devastating conducted by the Confederate General, Van Dorn. This was in 1862. Generals Grant and Sherman were launching a convergent

MAIN STREET AND COURTHOUSE SQUARE

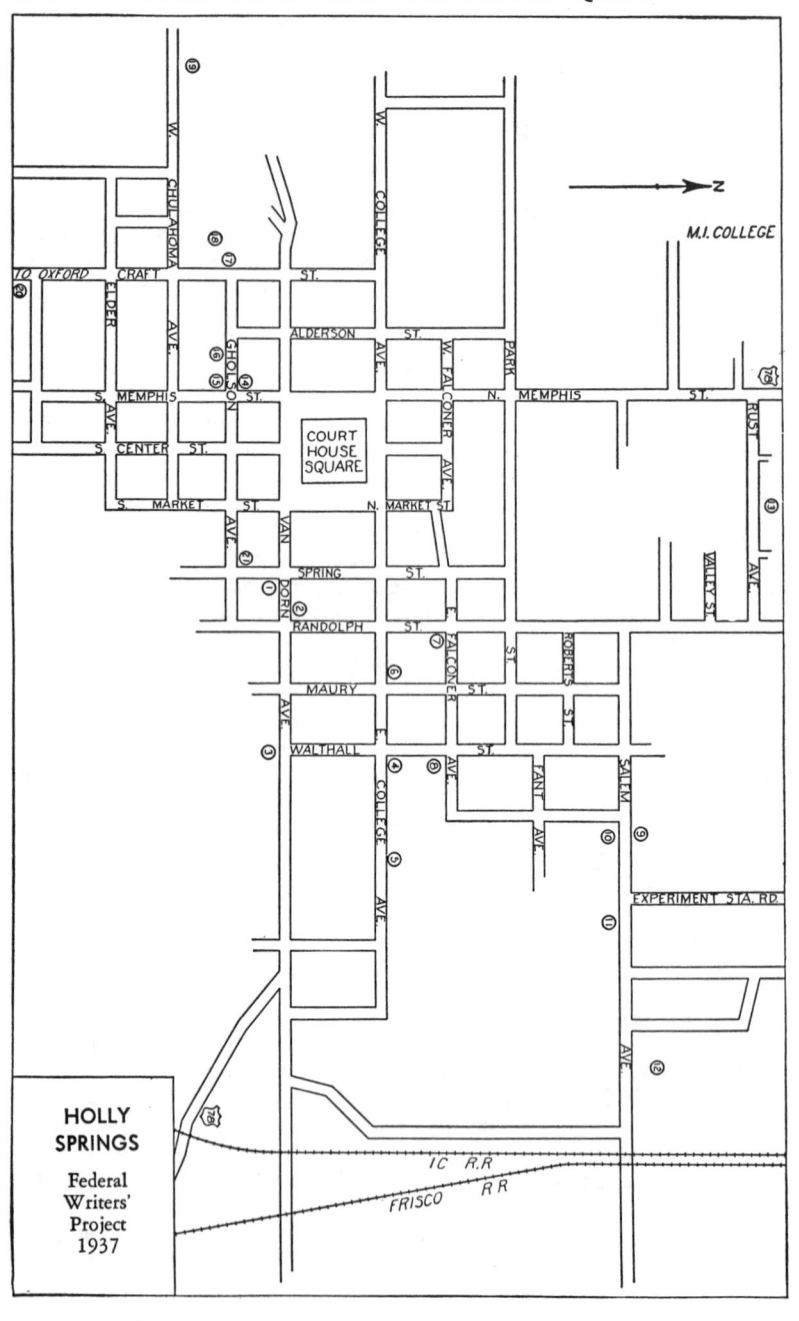

HOLLY SPRINGS

Federal Writers' Project 1937

attack upon Vicksburg, and Grant had moved his base of supplies from Memphis to Holly Springs. With Grant on his way to meet Sherman before Vicksburg, Van Dorn burst in upon the town unexpectedly, wrecked Grant's winter stores, and took the town for the Confederacy. The effect of this raid was to delay for a year the fall of Vicksburg *(see VICKSBURG).*

Hardly had the town recovered from war and reconstruction when it was struck by the yellow fever epidemic of 1878, which reduced the population by about half. At the time the epidemic broke out in bordering counties there was not a single case in Holly Springs, and authorities, believing the germ could not live in a high dry altitude, threw open the doors of the highest town in the State to fever refugees. Within a few months 2,000 fever victims were dead.

Neither war nor pestilence drained the vitality of the town so steadily and permanently as did the rapid erosion of the land. Behind the decline of Holly Springs as a wealthy agrarian center was the slump of the section's basic industry, cotton cultivation. Year after year, planters squeezed the fertility from one tract of land, then discarded it to repeat the operation on another, until at last the virgin strength of the land was gone. With the topsoil washed away, great gaping red gullies ate cancerously through the plantations, and the second generation of planters forsook the land for the professions. They became lawyers, doctors, ministers, and tradesmen, but their power was gone with their wealth.

Concerted efforts are being made to prevent further erosion. The conservation headquarters for northern Mississippi are set up in Holly Springs, home of Congressman Wall Doxey, who is much interested in this work. Also, a comeback to industrial prominence is being attempted in other fields; dairying is slowly taking the place of cotton growing, and clay deposits in the vicinity are being commercialized. But in spite of this new trend, it is the faded tapestry of ante-bellum grandeur that gives Holly Springs its tone today.

KEY TO HOLLY SPRINGS MAP

1. Methodist Church
2. Christ Church (Episcopal)
3. Strickland Place
4. The Freeman Place
5. Gray Gables
6. The Watson Building
7. The "College Annex"
8. The Rufus Jones House
9. Clapp–Fant Place
10. The McGowan–Crawford Home
11. Coxe–Dean House
12. Bonner–Belk Home
13. Rust College
14. Presbyterian Church
15. Craft–Daniel Home
16. The Crump Home
17. Featherstone–Buchanan House
18. The Polk Place
19. Walter's Place
20. Mason–Tucker Home
21. Waite–Bowers Place

Tour 1–3.1m.

E. from Courthouse Square on Van Dorn Ave.
1. The METHODIST CHURCH, SE. corner Van Dorn Ave. and Spring St., was completed in 1849. Except for the wooden spire and front entrance added in the 1870's, the structure is of brick covered with time-grayed stucco. After the courthouse was burned by the Federals, court sessions were held in its basement.
2. CHRIST CHURCH (EPISCOPAL), NW. corner Van Dorn Ave. and Randolph St., was built in 1858. Of Gothic Revival architecture, the edifice is constructed of brick covered with cream-colored stucco. The auditorium has delicate open beams and windows of stained glass. Facing the pulpit across the auditorium is a slave gallery. The lot was presented to the church by the county police.
3. The WILLIAM STRICKLAND PLACE, 800 Van Dorn Ave. *(open during Pilgrimage)*, is lovely but not well preserved. The date, 1828, found on one of its beams, is cited as proof that it was the first two-story house in this section. Among the old furnishings is a hand-carved rosewood tester bed built to accommodate nine persons. Jefferson Davis often visited here, and it is said that when Van Dorn recaptured the town from the Federals, the owners of the home hid a Northern officer within its walls to repay him for having earlier prevented Federal authorities from making a hospital of the house.

L. from Van Dorn Ave. on Walthall St.; R. on E. College Ave.
4. The G. R. FREEMAN PLACE, 810 E. College Ave. *(open during Pilgrimage)*, a small vine-covered frame cottage, was the home of Gen. Edward Cary Walthall, Mississippi's great conservative and perhaps Holly Springs' most distinguished citizen. Soldier, statesman, and patriot, Walthall (1831–98) was a corporation lawyer of the Tory tradition. Believing implicitly in the Constitution and defying political experiment, he was a great stabilizing force during the period of reconstruction, when civilization in the South reached the breaking point. He never sought political office and seldom spoke in political campaigns, yet he was U. S. Senator for four terms. Paying tribute to his memory in the U. S. House of Representatives, John Sharp Williams spoke of him as the "last of a long line of Mississippians of historic type and fame." Walthall is buried in the Holly Springs cemetery. The house is owned by the artist, Kate Freeman Clark.
5. GRAY GABLES, 871 E. College Ave. *(open during Pilgrimage)*, is a twin-gable, two-story structure of stucco-covered brick. The interior is characterized by a delicate spiral stairway with hand-carved woodwork that repeats the decorative motif of the ceiling design. Openings are of stained Venetian glass. The house was built in 1830.

Retrace E. College Ave.
6. The WATSON BUILDING, 601 E. College Ave., home of the jurist, Judge J. W. C. Watson, was built in the early 1850's. In it Elizabeth D. Watson, his daughter, established the Maury Institute, a school for girls. Later the school was made the Presbyterian College, and it is now a unit of the Mississippi Synodical College, a junior college established in 1883. Anna Robinson Watson, stepdaughter of Judge Watson, was poet laureate of the United Daughters of the Confederacy.

R. from E. College Ave. on Randolph St.
7. The "COLLEGE ANNEX," SE. corner E. Falconer Ave. and Randolph St., was the town house of Maj. Dabney Hull. Once, during the War between the States, Hull's nephew, Capt. Edward H. Crump, had tied his horse at the gate and was sitting on the veranda when he heard the cry, "The Yankees are coming!" Mrs. Hull called, "Quick, Ed, bring the horse into the parlor!" This the young soldier did, escaping the Northern troops while his horse pawed the parlor. The house is a part of the Mississippi Synodical College.

R. from Randolph St. on E. Falconer Ave.
8. The RUFUS JONES HOUSE, 800 E. Falconer Ave. *(private)*, built in 1857, is a handsome two-story frame structure of Greek Revival design. The entrance opens into a square, richly-decorated reception hall, flanked by rooms on three sides. The furniture and fixtures express the fineness of the homes of this period.

L. from E. Falconer Ave. on Walthall St.; R. on Salem Ave.
9. The CLAPP-FANT PLACE, 221 Salem Ave. *(private)*, was built of slave-made brick in the early 1840's and is probably the State's finest example of Georgian Colonial architecture outside of Natchez. Judge J. W. Clapp was so careful in the building of the house that he would tear down half a wall, if necessary, to take out a faulty brick; to prevent moisture he had charcoal placed between the outside walls. The interior is distinguished by a circular staircase, an oval dining room, white marble mantels, hand-carved cornices, and light grey rosettes centered in the ceiling. During a Northern raid Judge Clapp escaped capture by hiding in one of the hollow Corinthian columns supporting the roof of the front veranda. After the war Gen. A. M. West, who was twice nominated for the presidency of the United States, became the owner of the house.

10. The McGOWAN-CRAWFORD HOME, 222 Salem Ave. *(open during Pilgrimage)*, is a brick mansion containing parquetry floors, fine interior cornices, and a spiral stairway with a niche for statuary. It was built in the "grand manner" by Alfred Brooks as a gift to his daughter in 1858.

11. The COXE-DEAN HOME, 330 Salem Ave. *(open during Pilgrimage)*, designed in the manner of a Swiss chalet, was built in 1859 by William Henry Coxe. Through the house runs a 50-foot central hall with a stairway ornamented with elaborate woodwork. Materials for the house were brought from abroad. The house has etched glass windows, silver door knobs, and well preserved marble mantels. Its bathroom had a solid lead tub and a marble lavatory. The tub, when removed, had to

be taken out in sections. Situated on a 12-acre lot, the house is surrounded by numerous shade trees and magnolias; forming the entrance to the grounds are three massive iron gates. General Grant had his headquarters here when he occupied the town during the War between the States, and on its stairway three Confederate soldiers are said to have been shot as they made a dash for liberty.

12. The BONNER-BELK HOME, 411 Salem Ave. *(open during Pilgrimage)*, is a commodious Gothic Revival mansion built in 1858 by Dr. Charles Bonner. On spacious grounds, the house is notable for its ornamental windows and wrought-iron work. The outside walls are of four-brick and the inside walls are of three-brick thickness. The furniture in one of the front bedrooms was brought from France; the woodwork is hand-carved. Dr. Bonner's oldest daughter, Sherwood (1849-83), a first writer of Southern dialect stories, was born here. During the War between the States the place was occupied by General Ord.

Retrace Salem Ave.; R. on Randolph St.; L. on Rust Ave.

13. RUST COLLEGE, NE. corner Rust Ave. and N. Memphis St., has been one of the leading liberal arts Negro colleges of Mississippi since it was founded by the Methodist Episcopal Church in 1868. The property value is $125,000; its equipment is valued at $15,000. The school is supported by the Board of Education of the M. E. Church and the Woman's Home Missionary Society of the same church. With an enrollment of 177 students (1937), the school has an exceptionally good science department and is listed by the University Senate, an accrediting agent of the Methodist Episcopal Church. One of the oldest Negro schools in the State, Rust has given the Negroes of Mississippi many of their outstanding religious and educational leaders.

Tour 2—*1.9m*

S. from Courthouse Square on S. Memphis St.

14. PRESBYTERIAN CHURCH, NW. corner S. Memphis St. and Gholson Ave., is a Gothic Revival structure with stained glass windows, of Isle de Fleur design, imported from Europe in 1858. Two lovely spiral stairways lead to the second floor auditorium, and paralleling these "white folks' stairs" are narrow flights leading to a slave gallery. Though not quite finished at the beginning of the War between the States, the congregation was preparing to dedicate the church when the Federal army arrived in 1861 and used the lower floor for a stable.

R. from S. Memphis St. on Gholson Ave.

15. The CRAFT-DANIEL HOME, SW. corner S. Memphis St. and Gholson Ave. *(private)*, is one of the Holly Springs homes remaining in the hands of the original family. A two-story stucco house similar in design to Mount Vernon, it is occupied by the fifth generation.

16. The E. H. CRUMP HOME, 140 Gholson Ave. *(open during Pilgrimage)*, one of the earliest homes of this section, was built entirely of hand-hewn timber. Of Southern Colonial style, the one-story house is well preserved and has the original wallpaper and furnishings. The house is thought to have been built in 1830 by Samuel McCorkle, first land commissioner to the Indians and first banker in the county. This is the birthplace of E. H. Crump, Memphis political leader.

L. from Gholson Ave. on Craft St.

17. The FEATHERSTONE-BUCHANAN HOUSE, 290 Craft St. *(open during Pilgrimage)*, was built in 1834 by Alexander McEwen. A white, two-story, clapboard structure, the house is of the Planter type of architecture; the ground floor or basement contains the living room, dining room, and servants' quarters; the second floor is given to bedrooms, the back ones of which are raised above hall level. The original pegs are in all the doors.

18. The POLK PLACE, 300 Craft St. *(open during Pilgrimage)*, joins the Featherstone home by an oval driveway and is similar to it in color, style of architecture, and floor plan. The house was built in the 1830's by Gen. Thomas Polk, brother of the "Fighting Bishop," Leonidas Polk, and kinsman of President Polk.

R. from Craft St. on W. Chulahoma Ave.

19. The WALTER PLACE, 331 W. Chulahoma Ave. *(open during Pilgrimage)*, was begun by Col. Harvey W. Walter in 1854. This two-story brick house is a fine example of the more luxurious homes of the 1850's. The central motif of the façade is in the form of a Corinthian portico flanked by two battlemented octagonal corner towers. The broad, high central hall leads to a grand double staircase. On the east side of the lower floor is a large parlor containing unusually large pieces of furniture. In 1862 Mrs. U. S. Grant awaited her husband here, and it is told that when General Van Dorn raided the town she appealed to him to protect the privacy of her room and thus saved her husband's papers. In return for the courtesy, when Grant retook the town, he gave an order that no Federal soldier could go within a block of the place—unwittingly making the house a rendezvous for Confederates passing through the town.

Retrace W. Chulahoma Ave.; R. on Craft St.

20. The MASON-TUCKER HOME, 601 Craft St. *(private)*, is an example of the early affluence of Holly Springs. It is a fusion of the Georgian and Gothic Revival types, with a wide front gallery. Of especial interest are its double parlors, spiral staircase, iron hearth in the living room, and iron grille work.

Retrace Craft St.; R. on Elder Ave.; L. on S. Market St.; R. on Gholson Ave.; L. on Spring St.

21. The WAITE-BOWERS PLACE, NW. corner Spring St. and Gholson Ave., is a log house remodeled into a frame residence. Two log rooms are hidden within the house, built more than 100 years ago by Judge Godentia White, the first probate clerk of this county.

POINTS OF INTEREST IN ENVIRONS

Galena, *12.1 m.,* Goodman Home, *8.3 m.,* Austin Moore Home, *8.4 m.,* Martha Gardner Home, *8.3 m. (see Tour 9).*

◄◄◄◄◄◄◄◄◄◄◄◄◄◄◄◄✹►►►►►►►►►►►►►►►►►►

Jackson

Railroad Stations: Union Station, 301 E. Capitol St., for Illinois Central System, Yazoo & Mississippi Valley R.R., Alabama & Vicksburg R.R., and Gulf & Ship Island R.R.; E. Pearl St. for Gulf, Mobile & Northern R.R.
Bus Stations: Central Motor Coach Depot, 117 E. Pearl St., for Tri-State Transit Co., Varnado Bus Lines, and Thomas Bus Lines; Union Bus Depot, 118 N. Lamar St., for Greyhound, Dixie-Greyhound, Teche-Greyhound, and Oliver Bus Lines.
Airport: Municipal Airport, Woodrow Wilson Ave., bet. Rozelle St. and Sunset Drive, for Delta Airlines and Chicago & Southern Airlines, taxi fare 20¢, time 10 min.
Street Busses: Fare 5¢.
Taxis: Fare 10¢ per person first zone, 20¢ per person second zone. Cabs 25¢.
Traffic Regulations: Speed limit 20 mph. business district, 30 mph. other districts. No left turn at designated intersections; limited parking, 1 hr. between 8 a.m. and 6 p.m., all-night parking prohibited.
Street Arrangement: Capitol St. divides N. and S. portions of city, Farish St. divides E. and W. portions.

Accommodations: Five hotels; tourist camps; boarding and rooming houses.

Information Service: Chamber of Commerce, Lamar Life Ins. Bldg.; hotels.

Radio Stations: WJDX (1270 kc.); WTJS (1310 kc.).
Theaters and Motion Picture Houses: City Auditorium, S. Congress St.; occasional road shows. Six motion picture houses.
Athletics: Y.M.C.A., 303 E. Pearl St.; Y.W.C.A., 117 N. West St.; Livingston Park, 2918 W. Capitol St.; Millsaps College, N. West St.; professional baseball, Cotton States League, State Fairgrounds, end E. Amite St.
Swimming: Livingston Park; Y.M.C.A.; Crystal Pool, 2 m. E. out High St. near Pearl River.
Tennis: Y.W.C.A.; Armory, near Fairgrounds; Millsaps College; Belhaven College, Belhaven St.; Livingston Park; Portwood Tennis courts, 515 N. West St.
Golf: Jackson Country Club, 4 m. from Union Station, W. Capitol St. (US 80), 18 holes, greens fee $1.10; Municipal Course, Livingston Park, 18 holes, greens fee 44¢. Weather permits year-round playing.

Riding: Robert M. Stockett Riding Academy, east end Mississippi St.; minimum charge $1.
Skeet Club: 5 m. from city, US 51, minimum charge $1.15, April 1–Nov. 1, Sun. and Wed.

Annual Events: Southern Intercollegiate Athletic Association Basketball Tournament, City Auditorium, Mar.; Music Festival, City Schools, City Auditorium, no set date; the Follies, Junior Auxiliary benefit for underprivileged children, City Auditorium, Spring; May Day Festival, City Schools, Fairgrounds; Mississippi Championship Tennis Tournament, Livingston Park, second Tues. in June; Red Cross Water Pageant, Livingston Park, Aug.; Mississippi State Fair, Oct.; Junior Auxiliary Style Show, Edwards Hotel, Oct.; Horse Show, sponsored by Girl Scouts, Oct.; Feast of Carols, Dec.

JACKSON * (294 alt., 48,282 pop.), spreading along a high bluff, with the Pearl River forming its eastern boundary, is Mississippi's largest city and its capital. Viewed from an upper story window of an office building it is an unconsolidated city of breadth and space. Nowhere is there an over-concentration. On the south, well-spaced civic buildings surround a block-long flower garden. Near the center, the Governor's mansion, occupying an entire block, looks out upon the business district from a lawn that is wide and shaded with trees. The business district, confined almost exclusively to Capitol Street and characterized by modern façades, is unbegrimed and fresh. To the north and west are the residential districts. The northern section contains a few examples of ante-bellum architecture; the western area is a heterogeneous group of bungalows and English cottages. Strung along the railroad tracks northwest of the business district are the "heavy" industries, lumber, oil, and cotton. Forming concentric ellipses around the north, west, and south edges of the city are the new subdivisions. Planted along the neutral grounds and in the city parks are more than 7,000 crapemyrtle trees, Jackson's loveliest natural attraction.

In character with its position as a capital, a majority of Jackson's white population find employment in governmental service, either national, State, or county. Yet commercial and industrial employment does not lag far behind, for with cheap fuel and transportation facilities Jackson's growth is not based on government alone. Lumber, cottonseed oil, and textile factories have brought to it industrial solidity.

Approximately 40 percent of the population are the Negroes who furnish the bulk of the city's unskilled labor. A majority of their families live in the northwest section, in three- and four-room frame houses. Crowded together, these houses are in clean-swept yards; a few have garden patches at the rear. More familiar than the garden, however, is the clothes line upon which hangs the week's washing of some white family. For Jackson has not yet abandoned its washerwomen in preference to laundries, and many Negro women, who often are employed as cooks and nursemaids, take in washing on the side.

Yet not all of the city's Negroes are unskilled laborers; many of the State's leading Negro lawyers, doctors, and educators live here. With homes on the opposite side of the city, these professional men maintain a standard of living superior to their humbler neighbors, who mow lawns,

* A map of Jackson is on the back of the State map in pocket at end of book.

MUNICIPAL GARDEN AND CIVIC CENTER, JACKSON

work gardens, or do manual labor for the industrial plants. They own substantially built homes, make themselves a part of the city's economic life, and follow the sophisticated trends of the white population.

Founded and platted as the seat of government, and for 116 years the funnel through which all the turbulent events of the State's history have poured, Jackson has a background which is, in turn, murky with political intrigues and bright with historic associations. Its position as the democratic heart of the State accounts for its tone and prestige; the skyscrapers spaced along Capitol Street and the new outlying subdivisions are evidences of its rapid expansion on the surge of an industrial and governmental boom. For Jackson is the crossroads to which all Mississippians gravitate; and in a State that is predominantly rural, it alone has the metropolitan touch.

Jackson had its beginning as Le Fleur's Bluff, the trading post of Louis Le Fleur, adventurous French-Canadian who had his cabin at what is now the intersection of South State and Silas Brown Streets. When the Treaty of Doak's Stand expanded Mississippi by breaking the bounds of the Natchez District in 1820, the legislature decided that the capital city should be located near the center of the State rather than at Columbia or Washington. From Columbia, the temporary capital, a three-member commission composed of General Thomas Hinds, hero of Andrew Jackson's coast campaign against the British, William Lattimore, and James Patton made their way up the Pearl River to select a suitable location. Le Fleur's Bluff, with its extensive fertile flat to the east and rich prairie to the west, plus its strategic location with regard to river transportation, was the commission's choice. In 1821, three days after Thanksgiving, the legislature appointed Peter Van Dorn to work with Hinds and Lattimore in laying out the city, assisted by Abraham DeFrance, superintendent of public buildings at Washington, D. C.

The first statehouse was completed in 1821. It was a two-story building with outside dimensions of 30 by 40 feet, and was constructed of brick, clay, and limestone found in the vicinity. Shutters on each window, upstairs and down, added the 19th century modern touch, and large chimneys flanked each end. The first session of the legislature convened here in January 1822.

The name of the newly created city was changed to Jackson in honor of Andrew Jackson, then the idol of Mississippi and later President of the United States. The area around the city became Hinds County, named for the chief of the capital commission who had been Old Hickory's associate in military campaigns in the South. The new statehouse was erected at the approximate center of the town site, which embraced two adjoining half sections of land deeded for the purpose, and which had been laid out on the checkerboard plan in accordance with Thomas Jefferson's suggestion to Territorial Governor Claiborne 17 years before. Each square designated for building purposes was alternated with a square reserved as a park or green. Evidence of this plan remains in downtown Jackson and on College Green, which extends east of the New Capitol. The original boundaries were the bluffs on the east, and South, West, and High Streets, the town including College Green, Court Green, and Capitol Green. Among the first settlers was Lieutenant Governor Dickson, who was appointed postmaster soon after his arrival. In 1823, 100 lots were offered for sale.

Records of early Jackson were burned during the War between the States, but it is known that there was agitation for removal of the statehouse. In 1829 the Senate passed a bill authorizing the removal to Clinton, but the measure was defeated by a tie vote in the House. In the next year the House voted 18 to 17 to move the capital to Port Gibson, but immediately reconsidered. The following day they voted 20 to 16 to move it to Vicksburg, but still no action was taken. Then, to avoid the question for a number of years, the constitution of 1832 designated Jackson as the capital until 1850, when the legislature should name a permanent seat of government. By 1850 Jackson was well established and the legislature made no change.

The Old Capitol, though incomplete, was occupied in 1839, and the following year Andrew Jackson addressed the legislature here. Five years later, Henry Clay was entertained under its roof. In half a dozen more years a convention was called here to consider Clay's last compromise, that of 1850; and in January 1861, the building was the scene of the Secession Convention that severed Mississippi from the Union.

During the 1830's and early 1840's much of the groundwork for the

NEW CAPITOL, JACKSON

city's future prosperity was laid, even though this was a period when the State's currency was rapidly depreciating from the flush times that preceded the 1837 crash. A railroad linking Vicksburg to Jackson was begun in 1836. In 1837 the Jackson & Natchez R.R. laid its first track. Through this Jackson became, just prior to the war, the junction of two through railroads, the New Orleans, Jackson & Great Northern connecting with the Mississippi Central to give a route from New Orleans to Jackson, Tennessee, and the Southern, which completed the road east and west from Vicksburg to Meridian.

Early newspapers printed in Jackson were the *Pearl River Gazette,* published by G. B. Crutcher; the *State Register,* edited by Peter Isler; two political papers, the *Flag of Our Nation* and the *Reformer;* the *State Rights Banner;* the *Mississippian,* at one time the most influential paper in the State, published by Henry Foote and moved to Jackson from Vicksburg and Clinton; and the *Eastern Clarion,* organized at old Paulding in 1837, purchased by Col. J. J. Shannon in 1862, moved to Meridian until after the war, and then to Jackson where it is known now as the *Daily Clarion-Ledger.*

As the capital and as a railroad center Jackson played an important part in Mississippi's military history during the War between the States. After the Ordinance of Secession in 1861, the city remained the Confederate capital of Mississippi until just before it was besieged in 1863, when, under pressure of war, it lost its place as a seat of government until the spring of 1865. The siege of Jackson was closely connected with the campaign and siege of Vicksburg. When Vicksburg was attacked, Gen. Joseph E. Johnston collected troops at Jackson and moved them against the Federals across the Big Black River. But his campaign was halted when Vicksburg surrendered, July 4, and he was forced to retire to his entrenchments and base at Jackson. On July 9 General Sherman, marching across the State, reached the Confederate entrenchments. There was a spirited two-day engagement during which the Federals were repulsed, with a loss of about 500 men and three battle flags. Under continuous bombardment Johnston evacuated the city on the night of July 16, moving on toward Meridian, and Sherman took possession. It was then that Jackson's records were destroyed, for the city was gutted by fire and became known by the dismal sobriquet of Chimneyville. The governor's mansion, built in 1842 and occupied by Sherman, and a few private homes were saved from the general destruction. In Sherman's report to Grant on July 18 he stated: "We have made fine progress today in the work of destruction. Jackson will no longer be a point of danger. The land is devastated for thirty miles around."

Though retarded by the war and the fact that it kept a city government of carpetbaggers long after the State as a whole had restored white supremacy, Jackson's growth continued during Reconstruction. In 1869 Tougaloo College for Negroes, seven miles north, was founded by the American Missionary Union of the Congregational Church of New York City, aided by Mississippi; in 1884 Jackson College for Negroes, founded in 1877, was moved here from Natchez; in 1898 Campbell College, also for Negroes, was moved to Jackson from Vicksburg. The leaders of the Negro race developed by these schools helped Jackson to forgive the "Black and Tan" Constitutional Convention of 1868 under "Buzzard" Eggleston, and the use of troops to drive Governor Humphreys from the executive offices and mansion in that same year. In 1887 Jackson sponsored the Kermis Ball lasting three days, staged by a group of Jackson women to raise money for a monument to the Confederate dead. The monument, one of the handsomest in the South, was unveiled on the Old Capitol grounds in June 1891. In 1884 Jackson was the scene of Jefferson Davis's last public appearance. He spoke at the Old Capitol in response to an invitation of the legislature; and in 1890 Mississippi's greatest convention met at Jackson to draw up the present State Constitution.

Railroads continued to radiate from Jackson. In 1882 a line was completed from Jackson to Natchez; in 1885 a line to Yazoo City; then followed at intervals the Gulf & Ship Island, the New Orleans & Great Northern down the Pearl River valley, and the Gulf, Mobile & Northern, running northeast. The Gulf & Ship Island meant the beginning of south Mississippi's lumber boom.

Completion of the railroads and the end of the troubled days of reconstruction gave the city opportunity for new growth. In the first five years after 1900, Jackson nearly doubled its population and tripled its business, having a population in 1905 estimated at 15,000. In 1903 the magnificent New Capitol was completed. Millsaps College, opened by Major Reuben W. Millsaps in 1892, has become one of the State's leading institutions for higher education.

The latest period of the city's development began with the opening of the Jackson natural gas field in the 1930's. With cheap fuel for factories, and excellent transportation facilities, Jackson began to draw industries other than governmental. Starting almost with the crash of 1929 and continuing through the depression, it grew faster than any major city in the United States, with the possible exception of Los Angeles. The estimated population in 1937 was 60,000.

It is impossible to separate Jackson's history as a city from its history as capital of the State. In a governmental sense, all that has happened in Mississippi since 1822 has centered in Jackson; and today, government, including Federal, State, county, and city branches, is its biggest business.

‹‹‹‹‹‹‹‹‹‹‹‹‹‹‹‹‹‹☼›››››››››››››››››››››

Tour—*12.4m.*

S. from Capitol St. on S. Congress St.; L. on E. Pascagoula St.

1. HINDS COUNTY COURTHOUSE, E. Pascagoula St. (R) bet. S. Congress and S. President Sts., is a million-dollar four-story stone structure of distinctly modern design, occupying the entire square south of the municipal flower garden. It was erected in 1930, C. H. Lindsley, architect.

2. CITY HALL, E. Pascagoula and S. President Sts., a dignified classic Revival structure of gray stucco over brick, was erected in 1854, probably by A. J. Herod. The square it occupies was originally the city's musterground and market place. By an agreement the top floor is reserved for certain of the city's lodges. During the war the hall was converted into a hospital. Janus-like, the front and rear façades are similar; but the building is two stories on one side, three on the other. The narrow front lawn is shaded by oak trees. The back entrance faces the municipal flower garden. The structure is in an excellent state of preservation, and houses all municipal offices under Jackson's commission form of government, adopted in 1912.

L. from E. Pascagoula St. on S. State St.

3. The OLD CAPITOL, State St., facing Capitol St., is the city's most historic building. The architecture of the Capitol, designed in the style of

OLD CAPITOL, JACKSON

the Classical Revival, exemplifies the taste for classic form developed by Jefferson and his contemporaries during the early days of the Republic. Its design is based upon the abstract qualities of the classic ensemble—the temple and rotunda. Symmetrical in plan, the simple rectangular mass of the structure is broken by the graceful lines of a pedimented central pavilion, two smaller pavilions at each end, and a gleaming silver dome. The central pavilion is in the form of an Ionic colonnade, rising two stories above a high arcaded base. The dome is topped with a large circular lantern. The somber, gray stone walls of the exterior are somewhat relieved by the accented courses of the rusticated first story and the heavy lines of the classic cornice.

Within, two long halls branch from the central rotunda. Directly opposite the vestibule is a semicircular stairway which dates only from 1916, and in the center of the rotunda is a statue of Jefferson Davis that formerly stood on the grounds. This statue is lighted from the lantern of the elaborately decorated dome 50 feet above. Originally the second and third floors of the north wings were one, and housed the assembly and gallery. The third floor, however, has been extended and both floors divided into offices. The old rostrum and its beautifully decorated windows are yet visible. Directly above the entrance on the second floor are the offices once occupied by the governors.

In February 1833 the legislature appropriated $95,000 for the construction of the statehouse. It was not finished until 1842 and only after the total cost had reached $400,000. Much of the construction work was done by slave labor. Brick in the massive walls were burned in nearby kilns, and the longleaf yellow pine lumber was sawed from the then virgin forests of Simpson and Smith Counties and transported to Jackson by ox teams. Copper used in covering the dome, still in perfect preservation, was brought by ox team from New Orleans. By 1865 repair was necessary and in 1903 the place was abandoned as unsafe, not to be used again until 1916, when it was put into its present state of repair.

A major portion of Mississippi's early history has centered in the Old Capitol. Andrew Jackson in 1840 and Henry Clay in 1844 visited Mississippi and addressed the legislature within its walls. Jefferson Davis, triumphantly returning from the Mexican War at the head of his regiment in 1847, addressed a multitude from the second floor balcony. The Ordinance of Secession, which made Mississippi the second Confederate State, was enacted in the house chamber in 1861. An Irish comedian then playing in Jackson, Harry McCarthy, was inspired to write three verses of the "Bonnie Blue Flag," battle song of the Confederacy, and the flag was unfurled in the Secession Convention as a symbol of Mississippi's independence. Governor Clark was arrested in the executive offices in 1865 and taken to the Federal prison at Fort Pulaski. Governor Humphreys was ejected from the executive offices in 1868 to mark the beginning of the carpetbag reign. Governor Adelbert Ames, last of the carpetbag governors, threatened with impeachment by the legislature, resigned in 1876. In 1884 Jefferson Davis made his last public appearance here in an address to the State legislature. The building is used to house departments of State government, including those of Education, Insurance, Health, and Agriculture.

On the grounds south of the building is the Confederate Monument unveiled by Jefferson Davis Hayes, grandson of Jefferson Davis, the only

President of the Confederate States of America, in 1891 during the second Confederate Veterans Reunion.

L. from N. State St. on Amite St.

4. The JUDGE BRAME HOME, NW. cor. Amite and N. President Sts. *(private)*, marks the center of Jackson's earliest residential section. The exact date of erection is unknown, but the house was standing in 1836 and at that time was occupied by Silas Judd. For many years it was owned by Judge Lex Brame. It is a one-story Georgian Colonial structure, pleasing in its extreme simplicity and lack of distracting ornamentation. Dormer windows front and back, fluted classic columns supporting the roof of a square portico, and full-length windows are in keeping with its architectural style. Inside the house is a trap-door, which, though its significance is unknown, gives color to its story. During the early days of Jackson, State politicians used the house as a rendezvous, and it has been suggested that the secret door was for their convenience.

5. The J. L. POWER HOME, 411 Amite St. *(private)*, a wide, low-roofed frame structure, was built nearly a century ago within the original checkerboard plan of Jackson. The long gallery and ornamental grilles are original, but extensive improvements have been made within recent years. Jefferson Davis, a friend of Col. J. L. Power, was a frequent visitor. During the first gathering of the United Confederate Veterans in Jackson in 1891, all Confederate generals were entertained here.

R. from Amite St. on N. Congress St.; L. on Mississippi St.

6. The NEW CAPITOL, fronting on Mississippi St. (R), bet. N. President and N. West Sts., is the product of a new century, a place of power and utility rather than of tradition. Constructed of Bedford stone and similar in design to the National Capitol, it stands with formal dignity on a high terrace. The symmetrical building, four stories in height, is surmounted by a high central dome and lantern. The lantern is topped with a copper eagle, covered with gold leaf. The eagle stands eight feet high and has a wingspread of 15 feet.

Inside, a large central rotunda opens upward to the ceiling of the dome. Around the rotunda are built the wings which comprise the second, third, and fourth floors. On the first floor are the Museum, Hall of Fame, and the Archives. The Supreme Court occupies the east wing of the second floor, the State Library the west. On the third floor are the Senate and House Chambers and the Governor's suite.

On February 21, 1900, an act of the legislature authorized the creation of a Statehouse Commission to supervise the building of a new Capitol, which was to be built on the old penitentiary grounds, at a cost of not more than $1,000,000. Fourteen architectural plans were submitted. That of Theodore Link was finally adopted and a contract for $833,179 awarded. The Illinois Central R.R. laid a track at its own expense from its lines to the site to save the State time and money. The building was dedicated and opened for use on June 3, 1903.

The penitentiary, which had occupied the grounds, was built in 1840, and during the war was used as a munitions factory until Sherman's occupation of the city. It is said that part of the penitentiary's walls, too difficult to demolish, are buried under the man-made hill from which the Capitol now rises.

The *DEPARTMENT OF ARCHIVES AND HISTORY AND STATE MUSEUM*, on the ground floor *(open weekdays 9-5)*, is one of the first State-supported historical departments in the United States. Since its establishment in 1902, it has assisted actively in creating 15 State departments of history, and has originated the idea of a State hall of fame, adopted by other States. The Hall of Fame is a collection of portraits, assembled without cost to the State, and valued at $5,000,000. Many prominent Mississippians are represented there. Two of the most valuable portraits of the collection are the original paintings of Gov. George Poindexter by Benjamin West, and of David Holmes by Gilbert Stuart. The Manuscript Collection of the department includes the archives from 1678 to the present. The department's translations of European provincial archives are a standard source for the early history of this section. The museum has a fine collection of historical flags and a notable Indian display. Dr. Dunbar Rowland was the first director. Upon his death in December 1937, Dr. Wm. D. McCain was appointed to the office.

R. from Mississippi St. on N. West St.

7. GREENWOOD CEMETERY, N. West St. (L) bet. George and Davis Sts., is Jackson's first burial ground, and one of the few cemeteries in the South where both white and Negro dead are buried. One of the earliest graves is that of Gov. A. M. Scott who died in 1833. Perhaps the most famous monument is that at the grave of George Poindexter, Whig Senator. An interesting tomb is that of John R. Lynch, Negro Secretary of State during the carpetbag regime. Two Confederate brigadier-generals, four Confederate colonels, and more than 100 Confederate soldiers are buried in the cemetery.

8. The CHAS. H. MANSHIP HOME, NE. cor. N. West and Fortification Sts. *(private)*, has both architectural beauty and historical significance. Built in 1857, the one-story gray frame house preserves with accuracy the characteristics of Southern Colonial architecture. Beneath a steeply-pitched gable roof are seven spacious rooms, separated by a wide hall. A gallery runs the length of the house and iron balustrades are designed with a grapevine motif. Fortifications thrown up by the Confederate army extended across this lawn. On the front lawn is a Fire Bell, which originally belonged to Jackson's first fire company. The bell, similar to the Liberty Bell, is half-silver and was the only bell in the city to escape being melted and molded into cannon balls during the war. Instead, it was rung for curfew, fires, funerals, and news of battles. In 1888 it was presented to Mr. Manship, the last survivor of the volunteer firemen. Beginning with news of the Armistice, Nov. 11, 1918, the bell, removed from the Manship lawn to the Old Capitol, was rung continuously for 24 hours.

FORTIFICATION STREET, extending east and west through the northern portion of Jackson, derives its name from the fact that Confederate fortifications were built along its course. Crossing the yard of the Manship home, following Congress Street south, the lines turned into

MANSHIP HOME, JACKSON

what is now Fortification Street, and extended west between the Raymond and Clinton roads.

9. MILLSAPS COLLEGE, N. West St. (R) bet. Marshall St. and Woodrow Wilson Ave., is a fully-accredited, four-year, liberal arts college for men and women under the control of the Methodist Episcopal Church, South. The first senior college in the State approved by the Association of American Universities, it has a student body of 415 and was opened in 1892.

R. from N. West St. on Woodrow Wilson Ave.; R. on N. State St.; L. on Belhaven St.; R. on Peachtree St.

10. BELHAVEN COLLEGE, NE. cor. Peachtree and Pinehurst Sts., is a fully-accredited, four-year, liberal arts college for women. It was founded as a private school in 1894 by Dr. L. T. Fitzhugh. Since 1911 it has been under the auspices of the Presbyterian Church.

Retrace Peachtree and Belhaven Sts.; L. on N. State St.

11. MISSISSIPPI INSTITUTE FOR THE BLIND, N. State St. (R) bet. Manship and Fortification Sts., was founded in 1847 through the influence of James Champlain, blind philanthropist of Sharon, Mississippi, and became a State institution by legislative act, March 2, 1848. The school's purpose is to train blind children and those with defective sight, between the ages of 6 and 21, who can not be educated in public schools.

12. The MUNICIPAL CLUBHOUSE ART GALLERY, 839 N. State St. *(open weekdays 8-6),* houses a permanent collection owned by the

Mississippi Art Association and offers special loan exhibits monthly. The building was a gift of Thomas Gale in 1927. Among the Mississippi painters represented are Marie Hull, William Woodward, William Hollingsworth, Bettie McArthur, Bessie Cary Lemly, and Karl Wolfe. Karl Wolfe and John McCrady are Mississippi's foremost contemporary painters.

13. The NUGENT-SHANDS HOME, 607 N. State St. *(private)*, exemplifies the Southern ante-bellum architecture. The wide entrance porch is supported by Classic columns; double doors, outlined in side lights and with a transom of colored glass, lead into a wide hall. Noticeable features of the exterior are the three small balconies on the front, executed in delicately wrought iron. A wing at the left has its own porch and entrance, with railings on the upper porch similar to those of the front balcony. Inside, the house follows the Colonial plan of arrangement, with large rooms divided by a central hall both upstairs and down. It is furnished with antique furniture, some of which was brought by Colonel and Mrs. Nugent from Alabama in the 1830's. The original home on this site was badly damaged by fire and this house, a practically new structure, was built to encase the remnants of the old. The original flooring is still in place under the present covering of hardwood.

L. from N. State St. on Amite St.

14. BOWMAN HOTEL SITE, Amite St. (L) bet. N. State St. and North St., is now occupied by the Standard Oil Building. A five-story brick building, formerly the Eagle Hotel, it was the gathering place of the State's ante-bellum politicians. In 1855 Col. Alexander McClung, the Black Knight of the South, fulfilled the prophecy of his own melancholy "Invocation to Death" by committing suicide here, supposedly because of adverse public opinion resulting from the death of a youth in one of McClung's many duels. The hotel was burned by Federal troops in 1863.

15. MISSISSIPPI STATE FAIRGROUNDS, end of Amite St., is the place where Mississippi's largest fair is held in October of each year.

Retrace Amite St.; L. on N. State St.; R. on Capitol St.

16. SITE OF FIRST STATEHOUSE, NE. cor. Capitol and President Sts., is marked by a tablet on the side of the Baptist Bookstore building.

17. The GOVERNOR'S MANSION, Capitol St. (R) bet. N. Congress and N. West Sts. is situated amid a grove of trees at Jackson's busiest corner. The design of the building was intended to "avoid a profusion of ornaments and adhere to republican simplicity as best comporting with the dignity of the State." Appropriation of funds for the mansion was made in 1833, but construction was not begun until later, and the building was not completed until 1842. Its first occupant was Governor Tucker, although it is claimed that Governor McNutt occupied it temporarily during construction. The long list of governors it housed has given it personality, and the admirable arrangement of the lower floor makes it well suited for the occasional receptions that are highlights of Jackson's political society. In 1908 the building was repaired under the supervision of William Hud, and a new wing added on its center axis. As it stands today, however, it is almost indistinguishable from the original structure designed by William Nichols.

GOVERNOR'S MANSION, JACKSON

R. from Capitol St. on N. Farish St.

FARISH STREET is the spinal cord of the Negro business district. Though a great many Negroes patronize the cheaper stores maintained by white owners, a large part of their trading is done in their own section. On Saturday nights this street, swarming with shoppers and pleasure seekers, has a carnival atmosphere. The shingles of Jackson's Negro lawyers and doctors compete with lodge signs such as "The Sons and Daughters of the I Will Arise Society." Gallery space is reserved for Negroes at the civic auditorium for all public performances, but the number who attend is negligible; the Negro's social life, for the most part, is confined to the picture shows, dance halls, and pool rooms on or near this street.

Retrace N. Farish St.; R. on Capitol St.; L. on S. Gallatin; R. on Hooker St.; L. on Terry Rd.; L. on Porter St.

18. BATTLEFIELD PARK (R), formerly known as Winter Woods, includes 5.5 acres of natural woods in which tall oaks and slender pines predominate. Here nature has been left almost undisturbed since the days when Confederate troops abandoned their fortifications on this site. Parts of the trenches remain, and several cannon are on the ground. The woods form a children's playground maintained by the city.

Retrace Porter St.; R. on Terry Rd.; L. on Poindexter St.; L. on Lynch St.

19. CAMPBELL COLLEGE, W. end of Lynch St., is one of the two Negro schools in the State supported by Negroes. The school, composed

of two brick buildings three stories in height and several frame buildings, including the residence of the president, is affiliated with the African Methodist Episcopal Church. It has a high school department and offers a four-year college course leading to the Bachelor of Science degree. Connected with the school on the west are 36 acres which are farmed by students to help pay their tuition fee. The guiding hand behind the school is the native Mississippi Negro, Bishop S. L. Greene of the African Methodist Episcopal Church. The school, founded in 1885, has an enrollment of approximately 417 students.

Retrace Lynch St.; L. on S. Gallatin St.; L. on W. Capitol St.

20. The DEAF AND DUMB INSTITUTE, Capitol St. (R) bet. S. Green Ave. and Magnolia St., was erected in 1904 and is training 275 boys and girls of both races to overcome their handicaps. The State's first deaf and dumb institute was established in 1854, but its buildings were destroyed during the war.

21. LIVINGSTON PARK, 2918 Capitol St., comprises 79 acres of landscaped rolling park on which are a municipal 18-hole golf course, an artificial lake, tennis courts, pavilion, and a zoo. The lake, used for swimming during the summer months, is chlorinated twice daily. The zoo and bird sanctuary are the outgrowth of a pet animal collection begun by the Jackson Fire Department.

POINTS OF INTEREST IN ENVIRONS

Insane Hospital, 7.9 *m.*, Lakewood Cemetery, 12.2 *m.*, Mississippi College, 14.9 *m.*, Hillman College, 15 *m.*, Rankin County Natural Gas Fields, 2 *m. (see Tour 2)*; Radio Station, 7.4 *m.*, Tougaloo College, 8.9 *m. (see Tour 5, Sec. a).*

◄◄◄◄◄◄◄◄◄◄◄◄◄◄◄◄◄◄☼►►►►►►►►►►►►►►►►►►

Laurel

Railroad Stations: Maple and Oak Sts. for New Orleans & Northeastern R.R.; Central Ave. and Walters Ave. for Gulf, Mobile & Northern R.R.; Central Ave. and Commerce St. for Gulf & Ship Island R.R.
Bus Station: Central Ave. and Commerce St. for Teche-Greyhound, Tri-State Transit Co., Gulf Transport Co.
Local Busses: Fare 5¢.
Taxis: Intra-city rates 10¢.

Information Service: Chamber of Commerce, Civic Center, Ellisville Blvd.

Accommodations: Two hotels, tourist camps.

Radio Station: WAML (1310 kc.).
Motion Picture Houses: Three.

Athletics: Baseball Park, Beacon and Royal Sts.; Civic Center, Ellisville Blvd.
Swimming: Municipal Pool, Daphne Park, 6th St. and 10th Ave., adm. 25¢ and 15¢; Freeman's Amusement Park, Washington Road.
Tennis: Daphne Park; Y.M.C.A.
Golf: Laurel Country Club, 1 m. W. on US 84, reasonable greens fee.

Annual Events: Garden Club Festival, April.

LAUREL (243 alt., 18,017 pop.), seat of Jones County and situated on the northeastern edge of the vast yellow pine forests of southeastern Mississippi, is a new city. When Newt Knight and his followers were organizing a "Free State of Jones" and waging a private battle against Confederate troops in the 1860's, the site of Laurel was a gallberry flat separating two grassy ridges. Hence its story is not, like that of many Mississippi towns, richly flavored with the essence of the ante-bellum South, but reveals in a few fast-moving chapters a swift transition from forest through lumber camp to a stable industrial city in the course of fifty years.

Laurel dates from 1881, when the Southern Railroad, pushing northeastward, laid its course directly through the heart of Mississippi's great belt of virgin pine timber. In that year two sawmill men, Kamper and Louin, followed the tracks to a point which they considered the center of the forest. Here they built a sawmill and a railroad station, which they named for the flowering laurel shrubs, so abundant among the pines, and so soon exterminated because they were poisonous to livestock. Kamper and Louin had but one purpose, to cut as much timber as possible to keep their mill supplied. The settlement, therefore, became a typical Piney Woods lumber camp, rowdy in character and forlorn in appearance. The pines about the camp were considered a menace in windy weather, so they, too, were cut down, leaving the few cabins and mill in the midst of a half-mile strip of gaunt, girdled trees and stumps.

When, in 1891, the sawmill passed into the possession of the Eastman-Gardiner Lumber Company a new regime began. Laurel was transformed from the spirited child of the Piney Woods into a pampered ward of eastern capital. The first earnings of the mill were used to build a school, and mill hands were encouraged to buy property and build permanent homes. Soon a row of neat frame houses with picket fences and gardened lawns replaced the box-car cabins. Tough-fibered lumberjacks, whose previous experience with music had been bawdy songs around the campfire or a hymn sung lustily in church on Sunday, made down payments on pianos for their children's music lessons. And, as if to retract the injustice to the flowering shrub for which the town was named, the first garden club in the State was organized. When Laurel was incorporated, only the crooked narrow downtown streets that followed the cowpaths of the first-comers bore resemblance to the mill camp from which it had sprung.

Yet it was not until the Gulf & Ship Island R.R. was completed through Hattiesburg to Jackson, with a branch line to Laurel, and the opening of the harbor at Gulfport in 1902 that the town's real prosperity began. The Eastman-Gardiner Co. grew wealthy, and spent part of its money in playing godfather to the town it had fostered. Asphalt streets were laid among the pines; squares were developed into parks; and schools and churches re-

PULPWOOD READY FOR PROCESSING, LAUREL

flected the lavish expenditure of money, the latter in Gothic architecture, stained glass windows, and ivy-covered brick walls. In character with the fact that the early mill hands had spent their first pay checks for second-hand pianos, the first and only art museum in the State was established.

Continuing the development of the cultural side of Laurel to the large percent of the population who were employed as unskilled laborers by the mills, white families fostered a movement for an adequate school for Negro children. Prof. J. E. Johnson, educational leader of his race and principal of Prentiss Normal and Industrial Institute, was brought to Laurel to help Sandy T. Gavins, then leading Negro teacher at Laurel, in directing the work for founding the school. The drive resulted not only in the Oak Park Vocational School, which is one of the best Negro high schools in the State, but later in a $35,000 grammar school building for Negroes. Both schools are now a part of the city school system. As part of this program, *The Leader,* founded in 1897, continues to be one of the State's two newspapers carrying a column on Negro activities.

While other lumber towns despoiled themselves by cutting all the timber, Laurel created a permanent community. As the timber that fed its mills was cut, the mill hands were urged to buy the cutover land and, with homesteads of their own, to farm in their off time. So with this two-way means of livelihood for its citizens, the city developed a stability which not even the crash of the yellow pine industry in the late 1920's could shatter. After the World War, when other towns of the Piney Woods section reached the nadir of their fortunes, the same foresight which had made the mill hands buy farms prompted the development of industries to take the sawmills' place. A reforestation program was inaugurated to offset the former profligate tree cutting, and a balanced industrial program was given serious trial. Laurel is apparently on its way to a happy mean between the land and the machine. Its cultural side has developed with its industrial side, and this pattern of 20th century culture impressed upon it by its foster parents is its dominant feature.

POINTS OF INTEREST

1. The MASONITE PLANT, NE. cor. S. 4th Ave. and Johnson St. *(open weekdays 8-4; tours)*, is the largest single manufacturing plant in Mississippi, and the only plant of its kind in the United States. The plant buys second growth pine as small as two inches in diameter, chews it into small chips, then explodes the chips into fibre from which the Masonite process fashions a trade-marked fibre board. This board has more than 300 uses, ranging from panel ceilings to children's toys; from concrete forms to radio cabinets; and is exported to more than 30 foreign countries.

2. The SWEET POTATO STARCH PLANT, end of S. 4th Ave. *(open weekdays 8-4; tours)*, manufacturing starch to supplement that produced by the cereal starch industry, is the only plant of its kind in the country, and it annually supplies a domestic market with 420,000 pounds of starch. The factory, which is in an abandoned sawmill, began operation in 1934 as a result of a FERA project to assist the people of south Mississippi. In that year, $150,000 was allotted for the construction, equipment, and operation, on a commercial scale, of a plant that would provide not only emergency relief work but a market for sweet potatoes the farmers produce. The Laurel plant, with a capacity of 200,000 bushels and 2,000,000 pounds of starch per 100-day season, has been deeded to the Mississippi Agricultural Experiment Station, and leased to a self-help cooperative organization of farmers, at least 51 percent of whom are being rehabilitated. The plant pays the farmer a minimum of 20 cents a bushel for culls, at the same time competing adequately with imported white potato starch.

3. The MAYHEW CANNING PLANT, Commerce St. bet. 6th and 7th Aves. *(open weekdays 8-4; tours)*, encourages diversified farming on the cutover timber lands. Corn, beans, and cucumbers are packed here, enabling the farmer to grow at least three profitable crops from his land each year.

4. The LAUREN ROGERS LIBRARY and MUSEUM OF ART, 5th Ave. and 7th St. *(open weekdays 10-5; Sat. 7-9 p. m.; Sun. 3-6)*, grew out of the Eastman Memorial Foundation, established by Lauren Chase Eastman, lumberman of Eastman-Gardiner Co., in memory of his grandson, Lauren Rogers. It houses the State's only art museum. The building is of Southern Colonial architecture with a broad front portico having slender, coupled columns. The iron grille work, gates, and railings are the work of Samuel Yellin of Philadelphia. The paintings in the gallery are

ART MUSEUM AND LIBRARY, LAUREL

by such artists as Reynolds, Rousseau, Constable, Inness, Millet, and Whistler. Exhibits in the museum include a collection of baskets from all parts of the world; statuary by Anna Hyatt, Herman McNeil, Jeanette Scudder, and Ary Bitter; Chinese, Japanese, and Persian pottery; English, Ameri-

MERIDIAN 227

can, and Flemish tapestries; and antique furniture of different periods. In addition to the Memorial Library the building houses the circulating library of the Laurel Library Association.

5. The CITY PARK, bet. 7th and 10th Sts. and 8th and 10th Aves., is the beauty spot of Laurel. It is landscaped and has an attractive artificial lake with mimosa bushes along the shore.

POINTS OF INTEREST IN ENVIRONS

Bogue Homo Indian Reservation, *12.1 m. (see Tour 8);* Big Creek Baptist Church, *12.6 m.;* Buffalo Hill, *12.6 m.;* Laurel Country Club, *2.6 m. (see Tour 11).*

Meridian

Railroad Stations: Union Station, Front St. and 19th Ave., for Mobile & Ohio R.R., Yazoo & Mississippi Valley R.R., and Southern R.R.; 22nd Ave. and D St., for Gulf, Mobile & Northern R.R.
Bus Station: Union Station, 2306 6th St., for Tri-State Transit Co., Teche-Greyhound, Magnolia Motor, and Capital Motor Lines.
Local Busses: Intra-city, 5¢ per person.
Taxis: Intra-city, 10¢ per person.
Airport: Key Field, 2 m. SW. of city on US 11, for Delta Airlines, taxi fare 15¢, time 10 min.
Traffic Regulations: Speed limit 30 mph. Turns may be made in either direction at intersections of all streets except where lights direct otherwise. Parking limitations marked in yellow on pavement.
Street order and numbering: Streets run east and west, avenues north and south. Front (3rd) St. parallel to and north of railroad starts numbering at 100.
Information Service: Chamber of Commerce, Threefoot Building, NW. cor. 22nd Ave. and 6th St.
Accommodations: Four hotels; five tourist camps.
Radio Station: WCOC (880 kc.).
Motion Picture Houses: Three.
Golf: Northwood Country Club, Magnolia Drive, 2 m. N., moderate greens fee; Meridian Country Club, 4.5 m. N. on Poplar Springs Drive, moderate greens fee.
Swimming: Municipal Pool, Highland Park, 38th Ave. and 16th St.
Tennis: Municipal courts, Highland Park.
Riding: Massey Academy, Highland Park.

Annual Events: Mississippi Fair and Dairy Show, first wk. in Oct.; Confederate Memorial Day, April 26th at courthouse and Rose Hill Cemetery; Intercollegiate Athletic Association Event, Stadium, Magnolia Drive, Thanksgiving Day.

MERIDIAN (341 alt., 31,954 pop.), Mississippi's second largest city, lies among the most southerly of the Appalachian foothills, a region characterized by heavy forests and outcroppings of buff-colored limestone. In harmony with the surrounding hills, native rock is used for building material, and elms and live-oaks like giant grenadiers line the walks. Yet it is a railroad and industrial town, and as such has its shops and districts where the poorer workmen live.

Laid out with singular lack of design, Meridian, viewed from the air, is like a vast spider web with a multitude of streets intersecting at curious angles and coming to abrupt endings. Cutting through the web near its center are numerous railroad tracks, dividing the business section from the industrial district. At the heart of the web is the city's most salient piece of architecture, the Threefoot Building. The only skyscraper in Meridian, this building rises 17 stories, its brightly decorated tower dwarfing the buildings dotted below. The southern and eastern boundaries of the city are arched by the humped ridges of the foothills, known locally as Mount Barton. This is Meridian's playground, with stone and log cabins, lodges, and fishing camps stuck along the rugged slopes. Between the mountain and the city proper are the mill districts, Southside and Tuxedo, where a great part of the city's laboring class lives in two- and three-room rented houses. The wealth of the city's merchant class expresses itself in attractive residential suburbs fringing north Meridian. Every architectural style is being tried here, with the English cottage and manor house of native limestone the most conspicuous. The rugged topography of this section lends itself to both sunken and rock gardens, and the charming effects created with stone and flora are noteworthy.

In 1831 Richard McLemore migrated from South Carolina to clear a plantation on the present site of Meridian. Soon he was offering free land to settlers who he thought would make desirable neighbors. In 1854, when Mississippi's pre-war railroad building was nearing its climax, plans were made for the Vicksburg & Montgomery R.R. (Alabama & Vicksburg) to cross the Mobile & Ohio line. The former was to cross the State east and west, the latter to follow close to the eastern boundary from north to south; their junction was to be on McLemore's plantation. McLemore sold his plantation to L. A. Ragsdale and J. T. Ball, pioneer railroad men, and they immediately built the one-room, red and yellow "union station." But it was not until 1861, one year after Meridian had been incorporated as a town, that the Vicksburg & Montgomery train arrived from Vicksburg.

Other railroads became interested in the junction which, though small, quickly assumed the air of an important railroad center. But this attitude of suddenly acquired importance made the future city's first year extremely difficult. The farmers who lived on the plantation before the railroads were built pridefully considered themselves the junction's first citizens; the families who came in with the railroads boasted that they were building the town, and, with the pride of achievement, assumed the rank of leaders. The contest between farmer and mechanic was intensified when one of the two city fathers, believing the word "meridian" to be synon-

TEXTILE MILL, MERIDIAN

ymous with junction, determined on that name for the village, while the other, supported by the farmer families, chose "Sowashee" (Ind., *mad river*), name of the nearby creek. Each morning the first would nail up the sign "Meridian," and each night the second would tear it down to make way for his own "Sowashee." Instead of compromising, the two fathers selected different plans for laying out the city streets. One day one of them would drive stakes in line with his plan. The next day the other would pull up his rival's stakes and drive some of his own. It was a struggle that has affected the city to this day. For even though the continued development of the railroads and the consequent influx of railroad workers overruled contrary opinion and left "Meridian" on the union station permanently, the confused plans for laying out the city have given Meridian the appearance of having been formed by some giant who playfully gathered up a handful of triangles and dropped them at the junction of two railroads.

Railroads with their noisy shops, and trains with their screaming whistles and their engines puffing steam and smoke, changed the quiet plantation life in Meridian to one of excitement. Government mail contracts, the lifeblood of the early railroads, were awarded to the trains that could make the fastest time, and were determined by racing these trains from one terminal to another. In 1883 the Louisville & Nashville's crack train left Cincinnati on the dot with the Queen & Crescent, both bound for New Orleans. Excitement ran high, especially at Meridian where the Queen & Crescent changed engines. The latter train steamed into New Orleans eight hours ahead of its rival and established the fastest time then on record. A few years later the Meridian shops despatched a special train to Lumberton to carry a physician on an emergency call. This train covered the 112 miles between Meridian and Lumberton in exactly 112 minutes, and set a new record. Once a month Meridian's railroad men went to the banks of Sowashee Creek to enjoy a beer party and poker game. But the pride of the shops was the old wrecker car that had been reconditioned as a sort of restaurant and bar and was presided over by a Negro named "Bob," the best cook in east Mississippi. The wrecker held open house each day in the week and when the higher officials visited Meridian it was to the wrecker they went to order one of "Black Bob's" specials.

When the War between the States began, Meridian, with a population of about 100, was made a Confederate military camp and division headquarters. Troops were stationed here and arsenals and cantonments were built. In 1863 the State records were moved here for safekeeping, and for one month the town was the State's capital. In February 1864, General Sherman's troops, marching across the State from Jackson, entered the town. Several days later Sherman made his official report: "For five days, 10,000 men worked hard with a will in that work of destruction with axes, crowbars, sledges, clawbars, and fire, and I have no hesitation in pronouncing the work well done. Meridian . . . no longer exists."

Rebuilt after the war, Meridian, as a railroad center, grew rapidly, becoming a magnet that attracted a rabble of adventurers who came into the State seeking to share in the spoils of radical reconstruction. In 1871 a riot—prominent in Mississippi's reconstruction history—took place when one of several Negroes on trial for urging mob violence shot the presiding judge. A party of whites who were interested in the trial immediately formed a mob, killed between 25 and 30 Negroes, and burned a Negro school. This riot was followed by a yellow fever epidemic in 1878, which almost depopulated the town, and in 1906 a cyclone struck the city with considerable damage to life and property.

But Meridian survived these disasters and again achieved prominence as a railroad center. By the end of the century, however, manufacturing was competing with railroading for first place. A cotton mill established late in 1890 was the initial effort. In 1913 the commission form of government was adopted, and under the guidance of a mayor and two commissioners 90 industrial plants, including a large shirt and garment factory and three hosiery mills, have been established. These industries have done much to modify the city's railroad tone and have brought into it a new type of labor, the farm boy and girl. Drawn from the farms and villages of the environs by the attractions of city life these young people have been swallowed up by the factory system. A few commute daily from their homes to the factory, but the majority find cheap lodgings in the city's Southside. To the Negroes, who make up 35 percent of Meridian's population, fall the jobs requiring unskilled labor. They are used especially in sawmills, cottonseed oil mills, and gins, where strength and hardiness are requisite. As in most southern cities, the servant class is exclusively Negro, and, though Meridian is well dotted with Negro districts composed of one- and two-room rented cabins with tiny dirt plot yards, a few white people maintain servants' quarters in the rear of their homes for their cooks, nurses, or chauffeurs.

Not until recent years did agriculture attempt to regain the prestige it early lost to railroading and manufacturing. With the encouragement of diversified farming, stock, and poultry raising in the surrounding country, Meridian has gained recognition as an important market for vegetables, fruit, poultry, and livestock. With a view to building up the livestock industry of the county, the Meridian Union Stockyards were established in 1935. This plant occupies 14 acres of a triangle bounded by the tracks of the Southern, Mobile & Ohio, Illinois Central, and Gulf, Mobile & Northern railroads, and its buildings and pens accommodate approximately 5,000 head of stock. This is the State's largest stockyard.

Second to agriculture in importance is the lumber industry. Given a fresh impetus by the maturity of second growth stands of timber, six large and numerous small lumber mills operate full time, cutting pine timber. One company, the only hardwood mill in the city, cuts a daily average of 35,000 feet of gum, oak, poplar, ash, hickory, and magnolia.

Tour—*10m.*

N. from the World War Monument on 23rd Ave.
1. SCOTTISH RITE CATHEDRAL, NW. corner 23rd Ave. and 11th St., is based upon the design of the Temple of Isis at Philae, Egypt. The two-story structure is built of brick and concrete, faced with native Bowling Green limestone and ornamented with polychrome terra cotta. The symbols on the terra cotta decorations of the façade, as well as the obelisks, are typically Egyptian; on each side of the long flight of steps leading to the entrance are buttresses with a Sphinx and obelisk on each, the four sides of the obelisk being cut with Egyptian characters. The two massive round columns surmounting the steps are conspicuous for their bell-shaped capitals as well as for their monumental proportions. The interior contains banquet hall, ballroom, pool room, library, offices, assembly room, organ room, and kitchen. Striking and colorful Egyptian designs cover the walls of the foyer.

R. from 23rd Ave. on 11th St.; R. on 18th Ave.
2. McLEMORE HOUSE, 1009 18th Ave. *(private)*, is built around the original log home of Richard McLemore, the town's first settler. The present house is a mixed style of architecture and the original design of the McLemore house, built in 1837, has been obliterated. The site, however, is interesting as a landmark of the town's birthplace.

R. from 18th Ave. on 4th St.
3. The SOULE STEAM FEED WORKS, NE. corner 4th St. and 19th

Ave. *(open by permission)*, is a machine shop and foundry with international distribution. Organized in 1893, it manufactures sawmill and oil well machinery, and forges cast and wrought iron and brass products.

L. from 4th St. on 22nd Ave.

4. MERIDIAN GARMENT FACTORY, 22nd Ave. S. between B and C Sts. *(open weekdays 8-4; tours)*, is a square, two-story building of concrete and structural steel. The outside walls are broken by 11,500 window lights framed by projected steel sashes. The central hall is reached by five entrances, each with fire-latch doors. The interior columns and floors are of hardwood. The first floor is divided into offices, laundry, and shipping department; on the second floor are cutting, sewing, and first-aid rooms. Employing between 500 and 600 operators, this factory produces approximately 900 dozen shirts a day.

5. HAMM LUMBER MILL, 22nd Ave. S. *(open weekdays 9-5; tours)*, began operation in 1917 to plane and process hardwood timber. Cutting hardwood exclusively, it has a daily capacity of 40,000 feet, and employs approximately 60 persons.

Retrace 22nd Ave.; L. on A St.

6. MERIDIAN GRAIN ELEVATOR PLANT, A St. between Rubush and Grand Aves. *(open weekdays 8-4; guides)*, is the only milling plant in the State using the de-germinator method of manufacturing grits and cream meal, and the only one requiring a health certificate semiannually from its employees. Surrounded by a forest of elevators, 22 of which are used in making grits, this plant can mill 300 bushels of corn per hour. Because of the uniformity required in the grain, the corn used is shipped in from the Corn Belt. In general, the season for making meal starts in January and extends through September; for grits, the season is from September through May.

L. from A St. on Rubush Ave.; R. on B St.; R. on 31st Ave.

7. SWIFT & COMPANY OIL MILL, 31st Ave. at railroad tracks, *(open by permission)*, is housed in two adjoining buildings, each constructed of sheet iron and two stories high. The company manufactures cottonseed oil with its byproducts, hulls, meal, and cotton linters.

8. The J. H. GARY HOUSE, 905 31st Ave. *(private)*, in a somber setting of magnolia trees, is a white, two-story frame house with a broad gallery and classic columns. Similar columns uphold a porte-cochère at one side. The single story ell, which extends to the rear, was the headquarters of Gen. Leonidas Polk, Commander of the Confederate troops stationed in Meridian.

Retrace 31st Ave.; R. on 7th St.

9. In ROSE HILL CEMETERY, 7th St. and 40th Ave., is *GYPSY QUEEN'S GRAVE*. In a concrete vault armored with steel, is the burial place of the wife of Emil Mitchell, King of all gypsies in the United States. The Queen, Kelly Mitchell, who died in 1915 in Lititia, Ala., was buried here in her Romany dress strung with gold coins dating back to 1750. Until the King's remarriage gypsies from all parts of the country made periodic pilgrimages here.

Retrace 7th St.; L. on 38th Ave.; L. on 16 St.

10. The ARBORETUM, Highland Park, intersection of 16th St. and 38th Ave. (R), displays native shrubs, ferns, and wild flowers in a natural setting.

R. from 16th St. on the Asylum Road, graveled, to 20th St.

11. The EAST MISSISSIPPI INSANE HOSPITAL, entrance L. *(visiting hours 9:30-4:30 daily)*, was constructed in 1882. The buildings, half hidden in a great grove of trees and reached by a circular drive, are grouped about the administration building, which is constructed of brick, four stories high, and designed in the form of an E. The majority of the smaller buildings also are of brick and have more the appearance of large gingerbread style houses than of institutional designs. The landscaped grounds are one of the showplaces of Meridian. The hospital, with land, buildings, and equipment, is valued at $814,457. There are approximately 850 patients at the institution; the average yearly cost per patient is about $258.

POINTS OF INTEREST IN ENVIRONS

U. S. Horticultural Experiment Station, *3.5 m. (see Tour 4)*; Grave of Sam Dale, pioneer scout and soldier, *19.2 m. (see Side Tour 4B)*.

Natchez

Railroad Stations: Broadway, near river, for Yazoo & Mississippi Valley R.R.; Union Station, 212 Washington St., for Mississippi Central R.R., Missouri Pacific R.R., and Natchez & Southern R.R.

Bus Stations: Union Station, 515 Main St., for Teche-Greyhound, Tri-State Transit Co., and Interurban Transportation, Inc.; Missouri Pacific Branch Office and Bus Station, 107 N. Commerce St., for Bobs Bus Line and Parsons Bus Line.

Ferry: The Royal Route. Landing on Silver St. and Mississippi River. Fare 10¢ per person, 50¢ and up for car and driver depending on weight of car.

Airport: One mile east of city limits on Liberty Rd., taxi fare 50¢, time 15 min. No scheduled service.

Taxis: Fare 15¢ per passenger within city limits.

Traffic Regulations: Speed limit 15 mph. East and west traffic has right-of-way. All turns on green lights on congested streets. See signs on less important streets. One hour parking in business section. All night parking prohibited.

Street Arrangement: Main St. divides the city into N. and S. sections.

Accommodations: Four hotels; boarding houses; tourist homes and rooming places. Rates higher during Pilgrimage Weeks.

Information Service: Garden Club Headquarters at Ellicott's Inn, 215 N. Canal St.; Natchez Association of Commerce, 403 Franklin St.; *Natchez Democrat*, 106-108 S. Pearl St.; all filling stations and hotels.

234 MAIN STREET AND COURTHOUSE SQUARE

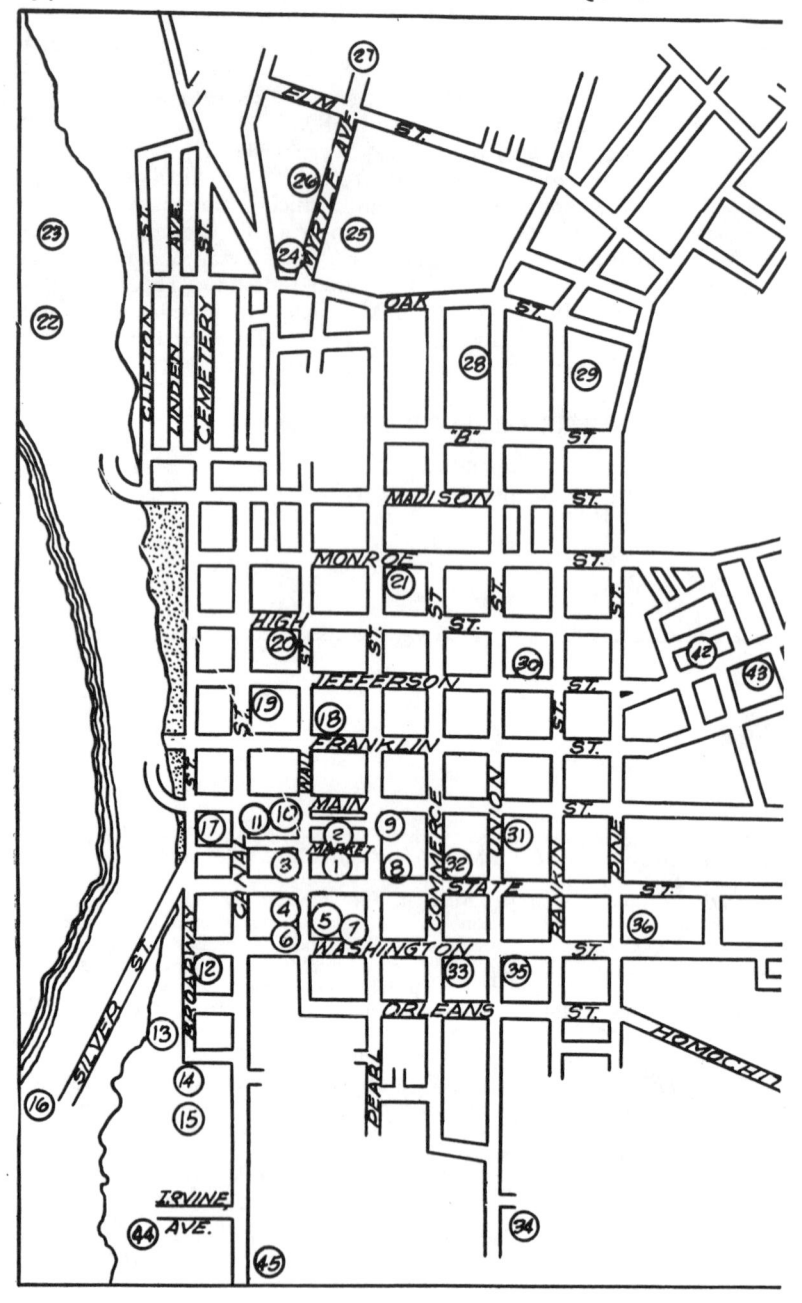

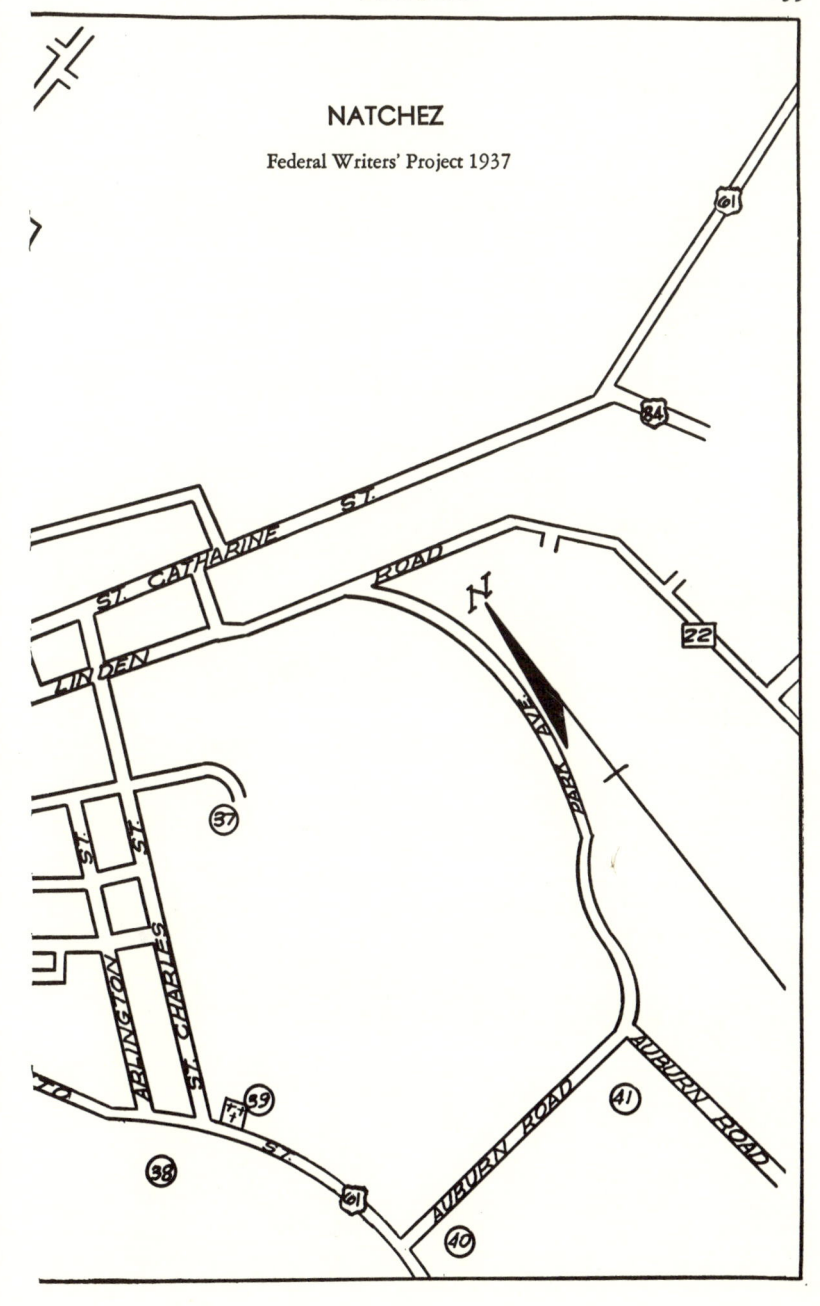

NATCHEZ

Federal Writers' Project 1937

236   MAIN STREET AND COURTHOUSE SQUARE

Motion Picture Houses: Three.
Swimming: Carpenter School, No. 2; Elks Pool; Crystal Pool, Washington Rd., 5 m. E.; Beverly Beach, 10 m. S. on Lower Woodville Rd.; Cool Coosa, 12 m. across Mississippi River in Lake St. John, La.
Tennis: Duncan Memorial Park, eastern limits of city 1 block N. from Homochitto St.; high school athletic field, Homochitto St.; Cathedral grounds, S. Union St.
Golf: Duncan Memorial Park, all year-round playing reasonable greens fee.
Skeet Club: On US 61, 1 m. N., April 1st to Nov. 1st, Sundays.

Annual Events: Pilgrimages to old estates, in March, 1st wk. in April; American Legion Fall Fair, held on Broadway, facing the Mississippi River, no definite date.

NATCHEZ (202 alt., 13,422 pop.), overlooking the Mississippi River from a series of lofty, alluvial bluffs, conscientiously presents its age in the appearance of its low-roofed, time-worn buildings and in what its people say and do. It is one of the earliest white settlements in the State, and was at one time the center of ante-bellum culture. Its people, its buildings, its aged trees, and its general Old South atmosphere conspire to keep these facts evident. Beginning with three narrow parks that overlook the docks and river front, the city proper spreads fanwise, with the Confederate Memorial Park as its center. The streets are slightly rolling, with restored or carefully preserved mansions rising unexpectedly from the midst of dilapidated, heavy-timbered houses whose flush fronts and steep roofs

---

KEY TO PRECEDING MAP OF NATCHEZ

1. Adams County Courthouse
2. Parish House of San Salvador
3. Mercer House
4. Lawyers' Row
5. Governor Holmes or Conti House
6. Old Spanish House
7. Britton Home
8. First Presbyterian Church
9. Memorial Hall
10. Old Commercial Bank Building
11. Banker's Home
12. Metcalfe House
13. Esplanade
14. Rosalie
15. Site of Fort Rosalie
16. Natchez-under-the-Hill
17. Buntura Home
18. Marschalk's Printing Office
19. Connelly's Tavern
20. Choctaw
21. Stanton Hall
22. First Lumber Mill
23. Magnolia Vale
24. Wigwam
25. The Towers
26. Cottage Garden
27. Airlie
28. Protestant Orphanage
29. Melmont or Sans Souci
30. King's Tavern
31. St. Mary's Cathedral
32. St. Joseph's Academy
33. Trinity Episcopal Church
34. Ravenna
35. Greenleaves
36. The Elms
37. Arlington
38. Dunleith
39. Routh Cemetery
40. Hope Farm
41. Auburn
42. Hospital Hill
43. Home of Don Estevan Minor
44. The Briars
45. Richmond

speak definitely of days past but not dead. Surreys and two-wheeled dump carts driven by white-haired Negroes are seen on the streets.

So deeply has the patina of the past been impressed on Natchez that it is the modern rather than the aged that stand out as anomalies. The downtown district, with the Gothic spire of St. Mary's Cathedral rising above the low skyline, and the historic courthouse hemmed in by stucco and brick, or yellowish frame structures, is definitely dated. Here is a marked conflict between careful preservation and decay. Standing flush with the sidewalk are structures whose uncompromising severity tie them to the Spanish period. Interspersed among these ill-preserved buildings, which often are occupied by Negroes, are modern one- and two-story structures that house up-to-date business firms.

The residential districts, emerging with uncertain plan from the downtown area and somewhat softened by the shadows of Spanish moss and magnolias, are marked by restoration rather than by change. Homes that are little more than ruins stand proudly beside mansions whose beauty and lines have been carefully cherished and preserved. Varying features of architecture indicate the survival of French and Spanish influence, while many of the houses were remodeled in the early 1800's to conform with the classic order dictated by the Greek Revival. Sprinkled among these homes are modern bungalows and cottages; but the sprinkling is so light it produces little discord between the old and the new.

Aloof from the city and yet a part of it are its industries. The cotton mill runs only spasmodically. The cottonseed oil mill is one of the city's oldest industries. Here are also a box factory and the oldest sawmill in the State. With the shirt factory excepted these industries draw their labor from the 53.3 percent of the population that are Negroes. The textile labor class is not well defined, but is a transitory group of white people who come in from and return to the outlying plantations as the routine of farm, or factory, becomes monotonous.

Natchez is still the trade center for its district and an important shipping point for cotton and for beef cattle. It is from this trade that a majority of its white population derive their income. Many of the older families are still large landholders and, like their grandfathers, live in town on incomes from their plantation operations. As in any plantation town, Saturday is trade day in Natchez, and fall, cotton picking time, is the busy season for growers, ginners, buyers, merchants, and bankers.

The wealth, the rich background, and the intelligence of the Natchez Negro leaders have made Natchez the Negro cultural center of the State. Among them are leading Negro physicians, several outstanding ministers, and a musician who presents "Heaven Bound," a production with a chorus of fifty voices, each year to a large white audience. The African Methodist Episcopal Church includes cultural and intellectual activities in its religious program, and the Negro Baptists support Natchez College, a coeducational four-year institution with a high school department. The Negroes of Natchez, unlike the Negroes in other Mississippi towns, trade almost exclusively at stores owned by members of their own race. This has created a comparatively wealthy business and professional class, families who send their children out of the State for education. Neither the Negroes' residential nor business districts are well defined but are scattered about the city in the midst of other residential and business districts. St. Catherine Street, however, may be said to be the focal point. Here, interspersed among the houses left from Spanish days, are many of the commercial and business establishments, and a majority of the churches. It is also to this street that Negroes from out of town gravitate.

The history of Natchez is the variegated story of a frontier town, raw and polished, crude and elegant: a town that absorbed the best and the worst of Mississippi River pioneer days. It has been ruled by the Natchez Indians, France, Spain, England, the Confederacy, and the United States. The town was settled as part of the French colonization development after Iberville landed on the Mississippi Gulf Coast in 1699. Land grants were made as early as 1702, but it was 1716 before Bienville built and garrisoned Fort Rosalie, named in honor of the Duchess of Pontchartrain. Two years later 15 laborers opened the first plantation at Natchez—a farm on St. Catherine's Creek. The settlement prospered, with ships plying to the Gulf Coast colony and back, carrying tobacco, pelts, and bear's grease in exchange for staple supplies.

In November 1729, the Natchez Indians (who inhabited the region and whose name is commemorated in the name of the city) attacked the fort and massacred the garrison and settlers. The following year the French colonists of the Gulf area retaliated by exterminating the Natchez Indians. Then they attacked the more warlike Chickasaw and were defeated. This defeat ended the French scheme of uniting the French of the Ohio Valley with the French of the lower Mississippi Valley, thus forming a line of defense against the westward-moving English.

After the French and Indian War, Natchez became a part of the region east of the Mississippi River which France ceded to Great Britain in 1763. The British settlers who followed were hardy veterans of the Colonial wars and established permanent homes on large tracts of land granted by the English king.

Natchez, as an English possession, was in reality a fourteenth colony of Great Britain. However, its people remained neutral during the Revolutionary War, indifferent to the struggle on the Atlantic seaboard a thousand miles away. It was this isolation that enabled Galvez, Spanish Governor of New Orleans, to take Natchez in 1779 in the name of the King of Spain. During the first year of Spanish occupancy, British veterans made an abortive attempt to retake Natchez.

Under the ambitious Dons the town began to prosper again. The Spaniards who occupied Natchez between 1779–98 were efficient and fair. They loved punctilio and all the trappings of lavish living, and they introduced a rigid caste system which prevails to a certain extent today. Until their coming few buildings stood on the bluffs, the settlement having grown up along the water front. So the town, much as it is today, was laid out in a square by Collel, a Spanish engineer. Choice streets were reserved for the residences of Spanish grandees and a church called San Salvador stood on a broad esplanade extending across the front of the city overlooking the river. But of all their magnificent buildings erected during this period not more than 20 remain.

By the treaty of Madrid, 1795, parallel 31 was agreed upon as the boundary between the newly formed United States and Spain's possessions, with free navigation of the Mississippi guaranteed by the Spaniards who still owned New Orleans. In 1797 Andrew Ellicott, a Pennsylvania surveyor, arrived in Natchez to run the new boundary line, and unofficially raised the American flag. But another year passed before Spain could be forced to evacuate this rich territory according to the terms of the treaty. On March 30, 1798, however, the last Spanish soldier withdrew, leaving the fort to Maj. Isaac Guion, who officially raised the American flag. In that same year, the Territory of Mississippi was organized and Natchez was made the capital.

The opening of the Mississippi River started the turbulent flatboat era that lasted until the steamboat brought it to an end. Down the river came the flatboatmen, swearing, drinking, fighting; bringing on their clumsy rafts, tobacco, grains, fruits, pelts, molasses, hams, butter, flour, and whisky. Many of them stopped at Natchez to sell their goods and their boats; most of them continued to New Orleans; but all returned through Natchez, since it was too difficult to return to the upper country by water. Banding together for protection against prowling savages and murderous outlaws, they returned home, carrying their money in money belts or in saddlebags. They followed the 550-mile road to Nashville, a road that was a mere trace or bridle path. This road became famous as the Natchez Trace *(see TRANSPORTATION)*.

A frontier city, capital of a rich territory, Natchez soon grew important as a supply depot and the gathering place for the intellectuals of the Southwest. It became an opulent, suave, and aristocratic community, maintaining a social and political prestige that influenced the entire Mississippi Valley.

Men of all degrees of wealth and intelligence were drawn to this new region where land was cheap and fortunes were quickly made. Hundreds of families drifted down the river from the upper valleys in fleets of flatboats. These pioneers came to a rich and fertile country that had a mild climate featured by a growing season nine months long. They tried raising indigo but the refuse accumulations, with the poisonous drainage from them, made it unhealthful. They tried raising tobacco and found it unprofitable. After the invention of Whitney's cotton gin in 1793, they turned to growing cotton. Slave labor, together with natural advantages, enabled them to create in a remarkably short time a system of great plantations and luxurious living. The *Mississippi Gazette,* first newspaper in the State, began publication in 1800. On April 9, 1803, Natchez was incorporated as an American city. In 1810, when the population of Natchez was 9,000 persons, it was estimated that the aggregate cotton sales exceeded $700,000.

Increasing prosperity made it necessary to establish an overland line of communication with the East. Hitherto, the Mississippi River had been the one route of travel. In 1801 the Treaty of Chickasaw Bluffs was made with the Chickasaw Indians whereby the Indians agreed to permit immigrants, the United States mail, and soldiers to pass through their lands. The immediate effect of this agreement was a sudden growth in the population of Natchez and the lower Mississippi Valley. Droves of settlers toiled down the Natchez Trace from the Atlantic seaboard, bringing new blood, new ideas, and new wealth in money and slaves.

In 1802, however, Natchez lost much of its prestige when the Territorial Assembly ordered the seat of government moved from Natchez to Washington, a small, gay, wealthy, inland city situated about six miles to the east.

Because of the growing importance of Natchez as an entrance to the West, Aaron Burr and Harman Blennerhassett selected it as the base from which to operate their mysterious colonization scheme. The plan was broken up when both were arrested, charged with treason.

During the War of 1812 the city was threatened frequently by Indians who lived in the wilderness east of the river. All able-bodied men became soldiers, and when the Battle of New Orleans was fought in 1815, the Natchez Rifles was present. One historian related that nearly all the male citizens of Natchez took part in the battle.

In 1817 the Mississippi Territory was organized as a State. The convention met at Washington and decided to move the seat of government from Washington to Columbia, then to a more central location at Le Fleur's Bluff *(see JACKSON).* From this time on, the political eminence of Natchez declined.

The booming steamboat era, however, had just begun with the arrival of the *New Orleans,* first steamboat to stop at Natchez, and within a few years the city recovered its prominence by becoming one of the great cotton ports of the world. In this period fabulous fortunes were made by cotton planters, and Natchez reached a pinnacle of wealth and culture with liberal, open-handed living prevailing. Planters spent their money building distinctive homes and accumulating libraries and art collections *(see ARCHITECTURE).* They speculated in land, slaves, cotton, and credit. While much in their lives was gracious, their code demanded exaggerated standards of honor. Duels were fought frequently on the sandbar across the river.

At the outbreak of the War between the States Natchez was still a rich agricultural center. It furnished many soldiers to the Confederate cause, most prominent of whom was Maj.-Gen. William T. Martin. Natchez was bombarded by the U. S. S. *Essex* in July 1863, and occupied by Ransom's brigade. Civil government was suspended from November 1863 to August 9, 1865. The war destroyed the fortunes, slaves were freed, and the economic and social structures were overturned completely. Natchez has never regained the river trade that once had helped to make it rich, one of the queen cities of the lower Mississippi.

For three generations the population increased little. The changes made were material improvements that blend with rather than destroy the still cherished past. In 1881 telephone lines were installed, and five years later Judge Thomas Reber built a street railroad from the ferry landing on

Main and St. Catherine Streets to the "Forks-of-the-Road." The Judge also installed the first electric light plant, in 1886, to furnish lights for a casino. In the same year, the Adams Manufacturing Company plant was built to manufacture cottonseed oil.

Natchez does not boast of its material progress, but prefers to keep its industries in the background. Yet the income from the sale of its manufactured products amounted to $2,121,755 in 1935.

The old Spanish portion of Natchez can be seen either on foot or by car. It was centered around an esplanade that faced the river. Many other interesting examples of Spanish architecture survive here and there in all parts of the city.

Tour 1–*3m*

W. from Pearl St. on Market St.

1. The ADAMS COUNTY COURTHOUSE, Market St. (L), stands in the exact center of Natchez as it was laid out by the Spaniards. Erected in 1819, and constructed of soft cream stucco-covered brick, it has three porticos with large fluted columns. In its vaults are stored records dating back to 1780, compiled in Spanish, French, and English. Its rectangular grounds are the site of the old Spanish market and, presumably, the Church of San Salvador.

2. The PARISH HOUSE OF SAN SALVADOR, 311 Market St. *(private)*, is a three-story frame structure erected by order of the King of Spain in 1786. It was first occupied in 1788 by four Irish priests, brought to Natchez to instruct the English-speaking population in the Roman Catholic religion. Though the house is gray and dilapidated, evidence of its beauty can be seen in its simple, hand-carved doorway and woodwork, and in its severe, plain lines.

L. from Market St. on S. Wall St.

3. The MERCER HOUSE, NW. corner S. Wall and State Sts. *(private)*, is a two-story Georgian Colonial structure built in 1818 and distinguished by dormer windows, spacious floor plan, and a fanlight filled with early, imperfect glass. Constructed of gray stuccoed brick, the lower front portico is supported by arches and the upper by slender columns. On the north side of the house is a garden enclosed by a well-patterned hand-wrought iron fence. Andrew Jackson, on his way to take part in the unveiling of his equestrian statue in New Orleans in January 1840, stayed

CONTI HOUSE, NATCHEZ

in this home. He was joined by Gen. Thomas Hinds and other veterans of the Battle of New Orleans, and from the porch addressed a throng of admirers gathered in the courthouse yard.

4. LAWYERS' ROW, SW. corner S. Wall and State Sts., is a low L-shaped stuccoed brick building with two adjacent wings extending for approximately half a block from the corner. The wings are broken into small, bin-like offices whose front entrances stand flush with the street. The rear entrances open into a court. Erected by the Spaniards before 1796, it is thought that the building was used first as a commissary for the old fort. After Mississippi became a territory the bins, converted into offices, were occupied by bachelor lawyers. Because many of these young men were later famous the building became known as Lawyers' Row.

5. CONTI HOUSE, 207 S. Wall St. *(open daily 10-4; adm. 25¢)*, is a rectangular, two-story stuccoed brick house, built prior to 1788. Of Spanish Provincial architecture it stands flush with the street, with Spanish slate steps and no eaves to break the line of wall or roof. Two green-shuttered windows and a central door open on the sidewalk. A two-story service wing extending to rear—with four slave rooms upstairs and down—forms a setting for an old-fashioned garden. First used as a home by Don Lewis Favre, surgeon of the King's galleys, the house was from 1825–35 the home of David Holmes, last Territorial and first State Governor of Mississippi.

6. The OLD SPANISH HOUSE, NW. corner S. Wall and Washington Sts. *(private)*, is a good example of the average home of the Spanish

Dominion. Brick and stucco trimmed in green, it is two stories high, with dormer windows, outside stairways, and a kitchen attached by a wooden hyphen. At the rear of the kitchen are the slave quarters, a two-story, rectangular structure built of cedar joined with wooden pegs. The house was built in 1796 or earlier.

L. from S. Wall St. on Washington St.; L. on S. Pearl St.

7. The BRITTON HOME, NW. corner S. Pearl and Washington Sts. *(open by appointment),* erected in 1858, is an imposing two-story brick house with Corinthian columns and a classic two-story portico. Wrought-iron railings enclose each gallery. The house was struck by a shell during the bombardment of Natchez in 1863.

8. FIRST PRESBYTERIAN CHURCH, NE. corner S. Pearl and State Sts., was designed by Levi Weeks of Boston and built in 1829. This simple, cream, stuccoed brick building has a classic portico with large Tuscan columns and pedimented headings over the doors. The interior is plain, with slave galleries, enclosed with handmade banisters, on both sides of the auditorium. Small wooden doors open into the cushioned box pews.

9. MEMORIAL HALL, 111-115 S. Pearl St. *(open daily 10-5),* flanked on each side by small landscaped grounds and protected by an iron fence eight feet high, is a stuccoed brick structure of modified Spanish architecture. Built in 1852 for public meeting purposes, it was first called Institute Hall. It is two stories in height, with recessed columns made in the masonry. The main floor is at street level. The entrance opens into a central hallway from which twin stairways rise to the second floor auditorium. After the World War, memorial tablets were placed on each side of the entrance and the name of the building was changed to Memorial Hall. Here balls and other social affairs of importance are held each year. The right wing houses the *FISK MEMORIAL LIBRARY,* separate entrance *(open weekdays 8-4).*

L. from S. Pearl St. on Main St.

10. The OLD COMMERCIAL BANK BUILDING, 206 Main St., was erected about 1809. It is of brick construction and has a stuccoed front with four graceful Ionic columns supporting a classic pediment. John Hampton White of New Jersey was the architect. Until the founding of this bank all currency used in Natchez was Spanish "hard money" and cotton gin receipts. The bank issued notes but none of them is known to exist.

L. from Main St. on S. Canal St.

11. BANKER'S HOME, 107 S. Canal St. *(open by permission),* attached to the Commercial Bank, was built in 1809 as the home of the bank's president. Set in the remains of a garden, the house is of stucco and brick construction and two stories in height. In front is a small portico with two slender fluted columns; a deck to the portico is enclosed with an iron railing. In the garden is a walk of Spanish flagstones brought to America in sailing ships as ballast. The custom of having the banker's home as part of the bank itself is said to have been a heritage from the Spanish regime.

R. from S. Canal St. on Washington St.; L. on S. Broadway.

12. The JAMES METCALFE HOUSE, facing the river at SE. corner S. Broadway and Washington Sts. *(open during Pilgrimage)*, is a raised brick building with a portico. Built about 1849 by Peter Little, pioneer lumberman in Mississippi, this home is well preserved and contains many of its original furnishings. The story is that Peter Little grew tired of his wife's continually entertaining preachers in his home, and erected this house and deeded it to a church on condition that entertaining in his home cease.

13. The ESPLANADE, extending along the bluff in front of the James Metcalfe House, was the parade ground attached to Fort Rosalie. It affords a view of the river and the remains of the old river town, Natchez-under-the-Hill.

14. ROSALIE, foot of S. Broadway *(open daily 10–4; adm. 25¢)*, is a square red brick home of the late Georgian (or Post-Colonial) type; its two-story, pedimented portico has four white Tuscan columns. Double doors, with fanlight transoms and side lights, are at each gallery. The windows are five feet wide, their huge wooden shutters held in place by slender wrought-iron hinges 26 inches long. The rooms are 21 feet square with 14-foot ceilings and mantels seven feet high. Double parlors contain hand-carved rosewood furniture. A stairway rises from a recessed hall. The house was built by Peter Little in the early 1800's and stands partly on the site of old Fort Rosalie, scene of the Indian massacre in 1729. Brick for this home was burned on the place by slaves. The house was used in 1863 as Union headquarters and later General Grant and his family spent several days in it.

15. The SITE OF FORT ROSALIE, an elevation directly back of Rosalie, is marked by a tall iron pole.

Retrace S. Broadway; L. on Silver St.

16. At the foot of Silver St. and below the Natchez bluffs, lies a strip of land called THE BATTURE. This is the only remnant of dissolute Natchez-under-the-Hill, known throughout the Mississippi Valley during flatboat days and the steamboat era. This colorful, ribald old river port with its brothels and gambling dens and its heterogeneous population of flatboatmen, Negroes, Indians, bandits, pirates, scented quadroons, courtesans, and gamblers held sway for many years. There were times when flatboats were tied to its banks 14 deep in a stretch two miles long. Ships from Liverpool and other foreign ports came to its wharfs. All that remains is a single desolate street and a few moldy buildings; year by year the river eats away the soft, rockless land.

The ferry line at the Batture that operates between Natchez and Vidalia, La., has maintained service since 1797.

Retrace Silver St.; L. on S. Broadway St.

17. The BUNTURA HOME, 107 S. Broadway St. *(private)*, midway between State and Main Sts. and facing the river, is a two-story, L-shaped house built in 1832. The galleries on its narrow front are ornamented with delicate lace ironwork. The ell faces on a courtyard garden with an old cistern in the center. A vaulted driveway through the rear of the house permitted the passage of vehicles into the courtyard.

CONNELLY'S TAVERN, NATCHEZ

R. from N. Broadway St. on Franklin St.; L. on N. Wall St.

18. MARSCHALK'S PRINTING OFFICE, NE. corner N. Wall and Franklin Sts. *(private)*, is a small two-and-a-half-story brick building where Andrew Marschalk, an officer in the American Army during the Revolutionary War and the pioneer of printing and publishing in Mississippi, issued the third newspaper in the State, on July 26, 1802. This paper, *The Mississippi Herald,* was in reality the first news sheet of any stability. *The Mississippi Gazette,* published by Benjamin Stokes, was established in Natchez in 1800 and was followed there in 1801 by *The Mississippi Intelligencer.* It was Marschalk's press that turned out both these papers. He conducted the *Herald* for many years but changed its name often. He was first territorial printer and printed the first territorial laws. Before Marschalk came to Natchez in 1800 he had been stationed at Walnut Hills, now Vicksburg, and while on duty there he printed a ballad on his small press, the first piece of printing done in Mississippi.

L. from N. Wall St. on Jefferson St.; L. on N. Canal St.

19. CONNELLY'S TAVERN or ELLICOTT'S INN, SE. corner N. Canal and Jefferson Sts. *(open by permission)*, is on the top of a steep, terraced hill. This old frame house, restored by the Natchez Garden Club, was built in 1795 during Spanish rule in Natchez. It stands on the old

Natchez Trace and is a notable example of Spanish Provincial architecture. Long, narrow, double galleries with slender columns overlook the Esplanade and the river. The lower floor is brick paved. Though the ceilings throughout are low, several rooms are vaulted. It is thought that some of the materials used in its construction were timbers taken from dismantled flatboats, and the vaulted rooms indicate the influence of a ship's carpenter in the construction of the house.

In 1797 the American flag was first raised on this site by Andrew Ellicott, sent from Washington to survey the line between the United States and Spanish territory. Ellicott kept the flag flying a year in defiance of Spanish objections. It was also on this hill that Maj. Isaac Guion, on March 31, 1798, raised the American flag after the Spaniards had evacuated the fort the night before. Tradition says that Aaron Burr and Harman Blennerhassett met here to plan their defense following their arrest for treason in 1807.

Retrace N. Canal St.; R. on High St.

20. CHOCTAW, SW. corner High and N. Wall Sts. *(private)*, was the home of Alvarez Fisk, wealthy cotton broker and philanthropist in the 1830's and 1840's. Though in bad condition, it is a notable example of Greek Revival architecture. It is built of brick with a large Ionic portico. The galleries of the portico are enclosed with a wooden railing. Unlike many of the manor houses of its period, Choctaw rises from the street, its first floor flush with the sidewalk. Double transverse steps lead to the lower gallery. Steamboats tied up at the wharfs to allow passengers time to inspect its gardens. Fisk donated land for the first school in Natchez and erected the first school building.

21. STANTON HALL and its grounds, enclosed by a high iron fence, occupy the entire block on High St. between N. Pearl and N. Commerce Sts. *(open daily 9-4; adm. 25¢)*. This huge brick house, with its Corinthian two-story portico, was built by Frederick Stanton, an Irish gentleman who became rich as a cotton broker. It was completed in 1857 after five years' work. Some of the ceilings are 22 feet high. Mahogany doors, carved Carrara marble mantels, heavy bronze chandeliers, and gigantic inset mirrors were imported from Europe on a chartered ship. The east side of the house can be opened by sliding doors into one long suite. Tremendous matched mirrors balance each other at front and rear of suite. The frieze in the music hall bears names of old masters.

Tour 2—3.3 m.

N. from Main St. on N. Canal St.; L. on Madison St.; R. on Clifton St.
From the corner of Clifton and Oak Sts. is one of the best river views in the city. To the west are the alluvial plains of Louisiana, where many Natchez planters owned cotton lands that made them wealthy. To the left is the canal completed by the Government in 1935 to shorten the Mississippi River 18 miles. When this canal was dug, Army engineers found petrified trees too large to be dredged out; they were pulled to one side of the channel. The great, sweeping curve of the Mississippi as it turns west above Natchez to flow east again will soon become another river-bed lake. The canal is depositing a sand bar across the river in front of Natchez and it is estimated that the stream eventually will be completely dammed up. (The canal is expected to send the river past Natchez on a straight course that will eliminate much of the eroding done by the river).

The two points following can be reached by an unpaved street extending down the bluff from the foot of Madison Street.
22. From this corner is also the best view of the FIRST LUMBER MILL in Mississippi, situated at the foot of the cliffs. The mill was started in 1809 by Peter Little. Its operating capacity is 40,000 feet a day. On the Louisiana shore opposite the mill is an old sandbar where many famous duels were fought. Here George Poindexter killed Abijah Hunt in 1811.
23. North of the lumber mill is MAGNOLIA VALE *(private)*, a two-story brick and stucco house with gardens that have been a Natchez attraction for more than 100 years. In steamboat days river travelers could see the gardens from the decks, but often the period allowed on shore was extended so passengers could hire a hack and drive through the gardens. It was built in 1831 by Andrew Brown, a Scotsman who came to Natchez in 1821. The land had in turn belonged to Stephen Minor and Peter Little.

R. from Clifton St. on Oak St.
24. The WIGWAM, 307 Oak St. *(private)*, back from the street on a lot elevated 10 or 12 feet, is enclosed by a brick wall. The walk from the entrance is shaded by a double row of live-oak trees. In the center of the walk is a fountain, a silent reminder of the days when the home was the center of culture and gay social life. The date the house was built is not known but it is shown on a map made in 1819 by Col. John Steel, first secretary of the Mississippi Territory and later Governor. It is a story-and-a-half, "H-shaped" frame structure to which several additions have been made. The eaves of the projecting wings are trimmed with graceful iron

work that is given emphasis by iron columns, ornamented with four-leaf clover designs, which support the recessed gallery. The interior is planned with a large central hall and with spacious chambers.

L. from Oak St. on Myrtle Ave.

Myrtle Avenue was once the most elegant neighborhood in Natchez. On it lived five governors: Vidal and Minor during Spanish sovereignty; John Steel, George Poindexter, and Robert Williams during the time Mississippi was a Territory. Harman Blennerhasset, Aaron Burr's co-conspirator, also lived here.

25. THE TOWERS, 803 Myrtle Ave. *(private)*, in a dense grove, is an old home pictured in Stark Young's *So Red the Rose*. The house, built about 1818 by Wm. C. Chamberlain, was first called Gardenia. The Towers is a two-story frame dwelling built on a brick foundation. It has recessed upper and lower galleries in the center, and a square tower on each side. At the time of Federal occupancy of Natchez during the War between the States the house was used as headquarters by Colonel Peter B. Hays, Union engineer in charge of fortifications. Several years ago it was badly damaged by fire.

26. COTTAGE GARDEN, 816 Myrtle Ave. *(private)*, is a frame structure of Southern Planter architecture. It is one-and-one-half stories high with a low, sloping roof extending across the front to form a long gallery. The gallery has slender square columns. The central columns support a pediment. Cottage Garden was erected in 1793 by Don Jose Vidal. It stands on lands first granted him when he was acting Spanish Governor of Natchez in 1798. The chief features of the house are its curving mahogany stairway and a fanlighted entrance door. Huge brick chimneys rise at each end, and there is a frame and brick gallery in the rear. A large, underground reservoir or cistern, used to furnish water and to cool wine and milk, is under the main part of the building.

27. AIRLIE, N. end of Myrtle Ave. *(open during Pilgrimage)*, is a simple frame home of Spanish Provincial design to which wings have been added. It was built in 1793 and was once a home of Don Estevan Minor, Civil Governor under Spain in 1798. The interior of the house is filled with heirlooms: silver, china, paintings and furniture. The grounds are laid out with old-fashioned flower gardens.

R. from Myrtle Ave. on Elm St.; R. on N. Union St.

28. The PROTESTANT ORPHANAGE, N. Union St. (R) between Oak and B Sts., is the last of three buildings bought by the "Female Charitable Society of Natchez." The building, erected as a country home in 1820, was bought from Ann Dunbar Postlewaite for $10,000. It is a large building with long galleries across front and rear.

L. from N. Union St. on B. St.; L. on Rankin St.

29. MELMONT (SANS SOUCI), N. Rankin St. (R) between B and Oak Sts. *(open during Pilgrimage)*, built in 1854, is an unpretentious brick home having double-decked porticos with fluted columns, and a steep-gabled roof. The brick was burned of Natchez clay, but the hardware and mahogany woodwork were imported. At present Melmont is owned by descendants of John Henderson, first great commission mer-

chant in Natchez. Many of the Henderson heirlooms are in the house. In 1863 this home was used as a residence for Union officers and breastworks were thrown up on its grounds.

Retrace N. Rankin St.; R. on Jefferson St.

30. KING'S TAVERN, Jefferson St. (R) between N. Rankin and N. Union Sts. *(open daily 9-5; adm. 25¢)*, is conceded to be the oldest house in Natchez. It abuts the sidewalk and is thought to have been a blockhouse on the old Natchez Trace. Built of ship's timbers, its huge sleepers and beams filled with holes and rounded pegs indicate they were part of a flatboat. For many years the inn was the mail and stage coach station on the Trace.

◄◄◄◄◄◄◄◄◄◄◄◄◄◄◄◄◄◄☼►►►►►►►►►►►►►►►►►►►

Tour 3—4.7 m

E. from Pearl St. on Main St.; R. on S. Union St.

31. ST. MARY'S CATHEDRAL, SE. corner S. Union and Main Sts., was built during the years 1841-51. Of Gothic Revival design, it is constructed of red brick with a tall spire surmounted by an illuminated cross. The altars are of Carrara marble, and behind the main altar is a copy of Powell's picture of Christ. The bell, weighing 3,000 pounds and made by Giovanni Lucenti, was given to St. Mary's by Prince Alex Torlonia of Rome in 1849. The Princess Torlonia threw her wedding ring into the molten metal as the bell was cast. The early history of Natchez was connected closely with the Roman Catholic Church. Missionary priests, both Capuchin and Jesuit, came and went. The edifice is now the Cathedral for the Catholic Diocese of Mississippi, and improvements costing more than $100,000 recently were made. The *CEMETERY* adjoining the church, and now called Memorial Park, is a portion of the old cemetery that was attached to the Spanish church of San Salvador. Until the 1890's it stood in the center of town, dilapidated, with crumbling tombs overgrown with weeds. At that time, it was decided to level the cemetery. All remains were carefully gathered and placed in one vault in the center of the grounds. Tombstones and markers were placed around it, and a monument to the Confederacy was erected. It was then that the name was changed to Memorial Park. The vault contains the dust of seamen, scouts, adventurers, distinguished Revolutionary War veterans, and two of the wives of Spanish Governor Manuel Gayoso de Lemos.

R. from S. Union St. on State St.

32. ST. JOSEPH'S ACADEMY, NE. corner State and S. Commerce

Sts., was organized in 1867 by the Sisters of Charity. In that year the nuns purchased a large house with extensive grounds from a Dr. Chase, Presbyterian minister, and moved their school to these quarters. Later the other buildings were added.

L. from State St. on S. Commerce St.

33. The TRINITY EPISCOPAL CHURCH, SE. corner of S. Commerce and Washington Sts., was erected in 1822. It is a rectangular brick building with a gallery extending across the front. Tall Corinthian columns are a part of the wide portico, and two heavy shuttered doors open into the beautiful interior. Here is a small slave gallery built over the entrance.

L. from S. Commerce St. on Orleans St.; R. on S. Union St.

34. RAVENNA, 601 S. Union St. *(open during Pilgrimage)*, is a simple, two-story frame building erected in 1835 by William Harris. Approached through a large iron gate, it has long, colonnaded galleries both front and rear. The interior woodwork is carved in geometric designs of squares, angles, and wedges. From the back hall a graceful stairway with mahogany hand rails curves upward. The furniture is of rosewood.

Retrace S. Union St.; R. on Washigton St.

35. GREENLEAVES, SE. corner of Washington and S. Union Sts. *(open during Pilgrimage)*, is a raised, brick and frame house built before 1812. Of Greek Revival architecture, it has a narrow, classic portico with Corinthian columns. In the rear is a detached brick kitchen erected in the Spanish era. In the patio is a giant live-oak beneath which the Natchez Indians are believed to have held their pow-wows. The 14 rooms of Greenleaves are furnished as they were in the 1840's with carved rosewood, gilt frame mirrors, and china said to have been painted by Audubon.

36. THE ELMS, NE. corner Washington and S. Pine Sts. *(open during Pilgrimage)*, is thought to have been built by the Spanish Governor, Don Pedro Piernas, in 1785. Low ceilings, narrow window facings with deep reveals, large chimneys, and heavy, hand-made iron hinges indicate its Spanish origin. Galleries with slender columns extend across the front and north sides. An iron stairway, once on the outside of the building, is enclosed in the north hallway. A feature of the interior is the set of old slave bells, each different in tone. Each house slave had his own bell with its particular tone to call him to his duties. The garden contains a lattice work eagle house and a brick archway thought to have been part of an early Spanish mission, for the mission was usually part of the official group of buildings in a Spanish settlement.

L. from Washington St. on St. Charles St.; R. on Main St.

37. ARLINGTON, E. end of Main St. *(open during Pilgrimage)*, reached through a large gate and down a long driveway, is considered an excellent example of Greek Revival architecture. A square red brick mansion, it has four tall, white columns supporting a classic pediment, and a double portico. The upper gallery is enclosed with delicate banisters, and the lower gallery is paved with marble mosaic. Delicate fan-

ARLINGTON, NATCHEZ

lights both front and rear open into a long central hall. The interior contains many of the original furnishings: gold brocades, carved rosewood, large mirrors, paintings by Vernet, Sully, and Audubon, and a library. Arlington was built by Mrs. James Surget White, daughter of Pierre Surget, who settled in Natchez during Indian days. The architect was James Hampton White, of New Jersey.

Retrace Main St.; L. on Arlington St.; L. on Homochitto St.

38. DUNLEITH, Homochitto St. (R) at S. end of Arlington St. *(open during Pilgrimage)*, is a stately, white-columned, Greek Revival mansion. It is a square building with tall Greek Doric columns surrounded by galleries enclosed with wrought-iron railings. At the rear is a kitchen wing attached to the house, and farther back are brick carriage houses and stables. Dunleith was built by Gen. Charles Dahlgren in 1847. The grouping of the buildings is typical of the period.

39. The ROUTH CEMETERY (L), on Homochitto St. *(not open)*, is the private burial ground for the Routh family.

L. from Homochitto St. on Auburn Rd.

40. HOPE FARM, intersection of Auburn Rd. and Homochitto St., is a notable example of the hybrid English-Spanish style of architecture. The rear wing, built in 1775, is one of the few architectural relics of the English period. The front portion was built in 1790 by Carlos de Grandpré, Spanish Governor from 1790 to 1794, and shows in its severe

lines the influence of Spanish Provincial architecture. Wooden pegs and tongue and groove method of construction were used in building both sections. The garden has a collection of flowering bulbs and camellia japonica.

R. *on Auburn Rd.*

41. AUBURN, Auburn Rd. (R) at Park Ave. *(open to public)*, was built in 1812 by Judge Lyman G. Harding, first attorney general of Mississippi Territory and of the State. Levi Weeks of Boston was the architect. The plainness of Auburn's red brick walls is broken by long triple hung windows with green shutters and the four heavy Ionic columns of the two-story pedimented portico. The entrance door is imposing, with side lights and a canopied fanlight transom. The lower floor contains a front hall opening at right angles into a long vaulted back hall, a drawing room, a banquet room and office, and a ladies' tea room. The outstanding feature of the interior is the spiral stairway. A detached brick kitchen faces a courtyard in the rear. A brick carriage house and a billiard hall are still standing. Auburn and its grounds were deeded to the city of Natchez in 1911 by the Duncan heirs as a memorial to Dr. Stephen Duncan, who purchased the estate in 1820. The grounds were converted by the city into *DUNCAN PARK.* The park contains swings, tennis courts, and an excellent 18-hole public golf course.

Tour 4–*1m.*

E. from Wall St. on Main St.; L. on N. Pine St.; R. on St. Catherine St.

42. HOSPITAL HILL, 70 St. Catherine St., is the site of the first charity hospital in America. The hospital was incorporated in 1805, and five acres of land surrounding it were deeded to the trustees by Don Estevan Minor in 1813. The site is now occupied by the electric light company.

43. HOME OF DON ESTEVAN MINOR, 42-44 St. Catherine St. *(private),* a small, dilapidated, two-story, stuccoed brick house, retains its severe Spanish line. Don Minor, a captain in the Spanish Army, came to Natchez in 1783 as a subordinate under Governors Miro and Gayoso. Later, he was Commandant at Natchez and, for a year preceding the Spanish evacuation in 1798, Civil Governor. Minor was well liked by the American settlers and, after the evacuation, remained at Natchez, became an opulent planter, and died in 1815.

Tour 5—2m.

S. from Main St. on S. Canal St.; R. on Irvine Ave. (an unpaved, winding alley-like street).

44. THE BRIARS, W. end Irvine Ave. *(open daily 9-4; adm. 50¢)*, is the best example of Southern Planter type of architecture in the Natchez district. A white frame structure with green blinds, its sloping roof, forming a 90-foot gallery, is supported by slender columns. Dormer windows light the upper floor. Three doors with fanlight transoms open on the front gallery. The rear gallery is upheld by an arcade and has a mahogany stairway at each end. Slave rooms are in the basement. The Briars was built between 1812-15, and was later owned by William Burr Howell, whose daughter, Varina, married Jefferson Davis here in 1845. The Briars commands a view of the Mississippi River.

Retrace Irvine Ave.; R. on S. Canal St. 0.5 m. to private drive (L).

45. RICHMOND, end of long circular driveway *(open daily 9-4; adm. 25¢)*, represents three distinct periods in architectural development. The frame and brick central portion was built in 1786 by Juan San Germaine, interpreter for the Spanish King. It is Spanish Provincial. The timbers are hand-hewn, and the gutters are made of hollowed logs. The lower or ground floors are bricked. The front, built in 1832, is Greek Revival, with a pediment and four tall columns. The brick wing of modified Empire design was added in 1850. Legend says that in the Spanish regime the central portion of the house was a rendezvous for river pirates.

POINTS OF INTEREST IN ENVIRONS

Longwood, *2.9 m.*, Homewood, *2.7 m.*, Lansdowne, *3.2 m.*, Monteigne, *1.5 m.*, Oakland, *1.7 m.*, Windy Hill Manor, *7.2 m.*, Monmouth, *1.4 m.*, Melrose, *2 m.*, D'Evereux, *1.5 m.*, Washington, *6.5 m.*, Site of Elizabeth Female Academy, *8 m.*, Foster Mound, *9 m.*, Pine Ridge Church, *11.5 m.*, Mount Repose, *11.9 m.*, Peachland, *13 m. (see Tour 3, Sec. b).*

Oxford

Railroad Station: W. end of Jackson Ave. for Illinois Central R.R.
Bus Station: Mack's Cafe, Lamar Ave., for Tri-State Transit Co.
Taxis: 10¢ per person within city limits.
Accommodations: One hotel.
Information Service: Service stations.
Motion Picture Houses: Two.
Swimming: University, adm., 25¢.
Golf: University, greens fee 50¢.
Annual Events: Spring festival on University Campus.

OXFORD (458 alt., 2,890 pop.), on a small wooded plateau overlooking the snug valleys of the Central Hills, retains the persuasive charm and culture of the Old South. Its character, like the essence of its appeal, is compounded of intangibles as elusive as the scent of its jasmines and as delicate as the humor of its town clock, the four faces of which seldom agree. It has been the county seat of Lafayette and the site of the State university for nearly a century, and it is these two factors, education and law, that give to it its tone today. The white stuccoed courthouse, with its green roof and clock cupola, centers the town. About the small grass-free courtyard, shaded on the west by heaven trees, is a low iron fence—handy for farmers to hitch their horses after having watered them at the nearby trough. Facing the courthouse on four sides are the low red brick and stucco commercial buildings that form the business district which Oxford's leisured trade has not outgrown. Leading from the square, shaded residence streets climb a slight ridge or two before changing into highways or country lanes. Cloistered behind the cedar, magnolia, and oak trees along these streets are the homes that make Oxford today seem as it has always been, a town dedicated to the cultural and social life revolving around the university.

Tradition is important; the current of Oxford's life is not swift but deep. The people are not prosperous as in the days "before the war," but they are comfortably sustained by the university and by the farmers who come in on Saturdays to do business on the square. It is the headquarters of the Northern District of the United States Court, and the headquarters of the northern division of the State highway department. As yet no industry has intruded upon its serenity, nor has the town felt the pain of expanding beyond original boundaries. In 1928 it received a silver cup for being the cleanest and best kept town in the State.

Oxford's unskilled and domestic labor is drawn from its Negro population, approximately 900. Negro men mow the lawns, trim the boxwood hedges, and work the gardens of the white townspeople; their wives are cooks, nursemaids, and washerwomen. Many of them feel the pride of belonging, boast of lifetime service with one family, and live in quarters that their parents and grandparents occupied before them. Others are confined to districts fringing the town, their homes the small cabins common to Mississippi Negro families.

In 1835 John Chisholm, John J. Craig, and John D. Martin made their way into the territory ceded by the Chickasaw Indians and, stopping in the section now comprising Lafayette County, set up business in a log store they built near what is now Oxford's town square. Close on their heels came Robert Shegog and Thomas D. Isom, the latter obtaining a position as clerk in the store built by the former. The influx of settlers was rapid; stimulated by the enthusiastic descriptions of early traders, there swarmed into the ". . . fairy land (of) park-like forests and waving native grasses . . ." adventurers, speculators, and would-be landowners. On June 12, 1836, Chisholm, Craig, and Martin bought from Ho-kah, a Chickasaw Indian woman, section 21, township 8, range 3 west. Ho-kah affixed her signature to the deed by making a cross mark, and to make the deed legal beyond doubt two other citizens certified ". . . that the above named Ho-kah is able to take care of her own affairs." After securing the land, the three traders donated 50 acres to the board of police to establish a county seat. The following year the village was laid out and incorporated, the first city minutes bearing the date May 11, 1837. Isom, voicing the hope that such a promising spot would catch the plum of the State university then under consideration, suggested the name Oxford. In 1838 the inhabitants numbered 400. There were no churches but arrangements had been made for two; there were two hotels, six stores, and two seminaries of education. Beasconn, a contemporary writer, described it as one of the most pleasant towns in the whole region.

The hope of Oxford's citizens was fulfilled when the State university opened in 1848. Eight years earlier the Mississippi Legislature had passed an act providing for the State university and, with a commission appointed to select the site, Oxford had been chosen by a margin of one vote. The institution under the administration of Dr. Augustus B. Longstreet, elected president after the first session, drew some of the South's most brilliant minds to Oxford, and until the outbreak of the War between the States, a society of culture and gaiety flourished. An opera house was built, bringing many famous entertainers to the town. Young men held tilting tournaments that resembled in their color and pageantry the jousts of Scott's romances. Sober-minded scholars divided their attention between their books and addresses to the crowds gathered on the courthouse square.

The War between the States, however, put a blight upon the gay little town. No major battles were fought in Oxford, but it suffered from Federal raids and from the necessity of helping supply troops and provisions to the Confederacy. By August, 1861, nine companies of infantry and cavalry had been drawn from the town and sent to Florida, Kentucky, and Virginia. Breaking the precedent of enlisting for 12 months, three of these companies enlisted for service "during the war." After the Battle of Shiloh the buildings of the university were used as a hospital for the sick and wounded. General Grant's forces occupied the town from early in December 1862 until Christmas Day. On August 22, 1864, the court records say, "The Public Enemy under A. J. Smith came to Oxford . . . and burned the town, including the courthouse." In reporting the destruction the Oxford *Falcon* quoted travelers as saying that Oxford was the most completely demolished town they had seen.

Oxford, before the war, possessed new lands and a new university to draw wealthy and brilliant persons from the older States. Oxford, after the war, accepted more than its share of the economic problems of reconstruction and the social problems of reconciliation on which to prove the leadership of its still brilliant but no longer wealthy citizens. For 25 years, from the end of the war until 1890, the town furnished Mississippi and the Nation with many influential leaders. Isom, Hill, Thompson, Lamar, and others gained State and national recognition for their work. But since 1890, when new political ideals and leaders came into power in the State, Oxford, like a sensitive plant, has refused to spread. There is a dreamy lethargy about the place that even the post-war progressiveness of the university cannot penetrate. Static and preoccupied, it has remained at ease while a native son and two of its one-time citizens have limned it for the public. It is the "Jefferson" of William Faulkner's novels and the scene of several of Stark Young's stories *(see ARTS and LETTERS)*; its courthouse square was the subject for John McCrady's painting, *Town Square*.

POINTS OF INTEREST

1. The HOME OF WILLIAM FAULKNER, 900 Garfield St. *(private)*, was built in 1848 by Robert Shegog. It is a two-and-one-half story clapboarded house of modified Greek Revival design. Its pedimented front portico has slender square columns and a balcony above the entrance doorway. The house is approached by a long tree-bordered walk. Faulkner, who still maintains his home here, has made several additions, but fundamentally the house remains as it was when built.

2. The SITE OF JACOB THOMPSON'S HOME, Garfield St. diagonally across from the Faulkner home, is marked by offices, carriage houses, and a gatekeeper's lodge that escaped destruction by Union soldiers in 1864. Thompson, Secretary of the Interior in the cabinet of President Buchanan, built the house, a 20-room mansion, for his young wife, Kate Jones, daughter of a Revolutionary soldier. Kate was so beautiful that, immediately after their marriage, Thompson placed her in school in France instead of taking her with him to Washington. When he finally permitted her to join him in Washington, the Prince of Wales, then on a visit to the States, asked her to lead a ball given in his honor. Kate's presentation at the English Court so pleased Queen Victoria that she gave the young girl a gold thimble set with diamonds, a gift that became part of the loot of a Federal raider. In 1863 Thompson at the request of President Davis headed a secret mission to Canada, where, in cooperation with Vallandigham of Ohio, he was to foment insurrection in the Western States, a plan of which nothing came.

HOME OF WILLIAM FAULKNER, OXFORD

3. The HOME OF L. Q. C. LAMAR, 616 N. 14th St. *(private)*, is a simple cream-colored frame cottage built prior to the War between the States. Lucius Quintus Cincinnatus Lamar was a member of Congress, Secretary of the Interior in Cleveland's cabinet, and a U.S. Supreme Court Justice. He is famous for the memorable eulogy he gave Charles Sumner. This speech made while in Congress was a prime factor in reconciling the North and the South *(see Tour 14)*.

4. ST. PETER'S CEMETERY, E. end of Jefferson Ave., surrounded by a low vine-covered fence and shaded by soft evergreen trees, has been the town's burying ground since the settlement began. Here is the grave of Lamar, bearing the inscription "L.Q.C. Lamar, 1825–1893." By the side of Lamar's grave is that of Augustus Baldwin Longstreet, Lamar's father-in-law. Longstreet, the author of *Georgia Scenes,* a book that set the pattern for Southern humor in the generation before the war, was made president of the newly opened University of Mississippi in 1849, and was instrumental in bringing Lamar to Oxford shortly after he himself had arrived. Here also are the graves of Senator Sullivan, Judge Hill, and Dr. Isom.

5. DR. T. D. ISOM HOME, 1003 Jefferson Ave. *(open by permission)*, is a white clapboarded two-story Planter-type house with a wide gallery and six square white columns across the front. Over the entrance door is a small frame balcony. The exact date at which the house was erected is

unknown, but it is said to have been standing in the latter part of the 1830's. The jig-saw brackets on the caps of the square gallery columns are of later date. Thomas Dudley Isom was one of the earliest settlers of Oxford, having arrived here in his youth; after some years of study of medicine in Kentucky, he returned to practice his profession. Of all Oxford's early citizens he is perhaps the best remembered. Dr. Isom's redheaded daughter Sarah was the only woman member of the university faculty. Known as "Miss Sally," Sarah had a magnificent deep voice and gained international recognition as a "reader." Her reading of Poe's *Raven* brought her an invitation to read in England.

6. The R. A. HILL PLACE, 419 N. Lamar St. *(private)*, a gray two-story structure, of modified Victorian Gothic design, with a gallery on each floor and a bay on the right, was the home of Robert A. Hill, one of the most influential personalities in reconciling the North and the South. Born March 25, 1811, in Iredell County, N. C., Robert received only a few weeks schooling each year; further education he acquired at home with his father's help. In 1855 he moved to Mississippi and the following year was appointed judge of united courts of Mississippi. Two years later he was elected probate judge, serving in this capacity until the end of the War between the States, when he was apointed chancellor by Provisional Governor Sharkey. Judge Hill was no politician and, opposed to secession, took no part in the war. By sheer personal integrity he retained the confidence of both factions, and was elected by his county as delegate to Governor Clark's constitutional convention in May 1865 and, after this convention was prevented from meeting, to the one called by Governor Sharkey in August of the same year. A personal friend of President Johnson, he was appointed judge of the Mississippi Circuit in 1866 and was the only "operating" judge in the State until 1869. Judge Hill was a trustee of the University of Mississippi and several other educational institutions. He died in 1900. The house was bought by D. I. Sultan, merchant and lumberman.

7. The OLD OPERA HOUSE, 106-108 S. Lamar St. *(open)*, one of a long line of attached commercial buildings, was once the center of Oxford's civic culture. It is a square, two-story brick structure with a flat roof, and a balcony across the front. The second floor auditorium, unused for years, is approached from the sidewalk by a stairway which divides the lower floor into equal parts. For a decade before and after the War between the States the country's leading singers, musicians, and lecturers appeared here. Because the university did not permit dancing in its halls, the students held their balls in the opera house.

8. The LAW OFFICE OF SEN. WILLIAM V. SULLIVAN, 1013 Jackson Ave. *(private)*, sits back from the sidewalk, a typical mid-Victorian brick structure resembling a small cottage more than an office building. The right side, half hidden by foliage, is softened by the dense shade of a red magnolia. Born in Montgomery County December 18, 1857, William V. Sullivan first attended the University of Mississippi then was graduated with the first law class of Vanderbilt University, Nashville, Tenn. Admitted to the Mississippi bar, he moved to Oxford in 1878; here he became a member of the Board of Aldermen. Sullivan served in Congress as

Representative from March 4, 1897, to May 31, 1898, when he was appointed as Senator to fill the vacancy caused by the death of Sen. Edward C. Walthall *(see HOLLY SPRINGS)*. Subsequently elected to the U.S. Senate, he served until March 3, 1901. Senator Sullivan died in Oxford March 1, 1918.

Of Senator Sullivan's five children, only his daughter, Ellen Sullivan Woodward, has followed in his footsteps. In 1925 she was elected to the State Legislature, the second woman to serve in the House of Representatives. This was the beginning of a career of outstanding service to her State in key positions: on the State Board of Development (1926–33); on the State Research Commission (1930); on the State Board of Public Welfare (1932). These activities led to her being chosen to organize and head the Women's Division under Harry Hopkins, Administrator of the Federal Relief Program (1933) and to become the only woman Assistant Administrator of the Works Progress Administration (1935).

Mrs. Woodward's interest in and work for library extension service began while she was in the Mississippi Legislature, and it is largely to her credit that Mississippi has library facilities in every county of the State (1937).

From the beginning of her career, Mrs. Woodward has stood consistently for the principle that women should receive equal pay with men for equal services.

9. The NEILSON HOME, 11th and Fillmore Sts. *(private)*, is one of the best preserved ante-bellum homes in Oxford. Built in 1855 by W. S. Neilson, this massive square house is flanked on two sides by porticos with slender square columns two stories in height, and fine classic pediments. The interior is planned in the form of a Maltese cross. In the yard, shaded by cedars and magnolias, occurred an incident mentioned in *So Red the Rose:* a small Negro boy who climbed into a tree to hide from Federal raiders was shot and instantly killed.

10. The KATE SKIPWITH HOME, 508 University Ave. *(private)*, on a spacious lawn overlooking the street, is a peak-roofed cream frame house. In the Skipwith art collection is a portrait of Ellen Adair Beatty, daughter of John Adair, Governor of Kentucky 1820–24, and celebrated Oxford beauty. Ellen was presented at many of the courts of Europe, including that of St. James.

11. HILGARD'S CUT, under the University Ave. bridge, was dug by Dr. Isom's slaves to bring the Mississippi Central R.R. through Oxford. It was hoped that by bringing the trains past this point the passengers would have an opportunity to see the new university. But the cut was made too deep; when the trains passed through, the passengers saw only the bright red clay banks. It is the deepest cut on the Illinois Central line and is named for Dr. E. W. Hilgard, an early State geologist.

12. The UNIVERSITY OF MISSISSIPPI, foot of University Ave., occupies 640 acres of wooded hill lands, with the campus and the older, red brick, white-columned buildings half-hidden by the shade of great oak trees. The Lyceum building, erected in 1848, is the center. Greek Revival in style, its wide spreading wings and towering white columns set the ar-

chitectural theme of the campus. The other buildings are grouped in the form of two great tangential circles. The east circle, swinging around a low forested bowl of natural beauty, is formed by the older structures. The west circle, swinging up into the more open hills, includes the latest additions to the university's physical equipment. These newer buildings, erected with the $1,600,000 appropriated by the legislature in 1929 and designed by Frank F. Gates, are of Classical Revival design with the simple classic details. Constructed of light red brick, two and three stories high, they have pedimented porticos with white columns. To avoid the monotony of a single perspective the porticos vary in design; some are Doric, some are Corinthian.

The founding of the university was provided by an act of the legislature of 1840. Four years later the college was chartered and the first board of trustees of 13 members was appointed. In another four years the four-member faculty received the first enrollment of 80 students. These early students, sons of planters, brought their horses and slaves to college with them. The records indicate that the majority of them were poorly prepared for college work. Under a wise administration, however, the university grew in numbers and in public confidence, soon taking rank as one of the best equipped institutions in the country.

The advent of the War between the States in 1861 seriously interrupted the progress of the university. The students organized a company that became historic as the University Grays. The faculty, cancelling an order for the world's largest telescope, resigned. The university closed its doors. In the following four years the buildings sometimes were used by Confederate and sometimes by Federal troops. After the Battle of Shiloh they were used as a hospital for approximately 1,500 sick and wounded Confederate soldiers, 700 of whom are buried in the little cemetery near the campus.

From the opening of the university in 1848 to the year 1870, the "close curriculum" was in use. The university was handicapped by the tendency to keep it as a liberal arts and law school and to relegate vocational subjects to the land grant colleges. There was a prescribed course of study leading to the B. A. degree and a prescribed course of study leading to the LL.B. degree, and the student took precisely either one or the other of these courses. This classicalism caused the university gradually to be known as a rich man's school, an unfortunate position for an institution in a farming state. In the year 1870 the principle of the "elective" system was adopted, but so deeply had the idea of a rich man's school embedded itself in the minds of Mississippians that they sought to democratize the institution by condemning the fraternity system in a legislative committee's report. In 1912 the fraternities were abolished, not to return until 1926.

Beginning with the session of 1882–83, women have been admitted to the university on the same terms and conditions as men. In 1892 preparatory courses were discontinued and since that time the grade of educational work has advanced fully one year. The enrollment has increased from 167 to 1,361 (1936–37).

The university, in 1937, included nine divisions, ranging from the original College of Liberal Arts through the Extension Division to the Graduate School, founded in 1927. The majority of the graduate students enter the profession of law, with approximately 90 percent of the State's lawyers and politicians receiving their education at "Ole Miss."

◄◄◄◄◄◄◄◄◄◄◄◄◄◄◄◄◄◄☼►►►►►►►►►►►►►►►►►►

Tupelo

Railroad Station: Union Station, foot of Spring St., for St. Louis & San Francisco R.R. and Mobile & Ohio R.R.
Bus Station: Courthouse Square for Tri-State Transit Co. and Greyhound Bus Lines.
Taxis: Intra-city rates 10¢ per person.
Airport: Municipal, 3½ m. W. on Chesterville Pike, taxi fare 50¢, time 10 min. No scheduled service.

Information Service: Chamber of Commerce, Lyric Theater Bldg.

Accommodations: Four hotels; tourist camps.

Motion Picture Houses: Two.
Swimming: Municipal pool, N. Madison St. between Franklin and Jackson Sts. Rates 15¢ per person.
Golf: Tupelo Country Club, 1½ m. NW. on US 78 (R), 9 holes, moderate greens fee.

Annual Events: Northeast Mississippi-Alabama Fair, last of September or first of October.

TUPELO (289 alt., 6,361 pop.) is perhaps Mississippi's best example of what contemporary commentators call the "New South"—industry rising in the midst of agriculture and agricultural customs. It has a pattern-like consistency of one-story, clapboard residences and two- and three-story red brick business buildings. These business houses, with stores on the street level and offices or factories in the upper stories, lie knotted in the angle formed by the crossing of the Mobile & Ohio and Frisco railroad tracks. The main residential section, emerging gradually from the business district, stretches into the slowly climbing hills north and west. A number of the houses, rebuilt after the tornado of 1936, were constructed with the advice of a planning commission. They are mostly white, one-story Colonial in type, with green roofs and shutters. Yet here and there the line of bright new green against glistening white is broken by a deep brown roof or a two-story home of faced brick.

South of the Union Station, which forms the angle's apex, lies another residential section. This is a small, unpaved district of standardized four- and five-room houses sheltering the mill folk. The houses, painted alternately yellow trimmed in white and white trimmed in yellow, are set in unsodded yards behind sagging picket and wire fences. They were built by the cotton mill and are rented to its employees. Biting off the northeast corner of the district is the recreational ground with a diminutive baseball diamond and grandstand. Facing South Spring Street across the ballground is the low, one-story red brick grammar school built especially for the children of cotton mill employees. This section of Tupelo is referred to either as "South Tupelo" or "Mill Town."

Looking down upon the residential section proper from the northern ends of Madison and Green Streets, and fringing the town eastward into the flat bottom land, which lies across the Mobile & Ohio tracks, is the Negro section. The houses on the hilltops are more or less substantial five- and six-room structures and, in a great many instances, are owned by their occupants. Here, too, are the two Negro churches, of red brick construction, with square spires and Gothic windows, and the Lee County Training School, an accredited high school for Negroes. But, as if influenced by the topography, the quality of the houses drops with the land, until those around Park Lake and in the low flats are hardly more than shacks. It is in the latter section, called "Shakerag," that a majority of the cooks, nurses, and house servants of Tupelo live. A few of the Negro men of Tupelo are professional men but the majority are unskilled laborers. The Negroes compose 39.5 percent of Tupelo's population.

Key city to an agricultural area circling on a 25-mile radius, Tupelo took its early wealth from rich black land and, never quite breaking with the land, invested in industry. It is a pioneer city at heart and was among the first to practice successfully the economic philosophy that factory employees should live on subsistence farms outside of town and commute to and from their work. Widely publicized as the "First TVA City," it earlier achieved distinction among Southern cities for the concrete roads approaching it. In its courthouse were written the first drainage laws in the nation.

With those who work at the cotton mill excepted, the majority of factory laborers in Tupelo are girls and young women who form a surplus supply of labor on surrounding farms. Each morning a fleet of busses gathers up the workers and brings them into town; each afternoon the same busses return the workers to their homes. The cotton mill laborers are stable, many of them of the group who moved into the new mill houses built for them when the mill was first opened; others are the children, now grown, of these workers.

The region around Tupelo was a part of the land obtained from the Chickasaw Indians by the Treaty of Pontotoc in 1832. Immediately after the opening of the land, settlers from the eastern seaboard States moved in and by 1848 had established themselves as well-to-do farmers. In that year, C. C. Thompson built a store on land belonging to Judge W. R. Harris, one of the wealthy prairie planters, and named the site Harrisburg. Within three years two stores were built. The village continued to thrive until 1859, when the tracks of the Mobile & Ohio R.R. were laid two miles to the east and a gradual abandonment of Harrisburg began. The people moved east, down from the upper slope of the ridge into the flat, marshy bottoms, where there were no stores or dwelling houses, but a railroad and plenty of tupelo gum trees. By the end of the first year, the first arrivals had built a store, a temporary railroad station, and two saloons. These stood opposite the present freight depot, on the east side of the railroad. Because of the nearness of a small pond lined with tupelo gum trees, the new station was called Gum Pond. But later the first citizens wished to honor the trees that had supplied the timber for their homes, so they changed the name to Tupelo (Ind., *lodging place*).

During the War between the States General Beauregard retreated to Tupelo after the battle of Shiloh, and encamped here during the summer of 1862. Later General Forrest made his headquarters in the Younger home. On July 14, 1864, the Confederate army under the command of Stephen D. Lee paused at Tupelo to give battle to the pursuing Union army commanded by A. J. Smith. The two armies met on the hilltop where the village of Harrisburg had been. It was the last major battle and one of the bloodiest fought in Mississippi. Cavalry General Forrest, whose wounded foot forced him from horseback into a carriage, drove madly up and down the Confederate lines, swearing at officers and giving orders wholesale. One of the orders miscarried, and the battle was lost for the Confederates—an incident which Joe Smith, once of the Forrest cavalry, described as "making the General so mad he stunk." But though the Confederate troops were beaten back, the Federals retreated two days later. Robert S. Henry, in his *Story of the Confederacy*, says: "General Smith was uneasy in his mind. That night he burned Harrisburg and started on his retreat to Memphis. He left so hurriedly that he abandoned 250 of his seriously wounded, their wounds undressed, to be found by the Confederates in Tupelo, a ghastly sight with open wounds fly-blown and festering.... It was a strange spectacle, an army which had just won a pitched battle drawing back from an enemy of half its own size which it had just beaten." In the winter of 1864–65, 20,000 Confederates rested at Tupelo.

On October 6, 1866, Lee County was formed from Itawamba and Pontotoc Counties, and after considerable wrangling on the part of the older towns, Tupelo was selected as the county seat, and a courthouse was built. This raised Tupelo from the category of village to that of town, and brought to it the adventurous young men who cut themselves off from established families in other communities, and who later forsook the land for the machine, thus shaping Tupelo into an industrial city. Cultural progress was manifested on September 1, 1871, when, according to John Thompson's announcement in the Tupelo *Journal*, "school was opened today in the new building near the Baptist Church with 30 pupils."

In 1875 the town was grouped around Main Street, with three brick store buildings, a brick bank, a courthouse, and several business houses. The population was slightly less than 100. There were no sidewalks or paved streets, and the large area between Main Street and the courthouse square served the farm people in town to trade as a "hitching yard." In wet weather the little holes caused by the restless pawing of horses' hoofs on the earth would fill with water and turn green. The hitching yard was also the "swapping ground," where farmer met merchant and traded produce for merchandise.

In 1887 the Memphis & Birmingham R.R., now the St. Louis & San Francisco, called the Frisco, swerved slightly out of a more direct course to cross the Mobile & Ohio tracks at Tupelo. This gave the town rail transportation in four directions, and enabled it to develop in a more substantial way. Connecting streets, now called Spring, Broadway, and Green, were cut, and Main Street was extended. In 1890 electric lights were installed and one year later a charter of incorporation was granted by the State. Then, with electric lights, a city charter, and thousands of "bottom acres" made available for farming by a system of 36 drainage canals (the latter of which were the outcome of the first drainage laws passed in the nation), the citizens financed one of the first cotton mills in the State.

The cotton mill was Tupelo's first step away from the land, but since its establishment the growth of the city has been largely identical with the growth of the cotton goods manufacture in the State. With money dug from the earth rather than with "outside capital," a work-shirt factory was built, as well as a woman's dress factory, a factory for making baby clothes, and finally, a cottonseed products plant. Outside capital was represented in a compress and a fertilizer factory.

Tupelo still retains its ties with the land. Cattle breeding and dairying led to the establishment of a condensery, whose trucks return each afternoon loaded with cans of milk picked up at surrounding farms. Each Wednesday and Thursday cattle auctions draw buyers from as far as North Dakota.

On October 11, 1933, the city entered into TVA's first contract for the purchase of power to be generated at Wilson Dam, 75 miles northeast of Tupelo. Initial service was inaugurated February 7, 1934. With a total first year's saving to residential and commercial consumers amounting to $53,000, consumption for residential users increased 114 percent and for commercial users 77 percent.

On April 5, 1936, a violent tornado struck old Harrisburg, now a subdivision, swept through Willis Heights, another subdivision, and roared down into the hitherto hill-protected city of Tupelo. In 33 seconds, 201 persons were killed, 1,000 injured; hosts of others wandered helplessly, without homes, schools, or places of worship. The great oak trees lay broken or uprooted. In less than a minute Tupelo received the most disastrous blow ever delivered to a Mississippi town. Within six months, however, Tupelo had built new homes, repaired the churches, and designed new, modern schools.

On April 8, 1937, approximately 100 cotton mill employees struck for higher wages, the first strike in the history of the mill. Unable to reach an agreement with the strikers, the board of directors of the mill voted to liquidate, throwing not only the strikers but also an additional 350 employees out of work. The cotton mill workers were not organized, but since the strike the garment workers have formed a local union.

Tupelo's history and character are epitomized in the view from the south front of the Union Station. In autumn, the bottom lands just over the tracks at the left are white with bolls of growing cotton; directly to the right, South Spring Street is blocked with trailers, trucks, and wagons piled high with dusty bales. Swarming about the bales, in and out among the vehicles, are buyers and sellers, who pull a large handful from each bale, hastily grade the fiber, and, again hastily, drop the fiber to the street to bargain with the farmer. Within a two-block area of the Union Station the cotton is ginned, compressed, dyed, made into yarn, into thread, into cloth, and finally into shirts, dresses, and baby clothes. Within the same area, the seed is milled for oil, hulls, and meal.

Tour—*1.2m*

S. from Main St. on S. Spring St.

1. TUPELO COTTON MILL (R) S. Spring St. *(open weekdays 8-4; tours),* one of the largest cotton producing units in the South, manufactures more than 25 miles of cloth per day. The mill operates in two buildings, one on each side of the street. The building on the left, where the cotton is dyed and spun into thread, is a two-story, dilapidated red brick structure with a flat roof and many windows. Adjacent to it is a one-story addition called the dyeing shed. The building on the right is well ventilated, of brick, and two stories in height. In this building the thread, conveyed by cable across the street, is respun for the looms, then woven into cloth. In front of the building is the small, brick, bungalow-shaped office building.

L. from S. Spring St. on Elizabeth St. across the M. & O. R.R.

2. TUPELO FISH HATCHERY (R) Elizabeth St. *(open weekdays 8-4; tours),* owned and operated by the U.S. Government, is the only fish hatchery in the State. Here in artificial pools of fresh water among green lawns and weeping willow trees, the Government propagates fish for the lakes and streams of the State. The well-kept grounds are Tupelo's favorite picnicking resort. The hatchery is often called "Private" John Allen's Hatchery, because his influence while a member of the House of Representatives helped procure it for his home town, Tupelo.

R. from Elizabeth St. on Green St.

3. TUPELO GARMENT PLANT (R) Green St. *(open weekdays 8-4; tours),* manufactures work and dress shirts in a three-story rectangular red brick building paralleling the Frisco railroad tracks. On a lower floor of this building, cloth, in many layers, is cut to pattern by a keen-bladed electric knife; then sent to an upstairs sewing room to be stitched on machines by women operators. Each operator performs a single operation. When the shirt is completed it is inspected, ironed, and wrapped for shipment.

R. from Green St. on Clark St.; L. on S. Spring St.

4. REED'S MANUFACTURING PLANT, S. Spring St. (R) bet. Magazine and Clark Sts. *(open weekdays 8-4; tours)*, occupies the second and third floors of a three-story red brick building of modern design. Six hundred or more women operators produce women's work dresses, smocks, and aprons.

L. from S. Spring St. on Main St.

5. MILAM MANUFACTURING PLANT, Main St. (L) bet. Broadway and Green Sts. *(open weekdays 8-4; tours)*, operates on the second floor of a commercial building. This is the only factory in the State that produces children's wear. Various garments are shipped to retail and department stores, the majority being the baby aprons which this company originated.

6. The BOULDER, parkway at intersection of Main and Church Sts., is a granite stone commemorating De Soto's alleged march through here in 1540-41. It was placed by the Colonial Dames.

L. from Main St. on S. Church St.; R. on Carnation St.

7. CARNATION MILK PLANT (R) Carnation St. *(open weekdays 8-4; tours)*, occupies a modern two-and-a-half-story building of white stucco, with a tall white smokestack. The building stands on a terrace. The plant receives approximately 17,500,000 pounds of milk from the surrounding farms each year and condenses it into about 30,000,000 cans of condensed milk. The milk is poured into large vats, then passed through copper condensers to the tin containers or cans.

POINTS OF INTEREST IN ENVIRONS

Tupelo Homestead Resettlement Project, *5.9 m. (see Tour 4)*; Tombigbee State Park, *7.4 m. (see Tour 9)*; Old Walker Home, *4.2 m. (see Tour 14)*.

Vicksburg

Railroad Station: Cherry St. for Illinois Central System.
Bus Station: 800 South St. for Tri-State Transit Co., Dixie Greyhound Lines, Oliver Coach Line.
Airport: Municipal, 6 m. NE., on Vicksburg-Oak Ridge Road. No scheduled service.
Ferry Line: Mississippi River Ferry Co. between Vicksburg and Delta, La. Landing at foot of Clay St. and Mississippi River. Fare for automobile and driver, 50¢; additional passengers, 15¢ each.
Bridge Service: Mississippi River Bridge, fare for automobile with driver, $1.25; additional passengers, 15¢.

Taxis: 10¢ up.
Intra-city bus line: Fare 5¢.
Traffic Regulations: Turns may be made in either direction at intersections of all streets except where traffic lights direct otherwise. Right turn on red traffic light. Downtown parking space free.
Accommodations: Three hotels; rooming and boarding houses; tourist camps.
Information Service: Chamber of Commerce, Carroll Hotel, Clay St.
Radio Station: WQBC (1360 kc.)
Motion Picture Houses: Four.
Athletics: Y.M.C.A. on Clay St.; City League Baseball, City Park, Drummond St.
Swimming: Mount Memorial Swimming Pool, municipal, Drummond St.
Tennis: City Park, Drummond St. *(free).*
Golf: National Park Golf Course, 18 holes, reasonable greens fee, Union Ave. just outside Vicksburg National Military Park.
Parks: Vicksburg National Military Park, free guides, Administration Bldg., Pemberton Ave., or Contact Station, at Memorial Arch, Clay St.
Fishing: On rivers and nearby lakes.
Annual Events: Historic Tour Week, held in Spring; Annual National Assembly of Descendants of Participants of Campaign, Siege and Defense of Vicksburg, held in Spring.

VICKSBURG (206 alt., 22,943 pop.), Mississippi's third largest city and major river port, is a leisurely town, rich in historic associations and natural beauty. Sprawling over the highest of a line of bluffs and overlooking the junction of the Yazoo Canal and the Mississippi River, it is a city of precipitous streets, natural terraces, and wooded ravines. During the War between the States Vicksburg was called the "Gibraltar of the Confederacy" and was the objective of the western campaigns. Since the war, and without relinquishing the customs and traditions of a river community, it has emerged from reconstruction and yellow fever into the "Hill City," an inland port of the New South.

The business district, dominated by the tall, sandy-colored cupola of the ante-bellum courthouse, parallels and climbs abruptly from the river front, an architectural mixture of ante-bellum porticos, gingerbread ornaments of the 1890's and modern steel and concrete buildings two and three stories high. Higher among the bluffs, clinging in scattered groups to the less precarious terraces, are the residences. Both the ante-bellum homes, placed by right of priority on the comparatively secure terraces, and the newer homes, built after the War between the States on streets that often are almost sheer, have a stern, militaristic appearance. Scattered about the city, clustered in the ravine bottoms, and facing the river from north Washington Street, are the Negro quarters. Infrequently these homes are solid brick houses abandoned by white persons; more often they are two- and three-room cabins, dwarfed by the backdrop of towering, steep-sided cliffs.

Vicksburg is the seat of a cotton county that supports gins, compresses, and warehouses; as a start to a new industry a garment factory was built in 1936. But as yet the city's chief business comes from the river that shaped its destiny. Barge lines have their terminals here for the shipment of hardwood lumber, cotton, and cattle; the Government main-

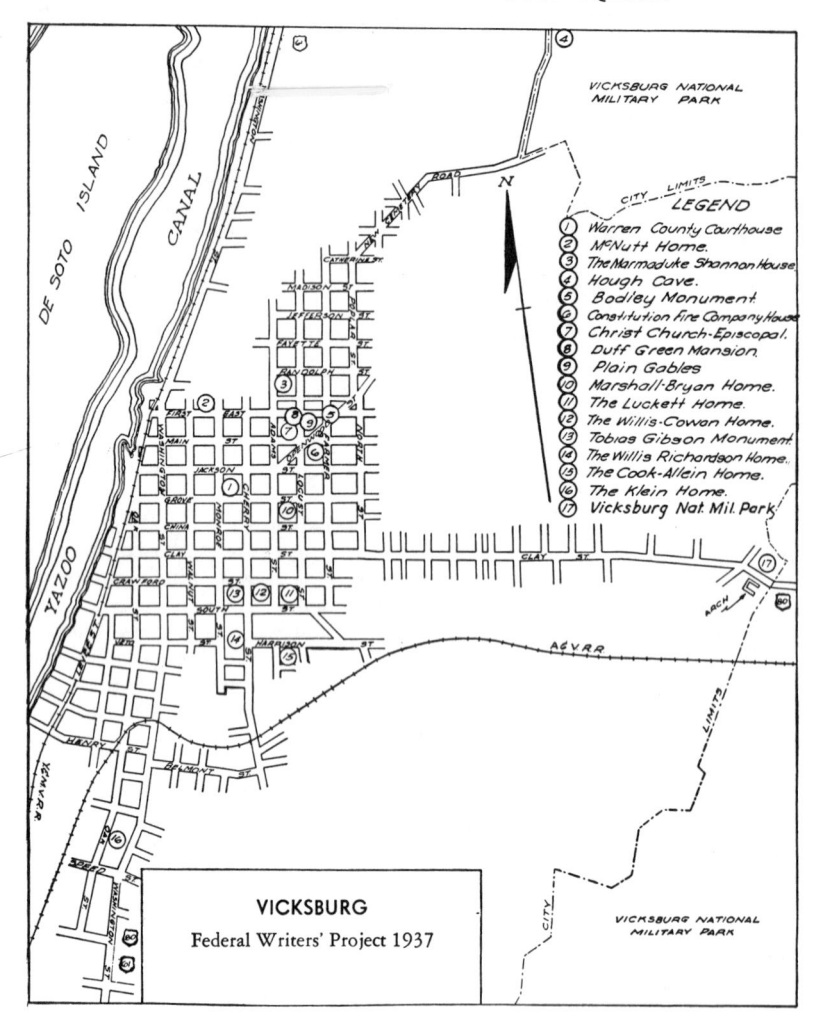

tains here the river fleet and the general headquarters of flood control work on the Mississippi and its tributaries; nearby is the United States Waterways Experiment Station *(see Tour 2)*. This government work requires skilled machinists and mechanics, technical engineers and draftsmen, while the handling of cotton, shipping, and levee building demand hardy, unskilled labor. Because stevedoring and roustabouting are jobs still left to the Negro, Vicksburg's Negro population is 51.9 percent of the total, the third largest urban percentage in the State. Under the leadership of Bishop Green, one of the outstanding Negro leaders of the State, the Negroes of Vicksburg were given an impetus to social and educational improvement. Today they have their own professional group, a modern, well-equipped Y. M. C. A., a private school of approved high school standing (St. Mary's), and two high schools, units of the city school system. But "Catfish Row" along the river still exists, and it is here that a majority of the Negroes spend their leisure hours.

The bluffs over which Vicksburg is spread are formed in part of a peculiar loess formation, a brown dust, or more accurately, a rock flour, blown eons ago from the Mississippi basin. The loess, caked 20 to 40 feet thick on all elevations and covered with jungle-like vegetation, often rises in sheer precipices. This makes a wild, rugged contour that has the appearance of distant castles, and gives to Vicksburg the air of a city in perpetual siege. This is not inappropriate, however, for by a siege Vicksburg is best known; and a pattern of violence following land speculation and turbulent river trade stands out, like the bluffs themselves, in the city's history.

In 1790 the Spaniards recognized the military advantages of the bluffs, obtained a land grant from the Indians, and established an outpost here. The following year, they built a fort on the highest hill and called it Nogales, for the many walnut trees that grew on it. Later, the flatboatmen and other voyagers, who sighted the point above the great bend in the river, renamed it Walnut Hills. In 1814 the Rev. Newitt Vick, a Methodist minister, came from Virginia and established one of the first missions in Mississippi in "the open woods." This was a clearing, six miles east of the present city, denuded of its timber by the Indians who had made the Walnut Hills their camping grounds.

Vick, evidently, was as good a business man as he was a minister. The War of 1812 was over; cotton culture had been made highly profitable by the introduction of slaves and the invention of the cotton gin. The first steamboat appeared on the Mississippi River, and settlers poured in from Virginia, the Carolinas, Kentucky, and the uplands of the Eastern Seaboard States—so Vick bought another tract of land, this time a piece that fronted the river, and planned to lay out a city. In 1819, however, before his enterprise was well begun, he and his wife died of yellow fever and his son-in-law, John Lane, as executor of the estate, sold the city lots and started the town. In 1825 the people named their sprawling village Vicksburg in Vick's honor.

True to its founder's expectation, Vicksburg became the export point for central Mississippi and the settlement, like other frontier river towns, expanded rapidly. Wagons, pulled by six and eight yokes of oxen, hauled bales of cotton from a radius of 100 miles to the little inland port, where it was stacked high on the cargo decks of river boats and shipped downstream to New Orleans. Merchandise from Europe was tugged laboriously upstream by churning "paddle wheelers" to be landed here, then hauled across the hills and through the bogs to inland communities. With the crops and water routes and slave labor to be metamorphosed into wealth

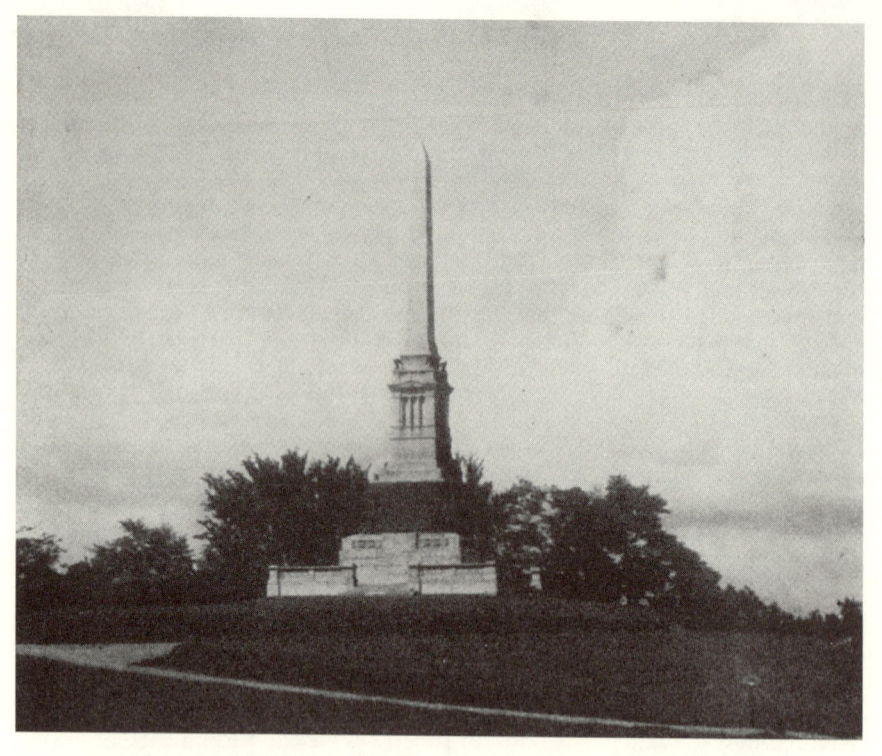

MISSISSIPPI MONUMENT, VICKSBURG NATIONAL MILITARY PARK

and culture, men of means came down the river and down the Natchez Trace to add new energy to the thriving community.

The first settlers, full of years and prosperity, soon lost themselves in their "segars," their families, their palatial homes, and their gardens which stretched beyond the rugged terraces down to the river itself. But by 1830 newcomers composed a majority of the 3,000 population. They were second sons of families well established in Eastern States, mostly lawyers, doctors, and professional men, alone in a frontier society with a tendency toward a more energetic and unrestrained mode of life. They lived well but recklessly, speculated in land, indulged in oratory, and took the chances of surviving a duel. They lived in the hotels and office buildings and spent their leisure hours lounging in each other's rooms, in the bars and gambling houses, or in drilling away the hours in aristocratic military companies. Their day was colored by an extravagant form of chivalry, but they opened new lands and built the town which became famous in the golden age of the old Deep South.

Like a strenuous boy, Vicksburg suffered violently from the pangs of eating too well and growing too fast. With trade and expansion came speculation, embezzlement, and graft. With prosperity came lawlessness and vice. The scum of the river gamblers gathered at the foot of the

Walnut Hills, and became an open menace. Wagon drivers, more often white farmers conveying their whole crop into Vicksburg in a single wagon, hated broadcloth coats and tall beaver hats. They wore coarse, dingy, yellow or blue linsey-woolsey and broad-brimmed hats, and with long rawhide whips in their hands and plenty of whisky under their belts, they blustered and roared through the town. Flatboatmen joined the wagoners in their blustering and the young professional gentlemen in their gambling. These "ring-tailed roarers" from the river spent their working hours fighting swift currents and hairpin bends, and their time on shore swearing they could "throw down, drag out, and lick any man in the country," and proving it. Beatings, knifings, and shootings occurred daily, and women appeared on the streets at the risk of insult.

On the 4th of July, 1835, a drunken gambler wandered into the Springfield section of the city and while there insulted Captain Brungrad's military company. The indignant officers of the company placed him under guard but, upon his threats of dire vengeance, released him. That evening the company returned to the courthouse to find him heavily armed and prepared to fight. He was seized, disarmed, and carried to the outskirts of the town. There he was whipped, tarred and feathered, and ordered to leave immediately. His enraged associates, encouraged by the number and reckless character of their patrons, denounced and threatened the citizens who had heretofore patronized them. Sentiment against the gamblers increased and at a public meeting the citizens decided to run the leaders of the gamblers out of town. They appointed a committtee to serve notice on the gamblers. But when Dr. Bodley led his committee down the steep incline to the river front and called out the warning, the gamblers, barricaded in a house, answered by shooting and killing Dr. Bodley. In retaliation the citizens lynched five of the gamblers in the city cemetery and gave a sixth back to the river from which he had come, setting him adrift in a small skiff with his hands pinioned behind him.

With the gamblers under control, Vicksburg next had a "war" with the flatboatmen. In order to collect a heavy tax from the flatboatmen, a company of soldiers was sent down to the waterfront with instructions either to get the tax money or, failing in that, to blast the flatboats from the river. But the flatboatmen, tougher and braver than the gamblers, were also shrewder. They fraternized with the soldiers, passed around several jugs, and swapped tall stories until the soldiers forgot their mission.

The first newspaper issued in Vicksburg was *The Republican* in 1825. In 1837 the Vicksburg *Tri-Weekly Sentinel* began publication. But the pattern of violence extended to the press. Within 22 years the vituperations of the first five editors of the *Sentinel* caused their violent deaths.

When the Union was severed, Federals and Confederates alike recognized the strategic importance of the Mississippi River. With the South in control of the river, Middle Western commerce would be stagnant; with the North in control, the Confederacy would be split in two. Because its strategic position on the Walnut Hills commanded the river,

Vicksburg ceased commercial activities early in the war and became an armed camp.

In June 1862, Admiral Farragut ran the Federal gunboats up the river to the great bend at Vicksburg. After several unsuccessful long range bombardments he withdrew his forces. In November of the same year, General Grant at Corinth and General Sherman at Memphis planned a converging attack from the north. Grant's line of communication was cut by Forrest's Cavalry and his supply depot *(see HOLLY SPRINGS)* was destroyed by Van Dorn, so that he, too, was forced to withdraw. Sherman hardly fared better. Descending the river in December with 30,000 troops, his command was hurled back with heavy losses by Confederate shot from the bluffs in a short, decisive charge on Chickasaw Bayou, just north of the city.

The new year, 1863, found General Grant in command of the Union forces with orders to compel the fall of Vicksburg. With the city seemingly impregnable from the north and from the river, he made numerous attempts to reach the rear of Vicksburg by a series of bayou expeditions. But these failed and during the remainder of the winter he sought to avoid exposing his army to the Confederate fire from the bluff, even attempting to cut a new channel for the river across the narrow tongue of land opposite the city. Spring floods kept the lowlands under water and President Lincoln lent every possible assistance, but the General's engineers could not persuade the river to change its mind.

In April, however, Grant decided to risk running the batteries. He ordered Admiral Porter to slip his gunboats and transports past Vicksburg by night, while he marched his army on a wide detour down the river through Louisiana. Although the Confederates fired part of the town to throw light on the river and the night was punctured with the bellowing fire of siege guns, Grant's desperate maneuver was successful. On April 30, 1863, under the protection of Porter's 80 vessels, he recrossed the river with his army at Bruinsburg *(see Tour 3, Sec b)*, 30 miles below the city. Cut off from the north and forced to live off the country, his strategy lay in clearing the territory south and east of Vicksburg and then carrying the fight to the city itself. This he accomplished by a series of brilliant maneuvers *(see Tours 2 and 3, Sec. b)*, which drove the Confederates and their general, J. C. Pemberton, into Vicksburg. A young girl's diary aptly describes the situation: "I never hope to witness again such a scene as our routed army. From twelve o'clock until late in the night the streets and roads were jammed with wagons, cannons, horses, mules, stock, sheep, everything that you can imagine that appertains to an army, being brought hurriedly within the retrenchment. Nothing like order prevailed, of course, and divisions, regiments and brigades were broken and separated. . . . What is to become of all the living things in this place, when the boats begin shelling, God only knows."

In Vicksburg, however, the Confederate lines were reformed on the innermost of the two parallel ridges that rim the city, and the Federals were halted. Twice, on the 19th and 22nd of May, 1863, the encircling

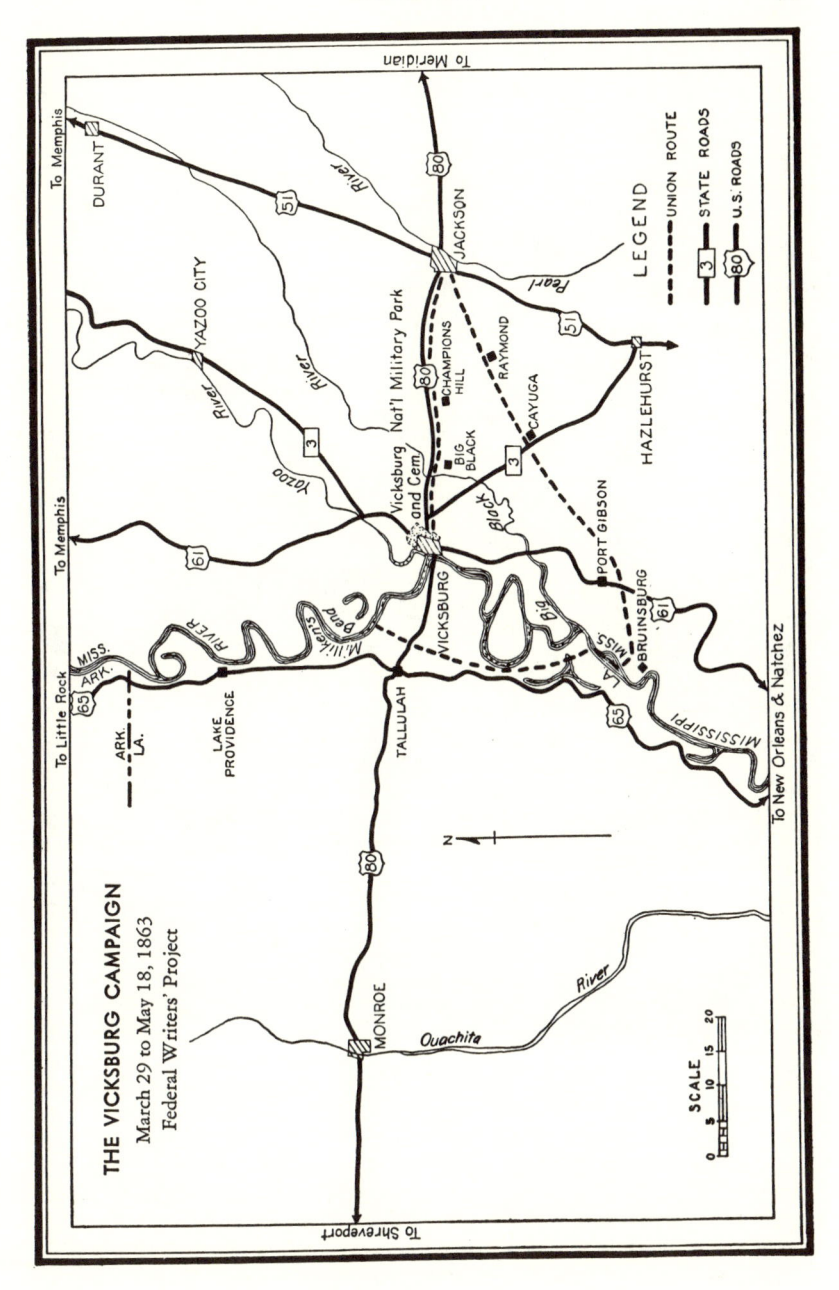

VICKSBURG

THE VICKSBURG CAMPAIGN
March 29 to May 18, 1863
Federal Writers' Project

WARREN COUNTY COURTHOUSE, VICKSBURG

wave of blue charged up the steep western rims to dash itself to pieces against the stubborn gray line. Met with such repulses, Grant, with characteristic stubbornness, decided to starve the defenders into submission. For 47 days and nights his land and water batteries hammered incessantly at the city. Many residents fled to caves in the hillsides. Food became scarce. Mule meat was a delicacy to starving inhabitants, and the soldiers were put on rations of fat bacon and stale bread. With the ranks of his army depleted by hunger, disease, and exposure, and with no indication of succor in sight, General Pemberton surrendered on the 4th of July, 1863. Five days later the Confederate garrison at Port Hudson also capitulated, and the Mississippi River was open.

The siege and aftermath of the war paralyzed the city for many years. During the carpetbag and reconstruction era that followed, the town was plunged into debt by mismanagement. Negroes in civil office had the support of the State "carpetbag" government in their defiance of old laws and the making of new ones. The white citizens differed politically and, at first, could not unite. But in 1875 they met and as one united party demanded the resignation of Negro officials. The Negroes refused to resign. One Negro, named Crosby, carried the matter to Governor Ames in Jackson and was advised by the Governor to defend his office with bloodshed if necessary. Returning to Vicksburg, Crosby circulated handbills over the county, urging all Negroes to be in Vicksburg on a specified Monday morning. Rumor that 1,400 armed Negroes were marching upon the town by three different roads spread through the city. Once more Vicksburg armed itself against attack. Streets were filled with weeping women and terrified children. Squads of armed white men hurried to the three approaches. Groups of Negroes appeared on the roads, some orderly, others disorderly. After the fight, white men claimed that the Negroes fired first, but the records are not clear. Fifteen Negroes and one white man were killed; 30 Negroes were taken prisoners. It was the end of Negro and carpetbag rule in Vicksburg.

This fresh start, however, was followed by cataclysms. In 1876 the erratic Mississippi River, which had so successfully defeated General Grant's efforts to cut a new channel, broke through the narrow tongue north of Vicksburg and made a new channel for itself. The city was left high and dry and Vicksburg seemed destined to disappear as had other towns that the "Father of Waters" sired only to abandon. However, one day a little boy suggested the possibility of bringing the Yazoo River down in front of the city through a chain of lakes where the boys went fishing. The idea was found practical. Under Government engineering, the Yazoo's mouth was closed and its waters were diverted through a canal into the old Mississippi River bed; on December 22, 1902, Vicksburg again had a river coursing along the base of its bluffs. Thus Vicksburg achieved the distinction of being moved from a river to a canal by an Act of Congress.

The financial depression of 1873, followed by a frenzied era of railroad building in the 1880's, was the death knell to river trade. By the end of the century the railroads had driven out the steamboats, and up to 1917 there was little or no river traffic. In that year the United States entered the World War and the Government, seeking to relieve the terrific strain upon the railroads, subsidized a barge line to operate on the Mississippi River. After the war, the subsidy was not withdrawn,

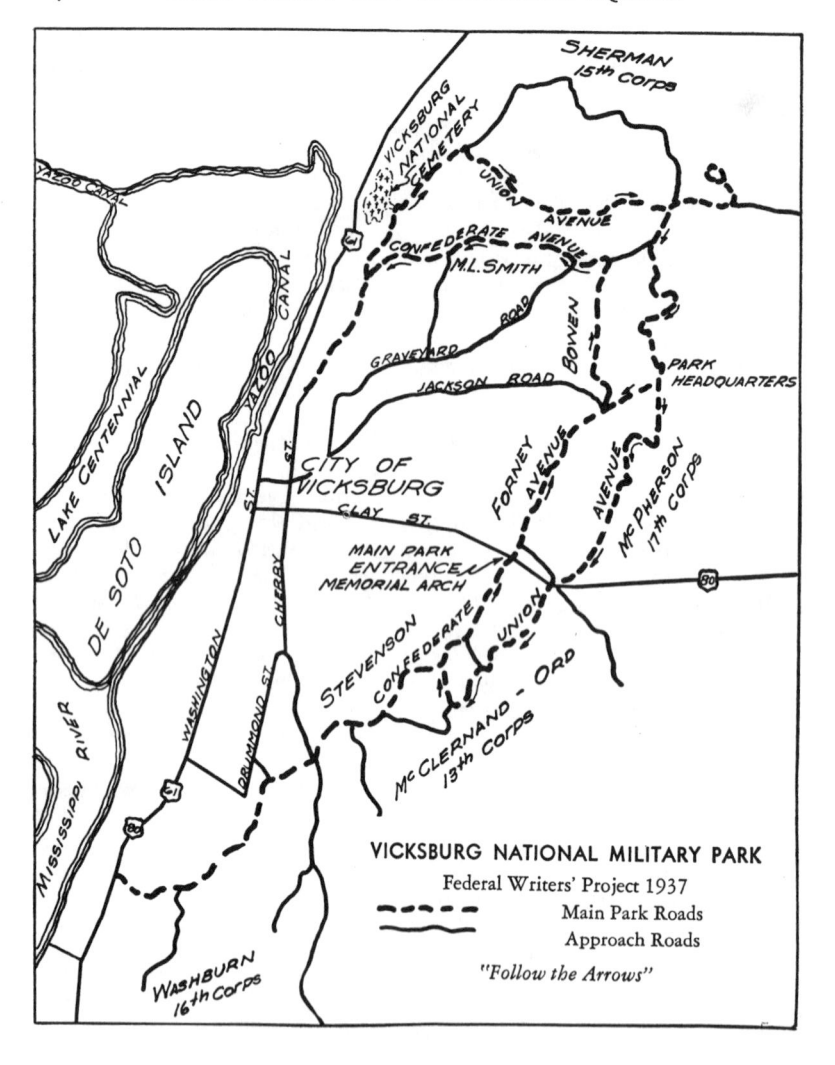

VICKSBURG NATIONAL MILITARY PARK
Federal Writers' Project 1937
- - - - - Main Park Roads
———— Approach Roads
"Follow the Arrows"

but was left to develop further river traffic. The profits made by the Government line led to the establishment of private lines, and at present (1937) the river is making great strides in regaining its prestige as a transportation route.

On June 28, 1879, Congress created the Mississippi River Commission to survey and improve the river channel and banks for better navigation, to prevent floods, and to promote commerce and postal service. By 1882 the commission had organized four operating engineer districts with Vicksburg in the third district.

When the Mississippi River overflowed in the devastating flood of 1927, Vicksburg again became a Gibraltar, with thousands of refugees rushing to its hills to escape the raging waters. Largely because of the flood damage to the lower valley and the menace of the river, the headquarters of the Mississippi River Commission were moved from St. Louis to Vicksburg in 1930. Shortly afterward, the United States Waterways Experiment Station, where the problem of controlling the mighty Mississippi is studied in a special laboratory, was established. The river commission's fleet and shops, known as the "U. S. Government Fleet," are on the river front just north of the business district.

◄◄◄◄◄◄◄◄◄◄◄◄◄◄◄◄◄☼►►►►►►►►►►►►►►►►►

Tour 1–*3.6m.*

E. from Washington St. on Grove St.

1. WARREN COUNTY COURTHOUSE, Grove St. (L) between Monroe and Cherry Sts. and extending to Jackson St., dominates Vicksburg from one of the highest points in the city. Designed by William Weldon and constructed by George and Thomas Weldon, who used slave labor, the structure is of Greek Revival architecture. Four identical façades having broad galleries, upper balconies, and fluted Ionic columns extend the full length of each side of the building. Begun in 1858, it was completed in 1861. During the siege of 1863 the courthouse was struck often by cannon balls and the original cupola was riddled by gunfire from Admiral Farragut's gunboats. The present cupola was added at a later date.

L. from Grove St. on Monroe St.

2. McNUTT HOME, NW. corner Monroe and First East Sts. *(open by appointment)*, built by Alexander McNutt, former Governor of Mississippi (1838–42), is said to be the oldest home in Vicksburg. A white frame house, two stories high, it has the straight, boxlike lines and steep roof of the Colonial New England type. The house contains a fine collection of antique furnishings, including a set of Dresden china more than 100 years old and other pieces handed down from one generation to another. In the side yard overlooking the river is the grave of a Confederate soldier, Lieut. D. N. McGill, who died June 4, 1863, from injuries received in the defense of Vicksburg.

McNUTT HOME, VICKSBURG

R. from Monroe St. on First East St.; L. on Adams St.
3. The MARMADUKE SHANNON HOUSE, 701 Adams St. *(open by appointment)*, was the home of one of Vicksburg's first crusading editors. In this low, one-story frame house, according to Vicksburg legend, on dark and blustery nights stalk the ghosts of the notorious gamblers who murdered Dr. Hugh Bodley. The large dormer window on the north and the portico with its gable roof, supported by plain square columns, are the most noticeable features of this century-old house.

R. from Adams St. on Fayette St.; L. on Farmer St.; R. on Catherine St.; L. on New Cemetery Road 0.5 m.; L. on Lovers' Lane 0.4 m.
4. HOUGH CAVE, Lovers' Lane at sign *(open by appointment)*, is one of the three remaining caves used by citizens of Vicksburg when seeking protection from gunfire and cannonball during the siege. Apparently this cave was private (though many were communal) and was ideally situated, well protected from fire from the Federal fleet on one side and from the rain of bullets from land forces on the other. It was easily accessible from a nearby road.

Retrace Lovers' Lane, New Cemetery Road and Catherine St.; L. on Farmer St.
5. BODLEY MONUMENT, intersection of Farmer and Openwood Sts., is a plain granite slab erected by the community to the memory of Dr. Hugh Bodley, murdered by gamblers July 5, 1835, "while defending the morals of Vicksburg." The monument was first placed in the yard of the old Presbyterian Church; later it was removed to the triangle.

R. from Farmer St. on Main St.

6. CONSTITUTION FIRE COMPANY HOUSE, 1200 Main St., is a gray brick building with tall arched doors and bell tower. It was built in 1835 for the volunteer fire company, composed of the city's most aristocratic young gentlemen. Motorized equipment has replaced the faithful horse, and the company is employed by the city.

R. from Main St. on Locust St.

7. CHRIST CHURCH (EPISCOPAL), NW. corner Locust and Main Sts., is the fourth oldest church in the State. Of brick construction, with ivy-covered walls, it is of English Gothic design. The cornerstone was laid in April 1839 by the fighting bishop, Gen. Leonidas Polk, later killed in the service of the Confederacy. The edifice was completed between 1842 and 1845.

8. The DUFF GREEN MANSION, SW. corner Locust and First East Sts. *(open)*, famed for its magnificent balls in ante-bellum days, has been in turn a private home, a Confederate hospital, a domicile for dependent old ladies, and (1937) a Salvation Army home. Built in the 1840's by Duff Green, the design of the four-story, red brick mansion, with its exquisite iron lacework galleries, is one of the finest examples of the Queen Anne influence that crept into Vicksburg's ante-bellum architecture.

9. PLAIN GABLES, 805 Locust St. *(private)*, was built in 1835 by a brother of Dr. Hugh Bodley. The Greek Revival structure, Doric in style, graces a high terrace surrounded by well-kept grounds in which is an old hand-turn bucket pump. Although considerably damaged by shell fire during the siege, the house has been completely restored. A notable feature is the flight of steps leading up to the terrace with its ancient iron railing and entrance gate.

◄◄◄◄◄◄◄◄◄◄◄◄◄◄◄◄☼►►►►►►►►►►►►►►►►►►

Tour 2—*5.3m.*

E. from Washington St. on Grove St.

10. The MARSHALL-BRYAN HOME, 1128 Grove St. *(open by appointment)*, was built about 1835 by the Rev. C. K. Marshall. son-in-law of the founder of Vicksburg. The original building consists of four large, square rooms and a reception hall but later two other units were added. Six graceful Ionic columns support the roof of the front gallery and the elaborately carved front entrance is a good example of

Greek Revival architecture. The house was untouched during the shelling of the city in 1863.

Retrace Grove St.; L. on Adams St.; L. on Crawford St.

11. The LUCKETT HOME, 1116 Crawford St. *(open by appointment)*, was built in 1830. Originally, the house was a one-story structure atop a small hill. Later this part became the upper portion of a two-story building, the hillock having been dug away and a sturdy ground floor built. This older portion now has an outside stairway from the pavement to the upper gallery. During the bombardments in 1863 a shell tore through the upper portion of the house. Following the surrender of the city, officers of the Federal army were billeted in the upstairs rooms, while their horses were stabled downstairs.

Retrace Crawford St.

12. The WILLIS-COWAN HOME, 1018 Crawford St. *(open by appointment)*, is on a high terrace, almost flush with the sidewalk. An austere two-story brick house painted gray, built about 1840, it was one of Vicksburg's most notable ante-bellum homes. During the siege, it was lent by its owners to General Pemberton for his headquarters and remained so until the fall of Vicksburg. It was also one of the childhood homes of Vicksburg's philanthropist, Mrs. Junius Ward Johnson.

13. In the METHODIST CHURCHYARD, SW. corner Crawford and Cherry Sts., is the *TOBIAS GIBSON MONUMENT*. A white marble shaft marks the grave of the Rev. Tobias Gibson, pioneer Protestant preacher of the Walnut Hills and founder of Methodism in Mississippi. Gibson, a South Carolinian, early caught the flame of evangelism spread by John Charles Wesley, and at the age of 23 made his way down the Natchez Trace to the bluffs. He found only a military outpost, evacuated the preceding year (1798) by the Spaniards. The minister worked hard and his influence was keenly felt during the early days of Vicksburg. He died in 1804 and was buried four miles south of the present city. In 1935 he was reburied in this churchyard.

L. from Crawford St. on Cherry St.

14. The WILLIS RICHARDSON HOME, 1520 Cherry St. *(open by permission)*, is the most pretentious early home of the Vick family in Vicksburg. Built in the 1830's of brick, it is of Greek Revival architecture. The portico, extended around three sides of the house, has beautiful fluted columns. The original grounds covered two city blocks.

L. from Cherry St. on Harrison St.

15. The COOK-ALLEIN HOME, 1104 Harrison St. *(open by appointment)*, was built by Col. A. J. Cook, about 1862. It is occupied by his niece, Mrs. Thomas Allein, and her family. The house, with octagonal brick columns, has woodwork of cypress and is constructed of brick imported from England. After the fall of Vicksburg, it was converted into a Federal hospital, and the soldiers left their U. S. insignia stamped on the floor in the living room.

Retrace Harrison St.; L. on Cherry St.; R. on Belmont St.; L. on Washington St.; R. on Speed St.; R. on Oak St.

16. The KLEIN HOME, 2200 Oak St. *(open by appointment)*, stands

about 1,500 yards from the Mississippi River and when built in 1856 was in the center of spacious grounds with lawns extending down to the river bank. A large brick house two stories high, it is of Greek Revival architecture, with an Ionic portico. On each side is a wing whose roof slopes gently from the second-story windows. During the Siege of Vicksburg a small cannon ball, fired from a Union gunboat, struck the front door. The owner had it replaced and there it has remained. In mansions of this type the first or main story was devoted almost wholly to entertainment. The Klein home has a ballroom, banquet hall, reception hall, and, as was typical in houses of the period, a guest room on the main floor. Family rooms were in the second story. On the spacious lawn is a fountain of the pre-war period. Originally there was a family burial ground on the estate directly east of the house, but the remains have been removed to Cedar Hill Cemetery. The house is well preserved and is now an apartment house.

L. from Oak St. on Henry St.; R. on Levee St.

LEVEE STREET *(railroad district along water front)* has at one time or another harbored all sorts and conditions of men and boats. Long before the first steamboat, the *New Orleans,* eased around the Mississippi's great bend in 1811, a continuous procession of Indian canoes, flatboats, and keelboats came to the foot of the bluffs. Steamboats sometimes anchored out four deep, and now the modern packets nose their barges away from the wharves and out into the river. Bleak, worn, and bare, stand houses once brimming with ribald laughter of men—white and black—with wine, women, song, and sudden death.

R. from Levee St. on Clay St.

17. VICKSBURG NATIONAL MILITARY PARK, entrance E. end of Clay St., at Memorial Arch *(open; guides)*, was established by Act of Congress in 1899 "to commemorate the Campaign, Siege and Defense of Vicksburg" and "to preserve the history of the battles and operations on the ground where they were fought." The park, consisting of 1,323.63 acres, comprises the battle area of the Siege and Defense of Vicksburg, May 18 to July 4, 1863. The visitor can walk among the remains of the Confederate army's trenches and see on the steep slopes rows of markers indicating the positions occupied by the Federal troops in their siege operations. Numerous places show outlines of the Federal approach trenches, once filled with soldiers determinedly digging their way towards the Confederate forts. The story is recorded on 898 historical tablets, 274 markers, and 230 monuments. Three equestrian statues, 19 memorials, and more than 150 busts and relief portraits memorialize the troops and officers who served here. Sculptors, such as H. H. Kitson, A. A. Weinman, C. C. Mulligan, F. C. Hibbard, and F. W. Sievers, are represented.

The park consists of two systems of ridges, running in a northerly and southerly direction, which hem in the city of Vicksburg like a crescent on the north, east, and south sides. Connecting the main systems of ridges are secondary ridges, at right angles to the former, with attending valleys. Approximately 40 percent of the park area is densely wooded, while the remainder is sparsely wooded or open ground.

Remnants of 9 major Confederate forts, 10 Union approaches, and many miles of breastworks, gun emplacements, and rifle pits are visible in the park, in varying degrees of preservation. Three distinct types of Civil War forts are preserved: the *redan,* or triangular fort, with its apex extended toward the enemy, the *lunette,* or crescent shaped fort, and the *redoubt* of various forms, of which the square is the most common type. Remains of Union trenches are of two types: the *parallel,* or regular trench running parallel to the enemy's lines, and the *approach,* or *sap,* an advanced trench, running at right angles toward the enemy's forts. From the ends of these approaches *mines* were dug under the Confederate fortifications and large charges of powder were exploded in an attempt to destroy them. The crater formed by the explosion of a Union mine is visible in front of the redan on the Jackson road.

At Fort Hill, at the northern end of the park, the view over Lake Centennial and the Yazoo Canal shows the course of the Mississippi River in 1863 and the dangers encountered by the Union gunboats and transports in passing the Vicksburg batteries.

The site of Fort Hill is also the original site of Fort Mt. Vigie which constituted a part of the Spanish military post of Nogales, 1791–98. Here also was Fort McHenry, an American military post established later to maintain the claim of the United States to this region.

Various services to help the visitor understand the military operations of the Siege of Vicksburg, by visiting in systematic order the various sites of historic interest and principal memorials, are provided free by the National Park Service. A staff of qualified historians is stationed in the Administration Building for this purpose.

Special provision is made at Vicksburg National Military Park for groups of students, clubs, patriotic and other organizations.

The Administration Building, Pemberton Ave. *(open weekdays 9-4:30),* is a one-story brick structure with wings extending on both sides. It was completed in 1937. In the left wing is the *HISTORICAL MUSEUM,* extensive in its scope. Through the medium of color charts, pictures, and relief models, the history of this area is graphically portrayed from the pre-human period to the rise of the New South. Literature on the park is available here. Illustrated lectures are offered periodically by members of the staff. Also in the left wing is a *HISTORICAL REFERENCE LIBRARY,* open to the public. Members of the staff will assist visitors in research on historical subjects.

POINTS OF INTEREST IN ENVIRONS

U. S. Waterways Experiment Station, *4.6 m. (see Tour 2);* Eagle Lake, *17.1 m.,* Blakely, *11.7 m.,* Vicksburg National Cemetery, *1.9 m. (see Tour 3, Sec. a).*

PART III
Tours

Tour 1

(Mobile, Ala.)—Biloxi—Gulfport—(New Orleans, La.). US 90
Alabama Line to Louisiana Line, 88 m.

Louisville & Nashville R.R. parallels route throughout.
Concrete and black-top paving two lanes wide.
Accommodations of all kinds available.
Bait, tackle, and small boats for fishing can be obtained along route. In the cities arrangements can be made for renting boats and equipment for deep-water fishing.

Caution: Do not attempt fishing or hunting in inland streams and bayous without experienced guides, or deep-water fishing without experienced boat pilots. Do not dive into the water without first ascertaining its depth. The Gulf along the Coast is shallow, particularly at low tide, and only in the channels or passes is there sufficient depth for diving.

US 90 breaks in upon a section of Mississippi that combines scenic and recreational attractions with legendary interests. Here in 88 miles of Coast country are the color and tone of the Old World and the Old South. Between Pascagoula and Bay St. Louis, US 90, called the mid-Gulf section of the Old Spanish Trail, passes through the oldest white settlements in the lower Mississippi River Valley. The beach front has been developed with fine homes and hotels, and is remarkable because the vegetation, instead of being sea-shrunk and wind-weathered, is profuse and subtropical. The combination of palms, pines, magnolias, oaks, Spanish bayonets, poinsettias, crapemyrtles, and azaleas gives the region a year-around, changing greenness.

Between Biloxi and Bay St. Louis, the highway follows the water's edge, with the sea wall, Gulf, and outlying islands on the L., and the homes on the R. The area between the highway and seawall, formerly a sloping beach, has been leveled and landscaped, and many residents have built pretentious summer pavilions here. Wooden piers, diving platforms, and small boat landings jut into the water.

While the Coast is covered by many separate communities, there is a geographical and spiritual unity that makes the Mississippi sobriquet, "the Coast," understandable. It has been a resort center for years. New Orleanians began coming here in the early 1800's to escape the yellow fever epidemics so prevalent in those days. Long before the War between the States, wealthy planters from upper Louisiana, Mississippi, and Alabama made their summer homes on the Coast because it was cooler here than on their upland plantations. In recent years Northerners have found it an agreeable winter resort. Freezing weather is rare and golf, fishing, and other sports can be enjoyed practically every day.

Though the French influence survives on the Coast in peculiarities of speech and pronunciation, its deepest impress has been on the character of the food, which is unlike that in other parts of Mississippi. The heritage of French cuisine shows itself in highly seasoned gumbo, *court-bouillon* *(koo-bee-aw,* a fish stew imported from the Court of France) and jumbalaya (a potpourri of shrimp, rice, and tomatoes), made famous by the creole cooks of New Orleans. Hard-crusted French bread and thick, fragrant French-drip coffee are served in almost all homes and restaurants along the Coast. Many hotels awaken their guests by serving morning coffee in their rooms. The grocery stores and the fruit and vegetable stands sell "soup bunches" which provide the base for home-cooked vegetable soup. As a rule these bunches consist of two carrots, some celery, a quarter of a head of cabbage, a large onion, a ripe tomato, a generous handful of string beans and fresh peas, a turnip or two, some pods of okra, several Irish potatoes, and a sprig of parsley—all for 10 cents.

Crossing the Mississippi Line, *0 m.,* 30.1 miles SW. of Mobile, Ala., US 90 runs about six miles from the Gulf shore (L) and parallels the Escatawpa (Ind., *dog)* River, which flows a mile or two to the R.

KREOLE, *8.1 m.* (118 pop.), is a clean mill town engaged in manufacturing kraft and white paper from pine cut from the woods around it. The mill was a pioneer in the manufacture of kraft paper from pine *(see* INDUSTRY*).*

MOSS POINT, *11.2 m.* (2,453 pop.), at the junction of the Escatawpa and Pascagoula (Ind., *bread people)* Rivers, is surrounded by lakes that in the 1880's and 1890's made it a center of the sawmilling industry of south Mississippi and during the World War a shipbuilding base. Here is the junction with State 63 *(see Tour 15).*

West of Moss Point US 90 parallels the Pascagoula River, a half-mile to the R.

PASCAGOULA, *15 m.* (15 alt., 4,339 pop.), is in reality four communities held together by a lotus-eating philosophy. History here becomes an old wives' tale as full of legend as of fact. About the rotting wharves and the aged fort, the marsh grass and Spanish moss grow as they have for centuries; and though destinies once were shaped in the shadow of the aged oaks, the events are accepted with charming unconcern.

Shut off from the world by a barrier of sterile pine ridges and marshy bayous, Pascagoula was left undisturbed by the American Revolution, the creation of the Government of the United States, the political bickerings between American and Spanish boundary commissions, and even the War between the States. Some dates and events, however, were influential in the town's destiny. These were the local events that tell a story of eight flags having waved over the place since it was first used as a summer camping ground by the Pascagoula Indians.

The first fort was erected in 1718, after Pascagoula Bay had been granted to the Duchess de Chaumont, a favorite of Louis XIV. In 1763, however, the British were given titular sovereignty, which they held until the territory was taken by the Spanish 16 years later. Though the settlers who poured in from the Ohio country and Orleans territories during this time were pro-American in attitude—as was made evident by border warfare against Spanish authorities in 1809 and 1810—the fort continued to be known as "Old Spanish Fort." In 1810 Pascagoula became a part of the new State of West Florida *(see AN OUTLINE OF FOUR CENTU-RIES)*. The following year, after the territory was taken over by the United States, Dr. W. Flood was sent by Governor Claiborne to organize the Parish of Pascagoula. Dr. Flood, a very learned man, had far more trouble with the illiteracy of the populace than with insurgency, but, as more settlers drifted into the newly acquired region and the industrial development began, illiteracy decreased rapidly and the town acquired culture along with physical charm. Indicative of this culture and of the popularity of Pascagoula as a summering place was a three-story hotel built to accommodate a thousand guests and serviced by a large staff of slaves. The town also published a newspaper, the *Pascagoula Democrat Star,* which was started in 1846 at Handsboro. It is characteristic of the town's neglect of formally recorded story that the files of this paper were burned a few years ago.

Of great importance were the four industries that developed from natural resources after the 1870's, which were to dictate the town's future. From the time the first yellow pine log was cut along the stream banks and floated down the river to Pascagoula, then the best loading point on the Coast, to the height of the business, lumbering was Pascagoula's most spectacular industry. It was largely responsible for the increase in population between 1890 and 1906. Closely related to the lumber business and almost as spectacular was shipbuilding. Pascagoula ships earned early fame for their ability to stand up under long Gulf crossings to the Mexican coast. During the World War the International Shipbuilding Yards here, combined with U.S. Shipbuilding Yards up and down the river, gave the town the most feverish boom it has ever known. But with the end of the war, business slumped suddenly, leaving the hulls of unfinished schooners half submerged in the river to mock the town's industrial death. Boat building, however, is still a fine art; the Pascagoula luggers are as traditional as the Gloucester fishing boats. Largely through the efforts of Congressman W. M. Colmer, Pascagoula has been retained as a base for the U. S. Coast Guard.

Commercial fishing has increased with the years. The native-made luggers bring in tons of deep-sea red snappers to be packed and shipped to Northern markets; smaller boats bring in shrimp and oysters. Apparently destined to be as important as the commercial fisheries is the pecan business, begun around 1900. Thousands of tons of local paper-shell pecans are now shipped annually, while Jackson Co., where many leading varieties of paper-shell pecans have originated, is recognized as the home of the paper-shells.

The SINGING RIVER (the Pascagoula), two blocks W. of the courthouse and fronting the docks of a fish company, produces a mysterious music. The singing sound, like a swarm of bees in flight, is best heard in the hot summer months in the stillness of the early evening. Barely caught at first, the music seems to grow nearer and louder until it sounds as though it comes from directly underfoot. Of the varied hypothetical scientific explanations offered for the phenomenon none has been proved. The music, so scientists say, may be made by a species of fish, the grating of

BOAT BUILDING, PASCAGOULA

sand on the hard slate bottom, a current sucked past a hidden cave, or natural gas escaping from the sand beds. Legend says the sound is connected with the mysterious extinction of the Pascagoula tribe of Indians. The Pascagoula were a gentle tribe of handsome men and shapely women with large dark eyes and small, well-shaped hands and feet. The Biloxi, on the other hand, were a tribe calling themselves the "first people" and extremely jealous of their position. Miona, a princess of the Biloxi tribe, though betrothed to Otanga, a chieftain of her people, loved Olustee, a young chieftain of the Pascagoula, and fled with him to his tribe. The spurned and enraged Otanga led his Biloxi braves to war against Olustee and the neighboring Pascagoula, whereupon Olustee begged his tribe to give him up for atonement. But the Pascagoula swore they would either save their young chieftain and his bride or perish with them. However, when thrown into battle against terrible odds, they soon lost hope of victory. Faced with the choice either of subjection to Otanga or death, they chose suicide. With their women and children leading the way into the river, the braves followed with joined hands, each chanting his song of death until the last voice was hushed by the engulfing dark waters.

Right from Pascagoula on N. Pascagoula St., *0.2 m.;* L. on Spring St. to crossroads at *0.6 m.;* L. on shady lane to narrower lane, *0.8 m.;* R. on narrower lane to *OLD SPANISH FORT, 0.9 m. (open).* Built in 1718, it stands on a low bluff and from the land side looks like what it really is now, a farmhouse set in a grove of pecan trees. From the lake it still appears much as it did in its early days

OLD SPANISH FORT, PASCAGOULA

as a fort, even though much of its color has disappeared. The clue to the age of the structure is best found in the attic. The walls of oyster shells, moss, and mortar masonry are 15 to 30 inches thick but are not stouter than the wooden timbers bracing the roof, hewn and joined by the early carpenters. The fort in late afternoon is an appropriate setting for a Maxfield Parrish sunset. Diagonally E. by the marsh-dotted lake is the Krebs Cemetery. Some of the graves are so old that the inscriptions on the headstones are effaced; each headstone is capped with an iron cross.

At *15.8 m.* US 90 crosses the Pascagoula River on a toll bridge *(car and driver 50¢; passengers 25¢; pedestrians free)*. On the banks of the Pascagoula are the *U.S. GOVERNMENT DRY DOCKS AND REPAIR*

YARDS, 16 m. (L). At the end of the marsh road is another major bridge, this one spanning the West Pascagoula River, 18.9 m.

GAUTIER (pron. *go-chay'*), 19 m. (116 pop.), named for one of its pioneers, is on the bluff of the Pascagoula bottoms, under fine oaks that overlook the marsh. Here was once a race track and a commodious summer hotel. At a fishing camp (R) near the second bridge guides can be obtained for reaching the Pascagoula lakes and bayous by outboard motor. *(Trip should not be made without guide.)*

West of Gautier US 90 runs through flat pine barrens now being reforested.

At 21.5 m. is the junction with a graveled road.

Left on this road at *1.4 m.* is the junction with a road; R. on the latter to Fairley's Camp, *2.7 m.*, at the mouth of BAYOU GRAVELINE. Here fishing for redfish, speckled trout, sheepshead, mullet, croakers, and drum is good.

At 21.7 m. on US 90 is the junction with a graveled road.

Right on this road at *2.5 m.* is the junction with a sandy local road; R. on the local road *1.7 m.* to the junction with a dim trail through a pine forest; R. on the trail *0.8 m.* to FARRAGUT LAKE and the SITE OF THE FARRAGUT HOME, *0.5 m.*, built about 1800. Here Admiral David Farragut passed his childhood, his father being the first Justice of the Peace for Pascagoula. Tradition has it that an orphan girl who lived with the Farraguts was jilted by young David and cursed the land, then drowned herself in the lake below the bluff. Now, when crops fail, the settlers remember the curse.

At 25 m. on US 90 is the junction with a narrow winding road.

Left on this road with one-way bridges to *NELSON'S CAMP, 3.4 m.* Here Lake Graveline is connected with the Gulf by small deep bayous and serves as a tremendous trap for seafish coming into it with the rising tide. Fishing here for redfish, speckled trout, sheepshead, mullet, croakers, and drum is perhaps the best on the Coast.

At FONTAINEBLEAU, 26 m. (22 alt., 19 pop.), is the junction with State 59.

Right on this road *10.2 m.* to VANCLEAVE (98 pop.), a backwoods settlement interesting because of the extreme age of some of the clearings along Bluff Creek. The first settlers found the Biloxi and Pascagoula Indians here; bears and wolves were so numerous that a century of the white man's domination has not killed all of them. It is said that the pioneers' first plowshares were made of wood sheathed with the tough skin of the scaly garfish caught in creeks and lakes in the wilderness.

At 16.1 m. on State 59 is the junction with a local dirt road.

Right on this road *0.3 m.* is the LIVE OAK POND SCHOOL, established to serve the children of mixed Indian, Spanish, French, and Negro bloods who live in the forests near Vancleave. These children are living racial history, showing the mark of every invasion into the swamps.

At 26.1 m. on US 90 is the junction with a graveled road.

Left *1 m.* along this road is the largest tract of VIRGIN PINE FOREST in the State, 3,000 acres, of which part belongs to the Government. Here is one of the scenes of the Mid-Winter National Fox Hunt, which is held every year the latter part of February. The drive through the forest extends to the point where the virgin pines go down to meet the waters of the Gulf.

West of Fontainebleau the highway is bordered with pecan groves.

At 28.8 m. is a bridge across DAVIS BAYOU, where bridge and bank fishing for bass is good.

At 29.3 m. is a bridge across HERRING BAYOU. Here fishing for bass and bream from the bridge or banks is fair.

OCEAN SPRINGS, 33.3 m. (19 alt., 1,663 pop.); occupies the site of Old Biloxi, the first European settlement in the lower Mississippi River Valley, made by Iberville in 1699. Today (1938) it is a quiet little village that makes its living by catering to tourists and in the pecan orchards that surround it. It is situated on a waterfront of extraordinary beauty, facing both the Gulf and the Bay of Biloxi on a curve between Fort Bayou and Davis Bayou.

Here the headland (R), N. of the Louisville & Nashville R.R. bridge, which crosses the bay, is doubtless the SITE OF FORT MAUREPAS, on what is now a private estate. While no traces of the fort remain, cannon balls have been dug up at the place and cannon have been brought up from the bay in front of it. The pieces of artillery mounted in the Biloxi Community Park *(see BILOXI)*, designated as *IBERVILLE CANNON*, were salvaged in the summer of 1893 from the shallow water near the fort site. Tiblier and son, Biloxi fishermen, while dredging for oysters in the bay, encountered the wreck of a submerged ship. Without diving suits they succeeded in raising four cannon, a number of cannon balls, musket barrels from which the stocks had rotted away, swords without scabbards, and several iron bars. The wrecked ship was built of mahogany timbers fastened with wooden pegs and was judged to be about 65 feet long with a 20-foot beam. About 40 feet astern lay a smaller ship. That these boats were part of Iberville's fleet in 1699 is legend; it is known that Iberville found the bay much too shallow to float his larger ships. It is possible, however, that the boats were driven into the bay by the storm of 1723, or that they were pirate ships of a later date.

As Old Biloxi, Ocean Springs was at one time capital of the vast watershed drained by the Mississippi River. After the seat of government was transferred to Mobile in 1702, the settlement around Fort Maurepas made little progress. With the exception of a few practical and experienced French Canadians who had joined the group, its members were soldiers and sailors who knew nothing of agriculture. They had come not to work the land, but with the belief that the ores of rich mines, the hides of wild buffalo, and the pearls of the Gulf would make them wealthy. The colony, reached only after a five months' sail from France, neglected by its King and dependent on the Biloxi Indians for food, somehow managed to survive. For two centuries the colonists' descendants, who lived on the Ocean Springs side of the bay, across from New Biloxi, made charcoal-burning and fishing their chief industries. In the 1880's the first summer visitors arrived. There is mention of a hotel built in 1835, but until 1852 Ocean Springs people sailed across the bay to get their mail at Biloxi. Among the many magnificent live oak trees that grow here is the *RUSKIN OAK,* with a spread of 139 feet and circumference of 25 feet, on the estate called Many Oaks. An Englishman bought the estate in 1843, and when

John Ruskin visited Ocean Springs after the New Orleans Cotton Exposition in 1885, the Englishman named the huge tree in Ruskin's honor.

SHEARWATER POTTERY, on east Beach, was founded in 1928 and takes its name from a variety of sea gull found on the Mississippi Gulf Coast. The products made here are sold throughout the United States, and are distinctive in the originality of design and variety of glazes used. Many of the designs are objects familiar to the Coast—gulls, pelicans, fish, and crabs. Figurines of Negroes are notable for their humor, grace, and character. The pottery is owned and operated by G. W. Anderson and his three sons.

> Right from Ocean Springs on a paved road and across Fort Bayou to GULF HILLS, 0.8 m., a $15,000,000 resort subdivision, club, and golf course, one of the show places of the Coast. The golf course *(open; greens fee $1.50)*, beautifully laid out, is one of the most difficult courses in the South.

At 34.9 m. US 90 crosses the mouth of the Bay of Biloxi on the mile-and-a-half long concrete WAR MEMORIAL BRIDGE. When this bridge was dedicated in 1930 it replaced the last ferry crossing between Ocean Springs and New Orleans. The view from the bridge, with Deer Island and the east and west channels (L) lying immediately offshore and the curving tree-lined bay shore (R) stretching to the N., is particularly good. Fishing from the bridge for sheepshead, speckled trout, and redfish is excellent.

US 90 enters on Howard Ave. to Main St.

BILOXI, 37.5 m. (22 alt., 14,850 pop.) *(see BILOXI)*.

> *Points of Interest.* Seafood packing plants, Back Bay Bridge, old homes, and others.

The route continues L. on Main St. to Beach Blvd.; R. on Beach Blvd. (US 90).

The boat trip across Mississippi Sound to Ship Island can be made from Biloxi *(see Side Tour 1A)*.

SOUTHERN MEMORIAL PARK, 42.4 m. (R), is one of the Coast's newest and most beautiful cemeteries.

BEAUVOIR, 43 m. (R), facing the Gulf, was the last home of Jefferson Davis, Confederate President. It is a State-supported home for Confederate veterans, their wives and widows. Surrounded by a grove of live oaks, magnolias, and cedars, Beauvoir is designed in the Mississippi planter tradition, a full story-and-a-half set high above a raised basement, with a wide central hall, a broad gallery on three sides, broad hip-roof, and long floor-to-ceiling windows. The square, paneled wooden posts of the gallery, joined by a delicate balustrade, rise in support of a simple dentiled cornice. The main doorway with its double glassed doors and slender side lights is approached by a graceful flight of steps, flanked by curving handrails. It was erected 1852–54 by J. H. Brown, and was the first beach home built in the vicinity. Brown planned the buildings himself, brought his skilled workmen from New Orleans, and, so the story goes, had the cypress pulled from the Louisiana swamps and carried to

BEAUVOIR, HOME OF JEFFERSON DAVIS, NEAR BILOXI

Lake Pontchartrain by camels. From there it was shipped to Beauvoir by schooner. The four original buildings are standing; the big house is planned with a cottage on each side and a brick kitchen at the rear. The cost of building and maintaining the estate impoverished Brown, and for some years before the War between the States the house was vacant. Finally it was bought by a planter named Dorsey from St. Joseph, La.

In 1877 Jefferson Davis rented from Mrs. Dorsey, an old friend of the Davis family, the east cottage called the Pavilion, and began to write his work, *The Rise and Fall of the Confederate Government*. In April 1878 Mrs. Davis joined him at Beauvoir, and for the next three years helped him write in longhand the manuscript of the book. Beauvoir, during the time the Davises lived in it, was a Southern social center. In the second year of his stay at the house, Davis bought the estate from Mrs. Dorsey for $5,500. Before he had finished paying her for it, Mrs. Dorsey died, willing the estate to him. In 1889 Davis, while on a business trip to his old plantation at Brierfield, in Warren Co., Miss., became ill and was never able to return to Beauvoir, dying that year in New Orleans, where he was buried. Four years later his remains were removed to Richmond, Va.

No story is more typical of post-bellum times than that of Winnie (Varina Anne) Davis, Jefferson Davis's maiden daughter, who gave up her Northern lover to remain her father's devoted and constant companion during his declining years. Within a year after his death Winnie and her mother moved to New York City. After again refusing to marry, Winnie died at Narragansett Pier in 1898.

Mrs. Davis sold Beauvoir in 1903 to the Mississippi Division of the Sons of Confederate Veterans. Until the Mississippi Legislature appropriated funds for the home's upkeep, the Daughters of the Confederacy maintained Beauvoir. The home is now controlled by a board of six directors appointed by the Governor of Mississippi, but it is still owned by the Sons of Confederate Veterans. The original buildings have been preserved without alteration. Many of the furnishings used by the Davises have been discovered and restored to their places in the great house. Exact reproductions of others have been obtained. The central hall and two large chambers have been dedicated as memorials to Winnie, while on the porch of the Pavilion is her skiff. On the front lawn near the entrance gateway is a statue marking the grave of Winnie's little dog. Twelve dormitories, a hospital, a chapel, and a few cottages have been erected. The number of inmates of the home is decreasing, the majority now being widows of veterans. In a shaded *CEMETERY*, N. of the cottages, are the graves of 1,000 men who, following Jefferson Davis through war, now sleep near their leader's home.

EDGEWATER PARK, *44.1 m.* (R), surrounds the *EDGEWATER HOTEL,* a great square building set in well-landscaped grounds, an impressive example of what Chicago capital did for the Coast during the real estate boom of 1926.

At *45 m.* is the junction with an unpaved road.

Right on this road to the *EDGEWATER GULF SKEET RANGE* and the *EDGEWATER GULF GOLF CLUB (open; nominal fees), 1 m.*

At *45.5 m.* is the *GREAT SOUTHERN GOLF COURSE AND COUNTRY CLUB,* one of the oldest in this section. In the clubhouse are the studios of WGCM, a 500 watt radio station operating on a frequency of 1,210 kilocycles.

GULF COAST MILITARY ACADEMY, 46 m., is an honor-ranking, privately supported school for boys of high school grade.

MISSISSIPPI CITY, *46.4 m.* (21 alt., 1,000 pop.), was before the War between the States the most important settlement in Harrison Co. The town had its beginning in 1837, when Scotch-Irish pioneers were issued a charter to construct a railroad from northern Mississippi to the Gulf. Although the effort failed, it initiated Mississippi City's flush pre-war period. In 1841 the little town lost by one legislative vote its fight to have the University of Mississippi located within its limits. A second attempt to build a railroad, in 1853, resulted in the construction of a number of fine beach homes and the building of a resort hotel, which was from that time until the 1890's the outstanding hotel on the Coast.

At *46.6 m.* is the Coast's *HAUNTED HOUSE,* a particularly good example of ante-bellum architecture adapted to the Gulf climate.

At *46.6 m.* is the junction with a macadam road.

Right on this road is HANDSBORO, *1.2 m.* (1,200 pop.), now as unruffled as the waters of Bayou Bernard that outlines its northern boundary, but before the War between the States an industrial and cultural center of the Coast. The community is peopled with descendants of the English and Scotch-Irish who settled here early in 1800. Handsboro shipped the first lumber to be exported from Harrison Co., and late in the war Federal troops raided the town for lumber to build their quarters on Ship Island. In 1902 the opening of the Gulfport harbor killed the lumber trade. More than a dozen houses built between 1840 and 1850, when Handsboro was a booming lumber town, are easily distinguished by the heavily morticed timbers of their framework. On the north side of Bayou Bernard are two houses, almost identical, built by Myles and Sheldon Hand about 1845. The houses are two-and-a-half stories high, with the broad expanse of their roofs broken by dormer windows. Broad two-story porches extend the entire length with square columns of heavy timber more than 24 feet high. Open hallways (now enclosed) on both floors of the houses provided a draft for Gulf breezes.

The *MASONIC HALL,* intersection of Cowan St. and Pass Christian road, (L) was built before 1850. Its square box-like architecture is undistinguished, but the building is pointed out as the place where Jefferson Davis attended lodge meetings.

PARADISE POINT, *47 m.*, was named by high-church Episcopalians who originally used it for their family burying ground.

At *47.4 m.* (L), half a block from the highway, is *ST. MARK'S CHAPEL*, a one-story frame Episcopal church building of fine proportions. Constructed in 1855, the church is celebrated because Jefferson Davis was once a vestryman and communicant. Along the beach opposite the chapel the blockaded Coast people during the War between the States boiled seawater in wide shallow kettles to obtain salt.

At *47.7 m.* (R), on Courthouse Road but visible from US 90, is the first courthouse of Harrison Co. Built in 1841, it is now a yellow brick apartment house.

At *47.9 m.* (R), on a vacant lot, stand the trees under which John L. Sullivan fought Paddy Ryan in 1882.

US 90 enters on E. Beach Blvd.; R. on 15th St.; L. on 21st Ave.; R. on 14th St.; L. on 24th Ave.; R. on 13th St.

GULFPORT, *50.9 m.* (19 alt., 12,547 pop.) *(see GULFPORT).*

Points of Interest. Harbor, U. S. Veterans Facility, Hardy Monument, and others.

Here is the junction with US 49 *(see Tour 7, Sec. b)*. A boat trip across Mississippi Sound to Ship Island *(see Side Tour 1A)* can be made from Gulfport.

The route continues on 13th St.; L. on 30th Ave.; R. on W. Beach Blvd. (US 90).

Between Gulfport and Bay St. Louis the beach is lined with well-spaced homes (R) of permanent residents. The houses for the most part are of planter and Victorian styles, with only a few small summer bungalows. Recreation here is simple; entire families golf, sail, swim, and fish. From the sea wall, piers, and boats, small nets baited with meat are lowered, a bushel basket being filled with crabs in a short time. Another diversion is gigging or spearing flounders, flat-bodied fish that swim in to the shore waters at night and burrow in the sand. The equipment for "floundering" includes a spear and a torch or flambeau. On still, moonless nights the flickering yellow light of flambeaux illuminates the dark along the water's edge as the flounderers wade about in the shallow water spearing the fish.

LONG BEACH, *53.4 m.* (25 alt., 1,346 pop.), stretches along the highway on the site of a former Indian village. *GULF PARK COLLEGE, 54.1 m.* (R), is a privately-supported junior college for girls, and the center of the Coast activities in music, painting, and drama. On the campus is *FRIENDSHIP OAK,* a live oak with a spread of 127 feet and a trunk diameter of 13½ feet. Vachel Lindsay, the poet, and one-time member of the college faculty, held classes on the platform built among the branches of this tree. The *MUNICIPAL ROSE GARDEN* is four blocks R. from the highway on Jefferson Davis Ave. On both sides of the avenue, N. of the Louisville & Nashville R.R., are the truck farms for which Long Beach is noted.

Between Long Beach and Pass Christian the desolate stretch of beach is known as White Harbor. Here, before the Gulfport harbor was built, lumber schooners loaded in a deep basin a mile and a half offshore. Legend is that the 18th century pirate who gave his name to PITCHER'S POINT, *56.4 m.* (L), pronounced a curse on this two-mile strip of land which has been effective to the present time. White Harbor is the only visible break in the line of continuous settlement between Biloxi and Henderson Point.

PASS CHRISTIAN, *58.4 m.* (11 alt., 3,004 pop.), for all its century-old importance as a recreation center, is in reality an unaffected community of the Old Deep South. Winter visitors furnish a livelihood to many of the natives, who retain great pride in the town's heritage and in a society whose brilliance dates from the 18th century.

Pass Christian took its name from the channel known as Christian's Pass, supposedly discovered by Christian L'Adnier, a member of Iberville's crew in 1699. Later, both the French and the Spaniards occupied this section, and with the opening of the Mississippi Territory the settlement became a trading center for the back country as far N. as Black Creek. Down the old Red Creek Road, now Menge Ave., came caravans of ox-teams, six and eight yokes long, loaded with cotton, hides, furs, venison, potatoes, honey, turkeys, gophers (dry-land burrowing tortoises), and "pinders" (peanuts). A U.S. garrison was stationed at Pass Christian in 1811. The Battle of Pass Christian, the last naval engagement against a foreign foe in American waters, was fought SW. of the town, near Bay St. Louis during the War of 1812. During the ante-bellum period "the Pass" with its delightful climate became noted as a resort, attracting the sugar, cotton, and rice planters of Louisiana, Alabama, and Mississippi, and the aristocrats of New Orleans. The first yacht club in the South was organized here in 1849, the year in which many of the present homes were built. In the 1880's, the influx of winter tourists from the North began.

Beach Boulevard rims the water, a narrow five-mile strip paralleling the seawall. Along the inland side of the drive are numerous hotels, filling stations, and antique shops built to attract tourists; they are in harmony with the old homes and cottages along the way. The homes are set in gardens of roses, oleanders, azaleas, crapemyrtles, palms, and camellia japonicas, and are enclosed with fences laden with honeysuckle, wistaria, roses, and trumpet vines. North of the Boulevard are the truck gardens that produce okra and other vegetables destined for the making of the famous creole dishes of the Coast.

Three miles offshore are approximately 30 square miles of shell banks, perpetually rebuilt by fishermen who are required by law to return a percentage of shells taken each year. Free of mud, these banks produce small oysters notable for their flavor. Before daybreak, in oyster season, people miles inland can hear the engines of the oyster-boats throb their way out to these reefs. In the evening the boats return, low in the water, their cabins covered with piles of oyster shells. During the winter months, residents and visitors are awakened each morning by the familiar cry, "Oyster ma-an from Pass Christi-a-an," announcing the approach of the oyster peddler.

OSSIAN HALL (private) is a white two-story frame Southern Colonial-type house with a wide, double-deck portico and large round columns. Set well back in Beechhurst facing E. Beach Blvd., the house is the scene of the motion picture, *Come Out of the Kitchen*, in which Marguerite Clark starred. The building was erected by Seth Guion in 1848.

The *ADELLE McCUTHEON HOME (private)*, 861 E. Beach Blvd., has in its front yard the Coast's most famous camellia japonica, originally cut from a Mt. Vernon bush and planted here by a great-granddaughter of Martha Washington, Mrs. Frances Parke Lewis Butler.

The *DIXIE WHITE HOUSE (private)*, 767 E. Beach Blvd., acquired its name in 1913 when President Woodrow Wilson visited here. The dignified two-story structure built in 1854 has the divided front steps characteristic of many houses of the period. The open ground floor is screened with ironwork banisters; the columns are covered with ornamental plaster. The second floor is frame, with a gallery across the front and arched windows extending from floor to ceiling.

The *MIDDLEGATE JAPANESE GARDEN (open daily 1-5; adm. 50¢),* St. Louis St. between Clarence Ave. and Pine St., is filled with plants, entirely Japanese, including flowering plum, quince, and peach trees, giant bamboos, and Japanese magnolias. The 174-year-old bronze Buddha and other Japanese figures came from Japan.

TRINITY EPISCOPAL CHURCH, NW. corner Second and Church Sts., was built in 1849 and stands in a magnificent grove of live oaks thickly hung with moss. The church is a small frame structure of the Gothic type with stained windows and a modern green roof. In the same moss-hung grove, but across the street, is the Live Oak Cemetery established simultaneously with the church.

The DOROTHY DIX HOME (private), 730 W. Beach Blvd., the summer home of the well-known syndicate writer, stands in a large garden shaded by live oaks. It is a rambling story-and-a-half frame structure with triple gables and a wide front gallery adorned with jig-saw latticework and a striking wooden railing. In the rear is a large rose garden.

Right at the second street beyond Miramar Hotel; L. between Trinity Church and the Cemetery, a macadam road leads to BAYOU PORTAGE, 2.1 m., where boat fishing for black bass, redfish, and speckled sea trout is good (boats and bait obtainable at pier). At 3.6 m. is the bridge over BAYOU ACADIAN, where fishing is also good. At 4.4 m. is the bridge over BAYOU DELISLE (pron. d'leel), the third good fishing stream crossed. DELISLE (150 pop.), near the mouth of Wolf River and known as Wolf Town until 1884, is one of the earliest settlements on the Gulf Coast. The name was changed to the present DeLisle to honor Comte de Lisle, lieutenant to Bienville and one of the first explorers of the Mississippi Coast. The land around DeLisle was first settled in 1712 by the Saucier, Necaise, Ladnier, Dedeaux, and Moran families, who tradition says were Acadian exiles. Until recent years the French language was spoken here exclusively, French being used in the schools. Communal life centers about the LADY OF GOOD HOPE CHURCH, a simple one-room frame building, containing valuable vestments and altar pieces from Europe. At 8 m. is the entrance to PINE HILLS, at the head of the Bay of St. Louis, a mammoth real estate enterprise undertaken during the boom of 1926. The pretentious hotel has long been closed, but the 18-hole golf course (open; greens fee $1) is still in operation. Pine Hills marks the highest elevation, 90 feet, on the coast between Pensacola, Fla., and Corpus Christi, Tex. The largest shell Indian mound on the Mississippi Coast is on the grounds. At 11 m. the road crosses ROTTEN BAYOU (Bayou Bienasawaugh), at Fenton. The bayou affords good fishing for bass and bream. The surrounding land is one of the best sections for fox hunting along the Coast, and hunters often follow the chase in automobiles. At 15.5 m. is KILN (165 pop.), named for the immense kilns in which the original French settlers burned charcoal for a living. Charcoal burning was soon superseded here by sawmilling, but Kiln did not come into the limelight as a lumber town until 1912. In that year, when the mill interests of the section were sold to a large eastern company, Kiln mushroomed from a backwoods community into a town with a high school, picture show, a 50-room hotel, and row after row of neat mill houses. In 1930 the mill closed and Kiln sank into near oblivion. During prohibition the territory around Kiln was the center of a moonshining industry known for the excellent quality of its whisky as far north as Milwaukee, Wis. Strange tales of giant stills hidden under sawdust piles and rumored connections of Kiln with Chicago's Capone gang still afford interest.

On HENDERSON POINT, 63.9 m. (L), is the entrance to the INN-BY-THE-SEA, an interesting adaptation of the Spanish mission style to the Mississippi Gulf Coast environment.

At 64.5 m. is the head of the two-mile-long wooden bridge across the BAY OF ST. LOUIS. Along the shore of the bay (L) is good salt-water bathing from the sand beach. Fishing is good from the bridge for speckled sea trout, sheepshead, and redfish.

The Bay of St. Louis was the scene of the misnamed Battle of Pass Christian in 1814. British Vice-Admiral Cochrane was following Andrew Jackson from Pensacola, Fla., as Jackson was hurrying to defend New Orleans. In an effort to delay Cochrane's fleet of 60 vessels and prevent his forcing a passage through Mississippi Sound, Lake Borgne, and Lake Pontchartrain to New Orleans, the American flotilla of 5 gunboats, commanded by Lt. Thomas Catesby Jones, waylaid the invaders. Jones had stationed his boats in the shallow bay where the enemy's heavier ships could not follow him. On December 14, the 5 American boats were attacked by 45 British launches and armed boats manned by 1,000 men, and, although Lieutenant Jones showed great bravery and excellent qualities as a commander, within an hour every American vessel was either captured or sunk. The casualties included 80 Americans and 300 British.

The town of BAY ST. LOUIS, 66.6 m. (21 alt., 3,724 pop.), at the time of the battle was known as Shieldsborough, for Thomas Shields, who obtained his grant from the Spanish Government in 1789. Bienville, however, had explored the bay in 1699, naming it St. Louis for the dead and sainted King Louis IX; and in 1720 John Law, Mississippi Bubble promoter, had given the land around the bay to Madame de Mézières. But the permanence of each of these colonization efforts was as uncertain as French policy. The French-Canadians living about the bay intermarried with the Indians, Spaniards, and Acadians expelled from Nova Scotia, forming the blood strain sometimes incorrectly called creole on the Coast. In the shuttling sovereignties of the 18th century, these forest dwellers around the bay ignored and were ignored by everything that smacked of government. Yet when the British overwhelmed Lieutenant Jones in 1814, Shieldsborough was an established summer retreat for wealthy Natchez planters. Because land titles in this section were based on claims that involved 23 different types of tenure, including claims of the State of Georgia, some of the ablest lawyers of the profession were drawn here. By 1825 Shieldsborough, then also known as Bay St. Louis, rivalled Pearlington as the seat of the Hancock Co. courts. The town was incorporated in 1854. The military road that Andrew Jackson had cut through the pine woods into Shieldsborough was bringing the town a substantial part of the back country trade W. of the Bay St. Louis streams.

The building of the New Orleans, Mobile & Chattanooga R.R. (now the Louisville & Nashville), completed in 1869, lent impetus to the development of the town as a summer resort. Since 1905 the growth of Bay St. Louis has been a paradox; the town has been a victim of progress. As long as it was isolated by the Louisiana marshes, the Jordan River, and the bay, it was a liberal, detached, and moneyed country community. But improved transportation facilities have resulted in making it more of a resort and less of a rural center.

The beach front includes a portion of the business section. Main Street follows a high ridge, which in turn follows the sea-wall. On the beach side of this street many of the frame buildings have entrances level with the street; the back parts, supported by heavy pilings, stand 30 feet above the base of the hill. Facing the Gulf from the first block W. of the Louisville & Nashville R.R. track is the CHURCH OF OUR LADY OF THE GULF, the center of the largest Roman Catholic parish in the State, with 3,000 communicants. The red brick structure, whose construction continued from 1908 to 1926, is designed in the Italian Renaissance style. The interior is beautifully furnished, the stained glass windows having been imported from Germany. West of the church and also facing the Gulf is ST. STANISLAUS COLLEGE, an accredited boys' boarding school of high school standing. The school was founded in 1854 by the Brothers of the Sacred Heart and named for Father Louis Stanislaus Marie Buteux, the first resident priest in the territory. Adjoining the church on the E. in a large white building of Romanesque design, three stories high, set well back from the beach, is the main building of ST. JOSEPH'S ACADEMY, a girls' school of accredited high school rank. The Sisters of St. Joseph are in charge of the school. At the rear of the academy, approached by an avenue of cedars, is the SHRINE OF OUR LADY OF THE WOODS. Honoring the Blessed Virgin, in fulfillment of a vow made for the salvation of the vessel on which he was returning from France, Father Buteux erected this shrine in what was then the wilderness. The statue, made of plaster of Paris and protected only by a small dome, has stood for more than 60 years without damage. ST. AUGUSTINE SEMINARY, 0.2 m. from bridge, is a Catholic school where Negro boys are trained for the priesthood. The school has several acres of landscaped grounds and a number of commodious buildings grouped about the two-story red brick administration building. It is said to have been richly endowed by a Northern woman.

Left from Bay St. Louis on the Hancock Co. sea-wall drive is WAVELAND, 2.4 m. (15 alt., 663 pop.), the home of many New Orleans people during the hot months from June to September. Since Waveland is closer to New Orleans than other Gulf Coast cities, hundreds of business men come here with their families to live in houses and apartments, commuting to New Orleans. Life in Waveland is simple, gravitating lazily around swimming, fishing, and house parties. Immediately after Labor Day the people return to New Orleans with the certainty, precision, and celerity of a regiment breaking camp. At 2.6 m. is the PIRATE'S HOUSE (open by appointment), built in 1802 by a New Orleans business man who is alleged to have been the overlord of the Gulf Coast pirates. At one time, legend says, a secret tunnel led from the house to the waterfront. Recently restored, the house is a perfect example of Louisiana planter type, with a brick ground story and an outside stairway leading to the first floor. The outer walls are covered with white stucco; square, white frame columns support the gallery, which runs the length of the house. The three dormer windows on the front are beautifully proportioned, and the iron grillwork forming the banisters is reminiscent of that in the French Quarter of New Orleans.

GULFSIDE, 5.6 m. (R), is an unusual institution. The plant, which includes several hundred acres of land, a number of buildings, and a mile and a quarter of Gulf frontage, is the only stretch of beach in Mississippi owned and controlled by Negroes. Gulfside is essentially a summer school; the only work done during the winter is by the pupils of the school for retarded boys, who pay their expenses by keeping grounds and buildings in order. During the summer, classes are held for teachers, pastors, and others, and camps are maintained for Boy Scouts and

PIRATE'S HOUSE, WAVELAND

Girl Reserves. The work done by the summer school is recognized by the State Departments of Education of Louisiana and Mississippi, and credits are allowed. Religious emphasis is strong, but no stress is placed on denominational lines. At a Song Fest, usually on the last Sunday in August, spirituals are sung by a chorus made up of Negro church choirs and college glee clubs.

At 7.3 m. is LAKESHORE and the mouth of BAYOU CADET, where fall and winter fishing for speckled trout is excellent.

Between Bay St. Louis and the Louisiana Line US 90 is a flat straight stretch of road running through cut-over pine lands. That the second growth pine is already being wellworked for turpentine is evidenced by the many slashed trees along the road.

At 75.5 m. is the junction with a graveled road.

Left on this road to the Gulfview School, 2.5 m.; R. here on a dirt road through pine and stump barrens, past the post office at Ansley, 5.8 m., and through two pasture gates, at 10.9 m. to a trail fork; R. on the trail to the old PLANTATION HOME, 13.2 m., once belonging to Col. J. F. H. Claiborne, Mississippi's pioneer historian. In 1712 John B. Saucier settled here on Mulatto Bayou, and in the 1780's had his title confirmed by the Spanish authorities. He built the house before 1800, taking timber from the pine woods about him and firing his own brick with the help of slaves. The house shows Spanish influence in its main floor, propped high on open brick piers in the West Indian manner. A single flight of steps rises to the gallery with toothpick columns, running across the front. The hipped tin roof is broken in front by two dormers and is topped by a plain box observatory. The rooms are large and open off a central hall.

At Jackson's Landing on Mulatto Bayou, just a mile from the house, is seen the long circle of earthworks thrown up by Andrew Jackson in 1814 to guard the mouth of Pearl River from British assault. Colonel Claiborne bought the house in the 1840's and lived in it until 1870, writing his best books during this period.

Back of the house are the ruins of the brick slave quarters. The piers that support the house itself are joined with bars to form cages. In these cages the Negroes who were brought from Africa were kept until they had been tamed enough to be moved into slave quarters in the rear.

Painted on the wall panels in the hall and in the front bedrooms are huge canvases of hunting and fishing scenes done by Coulon, a 19th century artist of New Orleans.

The estate now belongs to a New Orleans business man who has turned it into a cattle range. Brahma bulls, half again as large as the average bull, with shaggy humps above their shoulders, drink at the spring where the Choctaw Indians camped. Near the spring is a mound of clam shells left by the Indians.

At *82.4 m.* on US 90 is the junction with a wide graveled road.

Right on this road is the picturesque *NETTIE KOCH HOME, 0.4 m.* (R) *(private)*, erected before 1820. The original part of the house, consisting of two rooms, is constructed of logs. Lean-tos, ells, and wings that are connected to the main house by latticed porches have been added, giving it a rambling appearance. The kitchen floor is of timbers 30 inches wide and several inches thick, taken from a dismantled flatboat that drifted down Pearl River. The white-washed interior is furnished with old relics, some of them having been brought from Denmark, his native country, by Dr. Koch. The house is surrounded by live oaks, sycamores, and cedars. A red camellia japonica in the small courtyard rises higher than the house.

At *2.2 m.* on this same road is LOGTOWN (500 pop.). A sawmill here has been in continuous operation since 1850. It stands on the bank of Pearl River, was built with slave labor, and was worked by slaves for the first 10 years. BOUGAHOUMA BAYOU forms the dividing line between the white residential section and Possum Walk, the Negro residential section.

PEARLINGTON, *87.7 m.* (10 alt., 318 pop.), is a town which has been revived, the new US 90 short-cut to New Orleans having put it back on a main road for the first time in more than a decade. It was one of the pioneer lumbering towns in this once-important lumbering area, and later was the terminal for a Louisiana-Mississippi automobile ferry, now discontinued. Many large, Spanish-moss-covered live oak trees, and some of the largest and oldest camellia japonicas on the Mississippi Coast grow in and around Pearlington.

At *88 m.* a bridge crosses PEARL RIVER, the boundary line between Mississippi and Louisiana, 44 miles NE. of New Orleans. Free bridges at the Rigolets (pron. *rig-lees*) and Chef Menteur Passes in Louisiana; 47 miles by a toll bridge across Lake Pontchartrain in Louisiana *(car and driver $1; passengers 25¢)*. The river was given its name by the French because of the large pearl oysters found on the banks.

Side Tour 1A

Gulfport to Ship Island, 12 m.
Excursion boats leave yacht harbor and west pier at Gulfport twice daily during summer season. Round-trip fare $1.
Surf bathing and other aquatic sports.
No overnight accommodations.

SHIP ISLAND, a low white sandy bar lying between the Mississippi Sound and the Gulf of Mexico, is approximately seven miles long and half a mile wide, its length roughly paralleling the mainland east to west. The island has a strategic position, an excellent harbor formed by a "V" of deep water. The place is rich in early history and legend.

Intermittently from 1699 until the late 1720's Ship Island was the harbor for French exploration and settlement of the Gulf Coast from Mobile to the mouth of the Mississippi River. Iberville delayed here three days before he made his landing in small boats on the shore of Biloxi Bay *(see BILOXI)*, and later, using the island as a base, he explored the Mississippi River for nearly 300 miles from its mouth. Even after the capital was moved from Biloxi to Mobile, Ship Island continued to be the port of entry for vessels from France. To Ship Island came the first marriageable girls for the early colonists, bringing their chests, or "casquettes" with them. In 1717 the first fort and warehouse were constructed here near the present pass. In 1724 what was probably the first cargo of pine lumber to be sent from the Mississippi Coast was shipped from here.

In 1815, when the British general, Pakenham, tried to take New Orleans, Ship Island served as the base for the British Navy. From the island harbor the British fleet of 60 vessels sailed to what was to be the last naval engagement in which Americans fought a foreign foe in American waters *(see Tour 1)*.

On the extreme western tip of the island is *FORT MASSACHUSETTS,* used during the War between the States. As early as 1847 the island was reserved for military purposes; in 1858 the War Department, carrying out an act of Congress of 1857, authorized the building of a fort to protect the short cut into New Orleans, Rigolets Pass, the outlet of Lake Pontchartrain. In December 1860 work was still under way, and the Government had ordered 48 large cannon shipped from Pittsburg. The outbreak of the war in 1861 left the Union garrison isolated on the island, and in May 1861 they destroyed the fort in order to prevent its falling into Confederate hands. For three months, from July to September 1861, five companies of Confederates held the fort, having rearmed it with eight small cannon after its "destruction." Because of the constant threat of the Federal fleet then blockading the mouth of the Mississippi, the Confederates fired the fort and evacuated the island on September 16. In December Gen. Benjamin Butler moved into the damaged fort with a garrison of about 7,000 Federal soldiers, at which time it was named Massachusetts, in honor of Butler's home State, and partly rebuilt. As the war dragged on, the island was used as a prison for captured Confederates, some 4,000 of whom were held here in the course of the war years. A number of youths from a military school in Alabama, sent as prisoners, died and were buried in the sands. Subsequent washings of the sands have exposed a number of their skeletons.

From the time of the withdrawal of the Federal garrison in 1875 until the purchase of the old fort in 1935 by the Gulfport American Legion, the western end of the island was a desert, visited occasionally by boatloads of sightseers. The Federal encampment on the island had denuded its western half of protecting timber; rainstorms have washed away the ground in front of the fort.

Beyond the fort is the *SHIP ISLAND LIGHTHOUSE*, built in 1879 and maintained by the U. S. Government.

The present *QUARANTINE STATION*, 4 m. E. of the lighthouse, is an outgrowth of the station established in 1878, when the flourishing trade that sprang up between the Mississippi Coast and Cuba and Vera Cruz brought yellow fever into the country. Here all incoming vessels were inspected and fumigated. About 1886 the city of Biloxi vigorously protested that the proximity of the quarantine station was dangerous to the city, and as a result the station was removed to Chandeleur Island. Mississippi authorities then moved into the buildings left on Ship Island and established a quarantine station of their own. For a while incoming vessels had to be fumigated twice, once by Federal and once by State authorities. This situation continued until the storm of 1893 blew both stations away. The next year the present station on Ship Island was constructed by the Federal Government, and was active until yellow fever was definitely brought under control. The buildings are maintained in good condition for any emergency campaign against a contagious disease.

Surf bathing and boating are enjoyed on the outer beach of the island, where boats and swimming paraphernalia are for rent.

Tour 2

(Livingston, Ala.)—Meridian—Jackson—Vicksburg—(Monroe, La.). US 80.
Alabama Line to Louisiana Line, 157.7 m.

Alabama & Great Southern R.R. parallels route between the Alabama Line and Meridian, Yazoo & Mississippi Valley R.R. between Meridian and Vicksburg.

Concrete roadbed two lanes wide, well marked.
Accommodations of all kinds.

US 80 runs across the center of the State through Mississippi's three largest cities. It dips from the red clay hills on the east through the central prairie to climb again into the brown loam hills at Vicksburg. The only large stream crossed is the Pearl River at Jackson. The scene alternates between field and forest. Settlements are older in the western section. Meridian was insignificant at the outbreak of the War between the States; Jackson was small though the State capital; while Vicksburg was an important port on the Mississippi River. US 80 and US 11 *(see Tour 8)* are united through Meridian.

At *0 m.* US 80 crosses the Mississippi Line 21 miles W. of Livingston, Ala., and winds through red clay hills, pine and hardwood forests, and gully-threatened fields with unpainted houses.

KEWANEE, *1.8 m.* (150 pop.), is a sawmill and farm country hamlet, celebrated chiefly because it was the home of Chief Pushmataha. Pushmataha was the Choctaw who, by blocking Tecumseh's scheme for uniting the Indians, saved the Southern whites from annihilation. He was a friend of Andrew Jackson, and is buried in the Congressional Cemetery at Washington *(see ARCHEOLOGY AND INDIANS).*

Left from Kewanee on a sand and clay road is WHYNOT, *8.3 m.* (34 pop.), a backwoods farming settlement gradually acquiring improved roads and new fangled ideas from Meridian. "Why not?" is the native's retort to the visitor's query of how the community got its name.

TOOMSUBA (Ind., *rolling horse*), *6 m.* (292 alt., 350 pop.), on the creek of the same name, had an active Ku Klux Klan unit during reconstruction days. The cut through which the road passes at *10.1 m.* shows the red clay texture of the hilly soil and explains the poor landscape.

At *16.5 m.* US 80 follows B St. to 26th Ave.

MERIDIAN, *19.1 m.* (341 alt., 31,954 pop.) *(see MERIDIAN).*

Points of Interest: Industrial plants, Gypsy Queen's Grave, Arboretum, and others.

At Meridian are the junctions with US 45 *(see Tour 4),* US 11 *(see Tour 8),* and State 39 *(see Side Tour 4B).*

The route continues on 26th Ave.; L. on 6th St.; R. on 5th St. (US 80).

West of Meridian US 80 winds through hills.

CHUNKY, *33.8 m.* (312 alt., 268 pop.), is a sawmill town that takes its name from Chunky Creek, on which it is situated. Chunky is the Anglicized pronunciation of the name the Choctaw Indians gave to one of their games. It was the southernmost Choctaw town visited by Tecumseh in 1811 when he tried to unite all Indian tribes against the whites.

HICKORY, *39.7 m.* (322 alt., 736 pop.), another sawmill town, was named for Andrew Jackson, "Old Hickory," whose military road passed through the village. Jackson is supposed to have camped overnight in 1815 with his army on the banks of Pottoxchitto Creek just S. of the town.

NEWTON, *49.1 m.* (412 alt., 2,011 pop.), the seat of Newton Co., is the largest town in the county. A trading center for the farmers of a wide area, it has a compact, modern business district and wide residential streets, shaded with live oaks. Here is CLARKE MEMORIAL COLLEGE, a private school of junior college rating, with modern brick buildings. In the Doolittle family cemetery is a CONFEDERATE CEMETERY with approximately 100 graves.

At Newton is the junction with State 15 *(see Tour 12).*

Between Newton and Lake the hills gradually flatten to gently rolling swells, and the intense redness of the clay soil is modified to a light lemon yellow, with fewer pine woods and more truck farms visible.

At *59.1 m.* is LAKE (452 alt., 375 pop.).

Right from Lake on an unmarked graveled road to the PATRONS' UNION CAMP GROUND, *2.2 m* (R). The Lake Patrons' Union, an outgrowth of the National Grange, has held annual sessions in August since its organization in 1874. The first meeting was called under a rude brush arbor, but after two assemblies had been held, the arbor was superseded by a pavilion built to seat a thousand people. The granges of Newton, Scott, Lauderdale, Neshoba, Jasper, Smith, Leake, and adjoining counties elect the directors. The August programs of the union are varied. There are reports of committees on agriculture, horticulture, education, and other subjects embracing almost every topic of interest to the people of the State, and the sessions have many distinguished visitors. The daily attendance has varied from 2,000 to 6,000.

Since 1893 for several weeks prior to the August meetings, Teachers Normal Institutes have been held on the union property, with well-known educators serving as instructors.

On this same road is CONEHATTA, *8.8 m.* (152 pop.). The CONEHATTA DAY SCHOOL FOR INDIANS, under the supervision of the Government agent at Philadelphia, is the center of an Indian community of one-mule farms typical of the communities in this "Indian country" of Mississippi. The settlement is made up almost entirely of Choctaw, descendants of the Indians who made this their home after the signing of the Dancing Rabbit Treaty in 1830. A number of the Conehatta women and girls supplement the inadequate family income by making and selling baskets of dyed split cane. The Conehatta baskets are perhaps the most attractive in the State. Few tribal rites are practiced, the majority of the Indians being either Catholics, Baptists, Methodists, or Presbyterians. An outstanding feature of early Indian life that is retained is the bright-colored dress of the women. The men dress much as do the neighboring white farmers, but they are easily distinguished by their long hair and dusky color. The school is carrying on the Americanization process: although the girls are taught basket weaving and bead work along with their domestic science and basic subjects, Indian ball has been replaced with top spinning, marble shooting, and basketball. The Indians are shy and reticent.

At *62.7 m.* US 80 enters the eastern end of the BIENVILLE NATIONAL FOREST. This forest, established in 1934, covers an area of 382,820 acres in Scott, Smith, and Jasper Counties; in shape it is an irregular, squat L, extending W. approximately 20 miles from this point, and N. and S. more than 35 miles. The forest has not yet attained impressive height, but the shortleaf pine is restocking naturally and quickly.

FOREST, *68 m.* (481 alt., 2,176 pop.), is the seat of Scott Co. and the headquarters of the Bienville Forest supervisor. The town is so named because of the dense pine growth which once covered the site.

Here is the junction with State 35 *(see Tour 16)*.

MORTON, 79.4 m. (463 alt., 955 pop.), is the home of one of the largest sawmills between Newton and Jackson, and the shipping station for bentonite dug from a mine 18 miles SW.

Left from Morton on an unmarked graveled road to forks, *1.7 m.*

1. Right here to the ROOSEVELT STATE PARK, *2.2 m.*, named for President Franklin D. Roosevelt. It is on the western edge of the Bienville Forest in a 494-acre tract of natural forest and flower growth. The park includes several springs that have a combined capacity of around 3,000 gallons of water per day. There are rustic, overnight cabins, a clubhouse, a native stone lodge, and bath houses. A dam creates a 125-acre lake stocked with fish and used also for swimming. Foot trails for hiking and bridle paths for horseback, as well as camping and picnicking facilities, are available.

2. Left here on a graveled road, keeping R. at every fork for *14.9 m.;* L. to BENTONITE MINE, *15.2 m. (open by permission from office, 8:30 to 5 weekdays)*, utilizing the largest bentonite deposit in the State. The stratum averages three feet in thickness and underlies 100 acres. Because of its nearness to the surface the mine has the appearance of a great opened pit. In 1934 the State Geological Survey made a detailed examination of the field, which had been noted three years earlier, and in 1936 the Attapulgus Clay Co. began development of the mineral. The product is a grayish, clay-like mineral, or group of minerals, consisting of hydro aluminum silicates and alkalies. Bentonite mined here is shipped to Jackson where it is processed in the Filtrol plant *(see Tour 5, Sec. b)*.

At *80.7* US 80 crosses the western boundary of the Bienville National Forest.

PELAHATCHIE (Ind., *hurricane creek*), *89. m.* (409 alt., 1,599 pop.), is named for the creek it borders.

Between Pelahatchie and Brandon the highway runs past fine stands of pine and hardwood trees.

At *99.1 m.* (L) is the *CAPT. JAMES L. McCASKILL HOME (private)*, one of the few ante-bellum homes left in this section. A long one-story house with square columns, it was built in 1830 and was originally an inn and stagecoach stop. Because it was occupied by a Northern family during the War between the States, it escaped the fate of other homes in the vicinity. General Sherman made his headquarters here.

BRANDON, *99.6 m.* (484 alt., 692 pop.), is an old town, rebuilt since its destruction during the War between the States. It is said that Brandon has produced more State governors, senators, and representatives of distinction than any other town its size in Mississippi. The town was named for Gerard Brandon, who served as Governor of the State from 1825 to 1831. The *A. J. McLAURIN HOME (private)* was at different times the home of two governors, Lowry and McLaurin. It stands 100 yds. S. of US 80 at the W. end of town on a spacious lawn shaded by cedars. The house is of frame construction, painted white, and has a two-story colonnaded portico rising in front. By the door in the living room there was for many years a dark stain. Here, during the war, a Northern officer was slain as he answered a call at the door. In the attic is a charred spot, marking the attempted burning of the house by a young slave girl trying to escape. At PURNELL SPRINGS both Confederate and Union soldiers camped during the war.

US 80, W. of Brandon, slopes gradually downward toward the Pearl River bottoms.

At *109.3 m.* is the junction with a graveled road.

Left on this road to the new *MISSISSIPPI HOSPITAL FOR THE INSANE,* 5.6 m. (L), a $5,000,000 plant including 78 buildings. It is the handsomest and best equipped of Mississippi's eleemosynary institutions. The hospital plant covers 3,300 acres and was completed in 1935. In appearance it is more of a village than an institution, with roads passing fruit and pecan orchards and well-spaced buildings (none more than two stories high) of the Colonial Williamsburg type of architecture. In reality there are two plants, one for white patients and the other for Negroes, but no distinction is evident in the type of buildings, and all patients receive similar care. Each race has its own chapel. Because of the space available the patients of each race are segregated according to their types of disease. All non-violent patients march to a central dining room for meals served cafeteria style; most of the food is produced on the institution's farm, which is worked by patients. Treatment includes hydrotherapy, physio-therapy, and occupational therapy; one of the most successful aids for the women has proved to be a well-equipped beauty parlor. The landscaping, like the buildings, is free from institutional aspects. There are an artificial lake and several miles of shrubbery-lined walks and drives. The site was once the Rankin Co. Penal Farm.

Between Brandon and Jackson the highway is bordered with small but neat truck farms. Back of the truck farms (R) but not visible from the highway is the *RANKIN COUNTY NATURAL GAS FIELD,* a recently exploited source of much potential wealth.

At *110.1 m.* is the junction with a graveled road.

Right on this road to the *KNOX GLASS MANUFACTURING COMPANY, 1.9 m.* (R), *(visited by permission),* the only plant of its kind in the State. Here bottles of all shapes and sizes are manufactured for distribution to all parts of the United States. The plant is a modern building with recreational facilities provided for its employees.

At *110.6 m.* is the junction (L) with US 49 *(see Tour 7),* which joins US 80 to cross a levee running through the second bottoms of the Pearl River and over the Woodrow Wilson Bridge, *111.5 m.* The river limits Jackson on the E. From the bridge are visible the few skyscrapers of which Mississippi can boast.

At *111.5 m.* US 80 follows E. Silas Brown St. over bridge; R. on S. State St.; L. on South St. to S. Gallatin St.

JACKSON, *112.7 m.* (294 alt., 48,282 pop.) *(see JACKSON).*

Points of Interest. Old Capitol, New Capitol, Livingston Park and Zoo, Hinds County Courthouse, Millsaps College, Belhaven College, Battlefield Park, and others.

At Jackson is the junction with US 51 *(see Tour 5),* and US 49 *(see Tour 7).*

The route continues on S. Gallatin St.; L. on W. Capitol St. (US 80).

On US 80, Jackson, as it does on all the highways running through it, marks an end and a beginning. Over the section between Jackson and Vicksburg was fought one of the bitterest and most decisive series of battles in the War between the States. Over this ground the Confederates were gradually pushed by Grant to the earthwork defenses of Vicksburg, the last link binding the two halves of the Confederacy.

US 80 crosses the bridge over the Yazoo & Mississippi Valley R.R. at the western city limits of Jackson. At *117.4 m.* (R) is the entrance to the *JACKSON COUNTRY CLUB ($1.10 greens fee)*, of which the 18-hole course is the scene of Mississippi's major tournaments. At *119.3 m.* (R) is the *CRISMORLAND ROSE GARDEN*, a lovely country garden and nursery typical of the showy suburban places that contrast with the small truck farms along the road.

At *119.5* is the entrance to *LAKEWOOD CEMETERY*, in appearance more a park than a cemetery because bronze tablets set flush with the carpeting grass take the place of grave monuments. The cemetery, opened in 1927, occupies a 200-acre tract, 35 acres of which are developed. A pleasing conceit is a heart-shaped lake, divided by the graveled drive.

The highway W. of the cemetery is bordered with small truck farms, separated by hedges of honeysuckle and Cherokee roses, with an occasional clump of cedars denoting an older settlement.

At *121.3 m.* (L) is the *CLINTON CEMETERY*, marking the eastern limits of CLINTON (324 alt., 912 pop.), a small college town. Long before Mississippi became a State, Clinton was an Indian agency, known as Mount Dexter. About 1823 Walter Leake, formerly a Mississippi Territorial judge, who later became the third Governor of the State, bought land here and later erected a home called Mount Salus. The white settlement that grew up around his home was called Mount Salus. The first land office and the first post office in the State were in this place. The land office was established to dispose of lands acquired in 1820 from the Choctaw Indians by the Treaty of Doak's Stand. The post office was Governor Leake's "little letter-box." The spring waters at Mount Salus and the town's situation on the Natchez Trace made it popular as an early health resort. State roads to Vicksburg and Jackson were opened in 1820 and 1826.

In the fall of 1828 the citizens of Mount Salus changed the name of the village to Clinton in honor of De Witt Clinton, then Governor of New York. In the same year the town narrowly missed selection as the county seat, the honor falling to Raymond, and in the next year missed by one vote being selected as the State capital. The deciding vote was cast by Maj. John R. Peyton of Raymond, Clinton's rival town.

The Clinton & Vicksburg R.R. *(see TRANSPORTATION)*, the second oldest in the State, was incorporated in 1831. In 1835 the citizens had to organize hastily against a threatened raid of Murrell's desperadoes. In 1834 a Masonic lodge was organized, becoming the parent lodge to those of both Jackson and Vicksburg. Grant and Sherman each established headquarters here. Sherman pillaged, but there was little burning, and the two colleges were left unharmed. Immediately after the War between the States Clinton was shipping 20,000 bales of cotton a year, handling more than any market between Vicksburg and Meridian. In 1875 occurred the Clinton race riot, one of the bloodiest of the Reconstruction upheavals, in which white citizens rising against Negro supremacy gained the ascendancy, with the assistance of volunteer groups of armed men from Jackson and Vicksburg. The number of Negroes killed has been estimated at 50.

At *122 m.* (L) is the entrance to MISSISSIPPI COLLEGE, the Baptist school that has made Clinton a seat of learning since 1826. Next to Jefferson College it is the oldest school for boys in the State. It was founded as Hampstead (incorporated as Hamstead) Academy in 1826, but the year after its name was changed by an act of the Legislature to Mississippi Academy, and in 1830 to Mississippi College. The founders in changing the name hoped that it would become the State university, and this hope was realized to the extent of State recognition and support from the "seminary lands." Failure to achieve permanent State support, however, caused Clinton citizens to turn the school over to the Presbyterian Synod in 1842. The Presbyterians gave it back in 1850, and when it appeared that the school was about to become extinct, the Mississippi Baptist State Convention rescued it and has cared for it ever since.

The period of enthusiasm just after the Baptists took over the school resulted in the building of the COLLEGE CHAPEL, the only antebellum structure on the campus. The Baptists had succeeded in obtaining a $100,000 endowment fund; then in 1858 a building fund was raised, and from its $30,000 was created this Corinthian style temple. It is a square building constructed of red brick and stucco with a slate roof. The capitals, railings, interior columns, and other ornaments are of cast iron. The stuccoed ground floor is given to classrooms, but the chapel itself is lofty enough to include a balcony around three sides of the chamber. Particularly attractive are the triple-hung sash windows, fully 20 feet high. When the War between the States began, the Mississippi College Rifles was organized from the student body. The endowment decreased in value, and the school would have been sold for debt had it not been for the aid Mrs. Adelia Hillman gave in raising funds in the North. For a long period after 1877 the college faculty worked on a contingent basis instead of with guaranteed salaries. It has produced many of the outstanding men of the State, including three governors: Brown, Longino, and H. L. Whitfield.

Closely associated with Mississippi College in spirit as well as in organization is HILLMAN COLLEGE, the oldest existing school for girls in Mississippi. Almost hidden in a quiet tree-shaded campus, the brick and frame buildings are of no definite design. The school was begun by the Central Baptist Association in 1853 as the Central Female Institute, in 1891 it was renamed "in honor of those who have done so much for it, Dr. Walter Hillman and Mrs. Adelia M. Hillman, his wife." For 16 years it was under the direct control of the Baptist Association; it is said to have been the only educational institution in the South that held classes uninterruptedly throughout the War between the States. Even when the campaigns against Vicksburg brought the roar of the contending armies' cannon to the quiet campus the institute was enrolling a hundred pupils annually and was graduating classes ranging from nine in 1860 to two in 1865. Although the school remained open during the conflict and was unharmed by Federal troops, it was heavily in debt at the close of the war. In 1869 the Baptist Association turned the property titles over to the school's president, Dr. Hillman. It has since been operated privately, but has retained its denominational character. Dr. Hillman remained as president until his death in 1894.

At one time the school possessed the best natural history museum in Mississippi; it now shares science laboratories with Mississippi College.

At Mississippi College is the junction with the graveled Raymond road.

Left on the Raymond Road and on the westernmost of twin hills S. of Mississippi College are the ruins of the old *MOSS HOME, 0.6 m.* (R), formerly the home of Col. Raymond Robinson. The crumbling ruins are of a beautiful red brick, and enough is left to give a vivid idea of the original structure, built before 1810. Much of the original roof still protects the broken brick walls. The design of the structure, of somewhat hybrid type, is based upon Spanish and English Georgian traditions. This is notable in its H-shaped plan, raised basement story, the high central section with its low-pitched hip roof and tall flanking chimneys. The secondary roof of similar construction once covered the lower wings and deeply recessed front and rear porches. The porches, now gone, were in the form of loggias between the wings. At the eaves of the roof a heavy wooden cornice with modillion brackets is impaled with cut nails upon hewn joists and rafters. The great central hall on the second or principal floor, with its large window openings and graceful arched doorways, flanked by small half-length side lights, opens onto the porches. These, in turn, give access to the two rooms on each side. Each of the side chambers has corner fireplaces. The dining room, scullery and other services were on the ground floor. Facing N. on the crest of the hill, the house was originally approached by a drive crossing the ravine and circling the knoll. It is guarded and half hidden by two tall cedars on each side of what was once the entrance staircase. In 1818 Andrew Jackson, then land commissioner at Clinton, was a guest in this home.

Here the wealthy widow of Judge Caldwell *(see below)* was found murdered shortly after her re-marriage.

Between the Moss home and the Raymond road, on the other hill, are the *RUINS OF GOVERNOR LEAKE'S HOME,* Mount Salus, facing the lake across the road. When built Mount Salus was the first brick house in the county. It was burned in 1920.

In the middle of the road between the hill and the lake is the *SITE OF THE CALDWELL-PEYTON DUEL.* This duel, taking place in 1829, was the result of a quarrel between Judge Isaac Caldwell of Clinton and Maj. John R. Peyton of Raymond. As a member of the State legislature Peyton cast the deciding vote which established Jackson as State capital over Clinton. His action so enraged Caldwell that he challenged Peyton to a duel. Both men escaped uninjured, but in 1835 Caldwell fought a duel with Samuel Gwin, this time to defend the honor of his friend, George Poindexter. Gwin had hissed a speech of Poindexter's at a free-drinking inaugural levee for Governor Lynch. Caldwell and Gwin were each armed with six pistols and were advancing upon each other as they fired. Caldwell died that day; Gwin lingered in agony a year.

US 80, W. of Clinton, passes through cuts showing a pebbly clay outcropping. The land is not heavily wooded; the homes are poor. An occasional Negro is seen hoeing or plowing in fields which are separated by clumps of trees. There are pastoral landscapes, and at intervals groups of fine oaks.

At BOLTON, *130.2 m.* (216 alt., 441 pop.), the highway runs through an avenue of water oaks that shade the residences on each side. Bolton exemplifies the quiet, shadowy, old inland hamlet found in the prairie belt W. of Jackson. It has three steam cotton gins.

West of Bolton good farms lie on both sides of the highway, white folks' tractors alternating with Negroes' mules in the work. Fresh eggs and cool buttermilk can be bought at the roadside farmhouses.

At *139.2 m.* is EDWARDS (226 alt., 456 pop.).

1. Left from Edwards on a graveled road, the old Edwards-Bolton highway, to *CHAMPION'S HILL, 4.4 m.*, situated at the point where the middle Raymond road intersects the old highway. The old highway extends over the crest of the hill, an elevation 70 feet above the surrounding country. On the crest of this hill on May 16, 1863, Confederate General Pemberton's left wing was placed, facing E. against the far larger Union Army under Grant. The occasion was momentous. Grant was in possession of Jackson and was moving toward Vicksburg. The three divisions of Pemberton's army were trying frantically to unite with Johnston. Grant moved in between. South of Champion's Hill Pemberton's army stretched three miles, 15,000 Confederates fighting desperately to save Vicksburg from destruction, but it was for the hill that Grant and Pemberton fought. One of the most brilliant movements on either side was the charge of Cockrell's brigade of Bowen's division, preparing the way for the advance of the Confederate front to beyond the crest of the hill. This movement was accomplished in the evening of May 16, following an afternoon of steady contest for possession. The weight of the Federal forces, increased by fresh divisions moving up from Raymond, however, finally turned the Confederate wing and Pemberton retreated across the Big Black River. The Confederate loss was 324 killed, 3,269 wounded or captured, and all artillery. The Federal loss was 410 killed, 2,031 wounded or captured. One division of Confederate troops, consisting of almost 4,000 men, was cut off from the rest of the army and forced to flee in a southeasterly direction beyond Jackson. Grant's victory was the decisive stroke of the campaign. The Confederates were scattered and the Federals were rapidly nearing Vicksburg, their objective. The evening after the battle Grant received Halleck's order, sent five days before, telling him on no account whatever to undertake such a campaign. Grant could read the order with calmness; he had staked everything and had won.

2. Left from Edwards on a country road leading across the wooden bridge over the Yazoo & Mississippi Valley R.R. tracks to the *TILGHMAN MONUMENT, 3 m.* The monument is on the L. just beyond a church on the R. The stone is not 50 feet from the road and is easily visible, but is on the other side of a bordering gully. A path leads down into the gully and up to the railed enclosure. The road has every appearance of age, winding through a cut below the level of the fields, bordered with trees. A single small cedar shades the monument, whose inscription reads: "Lloyd Tilghman, Brigadier General C.S.A., Commander First Brigade, Loring's Division. Killed here the afternoon of May 18, 1863, near the close of the battle of Champion's Hill." Tilghman died defending the ford across Baker's Creek while the Confederates retreated. The story is that he was shot by a sharpshooter from the *HENRY COKER HOUSE, 3.3 m.*, on the next hill. It is a one-and-a-half-story country house, painted brown, with a central hall and a small four-columned porch. At the four corners are giant magnolia trees. Along the drive in front are cedars with moss hanging from the limbs. The house is on a knoll. In its front door and jambs are bullet holes made during the battle on Champion's Hill, three miles NE. across the hills and ravines.

The *SOUTHERN CHRISTIAN INSTITUTE, 140.2 m.* (L), a Negro college known as Mount Beulah, was established in 1875 on the plantation of the Cook family. Its 1937 enrollment is 222. The school structures, set on a hill just off the highway are grouped about a white, square

TOUR 2 313

frame building two stories in height, housing the administrative offices and the classrooms; the boarding students live in small one-story frame structures scattered over the campus. At the school the highway flattens out into the bottoms of the Big Black River.

At *145.3 m.* is the junction with the old road across the Big Black River.

Left on the old road leading under the Yazoo & Mississippi Valley R.R. to an old BRIDGE, *0.3 m.,* across the Big Black River. Near this concrete railroad bridge the Battle of the Big Black was fought, confirming the outcome of Champion's Hill. The Confederates were routed in panic, losing the fortifications of the bridge and 18 guns, in addition to 1,751 men taken captive by Grant. After the battle Pemberton concentrated his remaining forces in the bluff hills encircling Vicksburg.

US 80 climbs into the bluff hills immediately W. of the Big Black River. The cuts through which the new road passes are in some places 25 feet deep, showing brittle loess. The highway runs through a stretch of large and varied trees to come suddenly at *154.7 m.* upon a spider web of intersecting roads—the ENTRANCE TO THE VICKSBURG NATIONAL MILITARY PARK *(see VICKSBURG).*

US 80 follows Clay St. to Washington St.

VICKSBURG, *155.5 m.* (206 alt., 22,943 pop.) *(see VICKSBURG).*

Points of Interest. Warren Co. Courthouse, a number of ante-bellum, siege-marked homes, and others.

Here is the junction with US 61 *(see Tour 3).*

Left from Vicksburg on Clay St. to Cherry St.; R. on Cherry St.; L. on a local blacktop road that cuts an intricately winding path through the hills and bluffs of this section. The landscape is very rugged, with dense forests and undergrowth throughout, and contrives to give a scene of primeval beauty. The *U. S. WATERWAYS EXPERIMENT STATION (guides at Administration Building, 9-4 weekdays), 4.6 m.,* is a hydraulic laboratory installed for the purpose of building and operating small-scale models of the Mississippi and other rivers. The laboratory is on a Federal reservation containing 245 acres. In the valley at the entrance is the Administration Building, flanked with auxiliary buildings containing special laboratories, shop facilities, and warehouses. Back of these is an 80-acre lake, while spread in front across the valley are miniature reproductions of sections of rivers, bays, and harbors.

Beyond this valley a winding road up a steep wooded hill leads to a plateau that was levelled to provide a 100-acre experimental field. Here larger models are in operation. Among them and probably of greatest interest is the Mississippi River model, the largest of this type in the world. It represents a 600-mile stretch of the river—from Helena, Ark., to Donaldsonville, La.—including the entire main river channel and the backwater areas of its tributaries. The model, like all the others, is constructed of concrete and is covered with fluted screened wire that represents roughness such as trees and undergrowth or anything that hinders the flow of water. The model is 1,055 ft. long, has an average width of 167 ft., and covers 111,600 sq. ft., which represents 10,250,000 acres of the actual Mississippi area. One cubic foot per second of water flowing through the channel of the model is equivalent to 1,500,000 cubic feet per second in nature. The water is introduced into each of the tributaries by means of V-notch weir boxes, several of which are also scattered over the model to simulate run-offs from rainfall.

In seven small houses are gauges recording the height of the water surface in the models. Telephones installed in these houses enable all operators to keep in

HIGHWAY THROUGH LOESS BLUFFS TO VICKSBURG

touch with each other. An automatic timing device gives a signal with the passing of each "day," which requires five minutes and 24 seconds on this model. The purpose of this work is to test flood control devices, such as cut-offs, floodways, and storage reservoirs. This is carried out by running water into the model in which have been constructed proposed levees, dikes, or dredge cuts in order to determine if these constructions will produce the desired results. Two full-time photographers make pictures during these tests which need detailed study.

The station studies problems not only of the United States but also of foreign countries. The model of Maracaibo Bay in Venezuela, South America, shows the Pacific Ocean and the channel from the ocean to the bay through which heavily loaded oil barges must travel and are sometimes caught. The purpose of the study is to find a means of keeping the channel open without periodic dredging. In this model there is an apparatus that reproduces actual tides, and a machine that reproduces the waves, both of which are electrically operated and controlled. Thirty-five minutes of operation in this study of tides equals a 24-hour day. The model is on the plateau but is housed in a building 200 feet square.

The route continues L. on Washington St. (US 80-61). US 80 crosses the *VICKSBURG TOLL BRIDGE, 157.7 m. (cars $1.25, passengers 25¢, pedestrians free)* over the Mississippi River. A cantilever type and through truss spans, the bridge was designed and constructed by Harrington, Howard and Ash of Kansas City. It was opened for traffic in 1930. The river, the boundary line between Mississippi and Louisiana, is 73 miles E. of Monroe, La.

Tour 3

(Memphis, Tenn.)—Clarksdale—Vicksburg—Natchez—(Baton Rouge, La). US 61.
Tennessee Line to Louisiana Line, 334.6 m.

Two-thirds route hard-surfaced, two lanes wide, rest being paved.
Yazoo & Mississippi Valley R.R. parallels route throughout.
Accommodations of all kinds available; hotels chiefly in cities.
Caution: Look out for stock wandering on road at night.

Sec. a TENNESSEE LINE *to* VICKSBURG, *206.4 m.*

US 61 passes through the State's great alluvial plain, an extensive flat land with sluggish rivers, lakes, and bayous. The land, often lying below the level of the Mississippi River, which flows between a system of high man-made embankments called levees, is not strictly a river delta. But for thousands of years the river has deposited over it the rich topsoil of half a continent, giving it a fertility equaling that of the Nile and making it one of the world's finest cotton-producing areas. For this reason the section is colloquially called the Delta. Spreading leaf-shaped to the south, it is a land of cotton and cotton planters. In the fall, or cotton-picking time, it is a sea of white, broken at intervals by dark lines of trees that grow along the bayous. The plantation big houses are substantial but not pretentious; the tenant cabins are all alike. Smaller towns, hardly more than plantation centers, are of a single pattern; each is centered about a gin, a filling station, a loading platform, and a short line of low-roofed, brick stores. The points of interest, aside from the land itself, are the levees and the river, the lakes, the Indian mounds, and the cotton fields.

At *0 m.* US 61 crosses the Mississippi Line, 7.9 miles S. of Memphis, and, dropping from the hills to the Delta, gives an occasional glimpse of the green levee bank that is 25 ft. high (R) and of the wooded bluffs (L).

At *1.1 m.* is the junction with a graveled road.

Right on this road is LAKEVIEW, *0.4 m.* (222 alt., 200 pop.), a fishing resort *(buffalo, crappie, perch, bass, catfish, and trout)* by one of the lakes formed in an old bed of the ever-changing Mississippi River. The lake is six and a half miles long. Its front is privately owned *(no overnight accommodations; boats rented to fishermen, $1 a day).*

WALLS, *3.4 m.* (213 alt., 150 pop.), is a plantation town built near the Walls group of Indian mounds; so far as is known no post-Columbian material has been found in the mounds.

LAKE CORMORANT, *8.4 m.* (208 alt., 207 pop.), borders a lake of the same name, which is typical of the bodies of water left behind when the Mississippi River changes its course; it is four and a half miles long and only 100 yards wide.

Between Lake Cormorant and Robinsonville the highway cuts due southward while the levee (R) swings slightly westward and the bluffs (L) swing eastward; here the leaf-shaped Delta, at the northern end not two miles wide, begins to widen; further south it reaches a width of approximately 85 miles. At various points, plantation roads lead through the fields and over the levee. From any of these roads at the top of the levee the river is seen still farther to the west, and occasionally a cultivated field in the swamps between the levee and the river.

At *16.3 m.* is ROBINSONVILLE (204 alt., 150 pop.).

Right from Robinsonville on State 3, a graveled road, is COMMERCE, *4.8 m.* (201 alt., 50 pop.), once a rival of Memphis for the river trade, now a plantation centered around the big house built on the slope of a large Indian mound. The land was originally bought from the Chickasaw by Dick Abbay, who built his first log cabin in 1832. Other early settlers were Tom Fletcher, a Choctaw Indian, and Col. Tom Burns. By 1850 Commerce had become the seat of Tunica Co., but, just before the War between the States, the river, which had been responsible for the growth of the town, started destroying it. Abbay's log cabin was washed away. Trying to save their homes, the settlers built the first levees in this section of the Delta, Abbay being assisted by Gen. James L. Alcorn, later Reconstruction governor. But the river climbed the levees, spilled into the streets, and swallowed Memphis' rival. Today the old *COLONEL BURNS' STABLES* of whitewashed brick serve as commissaries on the Leatherman plantation which borders both sides of the five miles of road leading from Robinsonville to the big house. The present *LEATHERMAN HOME (private)* was not built directly on the 50-foot Indian mound because of the unwillingness of the builder to desecrate a mound "full of the dead." The mound rises behind the house. From its top, so the inevitable legend goes, Hernando De Soto in 1541 had his first glimpse of the great river that was to be his grave. The view of the river is now cut off by the levee and the trees. The Leatherman house is a modern structure, an impressive center for the silos, great barns, and Negro cabins on this typical Delta plantation.

At *5.7 m.* a great bend in the levee brings it close to the road. From the top of the great sloping green mound is a good view of the lowland that has been condemned for habitation by the Federal Government. Here is a 1,000-acre tract that gives a good illustration of what Delta planters have to fight again and again. This field is planted each year in corn, but if the planter breaks fifty-fifty with the overflowing backwater of the nearby river he considers himself fortunate. The river wins more crops than the planter, yet the yield per acre is so great that even one-third of a full crop pays for the effort and risk.

At *7.8 m.* on the plantation road is the *DE BE VOIS INDIAN MOUNDS,* nine small ones centered about one as tall as the Leatherman mound but much larger. Because of its size the center mound is believed to have been the place on which Chief Chisca of the Chickasaw tribe built his home, and the site of the skirmish De Soto had with the Chickasaw before he crossed the river.

TUNICA, *26.4 m.* (197 alt., 1,043 pop.), is the trading center for the stretch of the Delta between Clarksdale and Memphis. The river (R) near Tunica has changed its course so often that what was Mississippi shore 30 years ago is now Arkansas territory.

At *39.5 m.* is DUNDEE (190 alt., 300 pop.).

Right from Dundee on a narrow graveled road climbing over the levee *(road between levee and ferry is low; drive with care)* to a ferry, *6 m.*, crossing the river to Helena, Ark. *(18-hr. service, leaving on the half-hour; $1 for car and driver, 25¢ each passenger).*

At *44.6 m.* is LULA (180 alt., 448 pop.).

Right from Lula on a graveled road to *GRANT'S PASS, 2.5 m.* A small wooden bridge near the head of Moon Lake, here a bayou, marks the place where Gen. U. S. Grant dynamited a pass from the Mississippi into the Coldwater River in order to get his gunboats through the Coldwater into the Yazoo and then descend on Vicksburg from the rear. The scheme failed, however.

West of Grant's Pass for several miles lies MOON LAKE (R), a Delta recreational center (fishing, swimming, boating); the scene is delightful.

At *14 m.* on the graveled road circling Moon Lake is FRIAR POINT (171 alt., 988 pop.), lying in the shadow of the levee that conceals the Mississippi River from the town. From the levee's broad, flat top, however, is an extensive view of the river. The town is old, the only one of the towns established on the river in the 1830's that has not been swallowed by the waters that originally gave them importance. Nevertheless the river is a menace; because of it the county records were, in 1930, removed to Clarksdale, and Friar Point was abandoned as a county seat. Today the town lives by growing and ginning cotton, but it once had a steamboat trade that bustled and hummed in the days before the War between the States. Grant stopped here on his way with a fleet of transports to Vicksburg. The *ROBINSON HOME (open by permission)* has a hole in its façade made by a cannon ball when Federal and Confederate gunboats were skirmishing in the river at that time. Ferry to Helena, Ark. *(18-hr. service, leaving on half-hour; $1 for car and driver, 25¢ passengers).*

At *46.6 m.* is the junction with a graveled road.

Right on this road to COAHOMA, *3.5 m.* (177 alt., 295 pop.), a small plantation center. Directly across from the depot is the L-shaped, clapboard HOME OF MRS. BLANCHE MONTGOMERY RALSTON *(open by permission).* Mrs. Blanche Montgomery Ralston, prominent for many years in civic and social service work in Mississippi, is now Regional Director of the Women's and Professional Projects of the Works Progress Administration.

At *48.6 m.* on US 61 is the junction with a graveled road.

Left on this road *3.6 m.* is JONESTOWN (175 alt., 506 pop.).

1. Left from Jonestown *1.4 m.* on a graveled road to *MATAGORDA (open by appointment)*, a plantation with a home built by Col. D. M. Russell around a two-room log cabin constructed before the War between the States. Colonel Russell had attained notoriety by resigning from Yale in 1856 as the leader of the Southern students' rebellion against President Woolsey's anti-slavery remarks. Kept from fighting because of weak lungs, Russell was commissioner of the Confederate States for making purchases in England, and on his return planned the Confederate raid on the banks at St. Albans, Vermont. Colonel Russell's initials, D. M. R., C. S. A., are said to be carved on the top of St. Paul's Cathedral in London; Russell is supposed to have made the climb on a dare, despite a lung hemorrhage. The name Matagorda was given to the place by Colonel Russell for a special variety of long-staple cotton he raised, a variety well known on the Liverpool Exchange. The house contains 22 rooms and five baths, has one of the best private libraries in the State, a choice collection of old china, and one of the State's largest and finest private art collections. Although the house is two stories high, its length and wide porches give it a low, rambling appearance. Climbing roses, gnarled cedars, and water oaks grace the grounds.

2. Right from Jonestown *2.4 m.* on a graveled road to *EAGLES' NEST PLANTATION.* The plantation was the home of Gen. James L. Alcorn, whose persistence in fighting for a State levee system was finally successful. It was Alcorn who gave the plantation its name. Atop an Indian mound on the plantation is a *MONUMENT TO ALCORN* marking his grave. Alcorn served as Governor of

Mississippi from 1870–71. He died in 1894 *(see AN OUTLINE OF FOUR CENTURIES)*.

At *58.7 m.* is the junction with State 6 *(see Tour 14)*.

CLARKSDALE, *62.3 m.* (173 alt., 10,043 pop.), is a typical Mississippi Delta city with level surface, far horizons, and broad surrounding cotton fields. Viewed from a distance, the bare and treeless business district of stores, gins, warehouses, and loading platforms appears squat and dwarfed; yet silver-leaf maples and water oaks line the residential streets giving the homes a secluded air. As many of these streets end abruptly in the cotton fields, the sudden emergence from shade into open country offers a startling contrast of light and shade. Fringed by dark cypresses and bright willows, the narrow Sunflower River winds through the city eastward and westward. Along its banks are many of the oldest homes of Clarksdale—large, comfortable frame houses, with wide front galleries.

There is hardly a planter, tenant, or sharecropper on the surrounding plantations whose business does not bring him to Clarksdale every Saturday, the planter for business transactions, the tenant to buy supplies and fertilizer. These Saturday trips afford opportunity for much visiting on street corners; neighbors of the countryside call each other by their first names and with delightful informality extend invitations to foxhunting, fishing, or dancing. Weekends in the country form a large part of Clarksdale's social life.

Though a few French Huguenot families are said to have been established earlier in the locality, John Clark is given credit for founding Clarksdale, the seat of Coahoma Co. Clark was the son of an English architect, who was sent to Halifax by the British Government to help rebuild the city destroyed by fire. The elder Clark died of yellow fever in New Orleans in 1837 leaving John, age 14, to make his way. In December 1839 he landed at Port Royal near the present town of Friar Point in Coahoma Co., where he met Ed Porter who became his partner in the logging business. After several years both Clark and Porter quit logging for farming. Clark bought his first 100 acres of land from the Government in 1848. The land site was well-chosen, for though the Delta above the Lake Washington district was largely a trackless swamp at the time, here on the banks of the Sunflower was a narrow spot of dry ground. Formerly it was a point of intersection for two most important Indian routes: the Chakchiuma trade trail, which ran northeastward to old Pontotoc, and the Lower Creek trade path which extended westward from Augusta, Ga., to New Mexico. At the point of intersection was a fortification. After Clark's arrival, more Huguenot families came in, cleared land, and settled on plantations. In 1858 he began work on Hopedale, the original Clark home, and in 1868 opened a store and platted off a village on the site of the Indian fortification. In 1882 it was incorporated as Clarksdale. Frequent floods, a fire that swept away the business houses in 1889, and the lack of roads retarded the development of the town for many years, but since 1900 its corporate limits have pushed the cotton fields farther and farther back on all sides. A network of paved highways now connects it with the other parts of the State, and, perhaps more important, ties it close to other plantation centers. It is today the trading, ginning, compressing, and financial hub of a great cotton-growing area. Of secondary importance are lumber mills and planing mills, using timber cut from the Delta swamps.

The *CUTRER HOME (private)*, NW. of courthouse on Friar Point Road, occupies the site of one of the first houses in Clarksdale. Built by the daughter of John Clark and almost hidden by oak and cedar trees, on the bank of the river, it is a red-roofed, stuccoed mansion of good proportions.

HOPEDALE, adjoining the Cutrer home, is the original John Clark home. Begun in 1858 by workmen brought from Philadelphia, the house was not quite finished at the outbreak of the War between the States. Clark and his family moved in, however, and at the close of the war completed the construction. Though remodeled and modernized, the west side of the home, facing a large lawn studded with magnolia and oak trees, retains its earlier character. The interior trim is of solid walnut, the lumber having been whip-sawed from trees grown on the plantation.

The *CARNEGIE PUBLIC LIBRARY*, SE. corner Delta Ave. and First St., a red brick English Tudor type building, was completed in 1914 at a cost of $25,000, but within recent years additions have more than doubled its value. With 49,250 volumes, the largest public library collection in the State, and an annual book circulation of 167,982, it is one of the outstanding libraries in Mississippi. The collection of Indian relics on display here is also outstanding; excavated from the old fortification and from the many nearby mounds, are agricultural implements, hunting knives, beads, pipes, and pottery.

The Delta Staple Cotton Festival, held usually in late Aug. or early Sept., is an event that attracts visitors from a number of States. It is the social climax of the harvest season.

At Clarksdale are the junctions with State 1 *(see Side Tour 3A)* and US 49 *(see Tour 7, Sec. a)*.

Between Clarksdale and Cleveland the highway traverses cotton fields stretching for miles on each side. The cotton stalks grow taller than a man. In the few fields where it is cultivated corn reaches 15 ft. in height.

BOBO, *71.9 m.* (164 alt., 110 pop.), is an early plantation settlement.

ALLIGATOR, *75.4 m.* (163 alt., 278 pop.), was named for the alligators that formerly infested Alligator Lake by which the town lies.

DUNCAN, *77.3 m.* (157 alt., 337 pop.), like many Delta towns, has several Chinese families. In 1929 all buildings here were swept away by a tornado that killed 22 people. Since then the town has been completely rebuilt.

HUSHPUCKENA, *80.3 m.* (250 pop.), is a pecan-shipping center.

At SHELBY, *82.7 m.* (141 alt., 1,811 pop.), the two crews building the Yazoo & Mississippi Valley R.R. from Vicksburg to Memphis met in 1884.

WYANDOTTE, *85.7 m.* (142 pop.), also known as Chambers and Winstonville, is a suburb of Mound Bayou.

MOUND BAYOU, *88.7 m.* (143 alt., 834 pop.), Renova and Wyandotte are the only towns in the State populated entirely by Negroes. Mound Bayou was founded in 1887 by Isaiah T. Montgomery and Benjamin T. Green, Negroes. Montgomery was a former slave of Joseph Emory Davis, brother of Jefferson Davis, and purchased the Davis plantation at Davis Bend after the war, living there with his family until he moved to Mound Bayou. Later he, the only Negro delegate to Mississippi's Constitutional Convention of 1890, supported the provision whose effect was to bar Negroes from voting.

Montgomery and Green, accompanied by their cousin, J. P. T. Montgomery, and twelve families, most of whom came from Davis Bend, Warren Co., Miss., surveyed this site in Bolivar Co. and cleared it for occupation. Indian mounds NE. and SE. of the site gave the town its name. The population had reached 183 before the end of the first year of settlement. In February 1898 the Negroes petitioned the Governor to incorporate the village, and in August the charter was signed and sealed. The town has the usual mayor, sheriff, aldermen, and chamber of commerce; the inhabitants engage in farming, lumbering and merchandising and service businesses. Here is the *BOLIVAR COUNTY TRAINING SCHOOL,* a coeducational institution. Overnight accommodations for white visitors are available at the Montgomery Home (R), a red brick house.

Founder's Day, held annually in July, is attended by prominent Negroes from all parts of the country.

MERIGOLD, *91.4 m.* (804 pop.), with a population composed of whites, Negroes, and Chinese, has two white churches, three Negro churches, a high school for white children and a Rosenwald grammar school for Negroes. In the park are a swimming pool and tennis courts.

CLEVELAND, *98.8 m.* (139 alt., 3,240 pop.), is a growing Delta town made prosperous by the large planting interests of its inhabitants. Many of the white frame cottages in its residential section are perhaps the best examples in the State of the modern adaptation of the Greek Revival design for small dwellings.

DELTA STATE TEACHERS' COLLEGE is a modern plant, established in 1924 to serve the northwestern section of the State. It is a Grade A fully accredited senior college. The *NATURAL HISTORY MUSEUM (open),* though small, exhibits articles of interest. The Choral Club is outstanding in the State.

SHAW, *109.4 m.* (133 alt., 1,612 pop.), is a lively cotton ginning and marketing center. Its well-built frame cottages, paved streets, brick consolidated high school, and outdoor swimming pool *(open)* form a typical center of the new Delta.

At LELAND, *125.1 m.* (113 alt., 2,426 pop.), along the high sloping banks of Deer Creek is a charming residential section. Unlike the majority of Delta towns, which are dependent solely on the production of cotton, Leland profits from the growing of three other major products

—alfalfa, vegetables, and pecans. Leland, formerly Three Oaks Plantation, was settled in 1847 by Judge James Rucks, whose commodious home, with its surrounding slave quarters, smokehouses, cotton houses, barns, and stables, was a settlement in itself. At that time Deer Creek was navigable, and the fact that Three Oaks was in a bend on the high banks was responsible for its transition from a plantation to a plantation center, the change taking place in 1884 with the coming of the Yazoo & Mississippi Valley R.R.

Here is the junction with US 82 *(see Tour 6)*.

Right from Leland on an asphalt road along Deer Creek to the *DELTA EXPERIMENT STATION* at *STONEVILLE, 2.5 m.* established in 1906 and containing 760 acres under the supervision of Federal experts working in collaboration with Mississippi State College. The station has recently acquired 3,000 acres of sub-marginal land that is to be reforested.

At *132.2 m.* (R), facing Deer Creek, is a two-story stucco home with red tile roof and bright green lawn; it is typical of the new Delta big houses.

ARCOLA, *135.4 m.* (115 alt., 343 pop.), is a plantation trading center.

At *136.6 m.* (R) is a house, facing Deer Creek from a great oak grove, that is typical of the ante-bellum Delta homes. A square frame building two stories high, it sits on a high foundation and has a wide screened porch; at the rear is a one-story wing.

At ESTILL, *139.4 m.* (50 pop.), US 61 crosses the lower end of the 38,000 acres of the *DELTA AND PINE LAND CO. PLANTATION (see Side Tour 3A).*

At *143.1 m.* is HOLLANDALE (111 alt., 1,211 pop.).

Right from Hollandale on a marked dirt road is LEROY PERCY STATE PARK, *4.2 m.*, the first of the Mississippi State parks; it was opened to the public May 1, 1936. The administration building, the superintendent's home, and seven overnight cabins have been completed. Projects under way include additional overnight cabins, a swimming pool, development of the warm water pools, stables with horses for hire, two large lakes for fishing, canoeing facilities by Black Bayou, playgrounds for children, tennis courts, and trails. A hostess arranges for club meetings, parties, and dances; there is equipment to serve banquets to as many as 300 people. The entire area of 2,541 acres will be used as a game preserve and stocked by the Mississippi State Game and Fish Commission. The park is named for the late U. S. Senator LeRoy Percy (1860–1929), one of Washington County's most distinguished sons *(see Side Tour 3A).*

PERCY, *148 m.* (217 pop.), is the trading center and shipping point for a large plantation.

At *148.9 m.* US 61 crosses the northern boundary of *PANTHER BURN PLANTATION,* owned by McGee & Co. of Leland and typical of the large corporation-owned plantations in the Delta *(see AGRICULTURE).* This plantation has a total acreage of 12,400 and a population of 2,200. The frame tenant cabins (L) face Deer Creek across old US 61. The railroad (R) is said never to have been able to purchase this strip of land, making it the only privately owned right of way used by the Illinois Central System. At *151.2 m.* is the little town that forms the plantation center. At *151.7 m.* the highway crosses the southern boundary of the plantation.

The dark brown, one-story frame buildings, each flanked by a basketball court, that dot the roadside in this section are schools built by planters for the children of tenant families.

NITTA YUMA, *154.7 m.* (109 alt., 25 pop.), according to old settlers, was settled in 1768 by the Phelps family who were conducted up the Mississippi River by Indian guides. On the south bank of Deer Creek, W. of the railroad, is one of the cabins erected in 1768. It is constructed of cypress logs put together with wooden pegs. One end now houses a business office. West of town on the creek are the remains of several log cabins, slave quarters, and. brick cisterns, built before the War between the States. At the time of settlement much of this section was owned by the Vick family *(see VICKSBURG).* The large house (L) shows well the originality the early planter used in adapting current modes to his needs. Though having some Georgian characteristics, the house has a large archway through the center, furnished and used as a terrace.

ANGUILLA, *158.3 m.* (107 alt., 467 pop.), was settled in 1869 by William C. H. McKinney. In what was little more than a snake-infested canebrake he built the first store and later a post office. The town, however, was not incorporated until 1913. It is a plantation center slightly enlarged by a lumber mill, and several gins and compresses.

> Right from Anguilla on the graveled Deer Creek road to the BARNARD HOME, *0.4 m.,* an ante-bellum structure with fine old furnishings. The summer house is built upon an unexcavated Indian mound.

ROLLING FORK, *163.7 m.* (104 alt., 902 pop.), the seat of Sharkey Co., is named for Rolling Fork Plantation, which Thomas Chaney cleared in 1826. Chaney's daughter was the first white child born in Sharkey Co. Lying in the lowest of the bottom lands of the Yazoo-Mississippi Delta, the town has frequently been flooded by overflow from Deer Creek, but in spite of this menace it has a substantial trade. On the SE. bank of Deer Creek is a group of THREE INDIAN MOUNDS, one of which is said to be the tallest in the county.

Here is the junction with State 1 *(see Side Tour 3A).*

Between Rolling Fork and the Yazoo River the highway runs through one of the Delta's poorer and less interesting sections, part of which is to become a national forest. The so-called Delta Unit is the most recently purchased of the seven in the State, and is bound roughly by Yazoo City, Rolling Fork, and Vicksburg. Much of the area is under water when the Mississippi and Yazoo overflow, the backwater sometimes reaching a depth of ten feet. There are numerous Indian mounds scattered through the hardwood forests.

At *195.2 m* US 61 crosses the YAZOO RIVER (Ind., *river of death*). Here the Delta ends precipitately. South of the bridge over the Yazoo is the monument marking the SITE OF FORT ST. PETER, known during the siege of 1863 as Fort Snyder. In 1719 French missionaries erected here a stockade to protect settlers from raids of the Yazoo and Tunica Indians. Between the monument and Vicksburg the route is attractive, winding up through the Walnut Hills, heavily wooded with magnolia

TOUR 3   323

trees. Along the crest of these hills the trenches and earthworks thrown up by the Confederates in an attempt to turn back the Federal advance are plainly visible.
At *196.6 m.* is the junction with a graveled road.

Right on this road *1.9 m.* (L) to BLAKELY *(open by appointment)*. Reached by a narrow trail leading up a hillside, the house is the northernmost of the antebellum plantation homes that crown the Mississippi bluffs between the Walnut Hills and Woodville. The original cabin of sassafras logs became a refuge for Thomas Ferguson and his wife in 1833, when their home at Haynes Bluff burned. The cabin's site on a natural shelf halfway up the hillside and about 300 yds. W. of the Old Trace seemed to the Fergusons an excellent place for their new home, and they immediately ordered from Cincinnati a pre-fabricated one-room frame house that came by flatboat and was joined to the north end of the cabin. After Ferguson's death in 1838, Mrs. Ferguson married Benson Blake, who, in 1842, built a southern addition to the house. This entire structure was remodeled in 1873, when further proof of the cabin's great age was found in burials in lime discovered under it. While the yard and sunken garden were being graded the burial place of a horse with saddle and bridle was revealed, substantiating the story of old settlers that the cabin had once been a rendezvous of the highwayman, Murrel *(see TRANSPORTATION)*. During the War between the States Jefferson Davis and a large staff of officers, including Generals Smith and Breckenridge, breakfasted here in two relays on their way to inspect the fortifications at Snyder's Bluff. The first shell fired from Admiral Farragut's flagship at Vicksburg was presented the day it was fired to Mrs. Benson Blake; this shell now stands by the front steps at Blakely. During the siege of Vicksburg both Grant and Sherman dined here more than once, the dining room then as now being the original log cabin whose age not even Ferguson, who was interested to the point of making inquiries, could determine when he bought it in 1833.

Between here and Vicksburg the highway cuts across the foot of hills that give a good idea of the difficulties General Sherman faced toward the close of 1862, in the short but deadly Battle of Chickasaw Bayou when Grant was making his second assault on Vicksburg. In trying to gain the fortified bluffs (L), Sherman's two brigades were cut to pieces by the storm of Confederate bullets from the entrenchments along what is now the old highway. The flat land (R) was the scene of death, the total Federal loss being 1,929, the Confederate 206.

At *200.1 m.*, near a small lumber mill, is the junction with a dirt road.

Right on this road across the Yazoo River to EAGLE LAKE, *11 m.* This lake, formed when the Mississippi changed its course, is 17 miles long and in some places three miles wide. It is a well-known fishing place *(black bass, trout, bream, perch, buffalo, goggle eye, catfish)*. In winter the wild duck and geese flocking to the willows and marshes along its shore line make the lake a mecca for hunters. *(Hotel facilities; canoes, outboard motors, and fishing tackle for hire. Road to lake virtually impassable after heavy rains and under water when Yazoo River is at flood stage.)*

Between the junction and Vicksburg US 61 passes a number of large hardwood mills and through a "catfish row" of Negro shacks.
At *204.5 m.* (L) is the VICKSBURG NATIONAL CEMETERY, where more than 17,000 Union soldiers who lost their lives in the campaign and siege of Vicksburg are buried. Of this number, nearly 13,000 are unidentified. There are no Confederate soldiers buried in the cemetery; they lie in Cedar Hill Cemetery in Vicksburg. A few Spanish

American and World War soldiers are buried here. The much-visited grounds have been beautifully landscaped, with walks and drives, serpentine ravines, terraces, plateaus, long avenues of rare trees and shrubbery, and variegated tropical plants. The cemetery has no connection with the Vicksburg National Military Park.

Paralleling the highway (R) is the Yazoo Canal on which is a base of the United States Engineering Fleet *(see VICKSBURG)*.

US 61 enters on Washington St.

VICKSBURG, 206.4 m. (206 alt., 22,943 pop.) *(see VICKSBURG)*.

Points of Interest: Warren County Courthouse, Vicksburg National Military Park, a number of ante-bellum siege-marked homes, and others.

At Vicksburg is the junction with US 80 *(see Tour 2)*.

Sec. b VICKSBURG *to* LOUISIANA LINE, *128.2 m. US 61.*

The eastern bluffs rimming the circuitous Mississippi River between Vicksburg and Fort Adams are the wildest and most precipitous of the many hills in the State. The fertile loess, caked in giant hummocks of silt, supports a profusion of vines and trees. Moving with slow, measured grace at their feet, the river that has brushed the bluffs with the debris of half a continent gives them doubled beauty. It rolls by mile after mile of settlements that belong to the Deep South; south of the cliffs at Natchez its tawny waters have received the blood of Indians, Frenchmen, Spaniards, and British. For the 16 years before the accession of the Spanish the hills were a 14th colony of George III of England; but in 1779 the dons came back to the stream that had been De Soto's grave and restored to the bluffs the ceremony and punctilio to which the Natchez Indians had been accustomed. Wealth brought a renaissance. On escarpments appeared structures combining Spanish grace with classic proportions. The produce of the trans-Appalachian States drifted downstream in flatboats that tied up at Natchez Under-the-Hill; they were clumsy, blunt, and heavy with corn, whisky, and hides. But these, with the cotton raised on the bluff plantations, were the materials that enabled men to make fortunes almost overnight.

What Williamsburg is to Colonial Virginia, Vicksburg, Port Gibson, Natchez, and Woodville are to the Old Deep South. The story of this southwest corner of Mississippi is the bulk of the colonial and territorial history of the State, and is an integral part of the story of the Southwest. Of all the spots in the Territory none was tougher than Natchez Under-the-Hill, none more genteel than Natchez on the Bluffs. Both by antecedents and by way of life, many of the Natchez settlers were men of heroic characteristics, as great in strength as in weakness. The names of the plantations—Auburn, Richmond, Rosalie, Elmscourt, Melrose, Windy Hill, The Briars, Arlington—are indicative of the culture that developed here.

The death of this old culture did not efface all signs of the former life. Though many of the old homes are gradually falling into ruin, enough of them remain to stamp the scene with their character. The manner, too, survives, curiously expressed in the use of bric-a-brac cherished as evidence of the old way of life. The woods, festooned with vines and long gray moss, are as grand as they were to the first pioneer.

South on Washington St. in VICKSBURG, *0 m.*, US 61 and the river separate, the highway winding between the bluffs, and changing its character every few miles.

At *5.9 m.* the road temporarily flattens out on the Mississippi bottoms where, on plowed fields (R), is the *SITE OF WARRENTON*, founded in 1802, which became the first seat of Warren Co. The shelling and partial burning of Warrenton by Federal troops in 1863 put the finishing touches to a death that had been coming slowly since the river changed its course in the 1840's.

Opposite the fields of Warrenton the hills (L) almost touch the highway. The profusion of creeping vines and thick green shrubbery in the woods is striking. Perched in clearings on the slopes and facing the river bottoms are Negro cabins.

At *8.9 m.* US 61 comes close to the Diamond cut-off on the Mississippi River, approximately three miles W., the shortest water route to desolate Palmyra Island, for many years the plantation home of Jefferson Davis.

At YOKENA, *11.5 m.* (52 pop.), the highway climbs a wooded hill; long moss hangs from the cedars.

At *13.6 m.* US 61 crosses the Big Black River. South of the river the highway ascends as sharply as it descended and for several miles traverses rugged country cut by ravines, with the few visible habitations standing in hilly patches.

At *24.1 m.* (R), set against a bluff, is the northernmost of the fine plantation homes fringing Port Gibson, the *JOHN TAYLOR MOORE PLACE (open by permission)*, a large white frame two-story house with a broad double-deck front gallery and immense chimneys on each side. John Taylor Moore was the wealthiest of the old Port Gibson planters, the "Marse John" of Irwin Russell's verse, and the son-in-law of Resin P. Bowie for whom the bowie knife was named. It was Moore who donated the money to build the Catholic Church at Port Gibson *(see below).*

US 61 flattens out for Bayou Pierre. Leading from the highway on each side are sunken wagon roads worn deep into the loess, their depth an evidence of their age.

At *26 m.* is the junction with an old graveled road.

Right on this road to *THE HERMITAGE, 0.5 m. (open by permission)*, the home of Confederate Brig. Gen. B. G. Humphreys, first post-war Governor of Mississippi. The house, of Southern Planter type, with a broad front gallery and a wide enclosed central hall, was built about 1800 by George Wilson Humphreys, the general's father; it is well preserved. B. G. Humphreys was born here in 1808; he entered West Point in the same class with Robert E. Lee, but was dismissed for participation in a Christmas riot. Returning to Mississippi he represented Claiborne Co. at different times in both houses of the State Legislature, then moved to the Delta; in 1861 he organized a company known as the Sunflower Guards, which proceeded to Virginia without waiting for the State to organize troops. He rose rapidly in rank, serving at Chickamauga, Knoxville, in the Wilderness, and at Richmond until badly wounded in 1864, but when the war ended he was again on duty in Mississippi. In 1865 the conservative party in the State elected him governor. Increasing friction between Governor Humphreys and Congressional reconstructionists led to his expulsion from the mansion at Jackson. It is said that Andrew Jackson, entertained by the Humphreys on a visit to Port Gibson, remembered the charm of this place and named his own home The Hermitage.

West of the Hermitage the old road leads to GRAND GULF, *5.5 m.*, named for the whirlpools and eddies formed in the Mississippi by the current from the Big Black River and by a sandstone cliff jutting into the river. The danger of the Grand Gulf whirlpools was known to all early voyagers on the river, and a British settlement had been made at the mouth of the Big Black River before the American Revolution. On the level plain just above the eddy and cliff the town was laid out in 1828, was incorporated in 1833, and had a population approaching 1,000 by 1860. It was an important river landing, and to it cotton was barged down the Big Black River from as far as Jackson for transshipment. In 1835 Grand Gulf ranked third in commercial importance in the State, and for the next 20 years handled more cotton than any other town in Mississippi, not excepting Natchez or Vicksburg. A railroad, begun in the 1830's, was completed to Port Gibson to take the place of a wagon road so bad that Joseph Jefferson, the actor, commented forcefully on its discomforts. Huge stores, buying fancy goods in New York and selling cotton in Liverpool, were grouped near the wharf. Two of the store proprietors, Buckingham and Hume, were of the English gentry. Grog shops were plentiful and frequent duels were fought on the sand bar.

The decline of Grand Gulf started when the river began to cut into the bluff. There were times when the town was moved piecemeal away from the caving banks. Practically all that remained was destroyed by fire in 1862 when Federal gunboats were running the batteries in the successive campaigns against Vicksburg. General Grant said later that pistols would have been more appropriate— the gunboats and land batteries were so close together. The fall of Grand Gulf in 1863 was the prelude to the siege and fall of Vicksburg. Grant took the town and used it as his supply base for the remainder of the campaign. Traces of the Confederate fortifications, breastworks, and caves can be found on Tremont plantation back of the town, and trenches, still in good condition, are visible in the old cemetery. After the war, Grand Gulf's citizens attempted to revive the town life, but were again defeated by the river, which this time moved away toward the W. The river is now working in toward the one store and the few small houses that remain. The Federal Government has bought the cliff, from the top of which can be seen the Warren Co. Courthouse at Vicksburg, 25 miles away. A Geodetic Survey Station has been set up, and revetment work is planned.

At 27 *m.* US 61 crosses the big fork of Bayou Pierre.

At 28.4 *m.* (R) is the entrance to the *SITE OF GLENSADE,* one of the Humphreys homes, now destroyed. The towering grove of oaks under which the house stood is easily found. South of Glensade a curve of the highway gives a view of Port Gibson.

At 29.7 *m.* US 61 crosses the south fork of Bayou Pierre over the new *IRWIN RUSSELL MEMORIAL BRIDGE.* From the new bridge is visible, less than 100 yards away (L), the hulk of the bridge the Confederates burned in 1863 trying to check Grant as he pushed his armies toward Vicksburg. Of the old bridge only the pylons, cables, railings, and iron cross beams are left, and these are gradually rusting away. The flat-spring cables, however, remain to distinguish it as having been the only one of its kind.

PORT GIBSON, 29.8 m. (116 alt., 1,861 pop.), is today what it has always been, a small cotton-growing town that thrives without hurry. Purely ante-bellum in tone, it rests tranquilly in the curve of Bayou Pierre, its quiet oak-lined streets and well proportioned white frame homes supporting the story that General Grant said, when he passed through on his march to Vicksburg in 1863, "Port Gibson is too beautiful to burn."

The town's founder, Samuel Gibson, exemplifies the pioneer of his period. He came to this section in 1788 and soon became stockman, bee keeper, hunter, gardener, orchardist, planter, and operator of a grist mill and cotton gin. Salt, sugar, tea, and coffee were the only commodities with which Gibson could not supply himself. His plantation was a rendezvous for early travelers and circuit riding preachers, and in his backwoods library were a surprising number of volumes. *GIBSON'S GRAVE* is in the Protestant Cemetery at the east end of Greenwood St.

Harman Blennerhassett, an associate of Aaron Burr's in the Southwest conspiracy, brought his wife to Port Gibson in 1810, two years after he had been acquitted of charges of conspiracy against the United States. He had come to America because he had been ostracized in Ireland for marrying his young niece. The sensitiveness aroused by this ostracism and the collapse of his friend Burr's schemes made Blennerhassett name the plantation he bought here, La Cache, his hiding place. His ability and wealth made him a man of affairs in the community, but the same sensitiveness brought him continually in conflict with his neighbors. In 1818 he gave up La Cache, selling it and his 18 slaves for $25,000, and moved to Montreal.

The *IRWIN RUSSELL MEMORIAL,* SE. corner College and Coffee Sts. *(open),* is a square white brick house, originally the home of Samuel Gibson. During the War between the States it was used as a Confederate hospital; it had been used by the Port Gibson Female College for 104 years when the Irwin Russell Memorial Committee purchased it in 1933 for a community center. One room of the building is furnished with articles intimately associated with the life of Mississippi's outstanding poet, Irwin Russell; and there is an exhibit of some of his manuscripts. Russell, recognized as one of the South's three poetic geniuses, was born in Port Gibson in 1853. He was one of the first writers of genuine Negro dialect stories, *Christmas Night in the Quarters* being his masterpiece. His career, however, was cut short, for he died when only 26 years old, and it is only within recent years that he has received the recognition due him. Russell left Port Gibson early in his manhood to live in New York, but soon tiring of that city moved to New Orleans where he died in 1879. Various anecdotes revealing his quick and brilliant mind are still told by those natives who knew him intimately. The town hall and a library occupy the other rooms of the memorial.

The *L. P. WILLIAMS HOME (open by permission),* NW. corner Church and Walnut Sts., is a well-proportioned white frame house one story high. One of the finest of the old homes here, it was the birthplace of Constance Cary, the woman who made the first Confederate flag. Archibald Cary, distinguished lawyer and father of Constance, was a kinsman of Thomas Jefferson and was reared in Jefferson's household, moving to Port Gibson in the 1830's and becoming the editor of the town's first newspaper. His wife was related to Lord Fairfax. In the 1840's the Carys returned to Alexandria, Va., and it was there during the War between the States that Constance made the flags from "ladies' silk dresses." The flags were presented one each to Generals Beauregard, Van Dorn, and Johnston. It was from the porch of this home that General Grant made his announcement concerning the beauty of Port Gibson.

The *PRESBYTERIAN CHURCH,* NE. corner Church and Walnut Sts., has a steeple surmounted by an enormous galvanized-iron hand in place of the conventional cross. The original hand, fashioned by Daniel Foley and placed on the church when it was erected in 1829, was made of wood covered with gold leaf and was the hand of a scholar. The present hand, with the forefinger pointing to heaven, replaced the rotting original some years ago and represents the hand of a laborer.

Chandeliers in the church are a gift from the owners of the steamboat, *Robert E. Lee,* which in 1870 won the race with the *Natchez,* the most celebrated event of its kind in the history of Mississippi River packets. The church still has a slave gallery.

The *CATHOLIC CHURCH,* Church and Coffee Sts., was built with money donated by John Taylor Moore, the "Marse John" of Russell's dialect poems. The brick church, of Gothic design, has mellowed to a reddish-pink color with the years. The walnut altar rail and the heavy overhead beams were carved by Daniel Foley. On the wall above the altar is a portrait of Christ, painted by Thomas Healy, a brother of George Healy (1813–94), painter of portraits and historical pictures.

The *CATHOLIC CEMETERY,* Coffee St., contains the *GRAVE OF RESIN P. BOWIE,* inventor of the bowie knife. The original knife designed by Bowie was a deadly weapon fashioned by a Natchez cutler from a blacksmith's rasp. It was the first knife to have a guarded hilt and was first used by James Bowie, brother of the inventor, in a duel at Natchez. The original knife was on James Bowie's body at the Alamo when in 1836 James was found dead surrounded by 20 dead Mexicans.

THE HIL, S. end of town near Y.&M.V. R.R., is a large brick house erected early in the 19th century by the father of Gen. Earl Van Dorn, C.S.A. The house is in bad condition yet retains its dignity. On the hill opposite the house is the grave of Earl Van Dorn, one of the most dashing and brilliant of the Confederate Cavalry commanders. Born at Port Gibson Sept. 17, 1820, Earl Van Dorn later graduated from West Point and was given a lieutenancy in the 7th infantry in 1842. He took part in Scott's campaign in Mexico and won the brevets of captain and major for gallantry. He was wounded at the Belen gate of Mexico City. He served in the war with the Seminole Indians in Florida and, in 1855, received four wounds in a battle against the Comanche Indians in the West. Upon secession of Mississippi he resigned his commission to become one of the four brigadier-generals of the State's army. He later served with the regular Confederate army, becoming commander of the Army of the West.

RUINS OF WINDSOR, NEAR PORT GIBSON

His career was ended at Springhill, Alabama, on May 7, 1863, when a physician of that town assassinated him.

Right from Port Gibson on a graveled road are a number of relics of the Old South. For several miles the road is a mazy, tree-shadowed pathway leading past tangled woodlands and steep embankments. The embankments are covered with soft green moss, shaded by the long gracefully curled Spanish moss hanging in great gray bunches from extended tree branches. Around each curve is a new and pleasing vista.

At *1.4 m.* the road forks; R. here. The landscape gradually loses its secluded picturesqueness and emerges into open farming country. Bayou Pierre lies little more than 3 miles (R) from the highway; the black silt about it is unexcelled for growing cotton. When Vicksburg, Port Gibson, and Natchez were in their heyday as river towns, this section was a stronghold of plantation life. But now only the ruins of the splendid mansions are left.

The amazing RUINS OF WINDSOR loom up at *10.3 m.* (L). Twenty-two gigantic stone Corinthian columns remain as testimony to what was perhaps the supreme gesture of the grand manner of ante-bellum Greek Revival architecture. These columns, joined by Italian wrought-iron railings which were once at the upper gallery level, form a perfect outline of the house, which was rectangular in shape with a narrow ell, the service wing, at the rear. Windsor was built by S. C. Daniel, a wealthy planter who had holdings in the vicinity and across the river in Louisiana. When completed in 1861, it was considered the handsomest home in Mississippi. It had five stories topped by an observatory. The furnishings were imported and the library housed rare old books. Rich tapestries and velvet draperies adorned it. During the War between the States for a short period the Confederates used its lofty tower, which commanded a view of the Mississippi River, as an observation point; then the Federals used it as a hospital. Mark Twain, when a pilot on Mississippi steamboats, used to chart his course at this point by the peak of the tower. In 1890 Windsor was destroyed by fire. Except for a few pieces of jewelry nothing was saved.

At *10.8 m.* is a junction with an unmarked dirt lane *(impassable when wet);* R. here *3 m.* to *BRUINSBURG LANDING,* which affords one of the loveliest views of the Bayou Pierre. Before flowing into the Mississippi the bayou thrusts itself out in two giant arms to embrace cypress woodlands hazy with moss. The landing is a secluded spot today, its few inhabitants living in a primitive logging camp and in shanty boats moored to the shore. But in the days of river traffic, it was a lively port and cotton market. On April 30, 1863, Grant transported his 40,000 Union soldiers across Bayou Pierre, coming up the river to Bruinsburg. A fugitive slave that he brought with him from Louisiana guided him and his troops to meet an army of 5,000 Confederates at Port Gibson. Along the banks of the bayou at Bruinsburg are numerous Indian relics, flint, arrowheads, and bits of pottery. When wandering bands of Choctaw under Captain Chubby came here from their settlements in the eastern part of the State, efforts were made to get them to pick cotton, but they scorned the menial labor and its associations.

At *11.6 m.* is the BETHEL VOCATIONAL SCHOOL for Negroes, in a brown frame one-story building, sharing a small clearing with a little white frame church.

At *11.9 m.* is the junction with a graveled road; R. here *8 m.* is RODNEY (124 pop.), a ghost river town that died in 1876 when the Yazoo & Mississippi Valley R.R. was built. Prior to the War between the States, Rodney with a population of 4,000 supported a wharf, a boat landing, two warehouses, and numerous stores and dwellings. During the war the PRESBYTERIAN CHURCH was shelled by Federal gunboats, and the marks of cannon balls are visible on its walls. Because of the changes in the river's course, the village is now 3 miles inland.

At *13.1 m.* is OLD BETHEL CHURCH (L), a weathered red stuccoed brick structure that has faded to a salmon-pink. The stucco has peeled in many places exposing the brick. The Greek temple effect of the building is spoiled by a protruding square entrance tower surmounted by a small incongruous wooden spire. In the interior a broad, flat slave gallery faces the pulpit across plain pine pews. In the center of the auditorium is a modern, coal-burning heater. Dr. Chamberlain built the church in the early 1820's, and in it the first classes of Oakland College *(see below)* were held. General Grant's army passed here on its march to Vicksburg and riddled the belfry with bullets. The church is used by Presbyterians of the Bethel Community.

At *14.2 m.* is CANEMOUNT *(open by permission),* erected by John Murdock who died in 1826. Placed in a picturesque setting on sloping grounds planted in oaks and cedars, the one-and-a-half story white brick house is more elaborately designed than was the typical Southern Planter type of its period. A wide gallery extends around the first floor. The interior is divided by a wide hall, to the right side of which is the parlor and library, and on the left an unusually long dining room. The woodwork is cut in wedge-shaped patterns and the mantels, on both the first and second floors, are of white marble. In the library is a large triple-arched window that lends unusual charm to the room. The ceilings of the first floor rooms are ornamented with plaster arabesques, the dining room having a diamond shaped ornament in its center. The stairway has a mahogany rail, and the second floor hall is lighted by a dormer with triple-arched windows. Two frame wings extending from the main house form a rear court. These wings, used for guests, are typical of the lavishness of ante-bellum entertaining, when friends lingered weeks and sometimes years. Each wing contains four rooms, the front ones having open fireplaces. John Murdock, a native of Ireland and related to Robert and George Cochrane who settled in the Natchez area during the Spanish Era, amassed a large fortune and, like his kinsmen, was a man of considerable importance during the Territorial period.

At *15.2 m.* is the entrance to ALCORN AGRICULTURAL AND MECHANICAL COLLEGE, a Negro high school and senior college accredited and supported by the State. The college was established in 1871 during the administration of Governor Alcorn, and given his name. The first allotment made for its maintenance was $50,000. About 90 percent of the Negro teachers of Mississippi are graduates of Alcorn. Many of the buildings were once a part of old Oakland College, established in 1830 by the Rev. Jeremiah Chamberlain. Chamberlain came to Mississippi from Philadelphia, Pa., in 1823, sent by the General Presbyterian Board of Domestic Missions. The college was organized at a meeting held in the Bethel Church, the members of that church subscribing $12,000 toward the college fund. In 1851 Dr. Chamberlain, still acting president, was stabbed at the front gate of his cottage on the campus by a hotheaded Secessionist, who believed that the doctor was favoring the doctrines of the Unionist party in his teachings. The college gradually declined because of the war and yellow fever epidemics. The old buildings are distinguishable by their aged brick walls and large white wooden columns. The *CHAPEL* (R), a large, plain brick post-Colonial, Southern type structure, has been changed little since its erection in 1831; the original seats of solid walnut, hewn from trees in nearby woods, are still in use. The front steps of the building, of wrought iron, originally belonged to Windsor.

US 61 S. of Port Gibson crosses the fertile loess that made the town rich. The land is hilly with alternating woods and tilled fields. At *31.3 m.* US 61 enters the northern end of a tract of 29,000 acres being planted and terraced by the U.S. Soil Conservation Service.

LORMAN, *42.8 m.* (211 alt., 200 pop.), is a shaded village with a Sabbath-like quiet.

HARRISTON, *50 m.* (277 pop.), is a country village, grouped about a depot on the Yazoo & Mississippi Valley R.R.

FAYETTE, *52.1 m.* (292 alt., 848 pop.), is a typical southwest Mississippi village, interesting chiefly because its courthouse holds the records of the extinct County of Pickering, one of two Territorial counties founded in 1799. From the community have come many outstanding citizens, among them Gen. Thomas Hinds, who commanded the Mississippi Dragoons at the Battle of New Orleans, and Cato West, Secretary and Acting Governor of the Mississippi Territory (1803–05).

At *54.3 m.* is the junction with a sunken road.

Left on this road to *HOME HILL, 2 m. (open by appointment)*, which was the plantation of Gen. Thomas Hinds *(see JACKSON)*.

At *57.8 m.* is McGARRY'S FORKS.

Right from McGarry's Forks to the *SITE OF OLD GREENVILLE, 0.2 m.* On Feb. 8, 1804, in "Gallows Field" at Greenville, Wiley "Little" Harp and James Mays, notorious outlaws along the Natchez Trace, were hanged. They had been recognized at Natchez as they attempted to claim the reward for beheading their former partner, Samuel Mason *(see TRANSPORTATION)*, and had been recaptured here after they escaped. After the execution, the head of Harp was mounted on a pole at the north end of town along the trace, and the head of Mays at the south end. Their bodies were first buried in the town graveyard, but were later exhumed by outraged citizens and reburied in a spot now unknown.

At *58.8 m.* (L) is a monument marking a *CROSSING OF THE NATCHEZ TRACE (see TRANSPORTATION)*. The old road, leading off US 61 (L) from the monument, is deeply cut in the loess and arched with ancient trees.

The highway S. and W. of the monument rides the ridge, deep hollows dropping away on each side.

At *61.2 m.* (L) is *SPRINGFIELD (adm. 25¢)*, in a grove of lofty trees. This two-story Planter type house was erected in 1791 by Col. Thomas Marsden Green. Across its front extend wide upper and lower galleries supported by six Doric columns. The recessed doorways are simple, with side lights of plain design. The interior is spacious with woodwork carved by hand in a lacy design. The mantels, carved by Spanish workmen, are unusually large. According to tradition, Andrew Jackson and Mrs. Rachel Donelson Robards were married here in 1791.

West of Springfield US 61 winds through very beautiful woods, with moss six feet long hanging from trees whose trunks are almost hidden in a jungle of vines and shrubs.

RICHLAND (L), *61.7 m. (open by permission)*, was built in the 1840's by Robert Cox, whose wife had inherited the plantation from her grandfather, Col. Thomas M. Green, the owner of Springfield and of another large tract of land granted him about 1788. The white gracefully-proportioned house is built of brick and hand-hewn timber and there is a wide gallery with square columns across the front. The roof is broken by dormer windows. The front door is massive, with Corinthian pilasters on each side. The hall is unusually wide and, extending to an arch in the rear, meets a cross hall, from which rises a stairway. Set back from the highway in a grove of green cedars, and with a part of the original gardens remaining, the setting of Richland is particularly attractive. Among the camellia japonicas is a red variety that is rarely seen. The crapemyrtles have grown into shade trees, their venerable appearance enhanced by festoons of Spanish moss.

At *62.1 m.* is the junction with an unmarked road.

> Right on this road to *CALVERTON PLANTATION, 3.4 m.*, to which Aaron Burr was carried after his capture in 1807. The capture was as much a burlesque as was the excitement raised by the expedition. For two years after he had quitted the Vice-Presidency, Burr had plotted and planned, bringing into his scheme Gen. James Wilkinson, the man who was to betray him. Yet for all his preparation, Burr's flotilla when it arrived at the mouth of Bayou Pierre numbered but 9 boats and less than 60 men. Because of the politics involved and the excitement raised by President Jefferson's proclamation, Acting Governor Mead arranged for an interview with Burr at the plantation home near the mouth of Coles Creek, and it was here that Burr agreed to surrender himself to the civil authorities and await the action of the grand jury. The original plantation home has been destroyed.

At *66 m.* (R) on a hill stands *CHRIST EPISCOPAL CHURCH*, a small, gray stone, Gothic type structure, erected in 1857. Its exquisite exterior details and its silhouette against the sky are impressive. This congregation was established in 1820.

The *SHIELDS HOME* (R), *66.2 m. (open by permission)*, a two-story frame structure that is of no definite style but typical of many houses in the Natchez country, was built in the early 1830's. The Shields and Dunbar families were the first settlers in this community and influential in establishing Christ Episcopal Church, in which their descendants hold the largest membership today.

South of CHURCH HILL, as the community around the Christ Episcopal Church is known, US 61 follows a high winding ridge. There are fine views (L) of *COLES CREEK VALLEY*.

At *72.7 m.* is the junction with a graveled road.

> Right on this road to the *SELSERTOWN INDIAN MOUND, 0.7 m.* (R), covering nearly six acres. Roughly a pyramid about 600 ft. by 400 ft., it is considered

a giant among Mississippi mounds. It has been opened on many occasions, and articles of pottery and several implements of war have been found with human bones.

At 76 m. is the junction with a narrow dirt road.

Left on this road 0.7 m. to SELMA PLANTATION, settled by Gerard Brandon I immediately after the American Revolutionary War. Brandon had been forced to flee from Ireland because of his implication in an Irish uprising for independence. Reaching South Carolina just in time to join the Colonial forces in the revolution he was made a colonel under Gen. Francis Marion. In afteryears one of his proudest possessions was a rifle on the barrel of which was engraved "Given For Valiant Conduct At King's Mountain." At the close of the Revolution Brandon came to the Natchez district and settled first on St. Catherine's Creek. Later he married Dorothy Nugent and obtained a Spanish land grant of 600 arpens. The grant was later confirmed by the U. S. Government. Brandon's first home burned soon after erection and the present one was built on the site. This frame house, one of the oldest homes in Adams County, illustrates a stage in the development of the Southern Planter type; the structure sits on a high foundation, has wide eaves, and a front gallery more than 80 feet long. The entrance leads into an immense banquet room, suggestive of the ancient banquet halls of Ireland. The cooking was done in a large basement but a crane hung over the fireplace in the dining room. At each end of the dining room are two large rooms and on the back, under a sloping roof, are several smaller ones. Outside stairways lead from the back gallery to the top floor where the central room is of extraordinary size. On the plantation is a grove of 500 pecan trees, offshoots of what are said to have been the first pecans in the Natchez district. Brandon's son, Gerard Brandon II (1788–1850), was the first native-born Governor of Mississippi.

At 76.9 m. is the junction with a graveled road.

Left on this road 0.3 m. to PROPINQUITY (reached by private drive; open), a two-story white frame house with a hip roof and green shuttered windows. It was erected about 1810 by Gen. Leonard Covington and called Propinquity because of its nearness to the barracks at old Fort Dearborn. The house has old furnishings and the original hand-painted window shades are still in place.

At 77 m. (L) is the SITE OF FORT DEARBORN, where Propinquity's owner, Gen. Leonard Covington, was commander before he died in the War of 1812. Fort Dearborn was built in 1802 to protect Washington, the capital of the Mississippi Territory. All traces of the fort have vanished.

WASHINGTON, 78 m. (200 pop.), between 1802 and 1820 was in turn Mississippi's second Territorial and first State capital. On the hill (L) is the CLEAR CREEK BAPTIST CHURCH, a red brick building in bad repair, said to be the oldest Baptist church in Mississippi. Washington was the first station E. of Natchez on the Natchez Trace. That the United States land office, the Surveyor General's office, the office of the Commissioner of Claims, and the United States courts were here is evidence of its early 19th century importance.

JEFFERSON COLLEGE, entrance Main St. (R), founded in 1802, was the first institution of learning incorporated by Mississippi Territorial legislation, and the oldest endowed college in this part of the country. Audubon, the naturalist, and James Ingraham, the author of pirate tales and later a clergyman, were early members of the faculty. Here in 1815 Andrew Jackson camped going to and returning from the Battle of New

THE BURR OAKS, JEFFERSON COLLEGE CAMPUS, WASHINGTON

Orleans, and in 1825 Lafayette witnessed a drill of cadets. The two original square, brick buildings, two stories in height, were joined by a third building a few years after their erection, giving the appearance of one large building constructed of three types of bricks. The central portion is now used as a gymnasium. On the campus near the entrance are the BURR OAKS, in the shade of which Aaron Burr was tried for treason. Near the Burr Oaks is a white marble MONUMENT erected on the site of the old brick church in which Mississippi's first Constitutional Convention and first State legislature met.

The *SPANISH HOUSE (private),* with a raised red brick basement and a frame upper story (R), was built before 1800. The red brick *METHODIST CHURCH* (L), a large rectangular, box-like structure, was erected in 1825. Just behind the church, hidden from the highway by the trees surrounding it, is the former *HOME OF COWLES MEAD,* erected about 1800. It was Mead who gave the order for Burr's arrest. Later the house became the home of Mississippi's first geologist, B. L. C. Wailes. *INGLEWOOD* (R) was a home built in the 1850's by the Affleck family; Thomas Affleck was a scientist who did important botanical research. Some of his specimens are in the Smithsonian Institution. The Spanish influence is seen in the steep roof and severe walls of the rear parts of the house.

At Washington is the junction with US 84 *(see Tour 13)* which unites with US 61 between this point and Natchez.

1. Left from Washington *1.3 m.* on a graveled road to (R) the brick Southern Planter type HOME OF DR. JOHN W. MONETTE *(open by permission)*, author of the *History of the Discovery and Settlement of the Mississippi Valley*. Dr. Monette, typical of the cultured citizens of the Washington community before the War between the States, is remembered primarily for his history, for many years the standard source book of Mississippi students.

At *1.5 m.* (L) on this same road is a small roadside marker reading: "The first women's college in America. Chartered on Feb. 17, 1819, to confer degrees on women. Named in honor of Elizabeth Roach, through whose generosity the College was made possible. Audubon was on the faculty." The hill above the marker is the SITE OF ELIZABETH FEMALE ACADEMY, founded in 1818 with the support of the Methodist Church; it was the first girl's school in the United States to have legislative recognition of its authority to confer degrees. Mrs. Caroline V. Thayer, "a lady of scholarly attainments and literary reputation," and a granddaughter of General Warren, the hero of Bunker Hill, was governess here in the 1840's when the academy enjoyed its greatest reputation and when it was known for the thoroughness of its work. The site is marked by two sides of a former square of massive moss-hung cedars, which frame two ruined walls of brick. White-washed Negro cabins stand behind the ruins.

2. Right from Washington on a graveled road to FOSTER'S MOUND, *2.5 m.* (R), rising approximately 40 feet. The mound's base is circled by a low hedge of shrubs; its summit is crowned by a ring of magnificent oaks, within which is the FOSTER HOUSE, now used as an agricultural experiment station. Early maps point to a Natchez Indian village on this site. Within recent years the mound has been excavated by archaeologists from the Smithsonian Institution, and artifacts have been removed. The house, known today by the name of a comparatively recent owner, James Foster, was built in the Spanish era (1779–98). It is a long, low, white frame structure with three dormer windows. Its homelike appearance is accentuated by the narrow gallery, which runs its entire length, and by the old shrubs planted about the doorstep.

Year after year the intricately winding road has sunk deeper into the yielding loess, and the moss on the bordering forest oaks has grown denser. On each side of the highway, almost hidden from view by the trees, are some of the oldest homes in the Natchez district, varying widely in architectural designs. Many show Greek Revival and others Spanish influences; a few show both. The hybrids, for the most part, were built during the Spanish era; later cupolas, columned galleries, dormers, and other fashionable ornaments were added.

The PINE RIDGE CHURCH, *5 m.* (R), with a foundation and one wall that were a part of the second Presbyterian church built in Mississippi, is one of the last mementos of a Scottish settlement made early in the 1800's. It is a faded, red brick building with a steep roof.

Here is the junction with two roads that run like narrow tunnels beneath the branches of aged moss-covered oaks.

1. Right from the church on the first road, *0.1 m.* (R), to the PRESBYTERIAN MANSE *(open by permission)*. More than 100 years old, the manse was built at the same time as the Pine Ridge Church for the ministers who served that church. In spite of its bad repair, its architecture still suggests a characteristic Spanish-Georgian Colonial hybrid type. From the porch of the house is an excellent view of the church.

At *0.4 m.* (L) is EDGEWOOD *(open during Natchez Pilgrimage)*, a large two-story plantation home with a French style roof. The brick of Edgewood has mellowed to a faint salmon pink. The house was built in 1850–60, on the Juan Bisland land grant; eight slender fluted Doric columns support the flat roof of the gallery. In the house is a collection of portraits by Lamdin.

2. Right from the church on the second road *0.4 m.* to (R) the private lane leading to *MOUNT REPOSE (open during Natchez Pilgrimage).* Built in 1824 and recently restored, the house is a large, two-story structure of Southern Planter type with a grace that obscures its massiveness. The long double-deck gallery has six square columns supporting its roof, and the entrance is hand carved. The old brick kitchen, now painted white, has been converted into a garage. The lands were granted to the Earl of Ellington prior to the American Revolution, but during the Spanish Era were regranted to Juan Bisland, whose descendants own the place. Elizabeth Bisland was a novelist of the reconstruction period. Connected with the *Ladies Home Journal* for years and an early reporter of the old *Picayune,* Elizabeth gained international attention with her *Life of Lafcadio Hearn.* The Negroes who work on this plantation call it "Monty-pose."

At *1.5 m.* (L) is the entrance lane of *PEACHLAND (open by permission);* built in 1830 this house is a good example of post-Colonial architecture informally treated, with low hip roof, double-deck gallery, and wide chimneys flanking the sides. Dormer windows break the straight lines of the rear roof, but the downward sweep at the front is uncompromisingly steep and severe. The interior is simple, with a hall running the length of two rooms, low ceilings, and almost plain woodwork. There are six rooms on the first floor and four on the second floor. The walls of the hall and living room are papered in old-fashioned figured paper. The parlor mantel is delicately carved, and much of the furniture is of carved rosewood. It is said that the present name is a corruption of Pitchlyn, interpreter for the Choctaw Indian tribe, whose house once stood on this site.

At *83 m.* (L) on US 61 is *D'EVEREUX (adm. 25¢),* on a hill above the old trace. Though the gardens have been ruined, the house itself presents much the same appearance as it did when it was built. It is considered by many the most beautiful late Greek Revival structure in Mississippi. Designed by a Mr. Hardy whose initials are unknown, it is a large white mansion with fluted Doric columns two stories high, and is surrounded by enormous moss-hung oaks and magnolias. Because of its beauty it was used in the filming of scenes in *Heart of Maryland,* a recent movie. D'Evereux was completed in 1840 for William St. John Elliott, a close friend of Henry Clay. When Clay visited here the Elliotts gave in his honor one of the most elaborate balls ever held in the Natchez area.

The double drawing rooms were originally furnished in rosewood, of Empire design, with Duncan Phyfe tables, bronze sperm-oil lamps having crystal pendants, and magnificent chandeliers and bronze candelabra having long cut-glass prisms that reflected the light of sconced candles. The bookcases in the library were of the finest woods. The banquet hall walls had panels of soft green felt; the furniture was of hand-rubbed mahogany, the central table with an Italian marble top. The china was made on special order by E. D. Honoré of Paris.

The original grounds covered 12 acres, of which a large part was wooded. A double driveway crossed and recrossed under oak, catalpa, and magnolia trees to form designs that were further outlined by borders of luriamundi, an indigenous shrub. On each side were hedges of Cherokee rose. In the rear a courtyard opened into a terraced garden brilliant with camellia japonicas, roses, and massed azaleas. At the foot of the lower terrace was an artificial lake on which swans floated.

During the War between the States, Federal troops turned the garden into a camp ground and chopped down many of the oaks and magnolias

D'EVEREUX, NEAR NATCHEZ

for fuel. Opposite the front gate is a tree beneath which two Union soldiers were executed following their court martial for the killing of George Sargent at Gloucester in 1864. D'Evereux was the maternal family name of Elliott, whose uncle, General D'Evereux, was a Bolivian patriot and close friend of General Bolivar.

At *83.4 m.* is the junction with a marked paved road. Here (R) is the *SITE OF SLAVE BLOCK* from which Negro slaves were auctioned to the highest bidders.

> Left on this road is the *SITE OF THE OLD SLAVE BARRACK, 0.1 m.*, now occupied by a row of Negro cabins, many of which contain timbers taken from the original building. Negroes brought direct from Africa were delivered here, fed, clothed, and taught a few words. They were then sold on the block that stood on what is now US 61, then a part of the Natchez Trace.

At *0.2 m.* on the paved road is the junction with the Liberty Road and E. Franklin St.

> 1. Left on the Liberty Road *0.2 m.* to (R) *MONTEIGNE (open during Pilgrimage)*, a story-and-a-half brick structure smoothly stuccoed in pale pink. The steep hip roof is surmounted by a balustraded deck, the classic entrance is formed by a square portico with slender white columns. The floor of the portico is laid with mosaics. On each side of the building is a narrow gallery with delicately designed iron banisters. Tradition says the bricks were made by slaves and the heavy timbers were sawed by hand. Monteigne was begun in 1853 by William T.

Martin, later a major-general in the War between the States, and though the contractor never quite completed the building as it was designed, it was occupied in 1855. The architect is unknown, but as Monteigne originally stood it was an adaptation of a French chalet. When the house was remodeled by Weiss and Seiferth, New Orleans architects, the rear patio with its original service wings, camellia japonicas, and wistaria vines was left unchanged. The grounds include landscaped gardens and are shaded by giant, ivy-covered oaks. During the war the double drawing room was used by Federal troops as a stable; other horses were pastured in the gardens.

On the Liberty Road at *0.4 m.* (L) is OAKLAND *(open during Pilgrimage)*, a raised brick cottage erected in 1830 by a son-in-law of Don Estevan Minor, one time Acting Governor during the Spanish regime in Natchez. Oakland is furnished as it was in the 1830's. A fine portrait of Don Minor in Spanish regimentals, and other relics from Concord, mansion of the Spanish governors *(see ARCHITECTURE)*, are on display.

On the Liberty Road at *4.1 m.* is (L) the entrance to WINDY HILL MANOR, *1.8 m. (open Sun.; adm 25¢)*, a planter's house, one-and-a-half stories high with a portico having four irregularly spaced Tuscan columns. The dormer windows and the fanlight of the front entrance have panes of an early glass whose tints are opalescent and wavy. In the wide hall is a spiral stairway remarkable for its workmanship. The plantation was in the hands of Col. Benijah Osmun, a veteran of the Revolutionary War, by 1788. Colonel Osmun built the home that is now incorporated in the present manor. It was here in 1807 that the colonel invited his old friend, Aaron Burr, to stay when Burr was released on bail after his arrest for treason. Nearby, at the foot of Half Way Hill, lived Maj. Isaac Guion, who in 1798 raised the first American flag over Fort Panmure at Natchez. Both Guion and Osmun had served throughout the Revolution and both had known Burr intimately. Their continued friendship with and defense of the man who was branded a traitor is an evidence that many did not accept the popular judgment of Burr. As Colonel Osmun's guest he was treated with some of the respect he thought his due.

While there he met the lovely, unsophisticated Madeline Price, daughter of the Widow Price, who lived in a cottage on top of Half Way Hill. The admiration and devotion he won from Madeline pacified his wounded ego. When he forfeited his bond in February 1807, he risked capture by remaining at the widow's cottage in a fruitless effort to persuade Madeline to leave with him. The little cottage is gone, and Major Guion's lands have become a part of Windy Hill plantation, but Burr's desperate grasp at love at a time when his ambitions had been wrecked gives an aura of romance to the weather-worn timbers of Windy Hill, and to the avenue of moss-draped cedars and myrtles where he walked with Madeline.

In February 1817, a decade after Burr had fled into the night, the plantation was sold to Gerard Brandon I. The Brandons furnished Mississippi's first native-born Governor, Gerard Chittocque Brandon, and, according to historians, furnished the State more Confederate soldiers than any other family. One of the present mistresses of Windy Hill, Elizabeth Brandon Stanton, is the author of an historical novel on the Burr conspiracy, *Fata Morgana*. Windy Hill is in a state of poor repair.

2. Right from the paved road on E. Franklin St. *0.1 m.* to MONMOUTH *(open by appointment)*, a brick mansion with a well-proportioned portico having four square columns. Wrought-iron railings enclose the upper gallery. Monmouth was built in 1820 by John Hankinson of New York, who was related to the Schuyler family of that State. The house has beautiful old furnishings. It was the home of Gen. John A. Quitman, hero of the Battle of Chapultepec in the Mexican War, U. S. Congressional Representative, and from 1850–51 Governor of Mississippi.

At Monmouth is a junction with the Linden Road.

LINDEN, NEAR NATCHEZ

Left on the Linden Road *0.2 m.* (L) is *LINDEN (open during Pilgrimage)*, the older part of which was built in 1788-89. The frame wings that flanked the center were erected in 1825 by Thomas Reed, first U. S. Senator from Mississippi. A gallery 90 feet long with 10 slender columns extends across the front. The entrance with its beautiful fanlight, geometrically designed panels, and hand-carved decorations has been photographed frequently. The house contains old furniture, silver, and china, as well as paintings by Audubon. An old detached brick kitchen wing in the rear with posts of solid logs faces a patio.

On the Linden Road at *0.7 m.* is *MELROSE (open during Pilgrimage)*, one of the best preserved of the ante-bellum mansions in the area. The house, grounds, and furnishings are practically as they were in the 1840's. It is constructed of brick and its double portico has four huge Tuscan columns. The interior has elaborate furnishings of hand-carved rosewood, with flawless mirrors, and with the original draperies of green and gold brocatel imported from France. Candle shelves built over the front and rear inside doors of the central hall each hold a dozen candlesticks. A detached kitchen, a milk house, and a carriage house face a courtyard in the rear.

US 61 enters on St. Catherine St.; L. on N. Pine St.
NATCHEZ, *84.5 m.* (202 alt., 13,422 pop.) *(see NATCHEZ).*

Points of Interest: Historic and architecturally interesting homes and public buildings, exhibited especially during annual Pilgrimage, and others.

Right from Natchez on N. Pine St. which becomes the Pine Ridge Road *2.7 m.* (L) to *HOMEWOOD (private)*, a massive, three-story mansion topped by an observatory. Constructed of bright red brick the principal façade is dominated by a massive Ionic portico. Above the front doorway and under the porch roof is a long balcony with an elaborate iron railing. On each side is an octagonal, wrought-iron porch. The house was built in 1860-65, when the architectural trend was still to the Greek Revival in style. A Maltese cross is formed by the hallways on the ground floor. Scenes of the motion picture, *In Old Kentucky,* were filmed here.

The landscape between Homewood and Lansdowne is one of unmarred beauty. Vines and Spanish moss grow luxuriantly from spreading branches, giving the woodlands a story-book appearance.

At *3.2 m.* (R) is LANSDOWNE *(open during Natchez Pilgrimage; adm. 25¢)*, a simple buff brick cottage, with the graceful features designed in the Georgian Colonial style. Here, where all the furnishings are the originals, is a portrait by Sully. The house was built in 1853.

The route continues S. on N. Pine St. to Homochitto St.; L. on Homochitto St. (US 61). At *87.2 m.* is the junction with the Lower Woodville Road. The space between the fork is the SITE OF WHITE HORSE TAVERN, a rendezvous of bandits on the Natchez Trace. The road, narrow and winding in a deep cut, passes some of the finest plantation homes in the Natchez district; because of the woods and the low position of the roadbed few houses are visible from the highway.

Right on the Lower Woodville Road, which was the Natchez Trace, *0.2 m.* (R) to the entrance of LONGWOOD *(open daily; adm. 25¢)*. The house, an unfinished structure of oriental magnificence, stands at the end of a half-mile driveway cut through the hills. It was designed by Sloan of Philadelphia and was under construction when the War between the States began. The laborers on it dropped their tools to go to war and the work was never resumed. The eight-sided brick structure is six stories high and is topped by an octagonal drum with an enormous onion-shaped copper dome. It contains 32 octagonal rooms. Elaborate gallery porches on the exterior are adorned with lacy jig-saw ornaments. Niches were built to hold Italian and Grecian statuary. The fireplaces were to be made of Italian marble.

On the same road at *0.5 m.* is (L) GLOUCESTER *(open during Pilgrimage)*, which was the home of Winthrop Sargent, first Territorial governor of Mississippi (1798). The square house, erected between 1800 and 1804 of brick baked on the plantation, is the oldest mansion in the Natchez district and is a fine example of the Greek Revival style of architecture. Its pedimented double portico has four huge Tuscan columns. Two recessed entrances with arched fanlights lead into two long halls. Between the hallways is a cross hall that on each side opens into a hexagonal room. The floors have the original wide planking, and the door sills are cypress slabs two feet wide. The doors have inside bars, necessary in the days of Indian and bandit attacks. The basement windows are iron-barred and overlook a dry moat. The place is luxuriously furnished.

Opposite Gloucester is the SARGENTS' PRIVATE CEMETERY, in which is the tomb of Seargent S. Prentiss (1808-50), gifted Mississippi orator. The cemetery was reserved by a former owner in such a manner that only heirs of the Williams (Prentiss married a Williams) and Sargent families might use it. The first Territorial governor, Col. Winthrop Sargent (not related to Prentiss), is also buried in this graveyard.

South of Natchez US 61 is a route of picturesque beauty, cutting between high banks overgrown with green moss, and deeply shadowed by the overhanging branches of aged live oak trees.

At *87.3 m.* (L) is the entrance to INGLESIDE *(private)*, a Southern Planter type, one-and-a-half stories high with a roof extended to cover a low gallery. A large hexagonal room has been added since the original building was erected in 1832. Its windows somewhat resemble the *garconieres* seen on Louisiana homes. Ingleside was erected by Dr. Gustavus Calhoun, who was related to many of the prominent families of the period.

At *87.5 m.*, (L) and visible from the highway, is GLENBERNIE *(pri-*

vate), the scene of the murder of Miss Jennie Merrill in 1932 *(see below)*. The beautiful one-story house, with wide galleries supported by slender colonnettes, is more than a century old.

At 87.5 m. (R) is the entrance to ELMSCOURT *(open during Natchez Pilgrimage)*, reached by a long, winding roadway. The square, two-story, brick center of this commodious mansion, a reproduction of an Italian Renaissance villa, was erected in 1810 by Lewis Evans, first sheriff of Adams Co. When a later owner, Frank Surget, one of the first Natchez millionaires, presented the home to his daughter as a wedding gift, extensive improvements were made; two one-story wings were added, the banquet hall was extended, and many interior fixtures, including hand-wrought iron and bronze chandeliers and marble mantels, were imported for it. The double galleries, front and rear, are trimmed in fine, hand-wrought iron lace-work of grape design made in Belgium. The long, central hall is flanked on the left by double drawing rooms, a smoking room, and a billiard room. On the right are a music room, a library, and a banquet hall. The living quarters are upstairs. The house today has fine old furnishings: portraits, busts, chandeliers, Duncan Phyfe chairs and dining table, and a particularly beautiful pier table. Surget's daughter married Ayres P. Merrill, who became U.S. Minister to Belgium during President Grant's administrations. Elmscourt from the first was famous for its hospitality and entertainments; Jenny Lind, Gen. Andrew Jackson, Lafayette, and Thackeray were guests at different times. During Pilgrimage week Elmscourt is the scene of the Ball of a Thousand Candles, with the illumination the name implies.

At 87.9 m. (L), with only a bayou and a stretch of woodland separating it from Glenbernie, is GLENWOOD *(adm. 25¢)*. All that is visible from the highway is a large placarded gate and a dilapidated road house called Bucket of Blood. Glenwood itself is hidden in the dense thickets. It is much in need of repair, but still shows its substantial construction; though a corner column has fallen out, the roof has held its line.

The architectural design, a hybrid Georgian Colonial-Southern Planter, was characteristic of the country gentleman's house of the 1830's. It is constructed with heavy hand-chopped sills and joists fitted tongue and groove, and all woods used are fine and well seasoned. The rectangular mass of the edifice is crowned with a heavy cornice and paneled parapet, behind which a low hip roof is broken by arched and pedimented dormers. Across the principal façade is a double gallery with simple wooden balustrade and two tiers of slender columns. The central doorways at the first and second stories are set in deep elliptical arches with side lights and fan transom. Behind the big house is the kitchen, now tumbling down, with a brick floor, an old-time fireplace, and a Dutch oven. An outside stair once led to the servants' quarters above the kitchen. On the left of the central hall is the library, and behind it is a mildewed recess from which a mahogany staircase rises to the upper floor. A second room on the left, formerly the dining room, is now the dining room and kitchen. On the right are double drawing rooms. In the four second floor bedrooms are heavy, old-fashioned beds cased in dust.

The front of the house is stuccoed; to the N. is the now dilapidated schoolroom and tutors' apartment, a small building with pilastered doorways and a portico. The builder of Glenwood was Frances E. Sprague. In 1839 Glenwood was bought by Frederick Stanton and was his home until he erected Stanton Hall *(see NATCHEZ)*, with materials and furnishings brought from Europe in a chartered ship. In 1852 the place was sold to T. M. Davis, who was the first millionaire in Natchez and one of the founders of Mississippi's first bank. In time Glenwood became the home of Mrs. Mary Ker, a daughter-in-law of Territorial Judge David Ker.

In August 1932 the present owner of the now shabby old place had the misfortune to be arrested on a murder charge; he was later freed. During the period when he and his housekeeper were under arrest, newspapers exploited the case, and because goats were found living in the house, the papers renamed it Goat Castle.

At *92 m.* is the junction with a private road.

Right on this road to *ELGIN, 0.5 m. (open by appointment),* a two-story white frame house with a double-deck front gallery supported by two tiers of Doric columns. Built before 1838 it was later the home of the scientist, Dr. John Carmichael Jenkins. In ante-bellum days Elgin was noted for the beauty of its gardens; the place is still in excellent condition.

At *98.3 m.* is the junction with a graveled road.

Left on this road at *5.4 m.* (R) is the entrance to *HOLLYWOOD (private),* on the Spanish land granted to James Alcorn Gillespie about 1785. Various additions were made to the original house, making it architecturally one of the most peculiar houses in the Natchez country. It is composed of two separate buildings connected by a hip-roofed gallery extending the length of the house. The vaulted ceilings of the gallery were originally plastered and, except where large rooms have been added on each side, small hand-made balusters still enclose it. In appearance the house is reminiscent of the primitive dog-trot type. It sits on a knoll and through the open central hall is a charming view of meadow lands beyond.

The road, cutting narrowly through steep embankments covered with Cherokee roses, circles a tranquil countryside in the valley of the once navigable Homochitto River. One of the first English settlements in the area and the first Protestant settlement in Mississippi was made in this neighborhood in 1772, when Capt. Amos Ogden, retired naval officer, came to claim the 25,000 acres that had been granted him by the British Government in 1768. He was accompanied by Samuel and Richard Swayze, to whom he sold 19,000 acres at 20¢ per acre and by two surveyors, Caleb and Joseph King. The party went from New Jersey to Pensacola, Fla., thence through a chain of lakes into the Mississippi, and up the Homochitto. With them they brought 10 or 15 families including their own. Many old homes stand in this vicinity and their occupants, for the most part, are descendants of the early English settlers. These homes stand among the aged, moss-covered oaks.

At *6.4 m.* (R) is the lane leading to *WOODSTOCK (private),* set deep in an oak woods heavily festooned with moss. The brick red-roofed house has a recessed front entrance with fluted pilasters. The house was built in recent years, on the site of old Woodstock, but duplicates many features of the older house.

At *6.7 m.* is *MT. CARMEL CHURCH* (R), a toy-like, exquisitely designed structure with white walls, green-shuttered windows, a tiny porch, and a small cupola. The congregation was organized in 1825.

At 7 m. is the FOSTER HOME (L), known as The Hermitage. This is a dilapidated frame structure, standing gloomy and deserted on a high bank. Of Spanish Provincial type architecture, its timbers show great age. According to early records it stood here prior to 1834.

At 7.5 m. is the junction with old US 61; R. here.

KINGSTON, 11.4 m. (25 pop.), is an old community with a modern white, frame consolidated school and a general store. The original village, which developed around a blockhouse, was called Jersey Town until about 1777, when Caleb King, son-in-law of Richard Swayze, laid out lots around his plantation home. Until about 1825 Kingston prospered, having several stores, a tailor, a saddler, and a blacksmith. The Congregational Church, built in 1798, was the first Protestant church in Mississippi. Prior to this time services were held secretly in the woods or in private homes, the Spanish Government being opposed to any sect other than that of the Catholics. With the establishment of other towns in this district Kingston slowly began to decline. By 1830 it was little more than it is today.

At 12.5 m. on old US 61 is the junction with a graveled road; R. here.

At 12.8 m. is the KINGSTON METHODIST CHURCH, a typical plantation neighborhood church, built of brick with a small portico in front. Inside is a slave gallery. On the grounds are old steps from which riders mounted their horses. This church is the successor of the one founded by Lorenzo Dow in 1803, at which time he deeded land to the trustees for the erection of a church. The original church, according to tradition, was destroyed by a tornado in 1840, and the present one erected in the early 1850's.

In a field diagonally across the road from the church is the GRAVE OF CALEB KING, founder of Kingston, marked by an impressive monument rising high above tall meadow grass.

At 13.2 m. is the COREY HOUSE (open by appointment), formerly known as Hillside. It is a one-story, square, compactly built, Southern Planter type house, with galleries on all sides and green-shuttered windows that extend to the floor. Delicately painted shades as old as the house hang at the windows, and much of the furniture is the original. Sliding doors make it possible to convert the entire dwelling into one immense room. The Coreys came to the Natchez country with the Swayzes in 1772-73.

At 13.9 m. (L) is the OLD PUBLIC BURYING GROUND, enclosed by a sagging wire fence and overgrown with tangled weeds and flowering shrubs. The tombstones bearing names of early settlers—Swayze, Ogden, Foule, and King—date back to 1784.

At 15.7 m. is MANDAMUS (L), a simple country cottage, that has lost most of its original features in successive alterations. The house has a deep side porch, with small, square posts, and dormers breaking the steep lines of the roof at the front.

At 103.1 m. US 61 crosses the HOMOCHITTO (Ind., *shelter creek*) RIVER. Sand bars and masses of water plants form a swamp, choking a stream that in 1772 was navigable for sailing vessels.

Between the Homochitto River and Buffalo Creek US 61 climbs gradually but steadily for five miles to a hill giving an excellent view of the surrounding country.

At 113.5 m. the highway dips into the Buffalo Creek bottoms. The sand beaches on the inner bends of Buffalo Creek, 115.8 m., indicate that the loess is thinner toward the S.

Between Buffalo Creek and Woodville the highway runs over a loess mixed with clay and gravel; the dwellings are poorer.

WOODVILLE, *119.8 m.* (560 alt., 1,113 pop.), seat of Wilkinson Co., is on a watershed. Northeast of it are the former longleaf pine hills; W. and S. are the bluff hills of the Mississippi, so like and so much a part of the Natchez district that it is hard to draw the line between the two areas. Indeed, Woodville's most distinguished citizen, Judge Edward McGehee, was used in *So Red the Rose* to typify the best in the Natchez district planter. Judge McGehee gave the town its life and tone, and today it retains the marks of his influence.

The present *POST OFFICE* was formerly the station of the West Feliciana R.R., which McGehee financed and which was chartered in 1831. This was the first railroad built in Mississippi, the second in the Mississippi Valley, and the fifth in the United States. The railroad, the rails of which were made of cypress, cedar, and heart of pine hewn by McGehee slaves, is now a part of the Yazoo & Mississippi Valley R.R., a subsidiary of the Illinois Central System. It was among the first American railroads to use the standard gauge, the first to issue and print freight tariffs, and the first to adopt cattle guards and pits.

Facing the station is the two-story *COURTHOUSE,* 40 feet square, with massive columns on front and rear, each two feet in diameter, rising the full height of the walls.

The *METHODIST EPISCOPAL CHURCH SOUTH,* on a high oak-shaded bluff, SW. corner of Main St. and US 61, is a neat wooden structure, with tall windows and a large slave gallery facing the rostrum. The church was built in 1824 and is probably the oldest of its denomination in the State. Judge McGehee's name was the first on the roll of membership. At the rear of the building, in a small enclosure under some cedars, are the graves of the family of Col. John S. Lewis, whose wife donated the lot for the church. Prominent in the church's annals is the Maffit Revival. In the early 1840's John Newland Maffit so stirred the people that a group of young men, the "sons of Belial," determined to break up his meeting. They threatened to pelt his pulpit with rotten eggs if he preached again. He preached and one egg was thrown; the man who threw it was at the altar the next day pleading for forgiveness.

The *BAPTIST CHURCH,* one block diagonally SE. of the Methodist church, is possibly the oldest church building of any denomination now standing in Mississippi. It is a large well-preserved red brick structure with four round white columns on the façade, a tall bell tower, green shutters, and white trim. In 1806 the Baptist congregations in this area met at Bethel, a small community four miles SW. of Woodville, and formed an association that has grown into the present Baptist State Convention. The exact date of erection of the Woodville church is unknown; the first meetings of the congregation were secret because Roman Catholicism was the state religion of the Spaniards, titular sovereigns of the country N. of the 31st parallel until just before 1800, and of the country S. of the parallel (10 miles from Woodville) until 1810.

ST. PAUL'S EPISCOPAL CHURCH, corner Church and First Sts., erected in 1824, one of the oldest Episcopal churches W. of the Alleghanies. Impressive in its stately simplicity, the gray frame structure, built high on a terrace and surrounded by oaks, is now, except for minor repairs, as it was when built. Its architectural style followed that of St. John's Episcopal Church in Richmond, Va. No less impressive is its interior, with a massive crystal chandelier from an old monastery, a handsomely carved altar, and an organ, still in use, brought from England shortly after the church was built. In early days the novelty of Protestant services with a liturgy attracted great crowds. Indeed, so unfamiliar was the average Mississippian with the Episcopal form of organization and worship that the legislature, granting an act of incorporation to the church, changed the titles "warden" and "vestrymen" to the better-known "trustees." In 1862 the congregation of the church forwarded the church bell to General Beauregard to be melted into cannon, "hoping that its gentle tones, that have so often called us to the House of God, may be transmuted into war's resounding rhyme to repel the ruthless invader from the beautiful land God, in his goodness, has given us."

The *OFFICE OF THE WOODVILLE REPUBLICAN* is two blocks S. of the post office. The newspaper, the oldest in Mississippi, was founded by Andrew Marschalk, pioneer printer in Mississippi, and was first published in 1812. The *COL. JOHN S. LEWIS HOME (private)*, a block E. of the Republican office, is, with its massive columns, strikingly like Rosalie in Natchez. This Woodville structure has been the home of the Lewis family for more than a century. The Lewises, among the first English families to settle in the State, in 1808 built the first house in Woodville.

At Woodville is the junction with the Fort Adams Road *(see Side Tour 3B).*

Left from Woodville *1 m.* on the road that is a continuation of Church St. to (L) *HAMPTON HALL (private)*, the handsome old mansion formerly known as Ararat because it stands on a hilltop. Hampton Hall, built in 1832, later passed into the hands of Colonel Hoard, the engineer who constructed Judge McGehee's railroad and assisted in planning the Erie Canal. Oaks almost obscure the two-and-a-half-story, columned brick structure, and under them grow boxwood, sweet olive trees as old as the house itself, and camellia japonicas. The murals inside the house were painted by Grace McManus, sister of the present owner, before she had received the art training that later enabled her to illuminate the prayer-book for the coronation of King Edward VII.

At *1.5 m.* on the side road is the junction with a graveled road; L. here *0.6 m.* to *BOWLING GREEN* (R), a plantation holding the ruins of Judge McGehee's home. Four immense round columns shrouded by creeping ivy are all that remain of the big house. Nearby are the old brick carriage houses, the brick kitchen, and the brick office. The modest frame home now occupied by McGehee descendants was built by Judge McGehee after Federal troops had burned the original structure. In the present house is the grand piano saved from the fire. Under the moss and sweet olive trees a few hundred yards from the ruins are the McGehee family burial grounds. On the crest of a knoll and enclosed by a high wrought-iron fence is the monument marking the *GRAVE OF JUDGE McGEHEE.*

US 61, paved between Woodville and the Louisiana Line, is bordered by great hedges of Cherokee rose.

At *124.2 m.* (L) is *ASHWOOD (open by appointment)*, the former plantation of George Poindexter (1779–1855), author of the first Mississippi Code and second Governor of the State. The early history of Mississippi could not be written without mention of him. He was born in Louisa Co., Va., in 1779, and came to the Mississippi Territory to open a law office at Natchez when he was 23 years old. In 1807 he arranged the meeting between Aaron Burr and Territorial Governor Cowles Mead, and later was professionally connected with Burr's trial. As a Territorial delegate to the U.S. Congress Poindexter first won national fame in 1811, when he called Josiah Quincy of Massachusetts to order after Quincy's impassioned speech against the admission of Louisiana; Poindexter remarked that Aaron Burr had not gone as far in immoderate language as Quincy had gone. In 1817 Poindexter was the leading member of the convention that framed Mississippi's first Constitution for which he was almost wholly responsible. His code of laws, finished in 1822 while he was Governor, was subsequently described by Governor A. G. Brown as the best Mississippi "has ever had." In 1830 he was appointed U.S. Senator to fill an unexpired term, and it is evidence of Wilkinson County's early importance in the State's history that while Poindexter was Senator, Gerard Brandon was Governor, and a third Wilkinson Co. citizen, Abram Scott, was Lieutenant Governor. Poindexter's congressional career was marked by a break with his former ally, President Andrew Jackson, and an alliance with Calhoun, a realignment in accord with Poindexter's extreme doctrine of State sovereignty, in which he foreshadowed the course Mississippi would take for the next generation.

At *128.2 m.* US 61 crosses the Louisiana Line, 50 miles N. of Baton Rouge, La.

Side Tour 3A

Clarksdale—Greenville—Rolling Fork, 133.5 m. State 1.
Yazoo & Mississippi Valley R.R. parallels route between Sherard and Rolling Fork.
One-third hard-surfaced roadbed; rest graveled; two lanes wide.
Accommodations in cities.

This route roughly parallels the Mississippi River between Clarksdale and Greenville; it passes through the oldest and some of the most interesting of the Delta plantations and rims a number of beautiful lakes. The lakes, old beds left when the Mississippi River carved out new channels, have retained the horseshoe shape of the pronounced river bends. They are bordered by bright green willow brakes, and gnarled cypress trees that turn russet brown in fall. Part of this highway was under water in 1927 when

TAKING COTTON TO THE GIN

the Delta about Greenville was inundated in the greatest flood Mississippi has known.

State 1 branches W. from US 61 at CLARKSDALE, *0 m. (see Tour 3, Sec. a)*.

SHERARD, *9.3 m.*, is a typical large Delta plantation with 6,000 acres under cultivation. The northern end of Sherard is three miles from the big house (L) and commissary (R). In addition to the commissary two cotton gins, a sawmill, and a pecan cleaner and grader are operated. J. H. Sherard who cleared the plantation in 1874 lives (1937) in a low rambling house shaded by pecan trees. His sons, grandson, and daughter have separate dwellings grouped about his. One son, a doctor, practices almost exclusively among the families on the plantation. In the days when steamboats could leave the Mississippi at high water and go inland as far as Clarksdale, Sherard the elder used to sail by what is now his plantation. His story of clearing and draining the swamps that were the homes of snakes, alligators, and eagles, of building levees to hold the cleared lands, and of prospering through cotton-growing despite these difficulties, is the story of all the Delta.

At *11.3 m.* the levee is visible (R).

GREENGROVE, *13.5 m.*, was, from the 1850's until after the War between the States, the plantation of Confederate Cavalry Gen. Nathan Bedford Forrest *(see Tour 4)*. During the war Forrest brought his family here for safekeeping.

At *15 m.* is RENALARA (35 pop.), a hamlet that grew up on the plantation of John P. Richardson who owned 18,000 acres of Delta land.

HILLHOUSE, *18 m.* (157 alt., 75 pop.), is the center of the Beverly B plantation and the shipping point for the Delta Cooperative Farm.

The DELTA COOPERATIVE FARM, *22.8 m.* *(open: no fee, contributions accepted)*, has achieved some fame as a laboratory experiment in cooperative living. Organized in 1935 by Sherwood Eddy, New York writer and reformer, the farm is being used to improve the social, racial, and economic status of Southern sharecroppers *(see AGRICULTURE)*. On 2,138 acres of buckshot land were placed 19 Negro and 12 white families; the number has been increased to 33 families (1938). There is an 11-acre common garden in which vegetables are produced for immediate consumption and for canning; a hog farm, a poultry farm, a sawmill, a blacksmith shop, a school, and a commissary are collectively operated. Alfalfa as well as cotton is cultivated. The Rust mechanical cotton-picker is in use. Thirty frame houses have been erected, and nearly 200 acres of land have been cleared and reclaimed.

The board of trustees, holding a deed of trust on the investment of $25,000, is the supreme authority. Acting as a coordinator between the board and the tenants is an advisory council of five elected every six months from among the inhabitants of the farm; neither race may have more than three representatives. Under the direction of the council are operated the two cooperatives into which the colony is divided. The Producers' Cooperative supervises production—planting, cultivating, and building; the Consumers' Cooperative has charge of distributing the supplies to the tenants and selling the products to outsiders. After operating expenses and provisions for retiring the capital investment have been deducted, the net returns from all commercial crops and timber are prorated among the member producers according to the kind and amount of work done. Young social workers serve as directors and teachers without salary. On the board of trustees are Sherwood Eddy; Reinhold Neibuhr, a clergyman; William Amberson, a former professor of physiology at the University of Tennessee; and John Rust, the inventor.

The levee visible (R) between Hillhouse and Beulah was originally built with Irish labor behind wheelbarrows, but has since been improved, enlarged, and sodded many times to give what is now almost complete protection from overflow.

At DEESON, 26.3 m. (153 alt., 30 pop.), are the headquarters of the Delta Planter's Company, a Dutch organization operating a plantation of 8,800 acres, under the management of Oscar Johnston *(see below)*.

At *30.8 m.* is PERTHSHIRE (420 pop.).

Right from Perthshire is DENNIS LANDING, *4.3 m.,* a fishing colony just W. of the levee. The road runs through an extensive cotton field for two miles, meets a green, sluggish slough, and follows it through an Osage orange grove, supposed to have been planted by Indians, to top the levee at *4 m.* From the levee is a good view of the low damp land that lies between it and the Mississippi River. The landing is formed by a caved-in portion of the high bluff that is the bank of the river. The people live in frame houses built on a high secondary levee, and fish for a living. Carloads of buffalo and of giant river spoonbill catfish, valuable for their roe, are shipped weekly; the roe packed in ice is shipped in barrels. While Chicago takes a part of the yearly catch which amounts to several tons, other shipments go as far as New York.

At *31.7 m.* on State 1 is the junction with a graveled road.

Left on this road is the BLANCHARD PLANTATION, *0.9 m.,* that has been in the same family for four generations. Set off the road in the midst of the plantation's cotton fields is the big house, a spreading one-story frame structure typical of the Delta's better types of rural homes. On the place are five Indian mounds from which skeletons have been taken by Tulane University experts.

GUNNISON, *35.5 m.* (153 alt., 484 pop.), is larger than the usual plantation town, having several stores instead of one. Artesian wells here have shown traces of gas, the town hydrant shooting a flame 10 feet high when, after being capped for some time, it was ignited. Derricks of prospecting gas wells are visible from the town. On the northwestern limits of Gunnison is the old CONCORDIA CEMETERY, a significant survival of a prosperous river town that was so tough in its day that many of the grave markers bear merely the epitaph "Killed in Concordia."

ROSEDALE, *45.8 m.* (143 alt., 2,117 pop.), one of the seats of Bolivar Co., with a one-story cream-faced brick courthouse, is the only town of size on the river between Memphis and Greenville. The force of the currents from the confluence of the White and Arkansas Rivers opposite Rosedale keeps the Misssisippi pushing against the Rosedale levee. The view of the river from Rosedale landing, with shanty boats tied up here, is interesting. Catfish caught here are shipped as far N. as St. Louis and Chicago. At MONTGOMERY POINT, on the river, David Crockett is reputed to have crossed on his way to the Alamo. In the spring the town has the appearance of a well-kept garden, worthy of its name. Annually in October a Rose Show is held.

Perhaps the most noteworthy citizens of Rosedale and the surrounding area were Walter Sellers, Sr., who was born here, and Charles Scott, who came to Bolivar County shortly after the War between the States.

BEULAH, *51.4 m.* (143 alt., 506 pop.), is a fishing resort and farm town on Lake Beulah, which parallels the highway a half mile distant (R); the lake was formed by the capricious Mississippi River as early as 1863. Fishing for perch and crappie is fair.

At *56.3 m.* is LOBDELL (75 pop.).

Right from Lobdell on a dirt road to INDIAN POINT, *5 m.*, one of many points at which De Soto is supposed to have discovered the Mississippi River. At this point the gold seekers from Georgia and Alabama crossed the river in 1849 on their way to California. PRENTISS, on Indian Point, was the first seat of Bolivar Co. Because the old men and boys who remained at home took frequent pot-shots at the Federal gunboats on the river, the Federals burned the village in 1863. Only a few shacks now mark the site.

At *61.5 m.* is BENOIT (137 alt., 438 pop.).

Left from Benoit on a graveled road running along Egypt Ridge to the old *J. C. BURRUS HOME, 0.8 m.* (R). Egypt Ridge was so called because it was the only place on which corn grew during the unprecedented flood of 1844. The Burrus Home, called Hollywood plantation because of the grove of holly trees planted about the great house, is the only ante-bellum structure in Bolivar Co. It was built of heart cypress with slave labor. A portico with six slender columns having unusual spool-shaped capitals makes the entrance imposing. The pediment has generous proportions but simple detail. During the war it served as headquarters for Confederate officers, among them Gen. John Early.

At *64.7 m.* (R) is a view of LAKE BOLIVAR which parallels State 1 for several miles. Fishing here is excellent for buffalo, crappie, perch, and trout. Almost a mile wide, Lake Bolivar is somewhat larger than other river lakes. Cypress trees of great beauty outline its banks.

At SCOTT, *67.4 m.* (140 alt., 300 pop.), are the headquarters of the *DELTA AND PINE LAND CO. PLANTATION,* the country's largest plantation, containing 38,000 acres; it is owned by the Fine Spinners Association of Manchester, England, and is under the management of Oscar Johnston. Of the 38,000 acres, 11,700 are in cotton; the whole is under the supervision of 12 unit managers, and is worked by 1,000 Negro sharecroppers. The value of the property is about $5,000,000.

The company maintains a school, church, and hospital for tenants, the croppers paying a 75¢-per-acre hospital fee annually—thus a man who worked 12 acres would be assessed $9 a year for hospitalization. Women are encouraged to go to the hospital for confinement rather than to depend upon midwives. Vaccination for small-pox and typhoid, inoculations against malaria, and anti-syphilitic injections are offered as part of the medical service. Tenant cabins, unscreened but stoutly built, are above the Delta average in quality. The tenants eat the usual pork, molasses, and cornbread, but an attempt is made to make up vitamin deficiencies by supplying them with free yeast. It is estimated that the average tenant here clears about $300 a year above subsistence *(see AGRICULTURE).*

Oscar Johnston, a native Mississippian, took over the management of the company in 1928; since then the plantation has shown a notable profit for the first time since its establishment in 1910. Johnston was in 1933 Finance Director of the AAA, and later manager of the Federal cotton pool.

The road leading from State 1 to the Scott railway station is an experiment made to find new uses for cotton. A heavy coat of tar was applied to the old graveled roadbed, over this was laid cotton fabric, and this in turn was overlaid with an asphalt coating. Theoretically, the cotton mesh absorbs moisture, thus lessening the amount of expansion and contraction of the roadbed caused by changes in temperature. These changes are in some part responsible for cracks in paving. The half-mile cotton textile road was built in 1935.

At 74.3 m. is LOUGHBOROUGH, a low clapboarded structure, actually two cottages with long sweeping roofs carried down over its front and rear screened porches. The home was built in 1841 by Samuel Burks. In front of the house, the concrete roadbed is laid on top of the old levee that was built and maintained by the plantation owner before the war.

At 75.6 m. is WINTERVILLE (132 alt., 108 pop.).

> Right from Winterville on a trail to CARTER'S POINT, separated from the Delta by a cut-off which becomes a raging channel when the river is up. Since the cut-off forced the abandonment of the old plantations in 1900, duck, squirrel, and bird hunting has been good on the point. The three plantations, Woodstock, Salona, and Tarpley, were settled by the Carters and Randolphs of Virginia before the War between the States. The plantation barns still stand. Because of the river bend here, some Mississippi land is due W. of Arkansas.

At 76.6 m. (R) are the WINTERVILLE INDIAN MOUNDS, a group composed of a great central mound 55 feet high surrounded by an irregular ellipse of 14 smaller ones of various sizes. The view from the top of the tall mound is worth the climb, the mounds being the only elevations in this stretch of flat country.

GREENVILLE, 82.9 m. (125 alt., 14,807 pop.), the seat of Washington Co., spreads at random along the east bank of the Mississippi River and derives a brisk trade from the river. Tugs churn through the muddy water to the dock, and along the levee sweating stevedores strain at heavy cotton bales brought in from the surrounding plantations. The largest city in the Yazoo-Mississippi area, Greenville is a cotton planting, ginning, marketing, and financing center.

Laid out in broad avenues that run parallel to and at right angles with the river, Greenville has a business district with solid, modern well-spaced buildings interspersed with a few survivals of the past. In the residential sections the wealth of the city is evidenced in the homes which vary from Greek Revival, plantation-type dwellings to modern stucco and brick apartments; most commonly seen, however, are the large, roomy Victorian structures with bay windows, rococo cupolas, and gingerbread trim, their idiosyncrasies half-hidden in the shadows of magnolia and live oak trees. Greenville's early citizens were people of wealth and culture from Virginia, Kentucky, and the Carolinas who brought with them not only their household goods and their slaves but also bulky volumes of the classics, Greek and Latin textbooks, and tutors for their children.

The population is 56.5 percent Negro; the remainder are a cosmopolitan mixture. Five Protestant churches, a synagogue, a Roman Catholic church, and a Christian Science Church, in addition to 28 Negro churches, hold regular services. Separate schools for white, Negro, and Chinese children are operated. The Catholic church maintains a private school, St.

Rose of Lima Academy, for white children and the School of the Sacred Heart, under the supervision of German nuns, for Negroes.

The embryo of the present town was the Blantonia plantation on Bachelor's Bend. In 1828 the land was settled by Col. W. W. Blanton, and in 1866 sold by his widow, who was then Mrs. Harriet B. Theobold, for the third county seat; the first was destroyed by inundations of the river and the second was burned by fires from Federal gunboats in 1863. Greenville, incorporated June 24, 1870, is a mile NE. of this second site, which, after being burned, caved into the river. Block after block of the present town fell into the river until 1927, when for 70 days the town was under water. After this time levees were built higher and wider under Government direction; in 1935 the river was banished to a new course several miles westward and Lake Katherine was created at Greenville's western boundary. In 1937 its name was changed to Lake Ferguson. Boats still dock at its wharf here, and Greenville's river trade goes on. Greenville was the birthplace of Nellie Nugent Somerville (1863-   ), pioneer suffragist and WCTU leader, the first woman elected to the State Legislature. Her daughter, Lucy Somerville Howorth, an attorney, is a member of the Board of Appeals of the Veterans Administration.

The *PERCY HOME (open by permission)*, SE. corner Percy and Broadway Sts., is owned and occupied by William Alexander Percy (1885-   ), lawyer and poet *(see ARTS and LETTERS)*. He is the son of Senator LeRoy Percy and the grandson of Col. William Alexander Percy (1834-88), known as the Gray Eagle of the Delta because of his leadership of the Southern whites during the days of reconstruction. In the home are five works of Jacob Epstein: *Head of Christ*, bust of *David Cohn*, *Senegalese Girl*, *Indian Boy*, and *Baby Head*; two pieces of sculpture by Leon Koury, born in Greenville, Nov. 4, 1909; a Negro head in bronze, and a head of William Alexander Percy, the poet; and other notable objects.

In *GREENWAY CEMETERY*, end of Main St., is the *GRAVE OF SEN. LeROY PERCY* (1860-1929), marked by a bronze figure, the work of Malvina Hoffman. Possessed of the courage of his convictions LeRoy Percy became an able and forceful lawyer and in 1909 was elected to the U. S. Senate, serving until March 4, 1913. Senator Percy's private and public life was marked by the deep love for his home county that characterizes the three generations of Percys who have been active in building the Delta. His outstanding contribution to the Delta was his aid in organizing the Staple Cotton Association, his connections with the Federal Reserve System, the Drainage System, and his work for better roads development. During the World War Senator Percy went to France for the National Y.M.C.A.

In front of the *VALLIANT HOME*, NE. corner Central and Shelby Sts., a one-story dwelling built in 1866-67, is a large oak tree that illustrates the fertility of the Delta soil and the length of the Delta growing seasons. Planted by Mrs. Frank Valliant in 1867, it was recently estimated to have the growth of a tree 180 years old. Its spread of branches is magnificent.

The *STARLING COLLECTION* is housed in the *GREENVILLE PUBLIC LIBRARY*, SW. corner Main and Shelby Sts. This unusually fine collection contains 2,600 old and rare volumes in English, French, Spanish, Dutch, Persian, Arabic, Turkish, and Hebrew, and eight books belonging to the cradle age of printing.

In the steeple of the Episcopal Church, Main St., is a relic of early Mississippi River trade and old time plantation life, a *STEAMBOAT BELL* taken from an old steamer and used on the Woodstock Plantation until placed in its present position. It was the gift of Mrs. Harry Ball whose grandfather settled Carter's Point.

U. S. GYPSUM PLANT, on the Mississippi River, makes insulated wallboard from local cottonwood and willow trees. Established in 1930, it does considerable reforestation upon land purchased. Trees cut in the company forests are floated down the river to the mill at little cost.

CHICAGO MILL AND LUMBER CO. PLANT, on the river, also utilizes native woods to make boxes and dimension stock for radios, furniture, hoops, and staves. The mill was established in 1930.

Between Greenville and Rolling Fork, State 1 passes the oldest and most charming Delta plantations.

At *86.1 m.* is *WILDWOOD* (L), with a one-and-a-half story house used during the war as headquarters for Confederate scouts.

At Wildwood is the junction with a plantation road.

Right on this road past a large pecan orchard to *LOCUST, 1 m.* (L), a plantation home of historic value, built in 1846 by William Pinckney Montgomery, a pioneer Delta planter. Locust is a long low white structure raised, like many of its neighbors, on brick piers; it has wide wings and long windows. Though the kitchen at one side is of brick, the house is constructed of cypress. The servants' quarters and outhouses were made of brick for permanence, but the planters feared malaria, which they thought was hastened by the "brick-sweating," and used cypress in their own dwellings. In front of Locust is a levee built by slaves, and in the moat are cypress trees six feet through at the base. About the house are pecan and magnolia trees.

On *LONE PINE PLANTATION, 87 m.* (L), is a cypress log eight feet in diameter and 90 years old. The slaves from the old Montgomery plantation used the log as a bridge when they hurried to Greenville at the news of the Emancipation Proclamation. The banks of Ash Bayou, cutting through the plantation, are formed of cinder beds left by the Indians after burning their pottery.

At *88.2 m.* (L) is *SWIFTWATER (private),* built by Alexander B. Montgomery in the 1840's. With the exception of Longwood it is the best example of ante-bellum architecture in the Delta. Its red roof, broken by an open deck, matches in color the brick of the piers that lift it above the swift waters of occasional floods. The one-story building with full-length windows, wide doors, and a porch extending along three sides, is particularly well adapted for life in this area. The outside walls are white, the porch ceiling is blue. Swiftwater was the refuge of Mrs. Ann Finlay and her children when their home at Old Greenville was destroyed by Federal gunboats during the war. Before leaving, Mrs. Finlay collected quantities of quinine, calomel, and castor oil from the Finlay Drug Store in the old town, and, though some of it was confiscated on her way to Swiftwater, this small supply was the only medicine available in the community until the war ended.

At *93.1 m.* (L) is BELMONT *(private)*, a dull red two-story brick house, more French or Spanish in character than Georgian Colonial. In place of the traditional thick white columns it is fronted with slender gray posts, a feature quite in harmony with the wrought-iron railings and French bays. The hip-roofed structure is spacious with doorways 11 feet high. This house, finished in 1855, alone remains of those built by the pioneer Worthington brothers. The home of one, on a nearby plantation, caved into the river in 1885; that of another stood until 1932 when it was condemned by the Government in its levee-building program. The new levee rises in front of the remaining house; between the levee and the river is Lake Lee, the first lake, and one of the few lakes in the Delta, made by man and not by the river. It was formed in the 1850's when Marcellus Johnson, a planter, made a cut-off here.

LONGWOOD, *102.1 m.* (R), has been saved from the Mississippi only by moving it twice, in 1854 and 1885. The house was built in 1832 by Ben Smith, a planter, on a tract of 30,000 acres bought from the Government in 1822. Originally it had a raised brick basement, four rooms, an encircling frame porch ornamented with cast-iron stars, a balustrade, and a trellis. Four rooms were added in 1848 and four more in 1870. The hip roof of seamed metal, painted red, is surmounted by a long, low, glassed-in observatory. The porch is set, cantilever style, several feet out from the face of the piers. There are large chimneys, long, wide, well-spaced windows, and cleverly concealed cabinets. Longwood on its third site occupies an elevation that was once four Indian mounds, and is surrounded by prickly mock-orange trees.

At ELKLAND, *106.2 m.*, is the head of LAKE WASHINGTON, one of the Delta's most beautiful lakes, which parallels the highway to Glen Allan. Fishing and duck hunting here are excellent. About the lake are poules d'eau, called "poodle doos" by the Negroes. In southern Louisiana these birds are considered a delicacy, but Mississippians think their meat too fish-like. In the Lake Washington area is the nesting place for rare birds such as the great blue heron, the American egret, and the snowy egret. Members of the biology department of the Delta State Teachers College *(see Tour 3, Sec. a)* have here observed the water-turkey, the double-crested cormorant, the mallard, the green-winged teal, the wood duck, the Virginia rail, the purple gallinule, the sora rail, the least sandpiper, and the dickcissel. At the foot of the lake is a flat of cypress and water lilies that makes an ideal cover for ducks.

> Right from Elkland on a graveled road to LAKE JACKSON, *5.5 m.*, a long narrow body of water in the marshy land between Lake Washington and the river. It has none of the beautiful blue water of Lake Washington, but its jungle of moss-covered cypress, cane, and water lilies is attractive. Lake Jackson is noted among hunters for duck and alligator. Between Lake Jackson and the river are the sites of many former river landings, now extinct, among them Leota Landing *(see TRANSPORTATION)* and Princeton. From the latter the first barrel of cottonseed oil was shipped abroad.

Between Elkland and Glen Allan is one of the first settled parts of

MOONLIGHT ON LAKE WASHINGTON, ELKLAND

the Delta, called the Lake Washington Country and noted for its antebellum culture. A few homes are left to suggest the life of that period. Before the coming of roads, the lake provided the means of transportation.

At *107.9 m.* (L) is *ERWIN (private)*, with a plantation house that was built between the years 1827–30 by Junius Ward, one of the first settlers in the county. The story is that the 17-year-old Junius, while hunting with Indian guides, was shown Lake Washington and was so impressed with the "most beautiful lake in the world" that he preempted land and built a log cabin. The logs of the original cabin, now a part of the rambling frame house, are visible in the attic.

At *108.7 m.* (L) is *MOUNT HOLLY (private)*, a great red brick mansion of 30 rooms, as pretentious as Erwin is simple, built between 1855–59 for Margaret Johnson Erwin. The bricks were made on the place. Of special interest are the wrought-iron railings on the balconies. The interior is notable for its rosewood staircase, rounded niches for statuary, frescoes, walnut woodwork, and great oven. The walls of Mount Holly are 2 feet thick and the ceilings 14 feet high. Perhaps the most unusual feature is the asymmetrical plan, with a parlor projecting beyond the front line of the entrance porch, verandas and bay windows. During the 1927 flood the mansion was used as headquarters for relief committees, who were able to land their boats on the lawn.

LINDEN, 112.3 m. (L), is the site of the first white settlement in the county, made in 1825. The first settler, Frederick Turnbull, brought with him from South Carolina a plant called the Pride of India, now known as the chinaberry tree. Linden was for many years the home of Gen. Wade Hampton of South Carolina. The present home dates only from 1914, yet its Greek Revival effect and great Corinthian columns, half-hidden by trees, are strongly reminiscent of Melrose and Auburn *(see NATCHEZ)*. Visible across the lake from Linden is *EVERHOPE*, a red brick house built in 1841 by Andrew Knox. During its erection, bottles of wine were sealed in the walls of the house, these to be opened for the wedding of Knox's son who was then only a child. The boy died in his youth and in that same year Knox sold the house. He died soon afterward. But some say the marriage that never occurred was celebrated each December for many years by a phantom wedding party, using the wine. The bottles trotted out from hiding, placed themselves on great silver platters, and throughout the revelry kept the glasses brimming full. When all was over, the bottles, still full, hopped back to their hiding place.

At *112.8 m.* (R) is the landing pier for gravel barges. The barges are loaded across the lake with sand and gravel pumped from the lake's bed. The gravel that forms the bottom of Lake Washington is excellent for road building.

GLEN ALLAN, *113.6 m.* (275 pop.), is named for a plantation formerly on this site.

> Right from Glen Allan on a narrow paved road are the *RUINS OF ST. JOHN'S EPISCOPAL CHURCH, 1.8 m.* (L), completed in 1857, the first Episcopal structure in the Delta. The group of planters who settled around Lake Washington in the 1830's were of English descent; some of them were English born. Extensive landowners in the older Southern States, they had come to Mississippi in boom times and, from the proceeds of the sale of their former holdings, had invested in the fertile acres of what were then known as the Mississippi Bottoms. The mansions they built are the remaining evidence of their prosperity. To them in 1844 came Bishop Otey from Tennessee, and the fruit of his visit was the gift by Jonathan McCaleb of five acres of land to be used as a site for the church and a glebe. In October 1852, "at which time the families which leave that region in summer months generally return to their plantations," the building was begun.

There was delay because of the necessity for importing materials from England and an organ for the wilderness. When the church was dedicated in April 1857, the services were stopped by a snow storm. Slaves were given their own gallery, and the richly-carved chancel, pulpit, and altar were fashioned by the Negro sexton, Jesse Crowell, who was buried from the church, and was afterward given a place in the adjacent cemetery. After the War between the States the church began to decay, and a cyclone completed the ruin. Still evident is the outline of the corner tower with circular brick windows webbed in vines. Its design is based upon that of the English Gothic. The churchyard still bears the name of Greenfield, the plantation of Jonathan McCaleb. In its well-kept enclosure a number of iron crosses mark the graves of Confederate dead.

RICHLAND, 115.1 m. (L), with its face towards a bayou and its side to the highway, is a one-and-a-half story frame house on a high foundation; at the rear is a kitchen ell. The high, broken-roofed building has a cross hall separating the main building from the back ell. The house was erected by Jim Richardson, son of Edmund "Ned" Richardson, known as the Cotton King of the World. A politician who was in league with the carpetbaggers and renegade Confederates in both his native Louisiana and in Mississippi, Ned Richardson maintained convict labor gangs under the leasing system. With the labor gangs he accomplished the Herculean task of clearing the almost impenetrable morass of the central Mississippi Delta. Living on this rich soil and bringing Negro tenants from the central hills, Richardson was able to add link after link to his chain of plantations in Mississippi and Louisiana.

At *122.5 m.* (R) is a group of three Indian mounds, the tallest of them about 25 feet high.

EAGLE'S NEST, 122.8 m., is a plantation by Lake Lafayette. It was so named because eagles used to hatch in the great trees on the banks of the lake.

At *123 m.* is the junction with a graveled road.

Right on this road to *LAKESIDE PLANTATION, 2.7 m.* The home, built by the Turnbulls from South Carolina *(see above)* in the 1840's, is a simple dogtrot house built of wide boards throughout, with doors of plain paneling. The spacious front porch faces Steele Bayou, whose steep banks with big trees add dignity and beauty to the setting. Farther back from the bayou, but facing it in a row, are nine ante-bellum cabins. This plantation borders the bayou for two-and-a-half miles. Across the bayou is *HOPEDALE PLANTATION*, also established by Turnbull. At one time Steele Bayou was navigable, and cotton was shipped down it to the Yazoo River and into Vicksburg.

At *128.5 m.* is the junction with a graveled road.

Right on this road is MAYERSVILLE, 7 *m.* (136 pop.), county seat of Issaquena. Mayersville, settled in 1830 by Ambrose Gipson, was called Gipson's Landing until 1870, when the site was purchased by David Mayer. Five years later Mayer deeded a part of the land as a county site, and that same year the town was incorporated as Mayersville. Until the mid-century decline of river traffic Mayersville was the shipping point on the Mississippi for the cotton of Sharkey and Issaquena Counties. Showboats on the river during low water times and a shifting population of river crews, gamblers, and traders gave the village a gay existence that its present day quiescence belies. Since 1927 Mayersville has been adequately protected from caving river banks and floods, yet it has no railroad facilities.

ROLLING FORK, 133.5 m. (104 alt., 902 pop.) *(see Tour 3, Sec. a)*, is at the junction with US 61 *(see Tour 3, Sec. a)*.

Side Tour 3B

Woodville to Fort Adams, 20 m. Fort Adams Road.
Graveled roadbed, two lanes wide.
No accommodations.

This route winds through the bluff hills in the extreme southwestern corner of Mississippi, a tiny part of the State that holds more than its share of historic interest.

Fort Adams Rd. branches W. from US 61 *(see Tour 3, Sec. b)* at Woodville, *0 m.*

At *1 m.* is the SITE OF THE HILLS (R), the plantation of John Joor, a close friend of Andrew Jackson, under whom he served as an officer at the Battle of New Orleans. General Joor acquired two brass cannon captured in the battle, placing one in the courthouse square at Woodville and presenting the other to Natchez. During the War between the States both of the cannon disappeared.

At *2 m.* the road forks. Left here.

At *6 m.* (R) is the SITE OF LA GRANGE, the home of James A. Ventress, a graduate of Edinburgh University. In 1844 he was appointed a member of the first board of trustees of the University of Mississippi. Because of his interest and work in organizing the school he was called the father of the university. The house, burned recently, was a handsome place, similar in appearance to the Hermitage near Nashville, Tennessee.

SALISBURY, *12 m.* (L), reached by a lane, is a one-and-a-half-story structure built in 1811 and still in good repair. Live oaks shade the grounds.

WALNUT GROVE, *13 m.* (L), was built by a Nolan, believed by natives to have been a brother of the fictional character, Philip Nolan, the "man without a country."

The JOHN WALL PLACE, or the Evans Wall Place *(private)*, *13.5 m.* (R), stands at the corner where the old Lower Natchez Trace crossed the Fort Adams Rd. It was built in 1798 by John Wall, and in recent years was occupied by Evans Wall, author of "No Nation Girl." Andrew Jackson was a frequent visitor here.

The weather-beaten old structure, standing on a hill, is almost lost behind the locust trees shading the sunken road that was formerly the entrance lane. The forecourt is overrun with briars and lush grass, with smilax, wistaria, and other old garden plants that have run wild. The house has second floor porches on the front and rear, the ground floor on the front being open and paved with brick, and on the rear enclosed. The walls of the ground floor are of brick, deep rose and mellow with age. There are large outside chimneys at each end and the interior is divided into small rooms; each door has a very large wrought-iron lock and silver knob.

At *15 m.* is the junction with a graveled road.

Left on this road is PINCKNEYVILLE, 7 *m.* (100 pop.), once the seat of justice of Wilkinson Co. Oliver Pollock, a witness when General Wilkinson was being investigated for conspiracy with Aaron Burr, lived at Pinckneyville, as did a number of the first English-speaking settlers in the Natchez District.

The Kemper brothers *(see AN OUTLINE OF FOUR CENTURIES)* used Pinckneyville as a refuge after their forays into Spanish territory. Because the railroad never reached Pinckneyville, the village has retained many of the characteristics of the old Deep South.

The Whitaker Negroes here are a group with unusual racial characteristics; they have gradually decreased in number until only six remain in the vicinity. According to local physicians, the Whitaker Negroes have sub-normal sweat glands; consequently, in warm weather they have to be near a pool or creek in which they can immerse themselves. Frequently the Negroes take buckets of water to the field with them, turning the water over their heads to soak their clothing. Besides the peculiarity of the skin, which though dark has a shiny appearance, they have few teeth, perhaps two or three at the top and a few below, and these are fine and pointed. Their lips are large, thick, and protruding, making their speech a bit indistinct and giving their faces an odd look. Their hair is fine and silky but thin and short. They are perhaps slightly sub-normal in intelligence. Their peculiarities seem to be inherited only by the male children, the females being normal. The Whitaker Negroes are descendants of Louis Whitaker, a Richmond, Va., Negro, sold as a slave in the old market at New Orleans. They now live on Alto and Magnolia plantations.

In the vicinity of Pinckneyville are a number of typical old plantation homes. *ARCOLE,* the home of Gen. William L. Brandon, was built on a Spanish land grant received by General Brandon in 1790. It is constructed of blue poplar, hand-hewn and whip-sawed by slaves; it is a story-and-a-half high with a broad front porch, having heavy wooden columns. A mile N. of Pinckneyville is *DESERT,* built by Capt. Robert Semple in 1800, a two-story structure with porch columns supported by brick foundations and with elaborately hand-carved entrance doors.

Two miles SW. of Pinckneyville is *COLDSPRING PLANTATION,* one of the oldest in the section, with a house built of blue poplar on a brick foundation; over the flag-stoned, iron-railed back porch is an arch, from the center of which hangs a Masonic emblem, a relic of the decade when men of widely divergent character and views followed the Kemper brothers in throwing off Spanish rule in the country S. of the 31st parallel. Coldspring, built by Dr. Carmichael, an army surgeon, is perfectly preserved. Among its many legends is that of the maiden who sat so long at an upper window watching for her lover that a flash of lightning photographed her image on the glass—an image still visible, it is said. Coldspring has been in the McGehee family since it was bought in 1840 by Judge Edward McGehee, great-grandfather of the present owner.

At *COLUMBIAN SPRINGS PLANTATION, 16 m.,* is the *GRAVE OF GERARD CHITTOQUE BRANDON,* Mississippi's first native-born Governor, serving in that capacity for a brief period in 1825 and 1826, and in the latter year commencing a term of office which ended in 1832. Brandon, a typical planter, was an exponent of the conservative views later expressed by the aristocratic Whig party.

FORT ADAMS, 20 *m.* (55 alt., 200 pop.), a small farming center, is on the site of a mission conducted by Father Davion in 1698 and takes its name from a fort built here in 1798 and later named for

President John Adams. Its first commander was Gen. James Wilkinson (1757-1825), who was probably the center of more storms and mysteries than any other man who has held high positions in the American Army. Wilkinson, born in Maryland, entered the Revolutionary Army and advanced to high position as a very young man. His career was ruined, however, by his utter inability to keep out of conspiracies and intrigue. He was involved in the Conway Cabal but saved himself from complete disgrace by revealing the details; for a time he was inactive but after he went to Kentucky at the close of the war he became prominent in trade and politics there. The next major scandal came when he entered the Spanish conspiracy but he again managed to reestablish himself in the good graces of those in Washington and after he applied for reinstatement was rapidly promoted to the position of general-in-chief of the American Army. After two years in this position he was sent to Fort Adams. While in this area he performed several services of value. The settlers rapidly occupying the upper Mississippi Valley had to have free access to the sea, which meant that they had to pass through the Spanish-owned port of New Orleans. Wilkinson made valuable contributions to the development of the territory by completing treaties with the Chickasaw and Choctaw Indians for opening roads through the wilderness *(see TRANSPORTATION)*. He became involved in Burr's scheme for a southwestern empire, but exposed him, following his usual course in such matters. Burr's trial was in a sense a trial of Wilkinson. He was court martialed in 1811, charged with treasonable relations with Spain, with negotiations with Burr, and with maladministration in the transfer of troops. The court by its verdict turned the accusation into commendation. Throughout his stormy career Washington, Jefferson, Hamilton, and Adams defended him. Agreement on Wilkinson's motives and character may never be reached but the story of his various and complicated enterprises proved a colorful chapter in American history.

Only traces of the old fort remain but the place has yet other interesting associations; it was here that Philip Nolan, "the man without a country," was at one time stationed. There is also a legend that Richard Butler, an officer of the garrison, defied General Wilkinson; Wilkinson, having lost his own queue, ordered all the officers at Fort Adams to have theirs cut. Butler refused, telling his physician that when he died he desired that a hole be bored in his coffin and his queue be pulled through so that Wilkinson would know that he had been defied even in death.

In the vicinity of Fort Adams lived William Dunbar (1749-1810), Scottish scientist frequently called "Sir" William Dunbar, who was the first to recognize the value of cottonseed oil *(see INDUSTRY)*.

Tour 4

(Jackson, Tenn.)—Corinth—Tupelo—Columbus—Meridian—Waynesboro—(Mobile, Ala.). US 45.
Tennessee Line to Alabama Line, 298.6 m.
Route one-eighth paved; remainder, being paved.
Mobile & Ohio R.R. parallels route between Corinth and Shannon, between Macon and Meridian, and between Quitman and Waynesboro.
St. Louis & San Francisco R.R. parallels route between Aberdeen and Columbus.
Accommodations in cities.

US 45 in Mississippi runs from the foothills of the Tennessee River in the northeastern corner of the State to the red clay hills of Wayne County in the southeast. Between Tupelo and Scooba it traverses the Black Prairie Belt, formerly one of the richest cotton growing sections of the State but now supplementing that crop with diversified farming and dairying. Aberdeen and Columbus were prosperous ante-bellum centers and, being in the fertile prairie, they still hold their prosperity. Between Scooba and Waynesboro the highway winds through the uplands of eastern Mississippi, where a more typical Mississippi scene is evident with small terraced cotton patches scattered among the forests and between the gullies.

Crossing the Mississippi Line, *0 m.*, 44 miles S. of Jackson Tenn., US 45 follows the general route of the Union troops in their advance on Corinth after the Battle of Shiloh in April 1862. Markers at intervals indicate various positions of the contending armies. At *2.5 m.* is a line of earthworks paralleling the highway. The marker reads: "This earthwork, 1½ miles from the outer protective earthwork of the Confederate Army at Corinth, was thrown up by the Union Army between May 17 and May 29, 1862, in Halleck's advance from Shiloh to Corinth." The Union advance was an example of Halleck's generalship. Without risking an open engagement he brought an overwhelming force to the outskirts of Corinth and entrenched it as strongly as were the defending Confederates. From this earthwork the Federals could hear distinctly the movement of trains and the beat of Confederate drums in the town.

CORINTH, *4.5 m.* (456 alt., 6,220 pop.), Mississippi's only city in the Tennessee River Hills, was closely involved in an important engagement during the War between the States. Here soldiers fought in hand-to-hand combat, and for many years after the war, Presbyterians, innocently having built their church upon the site of an old Federal magazine, worshipped above a nest of mines. Yet the inhabitants find the future more absorbing than the past; they are more interested in the development of their poultry farms, dairies, and textile plants than in the fact that General Grant once occupied the town. They now ship more than a million dollars worth of products a year, and are beginning to produce milk commercially. A cheese factory provides a market for whole milk; quantities of butter fat are sold in other markets. The city has a hosiery mill and a garment factory. Industrial development is encouraged by the low rate of TVA electrical power.

In 1855 officers of the Memphis & Charleston R.R. and the Mobile & Ohio R.R. chose this site for the junction of their two lines, giving it the obvious name of Cross City. Two years later the editor of the weekly newspaper suggested that the community change its name to the more imaginative name of Corinth, the Grecian crossroads city.

But when war broke out between the States, the asset of being the crossing point of two trunk lines became a liability. From the beginning of the war the Federals planned to capture the town, and the Confederates kept it heavily fortified. After the Battle of Shiloh, April 6-8, 1862, Confederate General Beauregard retreated to the town, followed by Federal General Halleck. When Halleck, after slow marching, at last reached Corinth, Beauregard evacuated the town, permitting him to enter without opposition. The Union army occupied the place for five months, then General Grant, surmising that the Confederates under Van Dorn intended to attack, ordered Rosecrans, who was defending the town, to concentrate his troops. But Van Dorn and his forces swooped down from Tennessee with extraordinary speed, and on October 3 crushed Rosecrans' men three miles N. of Corinth. The Federals retreated into the city at dusk and spent the night preparing to renew the battle. The next morning Van Dorn hurled his troops against the entrenchments of the Federals, but his forces were disorganized and two battalions failed to attack simultaneously. In the second day of fighting Col. Wm. P. Rogers led his brigade in the charge against the Federal Battery Robinett. Rogers, after desperate fighting, succeeded in taking the almost impregnable position but paid with his life for the victory. Shortly afterward the Confederates were forced by the augmented Federal troops to retreat. After the battle Rosecrans had Rogers buried with military honors.

The *NELL CURLEE HOME (private)*, 711 Jackson St., was built in 1857 by Hampton Mask. Iron grillwork is used for exterior ornamentation. During the War between the States the house, then the showplace of Corinth, was occupied successively by Generals Halleck, Bragg, and Hood.

The *FRED ELGIN HOME (private)*, 615 Jackson St., was used for headquarters by General Grant; the large old bed in which he slept is now displayed with pride by the owner. A two-story structure set in a yard thickly planted with giant boxwood and magnolia trees, it is perhaps the most typical ante-bellum house in town.

The *A. K. WEAVER HOME (private)*, SE. corner Filmore and Bunch Sts., is a long low white cottage with pleasing lines. The recessed entrance is noteworthy. This home was occupied by Gen. Leonidas Polk at the time of the Federal invasion of Corinth.

The *NATIONAL CEMETERY*, 1 mile SW. of the courthouse, entrance on Meiggs St. *(open 6-6)*, is a plot of 20 acres enclosed by an irregular brick wall. Here are buried more than 6,000 Union soldiers from 273 regiments of 12 States.

The *CONFEDERATE PARK*, Polk and Linden Sts., holds the *SITE OF OLD FORT ROBINETT* and is maintained by the Corinth Chapter of the U. D. C. Within the park is a *MONUMENT TO COL. WILLIAM ROGERS*, who was killed attacking the fort.

The *JONES BOARDING HOUSE*, 815 Waldron St., was originally the Methodist church, and was at one time used as a Confederate prison.

South of Corinth is an area supplied with electricity by TVA. The TVA Bill was introduced in the House by Hon. John R. Rankin, of the First District.

At *18.3 m.* is the junction with a graveled road.

Left on this road to the *SITE OF DANVILLE, 1 m.*, the first white settlement in the northeastern corner of Mississippi. An abundance of fresh spring water suitable for tanning determined the site. It is said that the citizens of Danville were noted for their piety and their law-abiding natures. Danville lost its prosperity when the railroad skirted it, and, shortly after, completely disappeared when the Federal Army moved the houses elsewhere to use them as quarters for its troops.

BOONEVILLE, *24.5 m.* (509 alt., 1,703 pop.), was the scene of an all-day fight between Hardee's Confederate cavalry and Sheridan's Federal troops, July 1, 1862, after the Army of the Mississippi had retreated from Corinth and was reorganizing at Tupelo. A prosperous farm trading center, it now has a garment factory.

1. Right from Booneville on a graveled road into the *TIPPAH HILLS, 10 m.*, an extremely rugged section known for the number of wild flowers and dogwood trees, and for opossum, fox, and quail hunting.

2. Left from Booneville on State 30, a graveled road, to BOONEVILLE LAKE, *1 m.*, and WALDEN LAKE, *4 m.*, both favorite picnicking spots.

BALDWYN, *35.5 m.* (374 alt., 1,106 pop.), is on the line between Prentiss and Lee Counties, a division that has caused some amusing conflicts of jurisdiction. Until 1920 the town had a hotel named the Forrest House because Confederate Cavalry Gen. Nathan B. Forrest had used it for quarters after the Battle of Brice's Crossroads, his greatest fight.

Right from Baldwyn on a graveled road to the *BRICE'S CROSSROADS BATTLE MONUMENT, 5.8 m.* (R). Against a force of about 5,000 Federals, including cavalry, infantry, and artillery, Confederate Cavalry General Forrest interposed a much smaller force of mounted troops, defeated the column in a brisk engagement June 10, 1864, then turned its retreat into a rout along the road to Ripley, capturing 14 pieces of artillery, 5,000 stand of fire arms, 500,000 rounds of ammunition, and 250 wagons. The Federal casualties were 223 killed, 394 wounded, and 1,623 missing, as against Forrest's loss of 96 killed and 396 wounded. It was a signal victory for Forrest's peculiar strategy and method of fighting. The marshy terrain was to his advantage. He won a race for the crossroads, and, bluffing his way as usual, charged against the Federals before they could emerge from the woods. At one time he was in the front rank, pistol in hand, and his courage and aggressiveness carried his daring to victory.

At *40.5 m.* is GUNTOWN (381 alt., 369 pop.). According to local legend the village is named for a Virginia Tory, James Gunn, who fled here to escape the American Revolution. Gunn later married the daughter of a Chickasaw Indian chief. He continued to toast the King of England on his birthday as long as he lived.

At *49.9 m.* (L) is a double-pen timber house typical of the early homes of this section. It is particularly interesting in contrast with the *TUPELO HOMESTEADS, 55.3 m.* (L) and *55.5 m.* (R), a group of homes erected by the Resettlement Administration.

US 45 enters on Gloster St.

TUPELO, *55.8 m.* (289 alt., 6,361 pop.) *(see TUPELO).*

Points of Interest. U. S. Fish Hatchery, cotton mill, Carnation Milk plant, and others.

Here are the junctions with State 6 *(see Tour 14)* and US 78 *(see Tour 9).*

The route continues on Gloster St. (US 45).

South of Tupelo the change from hill country to rolling prairie and fertile bottom lands is evident.

VERONA, *60.6 m.* (301 alt., 554 pop.), is the old town that lost its leadership to Tupelo when the latter became the junction of the Mobile & Ohio R.R. and the St. Louis & San Francisco R.R. (then the Memphis & Birmingham) in 1887. After the Battle of Harrisburg General Forrest was brought to the *LUTIE McSHANN HOUSE* on Johnson St., 4 blocks E. of US 45, to be treated for wounds that had reopened during the battle.

SHANNON, *66.6 m.* (243 alt., 524 pop.) *(see Side Tour 4A),* is at the junction with State 23 *(see Side Tour 4A).*

NETTLETON, *72.6 m.* (252 alt., 834 pop.), is a small agricultural center. It was the birthplace of Dr. Felix J. Underwood, executive officer of the State Board of Health, and president of the State and Provincial Health Authorities of North America.

At *90.1 m.* (L), visible from the highway is a two-story white-columned house typical of the ante-bellum planter dwellings in the Black Prairie. At *96.8 m.* (R) on top of a knoll commanding Aberdeen is an old brick house with stepped end walls.

ABERDEEN, *91.6 m.* (203 alt., 3,925 pop.), is a lovely old town built on the western bank of the Tombigbee River at the edge of the prairie region. It was first named Dundee by Robert Gordon of Scotland. Objecting to the way the local people pronounced the name, Gordon changed it to Aberdeen. Near the head of navigation of the Tombigbee River and with the almost ideal cotton growing area to the W., Aberdeen was one of the most prosperous of the Mississippi ante-bellum plantation towns.

In 1836, after the Indian land cessions, Gordon, who founded the town as a trading post, auctioned building lots to new settlers, and in 1849 Aberdeen had grown so swiftly that it became the county seat. Steamboats on the Tombigbee carried cotton grown in the vicinity down to Mobile in the fall and carried back supplies in the spring. Negroes, brought from Virginia to work on the newly-created prairie plantations, made possible a swift transition from pioneer conditions to plantation comfort and Aberdeen became a social center with attractive town houses built by the planters for their womenfolk. Though many of the old structures need paint and repair, these ante-bellum homes, designed for the most part on traditional lines, evidence the substantial pre-war prosperity of the area. A good example is HOLLIDAY HAVEN *(private)*, on Meridian St., a white house with green shutters; its eight white Doric columns, hand-carved by apprenticed Negro slaves, are loftier than the classic rules of proportion demand, but they are not displeasing. There is a balcony over the front door and long windows opening onto the spacious gallery. Two immense magnolias frame the entrance; another magnolia (R) is draped with a freely-blooming wistaria vine. At the end of a sloping terrace (L) are the few plum trees remaining from the old orchard that is now a garden filled with crapemyrtle and syringa.

The finest of the homes is the REUBEN DAVIS HOME *(private)*, block C on Commerce St., just W. of the Mobile & Ohio R.R. Station. This white frame house, erected in 1847, in a Deep South variant of the Greek Revival style, is of monumental proportions. Judge Reuben Davis was born in Tennessee in 1813, the twelfth child of a Baptist minister who farmed to supplement his income. The child had little schooling except what he learned from adventurers who, temporarily penniless, acted as his tutors on the frontier. Before he was of age he studied medicine with his brother-in-law and began a practice in which he was more ambitious than learned.

Then he turned to the study of law and at the age of 20 was elected district attorney, making $20,000 in his first year. He moved to Aberdeen in 1838 and entered State politics. Starting as a Whig, he became a Union Democrat, then a rabid secessionist, and finally, in 1878, a Greenbacker. He dated all his mistakes and most of his troubles to the Mexican War, in which he contracted an illness that long stayed with him.

Throughout his misfortunes in politics in which he was continually being stranded by all parties, he maintained a lucrative connection as attorney for the New Orleans, Jackson & Great Northern R.R. and achieved success as a criminal lawyer. It is said that the use of red pepper in his handkerchief to induce tears at the decisive point in a murder trial heightened the drama of his courtroom oratory. In 1878 he was shot and dangerously wounded by a prosecuting attorney whom he had outdone in a criminal trial at Columbus, but he did not die until 1890. His *Recollections of Mississippi and Mississippians,* published in 1880, is an excellent source for Mississippi history of his time. In this home at Aberdeen his name is engraved in bold letters on the silver-plated doorbell.

The *OLD CEMETERY* on Cemetery Road is entered over a stile. Many of the inscriptions on the grave stones refer to wives as "consorts"; several of the graves are of Irish-born settlers who came to Aberdeen before the War between the States. A square of 30 graves of unknown Confederate soldiers recalls the skirmish at Egypt, Miss. *(see Side Tour 4A),* from which these wounded men were brought to die. One unusual monument carries the image of a woman surrounded by flames, the story being that an open fire caught her bouffant skirt and burned her fatally. A mausoleum in the middle of the cemetery carries a legend that the occupant, at her own request, was entombed in a sitting position.

At *99.5 m.* US 45 crosses the Tombigbee River and between Aberdeen and Columbus rides a levee in the Tombigbee Valley.

At *109.8 m.* a house (L) marks the *SITE OF HAMILTON*, first seat of Monroe Co. In the 1820's the county was separated from the other white settlements in Mississippi by over a hundred miles of Indian territory.

US 45 enters on 5th St. N., to 1st Ave. N.

COLUMBUS, *119.9 m.* (250 alt., 10,743 pop.) *(see COLUMBUS).*

Points of Interest. Mississippi State College for Women, a number of historic and architecturally interesting homes, and others.

Here is the junction with US 82 *(see Tour 6).*

1. Left from Columbus on State 12, which here approximates the route of the old Jackson Military Road *(see TRANSPORTATION)* to *BELMONT, 9 m.*, the home built between 1822 and 1825 by Capt. William Neilson on a 2,560-acre plantation granted to him as a bonus for his services in the U. S. Army during the War of 1812. Architecturally Belmont represents the transitional structure between the log cabin and the town house in the Black Prairie. Built of oak and heart pine, with hewn sills, hand-sawed lumber, and home-made brick, it is a lofty two-story house with a transverse roof ridge. The timbers are fastened with wooden pins. The hardware and window glass were brought from Baltimore, Md., by the skilled Baltimore Irishman who supervised the construction. The manual labor was performed by slaves. Although the formerly separate kitchen has been connected with the house, the main part of Belmont is as originally built, with much of the first plastering and many of the old window panes still in place. The house and 320 acres of the original tract have never passed out of the possession of the Neilson family. At the foot of the hill on which Belmont stands are two of what used to be a group of fine springs. Tradition has it that De Soto camped by these springs in 1540, and a marker placed on the Jackson road near them commemorates the camp.

2. Right from Columbus on old US 45, L. at every fork on a narrow road, and crossing the Tombigbee River on an old-style cable ferry, to *WAVERLY, 7.5 m.* This is an impressive mansion with an octagonal tower, colonnaded lower floors, and flanking wings. The years have ravished it of life and color, but its mantelpiece of delicately carved marble, its woodwork executed by a discerning English craftsman make it comparable to its Natchez forerunners. It is an architectural extravaganza, elaborately ornamented. The plan is an "H", the wings closing in Corinthian porches at front and back. The central octagonal hall rises a full 65 feet to the dome of the tower. Two rooms of monumental scale flank the hall on both sides for three stories. A massive double staircase winds up through the structure, touching narrow circular galleries on which open second and third floor bedrooms. So magnificent was the parlor that stories about it have become legendary. Damask curtains overdraped the lace at long windows. The rosewood chairs and divan were upholstered in blue and gold. Above the Italian marble mantel hung a gilt mirror of stupendous size.

Col. George Young, the builder, born in Oglethorpe Co., Ga., in 1799, was one of the first landowners with a large tract in the Black Prairie. At the bluff on the Tombigbee, where the river formerly made a great bend that almost brought it back on itself, he began the erection of Waverly in the 1840's, and continued its building until 1856. The velvet carpets, brocaded draperies, and handsome furnishings were imported from Europe, after a first order had been lost at sea. The colonel sank an artesian well, planted orchards and vineyards, laid out gardens, had extensive kennels of hunting dogs and a private boathouse on the river, operated his own ferry, built warehouses of brick and stone, built a gristmill, a sawmill, a tannery, a cotton gin, a brick kiln and an ice house, had a lighting plant for the big house (he burned lighter wood and resin to make gas), and made Waverly a small but complete village. A German gardener landscaped the bluff side. A cement swimming pool with marble steps was laid out below the house. As a planter he was well equipped for and devoted to entertaining; the hospitality of Waverly was as extravagant as its furnishings.

The War between the States cast its shadow on Waverly. Six sons of the house joined the Confederate Army, and Waverly became a refuge for men in gray. Cavalry Gen. Nathan B. Forrest and his staff spent one night here. Though impoverished by the war, the colonel's descendants kept Waverly open, with Captain Billy and Major Val entertaining more simply but not less genially than the colonel.

Waverly is still in possession of the family, but now needs repair. Some of the stained-glass side lights from Venice on the front entrance are cracked. The 30-foot hall has a wax-smooth floor and satin-smooth plastered walls, but the gilt-framed mirrors on the white marble consoles are covered with a film of dust, as is the piano with its mother-of-pearl keys. The draperies of the parlor windows are faded and drab as the outside paint. A massive bronze chandelier still hangs from the dome of the observatory, with cut-glass globes, but only the spaciousness of the rotunda is left to make it impressive. The boxwood hedge is covered with vines. The green shutters are faded, the garden rank with weeds, and the swimming pool dry. Unoccupied and dilapidated, it is still majestic.

Downstream two miles from Waverly *(not reached by road or trail)* at the junction of the Tombigbee with Tibbee Creek is the SITE OF PLYMOUTH, an extinct town that was formerly a rival of Columbus and Cotton Gin Port. It is said to have been a camping ground for De Soto on his passage through Mississippi, many scraps of armor and Spanish military equipment having been found here. It also is said to have been the scene of Bienville's operations against the Chickasaw, though Cotton Gin Port is usually given that credit. What substantiates Plymouth's assertion is that the first white settlers found a two-story fort of cedar logs standing on a slight elevation about 500 yards from the river and surrounded by a circular ditch and embankment. The building was approximately 20 feet square with windows in the first story. The first settlers tore it down to obtain material to build their cabins.

Tradition also makes the fort a base of operations for Gen. Andrew Jackson in his campaign against the Creek Indians. The site of Plymouth was well known as an Indian settlement and trading post even during French rule in this section, and was the home of Maj. John Pitchlyn. Pitchlyn, born on St. Thomas Island in 1765, was left among the Choctaw when his father, an English officer, died on his way from South Carolina to the Natchez district. John Pitchlyn's life with the Indians gave him extraordinary influence among them, which he exerted in favor of the United States. He had five sons, one of whom, Peter Perkins Pitchlyn, was described by Charles Dickens after a visit to the United States; he is buried in the Congressional Cemetery at Washington, D. C. John himself was buried at Waverly in 1835, though his body was subsequently moved by his sons to the Indian Territory.

After the Indian land cessions opened the west bank of the Tombigbee to settlement, Old Plymouth became an important cotton storage and shipping center chiefly because of a nearby shallow ford in the river. It was incorporated in 1836, but the low ground at the mouth of Tibbee Creek proved so unhealthful that the planters moved back to their plantations, and the merchants and lawyers crossed the river to Columbus. Nothing is left of the village though it is asserted that the embankment around the fort can be traced.

The route continues R. on 1st Ave. N., crossing the Tombigbee River, the western limit of Columbus. On the east bank of the river is a good view (L) of the bluffs on which Columbus is built.

Between Columbus and Macon US 45 runs past a number of hay fields breaking into the cotton in the prairie belt. The plowed fields and the sides of the creeks and drainage canals show rich black soil.

MACON, *155.1 m.* (114 alt., 2,198 pop.), is a pleasant old prairie town built on the bank of the Noxubee River and spreading fan-wise E., N., and W. from the river and courthouse. It was incorporated in 1836 on land ceded by the Choctaw under the Treaty of Dancing Rabbit Creek, and experienced a prosperity of which the big white-columned homes are the remaining evidence. During the War between the States, when Jackson was burned by General Sherman, the seat of the State government was moved for a short while to Macon. The executive offices of Governor Clark, whose home was on the outskirts of Macon, were in the buildings of the Calhoun Institute, a private school for girls established by W. R. Poindexter about 1856 on grounds now occupied by the Macon Public School. Two sessions of the State legislature also met in these buildings, and one of the buildings served as an improvised hospital, as did many of Macon's churches. Cotton growing and lumbering always have been industries associated with Macon; the town now has one of the largest cream condenseries in the South.

1. Right from Macon on Pearl St. which becomes a country road; at *1.5 m.* L. *0.5 m.* to SITE OF JACKSON'S MILITARY ROAD (*see TRANSPORTATION*), which crossed Noxubee River. The deep trench cut through the bluff on the east bank of the stream leads down to the ford and is plainly visible, though now overgrown with vines and underbrush.

2. Left from Macon on State 14, a graveled road, to the ancestral BANKHEAD HOME, *8 m.* (L), a dwelling that has been little changed in the 80 years since William Bankhead built it. In several rooms the original wallpaper remains. A number of inside windows open into the hallways, and, as they serve no apparent purpose, are rather mystifying. The Speaker of the National House of Representatives (1937), W. B. Bankhead, was married and several of his children were born in the house.

At *160.7 m.* US 45 crosses the Noxubee (Ind., *stinking water*) River with its steep and sometimes slippery banks.

At *161.9 m.* is the junction with State 14.

Right on this graveled road is MASHULAVILLE, *9 m.* (200 pop.), a village with a general store, a consolidated high school, two churches and a number of scattered homes, not visible from the highway. Mashulaville, named for Chief Mashulatubbee (Ind., *the one who perseveres and kills*), was once a famous Choctaw town. The Russell home, on the SITE OF THE HOME OF CHIEF MASHULATUBBEE, links the placid community with a lively past. Mashulatubbee succeeded his father Homastubbee in 1809 as District Chief of the Choctaw. Though he is said to have favored a coalition with the Shawnee chief, Tecumseh, who attempted to organize a general uprising against the whites in 1811, and gave his own race absolute loyalty, he was friendly with the white people of the section, receiving them in his home with courtesy and hospitality. Like many other chieftains of the day he vigorously opposed the Dancing Rabbit Treaty of 1830. A man of considerable wealth, he became dissatisfied with his simple cabin and, in 1819, hired Josiah Tully, a contractor from Pickensville, Ala., to build a house for him at Mashulaville that would be more in keeping with his dignity as a chief. The dwelling had four rooms, two below and two above, and was built of logs. He lived here with his two wives and a house full of offspring until the signing of the Dancing Rabbit Treaty. One of the chief's wives was partly white and very beautiful. When travelers stopped at his home he liked to show her to them, but the other wife, who possessed the stronger character and intellect, was his favorite. Upon his migration west, Mashulatubbee sold his home to Anthony Winston for $100. Several hundred yards from the Russell home is an old spring used by the chief, and on the property are numerous stone artifacts.

At *10.4 m.* on State 14 is the junction with an unmarked dirt road.

Left *8 m.* on this road to the DANCING RABBIT TREATY MARKER (L), erected to memorialize the consummation of the treaty in which the Choctaw Indians relinquished to the Government practically a third of north-central Mississippi in return for which they received certain annuities and land further W. Near here in September 1830, 20,000 Choctaw gathered to consider the proposed treaty. The Government sent agents to negotiate, and following them came white traders with whisky and trinkets to bribe the Indians to sign the treaty.

The first conference was held Sept. 18, 1830. Sixty Choctaw leaders seated themselves in a horseshoe on the ground. Facing them, seated on a fallen log, were the Government agents, John Eaton, William Coffee, and the interpreter, John Pitchlyn. Among the Indians a group of seven of the oldest women of the tribe squatted, muttering their disapproval throughout the deliberations. During the first day Government agents dominated the council. Only one Indian, Killahota, a young half-breed, addressed the gathering. He spoke in favor of the treaty, and the grunts and other signs of disapproval that had greeted the speeches of the white men swelled in volume as he spoke. At one point an old squaw, unable to control her indignation, rose and made a lunge at Killahota with a knife. For several weeks the negotiations proceeded. Every half-breed present advocated capitulation to the demands of the white men, and every full-blood Indian opposed it. The influence of Greenwood Leflore *(see Tour 6)* finally brought the Indians to accept the terms of a compromise treaty, which promised any Choctaw who cared to remain in the State a section of land and the protection of the Government. A hundred years passed before the Government formulated plans to keep the white man's promise.

At *10 m.* on this dirt road is an open field in which is BIG ROCK, *1 m.* off the highway (L), the traditional rendezvous of the Choctaw. This rock is at the foot of a hill which rises high above the surrounding country. Rough and cylindrical in shape, 10 feet in diameter and 20 feet high, it has the appearance of having been thrust into the ground by some giant hand. Legend is that the Indians had silver mines in the foothills of Noxubee and Winston Counties and that when they returned from work they gathered at the foot of Big Rock. Pow-wows between the Choctaw and neighboring tribes took place here, and once a treaty sponsored by Andrew Jackson to make peace between the Choctaw and Creek tribes was signed at this spot in Jackson's presence. At the foot of Big Rock is a small water hole that never runs dry. The water is stagnant, but year in and year out it remains at the same level.

SHUQUALAK (Ind. *hog-wallow*), *163.1 m.* (214 alt., 810 pop.), is between prairie and flatwoods. Several large lumber mills operate here. The cut-over timber land in the vicinity is the scene of annual field trials of bird dogs, an event sponsored by the National Field Trial Club and the Continental Field Trial Club, and held during the latter part of January. The National Club conducts two trials; the first a free-for-all championship stake in which any pedigreed dog can be entered, entrance fee $75, purse $1,000; the second is a derby for two-year-olds, entrance fee $50, purse $1,000 which is split on a three-quarter one-quarter basis, $250 going to the runner-up. The trials sponsored by the Continental Club differ from those of the National Club in only one important respect: a derby for two-year-olds is the only event run. Entrance fees and purses are the same. Saddle horses for following the dogs in the field are available at $3 a day.

At *170.4 m.* (R) is the southernmost of the Black Prairie Belt homes, and at *176.6 m.* are the southernmost white limestone outcroppings of the prairie. Between here and Scooba the highway passes half-timbered houses typical of the hill country.

SCOOBA, *181.1 m.* (192 alt., 933 pop.), is a small farming and sawmilling center. Here is EAST MISSISSIPPI JUNIOR COLLEGE, a public coeducational school established in 1927. The buildings of modern design are grouped on a 254-acre campus.

Left from Scooba on a graveled road to GILES PLANTATION, 5 m., (open by appointment), with a big house that is one of the few ante-bellum homes left in this section. Jacob Giles and his wife came here from the Carolinas in 1835 and built a typical story-and-a-half planter home. It has a guest room and ballroom on the second floor, and big fluted columns supporting the roof over the long gallery. The side walls are beautifully finished with hand-made plaster cornices and friezes.

ELECTRIC MILLS, *185.1 m.* (1,084 pop.), is what its name implies, an industrial village built around a large electrically-operated sawmill. Here are examples of the better type of grouped houses built by corporations for their employees. In contrast with the Piney Woods mill-owned houses, the houses here have four and five rooms and modern conveniences.

Between Electric Mills and Lauderdale the highway passes a number of aged dog-trot houses perched on the hills in the woodland clearings.

LAUDERDALE, *204.1 m.* (350 alt., 270 pop.), is the home of one of the oldest potteries in the State. Housed in a small, modern brick building, the work is done on an old hand-wheel pottery making vases and jugs from the white clays of the vicinity. The articles are in demand because their white surfaces can be painted.

At MARION, *216.6 m.* (358 alt., 54 pop.), the old seat of Lauderdale Co., an election riot occurred in 1874. Like many of the riots of the period, this one started with the killing of two white men by Negroes, and ended with a posse of white men pursuing the Negroes into the woods. A local anecdote has it that a totally blind Negro being led around by his son heard the bullets from the shooting whiz by his ears and immediately regained his sight.

Right from Marion on a local road to a CONFEDERATE CEMETERY OF UNKNOWN SOLDIERS, 1 m. The soldiers buried here died in a field hospital after they had been wounded in various battles, Shiloh, Corinth, Iuka, Jackson, Raymond, Vicksburg, and Bakers' Creek.

At *218.6 m.* is the junction with a graveled road.

Left on this road to the U. S. DEPARTMENT OF AGRICULTURE'S HORTICULTURAL EXPERIMENT STATION, 1 m., with a hundred acres planted to pecan trees, small fruits, and vegetables. Near the station is a group of 25 subsistence homesteads.

At *221.1 m.* US 45 enters on 14th St.; L. on 26th Ave.

MERIDIAN, *222.6 m.* (341 alt., 31,954 pop.) *(see MERIDIAN).*

Points of Interest. Industrial plants, Arboretum, Gypsy Queen's Grave, and others.

Here are the junctions with US 80 *(see Tour 2),* US 11 *(see Tour 8),* and State 39 *(see Side Tour 4B).*

The route continues on 26th Ave.; R. on C St.; L. on Grand Ave.

South of Meridian the highway winds along a high and rugged ridge for four miles. At *232.6 m.* (R) is a small country grist mill, and at *235.2 m.* (R) is the *NEW HOPE BAPTIST CHURCH.* Because several tornadoes have swept through this section, many of the houses on knolls have storm pits dug in the red clay banks around them.

At *246.6 m.* is the CLARKCO STATE PARK, a 750-acre tract being developed as a part of the State park system.

QUITMAN, *249.5 m.* (231 alt., 1,872 pop.), seat of Clarke Co., had until the 1930's one of the largest pine lumber mills in the South. But, after the cutting of the green pine forest the mill was moved to the Pacific Coast, and Quitman, like other somnolent Southern towns, was left dependent upon farm trade. Before the war Quitman had traded with Enterprise and the Gulf Coast by means of the Chickasawhay River, until the sinking of a river freighter stopped navigation. On Feb. 17, 1864, General Sherman completely destroyed the ante-bellum town.

At *254.2 m.* (L) are the ARCHUSA SPRINGS of fine red sulphur water, on the banks of Archusa Creek. Archusa, locally accepted as meaning *sweet water,* is probably a corruption of two Indian words meaning *little river.*

At *254.3 m.* (L) is a *CONFEDERATE CEMETERY.* Disregarded for 70 years, the cemetery was discovered when a Negro farmer plowed up a handful of buttons from a Confederate uniform. Now it has been cleared and provided with headstones and an arch.

At *255.2 m.* US 45 crosses the Chickasawhay, a large tributary of the Pascagoula River.

Between the Chickasawhay and Shubuta the highway passes a number of log houses with mud and wattle chimneys. Nearly every house has its rose bush and small one-mule-power cane mill.

At *262.5 m.* is SHUBUTA (201 alt., 720 pop.).

Left from Shubuta on a graveled road is LANGSDALE, *8 m.* (41 pop.); here is the old *C. L. LANG HOME,* a three-story plantation type house erected in the late 1850's. It has a third floor ballroom.

Right *3 m.* from Langsdale on a country road is MATHERVILLE (100 pop.); here is the *HORNE HOME,* the ante-bellum place of Col. J. H. Horne, who owned 800 slaves; he died in 1865.

Between Shubuta and Waynesboro the pines increase in number.

At *267 m.* the highway recrosses the Chickasawhay River.

WAYNESBORO, *277.5 m.* (191 alt., 1,120 pop.), near the dividing line between the hills and the Piney Woods, is a clay-stained town depending on the trade of the sheep-men, farmers, turpentine distillers, and sawmill hands in the country around it.

Here are the junctions with US 84 *(see Tour 11)* and State 63 *(see Tour 15)*.

WINCHESTER, *282.5 m.* (165 alt., 359 pop.), a village centered around its country store, stands near the site of old Winchester, at one time a political center rivaling Natchez. Old Winchester was near the Chickasawhay River S. of the present town. In 1813, when the Creek Indians rose against the white men, the settlers at old Winchester hurriedly built what came to be known as Patton's Fort. The ditches of the old stockade can still be traced. The town, incorporated in 1818, was the seat of Wayne Co. until the War between the States, and at one time contained about 30 business houses. Many prominent men were associated with it; Powhatan Ellis, a Virginian who said he was a relative of Pocahontas, was the first Judge of the Supreme Court District embracing the southeastern part of the State. He was described as "a man of very stately and courtly demeanor, of amiable temper and extremely indolent habits." Despite his reputation for laziness, he also served as U. S. Senator and as Minister to Mexico. The connection between the Chickasawhay settlements and the Gulf Coast through the Pascagoula River system is well illustrated in the life of John J. McRae, another Winchester citizen. McRae's father, a cotton buyer, was the first to use the Pascagoula River as a means of transportation for cotton destined for ocean shipment at New Orleans. In 1825 he moved to Pascagoula at the mouth of the river because the sea breezes were considered remediable for diseased lungs. A son, John J., was educated first at Pascagoula, then read law with Judge Pray at Pearlington. While still young, he, with a brother of President Tyler, was engaged to help move the Mississippi Indians to the West, and was the leader in agitation for the construction of the Mobile & Ohio R.R. He later edited a newspaper at old Paulding *(see Tour 8)* and in 1850 was one of the fascinating orators with Quitman and Davis in the States' Rights Party, which was even then advocating secession. He was Governor of Mississippi, U. S. Representative until the State seceded, and then a member of the Confederate Congress.

BUCATUNNA (Ind., *collected together*), *293 m.* (150 alt., 385 pop.), is in the center of one of the earliest settled parts of the Piney Woods. Many of the pioneers came in on the strength of land grants from the State of Georgia. In 1811 the "Governor of Georgia and Commander-in-Chief of the Army and Navy of that state and the militia thereof," gave William Powe a pass to the effect that he "with his wife, eleven children, and forty-six Negroes from Chesterfield district, South Carolina, have my permission to travel through the Creek Nation, they taking special care to conduct themselves peaceably toward the Indians and agreeably to the laws of the United States." Powe, one of the first settlers in the district, rolled his goods, packed in oaken hogsheads, along the ridges from the Chattahoochie River through the Creek Indian country to Bucatunna and settled on the creek about a mile N. of the present town. Other early settlers were the McRaes, McArthurs, McLaughlins, McDaniels, McDonalds, and Mc-

Laurins, the Scotch-Irish edge of the pioneer axe that was cutting a new center of civilization in the wilderness. At Bucatunna Gaelic was spoken as late as the 1820's.

The *RAILROAD BRIDGE* over Bucatunna Creek, *294.1 m.* (R), was in the 1880's the site of the Rube Burrows' holdup of a Mobile & Ohio R.R. train. Just before crossing the creek the train had to make a stop to take on water. One day Burrows and his men quietly boarded the train and ordered the engineer to pull out on the trestle and stop. Since no one could leave unless he dived into the creek, Burrows and his men took their time looting. When they were through they had $12,000. The saga of Rube Burrows is a part of the story of all early railroad outlaws, and has probably been colored with repeated tellings. The legend appears in Carl Carmer's *Stars Fell on Alabama.*

At *298.6 m.* US 45 crosses the Alabama Line, 64.5 miles N. of Mobile.

◄◄◄◄◄◄◄◄◄◄◄◄◄◄◄◄◄◄☼►►►►►►►►►►►►►►►►►►

Side Tour 4A

Shannon—West Point—Macon, 84.1 m. State 23, State 25.
Mobile & Ohio R.R. parallels route.
Graveled roadbed two lanes wide.
Accommodations in towns.

This route is a central artery through the gently rolling Black Prairie Belt, a dairying, and alfalfa and cotton growing country of warm black soil, good drainage, and long, mild seasons for cultivation. Except for the first few miles, where hills thinly forested with oak, gum, and elm furnish the landscape, the scene is typically prairie. From Okolona southward to Macon practically every acre of land is being used either for farming or dairying, and the careful economy of the country is everywhere evident. Unbroken stretches of furrowed fields, substantial barns, windmills, silos, and fat cattle cropping the grassy plains make a prairie picture that is more typical of Kansas than of Mississippi.

State 23 branches S. from US 45 *(see Tour 4)* at SHANNON, *0 m. (see Tour 4),* and moves through alternating farmlands and wooded hills. The hills often show white patches of limestone that appear bare and white in the midst of trees and cultivated land. As the hills lose themselves in the flat Chiwapa Creek bottoms, the trees thin out and the increasingly rich soil and the flattening landscape set the stage for the prairie country immediately S.

At *5.3 m.* the highway crosses Tallabinnela Creek.

OKOLONA, *8.3 m.* (304 alt., 2,235 pop.), wavers between the prairie and the hills, an old town inhabited almost entirely by natives. Originally called Prairie Mount and standing six miles N. on a stagecoach route, the town moved itself to the proposed line of the new Mobile & Ohio R.R. in 1848, adopting the new name Okolona at that time. In 1859 the railroad was built through. During the War between the States the town was raided several times. In 1864 the hospital, depot, and 100,000 bushels of corn were burned; in 1865 another detachment of Union troops visited the town and this time burned it completely. In the *CONFEDERATE CEMETERY* on the outskirts of town are buried 1,000 soldiers killed in the Federal raids. The older inhabitants have forgiven and forgotten the fighting and burning, but they still say that it was the Commissary Department of the Federals that first brought the bitterweed into the prairie. If eaten by cows, the weed gives a bitter taste to their milk, and because the prairie is a dairying section this often bitter-tasting milk is a constant reminder that Federal troops once fought their way across the flat landscape.

A *CHEESE FACTORY AND CREAMERY* to take care of milk products of the vicinity is the newest industrial plant. On the western edge of the city limits is an 80-acre *MUNICIPAL PARK*. Here are a swimming pool, skeet grounds, lighted tennis courts, a well-stocked lake, and a children's wading pool. In the center of the park is a large convention hall, more often used for dancing than for conventions.

EGYPT, *17 m.* (300 alt., 150 pop.), was established just prior to the War between the States when the Mobile & Ohio R.R. was built through in 1858. It was named for the variety of corn grown here. During the war corn was hauled here to await shipment to the Confederate army, but before this could be accomplished Federal troops passed through and burned it. The town has grown but little since that time.

At *18.9 m.* the highway crosses the northern boundary of the *NATCHEZ TRACE FORESTRY AND FEDERAL GAME PRESERVE*, which embraces 30,000 acres of submarginal land lying in Chickasaw and Pontotoc Counties. Headquarters of this area are in Okolona.

As the highway moves southward it penetrates the prairie's heart. This is wide and open country. The miles of earth rolling to meet far horizons make the houses, barns, and even the towns look dwarfed and squat. Dairy farms alternate with plowed acres of rich, black earth. Here the ancestors of the older families built a culture that equaled that of the Natchez district. But the younger families, those who have moved in after the War between the States, have felt not so much the pull of the land as the energy of a people who emerged apparently metamorphosed by the war. A few have proved themselves such exponents of change that they are willing to break with the land entirely and turn to industry, making the modern prairie Mississippi's laboratory for the New South.

At *32.7 m.* is the junction with State 25; State 23 and State 25 unite for several miles.

WEST POINT, *41 m.* (241 alt., 4,677 pop.), a roomy, prosperous town fed by the farms and dairies of the surrounding flat lands, epitomizes the prairie. Significantly, it developed on a section of land known as the

Granary of Dixie, which two Indian braves, Te-wa-ea and Ish-tim-ma-ha, sold to James Robertson in 1844. Though a battleground during the War between the States, the town, that once had moved itself from the extreme corner of the county to be on the new railroad, was considered so attractive by a number of Federal officers that they came back after the war and settled here permanently. In reconstruction days the town was the leader in Clay County's Ku Klux Klan activities, but immediately after white domination was restored, the people here opened one of the few private schools for Negroes. The school, *MARY HOLMES SEMINARY,* a fully-accredited junior college supported by the Presbyterian Church, is still a flourishing institution. On a large, shaded campus, the brick, one-story laundry, Music Hall, and Domestic Science Hall are grouped around the three-story red brick administration building which contains 112 rooms.

There are eight factories besides cottonseed oil mills, gins, and lumber companies in West Point. The *WEST POINT POULTRY AND PACKING PLANT* is the largest in the mid-South.

Between West Point and Artesia the highway passes between fields of waving alfalfa hay to descend into the marshy bottoms of Tibbee Creek. Here Tibbee often spills over its ill-defined banks to cover miles of surrounding flat lands, affording excellent fishing and hunting.

At 43.5 m. is a large stone that marks the *SITE OF AN OLD INDIAN CAMP GROUND.* Across the highway at diagonal angles N. and S. are two other markers on *INDIAN BURIAL GROUNDS.* The northern marker is backed by a large tree-studded burial mound of the Chickasaw; the southern sign marks the site of a Choctaw mound. Legend says that the Chickasaw and Choctaw tribes once fought a great battle at this spot and that after the battle each buried its dead in a separate mound. In 1934 Moreau B. Chambers, Field Archaeologist for the Mississippi Department of Archives and History, uncovered several burials in the Chickasaw mound. The markers were placed by the Horseshoe Robertson Chapter, D. A. R.

At 46.1 m. the highway crosses TIBBEE (Ind., *water fight*) CREEK on a steel and concrete bridge. Tibbee was named for the battle in which the Choctaw and Chickasaw annihilated the main part of the Chakchiuma tribe. The battle site is fixed by legend at Lyon's Bluff approximately five miles upstream from this bridge.

Rising almost imperceptibly from the creek bottom, the highway passes into country of peaceful pasture lands, where cattle and sheep graze in waist-high clover and alfalfa.

At 46 m. State 23 branches from State 25; L. here on the latter.

MAYHEW, 52.8 m. (207 alt., 172 pop.), is a small agricultural village that took its name from the mission established by the Rev. Cyrus Kingsbury of Massachusetts, who came here in 1818 to Christianize the Indians. The village is today the home of a very large *APIARY* containing 5,000 colonies of bees from which shipments are made to many places in America and Europe.

ARTESIA, 55 m. (223 alt., 612 pop.), is the junction point of the main line of the Mobile & Ohio R.R. and its Columbus and Starkville

TAKING THE QUEEN BEE

branches. It takes its name from an artesian well N. of the depot. Unusually large quantities of hay are shipped from this point.

Between here and Macon the dominant features of the landscape are the *HEDGES OF OSAGE ORANGE TREES* planted in fence-like rows along the prairie's edge. The highway runs like a narrow lane between their thorny, tangled branches. In winter these prickly trees are etched grayly against the sky, but in summer they burst into smooth green leaves and pale yellowish blossoms, which are replaced by orange-like inedible fruit. Many of these hedges were planted more than a century ago and constitute the pioneer planters' mark upon the land. They confined stock and kept prying Indians out of cornfields, and they conveyed to neighbors the idea that the land encircled by the thorny fences was private property. Sometimes called *bois d' arc* (Fr., *wood of the ark*), these trees, according to legend, furnished the sturdy wood out of which Noah built the ark. When lumber is cut from the trees, the tough wood often breaks the teeth of the saw.

At *74.9 m.* is the junction with a graveled road.

Right on this road *0.5 m.* is BROOKSVILLE (269 alt., 875 pop.), a quiet old prairie town of old-fashioned homes softened by an even spread of shade.

Southward from here the houses, cattle, barns, fields, and pastures are typical of the prairie country. In winter the landscape reveals the bare black soil; in summer and spring the land shows a soft, pastoral character, with orchards of peach and apple trees in bloom, fields of alfalfa, and grassy meadows that stretch across low-rolling hills to meet the sky.

At *84.1 m.* is MACON (114 alt., 2,198 pop.) *(see Tour 4)*, and the junction with US 45 *(see Tour 4)*.

◄◄◄◄◄◄◄◄◄◄◄◄◄◄◄◄❁►►►►►►►►►►►►►►►►

Side Tour 4B

Shuqualak—Meridian, 54.2 m. State 39.
Graveled highway two lanes wide.
Accommodations chiefly in cities.

State 39 between Shuqualak and Meridian is a less traveled but more scenic route than US 45. Climbing abruptly out of the flat, fertile Black Prairie, State 39 rides the backbone of a series of ridges that extend southward. The fresh greenness of the pines, which have found foothold in every ravine and on every hillside, and the intense redness of the sandy clay soil make for a landscape of extravagant color. This is a country of small patches of cotton and corn, of peach and pear orchards, and here and there a noisy sawmill.

At SHUQUALAK, *0 m.* (214 alt., 810 pop.) *(see Tour 4)*, is the junction with US 45 *(see Tour 4)*.

Southward from Shuqualak, State 39 for a few miles passes through the Prairie Belt with its characteristic black loam extending into country that is still apparently prosperous. In the rolling meadows are painted farmhouses with solid barns and herds of cattle, and near the barns the air has a pleasant smell of cattle and fodder. But at *5.5 m.* is a low flat of cut-over land, part of the cutting of a large lumber company, that marks the northern end of the highway's climb into the red clay hills. Passing through a primitive, heavily forested country it follows the humps of ridges for an excellent view of the countryside. The State has few sections where the pines have been so little touched or where the landscape retains such pristine freshness. There are no villages of any size, only an occasional sawmill settlement. Ancient split rail fences enclose the poor-looking farm patches, and the farmhouses built of dressed logs and flanked at each end with mud chimneys are good examples of early dog-trot structures.

North of De Kalb the soil takes a redness so lurid that it might have given rise to the county's sobriquet, Bloody Kemper.

DE KALB, *20 m.* (888 pop.), seat of Kemper Co., is responsible for the nickname. After the War between the States this formerly quiescent Southern town became the scene of one of the bloodiest of the Reconstruction massacres. Over a period of years from 1868 to 1876 certain elements of the county, under the carpetbag judge, William Chisholm, and the Ku Klux Klan of Kemper, waged a bitter contest for supremacy. Shooting was done from ambush, resulting in the deaths of members of both factions and making travel through the country unsafe.

In 1876 John Gully, a member of the Klan, was shot and killed as he rode horseback across the county one night. Judge Chisholm was accused of the murder and was held in the De Kalb jail, his wife, daughter, and two sons insisting on being locked in with him. In late December 1876 at this jail the Chisholm Massacre took place; a mob, with the cry, "Fire the jail," entered to take Chisholm. The judge seized a gun and prepared to escape with his daughter and son Johnnie. The three were shot and killed as they appeared before the crowd at the top of the steps.

De Kalb, named for the German baron who came to America in 1776 to assist in the fight for independence, is on the site of the old Choctaw village Holihtasha (Ind., *the fort is there*), and is often called by that name by Indians of the vicinity.

Two blocks off State 39 (L) is the *WILLIAM CHISHOLM HOME (private)*, a simple white frame cottage that is a constant reminder of the turbulent past of the county.

South of De Kalb the country drops off sheerly on each side of the highway, the pines thin out, and yawning gullies appear.

KIPLING, *27 m.* (30 pop.), was named for the English writer by an early settler of the 1890's when a feverish admiration for Kipling's books was sweeping the country.

DALEVILLE, *34 m.* (118 pop.), is a small agricultural village that swallowed up the population of old Daleville.

At *35.2 m.* is a *BRANCH STATION OF THE U. S. SOIL CONSERVATION PROJECT*, engaged in restoring eroded land, a work which is largely due to the efforts of Congressman Ross Collins.

LIZELIA, *37 m.* (20 pop.), was formerly known as Daleville and, except for one or two solidly built white frame houses, every remnant of the old settlement founded by Mississippi's picturesque general, Sam Dale, has vanished. Dale, the tales of whose daring have become legendary, is described as having been of giant-like stature, standing six feet three inches, and as having a hawk-shaped face and piercing black eyes. Born in Rockridge, Va., in 1772, he migrated with his family to Georgia when a lad of twelve. Here he associated with the Indians and learned Indian lore and warfare.

In 1799 Dale began trading with the Creek and Choctaw tribes and soon established a wagon line, which he used for transporting families of emigrants from Virginia and the Carolinas through Georgia into Alabama and Mississippi. During the War of 1812 the "Canoe Fight" occurred. Dale, traveling by canoe on the Alabama River, met a party of Creek Indians paddling downstream. In the ensuing fight on the river,

Dale killed 11 of the Indians. Two years later the most notable achievement of his career was accomplished. Carrying dispatches to Gen. Andrew Jackson from the Creek Agency in Georgia to Madisonville, La., he rode the distance on horseback in seven and a half days. Upon his arrival Jackson sent him back with replies to the Agency, though neither Dale nor his horse Paddy had an hour's rest. In 1831 Dale was commissioned by the Secretary of War to remove the Choctaw Indians to Indian territory in the West. In later life Dale purchased from the Choctaw Chief, Iocha-hope, two sections of land on the present site of Lizelia, and there made his home. Before his death in 1841 he represented Lauderdale Co. in the State House of Representatives for several terms.

Right from Lizelia on a graveled road to the *GRAVE OF SAM DALE, 2 m.*, in the old Cochrane Cemetery. For many years the grave of "Big Sam" was neglected, but recently the Government has marked it with a plain marble slab. It is said that the Choctaw chief, Greenwood Leflore, stood over this grave during his comrade's burial, and, when the last spade of earth had been turned, said: "Big Chief, you sleep here, but your spirit is a brave and a chieftain in the hunting grounds of the sky."

Between this point and Meridian the slopes of the hills are dotted with peach and pecan orchards, a few dairy farms, red barns, and whitewashed trees giving color to the landscape.

At 49.7 m. are the stone entrance gates of the *MERIDIAN COUNTRY CLUB.*

At 51 m. State 59 follows Poplar Springs Drive which becomes 24th Ave., to the Civic Center.

MERIDIAN, 54.2 m. (341 alt., 31,954 pop.) *(see MERIDIAN).*

Points of Interest. Industrial plants, Gypsy Queen's Grave, Arboretum, and others.

Here are the junctions with US 45 *(see Tour 4)*, US 11 *(see Tour 8)*, and US 80 *(see Tour 2).*

Tour 5

(Memphis, Tenn.)—Grenada—Jackson—Brookhaven—McComb—(New Orleans, La.). US 51.
Tennessee Line to Louisiana Line, 307.2 m.
Illinois Central R.R. parallels route throughout.

Route paved throughout, two lanes wide.
Accommodations in cities.

Sec. a TENNESSEE LINE to JACKSON, 208.3 m.

Cutting down the middle of the State between the Tennessee Line and Jackson, US 51 traverses a country with a fairly old, prosperous, and advanced culture. That in the bluff hills between Memphis and Jackson was not dissimilar to that of Natchez, and, though not scenically or historically as rich as US 61, the route is filled with points of more than local interest.

Crossing the Mississippi Line, *0 m.*, 16 m. S. of Memphis US 51 follows the approximate route of the old, planked, stagecoach road.

BULLFROG CORNER, *2.4 m.*, is a crossroads store so named because it was built at a hole in the road where strangers said only a bullfrog could live.

Left from Bullfrog Corner on a graveled road to the main office of *GAYOSO FARMS, 1 m.*, a stock ranch having one of the largest herds of Guernsey cattle and droves of Hampshire hogs in the South.

At *8.2 m.* is the junction with a graveled road.

Left on this road at *0.2 m.* (R) to the *WINNINGHAM PLACE (private)*, a square, three-story, frame house that was formerly an inn on the stagecoach road to Memphis. Here Jefferson Davis, Generals Grant and Forrest, and other notables stopped in their travels on the old plank road. Built in 1837, it is in an excellent state of preservation.

HERNANDO, *12.3 m.* (390 alt., 938 pop.), was named for the Spanish explorer, Hernando De Soto. The mark of a former importance is left in the formidable towers of the *DE SOTO CO. COURTHOUSE,* which is perhaps the most interesting public building in northern Mississippi. In its records are numerous transfers of land from the Indian chief Musacunna to the earliest white settlers. Hernando was incorporated in 1837 and its academy, opened the same year, was the first established in the Chickasaw land cession. At the home of Confederate Col. T. W. White, both Confederate and Federal prisoners were exchanged during the war. This house, completed in 1860, is now known as the *MILDRED FARRINGTON HOME.* Hernando's best-known citizen, Felix La Bauve, was born in France in 1809 and came to northern Mississippi in 1835. He served as a colonel in the war, grew wealthy as a cotton planter, and is remembered in the La Bauve Fellowship at the University of Mississippi. He is buried in the Hernando Cemetery.

SENATOBIA, *26.8 m.* (284 alt., 1,264 pop.), is a refreshingly clean town built near Senatahoba (Ind., *white sycamore*) Creek. The low hill S. of Hickahala Creek and N. of the town was evidently an Indian camp on the trail W. from Pontotoc toward the Mississippi River, and it is thought that De Soto traveled it on his westward march in 1541. Indian mounds can be traced under the cotton loading platform of the Illinois Central R. R. depot. The Illinois Central (then the Tennessee & Mississippi) was built in 1856 and gave the impetus for founding the town. Charles Meriwether, an influential planter and slave owner, named the new station Senatobia, a slight deviation from the Indian name for the creek. The town grew swiftly, but was burned by Federal troops after a skirmish near what is now the campus of the *NORTHWEST*

JUNIOR COLLEGE. The brick-constructed two-story RANDOLPH ROWELL HOME, of the Southern Colonial type, one of the few antebellum homes escaping the ravages of war, was the nucleus around which the junior college was built in 1926. Senatobia was first incorporated in 1860 in De Soto County, then became the seat of Tate Co. in 1873. The courthouse, built in 1875 of locally manufactured brick, is still in use.

Left from Senatobia on a graveled road to (1937) a UNIT OF THE U. S. SOIL CONSERVATION SERVICE, 0.8 m.

At 29.8 m. (R) the terracing on the hillside is evidence of an early attempt at erosion control in these easily washed bluff hills.

At 30.7 m. is the junction with a private lane.

Left on this lane to McGEHEE'S GATE, 1.7 m. (private), the ante-bellum home described by Stark Young, Mississippi author, in his *Heaven Trees* and *River House*. It is a white, two-story Greek Revival style house, with a square-columned portico. The delicate hand-wrought iron balcony over the front entrance, and the walks bordered by aged boxwood under the shade of great magnolias give it a typically Southern appearance. It faces away from the highway and toward the sloping valley of Senatahoba Creek, and from the highway approach it seems to be a farmhouse. The fanlights in the doorway are opalescent with age and, though the house still shows dully white through the burnished green of the magnolias, it has never been repainted. Col. Abner McGehee, the builder, was one of the largest land and slave owners in northern Mississippi. Treasures of a cultured family are housed in rooms whose size is reminiscent of another age. A rosewood piano inlaid with mother-of-pearl, a gift of Colonel McGehee to his bride in 1857, is the central piece of a collection of heirlooms which includes Sèvres vases, tester beds with posts carved in spiral whorls, and a rosewood dressing table with legs bent in the shape of a lyre. An unusual piece is a bathing machine, a shower and tub arrangement through which a slave poured water. The present owner of the house is Miss Caroline McGehee, a cousin of Stark Young.

COMO, 34.4 m. (367 alt., 851 pop.), established in 1856 when the railroad came through and named for Lake Como in Italy, was like other Mississippi plantation towns, wealthy just prior to the War between the States. The land upon which Como was built was formerly a part of the plantation of Dr. George Tait, one of the characters in *Heaven Trees*.

Right from Como on a graveled road at 1.1 m. (R) to WALLACE PARK (private), a square two-story house half hidden in a wandering grove of crape-myrtle, magnolia, and native cedar trees. This home was built in 1856 for Col. Thomas Wallace by the old stagecoach road. Wortz and Mayer, respectively from Indiana and Maine, were the architects, adding incongruous columns onto the New England type house; the plain substantial mass is entirely separate from its portico. The inside dimensions are more Southern, each room being a generous 20-foot square. In one of the big upstairs rooms, Gen. N. B. Forrest stayed two weeks during that trying period just before Grant took Memphis.

Between Como and Sardis the highway traverses a rolling, prairie-like section that is excellent dairy country.

SARDIS, 39.6 m. (384 alt., 1,298 pop.), established on the Illinois Central R.R. in 1856, took over the population of old Belmont, a river landing on the Tallahatchie River some five miles SE. The W. D. HEFLIN HOME (private) is Sardis' ante-bellum showplace. Sardis is now (1938) headquarters for the *SARDIS DAM AND RESERVOIR,* a Government project designed to control flood waters in the Tallahatchie River basin. The earth dam, to be erected five and a half miles SE. of Sardis, will be unusually large. The reservoir will cover approximately 100,000 acres and will give protection from overflows to nearly 800,000 acres in the Tallahatchie basin and in the Delta. The dam itself in places will be a quarter of a mile thick at the base. The road to be constructed from Sardis to the dam site will pass through old Belmont and near the old *DR. GEORGE W. LAIRD HOME,* built about 1846 and reputedly a rendezvous for Ku Klux Klan leaders during the Reconstruction Period. The first postmaster of Sardis gave the town the name of one of the churches mentioned in the Bible.

At *46 m.* US 51 crosses the Tallahatchie (Ind., *rock river*) River.

At *49.3 m.* is the junction with a graveled road.

Right on this road is BATESVILLE, *1.4 m.* (346 alt., 1,062 pop.) sitting on the arm of the Delta made by the Tallahatchie River. A typical country trade center, Batesville took over Panola's population when the railroad was put through in 1856. Here is the junction with State 6 *(see Tour 14).*

Right from Batesville on a graveled road *1 m.* to the *SITE OF OLD PANOLA,* marked by the old brick courthouse that has been remodeled into a residence. Panola was the rival town of Belmont, both of them important landings on the Tallahatchie River. Panola was incorporated in 1839, became a flourishing cotton shipping port in the 1840's, and struck a body blow at its rival, Belmont, by winning a long struggle for the county seat in 1846—through bribery, Belmont charged. When the Mississippi & Tennessee R.R. (Illinois Central) skirted Panola, many of the frame houses were put on rollers and moved to the new town of Batesville. The courthouse, its flaming red brick walls immovable, was left at the wharf. The rivalry that formerly existed between Panola and Belmont, however, is carried over into the friendly competition between Batesville and Sardis, both of them being seats of Panola Co., though but eight miles apart.

At *53.8 m.* is the junction with a graveled road.

Right on this road is COURTLAND, *0.6 m.* (263 alt., 230 pop.), incorporated in 1871, which took its name by popular vote from the fact that an unusually large number of the settlers were married the year it was founded. The first settler was Dr. George Randolph whose ante-bellum home is standing.

Right from Courtland on a graveled road *7 m.* to TOCOWA SPRINGS in woods of sugar maple, beech, and gum trees, where the hills meet the Delta. Above the springs, the bluffs rise from 80 to 100 feet. The springs are on the old Chickasaw-Choctaw boundary line and, having always been considered neutral grounds, were the meeting place for all Indians. The name is a combination of two Indian words, the Chickasaw *ptoco,* meaning *healing,* and the Choctaw *wawa,* meaning *water.* It was here at the healing waters that the Indians assembled after the cession of their lands in 1832, preparing for their trek westward beyond the Mississippi River. In the 1890's Tocowa Springs was a famous health resort; the old hotel still stands. The lines of trees planted as markers on the Chickasaw-Choctaw boundary line have grown to giant size.

At *63.1 m.* US 51 crosses the Yocona River to cut through hills beautifully laid out with farm patches, pastures, and wood lots separating substantially built, prosperous farmhouses.

At *83.2 m.* the highway leaves the hills to cut across black flat land that is a finger of the Delta extended eastward by the Yalobusha River.

At *89.9 m.* it rides a levee through swampland that is typical of what the Delta was before artificial drainage systems developed it into the South's best cotton fields.

At *92.1 m.* US 51 crosses the Yalobusha (Ind., *tadpole place*) River.

GRENADA, *92.5 m.* (193 alt., 4,349 pop.), is on the eastern edge of the Mississippi Delta and, though somewhat mellowed by great age, has the cotton-consciousness, the wealth, and the character of a Delta city. Cotton marketing and processing and lumbering are the leading industries.

The city embraces the two old towns of Pittsburg and Tulahoma, established on adjoining land grants by two rival speculating companies headed by Franklin Plummer and Hiram Runnels, Mississippi political gamecocks in the 1830's *(see Tour 13)*. Plummer's town, Pittsburg, was the western grant and was separated from Runnels' Tulahoma only by a line. The personal and political antagonism between Congressman Plummer and Governor Runnels kept the towns at white heat, and in the campaign of 1835 the excitement was so intense that bloodshed was narrowly averted. Tulahoma was the slightly larger town, having seven or eight grogshops (then called groceries) in addition to its seven or eight houses. Pittsburg had the part-time post office and, until the editor settled some of his personal debts by moving across the line and switching his politics, the only newspaper, *The Bowie Knife*.

By 1836 the towns had grown weary of quarreling, and in sudden penitence agreed to make up. It was decided to unite a couple in marriage as a symbol of the new friendship. Pittsburg furnished the groom; Tulahoma the bride; and a Methodist preacher joined the two in matrimony in July 1836. Both of the old names were dropped and a new one, Grenada, adopted. Line Street marks the division between old Pittsburg and Tulahoma. However, the troubles between the two were not definitely ended with the ceremony, Pittsburgers and Tulahomans finding it difficult to keep from backsliding until the common adversity of fire and the war created a civic unity. In the fall of 1862 Confederate General Pemberton made Grenada his headquarters while opposing General Grant in the second campaign against Vicksburg. Much more disastrous than the war, however, was the yellow fever epidemic of 1878, when out of a population of 2,500 there were 1,040 reported cases and 326 dead. In 1913 the city was a pioneer in the State in paving, covering its square with wooden blocks that are still in service. In 1917 it furnished Mississippi's first military company for the World War.

At Grenada is radio station WGRM, a 100-watt station operating on a frequency of 1210 kilocycles.

GRENADA COLLEGE, a Methodist junior college for girls, sits in a grove of oak trees and is centered about a red brick two-story building whose age shows in the mellow coloring of the brick. Behind and to the side are smaller brick buildings of more modern construction. The school was opened in 1851 as the Yalobusha Baptist Female Institute; the Methodist Church obtained control in 1882. The 1937 enrollment was 150. The IDA CAMPBELL HOME *(open by appointment)*, on Cuff's Hill, said to be the oldest residence in the town, was at one time the home of the Presbyterian Mission for the Indians. Hunly, the builder, was a clerk in the United States land office. Almost as old as the Campbell place is the *ESTELL ROLLIN HOME (open by appointment)*, 422 Doak St. Built in the 1830's of hand-hewn logs, the house is now covered with weatherboarding. The *JOHN NASON HOME (open by appointment)*, 410 College St., is said to have been used as a girls' school in the old town of Pittsburg. The *BRUCE NEWSOME HOME (open by appointment)*, 217 Margin St., is a two-story Southern Colonial type house with a great white-columned portico. Designed by John Moore, it is said to be the first house in Grenada planned by an architect. Here Confederate Gen. Sterling Price had his headquarters when Pres. Jefferson Davis reviewed the brigade under his command. It is said that the great pillars of the house were brought from England to New Orleans and thence up the Mississippi, Yazoo, and Yalobusha Rivers to Grenada. The *GOLLIDAY LAKE HOME*, 605 Margin St., was Davis' headquarters. The *IKE COHEN HOME*, 204 Cherry St., was constructed of material taken from a steamboat stranded by low water on the Yalobusha River in 1842. The *WALTHALL HOME*, on College Blvd., opposite Grenada College, is post-bellum but modeled after the Walthall home in Holly Springs. It was here that Edward Cary Walthall (1831–98), the embodiment of the ideal of Mississippi chivalry, lived when he moved to Grenada in 1871. Walthall, with Forrest and Gordon, was one of Mississippi's greatest volunteer leaders in the War between the States. He entered as lieutenant in the 15th Mississippi Regiment; was elected lieutenant-colonel of that regiment; in the spring of 1862 he was elected colonel of the 29th Mississippi; in December was promoted to brigadier-general, and in June 1864, was made major general. He was once appointed and three times elected to the United States Senate. He died in Washington, D. C., April 21, 1898, and is buried in Holly Springs Cemetery, at Holly Springs, Mississippi.

At 96 *m.* (L) is TIE PLANT (60 pop.), a mill community centered around the million-dollar creosoting plant in operation for 30 years.

GLENWILD, 97.5 m. (L), is the plantation of John Borden, wealthy Chicago sportsman. The original dwelling, on the brow of a hill overlooking an immense acreage, was a log house raised in 1839 by Col. A. M. Payne, an influential pioneer. Unusual for a log house, it had a cellar; 20 years later when Colonel Payne enlarged and weatherboarded it to nearly its present size, the house adapted itself easily to its greater prosperity. Six of the huge square two-story columns were raised in front to carry the roof out over a part of the wide lawn, to make a setting somewhat similar to Mount Vernon. With the additions made, the Paynes used the plantation as their summer refuge from yellow fever in New Orleans.

Just prior to the war, Colonel Payne succeeded in bringing the railroad through Grenada past his home and was rewarded by having the first locomotive dubbed the "A. M. Payne." But like many planters ruined by the war, he was forced to sell Glenwild in 1866. The contract for sale gives an idea of what the large Southern plantation included. The purchase price was $40,000 plus $25,000 for the stock and equipment. The plantation embraced 4,500 acres, 2,300 of which were in cultivation. With the real estate went 500 hogs, 200 head of cattle, 300 sheep, 9,000 bushels of corn, 30,000 pounds of meat, 15,000 pounds of cottonseed, and 4,000 bushels of Irish and sweet potatoes, all produced on the place in that year. In addition to the great house the deed of sale also listed: "Meat House, Smoke House, Blacksmith Shop and Tools, Carpenter's Shop and Tools, Good Grist Mill, Hospital, Overseer's House, 25 Negro Houses, Three Corn Houses, Ice House, Stable for Sixty Mules, New and Complete Cattle Stable, Carriage House, Horse Stable, Two Cotton Gins and Gin House, Four Hen Houses, Large Fruit Orchard Bearing Apples, Pears, Peaches, and Figs without limit." Colonel Payne urged the buyer to "take the place altogether, it is in better condition —better stocked than any plantation in the Confederacy." It was bought in 1920 by John Borden and greatly improved. Capacious—almost extravagant—barns and silos have been set up, and the great house made even greater. Its log façade now has ten widely-spaced columns which continue from the east front around to the original section of the south wing. To the N. another wing completes the plan of a rectangle to afford a delightful inner court. The present ensemble is in keeping with the original section.

ELLIOTT, 100.4 m. (235 alt., 128 pop.), established in 1818 as the result of a petition made by David Folsom, Choctaw Chieftain, was the first mission among the Choctaw Indians. The school was named for John Eliot of Massachusetts, the "Apostle to the Indians." John Smith of the same State was one of Eliot's disciples and the first teacher at the schools. In its time the mission was one of the most important in the Southwest.

DUCK HILL, *105.1 m.* (251 alt., 553 pop.), is named for the large green hill rising from a plain immediately E. of the town. This hill was where "Duck," a Choctaw Chief, held his war councils; and it was near this hill that Rube Burrows, notorious bandit *(see Tour 4)* killed the engineer and robbed the express car on the fast Illinois Central Express. In 1937 a double lynching occurred nearby that was given significant publicity owing to the fact that the Gavagan Anti-Lynching Bill was under consideration in the National Congress.

WINONA, *116.8 m.* (386 alt., 2,607 pop.) *(see Tour 6),* is at the junction with US 82 *(see Tour 6).*

VAIDEN, *128.1 m.* (325 alt., 648 pop.), is one link in a chain of small, comfortably prosperous towns, held together by a common dependence on the cotton crops of outlying farms. It is a static village whose population and character have changed but little in the 100 years of its existence. A street of one-story frame stores spreads along the railroad track (R) and homes of old-fashioned rambling architecture in the clumps of trees beyond are outward signs of the easeful life that the fertile surrounding cotton fields sustain. Ginning season sets a more lively tempo for the town, but after the last bale is marketed Vaiden settles down again into a placid, relaxed existence. Here is the junction with State 35 *(see Tour 16).*

Right from Vaiden on a graveled road to the SITE OF OLD SHONGALO, *1 m.,* the town taken over by Vaiden when the railroad was put through. Shongalo was settled by cultured people who established the old Shongalo Academy.

WEST, *137.9 m.* (290 alt., 370 pop.), was one of the towns raided by Grierson in 1863. The depot was burned, but Confederate soldiers drove off the raiders before any dwellings could be looted.

DURANT, *148.4 m.* (265 alt., 2,510 pop.), is a prosperous farming town in the rich second bottoms of the Big Black River. Founded in 1858 after the Illinois Central R.R. came through, it was named for Louis Durant, a Choctaw Chief who got his own name from the early French explorers along the Mississippi watercourses. In 1937 the town issued bonds for $25,000 for the erection of a *FACTORY,* the mill being leased by the Real Silk Co. The Durant mill was the first in the State to be established under the Industrial Act of 1936 *(see AN OUTLINE OF FOUR CENTURIES).*

Right from Durant on the lower Lexington Road *3.1 m.* to CASTALIAN SPRINGS (R), a watering place known for its natural beauty. The cures here are due as much to the rest as to the waters; there is a rambling hotel. The springs were used first by the Indians, and at one time a school for girls was here, the school being converted during the War between the States into a hospital. A number of Confederate dead are buried in a plot some distance from the springs.

At *151.1 m.* is the junction with a graveled ridge road.

Right on this road to the HOLMES COUNTY STATE PARK, *3 m.* (L), a tract of 419 acres of shortleaf pine now in process of development. This park will have a lake with facilities for swimming, boating, and fishing; a lodge, overnight cabins, bridle paths; picnic and camping grounds.

GOODMAN, *155.6 m.* (608 pop.), has the general aspect of central Mississippi towns; one long street is lined with single-story brick stores, and another street has attractive modern homes. Goodman's life is connected with the *HOLMES COUNTY JUNIOR COLLEGE,* established in 1925 as an addition to the Agricultural High School. The college, having seven modern brick buildings, operates an adjacent 40-acre farm with student labor. On the hill between the college and the highway is a single *GRAVE,* protected by a strong iron railing and marked by a monument with the inscription, "Here lies buried an old bachelor." The grave's occupant was a pioneer who was shot by robbers; at his dying request the monument with its singular inscription was erected to his memory.

At *160.8 m.* is the junction with a graveled road.

Right on this road *5.9 m.* to the *LITTLE RED SCHOOL* (L), marking the town of old Richland. The school is a two-story brick building, with its structural material so deteriorated that it has become necessary to brace the building with iron rods extending its width and fastened to the outside walls with huge iron washers. In this small building, now used as a schoolhouse, the idea

THE COUNTY AGENT VISITS

of the Order of the Eastern Star was conceived, and in it the greater part of the Eastern Star Ritual was written. Here in the 1840's the Masons of Lexington and Richland established a school of higher learning to keep their sons nearer home. The first teacher they obtained was Robert Morris, who conducted his classes in this building in 1849 and 1850. Morris was a beloved and honored Master Mason of Oxford, Miss. While teaching at Richland he worked out the plan of an organization for female relatives of Masons that became the Order of Eastern Star.

PICKENS, *162.4 m.* (234 alt., 635 pop.), in the days of keelboats and barges was a river landing on the Big Black River. The present name was not adopted, however, until the railroad was built through in 1858. The *JOSIE BURTON HOME (private)* is the handsomest of the remaining ante-bellum homes.

At *162.9 m.* is the main bridge across the Big Black River.

At *173.5 m.* is the junction with a graveled road.

Right on this road to the retreat of *ALLISON'S WELLS, 1.2 m.* (R), a low rambling frame building of many gables and continuous well-screened porches, a popular watering place. A State-wide bridge tournament is held here annually in June. The mineral waters at the wells are supplemented with hot sulphur baths and were celebrated before the War between the States for their supposed efficacy in preventing yellow fever.

CANTON, *183.3 m.* (224 alt., 4,725 pop.), the seat of Madison Co., was incorporated in 1836. Built on the low divide halfway between Big Black River and Pearl River, it achieved a character that was neither the Old South of the Big Black Valley nor the Piney Woods of the Pearl River Valley, and is dotted with homes distinguished by their variety of plan and appearance. The *COURTHOUSE,* raised in 1852, and the *SQUARE* come closest to fitting the groove of other Mississippi county seats. Its Georgian design is well suited to the ideals of those early settlers from Virginia, the Carolinas, and Georgia who obtained Canton's charter of incorporation. The old *JAIL* stands on a back alley off Center St. near the square.

Travel on the Natchez Trace and cotton culture gave Canton the wealth that was to express itself in the homes. The finest of those left standing is the *W. J. MOSBY HOME (private),* Center St., two blocks E. of the courthouse. Surrounded by formally landscaped grounds this imposing, square, red brick structure is designed with a massive Corinthian two-story portico and with two wings in the rear which enclose a courtyard. The roof is topped with a cubical observatory. In addition to the slave quarters in the basement, there are 15 large rooms, most of which have a natural grace that has not changed since the house was built in 1856 by Col. William Lyons.

Colonel Lyons, a pleasant but imperious landholder, left the task of building with an architect who, prior to one of the colonel's European excursions, implored his attention about a certain matter but was frustrated by the colonel's pleasantries. When the colonel returned, the greater part of the house was finished, but as he climbed the curved staircase he was amazed to find he could go no farther than the second floor—the architect had tried to tell him there was no stairway to the observatory. Subsequently the shaft was raised directly in the upper hall and a lovely winding stair extended to the roof. The upper floor of the home was used by General Sherman, the lower by his mules, during a temporary Federal occupation of Canton. When Colonel Lyons fell on evil days after the war, he went to his good friend, Mosby, the father of the present owner, expressing the wish to sell to him rather than to a less appreciative owner.

Next to the Mosby house is the *MARIE RUCKER HOME (private)*. The plan of the present two-story plantation house is a notable departure from its original Georgian Colonial H-shaped plan. Built in 1822 by Col. D. M. Fulton, a pioneer settler, a porch on three sides and a tower for scanning the cotton fields have been added, giving it an unusual appearance. The structure is painted red with a cream trim. This color scheme emphasizes the baroque cornice and window blinds. The interior is ornamented in the manner of an English house of the period of construction, the decorations having been done by English plasterers. The dining room is approached by low, broad steps leading down from the middle hall. A flagged brick terrace separates the detached kitchen, which looks now as it did originally except for the removal of the crane from the fireplace. The garden in the rear is laid out in scallops, and the formal treatment of lawn and hedges is as English as the interior. The original box hedge planted in a double heart design has grown luxuriantly around the ancient cistern.

Near the end of East Academy St. on the south side of town is the *GUS LUCKETT HOME*, a simple one-story white frame dwelling built by Major Drane, an early settler of Madison Co., prior to the War between the States. It was used as headquarters by Confederate Gen. Albert S. Johnston during the war.

The EPISCOPAL RECTORY was the birthplace of John McCrady, one of Mississippi's foremost contemporary painters. McCrady, the seventh child of a clergyman, spent his early years in Canton and in Oxford; his paintings are nostalgic scenes of the Deep South and show a quiet humor that combines fantasy with realism. His work has been exhibited in Manhattan's Boyer Galleries.

1. Right from Canton on the Flora road to *BELLEVUE, 11 m. (private)*, a good example of the plantation homes built in the rich cotton country around Canton.

2. Right from Canton on the graveled Madison Station road to the *GEORGE HARVEY PLANTATION, 5 m.*, comprising 3,000 acres of cotton and timber lands. The 102-year-old big house sits among large trees. The T-shaped house has an impressive Doric portico, designed with square columns and a crowning pediment, and a long one-story rear wing flanked by porches. From a central hall a semicircular stairway leads to the spacious living quarters on the second floor. The dining hall and scullery are in the rear wing.

Between Canton and Jackson US 51 passes through an increasing number of fruit and truck farms, the first large peach farm being at *182.6 m.*

At *195 m.* is the junction with a paved road.

Right on this road is MADISON, *0.2 m.* (335 alt., 325 pop.).

At *6.8 m.* (R) is *INGLESIDE*, in a setting of live oaks and an artificial lake. The house is a Greek Revival adaptation, with white stucco over brick, a red roof, and four large fluted columns upholding the portico. Ingleside was the home of the builder of the Chapel of the Cross *(see below)*.

At *7.3 m.* (R) on a slight rise well back from the road in a grove of hickory and oak trees is the *CHAPEL OF THE CROSS*, overgrown with green vines.

The ivy-clad brick structure is Gothic in style with a lofty bell tower. Wills, an English architect, drew the plans of the chapel. It was completed and consecrated in 1853. The arched main entrance is placed unobtrusively on the side; it has double wooden doors fastened with an iron latch. The dim interior with its long narrow windows, arched wooden trusses, and stone floor is decorated with charm and simplicity. It has a stone baptismal font and a carved altar of redwood decorated with gold leaf, both imported from Europe. Adjoining the chapel on each side and at the rear is the CHURCHYARD in which are graves grouped in family plots. Among them, close to the buttressed walls of the chapel, is the grave of Henry Crew Vick, marked by a rustic stone cross. To this grave belongs the story of the "Bride of Annandale," Miss Helen Johnstone, whose mother built the chapel. When John Johnstone, of a family from Annandale, Scotland, came here in 1820 he built in the wilderness the first Annandale, a log house, for his wife and daughter. Although he built Ingleside later, he continued to live in the weather-boarded log house until his death in 1848. Before his widow raised a finer Annandale, she built the chapel with brick and slave labor from her own place. Christmas of 1855 found Mrs. Johnstone and Helen visiting at Ingleside while the new Annandale was under construction. It was there that Helen met Henry Vick, son of the founder of Vicksburg. From the meeting developed love and then an engagement. The wedding was set for May 21, 1859. Four days before that date, Vick was killed in a duel in New Orleans, firing his own shot into the air to keep a promise to his betrothed never to kill a man. His body was brought to Annandale for burial, and work on the great house was suspended. Annandale was never actually finished, though descendants of the Johnstones occupied it until it burned on Sept. 9, 1926. Helen and her mother traveled for a while; then Helen returned as the bride of Dr. George Harris, who had come as minister to the chapel. The story is that Helen never gave her heart to her husband but remained the bride of a ghost, the sweetheart of Henry Vick. Annandale was a huge structure of French design planned by a New York architect and built with slave labor. During the war it was stripped for the Confederate cause. The carpets were cut into soldiers' blankets, the bronze and brass pieces were melted and sent to foundries to be cast into cannon, the Johnstone women's silk dresses were made into battle banners, and the imported linens torn into strips for bandages. In the later years of the war General Sherman and his staff made the home a headquarters.

At *199.9 m.* is the junction with a graveled road.

Right on this road to *TOUGALOO COLLEGE*, *0.5 m.*, an accredited school for Negroes founded by the American Missionary Association of New York in 1869. Tougaloo's red brick buildings are grouped in a natural woodland around the ante-bellum mansion of John Boddy, sold with a tract of 500 acres to the association in 1869 and since used as the *ADMINISTRATION BUILDING.* The largest of the halls is *HOLMES HALL*, housing the chapel, library, laboratories, and classrooms. Many of the other buildings were erected by students trained in the industrial department, with brick made in the school's own brickyard. Truck farming, orcharding, dairying, and trade shops supply the faculty and pupils and help support the institution. Various faculty members hold degrees from Columbia, Chicago, Yale, and Harvard Universities *(see EDUCATION).*

At *200.9 m.* are the *TOWERS OF WJDX*, the Lamar Life Insurance Company's radio station. The broadcasting studios are in the Lamar Building, Jackson. The station operates on a frequency of 1270 kilocycles.

At *203.7 m.* US 51 follows N. State St.; R on Pascagoula St. to S. Gallatin St.

JACKSON, *208.3 m.* (294 alt., 48,282 pop.) *(see JACKSON).*

Points of Interest. New Capitol, Old Capitol, Livingston Park and Zoo, Hinds

Co. Courthouse, Millsaps College, Belhaven College, Battlefield Park, and others.

Here are the junctions with US 80 *(see Tour 2)* and US 49 *(see Tour 7).*

Sec. b JACKSON *to* LOUISIANA LINE, *98.9 m.,* US *51*

South of Jackson, *0 m.,* US 51 follows S. Gallatin St.; R. on Hooker St.; L. on Terry Road. US 51 is the most direct route between Jackson and New Orleans. Centered around Crystal Springs and Hazlehurst is a truck farming area of importance. In the vicinity of Brookhaven dairying has supplanted lumbering, with cut-over lands now used for pasturage. Throughout the route the variety of wooded areas and the contrasting towns lend interest.

At *1.5 m.* is the junction with State 18.

Right on this paved road at *10.9 m.* is the junction with a graveled road. Left here *2 m.* to *COOPER'S WELLS,* a resort known throughout the State for the mildness of its waters. The frame hotel, a rambling informal structure, sits on a steep bluff, overlooking the well house in the ravine. From the front gallery is an excellent view of the alluvial hills encircling Vicksburg. The land was purchased in 1837 by the Rev. Preston Cooper, who, because of a recurring dream that there was a valuable mineral spring here, dug the first well. A resort hotel was built sometime later, but Federal troops burned it during the War between the States. The present building *(open in summer),* which was built in 1880, has undergone many alterations. The mineral waters of the well are of use in the treatment of several diseases. They are quickly purgative. Guests gather around the well before meals and engage in contests to see who can drink the greatest number of glasses. (Formerly the contest was with dippers of the water, everybody drinking from the same long-handled dipper. This was the custom as late as 1907. At that time in addition to the rambling old hotel there was another building a few feet away, called the Bull Pen, occupied by men only, where fortunes were lost and won at poker.)

On State 18 at *14.2* is RAYMOND (306 alt., 547 pop.), incorporated as the seat of Hinds Co. in 1829 with the advantage of being on the Natchez Trace. For several years it was a larger and more progressive town than the capital, and during the State's most prosperous days was the center of a flourishing plantation life. The Old Oak Tree Inn, now burned, was famous as the meeting place of ministers, doctors, lawyers, and scholars of Mississippi. From it Andrew Jackson made an address during his visit to the town, and so great was his ovation that linen sheets were taken from the beds and spread upon the board walks for him to tread upon. From a bed in this hotel Seargent S. Prentiss arose in the middle of the night and made a speech in defence of a bedbug that had bitten him. It was heard by a mock jury and judge, and the bedbug was formally acquitted.

Right *0.6 m.* from town water tank, to the *MAJOR PEYTON HOME (private),* one of the oldest houses in Raymond. Erected in the early 1830's with slave labor, it is an elaborate version of the type of plantation home popular at that time. When erected, it marked the center of Hinds County.

The *GIBBS BUILDING,* corner Main and Port Gibson Sts., was built in 1854–59. The lower story is now a filling station but the upper story retains its original iron railings and porches.

The *HINDS COUNTY COURTHOUSE,* a large gray building, green shuttered, is the outstanding structure in Raymond. It has Doric columns on the façade and a towering cupola.

The EPISCOPAL CHURCH, next to the courthouse, is nearly a century old. It is a small building of Gothic design.

The RATLIFF HOME (private), two blocks from the courthouse, corner Main St. and Dupree Road, was built in 1853 by Dr. H. T. T. Dupree from lumber given by John A. Fairchild to his daughter, Margaret, as a wedding present. Mr. Fairchild owned and operated the first sawmill in this section, and the lumber used in the home is heart pine cut in his mill. Cornices and mantels are hand-carved. When Raymond was occupied by Federal troops, the household furniture was thrown into the yard by Union soldiers, cotton was laid in thick carpets on the floor, and wounded soldiers were brought here for treatment.

Dominating the eastern entrance to Raymond are the red brick buildings of HINDS COUNTY JUNIOR COLLEGE (R) *(see EDUCATION)*.

At *31.1 m.* on State 18 is UTICA (285 alt., 652 pop.), an important vegetable shipping center.

At *35.4 m.* on State 18 to UTICA NORMAL AND INDUSTRIAL INSTITUTE, one of the State's outstanding institutions for Negroes. The school was founded in 1903 as a grammar school. Since that time its curriculum has been expanded to include high school and normal work, and many additional buildings have been erected to accommodate its 350 students (1937). The school is known outside Mississippi because of the Utica Singers, who have traveled in this country and Europe singing Negro spirituals. In 1905 the institute sponsored a Negro Farmers' Conference, the object of which was to encourage Negro tenants to buy land. At that time only one Negro in the Utica district owned his property. At present, with the Farmers' Conference an annual event, more than 35,000 acres in this area are owned by Negroes.

At *2.7 m.* is the junction with a graveled road.

Left on this road to the FILTROL CORPORATION PLANT, *0.7 m. (open by permission from office, 8:30 to 5 weekdays)*. Constructed of corrugated iron, the building is of modern industrial design, with two elevator towers rising from the center. The detached gray office building, surrounded by a grove of pecan trees, is of bungalow type, with an experimental laboratory in the rear wing. The corporation, established in May 1936, processes each week (1937) approximately 800 tons of bentonite clay mined in Smith Co. *(see Tour 2)*. Trade-marked Filtrol, the finished product is used chiefly to bleach and absorb impurities from vegetable and mineral oils. In the rear tower of the plant the crude clay is crushed, mixed with water into a slurry, and treated with acid for several hours under heat. This mixture then is piped into several large vats where the acid is washed out and left to settle in artificial reservoirs before being discharged into Pearl River. An Olivar filter press separates the clay from the water, and the clay, conveyed to the front tower, is further dried and pulverized. This product is supplementing the use of fuller's earth in chemical processes.

US 51 southward runs between fruit orchards alternating with suburban bungalows. Further S. are Negro cabins with walls of plank weatherboarding applied vertically. The cut at 7 m. (R) reveals the type of soil in the area, a mixture of clay and gravel with a warm yellow-red tint.

TERRY, *16.2 m.* (291 alt., 412 pop.), is the northernmost of the truck farming towns on US 51. Although the area had been settled before the War of 1812, a town was not established until the railroad came through in 1856 and put its depot on Bill Terry's land. Until 1910 Terry was an active cotton market, but since that time vegetable growing and shipping have become the main activities.

The best known early settler was Gov. A. G. Brown, whose home, the old *BROWN PLACE,* still stands, a primitive farm house whose simplicity suggests the hardships of the early settler. Brown, Governor from 1844 to 1848, was the most popular and influential man in the State at that time. As Governor he took the lead in repudiating the Union bank bonds and in working for free public schools and the popular election of judges. In national affairs he upheld State rights and all policies advocated by his small farmer constituents. He died at his Terry home in 1880.

The *DUBOSE HOME (private)*, a cottage, contains Waldo Beauregard Dubose's collection of oil paintings by American and European artists. By profession Dubose is a designer of elaborate and spectacular evening clothes for women, but his major interest is in the fine arts.

At *22.1 m.* is the junction with a graveled road.

Right on this road *0.2 m.* (L) to the *R. L. GANT HOME (private)*, a white frame house where lives the owner of Mississippi's most famous pack of bloodhounds. Between 1906 and 1933 the pack tracked down several notorious criminals. Gant has been successful in running down 85 per cent of the men he sought, and has 12 wounds to show for his man-hunting.

At *23.5 m* is the junction with a graveled road.

Right on this road to LAKE CHAUTAUQUA, *0.2 m.*, an artificial lake in a setting of pines and oaks. Here from 1903 to 1915 the Mississippi Chautauqua Association held annual sessions each July. Summer cottages and a community house were erected and a lake for swimming, boating, and fishing was made. Besides the Chautauqua programs, those using local talent were encouraged. During the height of its popularity the Chautauqua was widely attended by residents of Mississippi and of neighboring States. Cottages were rented for the season of two weeks and the hotel accommodated 100 guests. The site is now leased to the Illinois Central Railroad which uses the lake as a pumping station. The grounds are popular for picnicking and camping; in the summer political rallies are held here. On the elevation above the lake is the sturdy old tabernacle of the Hennington Camp Meeting, one of the oldest camp meeting sites in the State. Built before the War between the States, the tabernacle is constructed of hand-hewn logs.

At *25.2 m.* is the junction with a paved road.

Left on this road is CRYSTAL SPRINGS, *0.4 m.* (463 alt., 2,257 pop.), one of the largest tomato-shipping centers of the State. The story of commercial gardening in Crystal Springs begins in 1870 with the first shipment of peaches, grown by James Sturgis, to markets at New Orleans and Chicago. Tomatoes were still known as love apples at that time, but N. Piazza imported seed from Italy and with S. H. Stackhouse began scientific cultivation of tomato plants. With the help of a German emigrant, Augustus Lotterhos, the industry achieved success. In 1878 Lotterhos pooled the products of a number of tomato growers to ship the first full carload to Denver, Colo.

The shipping of other vegetables to Northern markets followed. Peas, beans, cabbages, carrots, beets, and asparagus began moving in carload lots, but strawberries had to await the development of refrigeration. To offset the occasional losses due to a glutted market, the farmers started a tomato-canning plant, Lotterhos being instrumental in its establishment. In 1927 the peak of shipping was reached with 3,342 carloads of vegetables moving to markets in the United States and Canada, of which 1,562 cars contained tomatoes. The vegetable growing industry now supports a box and crate factory and a refrigeration plant. These activities have made Crystal Springs different from Mississippi cotton towns. It has two rush seasons: the typical cotton-picking and corn-harvesting one, and the feverish weeks in the late spring when the truck crops are sent out.

The schools open earlier than usual so that the children can get through a full term and still work in the fields when crops, which perish rapidly, mature. The *CONSOLIDATED SCHOOL* brings its 1,300 pupils from truck farms within a radius of 15 miles.

Byron Patton Harrison, born in this town, has served Mississippi in one political office or another for 32 of his 56 years. Born at Crystal Springs in 1881, and educated in the Mississippi public schools and Louisiana State University, he began his law practice in Leakesville, Miss., in 1902. From 1905 to 1910 he was district attorney for the Second District. From 1911 to 1919 he represented his district in Congress. Since 1919 he has been U.S. Senator. He led the movement for flood control that resulted in the passage of the National Flood Control Act in 1928, and did outstanding work in the fight for the Agricultural Adjustment Administration. Senator Harrison's home is now in Gulfport.

At *33.9 m.* is the junction with a graveled road.

Right on this road *0.2 m.* to LAKE HAZLE, a favorite swimming and picnicking spot.

HAZLEHURST, *34 m.* (460 alt., 2,447 pop.), the seat of Copiah Co., is a fruit-and-vegetable-shipping town. Its history begins with the history of Gallatin, seven miles W., chartered in 1829; when the railroad was put through in 1857 the people of Gallatin moved close to the new depot, which was named for George Hazlehurst, chief engineer of the New Orleans, Jackson & Great Northern R.R. But because Copiah citizens had built an expensive courthouse at Gallatin just prior to that time, Hazlehurst did not become the county seat until 1872. Following the lead of Crystal Springs, the town is now chiefly concerned with growing, packing, and shipping vegetables. Like Crystal Springs, it has an ice plant and box factory and also a large fertilizer plant.

Right from Hazlehurst on State 20 is GALLATIN, *7.5 m.*, marked now only by a crossroads store, but in its day a town that lived up to what was expected of a Mississippi ante-bellum seat of justice. "It enjoyed the reputation of having a man killed once every week for pastime," and attracted to it some of the ablest members of the bar in Mississippi. The town became the seat of justice of Copiah Co. in 1824, and was named in honor of Albert Gallatin, Secretary of the Treasury under Madison. Here Albert G. Brown *(see above)* was born and reared, moving to Terry when a young man.

At *8.6 m.* (L) on State 20, perched atop a ridge above a cluster of trees is the old *WILEY HARRIS HOME (private);* it was here that Wiley Pope Harris, the younger, the power behind the achievements of many of Mississippi's greatest statesmen, was reared. He was a nephew of the Harris who had bought this home in the 1820's and died in it in 1845. The younger Harris practiced law at Gallatin in 1839, but soon turned his talents to wider fields, becoming a member of Congress in 1853, and a leading member of the Southern convention of 1861 that adopted the Ordinance of Secession. So influential was he in the troubled days at the outbreak of the war that he became the first delegate from Mississippi to the Montgomery congress that framed the Confederate Constitution. He was chosen a delegate by unanimous vote of the State convention. Throughout reconstruction he was scathing in his denunciation of the Ames Administration, and was openly an advocate of cooperation with the Liberal Republican movement. His last service to the State was as a member of the Constitutional Convention of 1890, where among men of tremendous stature he was still first in influence. His was the level head that determined many of Mississippi's decisions. This home in which he was reared is a simple one-story, central-halled dwelling with a long porch having six square columns.

At *10 m.* on State 20 is BROWNS WELLS (40 pop.), a health and pleasure resort built around seven wells containing large quantities of minerals. The first well was dug by Billie Brown before the War between the States, and shortly after the war a hotel and cottages were built to capitalize the wells' attractions. The resort is now a part of a 2,200-acre tract on which are week-end cottages, a dancing pavilion, a swimming pool, and a nine-hole golf course.

At *44.1 m.* on US 51 is a crossroad.

Left on this road is BEAUREGARD, *0.5 m.* (474 alt., 203 pop.), known as Bahala when the railroad was put through in 1857, but changed to Beauregard shortly after the war to honor Confederate General Beauregard. It is a lumber town formerly known for the number and size of its saloons; only three homes survived the cyclone of 1883, which destroyed most of the town. One of the three was on the estate of Benjamin King, a testy lawyer of Gallatin, who promoted the erection of the expensive courthouse at the latter town to protect his property rights against the railroad-made changes in population. The most interesting of the three houses, however, is the *DR. E. A. ROWAN PLACE*, with 23 rooms, first (1881) intended for a hospital but later made into a private home. Four sudden deaths in the Rowan family are responsible for the legend that the house is haunted. The story has been expanded and now includes the assertion that there is a standing reward for anyone who will spend a night alone with the ghosts in the dust-covered, cobwebbed place. A series of regular yet mysterious flaggings of Illinois Central R.R. trains in front of the house in 1926 grew so annoying as to call special detectives to the case, but the cause of the flaggings was never found.

WESSON, *46.7 m.* (799 pop.), is one of Mississippi's older mill towns, now devoting its attention to truck farming. It was named for Col. J. M. Wesson, who, when his plants in Choctaw Co. were destroyed by Federals in 1864, decided to make a new start in the pine woods. His first move was to build a sawmill. Soon he erected a cotton and woolen goods factory. The latter prospered, passing from the control of Colonel Wesson to a New Orleans company and growing rapidly between 1875 and 1891. One of the factories reached six stories in height and employed 1,200 people. In 1891, however, after the death of one of the backers, labor trouble began that culminated in the mills' going into receivership in 1906 and ceasing operations in 1910; during the World War the plant was torn down and the machinery and building material sold. Wesson is now the home of the *COPIAH-LINCOLN JUNIOR COLLEGE*, the largest junior college in the State. It is coeducational and State-supported.

At BROOKHAVEN, *54.8 m.* (500 alt., 5,288 pop.) *(see Tour 11)*, is the junction with US 84 *(see Tour 11)*.

Between Brookhaven and the Louisiana Line the pines grow thicker.

At *56.3 m.* is the model *DAIRY AND STOCK FARM*, on the former plantation of Samuel Jayne, who in 1818 came from New York State to clear a section of land for farming, and to operate a grist mill on the Bogue Chitto River. In time he built a one-room store, selling tobacco and calico to the little settlement around him and handing out the mail, which was delivered from Natchez. In 1851, when the New Orleans, Jackson & Great Southern R.R. came through, it missed the Jayne settlement by a mile and a half. Almost overnight the people began to move to the railroad, leaving Samuel Jayne, his little store, and his grist mill, but taking with them the name Brookhaven *(see Tour 11)* which Jayne had given the settlement. The Bogue Chitto River, which used to turn the little grist mill for Jayne, now supplies the cattle with water, and the old *JAYNE HOME,* with the long avenue of 100-year-old cedars leading to it, is used as a tenant house.

NORFIELD, 69.1 m. (1,399 pop.), once a prosperous sawmill town, has had a large exodus since the mill ceased operations in 1910.

Between the Pike Co. Line and the Louisiana Line, US 51 is a Memorial Highway for World War dead.

SUMMIT, 77.4 m. (430 alt., 1,157 pop.), like many Mississippi towns, was founded when the railroad was put through in 1857. Its elevation gave it its name.

Left from Summit on a paved road *1 m.* to the junction with another paved road; L. *0.7 m.* to the *SOUTHWEST MISSISSIPPI JUNIOR COLLEGE,* almost hidden in pines; it is one of the most attractive agricultural schools and junior colleges in the State.

McCOMB, *81.1 m.* (10,057 pop), is a railroad and manufacturing town, the largest on the Illinois Central R.R. between New Orleans and Jackson. Col. H. S. McComb, founder of the town, was president of the New Orleans, Jackson & Northern R.R. built in 1857 between New Orleans and Jackson. Colonel McComb's decision to establish the railroad shops here was responsible for the town's rapid growth. These shops were the biggest in the State and attracted a sturdy class of mechanics that became the backbone of the population. Also of influence in developing the town was the sawmill of Capt. J. J. White.

After the timber was cut, the settlers turned to raising cotton on the cleared lands, which caused the establishment of the *McCOMB COTTON MILL,* a block-long plant in South McComb employing 375 people and operating 20,000 spindles and 410 looms. Other mills in the town produce materials for upholstery and yarn, rayon, and silk garments. The *SOUTHERN UNITED ICE CO. PLANT* illustrates a fourth stage in the town's economic activities, from railroad servicing to sawmilling, to textile weaving, to truck farming. This ice plant has a capacity of 180 tons a day; it annually services the 5,000 refrigerator cars used in the truck-farming belt along the Illinois Central R.R. If necessary the plant can ice 50 cars at one time. The city school system is one of the finest in the State.

Here is the junction with State 24 *(see Tour 13).*

At 88.2 m. is the junction with State 48, a graveled road.

Right on this road to the PERCY QUIN STATE PARK, *3.5 m.* (L), a 1,480-acre tract now in process of development *(see Tour 13).*

MAGNOLIA, *88.7 m.* (415 alt., 1,660 pop.), the seat of Pike Co., has several times won a State prize offered for clean and well-kept streets. It was named for the number of magnolias growing on the banks of the little stream running through the eastern edge of the town. A large cotton mill is the town's chief industrial plant.

Between Magnolia and the Louisiana Line, US 51 runs through some of the loveliest pine forests left in Mississippi.

At *95 m.* is the junction with a graveled road.

Left on this road through oaks and pines so thick they make a twilight shade to *ST. MARY OF THE PINES, 1.2 m.*, a Catholic school for girls under the management of the Sisters of Notre Dame. These sisters came to Chatawa from Milwaukee in 1874 to open a day school for children of the village, and in 1879 they bought the present grounds and convent from the Redemptorist Fathers, who had closed their seminary after the yellow fever scourge in 1878.

Under the superintendence of Sister Charissia the pine-clad hills have been delightfully developed. The convent and the chapel are ante-bellum brick and stone buildings in Renaissance style. A dormitory and a music conservatory, a lake and outdoor swimming pool, and recreation courts have been built. The course of study is of high school rank, and St. Mary's is fully accredited. Half of the resident students are from Louisiana Catholic families.

OSYKA, *98.5 m.* (251 alt., 750 pop.), has the rustic stamp of Mississippi, though as a dairying town it is economically closer to New Orleans.

At *98.9 m.* US 51 crosses the Louisiana Line, marked by a cattle gap and a spreading liquor stand just on the other side, 100 miles N. of New Orleans, La.

Tour 6

(Tuscaloosa, Ala.)—Columbus—Winona—Greenwood—Greenville—(Lake Village, Ark.). US 82.
Alabama Line to Arkansas Line, 168 m.
Columbus & Greenville R.R. parallels route throughout.
Graveled highway for most part with a few miles of concrete. Paving in process.
Accommodations in larger towns.

US 82, cutting across north central Mississippi, makes clear the geographical and cultural divisions of the area. The eastern section runs through the lower Tennessee Hills, then descends into the low-rolling Black Prairie Belt, where is Columbus, the center of the prairie's antebellum culture. West of the land of cattle and corn the route winds through the flatwoods of shortleaf pines, crossing the Big Black swamp, where farms are few and logs are "snaked" from the bottoms by straining teams of mules. Ascending from the swamplands by a devious 30-mile climb into Winona, the route next traverses the loam-covered Bluff Hills, a wooded section with small farms producing diversified crops. West of Carrollton the route drops abruptly to end on the Delta's flatness where plantations are extensive and cotton is king.

Crossing the Mississippi Line, *0 m.*, 50.9 miles W. of Tuscaloosa,

TOMBIGBEE RIVER BRIDGE, COLUMBUS

US 82 descends from the lower Tennessee Hills to the even contour of the prairie.

US 82 enters on Military Road; L. on 9th St. N.; R. on 1st Ave.
COLUMBUS, 9.4 m. (250 alt., 10,743 pop.) *(see COLUMBUS).*

Points of Interest. Ante-bellum homes, Mississippi State College for Women, Friendship Cemetery, and others.

Here is the junction with US 45 *(see Tour 4).*

The route continues on 1st Ave. N., crossing Tombigbee River, the W. city limit.

Between Columbus and Starkville the route penetrates the heart of Mississippi's dairy and cattle country. The land is fertile and gently rolling. For miles little is visible except herds of cattle and meadows of alfalfa and corn. At harvest time when the grain turns gold the landscape is a monotone—a vast stretch of gold spreading to the horizon.

STARKVILLE, 32 m. (362 alt., 3,612 pop.), formerly the local capital of an old agricultural aristocracy, has become a center of the pioneer dairying and cattle raising farmers of the State. Serving the country around it, the town supports a condensery and a creamery, and ships more cattle than any other town in the State. The first settlers, wealthy slaveholders from the Seaboard States, grew cotton exclusively in the black loam and only after the War between the States turned to other sources of profit. The town's physical appearance is ante-bellum; it has long streets of old-style houses and branching avenues lined by oaks.

MISSISSIPPI STATE COLLEGE, foot of Main St., is a standard four-

TWIN TOWERS, MISSISSIPPI STATE COLLEGE, STARKVILLE

year coeducational college supported by the State. Founded Feb. 28, 1878, as a land grant college *(see EDUCATION)*, with Stephen D. Lee as its first president, it was until 1930 known as Agricultural and Mechanical College. Until 1887 the only courses offered were agricultural ones. Farm boys from all parts of Mississippi came here for scientific knowledge to be applied on the working of their own acres. Expansion of functions started in 1887, when, in order to gather scientific information for instruction in agriculture, a system of experiment stations was inaugurated. Since then branch stations have been established in five major soil-type sections of the State to augment the research program of the central station located at the college.

In 1892 the curriculum was revised, and later the Schools of Engineering and Agriculture were opened. The School of Science was established in 1911, the School of Business in 1915. In 1936 a Graduate School was added. The Agricultural Extension Service is a branch of the school's activities, being directly under the administration of the president. In addition, the State Chemical Laboratory, the State Plant Board, and the State Livestock Sanitary Board are housed on the college grounds.

The college occupies a 4,000-acre tract of gently rolling land, 750 acres of which are set aside as a campus, with 18 buildings and 70 residences. There are numerous farms and pastures for experimental and demonstration purposes. No specific style of architecture has been followed in the buildings. The oldest is Main Dormitory opened October 6, 1880; the estimated value of buildings, equipment, and grounds is $7,500,000.

Left at the rear entrance of State College on a graveled road and R. at the fork to (R) the *OUTLAW HOUSE, 4.8 m. (private)*, a white frame two-story dwelling built in 1835 by Dorsey Outlaw who migrated from New Jersey. It follows faithfully Georgian Colonial lines and has slender columns on its two-story portico. A one-story wing breaks its otherwise symmetrical balance. The entrance doorway and mantels in the drawing room are hand carved, the work of a slave convict, who, it is said, worked shackled in chains. Floors throughout are of native walnut. All work, including interior furnishings, was done by slave labor.

At *6.5 m.* (R) is the *RICE HOME (open by appointment)*, built in 1842. It is similar to the Outlaw House in design, a two-story frame home with a square hipped roof, long green blinds, and slender columns. The house was built by Capt. John W. Rice, who owned 5,000 acres. All labor on the house was done by slave carpenters.

At *9.1 m.* on the graveled road is a junction with an unmarked road; L. here *1.4 m.* to *GIBEON (open)*, the oldest house in Oktibbeha Co. It stands upon a knoll overlooking the wheel ruts of the old Robinson Road. No one knows the builder of either the house or the road. Gibeon is constructed of hewn logs morticed at the corners and with the cracks daubed with mortar, and stands today on the original wooden-block foundation in fairly good condition. Originally there were two rooms, one on each side of a wide dog-trot. Later a second story was added, a duplicate of the first, with an exposed stairway leading up from the downstairs central hall. Whatever its origin, Gibeon was a tavern stop on the Robinson Road in 1820, when the route became the chief artery of travel between Nashville, Tenn., and Jackson, Miss. At that time the owner was David Folsom, half-breed Choctaw chief, who had moved his family over from Pigeon Roost on the Natchez Trace to live on the newer highway. Here travelers rested overnight, and horses, jaded from the long trip through forest and swamp, were changed for fresh ones. After the Treaty of Dancing Rabbit Creek, Folsom sold the house to William Shaw and moved to Oklahoma with his tribesmen. Indian territory was being opened at the time, and the new host welcomed highway robbers and honest settlers alike, matching his customers glass for glass at the bar. Soon the place became notorious for its rowdy character. N. of Gibeon is a *CEMETERY* in which are graves of victims who died here in drunken brawls.

At *1.7 m.* on the unmarked road is the *SITE OF THE CHOCTAW AGENCY* (L), marked by a small frame store. The place today is a backwoods voting precinct.

At Starkville is the junction with State 23.

1. Left from Starkville on State 23 to the *MONTGOMERY HOME, 1.3 m. (open by appointment)*, built in 1839 by David Montgomery and modeled after a two-story 18th century English dwelling. It is marked by restraint of treatment, no unnecessary details detracting from its good proportion. Long green blinds hang at the small-paned windows, and walls and columns are white. Brick chimneys, mellowed to a faint rose, flank the ends. The house sits on a knoll in a grove of ancient and ivy-covered cedars. Beneath the cedars are beds of old-fashioned flowers.

2. Left from Starkville on Louisville St. to the *GILLESPIE HOME, 0.5 m.*, a two-story house designed in what is a good example of the Prairie's adaptation of the Greek Revival style. It was built in 1850 by Dr. James Gillespie.

Between Starkville and Mathiston are the dairy and stock farms that supply the Starkville market. Silos are as familiar a detail of this landscape as are the gins and compresses in the Delta scene.

MATHISTON, *53 m.* (405 alt., 484 pop.), is a railroad village where life revolves about the comings and goings of the daily train. At train time natives gather about the low frame depot; when the train arrives the bulky mail bag is tossed off, milk cans are packed in the baggage car, a few passengers climb aboard, and the train pulls away. Activity is then transferred to the post office. Young and old gather to visit while the mail is being put up—one of the pleasantest of village customs.

On the northern edge of the town is *WOOD JUNIOR COLLEGE*, organized in 1885 as Woodland Seminary, and known from 1900 to 1936 as Bennett Academy. At that time its name was changed to Wood Junior College in honor of Dr. and Mrs. I. C. Wood of Logan, Iowa, philanthropists. The school, with its frame and brick buildings grouped on a 48-acre tract donated by the citizens of Mathiston, is now under the management of the Women's Home Missionary Society of the Methodist Episcopal Church. In addition to the campus proper are several hundred acres used for farming and dairying.

At Mathiston is a *NATCHEZ TRACE MARKER* erected by the D. A. R.

West of Mathiston the prairie rises gradually, merging with the first ridges of the Central Hills. Cotton patches replace the cornfields, and the large painted farmhouses of the prairie disappear, dwellings here being of the smaller two-room houses of dog-trot type.

EUPORA, *61.4 m.* (1,092 pop.), is one of the largest poultry and egg markets in the State. A neat town with wide paved streets shaded by tall hardwood trees and vacant lots converted into well-kept parks, it now has a peaceful, smoothly flowing life antithetical with that of its past. At one time it was notorious for its feuds, killings, and lynchings. In the latter part of the 19th century feuds were constant and difficulties were settled without assistance of the law. Property rights, wills, love, and marriage were causes of violent family controversy; hot tempers were cooled by gunfire and arguments settled by a rope attached to the limb of a tall oak tree. The bloodiest feud was that between the Gray and Edwards factions—a feud that grew out of dispute over property rights and ended years later with the wholesale murder of the Grays at the Greensboro jail, eight miles from Eupora. Old-timers still spin stories of these violent days, and on the byways leading from town can point out trees that supported the body of a mob victim at one time or another.

West of Eupora the range of hills is wide. The highway skims the top of one ridge then another, and winds down through wooded hillsides to peaceful low-lying valleys. Terracing is necessary on the hillsides, where hardy cotton crops clutch at footholds in the thin top soil. Few tenant cabins are visible, for farm owners do their own plowing and reaping, or call in a neighbor to help when work is too heavy.

KILMICHAEL, *79.5 m.* (359 alt., 577 pop.), began as one small store built and operated by Sam Baines in 1845. The name was suggested by an early Irish settler. The *JAMES W. KNOX HOME*, 200 yds. E. of depot on US 82, was erected in 1858 with slave labor. Of the usual plantation type, the house has pillars and chimneys of homemade brick.

WINONA (Ind., *first born daughter*), *91 m.* (386 alt., 2,607 pop.), on the line between the swampland to the E. and the Mississippi-Yazoo Delta to the W., is the small center of a fertile hill-farms district. A majority of its stores were opened decades ago; its families are old; its comfortable quietness is broken only on Saturdays, when there are the bustling conversations and hand-shakings typical of a Mississippi trading center. The narrow streets are heavily shaded with elms, oaks, and locusts. Many of the houses were built in the latter part of the 19th century, though a few ante-bellum ones remain. Here are a cheese factory, a cotton mill, and a hickory mill.

On May 4, 1883, W. V. Money and James K. Vardaman took charge of the newspaper, *The Winona Advance,* with Vardaman as the editor. Shortly after 1890 the name of the paper was changed to *The Winona Democrat,* a change indicative of the feeling in the State at the time. As editor, Vardaman catered to the tenant farmers and working men of Mississippi, championing their cause in revolutionary editorials. When he entered politics late in the 19th century he carried his ideals with him and, after a heated campaign, became Governor in 1903. After his governorship he was elected to the National Senate where he remained until defeated by Byron Patton Harrison in 1918 *(see Tour 5)*. Vardaman's popularity was unrivaled in the State until he opposed Wilson's war measure in 1917, and lost his seat in the Senate. He returned to Mississippi, a broken old man, and died at his home in Greenwood, June 25, 1930. Known as the "Great White Chief," Vardaman, with his long white hair, wide-brimmed hats and frock coats, was a picturesque figure. He drove about the countryside in a buckboard during his campaigns and never failed to arouse his constituents with his cry of "Nigger, Nigger," symbolic of his racial prejudice.

At 316 Summit St. is the *OLDEST HOUSE IN MONTGOMERY CO.,* a two-story, rambling, white frame home, set far back from the street in a grove of willow, elm, and oak trees. Six thick columns reach to the roof from the front gallery. On the upper floor is a small balcony. The original log structure built nearly a century ago has been added to and remodeled, but the general outline of the original house has been retained. The two large front rooms have walls of sheathed logs; these rooms lead into a large hall from which rises a stairway; in the rear are the dining room, kitchen, and servants' stairway. The house was built by Col. O. J. Moore, who owned the land upon which the town was built. It was here that Miss Ella Moore, his daughter, gave Winona its name.

West of Winona the highway runs through thickly wooded hills.

At *93 m.* (R) are the slight *REMAINS OF OLD MIDDLETON,* the town that preceded Winona. On the site are a house and an old cemetery enclosed by a dilapidated brick fence. When the cemetery was laid out, Middleton citizens dug a deep ditch around it to keep wild animals away from the graves; traces of the ditch are still visible. Middleton's only remaining house, the *C. G. PACE HOME,* is a large, fairly well-preserved frame structure standing far back in a grove of cedars. Built with slave labor, the house has a chimney upon which is inscribed "1837 Harvey Merritt." The nucleus of the town of Middleton was a log cabin store owned by Ireton C. Devane in the early 1820's. Indian trails crossed here, and the first public road in Carroll Co., extending from Carrollton to Greensboro, ran by the place. The settlement was named for its central position between Carrollton and Shongalo (now Vaiden).

At its height of prosperity Middleton had 8 or 10 stores, a newspaper called *The Family Organ,* a girls' school called Judson Institute (later Middleton Female Academy) and a boys' school, People's Academy (later Middleton Male Academy). The female college was Baptist and the male Methodist; such a hot religious controversy arose between the two when a site for the State University was being sought that Middleton lost the honor. The town was almost deserted when the railroad established the station of Winona; the remainder was destroyed in a Federal raid during the War between the States.

NORTH CARROLLTON, *102.8 m.* (394 pop.), runs into OLD CARROLLTON, *103.7 m.* (229 alt., 523 pop.), one of the oldest towns in north central Mississippi, its written records beginning in 1834. Settled by a landed aristocracy, made wealthy by cotton, and now devitalized by the development of other towns in richer soils, Old Carrollton has still a certain pleasant charm salvaged from the glory of the past. The town was named in honor of Charles Carroll, a signer of the Declaration of Independence. Carrollton's weekly newspaper carries, significantly, the name under which it was first published, *The Conservative.* Carrolltown was the home of Hernando De Soto Money (1839–1912). A planter and editor by profession, Senator Money represented the State in the National Congress almost without interruption from 1875 to 1911.

1. Right from North Carrollton just E. of the railroad crossing, to COTESWORTH *(private), 1.6 m.,* home of the late Sen. J. Z. George, whose greatest achievement was the framing of the present constitution of Mississippi. The entrance to the 900-acre estate is marked by large iron gates hung from brick pillars. About 135 acres are farmed; the remaining acres are in pasture and timber land. The grounds immediately surrounding the house have beautiful formal flower and fern beds, and cedars and red oaks, some of which are more than a century old. The charming old home is two stories high with a columned portico. The furnishings are still those of Senator George. George named the place for his friend, Judge Cotesworth Pinckney Smith of the State's Court of Errors and Appeals, now the supreme court. The estate was willed to W. Cott George for life with the understanding that he, in turn, leave it to any other of the heirs of J. Z. George who were in good standing with the Baptist Church. Thus it came into the possession of Mrs. Lizzie George Henderson of Greenwood, who had it repaired.

2. Right from North Carrollton on the old Greenwood highway which winds picturesquely through forests green with pine and cedar to *MALMAISON (open, 25¢), 10.3 m.* This palatial old home of Greenwood Leflore, last Choctaw chieftain, was built in 1854 as a successor to the log house built by Leflore in 1835. Named for the home in which the Empress Josephine found refuge after her divorce from Napoleon, the house shows both French and Southern Colonial

MALMAISON, NORTH CARROLLTON

influences in its architecture. It is a two-story white frame structure with massive grooved columns on the porticos. Long narrow galleries extend the length of the house on both sides. Irregularly placed are iron grillwork balconies. On the roof is an observatory enclosed by elaborately designed iron railings. From here Leflore's beloved Teoc (Ind. *place of tall pines*) country is visible for miles.

Fourteen immense rooms, seven on each floor, open off the wide hallways that cross in the center of the house. Their furnishings were designed for Leflore by Parisian decorators. In the parlor is a Louis XIV suite finished in gold leaf and upholstered in rich red brocaded damask. On the walls large gold-framed mirrors alternate with murals of French and Swiss scenes. On the linen curtains are painted pictures of the French palaces, Malmaison, St. Cloud, Fontainebleau, and Versailles. The library contains portraits of Colonel Leflore, his wife, and daughter. Beneath the portrait of Leflore hang a sword and belt presented to him by the U.S. Government upon his election as Chief of the Choctaw.

Greenwood Leflore, the son of Louis LeFleur, French trader and trapper (*see JACKSON*), and Rebecca Crevat, niece of Pushmataha, was born at LeFleur's Bluff (now Jackson) in 1800 and named for an English sea-captain. He was adopted by Maj. John Donley, who owned a stage line on the Natchez Trace, and was educated in Nashville. In 1819 he married the major's daughter Rose and returned with her to Mississippi shortly afterward. In 1824, when for the first time a Choctaw chief was chosen by general election, the honor went to Leflore. He effected many reforms among his people, notable among which was abolition of witchcraft practices and the establishment of schools for Indian children. For 10 years Leflore was tireless in his efforts to raise the standard of living among the Choctaw. He was in his thirties, tall, handsome, and at the height of his power, when a conference was called at Dancing Rabbit Creek to decide upon the sale of Choctaw lands to the United States (*see Tour* 4). Because he realized that the treaty was inevitable and sponsored it, Leflore was condemned as a traitor by his tribe. It was through his influence, however, that an amendment was added whereby an Indian who desired to remain in the State received a section of land and enjoyed full protection of the Government. Leflore, after the removal of a majority of the Choctaw, lost face with the remaining members of his tribe. His later prestige came entirely from his standing with white men. As a cotton planter he prospered greatly during the period 1840–60. He was elected to the lower house of the State legislature in 1835 and to the Senate in 1844. For his third wife, Priscilla Donley, sister to Rose Donley, he built Malmaison, expressing in it both his Indian love of display and his planter wealth. Leading to Malmaison was a clay and cinder road, the first attempted hard-surfacing of a road in the State. With the outbreak of the War between the States, Leflore was ostracized by Indians and Southern whites alike. He refused to give up his United States citizenship and to support the Confederacy, and throughout the war the United States flag flew over Malmaison. On one occasion an attack was made on his life by Confederates; at another time a fire of incendiary origin broke out at Malmaison. When he died, August 21, 1865, he was wrapped for burial in the flag he loved and interred on a hillside near Malmaison.

US 82 turns L. on Carrollton Ave.; R. on Fulton St.
GREENWOOD, 117.9 m. (143 alt., 11,123 pop.) *(see GREENWOOD)*.

Points of Interest. Cotton gins, compresses, Terry collection of Leflore relics, and others.

The route continues N. on Fulton St., which crosses the Yazoo River to become Grand Blvd.; L. on US 82.

At Greenwood is the junction with US 49 E *(see Side Tour 7A)*.

Between Greenwood and the route's end the Delta's flatness increases. This is the State's last purely agrarian stronghold, with cotton-growing absorbing the interest of the people and the landscape.

ITTA BENA, (Ind., *home in the woods*), 123.2 m. (125 alt., 1,370 pop.), was named by Greenwood Leflore. It is the home of the *LEFLORE CO. TEACHERS' TRAINING SCHOOL FOR NEGROES.*

BERCLAIR, 124.2 m., is a fishing village on Blue Lake *(fishing free; boats, with Negro boys as paddlers, are rented at 50¢ a day)*.

MOORHEAD, 136.1 m. (1,553 pop.), one of the new Delta cotton towns surrounded by many small cotton farms, is situated "where the Southern crosses the Dog," an expression arising from the friendly rivalry that existed between the Southern and the Yazoo & Mississippi Valley Railroads, which cross at right angles in Moorhead; the latter was derisively called the Yellow Dog by its competitor. The town, so low that it is always threatened by floods, suffers whenever there is overflow in the Delta. In the latter part of the 1880's a timber man gave his own name to the bayou; soon afterward Chester Henry Pond of Illinois cleared 10 acres on the banks of the bayou and built a stave mill, a cotton mill, and, later, an oil mill. The town was incorporated as Moorhead in 1899. A college for Negro girls, established in 1891 by Pond's sister and supported by the Methodist Missionary Society of New York, was abandoned in 1928. The *SUNFLOWER JUNIOR COLLEGE,* established in 1912, became a junior college in 1926. This is a fully accredited, State-supported coeducational institution.

Between Moorhead and Indianola is an unending chain of cotton fields, dotted with tenant cabins, gins, compresses, and residences.

INDIANOLA, *144 m.* (117 alt., 3,116 pop.), *(see Tour 7A),* is at the junction with US 49 W *(see Tour 7, Sec. a).*

At *154 m.* is a junction with a graveled road.

Left on this road *0.6 m.* to DUNLEITH *(open by appointment),* once valued at $1,000,000, and considered one of the finest of the Delta's plantations, with a tile drainage system and every modern convenience. The rambling stucco constructed house, with a red tile roof, is built upon an Indian mound from which artifacts have been removed.

LELAND, *151.8 m.* (113 alt., 2,426 pop.) *(see Tour 3, Sec. a),* is at the junction with US 61 *(see Tour 3, Sec. a).*

Between Leland and Greenville the highway passes through a wealthy plantation section, with modern planter houses of brick and stone, and frame Negro cabins. Everywhere in this part of the Delta are signs of good years in which the planter has lived bountifully on the products of the land.

GREENVILLE, *162 m.* (125 alt., 14,807 pop.) *(see Side Tour 3A),* is at the junction with State 1 *(see Side Tour 3A).*

Between Greenville and Warfield landing, *168 m.,* on the Mississippi River, US 82 extends between two levees and, as it passes over the line of the first, the river is visible in a rolling yellow sweep. *(Ferry service 6 a.m. to 2 a.m.; leaves Mississippi side on the hour, Arkansas side on half hour; automobile with driver $1; 25¢ passengers.)*

Tour 7

Clarksdale—Indianola—Yazoo City—Jackson—Hattiesburg—Gulfport. US 49, US 49W.

Clarksdale to Gulfport, 317 m.

Yazoo & Mississippi Valley R.R. parallels route between Clarksdale and Jackson; Gulf & Ship Island between Jackson and Gulfport.
Route paved throughout; two lanes wide.
Tourist accommodations in larger towns.

Sec. a CLARKSDALE *to* JACKSON, *157.6 m.,* US 49, 49W.

US 49 swings southward through the Delta and, until it meets the bluff hills at Yazoo City, in a hundred miles gives a good presentation of the new Delta and the old. The rapidly growing towns in the northern section have for the most part been established since 1900; many of the extensive plantations lying between them are owned and operated by corporations. Southward, the route traverses a section along the Yazoo River that is part of a land grant settled by Alvarez Fisk in the 1820's. Here along the river's bank and in the network of lakes that cut this country into hundreds of small islands are a number of the Delta's oldest homes. In these durable houses live descendants of the original landholders, growing cotton on the same plantations their ancestors cleared more than 100 years ago. In the summer the Delta is first a great field of green plants, then, after the bolls appear, a vast whiteness of cotton with the shapes of Negro pickers silhouetted against it in bold relief. In the winter the land lies sluggish, a rich black bog of unending flatness, while the rivers and bayous rise to stand level with the levees. In early spring come the overflows. Southeastward from Yazoo City US 49 crosses the hills that separate the Pearl River valley from the Yazoo basin. The bluff country is studded with shortleaf pine and hardwood trees, with the bottom lands cleared for farming.

At CLARKSDALE, *0 m.* (173 alt., 10,043 pop.), is the junction with US 61 *(see Tour 3, Sec. a).*

The section S. between Clarksdale and Yazoo City is perhaps the most uniform of the State, the scenery, the evenly spaced towns, and the social and economic interests giving it the atmosphere of a large, friendly neighborhood.

MATTSON, *7.5 m.* (163 alt., 200 pop.). De Soto's expedition passed immediately S. of here, and Charlie's Trace cut directly through the center of the village. Charlie's Trace, alleged to have been made by a Choctaw Indian, was a short cut from Sunflower Landing on the Mississippi River to a point in the hills 12 miles S. of Charleston, Miss. It was often the route of the outlaws who marauded through this section in the early 1800's. An *INDIAN MOUND* in the center of the village is made conspicuous by a small cemetery perched on top of it. The mound, said to have contained approximately 50 burials, has been excavated by archeologists from the Smithsonian Institution and artifacts have been removed.

At TUTWILER, *15.8 m.* (157 alt., 873 pop.), US 49 forks into US 49W (R), which this route follows, and US 49E *(see Side Tour 7A).* Tutwiler is strung along Hobson Bayou in typical Delta fashion, the residences on one side and the stores on the other. The bayous, which run like veins through the Delta, are distinguishing marks upon a majority of the towns and, with grassy banks accented by willow and cypress trees, are spots of natural beauty. In the fall the cypress trees turn rusty red, giving color to an otherwise somber scene. Tutwiler, like all Delta towns, is liveliest on Saturday, when people from outlying plantations come in to trade.

ROME, *20.7 m.* (146 alt., 250 pop.), for all its grandiose name is a plantation town. The daily train of the branch line of the Yazoo & Mississippi Valley R.R., stopping here to pick up bales of cotton and an occasional passenger, is known locally as the Yellow Dog, commemorating the stray canine that used to chase the train through the village each time it passed.

At PARCHMAN, *24.0 m.* (140 alt., 250 pop.), is the *MISSISSIPPI PENAL FARM,* a prison operated on an agricultural system. The farm is a typical Delta plantation, consisting of 15,497 acres planted in cotton, corn, and truck, with cotton the leading crop. The prisoners, separated into small groups, live in camps. The present (1937) number of prisoners is 1,989. A brick yard, a machine shop, a gin, and a storage plant are operated by convict labor. The prison is self-supporting and operates at a profit when the price of cotton is good. The "fifth Sunday" of months that have more than four Sabbath days is visitors' day, and it is then that Parchman is best seen. A train called the Midnight Special brings the visitors to the farm, arriving about dawn and leaving at dusk. The Negro prisoners have made up ballads about the train, which they sing and chant while they work, waiting for fifth Sunday. One song is:

"Heah comes yo' woman, a pardon in her han'
Gonna say to de boss, I wants mah man,
Let the Midnight Special shine its light on me."

Between Parchman and Indianola the Delta's largest plantations are concentrated. In late summer the fields are solid with white bolls; in winter they are singularly colorless, the furrowed ground covered with the previous year's cotton stalks. Against the encircling sweep of skyline are blurred the bare branches of trees.

WHITNEY, *29.1 m.* (26 pop.), is headquarters for the Gritman-Barksdale plantation, owned and operated by a large Northern life insurance company. Divided into small tracts, the acreage of the plantation is worked by tenants on the sharecropper system.

Cotton fields stretching out interminably for miles on both sides of the highway are dotted with the tenants' cabins, each with its small front porch, a cistern, and a garden for growing vegetables, and each shaded by a chinaberry tree or two. The furnishings are few, usually consisting only of beds and chairs. When the families are large, the children often sleep on pallets on the floor.

DREW, *31.7 m.* (136 alt., 1,373 pop.), is a pleasant town typical of the new Delta in its lack of provincialism. Drawing a wealthy planter trade, the shops cater to expensive tastes for smart frocks, shoes, hats, and the latest novelties. Restaurants offer a good cuisine. Drew citizens have forgotten the roomy Southern Planter type of architecture to build compact English and Georgian Colonial cottages.

RULEVILLE, *37.7 m.* (131 alt., 1,181 pop.), like Drew, draws a substantial prosperity from the surrounding plantations. Here is a privately supported Chinese school for the children of the few Chinese families here and in Drew.

COTTONDALE, *40.2 m.*, is a group of neatly whitewashed tenant cabins clustered around a spreading, white frame plantation big house. The plantation bell in the yard is typical of the Delta, being used to summon hands from the fields. When rung its noisy clang is heard to the most remote corners of the plantation.

At *40.6 m.* is the junction with a graveled road.

Left on this road *0.9 m.* to an EXPERIMENTAL VOCATIONAL SCHOOL FOR NEGROES, established in 1914. The school consists of a one-story frame administration building, a professor's home, a frame bungalow type dormitory for faculty members and girl students, and 12 acres of land. Besides the regular vocational subjects, with emphasis on agriculture and home economics, the school offers a regular four year high school course. It is supported jointly by Federal and county funds and has approximately 230 students.

At *42.1 m.* is DODDSVILLE (124 alt., 317 pop.), a plantation center for trading and shipping cotton.

Toward the S. the preponderance of Negroes is striking. About the plantation stores a majority of the people are Negroes, and practically all the tenant cabins are occupied by Negroes. The Negroes' aged automobiles and slow-moving mule teams furnish a large part of the traffic along the highways.

At *50.4 m.* is the village of SUNFLOWER (117 alt., 530 pop.). On plantations in the vicinity perhaps more cotton is grown per acre than in any other part of the State.

South of Sunflower the highway passes through a swamp fairly well wooded with cypress, oak, and holly trees to cross Sunflower River at *36.8 m.*

At *55.3 m.* is the junction with a graveled road.

Left on this road *0.6 m.* to *FAISONIA PLANTATION* with a story-and-a-half Georgian Colonial type cottage, unpretentious but roomy and gracious appearing. A large veranda is screened against mosquitoes, and the house sits high on brick pilings to protect it from Delta floods. About the house are many things that make for comfortable plantation life—shade of live oak, cedar, and pecan trees, servants' quarters, a carriage house (now used as a garage), fruit trees, and an artesian well. The boat landing on the river is a reminder of the days when Sunflower River was navigable and cotton was shipped downstream to New Orleans by boats that came back laden with imported luxuries. The plantation was bought by George W. Faison during the War between the States.

At *58.5 m.* on US 49W is the junction with US 82 *(see Tour 6).*

INDIANOLA, *59 m.* (117 alt., 3,116 pop.), the county seat of Sunflower on cypress-shaded Sunflower River, developed on a clearing made near Indian Bayou in the late 1830's. Ginning and compressing, along with administering justice, are its chief businesses.

Between Indianola and Inverness, "red cotton," a variety recently imported and grown with success in this area, adds color to the landscape.

INVERNESS, *67 m.* (112 alt., 683 pop.), was named for the Scottish city by a native who gave the railroad a right-of-way through her plantation. Though many plantation settlements had been made in the vicinity much earlier, the town was not settled until 1904.

Right from Inverness on a graveled road to HOLLYWOOD, *2.2 m. (open by permission),* an early American 17th century type house built in 1855. It was erected exclusively with slave labor, and bricks, puncheons, floors, walls, and joists were hand-made. Logs used for walls are 50 feet long and are pinned together with wooden pegs, the cracks being filled with sassafras blocks and plaster to make them airtight. The house sits upon a high ridge, and when built was surrounded by a grove of holly trees. During the flood of 1882 all the cattle of the section were driven here for protection, and when hay gave out the holly trees were cut and fed to them. One of the owners of the house was killed in an upstairs room by a Negro slave, and his ghost is alleged to haunt the house today.

Between Inverness and Yazoo City the highway penetrates the lake country of the Delta. This is the rendezvous for fishermen and hunters throughout the State. In the labyrinth of streams game fish abound, and even wild turkeys, deer, and foxes are in the dense woods along their banks. Cotton fields still figure predominantly on the scene but, with the usual gins and compresses, large sawmills show themselves in the towns. At 71.2 m. is the junction with a graveled road.

Right on this road to the PRENTISS MOUND, 1.6 m., standing 20 feet high and well wooded. Built by the Indians in prehistoric times, the mound was given local fame when Seargent S. Prentiss addressed a group of Jackson lawyers from its summit in 1841. The lawyers were on a bear hunting trip and Prentiss' speech, in a light vein, was said to be "not for publication."

At 73.7 m. the highway crosses LAKE DAWSON, a narrow winding stream, its bank outlined by cypress trees. Fishing here is excellent.

ISOLA, 73 m. (107 alt., 519 pop.), on the banks of Lake Dawson, was established in what was then a wilderness abounding in deer, wildcats, foxes, turkeys, and bears. The name was given to suggest its remote location. Two years later a large sawmill was built on the banks of the lake and as the country was gradually cleared other mills were established. Lumbering gives the town its tone today.

The further S. the route goes, the more scenic it is, with frequent hardwood forests breaking the monotony of featureless cotton fields, and ribbons of lakes winding through the flat land.

BELZONI, 83.1 m. (124 alt., 2,735 pop.), is a part of the section purchased by Alvarez Fisk in 1827. Fisk laid out streets, measured off lots, named his town Fisk's Landing, and then waited for buyers to come, amusing himself meanwhile hunting and fishing on his plantation. The influx of settlers, however, was less than Fisk expected. At the time of the War between the States only a dozen or more families had arrived at Fisk's town, now called Belzoni in honor of the Italian archeologist, Giovanni Battista Belzoni, an acquaintance of Fisk's. When Grant was planning the siege of Vicksburg, he sent a fleet of 19 gunboats up the Yazoo River to open the way to that city. The boats gave out of fuel on the way, and the Federal soldiers stopped at the squat log HOUSE OF STEVE CASTLEMAN on the river, where they knocked down fences and took them away to burn for fuel. The W. S. KNOTTS HOME, Jackson St., faces the Yazoo River from the top of an Indian mound. The house marks the original site of Fisk's Landing.

The Yazoo River parallels the route between Belzoni and Silver City. In this section the watermarks on houses and trees tell the history of past Delta floods. During high water in the spring, when the river overflows its banks, a majority of the occupants of the cabins in the river flats "refugee" to the hills.

SILVER CITY, 89.1 m. (361 pop.), is sprawled perilously close to the banks of Silver Creek, but is protected from its high water by a steep levee. Formerly the village was called Palmetto Home for the plantation around which it grew. The first house was recently burned but palmettos growing luxuriantly around the marshes of the creek indicate why it was so called. The J. PARASOTT HOUSE, on Silver Creek, is a dogtrot duplex. Two brothers built the house of logs in the 1850's, separating

CULTIVATING A FIELD OF YOUNG COTTON

duplicate living quarters by a wide central hall. This hall has now been enclosed, and the logs have been weatherboarded, but the design of the house remains unchanged.

Between Silver City and Yazoo City the cotton fields fast lose themselves in densely wooded swamps, the country becomes more sparsely settled, and the Yazoo River constantly appears and disappears (L). An occasional gloomy stretch of swampland, rank with cypress, palmettos, and low thickets, and overshadowed with gray moss, gives a vivid conception of the old Delta area before clearings were made and levees built.

MIDNIGHT, *94.1 m.* (250 pop.), was born of a poker game played beside a campfire in the dismal swamp here 50 or more years ago by a party of hunters. One of the men laid claim to the land upon which they had stopped, placing it as a bet. He lost. The winner, looking at his watch, said, "Well, boys, it's midnight, and that's what I'm going to call my land." He settled here to build the first house upon the exact spot where they had camped that night.

At *99.5 m.* (R), visible from the highway, is an INDIAN MOUND. It is especially conspicuous because of a plantation bell perched on its summit.

South to Yazoo City the highway winds. Festooning moss drapes the trees, making the woodlands perennially picturesque, while their density makes them an excellent habitat for wild game.

As the highway crosses Yazoo River, *113.2 m.*, the Yazoo Bluffs, visible in the foreground, give a striking contrast of Delta with hills.

YAZOO CITY, *114.6 m.* (120 alt., 5,579 pop.), offers a contrast of Delta with bluffs, part of it being built on a low flat bordering the river, and the other perched precipitously on steep hills above. The town was established in 1824 as Hanan's Bluff, and for many years, with its booming river trade, was a more important town than Jackson. It was incorporated in 1830 as Manchester, in 1839 its name was changed to Yazoo City. During the War between the States major battles and a great many skirmishes took place on the river. At low-water periods the hulk of an old gunboat sunk by the Federals is visible. In 1904 fire swept the town and destroyed its ante-bellum homes and buildings. Rebuilt since that time, Yazoo City is modern in appearance. During the flood of 1927, a large Red Cross camp for refugees stood on the bluff above the river, sheltering people from the vast inundated area in northwest Mississippi. Yazoo City is the birthplace (1867) of Rear Admiral Thomas Pickett Magruder, D.S.M., now retired from active service.

1. Left from Yazoo City on the Benton road to CEDAR GROVE PLANTATION, *11 m.*, home of John Sharp Williams (1854–1932), who was for many years a leading figure in Mississippi politics. He served the State in the National Senate for 25 years, where he became famous for his oratory and racy repartee. In *An Old Fashioned Senator,* Harris Dickson has given a good characterization of Williams. The house at Cedar Grove, a rambling story-and-a-half dwelling with green shutters, red chimneys, and an entrance portico protected by a sloping shed roof, was built in 1838 by John Sharp, grandfather of Senator Williams. Sharp migrated from Tennessee, settling on a tract of 3,000 acres. Timbers for the house were cut from the woodlands, hewn, mortised, and pinned together by hand. The bricks were burned in a kiln on the place.

Originally the dining room and kitchen were separated from the main section, and in wintry weather it was necessary to wear an overcoat to breakfast. In late years the two parts of the house have been joined by a closed porch. A narrow stair climbs crookedly to the bedchambers above. Here John Sharp used to sit, shotgun in hand, guarding his sleeping wife and children from the Indians. His fear of the Choctaw, however, was unfounded, for it was their boast that no white person's blood was on their hands. The house sits in a deep cedar grove, and the grounds are informally landscaped with old-fashioned flowers and shrubs. Near the house in the family cemetery is the grave of Senator Williams.

2. Right from Yazoo City on State 3 is SATARTIA, *14.9 m.* (97 alt., 139 pop.), perhaps the oldest settlement in Yazoo Co. On the east bank of Yazoo River, during the early 1800's it was the shipping point from which the cotton of a wide area moved by steamboat to New Orleans. The climax of its importance was reached when General Grant sailed from Vicksburg on a gunboat and took the town during the War between the States. Since that time, like most Mississippi river towns, it has slowly receded in importance. Yet as long as the river curves around its western boundary, the memory of a romantic bustling river trade will endure. The *WILSON HOME (open by appointment)* is a two-story post-Colonial type house, with dormer windows front and back and square-cut columns upholding the front gallery. The house was built more than 100 years ago by Robert Wilson, who had cypress boards sent by steamboat from St. Louis to be used in its construction. Slaves on the plantation assisted a contractor in erecting the house, and the ornamental plaster in the interior is their handiwork. During the period of Grant's occupation of Satartia, the house was used as headquarters. On the walls of upstairs rooms are messages scratched in the plastering by Federal soldiers. Two of these are legible today: "How are you, Rebel?" and "To the owner of the house, your case is a hard one and I pity you." In spite of the downstairs rooms having been under water to a depth of 9 feet in past floods the house is in good repair.

TOUR 7   413

At *20.4 m.* on State 3 is CHURCHILL DOWNS PLANTATION. The plantation house *(open by appointment)* was built by Dr. Bonney in 1830, when he came from Kentucky to settle a tract of several thousand acres. It is similar to the Wilson home in architecture, with dormers on the second story and square columns on the gallery. Poplar timber, mortised and pinned together, is used throughout. Planking and weatherboarding were hand-sawed by the old whipsaw method. Brick for foundations were burned in a kiln on the plantation. All work was done by slaves. The place is named for the famous Kentucky racetrack, and on the old brick chimney, now ivy-covered, both the name and date of erection are scratched. During the War between the States jewelry, letters, and other valuables belonging to the Bonney family were hidden on the grounds. The hiding place has never been discovered.

South of Yazoo City the highway penetrates the bluff hills, where the loess has produced a jungle-like growth of vines and Spanish moss; US 49 then traverses a pleasantly rolling prairie, which is a fairly old and fairly prosperous truck farming belt.

FLORA, *137.6 m.* (250 alt., 513 pop.), between the hills and the prairie, retains something of its ante-bellum flavor in wide unpaved streets and rambling old-fashioned homes. It is, as it always has been, a trading center for outlying farms.

Left from railroad station in Flora *3.4 m.* to junction with a graveled road; R. here *0.6 m.* to the BELLE KEARNEY HOME *(open by permission)*. Set back from the road in a grove of cedars, the two-story rectangular white frame house has a double-decked gallery supported by six square columns across the front. The capitals of the columns and the second floor gallery railing are hand carved. The interior has four large square rooms on each side of a wide central hall. The house was built in the early 1850's by Col. W. R. Kearney, whose daughter, Belle, was associated with the prohibition and the woman suffrage movements. She was State president of the W.C.T.U., and later was commissioned to go around the world as a lecturer on temperance. In 1922 she was elected to the State Senate, the first woman in Mississippi to receive this distinction.

At *137.8 m.* is the junction with a narrow country road.

Right on this road to the PETRIFIED FOREST, *2.2 m. (open to public; free)*, on a ridge extending eastward that has been worn into a series of hills. The logs that give it its name project from a gully of ferruginous-sand and gravel in which they are buried. They vary in length from 3 to 20 feet. It is estimated by geologists that the logs became submerged during either the Pleistocene or near the end of the Tertiary Period. As no roots are evident, it is believed that the trees were swept into this region by prehistoric streams of great volume and violence. The rugged logs are subdued orange in color.

POCAHONTAS, *142.6 m.* (244 alt., 105 pop.), was named for the daughter of Virginia's leading Indian chief. Here is an INDIAN MOUND, rising 15 or 20 feet, that never has been excavated.

At *155.4 m.* US 49 enters on Bailey Ave.; L. on Monument St.; R. on N. Gallatin.

JACKSON, *157.6 m.* (294 alt., 48,282 pop.) *(see JACKSON).*

Points of Interest. Old Capitol, New Capitol, Livingston Park and Zoo, Hinds County Courthouse, Millsaps College, Belhaven College, Battlefield Park and others.

Here are the junctions with US 80 *(see Tour 2)* and with US 51 *(see Tour 5).*

Sec. b JACKSON to GULFPORT, 159.4 m.

South of Jackson US 49 passes through the Piney Woods, a long series of rolling red clay hills that were once covered with tremendous growths of longleaf yellow pine, but are now scattered with new trees, the skeletons of former mills, and mill towns. Near the southern end of the route the highway descends to a low coastal plain, and the resort section of the State.

East on South St.; R. on S. State; L. on Silas Brown St. in JACKSON, 0 m.

US 49 and US 80 run for a few miles through the center of a district of taverns and night clubs that are almost hidden in the gloomy Pearl River swamp. Fringing the swamp (L) is the State's largest gas producing field. In February 1930 the first well was brought in; the daily output is 3,640,000,000 cu. ft. These wells furnish gas for Bogalusa, La., Pensacola, Fla., and Mobile, Ala., as well as for many Mississippi towns.

At 2.3 m. US 80 (see Tour 2) and US 49 separate; R. on US 49.

At 18.6 m. is STAR (414 alt., 350 pop.), a town at the northeastern edge of the trucking belt. It was established in the late 1880's when the Gulf & Ship Island R.R. was pushing its way up from the Coast.

PINEY WOODS SCHOOL, 22.2 m. (L), a nondenominational Christian high school for colored boys and girls, was founded in 1909 by Laurence Clifton Jones. Diversified farming and industrial arts are taught here, 1,600 acres of land being used for experimental purposes. A side road leads to the administration building (guides furnished). The first building owned by the school, an OLD LOG CABIN donated to the founders when the school was established by a former slave, has been preserved and is protected by a wire fence. Much of the work on later buildings was done by students, who made the bricks and sawed the lumber by hand. The Piney Woods Singers, the name by which the school glee club is known, are famed for their rendition of Negro folksongs.

Between the school and the Coastal Meadow a few miles N. of Gulfport, US 49 shoots diagonally through the Piney Woods, a region of uneven topography originally covered by an unbroken expanse of longleaf pine timber and extending over the southern half of Mississippi. Until lumbering created fair sized towns in the wilderness, it was a primitive country, and this it remains except in the towns. The pines are still dense, and carpet the earth with pine needles in the few remaining areas where lumbering has not destroyed the trees. The people who settled here originally were uplanders, coming from Georgia and the Carolinas with the great migration of 1815. They were an independent-spirited people, brought no slaves with them, and settled far apart, clearing a few acres and building sturdy, compact log cabins. They made their living by raising sheep and by cultivating patches of potatoes and corn. After the War between the States, when the Gulf & Ship Island R.R. opened the country to the lumber industry, the Piney Woods became prosperous, then poor. Northern lumber companies bought

LONGLEAF PINES

vast areas, and the farmers, forsaking even small-scale agriculture, went to work in the lumber mills. The year 1911 saw the peak of lumbering; 360,000,000 feet of lumber were shipped from the harbor at Gulfport *(see GULFPORT)*. By 1930 the many widening acres of stripped timber lands had been united. The trees that gave the section its name were, for the most part, gone, and the great mills had closed their doors. Today the area tells its own story in the denuded hills, in the boarded-up ghost lumber towns, and in the gaunt, idle lumber mills; however, the small farms, the occasional dairies, the naval stores plants, and the efforts at reforestation offer evidences of reviving activity.

D'LO, *29.5 m.* (290 alt., 514 pop.), is a quiet little lumber town. Since the mill closed in 1930 there has been hardly more than a skeleton of the town that supported a hospital, a school, several streets of stores, and a great number of houses, all cut to a pattern. One story is that the early French explorers called Strong River, along which the town lies, *de l'eau* (Fr., *water*), and from their simple appellation, phonetically spelled, the town took its name; probably a more accurate one is that the name was chosen from a list submitted by the U. S. Post Office Department.

MENDENHALL, *32.1 m.* (334 alt., 919 pop.), is the center of an old farming community that has never been dependent upon the lumber industry. Once a month a Community Day is held here; farmers from a widespread area come together to take part in various contests. At the hotel on Main St. meals are served on a *REVOLVING TABLE,* one of the few left in the State.

SANATORIUM, *39.6 m.* (200 pop.), is an unusually large State-owned tuberculosis hospital *(guides; 9-4 weekdays)*. The sanatorium is in dry clean pinelands on a ridge, a spot well suited to the cure of the disease. Both Negro and white patients are cared for here. The modern fireproof buildings are in appearance rather like Southern Colonial homes. A library, a moving picture theatre, and an auditorium provide entertainment for the patients, and the sanatorium publishes its own newspaper, which is edited by patients. Operated in connection with the sanatorium, but separated from it, is a Preventorium for children under twelve years of age who have been exposed to tuberculosis but have not actually contracted it. Dr. Henry Boswell has been superintendent of the sanatorium since its founding.

MAGEE, *42.1 m.* (426 alt., 964 pop.), a substantial marketing town for truck and poultry, has a history that goes back to the 1820's, when the land in this section could be bought under the "Bit Act" for 12½ cents an acre. In 1859 Richard Farthing, a Virginian and a tanner by trade, came to Magee, then called Mangum in honor of Willie Mangum who had built the first grist mill here, and built a log house and tanyard near Mangum's Mill. In less than five years, Farthing was doing a thriving business. He contracted with the Confederate Government to make shoes for the soldiers and hauled wagonloads of them to headquarters himself. He became famous in south Mississippi not only for his army boots but for his red-top ones, which were kept for Sunday wear by the purchasers. *FARTHING'S HOUSE,* still in good repair, is an excellent example of the stoutly built pioneer cabin. At the home of Mrs. Mims Williams *(open by appointment)* is an unusually fine COLLECTION OF WOVEN PIONEER PRODUCTS.

MOUNT OLIVE, *50.6 m.* (325 alt., 812 pop.), takes its name from an old Presbyterian Church built on a hill N. of the town. It is a town gradually turning to farming after long dependence on lumbering.

South of Mount Olive the highway runs past a fairly good and fairly well-populated truck-farming section, contrasting sharply with the cut-over land immediately N. of Collins.

COLLINS, *60.7 m.* (274 alt., 935 pop.), stretches pleasantly along the slopes of a steep hill, with a courthouse that dwarfs the town. The town was wiped away in 1912 by a cyclone, but came to life again with the development of the lumber industry. Several large mills, built during the boom of the 1920's, stand idle today. Like most county seats, it is liveliest when court is in session. Virtually everyone in town attends the sessions, and court week is the occasion for a general holiday.

Between Collins and Hattiesburg is a country of small farms, peach orchards, and occasional areas with second-growth pine.

At *86.5 m.* the highway crosses the northern boundary of the LEAF RIVER FOREST RESERVE, a unit of the De Soto National Forest *(see Tour 8).* The reserve has 180 miles of graveled roads and five fire observation towers connected by 132 miles of telephone wires. The forest is being developed into game preserves and recreation centers.

At *85.6 m.* the highway crosses Leaf River.

HATTIESBURG, *88.2 m.* (143 alt., 18,601 pop.), is a town whose heart is in the noisy factory district from which rise the pungent odors of turpentine and cut pine; the city's sedate cultural life revolves around the campuses of two colleges. The community was established in the early 1880's by Captain Hardy, pioneer lumberman of Mississippi, and named for his wife. Unlike other towns of the longleaf pine belt, Hattiesburg was never wholly dependent upon the lumber industry for economic security. At the time of the lumber boom of the early 1920's, the city was well established as a railroad center and had several major industrial plants, which kept it from being affected appreciably by the period of inflation and the subsequent crash. With timber practically exhausted, Hattiesburg is following the trend of other New South cities in the encouragement of diversified industries. Recently, in addition to naval stores plants, several other factories have been established.

At 109 Walnut St. are the studios of WFOR (1370 kc.), radio station owned and operated by the Forrest Broadcasting Co. *(open).*

MISSISSIPPI STATE TEACHERS COLLEGE, on State 11, two and a half miles from the center of town, is a fully accredited, State-supported normal college, established by legislative act in 1910. On the grounds is a *BIRD SANCTUARY,* comprising 800 acres. At the college auditorium the week preceding Christmas the Vesper Choir presents Handel's *Messiah.*

MISSISSIPPI WOMAN'S COLLEGE, on Tuscan St., one and one half miles south of the business district, is a fully accredited, four-year college, established in 1912 and supported by the Mississippi Baptist Convention.

The *PIONEER SILK MILL,* NW. corner Edward and Tuscan Sts. *(guides; apply at office 8-4 weekdays),* is the only mill in the State that weaves cloth from raw silk. The low, squat mill with sides of glass and with a sawtooth roof looks like a mammoth greenhouse. The immense room shimmers with the myriad rainbow colors of threads shuttling back and forth in the looms. The bales of raw silk are received from China; the soft and pliable raw material, which is either white or yellow, arrives at the mill plaited into arm-length braids. Here it is soaked in an oil-and-water preparation, then stretched, combed, and hung upon tall shellacked poles in the mill to dry. After this treatment it has the feel of fine, clean hair. The skeins go now to the throwing mill where "fugitive color"—pink, lavender, green, blue, and yellow—is given for temporary identification of the grades of silk; this color remains in the threads throughout the process of weaving, but it is washed out by the manufacturer who eventually dyes and converts the woven cloth into wearing apparel. The tinted skeins go to the winding department, where the threads are wound on large bobbins similar to those of ordinary sewing machines. Next the threads are made into warp and harnessed on the looms, which make various types of cloth, such as crêpe de Chine, georgette, flat crêpe, and stocking crêpe. Millions of vari-colored threads are attached to a huge cylinder at the rear of each loom. As this cylinder revolves, the threads unwind, passing through the loom where the shuttles carry the filler in and out of the warp. The last process is the cutting and grading of the cloth for shipment.

At Hattiesburg are the junctions with State 24 *(see Tour 13)* and US 11 *(see Tour 8).*

South of this point the country has an appearance of greater fertility. Farms are larger and the economy of the land is evident in well-tended orchards, beehives, barns, and silos. The carefully nurtured young pines, in tracts fenced in by barbed wire, give the landscape a fresh greenness.

BROOKLYN, *109.1 m.* (155 alt., 300 pop.), is the center of a dairying, poultry, and truck-farming section. Here the South Mississippi Gun and Dog Club holds its annual field trials in March.

ASHE NURSERY, *116.3 m.* (L), is one of the agencies converting thousands of acres of cut-over lands in the State into future revenue-producing areas. This nursery, under the U. S. Department of Agriculture, operates with the aid of the Civilian Conservation Corps. The principal species grown here are the four Southern pines—longleaf, slash, loblolly, and shortleaf. In addition, a million black locust trees are being grown for planting to check soil erosion. The tiny trees are set out in fenced plantations, each covering several thousand acres; it is the practice of the Forest Service to clear the land of as much inflammable material as possible before planting, by selling pine stumps and "topwood" for turpentine distillation purposes. A system of fire breaks has been devel-

TOUR 7 419

oped by clearing lanes approximately 20 feet in width throughout the plantations.

The nursery covers a total of 300 acres of land. At present 75 acres are under cultivation. Although only 30,000,000 seedlings are now being grown, the capacity is 50,000,000. More than six miles of water pipe are used in the irrigation system, which is of the overhead sprinkler type. The seeds are extracted from pine cones collected in September and October, dried for three weeks in the curing sheds and then run through a kiln. After the cones open in the kiln, the seeds are extracted, cleaned, and stored until planting time.

As the highway nears the Coastal Meadow, a low plain lying between the Piney Woods and the Coast, the soil is increasingly sandy. Satsuma, peach, and pecan trees, which thrive here, have been set out in hundreds of acres of orchards. More and more the cut-over land is being used for dairy farming in this area, and, with cattle and sheep nibbling grasses in the rolling meadows, the landscape is becoming pastoral.

FRUITLAND PARK, *119.8 m.* (304 alt., 64 pop.), takes its name from the large number of surrounding pecan, tung, and fruit orchards. Practically every man in the village is a nurseryman or fruit grower, and in spring the homes are almost hidden behind the blossoms of the trees.

WIGGINS, *123.8 m.* (278 alt., 1,074 pop.), is the seat of Stone Co., which has the reputation of never having had a single slaveholder. It is a village that sprang to life with the lumbering era. One of the largest of the Mississippi mills was built here in 1919. When the mill had consumed all timber in the surrounding country, the company purchased redwood logs on the Pacific coast, shipping them by boat to Gulfport and thence to Wiggins by rail. This practice was abandoned in 1930, however, and the mill was closed. Recently a pickle factory, taking the produce of a wide area, has been established. Annually in June a pickle festival is held.

Left from Wiggins on State 26 to the *DOLL'S HOUSE, 1.5 m. (open by appointment)*, the home of Misses Emily and Marie Stapps, who are the authors of a number of childrens' books. The Cape Cod type cottage is named for the collection of 250 dolls that the sisters have on display. Each doll is authentically dressed in the style of a different people. Interesting paintings and furniture are in the house.

PERKINSTON, *128.9 m.* (123 alt., 275 pop.), once the scene of vast lumber and turpentine activities, is best known today for the State-supported *HARRISON-STONE-JACKSON JUNIOR COLLEGE*, established in 1925, a model institution of its kind. Approximately 250 students are boarded and housed here at a maximum cost of $17 each per month, which includes tuition and laundry. The buildings are modern fireproof structures.

At Perkinston the highway enters the Biloxi unit of DE SOTO NATIONAL FOREST, extending for several miles through an aisle of pines The gloom of the dense woods, its majesty, and its clean odor, are a reminder of what the Piney Woods formerly were.

McHENRY, *134.4 m.* (268 alt., 630 pop.), was incorporated as a town in 1902 to enable the inhabitants to rid themselves of seven flourishing saloons. The citizens could not outlaw these until the community became a legal entity. In time lumber and turpentine mills were established, and now pecan and peach orchards supplement the livelihood of the town.

As the road continues S. tung trees are seen in greater numbers, showing the increasing interest in this exotic tree, the culture of which began recently in Pearl River Co. *(see Tour 8).*

SAUCIER, *139 m.* (165 alt., 300 pop.), was settled by an exiled French Acadian, Phillip Saucier, when the nearest town, Pass Christian, was only a dot of a settlement. The homestead, erected by one of the Sauciers' sons on the present site of the town, is gone, but the large oak growing there when he erected his house and the roses and crapemyrtle bushes planted by his wife remain. The early Sauciers were prolific people and their descendants are found throughout this section and along the Coast.

LYMAN, *150 m.* (1,025 pop.), reached its peak of prosperity during the lumber boom of the 1920's and since then has turned its attention to growing citrus fruits and pecans. A few tung orchards have recently been planted as experiments. The GEORGE A. SWAN FARM, on the northern edge of town, was at one time the leading citrus farm of the section.

Right from Lyman on a graveled road to RINGOLSKY FARM, *3.1 m. (visited by permission of owner),* formerly stump land and now a valuable tung orchard. The first trees were planted in 1930 by the owner, I. J. Ringolsky. In 1934, 65,000 pounds of tung nuts were harvested. In addition both pecans and blueberries are produced here in commercial quantities. On the farm is a packing house for fruits and a warehouse in which equipment is stored.

US 90 enters on 25th Ave.

GULFPORT, *159.4 m.* (19 alt., 12,547 pop.) *(see GULFPORT).*

Points of Interest. Harbor, U. S. Veterans Facility, Hardy Monument, and others.

Here is the junction with US 90 *(see Tour 1).*

◄◄◄◄◄◄◄◄◄◄◄◄◄◄◄◄◄◄◄※►►►►►►►►►►►►►►►►►►►

Side Tour 7A

Tutwiler—Greenwood—Lexington—Pickens. US 49E, State 12.
Tutwiler to Pickens, 98.2 m.
Yazoo & Mississippi Valley R.R. parallels route to Tchula.
Paved highway to Greenwood; remainder under construction.
Accommodations in towns.

US 49E, branching southward from US 49W at Tutwiler, follows the eastern rim of the Delta to Tchula. At Tchula the route swings eastward to climb from the Delta into one of the oldest settled sections of the Central Hills and to end at Pickens. The Delta is flat and black, with numerous lakes and bayous; it is a cotton land divided into extensive plantations and cultivated by the labor of Negro tenants. The hill country is the stronghold of the small farm owner and of numerous though small sawmill interests. Here diversification has made headway in its fight against King Cotton, with dairying and cover crops becoming a part of every farm.

At TUTWILER, *0 m.* (157 alt., 873 pop.) *(see Tour 7, Sec. a)*, is the junction with US 49W *(see Tour 7, Sec. a)*.

SUMNER, *5 m.* (618 pop.), is divided by CASSIDY BAYOU. The bayou, the longest in the State, has its ghost. At intervals for 25 years the ghost has appeared at the home of Boone Jenkins, a farmer living one mile N. of Sumner. Each appearance is accompanied by weird voices and the shriek of a woman. Persons who have followed the voice say that it leads to the bayou and, in some instances, to the Indian mounds in the vicinity; the mystery of the Cassidy ghost has never been solved.

WEBB, *7 m.* (153 alt., 531 pop.), is the twin of Sumner, the interests of the two towns being almost inseparable. On the old highway between the two are a cotton mill and cemetery shared by both.

Left from Webb on a graveled road to TALLAHA SPRINGS, *3 m.* (overnight accommodations, boating, fishing, hiking).

At SWAN LAKE, *10.3 m.* (147 alt., 100 pop.), a low, white frame plantation house (R) is typical of the modern Mississippi planter home.

Left from Swan Lake on a dirt road to the *STATON HOUSE, 2 m.*, a typical ante-bellum plantation home, built with slave labor in the latter part of the 1820's by Eli Staton and given to his eldest son, James Harvey Staton. It is of the story-and-a-half post-Colonial type, with wide white clapboarded walls, two chimneys at each end, and a small square portico. The house faces a levee built before 1830; in the Negro quarters near the house is the first Staton home, a squat log structure.

South of Swan Lake there are 10 Negro cabins to every white cabin, and Negro schools, churches, and cemeteries predominate. Scantily clad children play in the cabin yards, men and women fish on the banks of bayous and lakes and in late summer pick the cotton.

Negroes make almost a ritual of the cotton picking. They stoop before the plants, pull the white seedy cotton from the bolls, and place it in long white sacks, which they trail behind them. Each movement is graceful and rhythmic, and is often performed to the accompaniment of song. These cotton-picking songs are rarely sung in chorus, but rather as a number of harmonizing solos. The tune varies from a minor note of despair to a triumphant major:

> "Old Massa say, 'Pick Dat Cotton! (oratorical tone)
> Can't pick cotton, Massa (whining tone)
> Cotton seed am rotten! Ha! Ha! Ha!"

MINTER CITY, *23.8 m.* (350 pop.), was settled when Delta land was selling for 25¢ an acre. The *J. A. TOWNES HOME*, the oldest in the county, on the western bank of Tallahatchie River, is a log house built near the ground with a breezy open hall.

At *35 m.* is the junction with a graveled road.

Left on this road to SHELLMOUND, *0.5 m.* (75 pop.), the site of a battle between the Chakchiuma and allied Choctaw and Chickasaw. Legend says the battle gave the Yazoo (Ind., *river of death)* River its name.

At *39.2 m.* is the junction with US 82 *(see Tour 6)*.

US 49E turns R. on Grand Blvd. which crosses the river and becomes Fulton St.

GREENWOOD, *43 m.* (143 alt., 11,123 pop.) *(see GREENWOOD).*

Points of Interest. Cotton gins and compresses, Terry collection of old relics, and others.

Right from Greenwood on Grand Blvd., here old US 82, to the WRECK OF THE STAR OF THE WEST, *2.4 m.,* visible in Tallahatchie River when the water is low. The ship was scuttled at Fort Pemberton during the War between the States to block the channel and prevent passage of Federals in their effort to get to the north side of Vicksburg. It was captured at Sabine Pass by General Van Dorn without a shot being fired; the officers and crew were ashore on a frolic. General Van Dorn, singularly enough, was in charge of a cavalry detachment at the time. On the same road is the SITE OF FORT PEMBERTON, *3.2 m.,* marked by a cannon. This fort was thrown across a narrow neck of land separating the Yazoo and Tallahatchie Rivers and delayed considerably the fall of Vicksburg. Confederate soldiers, not knowing the war was over, manned the fort for two months after peace was signed.

The route continues on Fulton St.; R. on Henry St.; L. on Mississippi Ave. (US 49E).

At *50.8 m.* (R) is ARCHERLEADER PLANTATION *(private),* a two-story white frame house with one of the best collections of fine old furnishings in the State; these were brought from Anchuka, the ancestral home of the Archer family *(see Tour 3, Sec. b).* This plantation has some of the better type tenant cabins of the Delta. Three and four rooms large, they are painted white with green trim.

Between Archerleader and Tchula the bluff hills are visible (L), contrasting sharply with the low, wide Delta horizon.

TCHULA, *67.8 m.* (130 alt., 907 pop.), is divided by Tchula Lake. The lake at one time was navigable, being known as Little River, and was the shipping point for an abundance of cotton. Though no longer used for river traffic, the lake now gives the town commercial importance in that it abounds in catfish. Thousands of pounds of fish are caught annually and marketed in neighboring towns or shipped to distant markets. Boats, with Negroes to paddle them, are available for 25¢ an hour, and in the vicinity are numerous camping sites equipped with cabins.

At Tchula is the junction with State 12. The route continues southeastward on State 12, climbing from the lakes and bayous of the Delta into the bluff hills that mark the central part of the State.

LEXINGTON, *80.8 m.* (209 alt., 2,590 pop.), the seat of Holmes Co., is one of the older towns of the Central Hills. Established as a trading post immediately after the Treaty of Doak's Stand, Lexington was incorporated on Feb. 25, 1836, and in 1906 was raised to the status of a city. Though a trading center for the surrounding farm country, shipping

12,000 bales of cotton and 300,000 pounds of butter annually, Lexington is largely dependent on the lumber and the sand and gravel industries.

Left from Lexington on the old road to Emory to the *J. H. ROGERS HOME, 8 m. (open by permission)*, a large rambling two-story house built by Col. J. H. Rogers in 1817. The construction of the house, built of hand-hewn lumber, was planned and supervised by Kirl Dixon, a Negro slave. Divided by a wide hall, open at each end, the house contains five bedrooms, a dining room, and a kitchen. The house, like the farm land surrounding it, has been in the possession of the Rogers family since its erection. Strangely, neither land nor house has ever been mortgaged.

The route between Lexington and Pickens passes through low-rolling hill lands, where small sawmilling interests supplement the incomes from small diversified farms of cotton and corn, and dairying.

At 96.6 m. is the junction with US 51 *(see Tour 5, Sec. a)*, 1.6 miles N. of Pickens *(see Tour 5, Sec. a)*.

Tour 8

(Livingston, Ala.)—Meridian—Laurel—Hattiesburg—Picayune—Santa Rosa—(New Orleans, La.). US 11.
Alabama Line to Louisiana Line, 181.9 m.

Highway two lanes wide; three-fourths paved.
New Orleans & Northeastern R.R. parallels route throughout.
Accommodations chiefly in cities.

US 11 runs diagonally across the southeastern corner of the State through the swelling ridges and red clay hills of east central Mississippi; through cut-over lands of the Piney Woods; and at the southern end across a small part of the Coastal Meadow. In the vicinity of Meridian great hills with unbroken forests of longleaf pines crowd to the edge of the highway. Then, almost abruptly, the route breaks from the forest into country where for some years the shrill cry of the circular saw against pine was heard until the larger mills had snaked their last virgin logs and moved to more profitable areas. The towns and cities that they so extravagantly sired remain lean as starved ghosts, some hopelessly depending on denuded lands, others, on the preparation of a limited quantity of naval stores until newly planted pines mature.

Southwest of Laurel and Hattiesburg the people have realistically faced the problem of cut-over pines, finding an answer in other products. Here, on low swells once dominated by the pines, are orchards of pecan, tung, and satsuma trees in long, regular, parallel rows. Between Poplarville and Picayune is a concentrated area of tung trees, where in the spring, when the waxy white blossoms stretch mile after mile, the landscape resembles

SECOND-GROWTH PINES

a Chinese countryside rather than southern Mississippi. At the southern end of the route the land drops noticeably into the flat, marshy meadow bordering the Coast, and the air suddenly is heavy and damp with a salty smell. Meadow land and orchards give way to rank and moss-hung oaks.

Crossing the Mississippi Line, *0 m.*, 21 miles SW. of Livingston, Ala., US 11 and US 80 *(see Tour 2)* are united to Meridian *(see Tour 2)*. US 11 follows B St. to 26th Ave.

MERIDIAN, *19.1 m.* (341 alt., 31,954 pop.) *(see MERIDIAN)*.

Points of Interest. Industrial plants, Gypsy Queen's Grave, Arboretum, and others.

Here are the junctions with US 45 *(see Tour 4)*, State 39 *(see Side Tour 4B)*, and US 80 *(see Tour 2)*.

The route continues on 26th Ave. to 6th St.; L. on 6th St.; R. on 5th St. (US 11).

For 10 miles S. of Meridian US 11 is paved, cutting between steep embankments of solid, creamy rock. This rock is used extensively in the vicinity for building purposes, with pleasing effects, as ROCK HOUSE, a tavern, *20.3 m.* (R), illustrates. Paralleling the route (L), undulating humps of ridges, western foothills of the Appalachians, are clearly visible.

At *20.8 m.* is KEY AVIATION FIELD, where Fred and Al Key, on June 27, 1935, broke the official world's endurance flight record set at Chicago in 1930. After 653 hours and 34 minutes aloft in their monoplane, "Ole Miss," the Key brothers landed here. In breaking the record the Keys flew more than 50,000 miles and made 75 refueling contacts.

The route curves into BASIC, *31.2 m.* (65 pop.), a railroad stop in the pine woods, with a single store and a number of comfortable white frame houses.

At *34.5 m.* is ENTERPRISE (258 alt., 792 pop.), its age revealed in gnarled clumps of cedars that formerly shaded houses that were burned during the War between the States. The low brick PRESBYTERIAN CHURCH (L) was used as a hospital for wounded Confederate soldiers. Enterprise's history began in the days when the muddy Chickasawhay River was navigable and boats would come up from Mobile. Then its lively river trade gave the town the energy and means to live up to the promise of its name; today it is quiet, with a single block of one-story buildings and two small depots, one at each end of town, a center for farm trading and shipping.

1. Right from Enterprise on a narrow country road that is impassable in rainy weather to DUNN'S FALLS, *3.2 m.*, formed by a spillway into Chunky River. Chunky River at this point is about 100 feet wide, its shallow bed lined with sharp stones. The water from the spillway drops about 45 feet over a rock wall, and at certain seasons of the year the cascade is picturesquely striking. At other times the water dwindles to a thin stream. Approximately 100 yards below the falls the river is deeper, forming an excellent swimming hole. An OLD WATER MILL at the falls is used as a dressing room for bathers.

2. Left from Enterprise on a graveled road is STONEWALL, *3.7 m.* (2,048 pop.), dominated by a COTTON TEXTILE MILL that rises giantlike above rows of low mill houses. The mill *(visitors permitted)* is one of the largest in the State.

Between Enterprise and Pachuta the pines gradually thin along the rugged slopes, giving way to hill farms producing corn and potatoes as the principal crops. The red clay soil is infertile and hard, and the primitive farmhouses, often no more than one-room cabins with mud-chinked chimneys, are indicative of the poverty of the section. The people who first settled here brought no slaves with them, and even today the absence of Negroes is noticeable.

PACHUTA, *44.1 m.* (267 alt., 338 pop.), has a railroad station, and a sawmill and a number of modern cottages to stamp it as a 20th century village.

Right from Pachuta on a narrow country road that is impassable in rainy weather is PAULDING, *10 m.* (155 pop.). One long red clay street, forming an aisle between immense live oaks, an ante-bellum home or two, a 100-year-old church, and a jail are all that remain of the town once called the "Queen City of the East." English pioneers of hardy yeoman stock settled here soon after the War of 1812 and by determined effort cut a town out of the wilderness. They built the courthouse with their own hands, digging the clay for bricks from the gully (L) at the entrance to the village, and baking the bricks in improvised kilns. When completed, it stood as fiery red as the soil of the gullies, and, according to James H. Street, was the only two-story building at that time between New Orleans and Chattanooga.

In spite of the sterility of the soil the settlers before the War between the States achieved sporadic wealth and a culture unusual in the Piney Woods. During court week especially the town sparkled. Every other activity was suspended. Aristocratic family carriages, stylish buggies, light sulkies, and battered farm wagons crowded the long shady street. Women wore their richest gowns and gayest plumes, the planters their fanciest waistcoats. But the lawyers held the center of the stage. Driving into Paulding in elegant carriages with Negro attendants, they attracted all eyes. The girls coquetted with them, and the youths imitated their mannerisms while noting the color of ties and the cut of waistcoats. Paulding of this ante-bellum period was a metropolis, its main street flanked with store buildings, its homes white frame mansions with comfortable slave quarters. Reconstruction, however, devastated it; and so deep were the scars left that, when the States were called upon to vote on the 13th Amendment, the Paulding delegation held out staunchly against ratification. To this day, because of their firmness, Mississippi has never ratified the Constitutional Amendment freeing the slaves.

Soon after Reconstruction it was proposed to build a railroad through Paulding, but Jasper Co. refused to pay the necessary tax and Paulding was too enfeebled to protest. Several years later its last remnant of prestige vanished when the county was divided into two districts and a new courthouse built at Bay Springs.

The *DEAVOURS HOUSE* (R) is now used as a home for Paulding school teachers. It is a story-and-a-half cottage, with four dormers and a square columned front portico. The ell was added after the house was built nearly 100 years ago. For many years this was the home of the Deavours family, many members of which have been admitted to the Mississippi bar.

Beyond the Deavours home is the *ORIGINAL PAULDING JAIL* (L), built at the same time as the courthouse and still in use.

Beyond the jail is the *CATHOLIC CHURCH* (R), more than 100 years old. This is a simple white frame structure, with a peaked roof and a spire. When the men of Paulding went off to fight in the War between the States, their wives visited with the women of Rose Hill, an Irish settlement, several miles N. It is said that when the men returned they found their wives converted to Catholicism, and since that time the population has been largely Catholic. The church is kept in good repair and mass is said here weekly.

The hills here S. of Pachuta become steep, stretching sheerly down to the highway, their slopes covered with a uniform expanse of seedling pines.

STAFFORD SPRINGS, *54.0 m.* (50 pop.), is one of the State's best

TOUR 8   427

known mineral springs. Before the coming of the white man, the Indians resorted here regularly to drink what they called bok-humma (Ind., *red water*). The rambling gray frame hotel *(open April through Sept.)* reflects the orange of the hills in its sloping roof.

Between Stafford Springs and Laurel US 11 traverses a land where farmers work hard, tilling unpromising soil. Here no acreage of any size is under cultivation, and not much farming is done commercially. The yield of beans, potatoes, and corn, however, is fair and the houses are painted and have a solid look.

SANDERSVILLE, *65 m.* (281 alt., 565 pop.), was settled by a group of Scotchmen who migrated from North Carolina and built the Good Hope Presbyterian Church in the 1820's. The town was named Sandersville in 1855 to honor one of its pioneer families, the Sanders. The houses have a noticeable number of cupolas, a survival of the Victorian period. The *ED PARKER HOME,* at the northern entrance (R), is the only remaining ante-bellum home, a roomy red-painted structure, with many cupolas and comfortable porches.

Right from Sandersville on a graveled road to BOGUE HOMO INDIAN SCHOOL AND RESERVATION, *3.1 m.* The school has been under Government supervision since its establishment in 1922. Dotted on a hillside are about 50 white cabins, a miniature frame church, and the school. In addition to farming the Indians weave baskets, which they sell on the streets of Sandersville, usually on Saturdays. The Indians wear ordinary modern clothes, but are recognizable by their dark skin, long braided hair, and childlike shyness.

Southward is typical cut-over land. Here and there second-growth pines rise stragglingly above the miles of waste land, with, almost miraculously, an occasional tall perfect virgin pine.

US 11 follows Cook's Ave., which becomes 15th St., to Magnolia St. LAUREL, *74 m.* (243 alt., 18,017 pop.) *(see LAUREL).*

Points of Interest. Masonite Corporation, starch plant, canning plant, art museum, and others.

Here are the junctions with US 84 *(see Tour 11)* and State 15 *(see Tour 12).*

The route continues on Magnolia St.; L. on Central St.; R. on Ellisville Blvd. (US 11).

US 11 is a concrete tie between Laurel and Hattiesburg whose interests have been the same. Poultry and dairy farms appear along the route, and small forests of second-growth timber, set out and carefully protected by the Civilian Conservation Corps.

ELLISVILLE, *84 m.* (240 alt., 2,127 pop.), is one of the Piney Woods' oldest villages. As the seat of Jones Co., a unit notable for the individualism of its citizens, the village had a stormy political history. In 1861, when the State was suddenly confronted with the problem of secession, the backwoodsmen of the county, who owned no slaves themselves, met in the Ellisville courthouse to voice their protest against what they called a "planters' war." They elected an anti-secessionist candidate to the State convention at Jackson, but the candidate, mingling with the soft-voiced planters at the capital, became confused and betrayed his electorate by voting with their opponents.

The citizens of Jones Co. gathered once more in Ellisville, this time to express their contempt for the candidate by burning him in effigy. They called their county the "Free State of Jones" with Ellisville its capital, and so staunchly did they hold out against war that Newt Knight *(see Tour 11)* was able to organize a band of followers and declare war upon the Confederate States of America. Operating from hide-outs in the Leaf River swamps fringing Ellisville, Knight and his men made raids upon Confederate troops and seized arsenals and supplies. The Confederacy sent General Lowry and his troops against Knight, but without success. Until the end of the war Knight carried on guerrilla warfare against the secessionists. After the war Ellisville resented the sobriquet given the county and petitioned the State legislature of 1865 to change the county name to Davis and that of the county seat to Leesburg, "hoping to begin a new history and obliterate the past."

At Ellisville is *JONES CO. JUNIOR COLLEGE,* coeducational institution established in 1927. Its 1936-37 enrollment (481) was the largest of the eleven State-supported junior colleges. On a rolling campus landscaped with water oaks, cedars, and shrubs, its three modern brick buildings overlook the southwestern edge of the town.

The *ISAAC ANDERSON HOME* is a substantial white frame structure overlooking Tallahala Creek. In the dining room of this house Capt. Amos McLemore, sent with a corps to round up Knight and his followers, was himself killed by Knight. Blood stains alleged to be McLemore's remain on the planked pine floor today.

ELLISVILLE STATE SCHOOL, *86 m.* (R), was established in 1920 as a hospital and training school for the feeble-minded. The present enrollment is 300. The institution has a farm, dairy, and fruit orchard where male patients capable of working find occupation. Female patients work in the kitchen and laundry.

Descending gradually into the Leaf River swamp, the highway flattens and crosses marshes where shiny-leafed bay trees are noticeable among the pines.

ESTABUTCHIE, *95 m.* (445 pop.), with its boxlike houses of pine timber, is a typical lumber mill town whose activity has decreased with the exhaustion of the timber.

The highway crosses Leaf River into the suburbs of HATTIESBURG, *103.2 m.* (143 alt., 18,601 pop.) *(see Tour 7, Sec. b).* Here are the junctions with US 49 *(see Tour 7, Sec. b)* and State 24 *(see Tour 13).*

At *110.4 m.* is the junction with a graveled road.

Left on this road to the SITE OF THE SULLIVAN-KILRAIN FIGHT, *3.7 m.* Here in a natural bowl below the spot where the road ends in a clump of trees, in 1889 John L. Sullivan met Jake Kilrain in what was the last bare-knuckle championship bout in American pugilism. The spectators, a mere handful, sat on the ground and watched the two men battle for 75 rounds, before Sullivan was declared the winner when Kilrain's seconds threw in a towel, although their man was still on his feet and apparently able to go on.

Sportsmen had tried to arrange the bout in New Orleans, but city officials barred it. Charlie Rich, in New Orleans at the time, told the promoters of a natural amphitheater near his home town Hattiesburg. When the Governor of Mississippi learned that a secret and illegal contest was to be held in the State, he summoned the militia to guard all main highways and to watch incoming trains. But promoters slipped Sullivan and Kilrain into Mississippi, threw up a ring in the middle of the clearing, sold tickets for $10 apiece, and proceeded to hold the match. After the fight Sullivan and Kilrain, as well as the sportsmen who promoted the bout, were arrested, carried to Purvis, and fined.

Between Hattiesburg and Purvis the hills increase in size, and the soil shows a faint reddish tinge.

It has been said that PURVIS, *123.4 m.* (363 alt., 881 pop.), is good for an hour's conversation on any front porch in the State. Near the turn of the century the town was thought by the preachers and reformers of the State to be headed for doom. They thundered from pulpit and platform about its gambling and drinking, prophesying its downfall. Then in April 1908 a cyclone came. It swept upward from the Gulf Coast, struck the town, killed seven people, injured several hundred, and stopped the hands of the courthouse clock at exactly 4 p.m. Half the State and all of Purvis felt assured the prophecy of the preachers had been fulfilled, and, lest the townspeople forget, the hands of the clock have remained at 4 p.m. ever since.

Two years after the cyclone Will Purvis, a relative of the Purvis who founded the town, brought it again into State-wide prominence. Purvis was sentenced to hang for murder, though he stoutly attested, and a large part of the State believed, his innocence. On the appointed day throngs of people poured into Columbia, where the hanging was to take place, and watched the noose being slipped around his neck. The trap was sprung, but in place of seeing Purvis dangling at the rope's end, the spectators saw the rope slip suddenly from around his neck. Someone excitedly shouted that it was an act of God, and the State joined in the chorus.

But what to do with Purvis was a problem. The State judges said he had been sentenced to hang and hang he should; the people said a miracle had proved his innocence. After much debating, a political campaign, and the election of a new State Governor, a compromise solution was reached in the commutation of his sentence to life imprisonment. Purvis served 15 years at the State farm; then another man, dying from the poison of a snake he had allowed to bite him to prove his sanctification and immunity from death, confessed to the crime, and Purvis was released, restored to full citizenship, and paid $5,000 for his inconveniences. Today he is a respectable farmer living on the edge of town; the scars left by the noose remain on his neck.

At *126 m.* the highway crosses the northern boundary of the Leaf River unit of the DE SOTO NATIONAL FOREST, a dense beautiful growth of pine, carefully protected from fire by lookout towers *(see Tour 7, Sec. b)*. The route begins to nose into the State's chief pecan-growing section. Long rows of symmetrical, broad-limbed trees become a familiar

GATHERING PECANS

sight. Growing in low evergreen clumps, satsuma trees are often planted beneath the pecan trees' spreading branches, making not only an attractive scene but also a profitable twin crop for the farmer. The *BASS PECAN ORCHARD, 132.6 m.* (R), is unusually large; the "Bass Special," a slender papershell nut, is well known in pecan markets.

LUMBERTON, *133.4 m.* (260 alt., 2,374 pop.), still retains its mill town appearance, though the industry that gave it its name is gone. Its pleasantly shaded streets are lined with rows of one-style mill houses; the large white frame *HINTON HOME,* residence of the former mill owner, is the show place. Lumberton was established, along with Picayune and Poplarville, in the early 1880's when the New Orleans & Northeastern R.R. opened up the Piney Woods and ruined the declining older mill towns on Pearl River.

South of Lumberton are occasional, squat, dome-shaped tung trees, planted experimentally with the pecans and satsumas.

The RANDOLPH BATSON HOME, *139 m.,* in a magnificent tract of virgin trees, is a good example of the mansions built by lumber magnates during the 1920 boom.

POPLARVILLE, *146.3 m.* (315 alt., 1,498 pop.), is a former sawmill town now concentrating its energies on tung-tree culture and the production of naval stores. Here is *PEARL RIVER JUNIOR COLLEGE,* the first State-supported junior college in Mississippi, established in 1922.

It was formerly the Pearl River Agricultural High School, the first in the State, established in 1909. The home of Sen. Theodore G. Bilbo (1877-), Poplarville finds its chief diversion in helping to elect this favorite son to whatever office he happens to seek. Before being elected to his present office in 1934, he served as State Senator, as Lieutenant Governor, and twice as Governor of the State. As champion of the common man, Senator Bilbo wears a red necktie and espouses the cause of the people in a drawling vernacular.

> Left from Poplarville on a graveled road to Senator Bilbo's DREAM HOUSE, 6 m. (L), in a large pecan orchard. The house gained both name and fame from the language of its colorful owner. This four-story red brick mansion with dormers and two-story pedimented portico was built largely by contributions from friends throughout the State and was opened with a housewarming in December 1935. The entrances have fanlights and side lights. There is a *porte-cochère* on one side and a sun parlor and sleeping porch on the other. Nearly opposite the house and of the same architectural style is the JUNIPER GROVE BAPTIST CHURCH, 6.5 m., built by the Senator and his friends. The Senator was at one time a Baptist minister. The church is supported by the people of Juniper Grove neighborhood.

Between Poplarville and Picayune lies Mississippi's "tung-oil frontier," with Picayune the tung tree capital. This important new crop was introduced largely through the intense enthusiasm of Lamont Rowlands. Rowlands, a lifetime lumberman, sold his sawmill interest after the decline of the lumber industry in the latter 1920's and turned his attention to developing the cut-over timberland of the section into tung orchards. Shortly before this time, as a result of the destruction of some of the best tung plantations in China, the oil of the tung nut was scarce and prices had risen. Tung oil has many uses, the most important of which is in the manufacture of paint; the hulls of the nut are used as fertilizer. Rowlands saw that it was a product in great demand, and of limited supply.

Before putting out a tree or buying a foot of land, he hired a horticulturist and agronomist, spending a year in investigating tung culture. It was found that these highlands back of Pearl River met all necessary conditions, having sufficient rainfall, acid soil, clay subsoil, a temperate range, and good drainage. Moreover it was found that fertilization was unnecessary, which greatly reduces the cost of growing. Rowlands then purchased 10,000 acres of land, which he planted with tung trees. Following in the wake of Rowlands other business men bought suitable land, and today in this concentrated area are an estimated 100,000 acres of tung orchards. The name of these trees (Chin., *heart*) is derived from the heart-shaped leaves, which resemble those of the catalpa. The tree is deciduous, shedding its leaves in October and leafing in March. The well-shaped white blossoms, which appear before the leaves, have deeply accented red centers. The flowers are staminate or pistillate (male or female), both appearing on one tree, and are formed at the tips of the branches of the preceding season. The fruit varies somewhat in size but the average is about that of a small apple. The kernel, which is very rich in oil content, is poisonous. Maturing early in autumn, the fruit drops to the ground and remains for weeks without deterioration. The trees flank the highway for miles and even in winter, when the branches are bare and sprawling, they have exotic beauty.

At *161.3 m.* is the McNEILL EXPERIMENT STATION, operated by the Federal Government to examine the problem of developing cutover land for agricultural use.

The naval stores activities are increasingly apparent in this area. Interspersed with the tung orchards are young forests of pines from which turpentine is extracted. During tapping season the oil that exudes fills the countryside with a sharp clean odor. Great trucks loaded high with pine knots and stumps, on their way to the naval stores plants at Laurel and Hattiesburg, are constantly encountered on the highway.

PICAYUNE, *171.3 m.* (50 alt., 4,698 pop.), now the tung tree center, is beginning to regain the wealth and prestige it attained during the lumber boom of the 1920's when the Crosby mill operated at full capacity and virtually every one in town was in some way connected with the plant.

Col. L. O. Crosby, the mill owner, was one of the early developers of the lumber industry of southern Mississippi. He operated the largest tung tree plantation in the State.

ROWLANDS TUNG MILL (visitors permitted), on Rowlands' plantation, is the fourth to be erected in the United States, and is the largest and most modern. The galvanized steel structure has storage and drying bins at one end. These bins having slotted floors and walls to facilitate the flow of air, are banked along the sides of a narrow passageway, the floor of which slopes to a foot-wide slot in the middle. Along the bottom of this slot runs a conveyor belt. The tung nuts are shoveled out of the bins into the alleyway and rolled onto the traveling belt, which carries them to a hopper from which a conveyor raises them above a hulling machine. Here a thick husk, enclosing the nut, is torn off. The nut meats emerge at the bottom, and the husks are blown out through a long pipe to a pile where they are loaded into wagons to be carried back to the orchard and spread around the trees as fertilizer.

The nut meats, again carried aloft, are dumped into a grinder and then into tanks, where they are heated. The meal is then fed into an expeller, which squeezes the hot meal with tremendous pressure forcing the oil out, to dribble into receiving troughs. The residue is also collected and used as fertilizer.

The oil is piped into a filter press, where dirt and impurities are strained out, and then is run into containers for shipment. Samples of oil from the Rowlands plant have been tested and adjudged the purest ever received.

On the banks of Hobolochitto River is the *HERMITAGE,* former home of Eliza Jane Poitevent, pioneer newspaper woman. A sturdy white frame ante-bellum structure, the house was first occupied by Colonel Poitevent, the builder, and then by his daughter, Eliza. Speaking of Eliza Poitevent in her book *Ladies of the Press,* Ishbel Ross says that she refused to appease her snobbish family, who thought that Eliza should bloom beside the magnolias until a good man arrived to take her into his home. She took charge of the bankrupt *New Orleans Picayune* and turned it into a fine paper with wide political power in the South. Eliza was born in 1849 in Pearlington, Miss., and was reared by her aunt. In 1860 she had some of her verse printed in the *New York Journal*, a debut that was a blow to her family. It was bad enough to write verses about the birds, but to let them appear in a newspaper was a social error of the worst order. Her verses, however, were liked by Col. Alva Halbrook, publisher of the *Picayune*, who gave her a job as literary editor of his paper. It was practically unheard of for a woman to work for a paper in the South, but Eliza, who had taken the pen name Pearl Rivers, made good. She married the colonel, and after his death became editor of the paper. Besides opening the journalistic field to women in the South and developing the Sunday newspaper as a medium of entertainment for the entire family, Pearl Rivers started Dorothy Dix on her extraordinary career. When she died in 1896 she left the *Picayune* a prosperous and well-established paper. At the time the little town that had grown up near the Hermitage was incorporated, it was named Picayune for the newspaper published by Eliza Poitevent.

South of Picayune the highway flattens gradually through eight miles of low Coastal Meadow, which lies between the Piney Woods and the Gulf. Here the land is for the most part covered with cut-over pine forests, but small wooded sections of giant oaks, festooned with the characteristic gray moss of the Gulf Coast, appear. Low, dank-smelling marshes from the banks of which local people fish skirt the highway. These people are descendants of the French Catholic immigrants who settled here in the latter part of the 18th century. The country was backwoods until the highway made it accessible from the Coast, and the people lived a life of almost pastoral simplicity, with many of the older among them speaking only a patois. Even today, along with the religion and language of their forebears, they cling to folkways, the most picturesque of which is the decorating of graves on November 1, All Saints' Day. Unable to cultivate flowers in the damp, marshy soil, they have developed the making of artificial ones. In the humble cabins barefoot women and children, often wearing clothes made of sugar sacks, express their love of beauty in the flowers they create to sell in shops along the Coast. On this holy day of the year, the people gather at local cemeteries with their home-made floral offerings to deck the covered graves. For weeks afterward the brightly colored flowers make gay spots in the quiet woods.

Between SANTA ROSA, *179.1 m.*, and Pearl River the highway crosses the Mississippi part of the HONEY ISLAND SWAMP (L), a wildlife refuge and for many years the hide-out of pirate bands as powerful, if not so notorious, as the LaFittes of Louisiana. The king of Honey Island and of all the outlaws in the swamps was Pierre Rameau; the swamp and the Pearl River bottoms provide good fishing and squirrel hunting *(dangerous without an experienced guide)*.

At *181.9 m.* the highway crosses Pearl River, which is the Mississippi-Louisiana Line, 54 miles NE. of New Orleans, La. In Louisiana the highway crosses free bridges at the Rigolets (pron., Rig-lees) and Chef Menteur Passes in Louisiana. A shorter route between Pearl River and New Orleans, 47 miles long, crosses a toll bridge on Lake Pontchartrain in Louisiana *(car and driver $1; passengers 25¢ each)*.

◄◄◄◄◄◄◄◄◄◄◄◄◄◄◄◄◄◄ ☼ ►►►►►►►►►►►►►►►►►►

Tour 9

(Hamilton, Ala.)—Tupelo—New Albany—Holly Springs—(Memphis, Tenn.). US 78.
Alabama Line to Tennessee Line, 124.6 m.
St. Louis & San Francisco R.R. parallels route between Tupelo and Tennessee Line.
Highway two lanes wide; three-fourths paved, rest graveled.
Accommodations chiefly in towns.

Cutting obliquely across the State, US 78 runs through country that illustrates the history of northern Mississippi's cultural and economic development. In the eastern part it drops rapidly away from wooded pine hills, where crops are small and farmers supplement their incomes by operating one-man sawmills, into the low-rolling fringes of the prairie. Here the new dairies and bottom-land pastures encircling Tupelo give what is probably the State's best example of the attempt to balance agriculture with industry. The highway then climbs through a rugged region of small dairy and cotton farms to reach at last a section of the north Central Hills, which before the War between the States developed a culture similar in its refinement and prosperity to that of the Natchez country. In the hills a number of fine homes remain as evidence of this culture, but the soil that produced it has been ravaged by erosion.

US 78 crosses the Mississippi Line, *0 m.*, 13.7 miles W. of Hamilton, Ala., to enter a vividly colored country characteristic of northern Mississippi. The highway constantly mounts and descends a series of steep wooded slopes; then it slowly sinks into Chubby Creek swamp, *5.1 m.* The swamp is gray with underbrush and boggy with still, shallow water. Then as the swamp continues (L) the highway climbs suddenly away from it, back into the steep rocky slopes, where numerous patches of cultivated land are scattered across the red clay clearings. The farmhouses are unpretentious but sturdy and well kept.

At *10 m.* is CLAY (22 pop.), a small crossroads community with a name that characterizes the area.

FULTON, *14 m.* (927 pop.), the largest town in Itawamba Co., is a lumbering and farming center. In the town square is the Itawamba

Co. courthouse, a red brick building dominating the encircling group of drug, grocery, and dry goods stores. From the town pump at the corner of the square a well-worn path leads to the courthouse steps; when court is in session, judges, attorneys, jurors, witnesses, and spectators gather at the pump to refresh themselves. The three modern brick buildings of the Itawamba County Agricultural High School are on the western edge of town.

At *16.3 m.* the highway crosses the Tombigbee River (Ind., *coffin maker*) to pass a number of sawmill communities; the one-man mills, usually powered by tractors, have cut spasmodically at the heart of the nearby woods. These mills, whittling away at the forest of shortleaf pine but scarcely making an impression on their density, contrast with the large mills of the longleaf pine belt of southern Mississippi, which have left hardly a tree in their wake *(see Tour 8)*. There is also a vast difference in the value of the two woods, with fortunes being made from the widely useful longleaf pine and only meager livings from the rough-grained shortleaf, useful principally as 2 x 4's and short stripping.

At *20.5 m.* is DORSEY (40 pop.), a truck farming community that absorbed the population of old Ballardsville when the highway missed the older settlement. Here is the junction with a graveled road.

Right on this road is MANTACHIE, 7 *m.* (188 pop.), named for the Chickasaw chieftain Man-at-chee, and formerly one of the largest of the Chickasaw towns. Until the Treaty of Pontotoc (1832) Mantachie was occupied entirely by Indians, but after their removal to western lands came a gradual influx of white settlers. Tishtony Creek which outlines the town's eastern boundary perpetuates in its name the memory of Tish-to-ni, an Indian warrior killed in a contest with another Chickasaw. Today this former Indian village is furnished with electrical power by the TVA.

MOOREVILLE, *24.7 m.* (150 pop.), is a rural village named for the Moore family, its first settlers.

1. Right from Mooreville on a graveled road is EGGVILLE, 6 *m.* (50 pop.), a rural farming settlement where the Northeast Singing Convention meets each year on the Saturday before the first Sunday in July.

2. Left from Mooreville on a graveled road to the *"HATTER" MOORE HOME,* 0.5 *m.*, a dog-trot house little changed since its erection in the 1830's. The builder served as hatter for the whole countryside, using this house for his hattery. Farmers, when they sheared their sheep, brought their wool to Moore who made them a hat "on the half"—that is, a hat for a hat. So enduring were the woolen hats that a farmer seldom needed more than two in a lifetime.

At *6.6 m.* on this road is RICHMOND, one of the oldest settlements in the county and before the War between the States the recreation center of this section. Here were a fair ground and other amusement facilities. The Baptist church is now in what was the center of the old race track.

At *29.6 m.* on US 78 is the junction with a graveled road.

Left on this road to TOMBIGBEE STATE PARK, *3 m. (follow signs)*, a tract of pine woodlands developed by the Government as a camping site and recreational center. The park is an excellent example of undisturbed rustic beauty, with a lake for swimming and fishing set among the hills, a bridle path, and a native stone and split-log community house for dancing. Overnight cabins are for rent.

Between Mooreville and Tupelo the highway breaks abruptly with the hills to drop into the fertile, rolling plain that is a part of the Black Prairie Belt. Here large-scale farming and dairying replace lumbering as the chief industries.

At *30.1 m.* is the junction with State 6 *(see Tour 14)*.

At *31.3 m.* is EAST TUPELO which began as a subdivision but, with a garment factory and a separate school, grew to independence. It is now a small corporate town.

US 78 crosses the bottom-land drained by a series of channels or creeks at *31.8 m. (narrow bridge)*. It was to drain this bottom that the first county drainage laws were passed in the South.

US 78 enters on Main St.; R. on Gloster St.

TUPELO, *34 m.* (289 alt., 6,361 pop.) *(see TUPELO)*.

Points of Interest. U.S. Government Fish Hatchery, cotton mill, garment factory, Carnation Milk Plant, and others.

Here is the junction with US 45 *(see Tour 4)*.

The route continues on Gloster St.; L. on Jackson St.; R. on Clayton Ave.

Between Tupelo and Belden the highway follows the eastern humps of the PONTOTOC RIDGE (L), a natural watershed that separates the hills to the N. and W. from the prairie to the S. On this line of hills the war-loving Chickasaw Indians had their chain of villages or "Long Town," where a great number of tribesmen lived in a concentrated area.

At *37 m.* is the junction with a narrow graveled road.

Left on this road *1 m.* to the probable *SITE OF ACKIA,* the Chickasaw fort attacked by the French under Bienville in 1736. By defeating the French here, and thus preventing their settlement in the Chickasaw territory, the Chickasaw Indians shattered the French scheme of forming a united barrier against the encroaching English settlers. This battle was important in that it opened this section to the English and at the same time closed it to the French *(see AN OUTLINE OF FOUR CENTURIES)*. The site has been excavated and the outlines of a fort charted by Moreau B. Chambers, State Field Archeologist.

The characteristic black soil of the prairie is visible (R) in the furrowed fields, and farms and dairies are numerous. In front of nearly every farmhouse are a bright tin mail box and a large galvanized milk can. The cans are filled with warm fresh milk during the early dawn; later in the day trucks from the milk plant in Tupelo pick them up for transporting to market. Between Tupelo and Sherman is perhaps the most thickly populated area on US 78.

BELDEN, *40.9* (271 pop.), has suffered because of its proximity to Tupelo. Much of the business of the cotton gin and poultry market here have been absorbed by the larger town.

SHERMAN, *45.6 m* (359 alt., 464 pop.), is curiously on the boundary of three counties, Pontotoc, Lee, and Union. The town was settled shortly after the American Revolution by Reuben Jones, who cleared a plantation on the present site and planted cotton and corn. The nearby Chickasaw Indians were friendly and left Jones and his family unmolested. The village that grew up around the Jones plantation was named Sherman many years later by a resident who had formerly lived in the Texas city of that name. On the school grounds (R) is the *SITE OF AN ANCIENT INDIAN VILLAGE* from which artifacts have been removed.

The highway rises NE. of Sherman, and as the hills grow steeper the landscape becomes more scenic. From the top of each ridge is a good view of the surrounding country, where small terraced farms grow truck, corn, and a little cotton. For generations the farmers, most of them independent landowners, have dug a living from the rocky soil. Their houses, roomy but unpretentious, sit in clean-swept yards and are, for the most part, unpainted.

At 50.7 *m.* is BLUE SPRINGS, named jointly for the "blue" soil and the deep artesian springs; it is situated on one of the highest of the Pontotoc hills. Dairying is the industry of the surrounding highlands, while in the creek and river bottoms corn and hay are grown.

WALLERVILLE, 55 *m.* (471 alt., 200 pop.), is said to have received its name from a fight in which two drunken men engaged on the village site, and smeared themselves with the clay-like soil in which they wallowed.

At 56 *m.* (R) is the entrance lane leading to *THE OAKS*, built in 1857 by Andrew Duncan on a section of land that had been purchased in 1816 by his grandfather, Wm. Duncan, from Pittman Colbert, a half-breed Chickasaw chieftain. The cedars growing about the doorway are from seeds brought from the battlefield of Manassas. The two-story frame house, perhaps the handsomest in the section, is a contractor's adaptation of a Greek Revival plan; the predominating exterior feature is the massive two-story front portico with its hand-carved columns. In the interior is a noteworthy hand-carved rosewood parlor suite, imported from England soon after the house was built. In the 1890's the Southern field trials were an annual event at the Oaks, attracting sportsmen from every State in the Nation.

NEW ALBANY, 59.3 *m.* (364 alt., 3,187 pop.), spreads laterally from the highway, which forms its main street, and is notable chiefly for the fact that it is one of the few Mississippi county seats that is not built around its courthouse square. Before the War between the States the town was a stagecoach stop on the Holly Springs-Pontotoc Line. After the war, when the Gulf, Mobile & Northern R.R. was literally built through the town, at right angles to and crossing Main Street in the center of the business district, it was incorporated as the seat of Union Co. Today it is a prosperous hub for farmers and dairymen who drive to town on Saturday, park their cars at every conceivable angle, and make the main street almost too congested for passage. The *COURTHOUSE GREEN* on a Saturday morning holds a representation of the population of the county, for everyone who has been able to obtain transportation into town eventually drifts to the green to sit in the sun on a wooden bench and chat with his neighbors.

At 60.5 *m.* the highway crosses the Tallahatchie (Ind., *river of rock*) River on one of the State's best examples of concrete-constructed bridges.

The highway between New Albany and Holly Springs winds deviously between high rocky hills, alternately windswept or densely covered with oak, beech, and shortleaf pine trees. The evergreen pines in winter give color to a 40-mile area that would otherwise be forlorn and drab; the sheep cropping the grasses on the slope make a scene uncommon in Mississippi. The extensive raising of sheep through this section is a recent development. For miles the country is unsettled, with only an occasional grist mill or a country store along the way.

MYRTLE, 68 m. (415 alt., 313 pop.), is known for the natural lakes in the vicinity where fishing is good, and for Hell Creek running southward from Myrtle to New Albany.

At 70.1 m. the highway crosses the eastern boundary of the HOLLY SPRINGS NATIONAL FOREST, covering an area of 350,520 acres in Benton, Tippah, Marshall, Union, and Lafayette Counties. The ranger headquarters is at Holly Springs.

HICKORY FLAT, 74.1 m. (401 alt., 337 pop.), sits placidly in a valley between two hills. Formerly a station on the Chickasaw trail between Pontotoc and Memphis, the town is today the marketing place for the produce of the surrounding country, and the place to which nearby farm families come to take a train.

Right from Hickory Flat on a graveled road to the *FOX HUNTERS' CLUB, 12 m.* (R), organized in 1925. The club owns 880 acres of highlands, a one-story frame clubhouse with bedrooms, a taproom, and a kitchen, and a 25-acre lake. The purpose of the club is to encourage fox hunting as a sport in north central Mississippi, where both the red and gray varieties of the animal still abound. Several hunts are held during the season each year.

Here the color of the soil begins to change. From a muddy dark brown, it turns first rusty then reddish orange, as if anticipating the fiery clay surrounding Holly Springs. In the banks of the hillsides various contrasting strata lie bare to the sunlight.

WINBORN, 78.3 m. (105 pop.), is the site of the only iron mine in the State. In 1912 a Birmingham, Ala., steel company built an iron foundry here to manufacture pig iron, and several stores and houses were erected. After three years of operation the manufacturers decided that the cost of shipping the product to Birmingham was too great to allow a profit, so the foundry closed. Since 1915 the town has slowly decreased in population until it is now hardly more than a ghost of its former self.

At 80 m. is a REFORESTATION CAMP, where the Government is creating a park of several hundred acres. From the *LOOKOUT TOWER* in the camp is one of the best views of Mississippi's Central Hills.

POTTS CAMP, 81.4 m. (334 alt., 326 pop.), is a sawmill town established as a levee camp in the 1870's by Colonel Potts. The building of the Memphis & Charleston R.R. (now Frisco) through in the 1880's brought in new settlers but the old name was retained.

Between here and Holly Springs the descent from the hills is gradual. Just south of the town are the first of the gullies that are to mark this

route through the State. These gullies, land laid open in sheer red caverns, look as if some giant hand had lashed the earth until it bled.
US 78 enters on Van Dorn Ave. to courthouse square.
HOLLY SPRING, 94.1 m. (602 alt., 2,271 pop.) (see HOLLY SPRINGS).

Points of Interest. Ante-bellum homes, churches, soil conservation bureau, and others.

1. Left from Holly Springs on State 7 at *1.9 m.* is the junction with a graveled road; R. here to GALENA, *10.2 m.* (L), the old home of the Cox brothers, connected with a story as bizarre as any William Faulkner has told. Low and broad, it is but one story high and rambles into a sturdy yet graceful H, its broad porch extending across the center hall and front rooms. Two identical sides and the enclosed hallway joining them are roofed in a dull red composition. The gray of the frame walls is so drab and blotched that even the remaining chips of paint are practically drained of color. Dulled to a lifeless blue are the heavy blinds that run the length of the many stained windows to shut out all light of the outside world. The original furnishings are in disorder, as if thrust aside in haste a half century ago when the house was vacated. Massive oak and walnut furnishings possess each room. In the front parlor an oil portrait of William Henry Cox looks down from above the heavy mantel upon a lovely old secretary and an old fashioned piano scattered with lyrics, none dating to more modern times than the "gay nineties." Staring back at the portrait are row after row of books along the opposite wall.

The story of Galena had its origin in the 18th century. Lord Ainsley's daughter married General Moultrie of Revolutionary fame and later Governor of South Carolina. From their union was a daughter who became the wife of a young Scotchman, William Henry Cox, who settled in Georgia. After the 1832 cession, the elder Cox purchased estates from the Chickasaw and sent his five handsome sons with several hundred slaves to Mississippi to cultivate them. William Henry, Jr., built Galena—from timber to brick, nails, and ironwork—all with the labor of his slaves. The slave quarters were so large that travelers often asked what village it was they were passing. The plantation name, given for the Scotch mineral symbolizing peace, is in contrast to Galena's history. Lavish entertainers, foppish dressers, heavy drinkers, dare-devil sportsmen, the Cox brothers came to violent ends. William Henry, Jr., on a drunken spree, rode a spirited horse up a stairway leading to the house and broke his neck. Toby, a younger brother said to have been more beautiful than any woman, killed his bride during a drunken orgy, then turned the gun on himself. Because his bride's family would not allow her body to be buried on the Cox lot, she lies in an unmarked grave; but Toby sleeps beneath a masterpiece of imported Italian marble, as do all the members of the Cox family. Another of the brothers, groomed to the last degree, drove a span of horses over the bluff at Memphis into the Mississippi River; a street in Memphis now bears his name. Of the five brothers, William Henry was the only one to have a child; his daughter, Lida, married Clark Brewer. At the death of her father and uncles she inherited the plantation. The post office located in her store was closed at her request; but when people living a mile or so from Galena asked for a post office, the Government obtained permission from Mrs. Brewer to use the stamp of Galena. Hence the community, like so many other Mississippi communities, took the plantation's name. During the War between the States, the battle of Cox's Cross Roads was fought nearby, and a number of family treasures were stolen. Other family heirlooms, however, are in possession of the descendants.

2. At *10 m.* on State 7 the U. S. FIELD TRIAL CLUB, considered the oldest in the United States, holds an annual field trial. The date is approximately the first week in February and is usually set so as not to conflict with other field trials. The club course, protected by a game warden, covers 10,000 acres.

The route continues from the courthouse square on N. Memphis St.

RED BANKS, *102.1 m.* (498 alt., 97 pop.), is one of northwestern Mississippi's oldest communities, having been settled between 1820 and 1825, while the territory was still owned by the Indians. At that time a group of North Carolinians came to settle near a Chickasaw trading post and to clear the land for planting. Until the Chickasaw Cession (1832), the whites and Indians lived amicably. After the removal of the Indians to the West in 1836, Red Banks, typifying its natural setting in its name, developed as a social and cultural center. The few antebellum homes that remain are but the shell of the proud little village that has died. The *G. C. GOODMAN HOME*, a two-story frame structure, was built by Henry Moore in 1840. During the War between the States, when Federal troops entered to search the house for Confederate soldiers, the house was set afire. But its mistress, Mrs. Eliza Moore, defied the soldiers and extinguished the flames. The *AUSTIN MOORE HOME* built during the same period is a slender-columned house of conventional ante-bellum type. After a century of service the lumber, planed by slave labor, remains sound. The *MARTHA GARDNER HOME* offers an excellent contrast. Built during the 1830's, it is a solid log house with brick chimneys at each end and an open central hall—almost a perfect example of early pioneer architecture. The house is owned by descendants of the original builder, who received his land grant from the Indians.

> Right from Red Banks on a graveled road *3.3 m.* to SUMMER TREES *(open during Holly Springs Pilgrimage)*, the old Sanders Taylor place, built between 1820 and 1825. This is a one-story house; the roof of the front gallery is supported by six slender grooved columns and the main roof forms a transverse ridge. The front and back walls are painted white, but side walls are a mellow rose, the color that bricks made from the clay of this section eventually turn. The house has been restored recently by Neely Grant.

North of Red Banks US 78 passes through some of the most eroded land in the State. The fields have great ravines that reveal a soil of startling redness. Except for occasional cotton patches, little land is under cultivation. It is used mainly for pasturage, dairying in this section being a growing source of income. A great many crumbling mansions, built during the flush times of the 1830's and 1840's, desolately face the encroaching gullies. These houses, gradually mouldering away as the earth slides from beneath them, are unpainted, with sagging porches and rotting pillars; they are often occupied by Negro families.

BYHALIA (Ind., *great oaks*), *110.2 m.* (386 alt., 565 pop.), lies on the old Pigeon Roost Road leading to Memphis. The settlement was begun in the late 1830's, soon after the Chickasaw Cession, by planters who belonged to the aristocracy of the seaboard States. Here on what had so recently been Chickasaw hunting grounds, they developed an elegant and prosperous society. Except for groves of scraggy cedars that mark the sites of the old plantations, all the landmarks of old Byhalia are gone. The town's chief industry is trading with farmers.

The *COL. WM. MILLER HOME (open by appointment), 118.1 m.* (L), is a two-story frame house designed with unusual restraint. Four slender tapering columns support the roof of the wide front gallery, and in the interior is an excellent spiral stairway. The house, more than 100 years old and held together by wooden pegs, has fine old furnishings. It is approached through a boxwood drive laid out when the building was erected; the place has been in the Miller family for four generations.

OLIVE BRANCH, *121.1 m.* (387 alt., 336 pop.), settled soon after the treaty of 1832 by which the Indians relinquished their land, symbolizes in its name the peace made between the white men and the Chickasaw Indians. The only landmark of the early settlement is the *MILTON BLOCKER HOME,* a one-story double log house, with four rooms and an attached kitchen. The logs were hand-hewn from native oak trees on the Blocker estate. The building was erected by slave labor. The logs have been weatherboarded and painted but the design remains unchanged.

MAYWOOD RECREATIONAL CENTER, 122.5 m. (L), is on the oak-shaded shore of a natural lake *(camping, boating, swimming, fishing, at nominal rates).*

MINERAL WELLS, *123.2 m.,* is the site of a large resort hotel built in the 1850's to accommodate visitors from Memphis who came to drink the waters of the springs. After the hotel burned, the popularity of the place waned, until today it is little visited except for picnic parties. A substantial log house built in the 1830's marks the site of the village, which at one time boasted of a depot, a telegraph office, and several residential streets.

At *124.6 m.* US 78 crosses the Tennessee Line, 9 miles S. of Memphis, Tenn.

Tour 10

(Florence, Ala.)—Iuka—Corinth—Walnut—Slayden—(Memphis, Tenn.). US 72.
Alabama Line to Tennessee Line, 103.4 m.

Southern R.R. parallels route from Alabama Line to Corinth.
Graveled highways two lanes wide.
Accommodations chiefly in towns.

Skimming across the northernmost part of the State, US 72 traverses a country of rugged contours, with sharp jagged ridges, rocky slopes, and sweeping views of forested valleys and distant purple hills. Corinth and Iuka, on the sites of two important battles of the War between the States, are beginning to prosper by the development of the natural resources of the area. This section—the State's experimental ground for dairying, road building, and power development—contrasts with the somnolent agricultural villages toward the northwest, where the farmers still plant cotton on the worn-out land, while the landmarks of an agricultural aristocracy fall in ruins about them.

Crossing the Mississippi Line, *0 m.,* 30.4 miles W. of Florence, Ala., US 72 enters the widest section of the State's highlands, the Tennessee River Hills. These hills are a part of the 2,000-mile "Catchment Basin," a high region of broken topography with outcrops of gravel and sand, and deeply cut by swift narrow streams. Large gravel beds shine through scattered oak, poplar, and sweet gum stands.

TIPPLE, *1.2 m.,* is a small community sitting at the foot of a mountain of gravel that provides excellent road-building material. The Southern R.R. operates a branch line along the crest of the mountain and as the rock has been dug through the years it has been necessary to move the track southward at intervals. At first convict labor was used to loosen the gravel, but now hired laborers aided by machines and dynamite do the work.

For a half mile W. of Tipple the almost inexhaustible deposits of silica, sandstone, and limestone break out on the sliced surfaces of red clay; then the highway crosses Clear Creek into a short stretch of bottom lands.

BLYTHE'S CROSSING, *5.2 m.,* was once considered as a site for the town of Iuka.

At *5.4 m.* is the junction with a graveled road.

Left on this road to SHADY GROVE CEMETERY, *0.4 m.,* where 261 Confederate soldiers are buried in one trench. The only marker is a low brick wall around the trench.

At *5.8 m.* are the IUKA MINERAL SPRINGS (L), whose medicinal value was first recognized by the Indians, who enclosed them with a fence of hollow logs. In ante-bellum days the place was a noted health resort. The springs today are in a landscaped park with century-old oaks, sweet gum, beech, and birch trees. They are of six distinct varieties, each with its traditional cure. Spring 1 has been exhausted only twice, first when Grant's army drank it dry, and later when the entire county attended a barbecue given here.

IUKA, *6 m.* (554 alt., 1,441 pop.). The town's chief resources are gravel and lumber, though lime, sandstone rock, and clays for the manufacture of paint are being utilized in increasing quantities.

Iuka is the site of a Chickasaw village named for one of the lesser chieftains of the tribe, a friend of the great chief Tishomingo, for whom the county was named. Little is known of the Indian settlement here, but it is thought to have been subordinate to one at Underwood Village on the Alabama Line and to Colbert's Reservation, approximately 12 miles W. The white settlement did not rise immediately after Indians abandoned the site, but sprang into being when the Memphis & Charleston R.R., now the Memphis branch of the Southern, was completed in 1857; the entire town of old East Port picked up business and belongings and moved to this place. Incorporated the same year, the community grew rapidly, building churches, a female college, a boys' military academy, and a fine hotel. The war, however, brought opposing forces to the little town; in one major engagement here between 1,200 and 1,500 were killed or wounded, and three skirmishes were fought within the city's limits.

Immediately after the Battle of Iuka, Sept. 19, 1862, practically all the homes and business buildings were transformed into emergency hospitals. The dead, separated according to the color of uniforms they wore, were buried, the Confederates in one long trench in what is now Shady Grove Cemetery, and the Federals at first on the grounds surrounding the buildings, then later in the National Cemetery at Corinth. At one period or another Generals Price, Forrest, Kelly, Van Dorn, and Whitfield of the Confederacy, and Grant, Rosecrans, Ord, and Hurbert of the Union made their headquarters in the town.

After the war, the first normal college S. of Mason's and Dixon's line was established here when Dean and Neuhardt built the Iuka Normal Institute, now gone. Ante-bellum prosperity did not return here and for more than a generation Iuka saw little activity. The recent building of Pickwick Dam and the opening of the Commercial Gravel Co. have brought new life to the place.

The *McKNIGHT HOME (private)*, Quitman St. (L), was erected first in the town of East Port, eight miles away on the Tennessee River, when that town was the shipping point for northeast Mississippi. Then, when the railroad town of Iuka replaced the river town of East Port and East Port citizens moved en masse, William McKnight even brought his house with him. Ox-drawn wagons hauled the pieces to Iuka over the rough mountain road and through the hollow that is still known as Long Hungry. In Iuka the house was re-erected. It is a low, one-story frame building of no definite architectural style, with four large rooms having ceilings 12 feet high, and with a wide hall.

The *METHODIST CHURCH*, NE. corner Front and East Port Sts., is the only remaining church of the early days of Iuka. This clapboard structure, built in 1857, was at one time used as a hospital. It has been remodeled several times; the slave gallery has been removed and the exterior walls have been covered with red brick. A two-story red brick wing has been added, but the tall Gothic spire, seen from every point in town, remains unchanged.

The *MATTHEWS HOME (private)*, SW. corner Main and Quitman Sts., was built in 1857 by A. T. Matthews, the president of the Iuka Townsite Co., who moved here from East Port. The white frame two-story structure has green shutters and a deep porch supported by four columns. Unlike a majority of the houses of its period, it has low ceilings and a narrow stairway. The servants' quarters and kitchen, connected with the house by a brick and latticed runway, have been converted into small apartments. During the many raids on and around Iuka, this house was the headquarters of Gen. Nathan Bedford Forrest. To it came the excited courier bearing the message that two gunboats and two transports loaded with Negro troops were steaming up the Tennessee River, expecting to land at East Port, march to Iuka, burn the town, and cut off connections with Forrest and his army, at that time in Alabama. The women, children, and men too old or too feeble for service gathered in the basement during the Battle of Iuka. From the house went an aged citizen carrying in his hands a broom stick with a white sheet nailed to it as a flag of truce, to ask protection from Rosecrans for the women and children of the town.

The *T. M. McDONALD HOME (private)*, adjoining the Iuka Public School, was built in 1858–59 by Col. Lawrence Moore of Alabama; it is of Southern Planter type, with deep verandas on four sides. The basement or ground floor originally contained the dining room with the kitchen and a servant room to the rear. On the main floor each room has a 15-foot ceiling and opens into a central hall 12 feet wide and 52 feet long. Painted side lights and a fanlight frame the double entrance doors, which are of oak 3 inches thick and 12 feet high. The walls and ceiling of the front and back parlors are painted, and in one of them are the carpet and draperies in use when Confederate Gen. Sterling Price and Federal General Rosecrans successively had their headquarters here. In another room is a carpet beneath which were hidden the notes of a Confederate scout sent by Forrest to gather information of Grant's army in camp at East Port; disguised as a woman selling gingerbread, the scout passed through the Federal lines, secured Grant's plan of battle, and returned to Iuka.

The *COMAN HOME (private)*, Quitman St. opposite the courthouse, is a one-story frame cottage built prior to the War between the States by Maj. J. M. Coman. Here John M. Stone married Coman's daughter in 1872 and lived until his death in 1900. Stone was one of the most conspicuous figures in the State during the Reconstruction Period. As president pro tempore of the senate he became Governor for the first time in 1876, after the impeachment of Governor Ames. During the six years of his first administration governmental affairs were re-established on a systematic and economical basis, and the last traces of the reconstruction corruption were removed. Mississippi State College was founded as Mississippi Agricultural and Mechanical College during this administration. His second administration, 1890-96, was marked by the Constitutional Convention of 1890 *(see AN OUTLINE OF FOUR CENTURIES)*. His grave is in the Iuka Cemetery.

The *BRINKLEY HOME (private)*, Eastport St., is a 12-room frame structure two stories in height, with a portico with Doric columns. The house, built on the site of Chief Iuka's home, was erected by Daniel Hubbard who settled here 20 years before the founding of the town. Hubbard later sold the house to Col. R. C. Brinkley, who made extensive improvements. Here, during the War between the States, Grant had headquarters, connected by a telegraph line with the house next door, occupied by General Sherman. On vacating the house Grant left a note telling the owners that he had taken good care of the property, even to a pin cushion in his bedroom.

A CABIN IN THE COTTON

The *CONFEDERATE MARKER* fronting the courthouse commemorates the 261 Confederate soldiers killed in the Battle of Iuka.

At Iuka is the junction with State 25 *(see Tour 17)*.

Between Iuka and Corinth the highway traverses a region where thickly wooded hills alternate with muddy bottom lands. At *11.7 m.* (L) is a particularly good view of hills and valleys glorified by pines. At *16 m.* (L) are visible the Tennessee Hills, contrasting with the rugged red-banked ones over which the road climbs. At *16.6 m.* compact growths of tall pine glow richly emerald-green; beyond are ridges of darker green, and beyond them are purplish-gray hills.

At CORINTH, *31.1 m.* (456 alt., 6,220 pop.) *(see Tour 4)*, is the junction with US 45 *(see Tour 4)*.

Between Corinth and Kossuth the highway passes into the northernmost fringe of the Black Prairie where the few elevations are topped with growths of stunted post oaks and lean pine saplings. Farmhouses and little plots of cultivated land are seen infrequently.

KOSSUTH, *40.2 m.* (224 pop.), has the aged yet ageless appearance of the country around it. It is much as it was in the 1840's, when the name of the village was New Hope and only 100 people lived here.

In 1852 the name was changed to honor the Hungarian liberal, Louis Kossuth, who visited the United States in 1851, after having been exiled from Hungary. His mission was to arouse sentiment in this country against the unification of Austria and Hungary. In 1857 the town had two churches and has since added one. Here are also a grist mill, a foundry, a machine shop, a plow factory, and a steam sawmill.

West of Kossuth the highway rolls through the hills, ascending into the higher altitude of the Pontotoc Ridge, where the cedar and pine forests are more depleted, the shacks more dilapidated, the people fewer, and the crops poorer, because of the sterility of the sandy red soil. Here and there is a two- or three-room shack, of old, unpainted wood, with a tin roof, a dog-trot through the center, a mud chimney, and a slack line across the porch for faded garments. The people often go barefooted and many are listless in manner.

CHALYBEATE, 56.2 m. (100 pop.), named for Chalybeate Springs in a ravine on the northern edge of town, is the center of a cotton, corn, and truck growing community.

WALNUT, 58.7 m. (219 pop.), was christened Hopkins in 1871. A mile S. lay another village, Hopkinsville, but no one minded the similarity of names until a keg of whisky intended for Hopkins was delivered to the station beyond. The train had to back a mile to adjust the error, and the recipient of the whisky, shuddering to think how nearly he had missed the keg, changed the town's name to Walnut on the spot. Since the village's incorporation in 1912, lumber mill interests have been making steady inroads upon the pines and hardwood trees of the vicinity.

At 62.1 m. US 72 enters HOLLY SPRINGS NATIONAL FOREST, which covers a gross area of 350,520 acres in Benton, Tippah, Marshall, Union, Lafayette, and Pontotoc Counties. Ranger headquarters are at Holly Springs.

West of Walnut is one of the State's most thinly populated sections. Almost every crossroad, however, has a country store and gasoline pump, serving some backwoods settlement. Bonneted women and overalled farmers walk here from farmhouses in the hills to buy coal oil and tobacco, and children sometimes stop to spend pennies for candies and chewing gum. In winter teamsters gather around the pot-bellied iron stove at the rear of the store to warm their hands and talk. The storekeeper is usually a man of ideas. His wits are sharpened by arguments with his customers; he has strong opinions on government, the weather and the universe at large.

CANAAN, 73 m. (50 pop.), sits upon land that belies the promise of its name. The soil is fast washing away from the scattered farms, and erosion has marked the woods and farmlands with blood-red scars.

At 74.3 m. the highway crosses the southern boundary of Holly Springs National Forest.

SLAYDEN, 92.9 m. (75 pop.), has a well-equipped agricultural high school, two churches, and several general stores.

West of Slayden US 72 passes a number of crumbling relics of ante-bellum culture. Before the war, when the now almost sterile soil was productive, planters grew rich on cotton and built homes in keeping with their prosperity. These houses, the majority of them Southern Planter in type, are ghosts of the past; but even with sagging blinds, columns, and chimneys, they are impressive.

MT. PLEASANT, 96.8 m. (107 pop.), keeps alive in its name the pleasant, smoothly flowing life lived here before the War between the States, when the red-gullied hills were white with cotton crops. The few mansions that remain are anomalies in the present village scene.

The *JESSE IVY HOME (visited by permission), 97.1 m.*, built in the 1850's, is a handsome red brick house designed with slender proportions in the manner of Georgian Colonial works. The double-deck portico has large square columns and the banisters and railings are of finely wrought ironwork.

The *DEMPSEY CURL HOME (visited by permission), 98.7 m.* (L), is a one-story clapboarded cottage of great simplicity. It has a square entrance porch, and chimneys on each side.

By the Curl home is the junction with a graveled road.

Right on this road 200 yds. to a junction; L. here on a dirt road to *SHILOH BAPTIST CHURCH, 0.4 m*. The church, a small though notable example of Greek Revival architecture, was built of hand-hewn timber with slave labor prior to 1836. It is in good repair and services are held occasionally.

Osage hedges line the highway. Here the gullies are very deep and gnarled cedars and water oaks clutch footholds.

At *101.4 m*. is the shell of an ante-bellum mansion, unidentified and without occupants. It is a good example of this section's ante-bellum adaptation of the Greek Revival style of structure. It is of frame construction, two stories high, and has a portico with four square columns that is perhaps too narrow and slender for the mass of the house.

At *103.4 m*. the highway crosses the Tennessee Line, 22 miles S. of Memphis, Tenn.

Tour 11

Waynesboro—Laurel—Brookhaven—Washington. US 84.
Waynesboro to Washington, 191.3 m.

Mississippi Central R.R. parallels route between Prentiss and Silver Creek, and between Brookhaven and Washington.
Graveled roadbed two lanes wide.
Accommodations in cities and towns.

US 84 in Mississippi runs through a backwoods country in the eastern part of the State and through the Natchez plantation area in the west. A great part of the country is rural; the highway skirts Sullivan's Hollow, brushes briefly the Pearl River communities and dairying and truck farms near Brookhaven.

WAYNESBORO, *0 m.* (191 alt., 1,120 pop.) *(see Tour 4),* is at the junctions with US 45 *(see Tour 4),* with which US 84 is united to the Alabama Line, and State 63 *(see Tour 15).*

At *2.1 m.* US 84 crosses the Chickasawhay River and meets the junction with a graveled road that borders the river.

> Right on this road to the unexplored *PITTS CAVE, 1 m.*, on the Pitts farm. The cave, with its entrance in the side of a hill, is a limestone formation. A number of stories are associated with the place. An Indian, said to have lost his dog in the cave, went in after it and was never seen again. Some say his skull was found years later. The dog, it is asserted, came out at another entrance with its body stripped clean of hair by the limestone gases. Another story has it that a Confederate detachment, pursued by the enemy, took refuge in the cave. The most enthralling story, however, is that of the exploration made by Capt. L. S. Pitts, father of the present owner, who many years ago decided to investigate the cave, using twine and candles in a Tom Sawyer manner. After four candles had been burned, Pitts was at the end of his twine and gave up his search for the end of the cave. He had traveled, he estimated, three miles. When he emerged, his eyes and face were swollen from the gas. Pitts believed the cave went under Chickasawhay River, for at a certain point in his trip he could hear running water above him. The river is about a mile in a direct line from the mouth of the cave.

US 84, between the Chickasawhay River and the Bogue Homo Creek, runs through a sparsely settled, marginal pineland and farm country. On both sides are log cabins with mud-and-stick chimneys, storm pits cut into red clay banks, and ancient, one-mule-power cane presses.

At *24.6 m.* the highway crosses Bogue Homo (Ind., *red creek*) Creek.

At *25.6 m.* is the junction with a graveled road.

> Right on this road to the first fork; L. here to a crossroads where is the *SITE OF THE RUSHTON POTTERY KILN, 1.9 m.*, an unusual concern for such a remote place as the "Free State of Jones." The Rushton brothers, who were potters by profession, came here from Staffordshire, England, and erected a kiln many years before the War between the States. The owner, B. J. Rushton, gained a reputation for himself throughout this section, fashioning pieces that ranged from five gallon urns to saltcellars.
>
> At the period of his greatest prosperity, between 1858 and the outbreak of the war, Rushton owned 20 slaves, one of whom was such a fine potter that Rushton is said to have refused $1,500 for him. Rushton mixed his clay with a log sweep pulled by a mule. He fired his ware without a temperature gauge, using peep holes in the top of the kiln to help him judge the color of the ware and the extent of processing. For fuel he used dried split pine. The ware was finished with a glaze called hickory pulp, made by a soupy mixture of clay and hickory ashes.
>
> On Feb. 2, 1864, Rushton was shot through the door of his cabin by Babe White, a member of the Newt Knight band *(see Tour 8).* For a time Rushton's 12 children operated the pottery, but they abandoned it after a new process of salt glazing, which they introduced, proved unsuccessful. The site today is well strewn with pieces of broken ware, and a mound of crumbling brick marks the place where the furnace stood.

The highway here passes through the undulating, prairie-like country

A ONE-MULE-POWER CANE PRESS

that appears at intervals along the northeastern edge of the Piney Woods.
At *30.5 m.* US 84 crosses the Tallahala (Ind., *smooth rock*) Creek.
US 84 follows Cook's Ave., which becomes 15th St., to 2nd Ave.
LAUREL, *31.5 m.* (243 alt., 18,017 pop.) *(see LAUREL)*.

Points of Interest. Masonite Plant, art museum, canning plant, and others.

Here are the junctions with US 11 *(see Tour 8)* and State 15 *(see Tour 12)*.

The route continues on 2nd Ave.; L. on 7th St.; R. on 8th Ave.; R. on 6th St.; L. on 13th Ave.; R. on 5th St. (US 84).

At *34.1 m.* is the *LAUREL COUNTRY CLUB AND GOLF COURSE (open to visitors by card)* with a long 18-hole golf course.

At *35.2 m.* US 84 crosses Tallahoma (Ind., *red rock*) Creek. Tallahoma and Tallahala Creeks are Laurel's legendary protection against tornadoes, the Indian tradition being that wind storms will seldom cross a running stream. The ridges around the plain and between the two creeks are apparent as US 84 climbs slowly W. of the Tallahoma. The timber stands on distant ridges are blue and hazy.

At *40.4 m.* is the junction with a graveled ridge road.

1. Left on this road to BUFFALO HILL, *3.7 m.*, a beautiful low ridge between Tallahoma and Big Creeks commanding Ellisville and the valleys of the Tallahala and Tallahoma (R) some 200 feet below. This ridge at intervals has outcroppings of salt that fashioned its history. Buffalo traveling the ridges of the Mississippi Valley made the salt lick a favored gathering place, meeting here in mating season. The sandy red clay soil began to wash, and torrential spring rains gradually cut deep ravines across the ridges, following the buffalo paths. Now more than half of the vast swelling hills are cut into deep gullies of fantastic shape and color. A legend tells of a terrible drouth that drove the buffalo to new feeding grounds shortly after the first white explorers came to Mississippi's Indian country. The buffalo are gone, but the gullies they started grow deeper year by year.

2. Right on this road is SOSO, *1.6 m.*, a farm community dying swiftly as Laurel drains its vitality. The *MOSS PLANTATION, 5 m.* (L), is an unusually fine hill-country cotton plantation. In the creeks and runs that border the road are cold, spring-fed, swimming holes, into which naked rural children dive from the branches of trees.

At *43.4 m.* (L) is a good example of the dog-trot log cabin, the original type of house in this hill country.

At *44.1 m.* the highway crosses Big Creek. On the bank of the creek is the *BIG CREEK CHURCH,* belonging to the oldest "Hard-shell" Baptist congregation in Jones Co., organized more than a century ago. The present white frame building, built about 1887, is a simple structure set in a quiet lowland with a churchyard across the highway. In April and May the creek banks at the rear of the church are a bower of laurel blossoms, and all summer long the flowers bloom in the churchyard. In the Lauren Rogers Library and Museum of Art in Laurel is a PAINTING OF THE CHURCH by Paul King, A.N.A.

Between Big Creek and Hebron US 84 traverses poor cotton and corn fields separated by woodland patches of scrub oak and surrounded by crooked, split-rail fences.

HEBRON, *48.5 m.*, was once the home of Capt. Newt Knight of the Jones County Free Staters *(see Tour 8)*.

At *50.8 m.* the highway crosses the Leaf River on Reddoch's Bridge. The shell of the old bridge remains (L). The crossing is possibly a century and a half old.

At Reddoch's bridge (L) is the entrance to DESERTER'S END LAKE, a horseshoe lake where Free-Stater Newt Knight and his band often hid out to evade the pursuing Confederate cavalry. The peninsula within the curve of the horseshoe was a strategic position at which to meet attacking forces.

At *54.6 m.* (L) is a country church and churchyard with graves covered by small wooden sheds. The church has gingerbread trimmings,

COVERED GRAVES IN A COUNTRY CHURCHYARD

reminiscent of the architecture of the 1890's and incongruous with the simplicity of its lines.

The highway in its tortuous descent of the ridge occasionally passes good stands of timber.

COLLINS, 62.7 m. (274 alt., 935 pop.) *(see Tour 7, Sec. b)*, is at the junctions with US 49 *(see Tour 7, Sec. b)*, and State 35 *(see Tour 16)*.

WILLIAMSBURG, 67 m., was the seat of Covington Co. when Covington included a large part of what is now Jefferson Davis Co. In the old county Williamsburg was at the geographical center and, before the railroad passed it by, was a political center of considerable influence. It is now unpainted and almost uninhabited. Cane presses, log cabins with separate kitchens, mud chimneys, and paling fences remain.

MOUNT CARMEL, 78.5 m. (218 pop.), marked by a half-dozen unpainted houses and unoccupied stores, was in the 1880's a thriving crossroads town grown rich from the farming country around it. When the railroad was carried through E. of the town, the white merchants' dwellings in their faded splendor were taken over by Negroes.

At *81.5 m.* (R) on the hill is *MOUNT ZION CHURCH*, typical of the hundreds scattered through this section of the State, where church service is one of the few diversions in the weekly routine.

PRENTISS, 85.4 m. (655 pop.), a stubbornly independent farm town, is the seat of Jefferson Davis Co.—the natives call it Jeff Davis. Like a majority of Mississippi county seats it is dwarfed by its courthouse. The farmers of Jeff Davis Co. were the first in the State to vote against beer after its legalization in 1933. The residents of Prentiss, with this same standard of morality, still refuse to sanction round dancing in the community house constructed with WPA assistance.

Perhaps the most recent of the many stories of Prentiss concerns what is locally called the Battle of Mississippi Run. The *BANK OF BLOUNT-VILLE* in the center of the town was held up in 1935 by Raymond Hamilton, a public enemy who had found a hide-out from G-men in the Jeff Davis Co. hills. When the bank sounded its alarm the citizens took out their squirrel guns and "Long Toms" and went after the fleeing bandit. All day through the dust, he was followed by an ever-increasing group of man-hunters, who were whooping at him from a respectful distance. The climax was reached when Raymond turned, waited for the vigilantes to catch up, and then held up and disarmed them. Two of the sturdy citizens were taken as hostages and stuffed in the rumble seat of the car in which Raymond made his get-away. He abandoned the car and hostages at Memphis, Tenn.

> Left from Prentiss on State 42 to the *PRENTISS NORMAL AND INDUSTRIAL INSTITUTE, 1 m.*, a privately controlled but semi-public training school for Negroes, non-sectarian and coeducational, with a self-perpetuating board of trustees. The curriculum, of four-year high school grade, aims particularly at teacher training. Approximately 400 students come from rural homes of 25 south Mississippi counties, and most of them work for their board and tuition. The property on which the school is situated was once a plantation, and the ante-bellum big house is now used as an office building. It is said that several grandchildren of slaves who belonged to the plantation have graduated from the school. The Prentiss Jubilee Singers have been used to publicize the work of the institution for more than 20 years, a third of the operating expenses usually being met from funds raised by the traveling singers; they have toured every section of the United States.

Between Prentiss and Silver Creek the highway passes through a remote section with small cotton farms, where farmers live almost independent of outside influences.

SILVER CREEK, *95 m.* (263 alt., 341 pop.), has wooden sheds over the gravestones in its graveyards.

At *101.6 m.* the planter-style house (L) is indicative of the influence of the Pearl River Valley.

At *101.8 m.* the road parallels the river (L), passing through a cypress swamp of considerable charm, and crosses Pearl River at *102.7 m.* The view (L) from the bridge is one of the finest in the valley.

MONTICELLO, *102.8 m.* (200 alt., 606 pop.), is a good example of a Mississippi inland river town. Fifty miles down the Pearl River from Jackson, it was a port for river steamers running to and from New Orleans as late as 1904. The town was founded in 1798, the year Mississippi Territory was created, and was made the seat of Lawrence Co. in 1815. From that time until 1880 it prospered, reaching its greatest population, 2,500, in the latter year. Just before the War between the States, the Illinois Central R.R. was built through Brookhaven 22 miles W. of Pearl River; this has been a drain on Monticello's business.

During its period of prosperity, however, the town furnished the State two Governors, Charles Lynch (1836-38) and Hiram Runnels (1833-35). Hiram Runnels was the son of Harmon Runnels, founder of Monticello and in 1817 a member of Mississippi's first Constitutional Convention. Harmon Runnels was described by Col. J. F. H. Claiborne, Mississippi historian, as a "Hard-shell" Baptist who had been a hard-fighting captain from Georgia in the Continental Army, decidedly a pugilist in temperament, and ready to flare up at anyone who slurred his religion, his politics, or his friend, Gen. Elisha Clark. He ruled the Pearl River country as long as he lived and died an octogenarian at Monticello. His son Hiram took office as Governor in 1833, then was defeated by Lynch in 1835.

In the second campaign as he toured the State Runnels was heckled by Franklin Plummer. As Colonel Claiborne, candidate for Lieutenant Governor on the Runnels ticket, described the scene, Plummer, the representative of the United States Bank interests, "having no principle, was able to keep provokingly cool and entertaining to the crowd," while poor Hiram "found his indignation and resentment beyond expression in parliamentary language." But the Runnells party were no mean hecklers themselves. Their press dubbed Lynch as the "alias Van Buren, alias Jackson, alias anti-Jackson, alias anything candidate." Both Lynch and Runnels were vocal in opposition to the bank and to Calhoun's nullification theory, their stand on these two national issues representing well the anti-capitalist and anti-planter views of their Pearl River Valley constituents.

Monticello was selected the State capital in the 1820's, but 24 hours later the legislature changed its mind. In the courthouse, which has been rebuilt three times, silver-tongued Seargent S. Prentiss, lawyer and orator, received his license to practice law in 1829. Several of the inscriptions in Monticello's two cemeteries, written in Hebrew and Greek, show the learning of some of Monticello's early citizens.

At *103.4 m.* (R) is the junction with a graveled road that borders the river. This cool, shaded drive through a hardwood forest suggests well the break the Pearl Valley makes in the typical culture of the Piney Woods.

Between Monticello and Brookhaven, US 84, passing isolated churches and churchyards, runs through the westernmost tracts of the Piney Woods from which the truck-farming belt has developed. The truck fields begin to appear near the *OAK HILL FARMS, 118.8 m.* (L), whose champion bulls have taken ribbons at many Southern stock shows.

BROOKHAVEN, *127 m.* (500 alt., 5,288 pop.), has practically outlived its ante-bellum character and with its dairying interests has become a lively modern town. Until 1851, when it was the first northern terminus of the New Orleans & Great Southern R.R., Brookhaven was little more than a straggling group of plantations centered about the crossroads store of Samuel Jayne, who had settled here in 1818. With the advent of the railroad, it slowly took shape as a village of wealthy merchants who ensconced their families in great white-columned homes to live leisurely but formal social lives. Until 1907 it was a place where ladies never made calls without hats and gloves, where the blinds were drawn for afternoon siestas, where streets were unpaved and shadowy with the arching branches of live oak trees, and where the daily arrival of the train and the mail were events to be anticipated. In that year, however, Brookhaven broke with its staid past to pioneer in a new activity in the State. The creamery established here was the first in Mississippi. Today the town is the hub of southern Mississippi's dairying country, supplying a great part of the milk products shipped to New Orleans. It has a well-knit business section and asphalt-paved streets; and sons and daughters have left outmoded rambling Colonial-style homes to follow every architectural fad in house building. Only burgeoning oaks and here and there a landmark are left as relics of the former easy village life.

The *HARDY HOME (private)*, S. end of Jackson St., is a good example of the type of house wealthy citizens built prior to and just after the War between the States. Constructed of red brick, the house follows the Greek Revival style, with imposing fluted columns simulating the stone ones of the Natchez district. The interior has ornamental plastering and fine old furnishings. Built by Capt. J. C. Hardy, it has for five generations been in possession of that family.

The *W. C. F. BROOKS HOME (private)*, near the courthouse (R) on Cherokee St., antedates the Hardy home by several years. It is a one-story frame structure built in 1858 in the plantation tradition. Its spread of rooms in long side ells, and the low sweeping lines of its roof give it an attractive informality.

WHITWORTH COLLEGE, facing South Jackson St., was built in 1858 as a successor to Elizabeth Academy. Today it is a Methodist junior college for girls that manages to retain a mellowed dignity in spite of modern-minded undergraduates. During the war the school dormitories were used as a hospital for wounded Confederate soldiers.

Here is the junction with US 51 *(see Tour 5, Sec. b)*.

Between Brookhaven and Meadville the highway passes through a country of pines and bluff hills. The pines are small but fairly thick. The cuts through which the highway runs show the yellow gravel-and-sand mixed clay that makes the section valuable for truck farming. The gradually increasing undergrowth in the woodland patches indicates the approach to the loess area. Split-rail fences border the road, and here are a number of oak-shaded churches and several small frame school buildings for Negroes. The rain-washed fields show the section's great need for erosion control.

At *143.3 m.* US 84 crosses the boundary of the HOMOCHITTO NATIONAL FOREST, first of the national forests to be established in Mississippi. This one is irregularly shaped and lies for the most part along the Homochitto River basin. It is used to demonstrate the control of soil erosion that has formed the large bars in the river. The forests have been cut over at least once, and most of the area has been severely burned.

The old cotton fields, abandoned at the outbreak of the War between the States, contain fine stands of second-growth loblolly pines.

Within the forest US 84 crosses the Homochitto (Ind., *big red*) River, *147.6 m.,* a clear stream meandering through great white sandbars.

The mill towns in the forest, QUENTIN, *149.5 m* (200 pop.), EDDICETON, *152.4 m.* (375 pop.), and BUDE, *156.7 m.* (1,378 pop.), are lively but stereotyped with their clustered cut-to-a-pattern houses.

At MEADVILLE, *161.1 m.* (341 pop.), is the FRANKLIN COUNTY COURTHOUSE. The county is named for Benjamin Franklin. On a well-chosen knoll at the west end of town, squarely blocking the highway, which serves as the main street, is the Meadville MASONIC HALL. In outline at a distance it is imposing, but closer inspection shows it to be plain. The town has no churches, religious services being held in the Masonic Hall by various denominations. The bell mounted on a scaffold at the side of the hall is rung before Sunday services.

Meadville is the home of Congressman Dan R. McGehee.

US 84 between Meadville and Washington shows well the fertility of loess. Vines running to the tops of tall pines are akin to those of the Natchez district. The great difference between these woods and the woods on the savannahs N. of the Coast is the undergrowth. Whereas the latter are park-like, these in the loess hills are jungles of tangled vines and shrubs. Through them the highway rides the comb of a ridge affording charming vistas of the National Forest.

At *171.2 m.* US 84 crosses the western boundary of the De Soto National Forest.

At *186.6 m.* is the junction with a graveled road.

Left on this road *0.1 m.* to old US 84; left on this road to entrance to TRAVELER'S REST, *1 m. (private),* the plantation home of Col. James Hoggatt. Hoggatt received his land grant from the Spanish authorities at Natchez in 1788 and built Traveler's Rest in 1797. At one time the Hoggatt holdings were perhaps the largest in Adams Co. Traveler's Rest is in reality two buildings joined by an immense open passage, with pointed arches at each end. It is an elaboration of the double-pen principle usually seen in log cabins rather than in planter's homes. Across the front and rear stretch galleries 84 feet long, supported by square colonnettes. Seven generations of Hoggatts have occupied this home.

WASHINGTON, *191.3 m.* (200 pop.) *(see Tour 3, Sec. b),* is at the junction (R) with US 61 *(see Tour 3, Sec. b),* with which the route unites between this point and Natchez.

Tour 12

(Bolivar, Tenn.)—Pontotoc—Bay Springs—Laurel—Lucedale—(Mobile, Ala.).
State 15.
Tennessee Line to Alabama Line, 330.5 m.
Highway one-third paved; rest graveled, two lanes wide.
Accommodations chiefly in larger towns.

State 15 reveals many phases of rural Mississippi life. For a hundred miles or more the scenes are typical of an upland: terraced corn and cotton patches clutching at the rugged Pontotoc Ridge; dog-trot houses with cool open hallways and clean scrubbed galleries; shortleaf pine woods and stumpy cut-over land dotted with nondescript grazing cattle. Between Louisville and Newton the ruggedness is modified but the scenes are more colorful. Sandy red soil and a sprinkling of glistening longleaf pines that shoot suddenly up among the duller shortleaf anticipate the Piney Woods to the S., where yellow pine forests, miles of cut-over land, promising young orchards, and farms alternate in rapid succession. Then abruptly the highway drops into the shadowy river country. Here in Arcadian tranquility and charm the Leaf and Pascagoula Rivers flow quietly to mirror in their waters the aged moss-hung oaks and gnarled cypress trees.

Crossing the Mississippi Line, *0 m.*, 15 miles S. of Bolivar, Tenn., State 15 immediately enters a region that becomes more populated the farther south it goes. On the rocky slopes fringing Walnut are a fair sprinkling of dairy and truck farms.

At WALNUT, *3.5 m.* (219 pop.), is the junction with US 72 *(see Tour 10)*.

South of Walnut for 25 miles the hills of the ridge are visible in a low blue line.

FALKNER, *11.1 m.* (466 alt., 275 pop.), is a typical upland farming village that supports, also, a hardwood lumber mill. Quiet all week, it is on Saturdays the center of a trade that brings a large number of wagons, trucks, and automobiles to crowd its unpaved main street. The town was named for Col. William C. Falkner, soldier, novelist, and grandfather of the novelist, William Faulkner who has made north central Mississippi live in fiction *(see ARTS and LETTERS)*.

Between Falkner and Ripley is the farming country where the Saturday traders live, growing cotton as an annual cash crop and raising sweet and Irish potatoes and hogs enough to feed the family.

RIPLEY, *19.1 m.* (508 alt., 1,468 pop.), was incorporated as the seat of Tippah Co. in 1837. Today the court square is the nucleus of the county.

Ripley's most colorful personality, Col. William Falkner, came to the

A HARDWOOD SAWMILL

village soon after the first courthouse was built, a barefoot boy of ten who had walked the several hundred miles from Middleton, Tenn., to see his uncle John Thompson with whom he wished to make his home. He arrived at dusk to find his uncle in jail, charged with murder. Disheartened and weary, he sat down upon the courthouse steps and wept. The story goes that in that moment of discouragement he swore he would some day build a railroad along the route he had walked. After the War between the States, in which Colonel Falkner became a local hero by assisting General Forrest in the defense of Ripley, he made his railroad something more tangible than a dream by building a line from Ripley to intersect the Memphis-Charleston line at Middleton. He first called his railroad the Ripley, Ship Island & Kentucky, but later, extending it southward through New Albany and Pontotoc, he renamed it the Gulf & Chicago. The railroad is now called the Gulf, Mobile & Northern.

Colonel Falkner fought many duels, and it is a family legend that when he made a bitter enemy of his old friend and railroad associate, Col. R. J. Thurmond, by defeating him for the State legislature in 1899, he refused to arm himself, saying that he already had killed too many men and did not want to kill any more. On the day of Falkner's second election to the legislature, Thurmond shot him dead on the main street of Ripley. A *MARBLE STATUE* marks Colonel Falkner's grave in the local cemetery. The Colonel is remembered not only for his railroad but for his novel, *The White Rose of Memphis,* the realism of which shocked his generation as much as his grandson's *Sanctuary* shocked present-day readers.

The *MURRY HOUSE (private),* two blocks (L) from court square, is characteristic of the more prosperous town houses built in the Central Hills before the War between the States. It was originally a frame two-story dwelling with a central hall. Later embellishments include the elaborately grilled balustrade of the long front gallery and upstairs balcony. The *JAIL,* Railroad St., memento of the War between the States, is now too weatherbeaten and dilapidated to be of use.

Left from Ripley on the Rienzi Road to the *THOMAS HINDMAN HOME, 1.3 m. (open by permission),* a two-story frame house, with greater width than depth, and a portico with balcony and four square columns. It is weatherboarded and twin brick chimneys flank the end walls. Thomas Hindman, killed in a duel with Col. Falkner, built the home in 1842. Hindman is buried in the cemetery 20 yds. W. of the house.

At *19.6 m.* on State 15 is the junction with a graveled road.

Left on this road to the *GILLARD HOME, 0.3 m. (open by permission).* A one-story cottage with a square portico and four slender square columns, it stands high on brick pilings. The house was bought in 1837 from the American Land Co. by H. W. Stricklin and sold in 1877 to A. M. Gillard. Perched upon a high bluff, the house, now in need of repair, is invisible from the road.

Between Ripley and Blue Mountain the highway climbs higher into the steep and rocky Pontotoc Ridge. Few farms are visible from the highway but pasturage is excellent. A substantial part of the milk that supplies the condenseries, creameries, and cheese factories of the Prairie belt is produced along this route.

BLUE MOUNTAIN, *25.8 m.* (461 alt., 569 pop.), sits in a valley between two of the highest Pontotoc Hills, drawing its subsistence from the colleges that cling to the slopes of these hills. *BLUE MOUNTAIN COLLEGE* (R) is a four-year accredited college for women, supported by the Mississippi Baptist Convention. Founded in 1873 by Gen. Mark Per-

TOUR 12 459

rin Lowrey, it is the oldest senior college for women in the State. The red brick administration building of modern design overlooks the town from the center of the campus. To the rear and side of it are seven other modern buildings including dormitories. *MISSISSIPPI HEIGHTS*, on the hilltop opposite, is a newer school established in 1905 as a privately supported preparatory school for boys. With a small enrollment, all school activities take place in the square red brick building that dominates the campus. From this is a sweeping view of the surrounding valleys. In spite of collegiate activities centered here, the town of Blue Mountain retains the dignity of age. It was established in the 1830's.

The ridges, having reached their height at Blue Mountain, level off between here and New Albany; with the rugged topography lost in gentle undulations, farm lands are better and more acreage is under cultivation. The scene is average Mississippi without the palpable signs of prosperity that the Delta and Prairie flaunt, yet with comfortable living from the land. This comfort is evident in well-tended vegetable gardens, cords of wood stored under the farmhouses, chickens, geese, turkeys, and pigs around the doorsteps and often a truck or automobile parked beneath a tree in the yard.

At *31.1 m.* is the junction with a local graveled road.

Right on this road is COTTON PLANT, *0.7 m.* (415 alt., 150 pop.), best known for the *PAUL RAINEY ESTATE*. In 1898 Paul Rainey, sportsman and big game hunter, bought 11,000 acres and stocked them with wolves, bears, foxes, and pheasants. During Rainey's lifetime sportsmen came here to hunt and to attend the annual field trials. The Rainey house, now occupied by a sister of Rainey, is a plain white frame farmhouse that has lost much of the glamor of gay parties, hunt balls, and breakfasts associated with it during Rainey's lifetime. Since his death in 1926 the game preserve has been abolished and the estate converted into small tenant farms known as Tippah Farms. Prevalent in the neighborhood is the belief that Rainey's death, reported to have occurred while he was en route to Africa on a hunting expedition, actually did not happen, and that the hunter now lives incognito in Europe.

Between here and New Albany large galvanized milk cans sit before the farm gates along the highway, giving a clue to New Albany's newest and most flourishing industry.

At *31.6 m.* is *TIPPAH-UNION SCHOOL* (R), a Smith-Hughes vocational high school.

At NEW ALBANY, *39.8 m.* (364 alt., 3,187 pop.) *(see Tour 9)*, is the junction with US 78 *(see Tour 9)*.

South of New Albany the well-built durable farmhouses are indicative of the living derived from cattle raising and truck and fruit farming. In peach time, when the upland orchards are bearing, the fruit is for sale at houses along the highway. The rocky, semi-fertile soil produces an excellent peach of the Elberta variety.

At *45.9 m.* is the junction with a graveled road.

Right on this road is INGOMAR, *1.3 m.* (364 alt., 241 pop.), established by Colonel Falkner as a stop on his Chicago & Gulf R.R. and named by him for a character in his novel, *The White Rose of Memphis*.

At *51.6 m.* is ECRU (560 pop.), also established by Colonel Falkner and named for the color of the depot. Formerly a lumber town, it is now dependent upon farming.

The lands encircling Pontotoc are closely associated with the history and legends of the Chickasaw Indians. Before the Treaty of Pontotoc (1832), in which northern Mississippi was ceded to the Government, few white settlers had come among the warlike Chickasaw to disturb their "long towns" scattered through the Pontotoc Hills *(see ARCHEOLOGY AND INDIANS).*

PONTOTOC, 57.3 *m.* (462 alt., 2,018 pop.), is the seat of Pontotoc County, a county well known in Mississippi for its individualistic point of view and manner of living. Here the courthouse does not dominate the business district by sitting solidly in the center of the square, but democratically stands in line with the business houses facing the square. Pontotoc is entirely dependent on rural trade.

In 1832 the Chickasaw Cession provided that a land office for the sale of Chickasaw lands be located in the center of the former Chickasaw Territory, and, with the establishment of that office, Pontotoc came into existence. In its name the town perpetuates the Chickasaw struggle to retain their territory, the word being a compound (Ind., *ponti* and *tokali, battle where the cat-tails stood*). The battle referred to is D'Artaguiette's defeat near old Pontotoc in 1736. The land boom of the 1830's brought settlers of English and Scotch-Irish blood from Virginia, Carolina, and Kentucky and before the War between the States made Pontotoc one of the most popular and prosperous towns in northern Mississippi. The culture produced at that time has not been effaced today.

CHICKASAW COLLEGE, a Presbyterian coeducational school founded in 1852, is on the site of the Pontotoc Female Academy established in 1836. The *JACK FONTAINE HOME,* 1210 S. Congress St. *(open by appointment),* is a frame two-story house with a high pitched roof and a square entrance portico supported by large round columns. It was built in 1850. The *TURNER THOMASON HOME,* 705 S. Congress St. *(open by appointment),* of Greek Revival design, has a one-story wing extending from each side of the two-story main unit. The fluted Ionic columns of the square portico and a double entrance door are its outstanding features. The house was built in 1856. The *FRANK A. CLARK HOME,* half a mile NE. of the courthouse on State 6, built in 1850, is on the site of the old land office. The house is a gracefully rambling one-story cottage, with low roof, porticoed entrance, and end chimneys that add to its informal appearance. Painted white, with a green roof and shutters, it has a freshness that belies its age. The *CAPTAIN BOLTON HOME,* in the first block of E. Marion St., is a tiny one-story brick house, interesting in that it was at one time the office of the New York-Mississippi Land Co.

Here is the junction with State 6 *(see Tour 14).*

At the southern limits of Pontotoc is the junction with a rough clay road.

> Right on this road to the *SPENCER HOME, 0.8 m. (open),* a low spreading dog-trot house built in 1836 and since greatly enlarged with rambling additions at the side and rear. The log walls are painted white and a narrow gallery runs

the length of the house. The house is occupied by descendants of the builder, and many pieces of the early family furniture are in use today. This structure is one of the best examples of the pioneer home of this section, and it shows how an increase in family and wealth enlarged it.

At *58.8 m.* on State 15 is the junction with State 41, graveled.

Left on State 41 at *2.9 m.* (L) to *STONY LONESOME (open).* The name is an eloquent description of the house that sits high on a ridge, its tall, straight uncompromising mass silhouetted against a landscape of unusual primitiveness. Judge Joel Pinson, one of the county's earliest settlers, used hand-hewn timbers 16 inches thick for the walls and six-inch heart pines for the flooring when he built the house in 1849. It is a two-story, frame dwelling with long gable, end chimneys, and narrow front gallery. The exterior is covered with weather-beaten clapboards, and the gallery with its slender wood posts has a shingled shed roof. The central hall on each floor is flanked by large square rooms. The house is occupied by Negro tenants.

At *3.9 m.* on State 41 is the *D'ARTAGUIETTE MARKER* (L), a plain rock slab bearing the following inscription:

"Pierre D'Artaguiette
French Commander, was defeated in battle
With Chickasaw Indians Sunday, May 20, 1736
A week later D'Artaguiette, Francois-Marie
Bissot De Vincennes, Father Antoine Senat,
Jesuit Missionary—in all 20 Frenchmen captured—
Were burned at the stake by their captors.
Father Senat
Scorning the offer to escape martyrdom,
Remained with his comrades and intoning the
Miserere, led them into the destroying flames.
Erected by the John Foster Society
Children of the American Revolution
Columbus, Mississippi 1934."

A map from the French archives, however, places the scene of this battle a few miles further E. nearer Belden and Tupelo.

Between Pontotoc and Ackerman farming gives way to small-scale lumbering. Hillsides thickly covered with shortleaf pine trees alternate with small clearings made by the tractor-run sawmills characteristic of northern Mississippi. The impress of the early pioneers remains here both in the architecture and in the wholesome, unpretentious manner of the people. The pioneers were Scotch-Irish mountaineers who moved out of the Piedmont through Kentucky and Tennessee and into Mississippi in ox-drawn carts. In their course of migration they did not touch the Tidewater country, so they brought no traces of Tidewater culture with them. They built dog-trot houses with no refining additions, and they centered their communities around square, box-like churches that had no slave galleries. A number of the early homes and churches remain scattered over the countryside as indications of the straightforward people who built them. Even the newer homes and churches, patterned on the old, show an inherent quality of plainness and independence that has not been colored by modernity.

The *JOHN PEARSON HOME, 59.3 m.* (L), resembles the Spencer home near Pontotoc in appearance, having been erected during the same pioneer period. The house stands directly upon the old Chickasaw Trail.

At *59.9 m.* (R) is LOCHINVAR *(private)*, built in the early 1830's by Robert Gordon, a descendant of one of Scotland's oldest families. Coming to Mississippi in 1800, Gordon settled in the prairie country near Aberdeen, which town he named. Here he amassed a fortune trading with the Indians and growing cotton *(see Tour 4).* With the opening of the land office at Pontotoc he migrated to the hills to build his mansion, designed more in the manner of the hybrid Georgian Colonial style of the Prairie Belt than that of the Central Hills area. Lochinvar is two-and-a-half stories in height and contains a broad central hall and eight high-ceilinged rooms, each 22 feet square. A spiral stairway leads to the third floor. At the rear, separate from the house, is a brick kitchen that contains the original brick Dutch oven. Timber used in the house is heart pine and the framework is of solid hand-hewn pine. The columns of the front portico are of the Roman Doric order and rise two stories in height in support of a classic pediment. A notable feature of the portico is the delicate detail of the balustrade at the second floor gallery. The columns were shipped to Mobile from a Scottish castle and were hauled overland in oxcarts. The house is flanked by broad side porches, one story in height topped with flat deck roofs. The house was designed by a Scotch architect.

At *64.9 m.* (R) is the *MONROE MISSION,* a small box-like frame building, gray with age, established by the Rev. Thomas C. Stewart. Sent by the Presbyterian Synod of South Carolina, Stewart came as a missionary to the Chickasaw early in 1821. Chief Colbert, leader of the Chickasaw Nation, helped the missionary to find a suitable site, though Stewart himself selected the name, calling the mission for James Monroe, then President of the United States. The mission is now a mortuary connected with the cemetery in the churchyard.

At *68 m.* is the junction with a graveled road.

Left on this road to the *TOXISH BAPTIST CHURCH, 1.7 m.* (L), built in 1840. With its white frame walls and square lines it is typical of Mississippi country churches. Inside, coal oil lamps, pine benches, colored glass windows, and a foot-pump organ are in keeping with exterior simplicity. The church occupies the site of the home of Col. John McIntosh, who migrated here from the Oglethorpe Colony in Georgia, and takes its name from an older church building.

At *73.3 m.* is OLD HOULKA (Ind., *sacred place).* Nothing is left of the town that at the time of De Soto's expedition in 1541 was well established as a seat of Chickasaw tribal culture and near which almost three centuries later an Indian agency was established. This agency became an important trading post on the Natchez Trace, which, running directly through the village, determined much of its early history *(see TRANSPORTATION).* After the cession of Indian lands in 1832, white settlers took over the town, cleared the land, and built their homes. The town prospered until the Gulf, Mobile & Northern R.R. was built a mile E. and New Houlka absorbed the older settlement.

Between Old Houlka and Houston the landscape is marked by extensive rugged pasture lands. Along the highway shiny milk cans wait beside farmhouse mail boxes for the milk truck that conveys them to Houston.

TOUR 12 463

HOUSTON, *83.5 m.* (324 alt., 1,477 pop.), the hundred-year-old seat of Chickasaw Co., is named for Sam Houston, Texas general and life-long friend of Joel Pinson who donated the land for the town's site. Closely tied to the Prairie towns that fringe it on the E. *(see Tour 4),* Houston is building its future on the newly developed dairying industry. Recently a *CHEESE PLANT* to handle the milk products of a wide area has been established. But tying it to the past are its ante-bellum homes of Georgian and Greek Revival types of architecture.

The *BATES TABB HOME* is a nine-room house with a portico having four ornate columns and, above the entrance door, a graceful balcony. Erected in 1845 the house is in good repair today; a detached kitchen remains as it was in ante-bellum days, with pothooks and cooking vessels intact. After General Grierson's raid on the town the house was used as a hospital for wounded Confederate soldiers.

The *J. M. GRIFFIN HOME* was built by General Tucker a few years preceding the War between the States. Although similar in floor plan to the usual Southern Planter type of dwelling, the style of the house is early Victorian. This is notable in its high hip roof, overlarge dormers, and lacy jig-saw ornament.

The *CARNEGIE LIBRARY,* Main St., was the first Carnegie Library to be established in the State.

GEOLOGY HILL, half a mile N. of the courthouse, is named for the unusual geological formations of various colors and sizes found here. Near the hill are *INDIAN MOUNDS* from which arrow points, pottery, and crudely fashioned jewelry have been removed.

As the highway climbs among the Central Hills, comfortable frame and log houses, country schools and churches, and crossroad stores are seen.

MABEN, *107.7 m.* (444 alt., 508 pop.), is a slightly enlarged edition of the numerous small communities that dot this highway. Its essential characteristic, that of being a trading place for farmers, is the same; only in the number of its stores, houses, and people does it differ. Suggestive of old-time horseswappings is the auction of livestock, poultry, and farm produce held here on Thursdays.

MATHISTON, *110.1 m.* (405 alt., 484 pop.), is the junction with US 82 *(see Tour 6).*

Between here and Ackerman small tractor-powered lumber mills have cut blank patches in the green wall of shortleaf pines.

At ACKERMAN, *127.6 m.* (522 alt., 1,169 pop.), two large sawmills give the inhabitants a substantial industrial life. Though few of the lumber towns of this section have attained a prosperity equaling that of the villages that mushroomed with the yellow pine dynasty in the Piney Woods, none has been left to lie like a ghost in the shadows of gaunt, deserted mills.

Ackerman is the home of Hon. A. L. Ford, Representative in Congress (1934–   ).

Here is the junction with State 9 *(see Side Tour 12A).*

South of Ackerman the scene slowly changes. This transition section between the Central Hills and the Piney Woods is known as the flatwoods.

A touch of the Prairie's roll creeps in to modify the rugged contour of the land, and the clay changes from light orange to red giving color to the landscape. The longleaf pines are visible in the wooded areas, and there are houses of both classic and dog-trot type.

LOUISVILLE, *142.7 m.* (536 alt., 3,013 pop.), represents both hills and prairie, combining in its interests the lumber mills of one and the large-scale farming and dairying of the other. The pattern upon which the town is planned resembles that of most Mississippi county seats: with a courthouse square and a Confederate monument in the center.

Left from Louisville on a graveled road to LEGION STATE PARK, *1 m.*, occupying a 424-acre tract of rugged woodlands. The park was built by the Civilian Conservation Corps as a camping site and recreational center. Hiking and bridle paths cut through it in a network of scenic beauty. A part of the acreage has been set aside as a bird and game preserve. The whole is enclosed by fences of native orangewood, a wood of great strength and durability, which add to the pleasantly rustic effect. In the center of the park is a recreation hall built of native rock; overnight cabins, equipped with running water, are available at moderate cost.

NOXAPATER (Lat., *dark father*), *152 m.* (487 alt., 526 pop.), is an old village near the heart of Choctaw Indian country.

Left from Noxapater on a graveled road to a narrow winding lane at *6 m.;* L. here to *NANIH WAIYA* (Ind., *slanting hill*) *9.6 m.* This, the sacred mound of the Choctaw, occupies a unique position in Choctaw tradition in that it is connected with both the creation and the migration of the tribes. It was the center of Choctaw life before the advent of the white men. The Indians call it "Great Mother" and look upon it as the birthplace of their race. Out of it ages ago, they believe, came first the Muskogee who sunned themselves on the rampart until dry, then went eastward. Next came the Cherokee, who, after having undergone the sunlight baking process, followed the trail of the older tribe. Then came the Chickasaw who settled and made a people to the north. At last came the Choctaw, who sunned themselves until dry, then settled about the mound, their "Great Mother," who told them that if they ever left her side they would die. When the Government remembered its century-old debt to the Choctaw *(see Tour 4)* and established the present Indian agency in 1918, most of the tribe who remained were found to be living near the sacred mound, clinging hopefully to the legendary promise of protection. Nanih Waiya is more than 50 ft. high and covers an acre.

North of Nanih Waiya 250 yds. is another mound, a small one where, according to Choctaw legend, corn was first presented to the world. Soon after the Choctaw had settled, a crow brought a single grain from across the great water (Gulf) and gave it to an orphan child who was playing near the mound. The child named it *tonchi* (corn) and planted it. When it came up he "hoed it, hilled it, and laid it by," and so began the cultivation of maize.

BURNSIDE, *158.9 m.* (399 alt., 100 pop.), was established in 1846 by the Burnside brothers. In the early 1850's a sawmill, purchased in Ohio and brought down the Mississippi River to Vicksburg and thence by way of Pearl River to Burnside, was erected. This was the first steam mill of its type in the State; its erection marked the beginning of the lumber industry in northern Mississippi. A large mill operates here today.

Between Burnside and Philadelphia the soil is increasingly red and sandy. The farms that the highway passes are splotched colorfully against it, making a gay and pleasing picture.

PHILADELPHIA, *167.1 m.* (416 alt., 2,560 pop.), settled soon after

CHOCTAW HANDICRAFT, INDIAN AGENCY, PHILADELPHIA

the Treaty of Dancing Rabbit Creek *(see Tour 4)* on the site of the ancient Indian town, Aloon Looanshaw (Ind., *bull frog place)*, is today the center of Mississippi's Indian country. In the Philadelphia area are concentrated the greatest number of the 1,745 Indians remaining in Mississippi, and in Philadelphia is the Choctaw Indian Agency, established in 1918. In direct control is a superintendent, and under him are a chief clerk, two stenographers, a farm agent, a farmer, and a field nurse. The superintendent also supervises the modern 30-room hospital, built especially for the Indians, and the seven scattered day schools for Indian children. The work is financed by an annual allotment of approximately $100,-000. The Indians are known today as "Mississippi Choctaw," meaning

MISSISSIPPI CHOCTAW

they are a remnant of the 3,000 Choctaw warriors who in 1830 refused to give up this land and their homes to the U.S. Government *(see ARCHEOLOGY AND INDIANS)*.

Approximately 75 families live either in small white houses, dotting hills purchased by the Government, or in small tenant houses on land owned by the Roman Catholic Church. Scattered among the settlements are 77 small farms that the Indians own and cultivate with implements, stock, and seeds furnished them. In addition, two farm experts are provided to help them plan, raise, and market their products. The farms are of necessity the chief source of Indian income, though the men make axe handles and split-oak-bottom chairs, and the women weave gayly colored baskets, which, when sold, supplement the incomes. These products are exhibited the first of August each year at the Neshoba Co. Fair, and can be purchased from the Indians themselves, from the agency, or from the Municipal Art Gallery in Jackson.

A YOUNG CHOCTAW

1. Left from Philadelphia on State 19 is *TUCKER, 6.3 m. (open)*, one of the seven Indian day schools. The Tucker school is well situated on a tract of seven acres, with a Roman Catholic Mission adjoining. The teacher's cottage is one-story with six rooms; the school building is a large, white frame building with two classrooms, a dining room, a kitchen, and two bath rooms. While morning classes are in progress, the teacher's assistant prepares a substantial meal which is

served at noon. The children receive baths at the school. The work done in this and other Indian schools extends through the first six grades and compares favorably with that done in white schools.

At 13.4 m. on State 19 is the HOUSE CONSOLIDATED SCHOOL, a two-story box-like frame building. Here is the junction with a graveled road.

Left 2.2 m. on this road to the JAMES WILSON HOME (L), with the good proportions and simple lines of the Southern Planter type of dwelling. Colonel Wilson was the first white settler in this location which was formerly the Indian village Emuchalushia (Ind., *our people are there*). He was living here in a log hut when "the stars fell" in 1833, and the next year built the present house to be used as a tavern for the stagecoach line he operated. Colonel Wilson drove the coach himself, contracted for a certain number of miles with the Government, and was paid by the mile. He drove four horses to a coach and would trot them as fast as they could go, changing horses with each ten miles. The old taproom of the hotel is known today as Traveler's Room. In it is a chimney stack 67.5 inches wide and 53 inches deep. Upon it hang the portraits of Washington and Andrew Jackson placed there when the house was built.

2. Right from Philadelphia on State 16 to WILLIAM'S STORE, 2 m., typical of the country store in the South. A rambling one-story building, it serves a widespread farm community with various commodities from plug tobacco to plows. Farmers' wives meet here and gossip while their children munch candy and drink soda pop. The farmers discuss crops, the weather, and politics with great heat, and often political convictions are formed over the counter. Political candidates find the country store of this type an excellent place to leave their cards for distribution.

At William's Store on State 16 is the junction with a graveled road.

Left 4 m. on this road to NESHOBA COUNTY FAIRGROUND. The fair originated in 1892 and is held annually the latter part of July or first part of August *(season tickets $1, single adm. 50¢; accommodations at two hotels on fair ground)*. The usual products of an agricultural county are shown. Concessions, sideshows, merry-go-rounds, and ferris wheels entertain the customers. What has made the fair unusual is that it has become the political ring into which State politicians toss their hats during election years. Often candidates for office make their first public announcement here. In a hall on the fairground, political speechmaking goes on continuously, and outside on the sawdust midway candidates dispense cards and food freely. The impression a candidate makes here at the fair often remains in the minds of the public on election day and greatly influences the vote.

One night of the fair is set aside as Indian night, at which time the Choctaw give exhibitions of tribal games and dances. Their colorful costumes, adorned with beads and horses' tails, and their dances contrast strikingly with the homely fair atmosphere. During fair week at least one Indian ballgame is played. It takes place in the afternoon, following the same procedure and rules as the peculiar game of the ancient tribe. This contest takes place on a field similar to a football field in size. The player is equipped with two sticks approximately three feet long, having loosely woven cups at each end. The object of the game is to hit one's pole or goal, located at the end of the field, with a small golf-like ball which is thrown by an opponent, caught by the player in the cup of his stick, and quickly hurled again. The Choctaw spectators enjoy this sport as much as the players, and betting is heavy. In the past the Choctaw would bet their ponies, their crops, their clothing, and often a large part of their territory if they met a rival tribe in a game. Several inter-tribal games in which territory was lost and won took place between the Creek and Choctaw tribes, and one, the game at Beaver Pond, resulted in war.

Between Philadelphia and Newton is open farming country. The red sandy soil is especially adapted to fruit growing, and where formerly grew longleaf and shortleaf pines and a variety of hardwood trees, now peach, apple, and pecan orchards stretch out in symmetrical rows. Indians are passed often on the highway through this section, the calico dresses of the women and children as gayly colored as the red clay hills that furnish their background.

At *182.7 m.* is UNION (471 alt., 1,705 pop.), occupying the site of the Indian village, Chauki. The town was settled by white men in 1829 because the Indians here grew corn with great success. At that time a stage line from Montgomery, Ala., to Jackson, Miss., ran through the village and assisted in the town's growth until April 1863, when General Sherman burned all but a few of the houses.

The *BOLER HOME,* a sprawling two-story frame house, is the one remaining example of ante-bellum architecture. It is in bad repair, but long, wide galleries on the first and second stories, mammoth brick chimneys flanking the ends, and a yard planted with magnolia trees still give evidence of the comfortable small-town living that existed before the War between the States. It was built by Wesley Boler in 1847.

Between Union and Newton the red clay hills, modified both as to degree of color and ruggedness, have been stripped of their trees by lumber mills.

DECATUR, *192.9 m.* (408 alt., 654 pop.), lost the records of its antebellum history when Sherman passed through and burned the courthouse in 1863. Since that time it has become so modern as to elect a woman for its mayor and to build one of the best equipped junior colleges in the State. Its interests are divided between hill farming and lumbering with a substantial income derived from both.

Here is the *EAST CENTRAL JUNIOR COLLEGE,* a State-supported coeducational school, established in 1928 (1936–37 enrollment, 345).

At NEWTON, *200.9 m.* (412 alt., 2,011 pop.) *(see Tour 2),* is the junction with US 80 *(see Tour 2).*

South of Newton the prosperous hill farms recede, and with the miles the Piney Woods scene is more and more evident. Here longleaf pines have crowded out other varieties of trees, and only a few small patches of corn and cotton appear; the country centers its interests upon lumbering.

At *217.8 m.* is MONTROSE (418 alt., 312 pop.), a village that achieved prestige in the 1840's when Montrose Academy flourished here. The school, after losing its president to the newly-opened University of Mississippi, was abandoned in 1848.

At *222.5 m.* is LOUIN (427 alt., 583 pop.), a country village and railroad stop on the Gulf, Mobile & Northern R.R.

BAY SPRINGS, *229.7 m.* (406 alt., 927 pop.), operates a sawmill, a stave mill, and a block and spindle mill, utilizing the material of the nearby forests. It administers justice for the county from the red brick courthouse on the crest of a steep hill at the northern edge of town.

Within the short span of less than 25 years the brief stretch of country between Bay Springs and Laurel lived and died, and today is struggling for a rebirth. Towns that mushroomed into prominence with the rise of the yellow pine lumber industry are now desolate, ghost-like guardians of abandoned sawmills. The land lies now scarcely touched by man, as if left free in its desperate struggle to replenish the once great forests of pine; but the scars left by mill owners when the cutting was exhausted show through the small, second-growth timber in miles of stump-covered fields. The cutting of the virgin trees also gave an impetus to erosion; hillsides and ridges, appearing a vague greenish-blue at a distance, have deep red gullies eating at their hearts.

State 15 enters on 5th St.; R. on 13th Ave.; L. on 6th St.; L. on 8th Ave.; R. on 7th St.; L. on 2nd Ave. to Magnolia St.

LAUREL, *253.6 m.* (243 alt., 18,017 pop.).

Points of Interest. Art Museum, vegetable canning plant, starch factory, Masonite Corporation, naval stores, and others.

Here are the junctions with US 84 *(see Tour 11)* and US 11 *(see Tour 8).*

The route continues R. on Magnolia St.; L. on Central St.; R. on Ellisville Blvd. (State 15).

The cutover lands that extend southward from Laurel to the marshes of the Leaf and Pascagoula Rivers are used as a laboratory for industrial experimentation. Fruit and tung tree orchards, turpentine farms, forests of young pines to be sold to pulp mills, poultry farms, and forest preserves are seen. Occasionally the highway passes miles of stumpy former timberland, to come upon the skeleton of some mill town left as a relic of the lumber dynasty. The hills of the Piney Woods then lose themselves in the low flat Coastal Meadow, and the highway descends to a setting of picturesque beauty with live oaks and winding rivers furnishing the scenery.

DE SOTO NATIONAL FOREST, *264.7 m.,* is the scene of reforestation efforts. A fine sprinkling of tiny seedling pines and a few remaining specimens of virgin timber are being carefully protected by the Government. Southward truck and poultry farms dot the landscape to vary the scene of seedling pines that extend for miles through this section and resemble Christmas greens in their perfect uniformity and diminutive size.

RICHTON, *281 m.* (160 alt., 950 pop.), abandoned a fast-dying lumber industry in 1927 to turn its attention to diversified farming.

Left from Richton on a graveled road to the *FARM HOMESTEAD PROJECT*, *2.5 m.,* the result of a "grown-in-the-county dinner," at which 47 articles of food were served to the guests by the Rotary Club at Richton, inspiring the people of the county to a back-to-the-farm movement. The outgrowth of this dinner was the erection of 15 houses in 1936. The houses were built on 80 acres of cutover land, the latter to be used for diversified farming. The houses contain five rooms each, are painted white with green or red roofs, and have their private wells, chicken yards, and barns. They have been erected by the Government and are for sale on small-term payments. On Beaver Dam Lake, near the center of the homestead project, is an *OLD WATER MILL* built in 1851. Formerly used for sawing lumber the mill today grinds meal and thrashes a little rice grown in the vicinity. Beaver Dam is alleged to have been built by Indians who came here to camp and to swim in its waters.

South of Leaf River, *293.5 m.,* the pines give place to sprawling live oak trees, overgrown in a luxuriance of gray moss. The soil shows an increasing sandiness.

At BEAUMONT, *294.5 m.* (93 alt., 350 pop.), is the junction with State 24 *(see Tour 13)*, the two highways uniting between this point and McLAIN, *301.9 m.* (76 alt., 350 pop.).

South of McLain the highway passes through LEAF RIVER SWAMP, a sandy white thread twining among woods of shadowy beauty.

At *304.2 m.* (L) the view of Leaf River Swamp, with moss-covered cypresses reflected in still green marsh pools, is more suggestive of the Florida Everglades than of Mississippi.

At *305 m.* Leaf and Chickasawhay Rivers join to form Pascagoula River. Right from the bridge the red sandy banks are a brilliant background for the limpid green waters. East of the river the highway rises out of the swamp to run through miles of pasture land thickly dotted with sheep and cattle.

At LUCEDALE, *318.8 m.* (185 alt., 834 pop.), is the junction with State 63 *(see Tour 15)*.

The highway is paved between this point and the Alabama Line, cutting through steep red clay banks. On both sides of the highway are rolling farms and pastures.

The *LUCE FARMS, 319.8 m.*, the best example the route offers of renascent cut-over land, were established in 1914 to furnish employment to men left idle by the closing of the mills in Lucedale. The farms supply the Luce Products Co. with vegetables, growing green beans, okra, tomatoes, turnip greens, peppers, English peas, beets, spinach, pineapple pears, pecans, corn, oats, and rye. Many farmers of George and Greene Counties are stockholders in the company.

The influence of the Luce Farms extends throughout the remainder of the route in a patchwork of small fruit and vegetable farms.

The highway crosses Escatawpa River which forms the Alabama Line, at *330.5 m.*, 27 miles NW. of Mobile, Ala. The hills of Alabama are visible as a dark humped outline.

Side Tour 12A

Springville—Calhoun City—Ackerman, 80.8 m. State 9.

Graveled roadbed, two lanes, short paved sections.
Accommodations only in larger towns.

This route breaks in upon a brief stretch of country dominated throughout by strong sectional flavor. Lying among the last outcroppings of the Pontotoc hills, the land is evenly spread with dark bristly growths of shortleaf pine, which furnish the main industry for the people. Independent landowners from the mountains of Virginia, Kentucky, and Tennessee homesteaded the hill lands here in the 1840's, settling in clans and neighborhoods. Remnants of these clans still exist and the pattern of life has changed but little since that time. Remote from a railroad the natives have retained their dog-trot houses, their ancestral quilts, and a great deal of their individuality. Their vocabulary has a direct, poetic quality; archaisms are present in their speech. They sing lusty old-time ballads and "cut the figures" of square dances far into the night.

At SPRINGVILLE, *0 m.* (200 pop.) *(see Tour 14)*, State 9 branches S. from State 6 *(see Tour 14)* and climbs to a hilltop view of forested hills and low-lying valley farms. The houses here are typical of the houses throughout the route. Some are new, some old, some spacious, and some compact, but, with few exceptions, all are weathered and unpainted, with overhanging roofs, log-sidings, and squat mud-chinked chimneys; and all are built around a roomy, open hallway or "dog-trot." This dog-trot is an outgrowth of the climatic needs and gives the habitations an air of homely comfort; it is an excellent place to hang the wash, to store a bale of cotton, or to "just sit" and catch the breeze when a day's work on the land is done.

RANDOLPH, *5.4 m.* (195 pop.), was named for the Virginia statesman by early settlers who were staunch followers of his belief in the importance of States' rights. Many years ago the village prospered from the sale of moonshine whisky, but today the terraced farms along the rugged hill slopes and in the more fertile creek bottoms are the chief sources of livelihood.

Between Randolph and Pittsboro are some of the densest shortleaf pine forests in the State. Visible and audible from the highway are numerous portable sawmills. Farmers in this area cut a few pines, sell the "billets," and plant a crop of corn where the trees formerly stood. The trees are the farmers' cash crops, for truck is raised in quantities sufficient only for their own needs.

At *8.5 m.* is GAREY SPRINGS BAPTIST CHURCH, where Sacred Harp Singings are held annually on the third Sunday in June.

As State 9 travels southward the density of the pines increases, their great height making long shadows across the road.

SAREPTA, *14.4 m.* (150 pop.), has lived down a bad name acquired during the 1880's when the swaggering backwoodsmen of the vicinity had the habit of coming to the village and taking the law into their hands. The memory of one infamous son, however, is kept green in the "Ballad of Dock Bishop," of local origin. The ballad, telling in endless, mournful verses of the crimes, the trial, and the hanging of Dock, is sung by the people at neighborhood parties. In Calhoun Co. these neighborhood parties are not only an institution but are in a large measure responsible for the perpetuation of the ballad here. Neighbors from miles around gather in the "front room" of some farmhouse, where the biggest feather bed is decked with the family's prize quilts, and standing around the organ entertain themselves with ballad and hymn singing and eating *(see WHITE FOLKWAYS).*

South of Sarepta in a low flat along Skuna (Shooner) River is BRUCE, *26.2 m.* (946 pop.), an anomaly in this section, with a large, prospering hardwood lumber mill. The town was established in 1927 when the lumber mill that gave it its name was built here. Until that time the forests had been a problem to the farmers, who saw them only as an impediment to planting the land in cotton and corn, and had burned much valuable timber as firewood and as waste after log-rollings.

At *27.3 m.* State 9 crosses Skuna River and runs for a short distance through low fertile bottom lands, which grow abundant corps of full-eared, long-tasseled corn, and climbs once more among the hills.

PITTSBORO, *30.2 m.* (249 pop.), has clung to the title of seat of Calhoun Co. through a long series of contests with larger and more accessible villages of the county. When Pittsboro's two-story brick courthouse, which had reverberated to the oratory of Democrats and Whigs of the county since 1856, burned in 1922, the other covetous villages thought surely Pittsboro's hold would weaken. But immediately the furnishings of the old structure were moved into an empty store building, and when the next session of court met, it met in Pittsboro, as before. Long associated with court week in Pittsboro is the custom or art of horse swapping. Formerly hundreds of tobacco-spitting, swearing, swashbuckling swappers poured into Pittsboro on the first Monday of court to spend the day haggling over the merits of their respective horses. All sorts of deals were made—an old worn-out horse might be traded for a jackknife. Occasionally a man would mount a wagon and auction his horse to the highest bidder. Today, much of the color and excitement is gone from the trading, but old-timers still listen for the tune of the jews'-harp that heralds the coming of the traders, and for the restless neighing of horses.

Between Pittsboro and Calhoun City the toll on the forest has been heavy, and the rugged stumpy hillsides have been converted into pastures. The slopes are dotted with grazing red and brown cattle, and the windmills of nearby farms whirl in the breeze.

CALHOUN CITY, *36.3 m.* (1,012 pop.), has the prestige that belongs to the largest town and only railroad station in a county. One-story drug and grocery stores and dress shops where women of the section buy their Sunday garments enclose a central parkway, which has been hopefully reserved since the town was laid out awaiting the time when Pittsboro will relinquish the county seat and courthouse. The town was settled on part of a 640-acre tract of land that T. P. Gore bought from an Indian, Ish-ta-hath-la. Tradition says that Gore obtained the entire section for a handful of bright beads and several quarts of whisky. Gore migrated here from Oklahoma, and, settling himself in a broad, squat dog-trot house, led an easy life in which horse-racing and cock-fighting figured prominently. Before his death Gore buried a great part of the gold he had amassed on his plantation, and died without revealing its hiding place. Hopeful persons still dig diligently near the plantation in search of the treasure. With three sawmills in operation and the opening of a railroad station on the Gulf, Mobile & Northern R.R. here, Calhoun City developed from a straggling backwoods village into a town that can offer smart clothing, exotic canned goods, and the diversion of a picture show to country people who come in to spend the day.

Right from Calhoun City, *0.5 m.*, on State 8 to the *GRAVE OF T. P. GORE*, the founder of Calhoun City. His tomb bears the date of his birth, 1776. Near the grave and marking the site of Gore Plantation is GORE SPRINGS.

On the same highway is BIG CREEK, *8 m.*, sectionally famous for the Fiddlers Contest held annually on or near the 15th of August. Selections range from old "break-downs" to modern jazz, and competition among the perspiring farmers is keen. Following the contest, dinner is spread on the school grounds.

Immediately S. of Calhoun City the town atmosphere lingers in spreading farmhouses, painted cheerfully red, yellow, and white, and in billboards displaying local advertisements. But the country is too primitive to be bound long by a townish atmosphere and soon again assumes its natural air. Dog-trot houses, usually with blue-jean overalls and calico dresses blowing dry in the open central hall, contrast with the modern bungalows outside the town.

SLATE SPRINGS, *44.3 m.* (375 alt., 190 pop.), is one of the oldest and highest communities in the county. At one time a college flourished here, also a flour mill and two churches; but today its chief claims to notice are the two nearby elevations known locally as Sand and Rocky Mountains.

BELLEFONTAINE, *53.8 m.* (129 pop.), originated in the early 1840's as a market town on the old Grenada trail. So dim was the trail that it was necessary to ring a bell every hour for guidance. This bell, a large noisy one, hung high in the air on a spot that later became the village. Near the bell a saloon was established, and here travelers stopped for relaxation.

At *54.9 m.* (L) is the *WILLIAM CASTLE HOME*, a large elaborate version of the dog-trot structure so commonly seen through this section. Bill Castle built the house himself in 1833, and all material was made by hand. The house is still in good condition and occupied as a home.

WALTHALL, *57.1 m.* (124 pop.), has all the elements of a country county seat—a courthouse, a jail, a town pump, and a store the sides of which are never without their colorful array of circus posters.

Between Walthall and Eupora the country is continuously high, hilly, and rugged, dotted with occasional tractor mills, squat log houses, corn and cotton patches, and dairies.

At EUPORA, *62.4 m.* (1,092 pop.) *(see Tour 6)*, is a junction with US 82 *(see Tour 6)*.

Between Eupora and Ackerman the highway flattens into low-lying dank bottom land, then rises to heights not surpassed elsewhere on the route. Close to its southern end State 9 enters a country in which the peaks of the hills, the sheerness of the slopes stretching to the valleys, the density and height of the pines and the view of distant ridges call forth superlatives.

At ACKERMAN, *80.8 m.* (522 alt., 1,169 pop.) *(see Tour 12)*, is a junction with State 15 *(see Tour 12)*.

◄◄◄◄◄◄◄◄◄◄◄◄◄◄◄◄☼►►►►►►►►►►►►►►►►►

Tour 13

Junction with State 63—Hattiesburg—Columbia—McComb—Woodville. State 24.
Junction with State 63 to Woodville, *206.4 m.*
The Gulf, Mobile & Northern R.R. parallels route between McLain and Hattiesburg; Fernwood, Columbia & Gulf R.R. between Columbia and McComb.
Graveled roadbed two lanes wide.
Accommodations in cities.

State 24 wanders through the heart of the Piney Woods, then, skirting the lower part of the truck farming belt between Columbia and McComb, it traverses the southern extremity of a section noted for its ante-bellum prosperity. With the exception of the Hattiesburg, Columbia, McComb, and Woodville areas it runs through a rolling country visited by few Mississippians and fewer out-of-state travelers.

State 24 branches E. from State 63, *0 m. (see Tour 15)*, 2.5 m. NW. of LEAKESVILLE *(see Tour 15)*.

McLAIN, *18.8 m.* (76 alt., 350 pop.), has an easy rural manner that is evidenced by the drinking fountain centering the crossroads around which the town is gathered. The town's favorite story concerns the revelation of buried Spanish gold a few miles northwest of the drug store. A century and a half ago, when the Spaniards ruled the territory then known as West Florida, an American named Gaines acquired a fortune by trading with the Spaniards and Choctaw. For safekeeping, he buried his treasure in five caches; then he died, taking his secret with him. Soon after the War between the States three of the caches were unearthed and still later a fourth, containing Spanish gold, jewelry, and a gold pocket knife. The fifth and last cache was revealed in 1934 to a farmer named Sylvester when the bank of a small tributary of the Leaf River washed away. This collection contained American coins and many old Spanish gold pieces of eight.

Here is the junction with State 15 *(see Tour 12)*.

Left from McLain on a forest firebreak road to the Progress School, *3.1 m.;* (L) from the Progress School to a *LOG CABIN*, *3.6 m. (private)*, one of the best examples in the State of the pioneer's cabin. The builder raised the logs 75 years ago, made a single pen room, rived his shingles of cypress, and to escape the heat and lessen the danger of fire built his kitchen apart from the house. The logs refused to die, and now their growth has cemented them as firmly as if they were rock. The kitchen, still separate from the main room, is now connected with it by a hewn plank walk. The main room has been papered with a white covering that bulges over the logs.

At *5.7 m.* on this same road is the junction with a fire trail.

Right here along a ridge to LITTLE CREEK, *4.7 m.* On the beech trees that hold the bridge in place are ax scars thought to have been made by Andrew Jackson's army returning from the Battle of New Orleans. Right from the bridge is a deep hole where Jackson's men watered and rested their stock.

Between McLain and Beaumont State 24 and State 15 are the same route *(see Tour 12).*

BEAUMONT, *27.2 m.* (93 alt., 350 pop.), is in the second bottom flats along Leaf River.

The highway runs between the river (R) and the Leaf River Unit of the De Soto National Forest (L). The sandy texture of the soil and the richer vegetation are indicative of the break made by the watercourses in the red clay and pine woods of the uplands.

NEW AUGUSTA, *34.7 m.* (350 pop.), is the seat of Perry Co. and a farm trading center.

Right from New Augusta on the Ellisville road to a bridge across Leaf River, *2 m.* On the north bank of the stream is a triangular open plat of ground shaded by tall oaks, the SITE of OLD AUGUSTA, *2.1 m.* Among the relics is a safe made of concrete and sheathed in rusted iron; this was a part of the old courthouse vaults. Under the trees, almost hidden from view and shrouded in creepers, is part of the old jail block. This cell, with a few iron bars left in the broken window, was the one in which James Copeland, leader of the Copeland Clan of outlaws, was confined before he was hanged in 1857.

Before the War between the States, the Piney Woods were not only an excellent hideout and ambush for highwaymen, but they also offered wealthy prey in the form of slave speculators on their way to New Orleans and the Natchez country, and in the gentlemen who traveled from tavern to tavern with saddle bags and money belts filled with gold. The story of the Copeland Clan is typical of the gangs that made this southern neck of Mississippi a part of their field of operation. James Copeland, the leader, was born in 1823 near the Pascagoula River about 20 miles north of the Gulf, and made his first theft when he was 12 years old. Before he was 15 he had burned the Jackson Co. courthouse to destroy an indictment against him. In 1839 the clan of which he was then a member raided Mobile. Thieving expeditions to Florida, Texas, and Louisiana followed. Retiring to a hideout somewhere on Red Creek near what is now Wiggins, Copeland and his cronies murdered a number of their clan whom they thought to be spies, and Copeland was made the leader. In Catahoula Swamp, Hancock Co., Copeland buried $30,000 in gold.

The decline and fall of the clan was climaxed with the battle of Harvey on Black Creek in which a small army of men outshot the outlaws. Copeland's running saved him temporarily, though he lost the key map to his buried treasure. Early in the 1850's Copeland was stabbed in an altercation, and a posse trailing him by the blood stains arrested and carried him to Mobile. After a number of trials and confusion over State sovereignties, he was hanged in 1857 at Old Augusta, on the edge of the pine forests that had been his former sanctuary.

Except for the old jail cell nothing is left to mark the town that was, in 1822, the Government land office and the most important settlement in the Piney Woods east of the Pearl River Valley. Its political importance as land office gave the town an impressive start but in 1841 signs of decay were evident. Augusta citizens managed to exist by rafting logs down Leaf River to Moss Point on the Coast. This period of existence as a river-landing was a part of the early history of all the older settlements along the watercourses in the Piney Woods. Shortly after 1900, the railroad having been built through in 1903, the few settlers left in Old Augusta moved across the river to the railroad settlement at New Augusta. The death of the old town is one of the best examples in Mississippi of the influence of the first railroads—the end of river town civilizations, and the beginning of a new era.

At *53.1 m.* (L) is a PINE FELT FACTORY *(visited by special permission),* a long, wooden shed with piles of pine needles around it. The factory, the only one of its kind, was opened in 1935. Pine straw, formerly wasted, is processed for use in pillows, mattresses, upholstering, etc.

At HATTIESBURG, *55.5 m.* (143 alt., 18,601 pop.) *(see Tour 7, Sec. b),* are the junctions with US 49 *(see Tour 7, Sec. b)* and State 11 *(see Tour 8).*

West of Hattiesburg State 24 becomes a broad, improved highway leading to the Pearl River valley, second only to the Natchez district in date of settlement and density of early population. Cotton patches and corn fields break the woodland stretches of oak and pine.

At *90.8 m.* is the junction with a graveled road.

Right on this road to the MISSISSIPPI INDUSTRIAL AND TRAINING SCHOOL, *1.2 m.,* a home-like institution for wayward, backward, and orphaned children of the State. The plant, centered by the large, rectangular shaped administration building, is scattered over a large landscaped campus and consists of 22 modern-design brick buildings, the majority of which are two stories in height. The boys and girls are taught various crafts and trades to fit them for useful lives. A large acreage of farmland surrounding the school supplies it with vegetables and fruits; a dairy and syrup mill are operated in conjunction with the institution. A swimming pool and ball park provide recreation for the children.

COLUMBIA, *92.4 m.* (145 alt., 4,833 pop.), until 1929 was a typical sawmill town with all interests centered about a large yellow pine mill. Then the mill closed its doors and Columbia became a dreary place of abandoned houses, a rotting mill structure, and a stagnant mill pond. Through the efforts of its citizens who were proud of their white-lighted main street and the other luxuries the mill had brought, the town, instead of dwindling to a ghost, in 1929 adopted the economic philosophy of balanced economy—already in practice to a certain extent in the prairie. The surrounding cut-over timber land, desert-like in its spread of cactus-like stumps, was cleared for farming and dairying. So effective has been Columbia's break with the past that few remember that in the early 1800's it was a river port, or that for three months it was the capital of the State. Here the legislative session of 1821 met to vote Jackson the permanent capital. But, with Jackson established, Columbia slipped back into the easy life of a village until recalled to industry by the lumber mill in the 1920's.

SOUTHERN NAVAL STORES PLANT, S. of Courthouse Square *(visited with permission),* known locally as the knot factory, manufactures pine knots and stumps into turpentine, pine oil, rosin, and disinfectant. This is the only use yet discovered for the stumps and knots left by the lumber mills. The steel and concrete buildings of the plant are equipped with six 8½-ton extractors and three 1,800-gallon stills for refining turpentine and pine oils.

The stumps and knots are first weighed by the ton, then, passing into the mill house, moved from the hopper into the hog and thence to the shredder, where they are reduced to particles the size of oats. These small particles of pine are stored in 100-ton chip bins in the extractor house until, in time, they are dumped into extractors where a steam and solvent process extracts from them a crude form of turpentine and pine oil. Rosin, being cut from the chips with naphtha, is sent to a refinery to go through six large washers each of an approximate 15,000-gallon capacity, and from there to evaporators where the processing is completed. The crude turpentine and pine oil go into tanks until they can be placed in stills and refined under the supervision of chemists. Certain grades of pine oil flow through copper tanks, never coming in contact with iron which would cause contamination. Rosin is stored in steel drums or wooden barrels and shipped. The drums are bought knocked down, and then reassembled at the plant. The barrels are made at the stave mill operated in connection with the plant.

The Southern Naval Stores Co. has under lease 75,000 acres of stumps, but, as an ample supply can be obtained from farmers, their supply remains untouched. Stumps from virgin pine timber stay in the ground indefinitely without rotting. By dynamiting the stumps approximately 18 inches below the ground, the soil is made better for farming and grazing purposes. In conjunction with a tour of the Naval Stores Plant, a trip by car to the cut-over lands, where the process of dynamiting stumps is being carried on, is of interest.

The *DORGAN-McPHILLIPS VEGETABLE PACKING PLANT (open 9-4 from March to Dec.)* cans peans, beans, corn, carrots, and sweet potatoes. Cleaning, paring, and cutting the vegetables are done by Negro women. After this preliminary work, the vegetables, under the supervision of white workers, are cooked at high steam pressure in vats, then electrically canned and sealed.

The *COLUMBIA BOX FACTORY (open 9-4 weekdays)*, across street, manufactures veneered strips to be used by Northern manufacturers in making packing boxes. The gum logs are soaked in water for three days, then a circular saw, cutting round and round the log until the heart is reached, shaves off strips ½ in. in width. The strips are glued in threes, the grain of the center strip running opposite to that of the outside strips to give the material additional strength.

The *HUGH WHITE HOME*, Broad St., 1 mile from courthouse, built during the lumber boom of the 1920's, is typical of the houses of Columbia's lumber magnates. Set among landscaped gardens on a 35-acre tract of pine woods, it is a fine two-story house of Spanish design. White was elected Governor of Mississippi in 1936 on a platform of balancing agriculture with industry. The son of J. J. White, pioneer lumberman, he was born in McComb in 1881. He early identified himself with the lumber industry in Mississippi, and until its closing in 1930 owned and operated the White Lumber Mill at Columbia. With the collapse of the lumber industry, he turned his energies toward rebuilding Columbia on a sounder basis. He was for many years mayor of the town, the only public office that he held before being elected Governor of the State *(see AN OUTLINE OF FOUR CENTURIES)*.

At *94 m.* State 24 crosses Pearl River, which gave Columbia, like Monticello *(see Tour 11)*, a character apart from the rest of the Piney Woods. The height of the road levee through the overflow bottoms and the mossy cypress and water hyacinths in the bed are worthy of notice.

At FOXWORTH, *95.3 m.* (200 pop.), is a water mill which now cuts lumber, gins cotton, and grinds corn. The mill rocks are more than 100 years old.

Left from Foxworth, on a graveled road by a number of planter houses, to BALL'S MILL, *9.2 m.,* an old-fashioned water grist mill.

At *15.8 m.* on this same road is the junction with a graveled road.

Left on the narrow road *2.5 m.* to the old *JOHN FORD HOME*, on a plateau approximately a mile from Pearl River. It is a rude but strong building, of ash-gray timbers and yellowed brick two-and-a-half stories high. In its architecture it shows the influence of the Spaniards, masters of the territory whose border was five miles S. John Ford, the builder, was a Methodist minister who came from South Carolina in 1805. Between 1805 and 1809, he built this first house in the region, and subsequently filled it with five sons and two daughters. Four of the five sons became Methodist circuit riders and the two daughters became wives of circuit riders. One of the sons, Thomas, organized the Mississippi Methodist Society and built the first church of that denomination in Jackson, the new State capital. The second Mississippi Methodist Conference was held in the house in 1814. So pronouncedly religious was the Ford family that when Gen. Andrew Jackson stopped here on his way to fight the British at New Orleans, the Reverend Mr. Ford, hearing that the general was a great man to swear, would not grant him shelter until he promised he would use no profanity and would attend family prayer.

The Pearl River Convention met in the home in 1816 and drew up a petition asking for admission of the State to the Union. The enabling act was passed soon after by Congress; the Constitutional Convention assembled the next year; and Mississippi Territory became a State in 1817. Long before, the site of the home had been identified with the Indians. Arrowheads, beads, and stone hatchets are found in the fields and woods around it. In the yard are traces of the old stockade that surrounded the house. In the ceiling of one of the upper rooms is a small trap door through which Tallapoosa, a friendly Indian, was hidden when a strange Indian approached the house. It was Tallapoosa who kept the white settlers informed of the movements of the hostile tribes.

The house is nearly square. Its ground floor has very thick brick walls and is paved with brick. The second floor is frame, with clapboards of heart pine, hand-cut and hand-dressed, and put together with hand-wrought iron nails made at the home forge. The roof is shingled. Not a drop of paint has ever been put on any part of the building, so the outside walls have taken on a soft gray shade often seen on old dead pines. The side now seen first was originally the rear, the house having been built to face the river. Two rooms at each end of the second or main floor open on a porch enclosed on three sides and approached on the open end by a straight stairway rising from the ground, with a round stair rail and slender balusters. The front has a long porch added in the 1840's. The medium-sized rooms are ceiled with narrow planks. The small windows are many paned. The effect is that of a blockhouse.

At *105.2 m.* is KOKOMO (100 pop.), a sawmill village that drew the life from China Grove when the railroad came through.

At *109 m.* is CHINA GROVE CHURCH, all that remains of one of the oldest settlements on the ridge between Pearl River and Bogue Chitto River. Built in 1854, it is a one-story, box-like frame building set in the grove of trees for which the village and church were named. Above the entrance in the interior is a slave balcony. China Grove was settled in 1815 by Ralph Stovall who used the power of Magee's Creek to run a sawmill, a cotton gin and press, a rice pestle mill and fan for cleaning, and a grist mill. Around these mills Scotch-Irish farmers from the Carolina Piedmont settled.

At *113.8 m.* is TYLERTOWN (1,102 pop.), a farming center and the seat of Walthall Co., in which it is the only incorporated town. The place was named for William G. Tyler, a settler from Boston, Mass., and an artilleryman under Gen. Andrew Jackson in the Creek campaign and the War of 1812.

Left from Tylertown to Collins Creek, on the bank of which is the *CHAUNCEY COLLINS PLACE, 2 m.,* the oldest house in the vicinity. This two-story house with square frame columns was erected about 1822. The remains of Collins' bark-tanning mill are evident.

Between Tylertown and McComb, the corn and cotton patches show pine stumps, a composition that clearly demonstrates the change made in the former Piney Woods. The shotgun houses, their rooms built one behind the other, have clean-swept dooryards, chinaberry trees, and rosebushes.

At *124.2 m.* State 24 crosses the Bogue Chitto (Ind., *big creek*) River on a bridge that is held in place by enormous moss-covered oaks.

At *129.1 m.* is the junction with a narrow graveled road.

Right on this road is HOLMESVILLE, *4 m.* (72 pop.), on the banks of the Bogue Chitto River. Doomed when the railroad was pushed through McComb to the northwest in 1857, it, like many other river towns in the State, is desolate except for the few fine old homes (*private*). The first seen is the *S. S. SIMMONS PLACE,* a two-story frame structure, one room wide and fully 80 feet long with a columned porch down its long side. The *HOLMESVILLE CEMETERY, 3.6 m.* (R), overgrown with weeds and flowers, has headstones with inscriptions dating back to 1824. The *CHANCERY CLERK'S OFFICE, 3.9 m.* (R), is a part of the old Holmesville courthouse, built in 1816, Holmesville having been the first seat of Pike Co. The office has recently been repaired and converted into a community center. Its sand rock foundation, with the original brick held together by a mortar made by mixing clay with salt, and the original hewn window and door sills are intact. In the yard a circle of cedars marks the site of the courthouse, burned in 1884. At *4 m.* (R) is the *DR. GEORGE NICHOLSON PLACE,* a small frame house almost hidden by a century-old camellia japonica. Near Dillon's Bridge on Kirklin Creek, one of the Bogue Chitto tributaries, is the *GEORGE SMITH PLACE,* settled as early as 1817. The low house, constructed of heart pine, and the old water mill are noted for their picturesque beauty. The *COL. PRESTON BRENT HOME,* constructed of hewn logs sheathed later with hewn lumber, stands in a grove of 1,000 crapemyrtle trees. The *THAD ELLZEY PLACE* was built in 1812 of hewn logs a foot in diameter joined with wooden pins and is unchanged except for a new roof.

TOUR 13 481

At *139.1 m.* State 24 parallels the railroad shops and yards (L) that made McComb prominent.

At McCOMB, *140 m.* (10,057 pop.) *(see Tour 5, Sec. b)*, is the junction with US 51 *(see Tour 5, Sec. b).*

At *144.3 m.* (L) is the junction with State 48.

Left on State 48 is PERCY QUIN STATE PARK, *1.4 m.* (R). This park is a rolling and slightly hilly tract of 1,480 acres lying along the Tangipahoa River. On it is being constructed a very large earth dam that will impound water for a lake of 540 acres. One hundred thousand cu. yds. of soil will go into the dam, and the lake will be big enough for swimming, boating, and fishing. A lodge, a boathouse, overnight cabins, trail-side shelters, and picnic grounds are available. Virgin and second growth pine timber and thickly-growing hardwood trees shade the grounds. The Percy Quin Park was named for the U. S. Representative, Percy E. Quin, who was born in Amite Co., Oct. 30, 1872, and died in 1932.

At *145.2 m.* (R) is the *SABINE HOME* on an elevated site. Constructed in 1812 of red brick, the house is two stories in height and has a double-deck frame porch with round columns. It is one of the oldest in Pike Co.

Between McComb and Liberty the highway passes through the westernmost part of the longleaf pine region. There is little good timber left, but the farms tilled on the cleared lands are above the average for the pine woods. The cuts show a mixture of the sandy clay of the truck farming belt and the loess of the bluffs of the Mississippi. The impression is of farms without the newness of the Piney Woods clearings east of Pearl River, even though the fields are dotted with stumps.

The *RED FRAME HOUSE* at *154.8 m.* (R) serves well to mark the division between the truck farming belt and the old south section.

LIBERTY, *163.2 m.* (300 alt., 551 pop.), is one point of the triangle which, with Fort Adams and Vicksburg, bounds the corner of Mississippi best epitomizing the deep South. The *AMITE CO. COURTHOUSE,* recently repaired, replaced in 1840 an earlier log structure that had marked the seat of the county since its organization in 1809. The square in which the early structure stood had been, before 1809, a ball ground for the friendly Amite Indians. Later, the square was the junction point of the Mobile-Natchez road with a road to Bayou Sara, La., both of them important arteries of travel in the Southwest. Men came 50 miles to attend court here. In 1816, the year before Mississippi became a State, a census of the town and county showed 3,365 whites, 1,694 slaves, and 19 free Negroes. Slaves were one of the most important commodities of the period, and the slave block where they were bought and sold was placed just north of the present courthouse. Streams of oxcarts, each cart loaded with three or four bales, carried cotton to the Natchez market, 60 miles northwest.

In addition to cotton culture, the town had industrial activities unusual for Mississippi. In the *GAIL BORDEN HOUSE* across from the courthouse on Main Street, Gail Borden condensed the first can of milk. Hiram Van Norman, who married Borden's step-sister, moved from Indiana to Liberty, bringing Gail, a small boy, with him. Young Borden attended the Liberty Male Academy, was made County Surveyor in 1825, and while teaching at Zion Hill near Liberty married Penelope Mercier in 1828. He later made a fortune from the perfected formula for condensing milk, on which he was working at the time of his marriage. Dr. Tichenor, who made and perfected Tichenor's antiseptic, began his experiments in Liberty before the War between the States, although it was not patented until 1883. A contemporary reports that Dr. Tichenor said, "I will use my antiseptic freely on southern soldiers, but want no d—— yankees to get it." He lived on what was known as the John Webb place, about 1½ miles E. of Liberty. After a few years in Liberty, he moved to a place on the Mississippi River in Wilkinson Co., and later to Baton Rouge, where he secured the patent for the antiseptic. Speculation Creek, on the banks of which the speculators established Liberty in 1809, became known as Tanyard Creek, when in the 1820's Van Norman built on it a shoe factory that he ran with slave labor. The water power supplied by the two prongs of the Amite River moved the wheels of the cotton gins and the first clumsy gristmills and sawmills. When the War between the States began there were 16 water power mills in Amite Co. Liberty was given a blow when, about 1882, the railroad was run to Gloster 15 miles northwest.

Beautiful homes were a manifestation of the wealth of the people. The first house in the settlement to have glass window panes, a carpet and a piano, the *E. N. SKINNER HOME* on a hill three blocks south of the courthouse, is in almost as good condition as when built in 1824. Its heart-of-pine timber was hand-sawn and put together with pegs, and all interior woodwork, including an elaborate mantel, was hand-carved by slaves. The carpet and piano were shipped down the Mississippi from Kentucky. The builder of the house, Dr. Edward Carroll, shipped in a steam sawmill also, but when he tried to run it with slave labor the engine exploded, killing five of his Negroes.

The *COURTHOUSE* was built in 1840 of brick fired by slaves. It is a square building two-stories high, with a low sloping roof. The flooring is of planks a foot wide, and the stone steps are deeply hollowed by wear. The first brick office buildings, also erected in the 1840's, were made from the same red and white local clays as was the courthouse. The *OLD OPERA HOUSE,* now known as the Walsh Building, on the corner of Main and East Girdle Sts. (formerly the street girdling the town), was built in 1840. Its enormous brick columns on two sides have retained a dusty yellow tinge, contrasting with the flame color of the other buildings. In it Jenny Lind sang to the planters from the surrounding country. The congregation of the present *PRESBYTERIAN CHURCH,* organized in 1848 with a slave as one of its 14 charter members, meets in a building erected in 1853 on the corner of East Girdle and Broken Sts. The brick, the high-backed pews, the altar, the walls of the commodious auditorium, and the slave gallery were hand-fashioned by slaves. The Amite Female Academy, founded in 1853, had a plant of several brick buildings until Federal troops destroyed all but one in 1863. The building left standing is a part of the *AGRICULTURAL HIGH SCHOOL* on the eastern edge of town.

When the War between the States had ended, Liberty began the task of raising a *MONUMENT* to its dead. It was made in New Orleans, hauled the last 30 miles to Liberty by oxen, and raised in 1871. The total cost was $3,322, representing hard-earned money in the post-war Reconstruction period It is classic in style, a single eight-sided shaft of Italian marble, 20 ft. high on a base seven feet square. A laurel wreath with the motto "At Rest" is topped with a raised star and a Grecian urn; there are four richly-carved tablets inscribed with the names of the Amite County soldiers who died in the war.

Left from Liberty on State 48 to an unmarked graveled road at *3.8 m.;* L. here to the *TOM STREET HOME, 6 m.* (R), a well-preserved house built in 1827. Two stories in height with a double deck entrance porch, it has unusually large rooms with high ceilings. Originally there was a ballroom on each floor.

At *174.4 m.* on State 24 is the junction with an unmarked graveled road.

Right on this road (L) to the *THOMAS TALBERT HOME (private), 1.8 m.,* a large, two-and-a-half story red brick structure, set high on a hill and visible a half-mile away. Finished in 1853, it is probably the best remaining ante-bellum home in the area. Thomas and Sally Talbert, the owners, were South Carolinians from the Edgefield District. The brick was made by slaves and burned on the place; the glass was shipped from Kentucky. The structure is of monumental proportions: ceilings are 14 ft. high; a hall 40 by 14 ft. is flanked by rooms 20 ft. square; and solid brick walls, a foot-and-a-half thick, are still sheathed in plaster that has neither cracked nor been repaired. The flooring is of heart pine, as are the mantels, stained to represent dark marble.

A slave with a lamp on a stick burned figures of animals and other objects in the stained pine of the second-floor ceilings; it now resembles tiling. The house contains some of the original pieces with which it was furnished: four-posted beds, old-fashioned dressers and chairs; a secretary; a large chest full of quilts; and a whatnot, a thing of beauty with spindling props, three shelves, and a mirrored back. There is a legend concerning a murder committed while a dance was in progress in the parlor. A jealous husband, advancing on his wife's dancing partner with upraised poker, was stabbed in the ensuing scuffle. The hill on which the house stands was formerly terraced and planted with rows of cape jessamine, some of which remain.

GLOSTER, *178.2 m.* (434 alt., 1,139 pop.), is a comparatively new railroad town named for the engineer who put the Yazoo & Mississippi Valley R.R. through in the 1880's.

CENTREVILLE, *188.6 m.* (374 alt., 1,344 pop.), is a small early settlement that did not become incorporated until 1880, when the Yazoo & Mississippi Valley R.R. ran along the border between Wilkinson and Amite Cos. Because the station was approximately midway between Liberty and Woodville and about midway between Natchez and Baton Rouge, it was appropriately named Centreville.

Right from the railroad station to the *WILLIAM DICKSON HOME, 0.8 m. (private)*, built in 1819 by William Winans, the eccentric and powerful Methodist circuit rider, whose voluminous papers are preserved in the State Hall of History. Of the usual Southern plantation type, it is a story-and-a-half high with a long wide gallery. A frame office is attached to the south end of the gallery. Brick and lime hauled by ox cart from Natchez were used in the foundations and chimney. Among the old relics is one of the seven pikes stolen from John Brown's arsenal.

Between Centreville and Woodville the richness of the soil indicates the approach to the Bluff Hills. The cabins and wooden churches in this stretch mark the last hold and former westward extension of the Piney Woods.

At *205.4 m.* is *ROSEMONT PLANTATION,* on which Jefferson Davis spent his boyhood. The house, built in 1830 for Lucinda Davis, his sister, stands in a grove of live oaks. It has a long wide gallery across the front and a spacious hall, with two rooms on each side. The half-story with its two front dormers has the floor plan of the lower story. The hand hewn timbers fastened by wooden pegs, as well as the plastered walls and ceilings, are well preserved. The old mantel in the living room is of black Italian marble. In the family burial ground near the house are the graves of Jefferson Davis' mother and his two sisters, Mary and Lucinda. In the house now owned by Henry Johnson is a large spinning wheel said to have been used by the mother of Davis.

At WOODVILLE, *206.4 m.* (560 alt., 1,113 pop.) *(see Tour 3b),* is the junction with US 61 *(see Tour 3, Sec. b).*

Tour 14

(Winfield, Ala.)—Amory—Tupelo—Oxford—Clarksdale. State 6.
Alabama Line to Clarksdale, 178.1 m.

Graveled roadbed, two lanes wide, with short paved sections.
Accommodations in larger towns.

State 6 is stamped by strong scenic contrasts, the result of varying soil types which, in turn, have exerted a pronounced influence upon the economic development of the inhabitants. It rolls down from the southern slopes of the Tennessee River Hills to cross the Tombigbee River into the Black Prairie belt, then climbs the crest of the Pontotoc Ridge to follow the cut-up surface of the North Central plateau for 40 isolated miles. Entering the Delta at Batesville the route follows snaky rivers and bayous past flat, featureless, and far-flung cotton fields into Clarksdale, a city under the rule of King Cotton. Amory, Tupelo, Pontotoc, Oxford, and Clarksdale are the key towns of the five sections connected by the route and furnish respectively a good cross section of the life of each.

Crossing the Mississippi Line, *0 m.,* 30 m. W. of Winfield, State 6 rides the ridges of the Tennessee River Hills past pleasant small farmhouses and clearings in the midst of thick hardwood forests.

GREENWOOD SPRINGS, *4 m.* (301 alt., 117 pop.), is a tiny village tucked away in a valley between two precipitous hills. The village derived its name and reason for existence from a mineral spring that for more than 100 years has been known by the hill people for its therapeutic values. The old-fashioned, latticed summer house enclosing the spring, the white frame hotel with rambling galleries, and the scattered village homes —all have a rustic simplicity representative of the Tennessee Hills.

At *7.1 m.* the highway ascends to give a good view of the farm-dotted valley below and the forest-covered ridges in the distance. The red clay swath made by the road is an intense contrast to the green of the pines on the slopes. Between this point and Amory the ridges are less precipitous and the valleys broader. Cotton and corn fields in the bottom lands are mixed with apple orchards and pasture meadows.

AMORY, *20 m.* (214 alt., 3,214 pop.), sits on the dividing line between hills and prairie and has taken its development from both. Established in 1887 as a station on the St. Louis & San Francisco R.R., it has been a shipping point for timber, cotton, grains, and dairy products; and it still retains the character of a railroad town. The discovery of a natural gas field at Amory in 1926 prompted a mild boom, but within a few years the imminent practical exhaustion of the field turned the attention of Amory's citizens back to farming and shipping.

Left from Amory on a graveled road to the SITE OF COTTON GIN PORT, *2.5 m.*, most important old town in northeastern Mississippi. Indians called the place Tollamatoxa, meaning *where he first strung the bow,* referring to Bienville's disastrous expedition against the Chickasaw in 1736. At the time the Chickasaw, allied with the English, were constantly attacking the French settlements on and near the Gulf and were blocking French attempts at expansion toward the interior. After the massacre of the French garrison at Fort Rosalie *(see NATCHEZ),* a number of the Natchez tribe took refuge with the Chickasaw, and Bienville laid immediate plans for a war of extermination. Outraged at the massacre, he transported men and supplies up the Mobile and Tombigbee Rivers, erecting a fort on the present site of Cotton Gin Port, at a distance of some 27 miles from what were then the Chickasaw towns. It was to this fort that Bienville retreated after the defeat of his expedition at Ackia *(see Tour 9),* the turning point in the history of French colonization in Mississippi. De Vaudreuil, successor to Bienville as Governor of the French colony, made a third attempt to conquer the Chickasaw in 1752, but was unsuccessful. De Vaudreuil used Bienville's old fort as his supply base. When he returned from the battle at the Chickasaw Old Fields near Tupelo, the Tombigbee had fallen to such an extent that he was forced to lighten his cargo by throwing his cannon into the waters. This point has since been known as Cannon Hole.

After the treaty with the Chickasaw in 1816, Cotton Gin Port became an important frontier outpost, river town, and cotton market, being on the Tombigbee and at the terminal of Gaines Trace *(see TRANSPORTATION).* Its decline came with the decline of river transportation and its death with the development of Amory. Remnants of the old mound and the earthen wall around the fort used by Bienville are visible; and 1 mile W. of the ferry, near the top of a hill, is the site of the cotton gin established by Pres. George Washington to encourage the cultivation of cotton among the Chickasaw. The town derived its name from this gin. In 1837 the Indians of northern Mississippi were sent by the U.S. Government to the Indian Territory. For three days and nights the line of mourning Indians marched through Cotton Gin Port. The town felt their departure, for trade with the Indians had been a source of income, and white settlers were not coming in fast enough to make up for their loss.

At *22.8 m.* the highway crosses the Tombigbee River. The white sand pumped from the stream here is used extensively in concrete construction.

Between the Tombigbee River and Tupelo the red clay hills are replaced by the rich lime soils of the Black Prairie.

At NETTLETON, *35.5 m.* (252 alt., 834 pop.) *(see Tour 4),* is the junction with US 45 *(see Tour 4).*

PLANTERSVILLE, *45 m.* (252 alt., 346 pop.), is a good example of the smaller prairie farm town. Vegetables and milk are picked up here and carried to Tupelo for marketing, and as a result Plantersville has become little more than an agricultural suburb of the latter city.

At *47.7 m.* is the junction with US 78 *(see Tour 9).* State 6 enters on Main St.

TUPELO, *52.9 m.* (289 alt., 6,361 pop.), first TVA city *(see TUPELO).*

Points of Interest. Garment company, dress factory, fish hatchery, cotton mill, and others.

At Tupelo is the junction with US 45 *(see Tour 4).*

The route continues on Main St. (State 6).

BISSELL, *57.1 m.* (50 pop.), is a small community that has grown from the Natchez Trace village known as Walker's Crossroads. The old WALKER HOME (L) *(private),* a one-story Southern Colonial type frame dwelling built in 1840 by William H. Thompson, occupies the site of Colbert's Tavern, a station for travelers on the Natchez Trace operated by Pittman Colbert, secretary of the Chickasaw Indian Council. Chief Colbert was a famous hunter and kept the tavern well supplied with fresh deer and bear meat until he migrated westward with his tribe. Today Bissell's population is composed largely of Tupelo workers who have taken advantage of lower suburban costs of living and whose tidy small homes have little connection with the former village.

At *60.9 m.* (L) State 6 crosses the old Natchez Trace.

Between the Trace Monument and Pontotoc, as the highway intersects the Pontotoc Ridge, the cultivated land on the steep slopes is gradually replaced by pastures and peach orchards.

ROSALBA LAKE, *67.7 m.* (L), was originally a mill pond of the Rosalba wheat mill, built in 1850 when north Mississippi farmers were so self-sufficient that they grew their own wheat. Col. Richard Bolton was the operator, having brought the mill engine from a cotton factory in Georgia. Colonel Bolton's house was near the mill and was called Rosalba for a beautiful white rose vine that rambled over the porch and for the snow white flour produced by the mill. Since Bolton's mill was the only one within a radius of 50 miles, the farmers often had to camp around it for days awaiting their turn. A rustic inn is on the site of the mill, supplying camping, boating, and fishing privileges for a small fee.

Between Rosalba Lake and Pontotoc the highway climbs one of the longest hills in the State to the summit of the Pontotoc Ridge. From the top of the ridge is a good view of heavily forested ridges and rocky pasture land.

At PONTOTOC, *71.3 m.* (462 alt., 2,018 pop.) *(see Tour 12),* is the junction with State 15 *(see Tour 12).*

Between Pontotoc and Batesville the highway crosses the rugged surface of the North Central Plateau, a once prosperous farming area now having its existence threatened by erosion and a one-crop economy. Farm houses weathering or abandoned, raw red gullies gnawing at the vitals of the swelling hills, fields reverting to forest growths, and villages with only the schoolhouse and gasoline station new, are evidences of the plight brought by the outmoded agricultural system.

TOCCOPOLA (Ind., *the crossing of the roads*), *85.9 m.* (288 pop.), was, before the white man came, an Indian village so old that in the annals of the Chickasaw the date is unknown. In 1840, however, two Carolinians, Tobias and Allison Furr, settled here. Tobias Furr built a water mill on the creek and Allison established a store at the crossing of two roads. Other settlers made homes in the vicinity, and eventually the Indian name Tok-a-pula was corrupted to Toccopola. Immediately following the War between the States, W. B. Gilmer, who was forced by a wound received in the war to forsake farming for school teaching as a profession, established Toccopola College, an academy for boys and girls. This college continued operation until 1907. Toccopola's future was shattered when the Gulf, Mobile & Northern R.R. passed it up in preference to Pontotoc, its rival.

There is a local tradition that when Pierre D'Artaguiette fought his disastrous battle against the Chickasaw in 1736 *(see Tour 12)*, his retreating army under the leadership of a 16-year-old boy named Voisin made their first stop at Toccopola. Here Montcherval, commander of the Arkansas force sent to reenforce D'Artaguiette, met the retreating army and returned with it to the Chickasaw bluffs.

On the campus of the high school a piece of concrete torn from an old side walk marks the GRAVE OF BETSY ALLEN. Betsy, whose real name was Susan, was a young Chickasaw woman who carried her legal fight for property right to the Mississippi Supreme Court in 1837. When very young, Betsy had been given another Indian as a slave by her mother. The gift was completed under Chickasaw law in 1829, a year prior to the extension of Mississippi jurisdiction over the Chickasaw. In 1837 Susan, alias Betsy, refused to relinquish her servant to her husband who had been ruined by debt and, carrying her fight to the court, won her case on the grounds that she, her mother, and her family were members of the Chickasaw tribe, that the gift had been completed under Chickasaw laws before the establishment of Mississippi jurisdiction, and that, therefore, the court did not have the right to deprive her of property gained in 1829. Betsy died in 1837 and, like the court decision, was forgotten. A hundred years later a newspaper columnist resurrected the case and gave it publicity as being the first decision in the United States to grant property rights to women. The newly created legend was widely circulated and prompted a woman's civic club to remove a plot of dirt, representing Betsy's remains, to the high school campus and there ceremoniously inter it in a new grave. Betsy, figuratively removed from the old Indian burial ground that had become a pasture, now rests near the white man's school, perhaps a little bewildered by all the belated honor that eventually blew her way.

State 6 enters on University Ave.

OXFORD, *107.6 m.* (458 alt., 2,890 pop.) *(see OXFORD).*

Points of Interest. University of Mississippi, old opera house, ante-bellum homes, and others.

The route continues W. on University Ave.; R. on S. 9th St.; L. on Jackson Ave. (State 6).

1. Left from Oxford *19 m.* on State 7 is WATER VALLEY (294 alt., 3,738 pop.) with all its business houses on one long street stretching N. and S. It was named for the meanderings of Town Creek in the narrow valley between the ridges E. and W. In this watered valley some stragglers of the Choctaw tribe, dispossessed by the Treaty of Dancing Rabbit Creek, had established a temporary village in 1843. With them was a young white boy, Bill Carr, who had been captured from the dispossessors. Turkey Bill, as he later became known, was Water Valley's first white settler, starting business with a blacksmith shop at the point where Town Creek met Otuckalofa Creek. Water Valley was incorporated in 1858; two years later the Mississippi Central R.R. was built through the town. This railroad was burned during the War between the States, and for several months the town was occupied by Federal troops. In the vicinity several important battles took place. Here, as in Oxford, there was a preponderance of white persons, making the upheaval of reconstruction less felt than in other parts of the State. In 1873 Water Valley was made county seat of Yalobusha, and in that same year the town was struck by a yellow fever epidemic. Early identified as a railroad town, Water Valley experienced an overnight development when, after the war, the Illinois Central System absorbed a number of smaller railroads and located the main division shops here. Until 1929, when the shops were moved to Grenada, the town, entirely dependent upon its railroads, drew from them a comfortable prosperity. The town now has replaced the shops with a cheese plant, a silage mill, axe handle factories, and a stave mill. Water Valley's major activity, however, is the growing and shipping of watermelons. The watermelon season is climaxed in August with a Watermelon Festival. The Festival Queen is selected from beauty queens of towns in Mississippi, Arkansas, and Tennessee.

The *CEDARS,* 211 Woods St. *(open),* is a white, brick and frame, two-story Spanish-type house with green shutters. Capt. S. B. Brown built the house in 1863 using slave labor. Sills, floors, and joists are hand-made. English ivy covers the outside walls, and the dwelling is surrounded by a grove of fine old cedars.

At Water Valley is the junction with the Batesville Road.

Left on this graveled road *5 m.* to a COVERED BRIDGE, with stout timbers wind-weathered and aged. The bridge is one of the few of this type remaining in the State.

2. Right from Oxford on State 7 is ABBEVILLE, *9 m.* (366 alt., 243 pop.), illustrating the changing fortune of the Tallahatchie valley settlements. A flower of the old South in its culture and prosperity of a century ago, it is now so poor that few of its inhabitants can afford to buy a mule with which to till the depleted soil. Abbeville was settled in the early 1830's by emigrants from Abbeville, S. C., who lived among the remaining Chickasaw with apparently little friction, and were especially friendly with Chief Toby Tubby who owned and operated a ferry on the Memphis-Oxford stage coach route. L. Q. C. Lamar was among those who settled at Abbeville during its pre-war prosperity. Lamar came from Georgia in 1849 on the strength of the statement of his father-in-law, Augustus Baldwin Longstreet: "It is a farmer's paradise. There are men here who left Newton Co., Ga., in debt no more than eight years ago, who now own their farms, have 15 or 20 slaves, and are buying more every year." A dozen years after Lamar came, however, this farmer's paradise was plunged into a war which marked the end of the southern planters' rule in the U. S. The war was particularly devastating in the Abbeville neighborhood. Wild grape and trumpet vines now hide the earth breastworks erected by Pemberton's Confederates in the valley, but the scars of

BUILDING A TERRACE TO CONTROL EROSION

the conflict can not be hidden. With the exception of two houses Abbeville was burned after the Battle of Tallahatchie Bridge, June 18, 1862, as Federal troops moved southward to Vicksburg. There was fighting on Tallahatchie River in February and November of 1862, and in August of 1864. The post-war history of Abbeville is one of slow decay. The building of the railroad meant the end of the village's importance as a river landing, and the destruction of capital made necessary the growing of an annual cash crop, which, in turn, speeded by the constant use of commercial fertilizer, ruined the land. Lamar's country home, Solitude, is a moldering heap on a local road 2.5 miles NE. of the village. The home used by General Grant as a headquarters is occupied by the Smith family.

Between Oxford and Batesville are some of the State's best examples of land erosion which year after year is eating into the foundations upon which the towns and villages rest and into the farm lands upon which they depend.

BATESVILLE, *136.4 m.* (346 alt., 1,062 pop.) *(see Tour 5, Sec. a),* is at the junction with US 51 *(see Tour 5, Sec. a).*

Between Batesville and Clarksdale the highway crosses a part of the Delta that has been particularly plagued with floods from the swiftly rising Coldwater and Tallahatchie Rivers. The Tallahatchie within the next few years will be robbed of some of its terrors by the Sardis Reservoir above Batesville *(see Tour 5, Sec. a),* but the Coldwater threatens its flat low valley each winter and spring.

At *143 m.* the highway crosses the Tallahatchie River. At this point the river is in summer a narrow green stream twisting between dense woods, but in winter it becomes a yellow spreading sea, filling the space between the low levees confining it.

State 6 crosses the Coldwater River at MARKS, *158.5 m.* (165 alt., 1,258 pop.), a flat Delta town with one street of stores ranging along the railroad tracks. The Quitman Co. courthouse, a modern stone building with a rounded dome, rises above the squat buildings to dominate the scene. As a trading center for the large plantations surrounding it, Marks, like other Delta towns, is dependent on the rise and fall of cotton prices; but flood control on the Coldwater is its greatest need.

The Delta between Marks and Clarksdale is a swampy tableland sprouting cotton on every foot of tillable soil.

At *175.4 m.* is the junction with US 61 *(see Tour 3, Sec. a).*

CLARKSDALE, *178.1 m.* (173 alt., 10,043 pop.) *(see Tour 3, Sec. a).*

◄◄◄◄◄◄◄◄◄◄◄◄◄◄◄◄◄☼►►►►►►►►►►►►►►►►►►►

Tour 15

Waynesboro—Leakesville—Lucedale—Moss Point, 114.8 m. State 63.

Graveled roadbed, two lanes wide.
Accommodations in towns.

State 63 twists through a remote backwoods section about which little has been written. Formerly the area was covered by unbroken pine forests, but now the virgin timber is gone, and the fields, barren except for scattered stumps, alternate with areas well-wooded with young trees. Between Waynesboro and Lucedale economic and social development has been slower, perhaps, than in any other part of the State. The soil is poor, and the small yield of cotton, corn, and truck from the farm patches provides for few comforts of life. The homes are often unpainted log structures of the dog-trot type. Ox teams, hoover-carts, wooden wash troughs, and bare feet are often seen. A sparseness of settlements and the primitive aspect of the country give the few small towns an importance out of proportion to their size.

Southward, between Lucedale and Moss Point, cultivation of the land is more evident, and the people appear more prosperous. The low rambling houses, painted and well-fenced, are more substantial. Well-tended orchards of pecan, peach, and tung oil trees, and young forests of second growth pines dominate the landscape. For a few miles N. of Moss Point, the highway runs along a low, marshy flat paralleling Escatawpa River.

At WAYNESBORO, *0 m.* (191 alt., 1,120 pop.), are junctions with US 84 *(see Tour 11)* and US 45 *(see Tour 4).* State 63 branches S.

At *2.5 m.* the highway crosses CHICKASAWHAY RIVER, which was

LONGLEAF PINE TAPPED FOR TURPENTINE

at one time navigable for 50 miles above Waynesboro; most of the early settlements were made along its banks. With few exceptions the first settlers were Scotch immigrants, and names prefixed with Mac are still prevalent in this section.

At *24.9 m.* is PIAVE (1,000 pop. rapidly diminishing), remains of a lumber town established during the lumber boom of 1927. One of the largest sawmills in the South was built here, bringing to the surrounding backwoods a prosperity never known before. Aside from the rows of stereotyped mill houses, a great many larger residences, a number of stores, and a picture theater were built. But prosperity was short lived. The mill is closed, practically every house stands deserted, and the remains of a once large forest stretch out for miles in each direction.

The lonesome, unfrequented country between Piave and Leakesville is one of the State's last strongholds of old folk customs. As all the early roads led to Mobile, and the people seldom went there more than twice a year, they were completely isolated from outside influences. In recent years the railroad and the highway have caused some changes in the lives of the inhabitants, but folkways endure. Stimulated by privation, the desire is keen for simple pleasures. Old ballads are covetously preserved. Square dancing is entered into with zest. Young and old alike dance all night, then walk the 5 or 10 miles home at daybreak, often carrying their shoes slung by strings across their shoulders. Often the spryest dancer and the lustiest ballad singer in the crowd is a man or woman nearing a hundred years of age.

At *47 m.* is the junction with State 24 *(see Tour 13).*

LEAKESVILLE, *50.4 m.* (105 alt., 662 pop.), the seat of Greene Co., is the center of a lumbering, farming, and stock-raising area. It was here that Kinnie Wagner, the sawmill worker who became Mississippi's last notorious outlaw, first "broke the law, and threw his life away," as the old ballad says. Kinnie killed Sheriff MacIntosh at Leakesville on May 2, 1925, then extended his operations into Tennessee, Arkansas, and Texas. In Texarkana a woman sheriff captured him and brought him back to Leakesville for trial. He was sent to the State penal farm at Parchman *(see Side Tour 7A).*

At *51.8 m.* the highway recrosses Chickasawhay River on a new concrete bridge.

LUCEDALE, *72.3 m.* (185 alt., 834 pop.), the seat of George Co., has, like many Mississippi towns, the composite character determined by a combination of tilling the soil and administering justice. Carved out of back country woodlands to become a bustling lumber town in 1898, it lost this identity with the decline of the industry in the 1920's. Today it has regained prestige with diversified farming. The *LUCE PRODUCTS CO. PLANT* is the largest vegetable packing house in the State. Main street here is named 15-26-63, for the three converging highways.

Here is the junction with State 15 *(see Tour 12).*

George Co. has been under seven flags, and the original land grants, many in the shape of long irregular sections, still exist unchanged in shape through this territory.

South of Lucedale the topography changes gradually. The roll of the hills is less pronounced, cavernous gullies disappear from the scene, and the soil becomes white and sandy. The increasing number of trim painted farmhouses, set among pruned and whitewashed orchard trees are in sharp contrast to the houses in the country northward. Both the vegetable canning plant at Lucedale and the recent development of the tung oil industry have brought a measure of prosperity. Along the road reforestation is evident, also, in the growth of young pines, almost wearying in its extent and uniformity.

AGRICOLA, *83.7 m.* (250 pop.), reveals its character in its name, being the center of a wide farming area. The largest and most productive fruit and vegetable farms of the county are near the village. Pecans and satsumas, growing well in the sandy soil, make the largest and most profitable crop.

HARLESTON, *92.9 m.* (30 pop.), bears a close resemblance to Agricola; they have a like interest in pecans and satsumas.

The highway at *113.8 m.* crosses Escatawpa (Ind., *dog river*) River, one of the tributaries of Mobile Bay, on a long, concrete draw-bridge.

Between here and Moss Point there is evidence of nearness to the Gulf of Mexico in a strong smell of salt water and fish, and in an increasing dampness of the air. Marshes, overgrown with sedge grass, lie dank and low on both sides of the highway.

At MOSS POINT, *114.8 m.* (2,453 pop.), is a junction with US 90 (*see Tour 1*).

╍╍╍╍╍╍╍╍╍╍╍╍╍╍╍╍╍╍╍╍╍╍╍╍╍╍╍╍╍╍╍╍╍╍╍

Tour 16

Vaiden—Kosciusko—Carthage—Raleigh—Junction with US 84. State 35.
Vaiden to Junction with US 84, 141.1 m.

Graveled roadbed two lanes wide.
Accommodations in towns.

State 35 cuts through a narrow slice of the State that until recent years was hemmed by pine forests and isolated by lack of transportation facilities. The lumber industry, following on the heels of the railroad, was the first outside influence to stamp itself upon it, destroying a large part of the barrier of pines. As the lands were cleared they were in the northern section converted into pastures and toward the south developed into farms with diversified crops. Thus, two new industries were ushered in.

The creamery and condensery at Kosciusko are among the largest in the State; the vegetable produce and watermelons of the southern section are noted for their superior quality. Throughout the area the rugged beauty of hills and the rich redness of soil contribute to wayside charm. Southward the highway skirts the notorious Sullivan's Hollow, the scene of more bloodshed and crime than any other part of the State, and around which extravagantly colorful stories have been woven.

State 35 branches S. from VAIDEN, *0 m.* (325 alt., 648 pop.) *(see Tour 5, Sec. a),* which is at the junction with US 51 *(see Tour 5, Sec. a).*

The highway runs through a region with broad cultivated fields, solid-looking farmhouses, and clustered tenant cabins, then through heavily forested hills and red gullies. At *4.1 m.* the route crosses the Big Black River, S. of which is a gloomy region deeply wooded with thick-leaved hardwood. Here and there is a paintless weathered cabin in a clearing with a small corn patch; occasionally smoke from a mud-chinked chimney is seen curling above the tall tree tops. The highway mounts steadily to the crest of a high ridge revealing a panorama of wooded valleys, and drops again at *9 m.* into a smaller swamp and crosses Scoopchitto River, a shallow meandering chocolate-colored stream. Between the river and Kosciusko lies a tableland free of trees and used for grazing. This is the heart of one of the State's best dairying sections.

KOSCIUSKO, *24.9 m.* (430 alt., 3,237 pop.), clings to the sides of a series of ridges, its narrow paved streets ascending tortuously to the courthouse square on the crest of the highest hill. Viewed from the grassy square, the town is a mixture of the old and the new; dilapidated frame buildings stand shoulder to shoulder with compact brick ones; rambling Victorian houses, with magnolia-littered yards, contrast with small new cottages and bungalows; neatly asphalted streets come to dead ends at the edges of deep ravines or wander beyond the corporate limits as country lanes.

The town was settled about Red Bud Springs, now dry, which, it is said, appeared after the earthquake of 1811, though the Indians asserted they were formed when the great chief Tecumseh stamped his foot in Detroit. When Andrew Jackson marched back from the defense of New Orleans, he followed the Natchez Trace and, because of an abundance of good spring water, pitched camp in what is now Kosciusko's principal business district.

Originally the little overnight station on the Trace was called Peking because its founder hoped that the connotations of a foreign name would prove attractive to settlers, but the meager food and poor accommodations provided by the taverns caused the town to be known as "Peakedend." The name was in time changed to Paris; but, once more, the effort to dignify the struggling village with a grand title was made in vain. The name was completed to Parrish, possibly because of a family of outlaws (members of the Murrell clan) living here; then it became Perish. Finally the present name was chosen, honoring the Polish hero of the American Revolution, under whom a grandfather of a council member had served. The village was incorporated in 1836.

In 1845 a girls' boarding school, Beechwood Seminary, was established here, and several years later a male academy. By 1859 the village had developed such cultural appreciation as to organize a stock company, the stock of which was sold at $10 a share in order to found a library which, when opened, had 389 well-selected books. The collection included histories, biographies, travel books, and general reference material but no fiction. The present Attala Co. Library was organized in 1931 under the direction of the Mississippi Library Commission.

Until 1920 the town's chief business was the marketing and shipping of produce of Attala and neighboring counties. At that time the lumber industry was clearing off the timber and in its wake dairying developed. In 1928 a creamery was established to care for the dairy products of the county and the next year the Pet Milk Co. built a condensery. Both industries speeded the development of the town, yet Kosciusko has been slow to relinquish its village ways.

Such pleasures as checker-playing and domino games are still a part of the social life. Each fall an Old Fiddler's Contest is held in the courtroom of the courthouse before judges and a large audience. While prizes are offered to the best players on various instruments, the fiddle receives the most attention. There are several prizes for performances on this instrument, the contestants being divided according to age. "Yankee Doodle," "Turkey in the Straw," and "Leather Breeches" are favorite tunes. The winners of the contests usually receive small amounts of cash and runners-up receive such commodities as flour, coffee, and sugar. The giving of the latter is a custom dating from a time when such everyday articles were luxuries.

Music of a more modern and standardized type is taught in the public schools.

KOSCIUSKO MOUND, on the schoolground, was built by 3,000 local children during the Centennial celebration of 1934; each deposited a small cupful of earth brought from their homes, duplicating a mound near Krakow, Poland, honoring Thaddeus Kosciusko. Near the mound is a NATCHEZ TRACE MARKER at a point where the old route formerly ran.

WILLIAMSVILLE, 28 m. (200 pop.), is built around a large yellow pine lumber mill, with the mill's commissary the only store. There are but few dwellings, a majority of the workers living in Kosciusko.

Between Williamsville and Carthage the highway threads its way through the densest forests along this route, much of it the virgin timber. The woodlands, covered with pine needles, have a clean appearance, and the smell of the trees is fresh and sharp. Every mile or so the highway climbs a ridge that presents a view of the rugged country. In autumn, when the red and yellow leaves of sweet gum and oak stand out against the evergreens, the scenery is notable for its vivid coloring.

HOPOCA (Ind., *final gathering*), 39 m. (5 pop.), is the site of an old Indian village. It was settled by Gen. Nathan B. Forrest in 1832, and is the point where the Choctaw gathered prior to their removal west of the Mississippi. Gen. Sam Cobb, Indian chief who led the faction opposing the Treaty of Dancing Rabbit Creek, made his home here. His log cabin, about which numerous Indian relics have been found, is standing but it is in poor condition.

CARTHAGE, *50.5 m.* (998 pop.), the seat of Leake Co., has a modern white stone *COURTHOUSE*. The whole of the village, from the courthouse to the frame store buildings and shaded dwellings, is seen at a glance, and only the steeples of two white frame churches break the low skyline. On Saturdays Indian families living on reservations to the E. and in the backwoods come here to buy supplies and to sell their gayly colored woven baskets. The town is known throughout the State because of the Leake Co. Revelers, a group of local musicians who are keeping alive the old folk songs of the section. Their instruments vary from the saw to the harmonica.

> Left from Carthage on State 16 at *1.5 m* (L) to *PEARL RIVER INDIAN DAY SCHOOL,* typical of the Government-controlled schools for Indian children. In addition to the basic subjects of reading, writing, and arithmetic, carpentry, agriculture, and home economics are taught. Recently attempts have been made to familiarize the Indian children with the folklore and legends of their race.

At *52.3 m.* the highway crosses Pearl River.

WALNUT GROVE, *63.3 m.* (753 pop.), is an old town that has received a new life with the establishment of a large lumber mill. Practically every white frame house has been built recently and sits behind a neat whitewashed picket fence.

South of this point the country gradually loses its shut-in appearance, the pines growing fewer, and many local roads intersect the highway. This is a section of small hill farms, where even before the War between the States the people were making comfortable livings from the soil. Their surplus vegetables and small amounts of cotton are marketed in Forest.

HARPERVILLE, *70.8 m.* (179 pop.), once a lively agricultural town, was burned by General Sherman on his march from Vicksburg to Meridian, and has never recovered. The *G. C. HARPER HOME,* the only antebellum structure and the village showplace, follows early architectural ideals in its straightforward two-story, square design. Of frame construction, it is sturdy but in bad condition.

HILLSBORO, *73.6 m.* (200 pop.), was formerly the seat of Scott Co., and a town antagonistic toward Forest because of the location of the latter on the railroad. When Forest was named the country seat in 1866, Hillsboro people tore up the first foundation for the courthouse, burned the second, and carted away the third, brick by brick. Only by a legislative act in 1873 was the seat permanently established at Forest. Hillsboro has dwindled to a store or two and a few scattered frame dwellings.

> 1. Left from Hillsboro on a graveled road to the *OLD JOE ROLAND HOME, 3 m.,* a log house held together by iron pegs and interesting as a good example of early dog-trot architecture.

> 2. Right from Hillsboro on a local dirt road is GUM SPRINGS, *4 m.,* seven springs within a few feet of each other, each with a different mineral content. They received their name because of the large gum trees growing around them. In 1863 Sherman's soldiers camped here for several weeks during his raid along the Alabama &'Vicksburg R.R. A Holiness Tabernacle is on the hill above the springs, and during the summer old-fashioned revival meetings are held.

FOREST, *81.7 m.* (481 alt., 2,176 pop.) *(see Tour 2),* is at the junction with US 80 *(see Tour 2).*

At *83.4 m.* is a NEGRO C.C.C. CAMP. In the woods two miles S. of the camp is the REFORESTATION LOOKOUT TOWER, not visible from the highway.

Between Forest and the southern end of the route the virgin pines have been cut away to a great extent. The rugged hillsides, thinned of their trees and split by huge crevices, show a magnificently colored clay soil that runs the gamut from a startlingly rich red to a deep bruised purple. Plowed fields, small farming communities, and infrequent sawmills are seen at intervals.

At 87 *m.* is a good example of a Mississippi hill farm with a comfortable farmhouse, painted outhouses, and several hundred acres of cotton.

The highway now climbs a steep ridge through fine stands of second growth pines and hardwood trees.

RALEIGH, *107.6 m.* (583 alt., 219 pop.), built on the top of a small plateau with orange-colored gullies surrounding and encroaching upon it, has discarded the colorful excesses of backwoods settlements and, according to James Street, has reckoned itself a cultural center. It has transferred its interests from the doings of the "hollow folks" to the south to politics. Court sessions are the inhabitants' chief diversion. Not seasons but court terms mark the annual cycle, thus: "I hope to see my corn up by spring court" or "I'm going to house-clean after court is over," or "Come and stay with me next court week." The *SMITH CO. COURTHOUSE,* a large red brick building Greek Revival in type, has a dignity out of keeping with the informal village clustered about it. *HARRISON HOTEL,* on Main St., is an ante-bellum building, used by Civil War soldiers as a recreational center and a hospital. The *JACK TULLOS HOME,* across the street from the hotel, is of the usual plantation type and was built of handhewn timbers, before the war. For many years the local Negroes have believed the *OLD RALEIGH CEMETERY* to be haunted, because of the strange noises that come from it. The phenomenon has been explained by the fact that a cave in the cemetery echoes the sound of approaching traffic on the highway, the noise strangely like the rustling of wings. Raleigh is the birthplace of Daisy McLaurin Stevens, onetime President-general of the United Daughters of the Confederacy.

> Right from Raleigh on a clay and sand road is COHAY, *7 m.* (1,092 pop.), a progressive farming and marketing center. Legend states that Jackson's men crossed Rahoma Creek south of town on their way to defend New Orleans, and on the bridge that spans the creek Jessie Craft served his volunteer troops a sumptuous banquet before they left to join the Confederate Army in 1861.

Between Raleigh and Taylorsville the landscape has the beauty of an unspoiled countryside. Small cotton and corn patches end on the edges of dark pine woodlands, where virgin trees stand clean, straight, and tall. Blackberry bushes and Cherokee roses grow lush beside the road. Farmhouses with adjoining orchards and vegetable patches evidence the dependence of the people upon the land.

TAYLORSVILLE, *124.6 m.* (805 pop.), was a static little village, backwoods in appearance and character until 1925, when the first lumber mill of this section was built. The town changed almost overnight; the main street was paved, a drug store was built, and filling stations were erected on the corners. But unfortunately the timber was soon exhausted and the mill ceased to operate except for short periods of the year. At present (1937) the remnants of the once fine forests are being used by the naval stores factories at Laurel, and the dynamiting and hauling of these stumps is the principal business at Taylorsville today. The so-called *INDIAN BATTLEFIELD* has not been explored, but the large number of arrowheads found here seem to indicate that it was once the scene of an Indian battle. On the schoolyard is the *GRAVE OF GENTLE SOUTH WIND,* a young Indian girl who was killed by her father Onubee in a drunken rage. Her youth and beauty made her fate especially pitiable, and sympathetic white settlers marked her grave, which they keep well-tended.

Right from Taylorsville on State 20, a graveled road, is MIZE, 8.4 *m.* (429 pop.), known by the nickname "No Nigger" and acknowledged the capital of SULLIVAN'S HOLLOW. Mize was reputedly settled by "Hog" Tom Sullivan, whose neighbors by the nickname suggested indirectly the reason for the disappearance of their hogs.

The Hollow, a long narrow valley lying south of Mize, has been the source of so many tales of feuds and bloodshed that it is now impossible to separate fact from legend. Every Mississippian knows of it and uses its name as a synonym for lawlessness. It was first inhabited by nine Sullivan brothers, fierce Irishmen who brought with them from the South Carolina mountains the clannish customs of that section. Moving into the Hollow in 1810, each brother homesteaded a 160-acre plot, and each cut a ditch around his land to separate it from his brother's. At the mouth of the stream along which the farms lay, they built a lumber mill, a gristmill, and a cotton gin. The collection of mills and farms was called Bunker Hill for some reason satisfactory to the Sullivans, but soon came to be known as "Merry Hell," because of the fights taking place there. The brothers continued to clear the land and to increase their farms until they had the entire valley under cultivation. Their arrogance, increasing with their prosperity, caused them to be hated and feared by the neighbors, many of whom moved away. "Wild Bill," a son of Hence, one of the nine brothers, was the most notorious of the clan. But though he brawled, fought, and caroused up and down the Hollow throughout his life, he managed to outlive the War between the States, the World War, and, more remarkably, the Sullivan Feud, dying peacefully in his bed. Alleged to have killed more of his kinsmen than any other Sullivan, he was given the title "King of the Hollow." Neace, brother of Wild Bill, was the most magnificent specimen physically. Tall, straight, gaunt, he had a dark beard that reached below his waist. Once after a rough and tumble fight at Shiloh Church in which two men were shot to death, Neace, with blood pouring out of his intestines exposed by knife wounds, got up and walked 200 yds. and mounted his horse. Stories of the efforts of officers to enforce the law on the Sullivans were favorite local jokes. A sheriff and his deputies once attempted to arrest Bill and Neace, but the brothers stopped their plowing and, forcing the officers into a barn, locked them in. On another occasion, Bill and Neace placed a sheriff's head between the rails of a heavy split-rail fence and left him there to starve. In 1874, however, after Bryant Craft was shot for some good Sullivan reason, a serious attempt was made to apprehend Bill and Neace, who took to the swamps and remained in hiding for four years. At the end of that time they gave themselves up for trial, but a fire of mysterious origin destroyed the courthouse and the records of indictment against them. They never came to trial.

Some of the earlier Sullivan men were very small, the youngest of "Small Jim's" children being called "Runty Bill." The boy hated the name and was extremely sensitive about his dwarf-like stature. Legend has it that Runty Bill on one of his solitary walks was given a drink from an acorn cup by a woodland elf; the liquid was an elixir promoting growth and strength. After that he and all his descendants were of splendid physique. Because of his superior size he was able to win from one of his smaller brothers the girl both loved, and it is said that the notorious intra-clan feud originated in the enmity which resulted. The fight broke out about 1860 and the offspring of the brothers were drawn into the argument. Fighting words were hurled, and the feud lasted until 1910. Fights, ambuscades, and wholesale executions were frequent. Brothers slew brothers and families arrayed themselves agains. in-laws. The fiercest battles were fought at Shiloh Church on Bunker Hill. Once, the members of one faction caught a member of the opposing faction and hitched him to a plow. Then, after plowing him all day, they locked him in the ox's stall and fed him fodder. Saturday afternoons, regardless of the weather, the men of the clan gathered in Mize and the wise citizenry remained at home, content with the knowledge that, come Sunday morning, fewer Sullivans would be in the world than had been the day before; the Sullivans bullied, swaggered, and insulted one another until the desired fight began.

One Sullivan reformed and reported not only his own sins but also those of his kinsmen to the preacher. Immediately his unappreciative kinsmen destroyed his mill, burned his farm house and timber, and rode him out of the Hollow on a rail. At a ball game in Mize in 1924 a squabble arose over a technicality and a fight supplanted the game. After the fight was finished two persons lay dead and a half dozen were seriously wounded.

Notwithstanding these activities the Sullivans were excellent farmers. They were always prosperous and raised good cattle. Wade Sullivan offers a reason for their success: "We watch all the times it thunders in February and, in April when them days come, we kiver our garden up. It will sho' frost on them days. Then, too, we allus plant all day on Friday before Easter."

While lawlessness is by no means a thing of the past in the Hollow, the Sullivans have become more cautious in their ways. Occasionally, at election time and during county fair week, someone will go berserk and act Sullivan, but community spirit is against such reversions. Many of the more peaceable Sullivans have moved away to less turbulent areas to make honored names for the family.

Between Taylorsville and Hot Coffee the highway makes a steady upward climb over the top of a chain of steep ridges. Far away are low-lying valleys framed in forests of longleaf pines, and more remote hills are a vague enchanting blue.

HOT COFFEE, *131.8 m.,* is hardly more than a gin, several frame houses, and a conspicuously new brick-constructed store building sprawling beside the road, but because of its name it is known throughout the State. According to James Street, immediately after the War between the States, J. J. Davis of Shiloh swapped a sabre for a sick horse, swapped the horse for a wagon, swapped the wagon for another horse, and after a week of such swapping found himself with enough cash to start a store. He gathered his possessions and came here, building a store by the old Taylorsville-Williamsburg Road. He hung a coffee pot over his door, and served coffee that was both hot and good, made of pure spring water and New Orleans beans. He used molasses drippings for sugar and the customer could have either long or short sweetening; he refused to serve cream, saying it ruined the taste. Politicians from Taylorsville and Williamsburg patronized the store, serving coffee to their constituents and anyone else that happened to be around. Travelers coming by on their way from Mobile to Jackson drank Mr. Davis's coffee while eating the food they brought with them. Old Mr. Davis died in 1880 and one of the boys from Sullivan's Hollow took over the management of the place. One day a drummer stopped and ordered coffee. "What's the name of this place?" he asked. "Ain't got no name. Just Davis' sto'," said the owner. The salesman started to drink his coffee, but it was too hot. He strangled and sputtered, "Mister, this is *hot* coffee," which was all right with the "sto'keeper." The same day another drummer came through. "Ever given this place a name?" he asked. "Yessir," came the answer quickly, "this is Hot Coffee." The present village store occupies the site of the one in which Davis made his coffee.

At *141.1 m.* is the junction with US 84 *(see Tour 11)*, 1 mile E. of COLLINS *(see Tour 7, Sec. b)*.

◄◄◄◄◄◄◄◄◄◄◄◄◄◄◄◄◄◄◄☼►►►►►►►►►►►►►►►►►►

Tour 17

(Pickwick, Tenn.)—Iuka—Fulton—Amory—Junction with US 45. State 25.
Tennessee Line to Junction with US 45, 108.2 m.

Graveled highway two lanes wide.
Accommodations chiefly in towns.

State 25 winds through the foothills of the Tennessee mountains, the most primitive and picturesque section of the State. Here tiny villages are perched perilously on peaks, and shallow plow marks crook dizzily down hillsides to cabins hanging miraculously to the edges of deep ravines. It is Mississippi's chief stronghold of the ballad and old time customs; the natives, of English, Scottish and Irish stock, are sturdy and self-sufficient, slow to accept changes. Many use the spinning wheels, wash troughs, and quilts of their forebears. Each householder cultivates his own limited acres with the aid of his sons and seldom hires outside help; there is less tenancy here than in any other section of the State.

Crossing the Tennessee Line, *0 m.*, 6 miles S. of Pickwick, Tenn., the highway runs southward through country that is rapidly being cleared for overflow by the Government. Within two years (1939), Pickwick Lake (a part of the Pickwick Dam Project of the TVA) will occupy the entire valley (L), flowing within four miles of Iuka. The dark humped shape of the Tennessee hills parallels State 25 through this section, and here and there the Tennessee River, tossed northward by the rugged hills, is visible through clearings in the woods.

At *6.2 m.* the winding highway crosses Yellow Creek bottoms, and for several miles follows the old Natchez Trace.

THE CARDER

ISLAND HILL, *12.1 m.* (L), not visible from highway, is a limestone bed belonging to the Paleozoic Period.

At IUKA, *15.8 m.* (554 alt., 1,441 pop.) *(see Tour 10),* is the junction with US 72 *(see Tour 10).*

At *16.8 m.* (R) is the *IUKA BATTLEFIELD* where General Rosecrans defeated Confederate troops on September 19, 1862, and brought the control of Iuka into Federal hands. A white frame country house known as "Battle Heights" marks the battlefield, and in the hills surrounding, relics of the battle, Minié balls, belt buckles, shrapnel, and shells have been found.

As the highway twists over the hilltops southward from Iuka, it runs through a fairly well populated area. Roomy log houses set on sheer hillsides appear every mile or two. Constructed of unpainted dressed logs with native limestone chimneys, these houses usually originate as two-room cabins and are expanded with the needs of the occupants. They often house married sons and daughters and their children as well as the parents. On Sunday afternoons family groups of a dozen or so people gather on the wide porches to rock and rest, giving evidence of the fact that here children are still of economic value. Without the aid of Negro servants and with practically no modern conveniences, these families raise their food, quilt their bedding, and often spin the cloth for their simple clothing.

At *17.2 m.* (R) is a good view of WOODALLS MOUNTAIN, a

heavily forested ridge whose top, 780 feet, is the highest point in the State.

TISHOMINGO (Ind., *warrior chief*), 30.4 m. (504 alt., 402 pop.), is an old-fashioned hill village in the heart of the richest mineral deposits in the State. Pottery clay, china clay, paint clay, sandstone, phosphorus rock, and bauxite are found in the immediate vicinity. At the northern entrance of the town is (R) GOOD SPRINGS, where Gen. Andrew Jackson camped on his way to visit the Creek nation. The Natchez Trace cuts directly through the center of Tishomingo, and is marked by a stone boulder in the heart of the village.

> Right from Tishomingo on a graveled road to BETHLEHEM CHURCH, 1.6 m., a narrow shell-like frame structure with a steep-pitched hip roof. Here the primitive or "Hardshell" Baptists annually hold an Old Harp Singing on the first Sunday in June. Old harp books with shaped notes are used, and, after the tune has been pitched, the congregation sings unaccompanied. After the singing, which usually lasts until midafternoon, the singers eat dinner on the grounds *(see WHITE FOLKWAYS).*

At 33.2 m. on State 25 is the junction with a graveled road.

> Left on this road to TISHOMINGO STATE PARK, 1.9 m., one of the nine parks being developed in the State by the U. S. Government. A 980-acre tract of highland forest, the park is divided by Bear Creek which flows northward and empties to the Tennessee River. In the bluffs above the creek is a ledge of limestone rock, at one time an Indian camping ground. Depressions in the ledge show where the Chickasaw formerly ground their corn into meal. Wild azaleas, japonicas, honeysuckle, violets, and many uncommon species of wild fern grow prolifically in the forest shade, and the park is being stocked with deer and other game. A limestone quarry is being worked by the CCC boys who have a camp here, and the rock quarried is used in the construction of cabins. These cabins, completely furnished and equipped with running water, are for rent at nominal cost.

Just S. of Tishomingo the FREEDOM HILLS of Alabama are visible from the highway (L). These far-flung ridges were so named because in the early 1800's they were the hide-out of outlaws of the Southwest.

DENNIS, 36.4 m. (605 alt., 238 pop.), is a sawmill village with a group of frame stores built like steps on the side of a steep hill. The two churches here are older than the village itself. The small frame METHODIST CHURCH is an out-growth of old Valley Church, whose congregation dates back 100 years; the PRIMITIVE BAPTIST PROVIDENCE CHURCH, also of frame construction, has a congregation equally old. At the latter, annual foot washing services are held on the second and third Sundays in May. The men sit on one long bench on one side of the church; the women are seated opposite. Each member of the congregation, a towel girdled about his waist, washes the foot of another and then dries it according to scriptural command. A sermon and communion follow the ceremony.

Between Dennis and Belmont the road winds around hills of gravel, limestone, and chert, and passes tracts of hardwood forests ruthlessly cut over in spots. Just N. of Belmont is (R) the narrow valley of Big Bear Creek with its ledges of sandstone rock.

BELMONT, 40.2 m. (570 alt., 703 pop.), perched on a high ridge between the Tombigbee River and Bear Creek, occupies the site of old Gum Springs, where one of the county's first schools was established. The ridges surrounding the village are rough and bare, having been stripped of their pines and hardwood trees to supply the Belmont sawmill.

South of Belmont State 25 threads through a heavily wooded and irregular highland, with few signs of habitation. A deep-bodied wagon filled with women and children is not an uncommon sight in this section where the hillman loads his family into his wagon and, accompanied by a flop-eared hound dog or two, drives them into town. This occasional trip to town is often the longest journey many of these hill people ever make. The home and the church are the centers of all social life. Log-rollings, quiltings, and serenadings are among the popular events. The principal musical expression is hymn and ballad singing and fiddling; a number of ballads of entirely local origin have been gathered from this section. Unlike the ballads of the southwestern part of the State, which have a medieval flavor dealing with knights, tournaments, and lordly manners and passions, the ballads of these healthy, hardy people are vigorous and earthy. Many have a broad vein of humor and many are "outlaw songs" brought from over Bear Creek by outlaws in hiding there. Often the ballads are sung formally by groups of neighbors gathered for a "singing," but it is not uncommon to hear them from the farmer as he plows, from his wife as she washes the family clothes, or from boys and girls walking along the country roads.

As the highway twists southward the hills gradually brighten until they become mounds of pure red clay against which evergreens and birches gleam sharply green and white.

At 64.5 m. is the junction with US 78 *(see Tour 9)*, with which State 25 unites briefly.

At 67 m. is FULTON (927 pop.) *(see Tour 9)*; L. here on State 25.

South of Fulton the Tombigbee (Ind., *coffin maker*) River parallels the highway (R) throughout and is never more than three miles away.

At TILDEN, 74.8 m. (118 pop.), the oldest town in Itawamba Co., are dilapidated buildings with half-fallen-in roofs, remnants of clay chimneys, and completely rotten steps. From a few fence posts straggle pieces of rusty barbed wire. Many of the people who live here hardly know of the existence of other places more than 30 miles distant. Tilden was settled in the early 1830's by a group of Scottish people from North Carolina, all with the prefix "Mc" to their names, and the present Tilden church is an outgrowth of the one these Scotsmen established.

Left from Tilden on a clay road to the *W. T. McNEECE HOME (private)*, 0.5 m., oldest house in the county, built by a McFadden about 1830 with slave labor. The house is a good example of the durable cabins of the pioneers of the period. The exterior walls are covered with log siding and the chimneys are chinked with mud. The enclosure of the central hall is a modern alteration. In the yard are aged rosebushes, shrubs, and a well-house.

Between Tilden and Amory State 25 skims the last outcroppings of the northeast Mississippi hills, dropping every few miles into a valley between

BOY, BROOM, AND BUTTERBEANS

the ridges. The pine woodlands through this stretch have been little touched and give the landscape a perennial greenness.

At *83 m.* the highway crosses the east branch of Tombigbee River.

SMITHVILLE, *84.4 m.* (401 pop.), settled by an Indian chief named

Chubby and included in the land purchase of 1836, is an old village which has been rejuvenated by the shortleaf pine lumber industry.

At AMORY, 93.8 m. (214 alt., 3,214 pop.) (see Tour 14), is the junction with State 6 (see Tour 14).

South of Amory the highway enters a section of the State as different socially and economically from the highlands as it is scenically. The country here evidences the Black Prairie prosperity, achieved by farming and dairying. Painted houses with firewood piled high in the yard, large red barns, and fat cows in the pastures are the outward signs of comfortable living.

Near the route's end are good examples of the white frame houses of proportions similar to those found in the more elaborate ante-bellum homes of the Black Prairie (see ARCHITECTURE). In contrast with these houses are the Negro tenant cabins, hugging the earth, with whitewashed walls, mud chimneys, and naked, clean-swept yards.

At 108.2 m. is the junction with US 45 (see Tour 4), 1 mile E. of Aberdeen.

PART IV
Appendices

Chronology
1528–1937

Early Explorations

1528   Panfilo de Narvaez explores interior, possibly the Mississippi region, from Tampa Bay. Expedition returns to sea and is dispersed by storm.

1536   Alvar Nunez Cabeza de Vaca, with three other survivors of Narvaez expedition, reach Spain after eight years spent among tribes of American interior.

1537   Don Hernando (Fernando) de Soto, obtaining permission to conquer Florida, organizes expedition.

1540   De Soto enters Mississippi, one year after his landing in Florida.

1541   De Soto discovers the Mississippi River; crosses, and explores country, but fails to find the mythical cities of gold.

1542   Returning, De Soto reaches the confluence of Red River with Mississippi. Dies (May 21), and is buried in Mississippi River.

1629–30   Charles I makes first Carolina grant to Sir Robert Heath. Grant includes what is now Mississippi.

1663   Charles II makes second Carolina grant to Clarendon, Carteret and others of all territory, from sea to sea, between latitudes 31° and 36° N.

1665   Grant of 1663 is enlarged to extend south to latitude 29° N.

1673   Joliet and Marquette descend the Mississippi River from about 42° to about 34° N. latitude (from the Wisconsin to the Arkansas River).

1682   LaSalle descends the Mississippi River from the Illinois River to the Gulf of Mexico.

French Dominion. 1699–1763

1699   Pierre le Moyne, Sieur d'Iberville, establishes the first colony on what is now Mississippi soil. The colony was Fort de Maurepas on the Bay of Biloxi.

1700   D'Iberville, de Bienville, and de Tonti ascend the Mississippi to the present site of Natchez.

1712   Louis XIV grants Antoine Crozat, Marquis de Chatel, a 15 years' monopoly of trade in Louisiana.

1716   Jean Baptiste le Moyne, Sieur de Bienville, French Governor of

Louisiana, builds Fort Rosalie, where the city of Natchez now stands.

1717 Crozat surrenders his charter to the King. The Mississippi Company (Compagnie des Indes Occidentales) is chartered, with exclusive privilege of developing Louisiana, but is obligated to introduce within 25 years 6,000 white colonists and 3,000 black slaves.

1718 The Mississippi Company grants land for settlements on the Yazoo, at Natchez, on the Bay of St. Louis, and Pascagoula Bay.

1720 Three hundred settlers locate at Natchez.
Collapse of the "Mississippi Bubble."

1721 Three hundred colonists, destined for the lands of Mme. de Chaumont, arrive at Pascagoula.

1723 Seat of government of Louisiana is removed from Biloxi to New Orleans.

1726 Bienville is recalled. Perier becomes commander-general of Louisiana.

1729 French settlers and soldiers are massacred at Fort Rosalie; 237 are killed and 227 made prisoners.

1730 French soldiers and Choctaw warriors practically annihilate Natchez tribe in retaliation for the 1729 massacre.

1732 Mississippi Company surrenders its charter. The English proprietary charter is included in that of Georgia.

1733 Bienville reinstated as Governor.

1736 Governor Bienville fails to subdue the warlike Chickasaw.

1762 France cedes New Orleans and territory west of the Mississippi River to Spain.

An English Province. 1763–1779

1763 By treaty with France, West Florida, including Mississippi Territory south of 31st parallel, becomes an English province, Captain George Johnstone, Governor.

1764 King in Council, in a second decree extends the boundaries of the province of West Florida north to the mouth of the Yazoo, thus including the Mississippi settlements.

1768–70 Scotch Highlanders from North Carolina and Scotland establish Scotia, about 30 miles eastward from Natchez.

1772 Richard and Samuel Swayze, of New Jersey, purchase land on Homochitto River (within present Adams County), and form a permanent settlement. It is claimed that Samuel Swayze, a Congregational minister, built the first Protestant church in Mississippi.

1775 Revolution of American Colonies begins. British West Florida remains loyal to Crown.

1778 Continental Congress grants to James Willing authority to descend the Mississippi and secure the neutrality of the colonies at Natchez, Bayou Pierre, etc.

By order of the Governor of West Florida, Fort Panmure, formerly Rosalie, is garrisoned by a company of infantry under Capt. Michael Jackson of the British Army.

A Province of Spain. 1779–1798

1779 The Spanish general, Don Bernardo de Galvez, storms Fort Bute (September 7), captures Baton Rouge from Lt. Colonel Dickinson, who surrenders West Florida (September 21) including Fort Panmure and the District of Natchez.

1781 The people of the Natchez District rebel against Spain, capture Fort Panmure, and raise the English flag (April 30). Don Carlos de Grandpré, appointed Spanish commander of the Natchez District (July 29), recaptures fort and inhabitants but drives many colonists from the territory.

1782 September 3. By definitive treaty of peace between the United States and Great Britain the southern boundary of the United States is fixed at the 31st parallel N. lat., from the Mississippi to the St. Mary's River. But in ceding Florida to Spain England specifies no boundary on the north; therefore Spain claims north to the mouth of the Yazoo River.

1785 Georgia organizes the County of Bourbon, which includes all lands east of the Mississippi, between latitude 31° and the mouth of the Yazoo River, to which the Indian title had been extinguished.

1788 February 1. Act erecting Bourbon County is repealed.

1795 The State of Georgia sells to four companies the territory in dispute, consisting of approximately 40,000,000 acres, at the rate of 2½ cents per acre. This act is known as the "Yazoo Fraud."
A Negro mechanic belonging to Daniel Clarke of Fort Adams, Wilkinson County, makes a cotton gin from a crude drawing and verbal description of the Whitney Gin, and Clarke introduces its use to county.
By treaty with Spain, the southern boundary of the U. S. is fixed at 31° latitude; the western boundary is fixed at the middle of the Mississippi River, and free navigation is agreed upon.

1796 Sale of land by Georgia rescinded.

1797 February 24. Andrew Ellicott, commissioned by the U. S. to fix the boundary line, with the Spanish commissioner, Don Manuel Gayoso de Lemos, arrives at Natchez.
July. Col. Ellicott secures the election of a permanent committee of public safety.
Andrew Marschalk, a soldier of the garrison at Walnut Hills, first uses the printing press in the Mississippi territory.

1798 January 10. Col. Ellicott is notified by Governor-General of New Orleans that the King of Spain had ordered the surrender of the territory.

March 23. Fort Nogales on Walnut Hill is evacuated by Spanish garrison.

March 29-30. Fort Panmure is evacuated about midnight.

Territorial Days. 1798-1817

1798   April 7. Act of Congress creates the Territory of Mississippi with bounds including the region now Alabama.

May 7. Winthrop Sargent appointed first Governor of the Mississippi Territory by President Adams.

August 6. Gov. Sargent arrives at Natchez.

Gen. Wilkinson reaches Natchez; makes headquarters on Loftus Heights, later Fort Adams.

1799   February 28. The first law made and promulgated by the Territorial authorities is signed by Winthrop Sargent, Governor, Peter Bryan Bruin and Daniel Tilton, judges. The law provides for the organization of militia.

1800   Population (U. S. Census) of Mississippi Territory, 8,850.

Benjamin F. Stokes publishes the *Mississippi Gazette,* the first newspaper in the Mississippi Territory.

Supplemental act of Congress regarding Mississippi Territory provides that settlement shall be made with Georgia for claims on or before March 10, 1803.

1801   May 25. William Charles Cole Claiborne is appointed Territorial Governor by President Jefferson.

October 24. Treaty of Chickasaw Bluffs, between U. S. and the Chickasaw Nation, gives road right-of-way between Mero Settlement to Natchez. This, with the Treaty of Fort Adams, opens the Natchez Trace.

1802   February 1. The seat of government is moved from Natchez to Washington, 6 miles east.

Port of New Orleans closed to American goods.

Jefferson College is established at Washington, Miss., by legislative act.

April 24. The U. S. Government agrees to pay Georgia $1,250,000 to relinquish claims to certain disputed territory, partly in the new Mississippi Territory.

Bandits infest the Natchez Trace. Governor puts price on head of one bandit, Mason. The head is brought in by Little Harpe and another bandit. They unsuccessfully claim reward. Little Harpe is hanged.

1803   March 10. Natchez is incorporated as a city.

March. Port of New Orleans reopened.

March. Congress provides for survey of land ceded by Georgia to U. S.

United States purchases Louisiana from France for $15,000,000.

1804	March 27. The territory north of Mississippi Territory and south of Tennessee, e.g., the land ceded by Georgia to U. S., is annexed to Mississippi Territory.
1805	March 1. Robert Williams, of North Carolina, succeeds W. C. C. Claiborne as Governor. By treaty with U. S. the Cherokee, Creek, and Choctaw Nations permit roads to be opened through their districts.
1807	January 12. Aaron Burr arrives at mouth of Bayou Pierre. He surrenders unconditionally to Mississippi Territory authorities. January 18. Burr, at Washington, Miss., gives bond to appear before the territorial court February 2. February 4. No formal court action having been taken, Burr demands release from recognizance. Refused, he breaks bond next day, but is arrested in Alabama. Judge Harry Toulmin's digest of the laws of Mississippi is adopted by the legislature; this is the first digest. Eleazer Carver begins manufacture of cotton gins near Washington, Miss.
1809	January 9. Congress extends the right of suffrage to Mississippi Territory. March 3. Gov. Williams resigns. Four days later David Holmes is appointed his successor. December 23. The Bank of Mississippi is established at Natchez.
1810	Population, 40,352.
1812	May 14. The District of Mobile, lying east of Pearl River, west of the Perdido River, and south of 31°, is annexed to the Mississippi Territory.
1813	August 13. Fort Mimms, in what is now the State of Alabama, is attacked by 1,000 Creeks under Weatherford, McQueen, and Francis; 260 of the garrison are massacred. December 23. Mississippi troops, under General Claiborne, attack and destroy Escanachaha, the Holy City of the Creek Indians.
1814	December. The naval battle of Pass Christian is fought near St. Louis Bay.
1815	January 8. Mississippi troops take valiant part in the Battle of New Orleans.
1816	Mississippi Territory gains new lands, ceded by Chickasaw and Choctaw Nations.

Statehood. 1817–

1817	March 1. Congress passes act enabling Mississippi Territory to prepare for statehood. July 7. Constitutional Convention in session at Washington, Miss., with 47 delegates representing 14 counties. August 16. President of the U. S. is notified that State Constitution has been adopted on the 15th.

CHRONOLOGY

September 1-2. David Holmes is elected State Governor and Louis Winston, Secretary.
October 6. State legislature opens first session.
December 10. Act of Congress admits Mississippi as a State into the Union.

1818   January 21. Legislature organizes the first Supreme Court.

1819   February 17. Legislature passes an act establishing Elizabeth Female Academy at Washington, Miss.

1820   Population, 75,448.
January 5. George Poindexter elected Governor.
October 18. The Treaty of Doak's Stand is made between U. S. and the Choctaw Nation with an exchange of territory.

1821   Legislature appoints commission to locate a permanent State Capital. Le Fleur's Bluffs on the Pearl River is chosen, and site of new capital is named *Jackson*, in honor of Maj-Gen. Andrew Jackson.

1822   January 23. Legislature convenes at Jackson—the first session in the new capital.
June 30. Poindexter's Code adopted in special session.

1824   January 23. Imprisonment for debt is abolished in Mississippi.

1830   Population, 136,621.
Planters Bank is chartered.
September 15. By Treaty of Dancing Rabbit Creek the Choctaw Nation cedes to U. S. remainder of their lands east of the Mississippi.

1831   The first Mississippi charter is granted for a railroad, to run from Woodville to St. Francisville, La.

1832   September 10. Constitutional Convention meets at Jackson.
October 26. Convention completes labors.
November. At general elections, people ratify constitution. Under new constitution the judiciary becomes elective.
October 20. By Treaty of Pontotoc Creek the Chickasaw Nation cedes its lands east of the Mississippi to the U. S. and agrees to move from State.

1833   February. Legislature creates the High Court of Errors and Appeals, and appropriates funds for erection of a statehouse and executive mansion.

1836   February 26. Erection of a State Penitentiary is authorized.

1837   January 21. Legislature charters the Mississippi Union Bank and agrees to subscribe the equal of private subscriptions to the limit of $15,500,000.

1839   Legislature sanctions the issuance of $5,000,000 State stock for the Mississippi Union Bank.
The New Capitol, though unfinished, is occupied.
February 15. Legislative act defines married women's right to property.

1840	Population, 375,651. Act of Legislature provides for establishment of a State university at Oxford. State Penitentiary is occupied.
1841	Gov. McNutt advises legislature to repudiate Union Bank bonds. This is done next year. Indebtedness, $5,000,000 with interest.
1844	February 24. The University of Mississippi is incorporated.
1845	March 6. Robert J. Walker is appointed Secretary of the Treasury of U. S.
1846	March 4. The State is divided for the first time into Congressional Districts. Law is passed establishing common schools.
1847	February 23. The Mississippi Volunteers, under command of Col. Davis, render distinguished service at Buena Vista.
1848	February 7. Chickasaw school lands opened for leasing for 99 years. March 2. Institution for the Blind, opened privately in 1847, is authorized. November 6. University of Mississippi is opened at Oxford.
1850	Population, 606,526.
1851	Gov. Quitman, arrested by U. S. authorities for violation of neutrality laws of 1818 by abetting an expedition against Cuba, resigns as Governor. Is acquitted and renominated, but withdraws before election.
1853	The Planters Bank bonds are repudiated. Indebtedness, $2,000,000 with interest. March 3. President Pierce appoints Jefferson Davis Secretary of War.
1854	August. Institution for the Deaf and Dumb is opened.
1855	January 8. The Asylum for the Insane is opened.
1856	February 6. Amendments (4 and 5) to constitution make first Monday in October the day for general elections.
1857	Jacob Thompson, of Miss., becomes Secretary of the Interior.
1859	Delegates from eight States meet in convention at Vicksburg, to consider reopening of slave trade. Whitworth Female College at Brookhaven is opened.
1860	Population, 791,305. November 26. Legislature in special session to consider withdrawing Mississippi from Union. Convention is called.
1861	January 7. Convention opens and two days later passes an ordinance of secession, 84 to 15. Is the second State to secede. January 20. Confederate force seizes an unfinished fort on Ship Island. January 21. Senator Jefferson Davis in the U. S. Senate announces Mississippi's withdrawal from the Union. February 9. Jefferson Davis becomes the President of the Confederate States.

	April. President Davis calls for 1,500 Mississippi troops to defend Pensacola. Ninth and Tenth Regiments respond. December 31. Federal naval force captures Biloxi.
1862	Mississippi invaded by Union Army.
1863	Vicksburg falls. The seat of government moved to Enterprise, later to Meridian, then to Columbus.
1864	Seat of government moved to Macon.

Reconstruction

1865	May 6. Upon surrender of General Taylor to General Canby, Gov. Clark recalls State officials, with State archives, from Columbus to Jackson. May 18. Legislature convenes in special session at Jackson to consider repeal of ordinance of secession. May 22. Gov. Clark is arrested and imprisoned in Fort Pulaski, Savannah. June 13. Federal Government refuses to recognize old State Government, and appoints Judge William L. Sharkey as Provisional Governor. August 14-16. Convention drafts and adopts amendments to constitution of 1832. Freedmen granted civil rights. October. Benjamin G. Humphreys is elected Governor; inaugurated on 16th.
1866–67	Legislature, in special session, refuses to ratify the 13th and 14th amendments of the Constitution of the United States.
1867	March 2. Mississippi by Reconstruction Act comes within 4th Military District, Major General Ord commanding. November 13. Gen. Ord orders W. H. McCardle, editor of *Vicksburg Times,* to be confined in military prison for obstructing the reconstruction acts.
1868	January 6. "Black and Tan" Convention meets in Jackson to form a constitution, adjourns May 18.
1868	January. Legislature rejects the 14th Amendment. June 4. Gen. Irwin McDowell succeeds Ord as commander 4th District. June 15. Gov. Humphreys removed from office by soldiers. Adelbert Ames is appointed Provisional Governor. June 22-30. People, by vote of 63,860 to 55,231, reject constitution framed by "Black and Tan" (Reconstruction) Convention.
1869	September 8. National Union Republican Party of Mississippi holds convention at Jackson and adopts State ticket, the majority of Democrats concurring. November 30–December 1. At State elections constitution drafted in 1868 is ratified, objectionable features having been removed.

	CHRONOLOGY 517
1870	Population, 827,922. February 17. Congress readmits Mississippi as a State into the Union. State Board of Education created; system of public schools established.
1871	First monument to Confederate dead in State raised at Liberty.
1873	General Adelbert Ames, with solid Negro vote, is elected Governor.
1874	December 7. Race riots near Vicksburg. Attacking Negroes dispersed with much loss of life.
1875	Political strife between office-holders and taxpayers continues intense through 1874 and 1875. Rioting at many places, notably at Yazoo City, September 1, and Clinton, September 4, 1875. Gov. Ames appeals to President for protection; is refused. At State elections (November) Democrats sweep Republicans from office, and gain control of both houses of legislature.
1876	February 16. T. W. Cordozo, Negro Superintendent of Education, is impeached; resigns and proceedings dropped. February 22. Resolution is reported to favor the impeachment of Gov. Ames. He resigns (March 29) and John M. Stone becomes Governor. March 13. A. K. Davis, Negro Lieutenant Governor, is impeached and removed from office.
1877	State Board of Health created.
1878	By legislative acts, a system of free public schools is established, and Alcorn University becomes Alcorn Agricultural and Mechanical College. February. Agricultural & Mechanical College for white students established. August–November. Yellow fever epidemic.
1879	Mississippi Valley Cotton Planters' Association is organized at Vicksburg. Labor convention meets (May 5) at Vicksburg "to consider the Negro-exodus question."
1880	Population, 1,131,597. Revised code of Mississippi laws is adopted by legislature.
1882	March 9. Legislature passes laws to foster industries and encourage immigration; also an act prohibiting sale of intoxicating liquors within five miles of University of Mississippi. June. Trustees open State University to women. Disastrous flood in Yazoo-Mississippi Delta.
1884	March 4. Act passed providing for railroad commission.
1885	October 22. The Industrial Institute and College is opened to the young women of Mississippi.
1886	March 11. General local option (liquor) law is passed.

CHRONOLOGY

Extensive immigration of Negroes from hill country to river bottoms in the Yazoo area basins.

1889   December 6. Jefferson Davis dies at New Orleans.

1890   Population, 1,289,600.
January 16. John M. Stone inaugurated Governor.
Australian ballot system of voting is adopted in all except Congressional elections.
November 1. New State constitution is promulgated, to take effect January 1, 1891.

1891   June 3. Monument to Confederate dead is unveiled at Jackson.

1892–3   State relief for Confederate soldiers and widows is authorized.
February 7. State flag and coat of arms adopted.

1897   Mississippi raises 3 regiments for Spanish War service.
Disastrous flood.

1898   Yellow fever epidemic.

1900   Population, 1,551,270.
February 21. New State Capitol, with total appropriations of $1,093,641, and to occupy site of old State Penitentiary, is authorized.
Pensions for Confederate soldiers are provided for.
Magnolia chosen State flower.

1902   February 26. Department of Archives and History created.
March 5. Department of Insurance created.

1903   June 3. Cornerstone of new State Capitol is laid.
August 6. First election held under new primary election laws.
Disastrous flood.

1904   A text-book commission is created.
Legislature passes laws requiring equal but separate accommodations for white and blacks on street cars; authorizing a new code of laws; creating Lamar County; providing for additional branch agricultural experiment stations, and a new institution for the deaf and dumb.

1906   Laws are passed which change the management of the penitentiary; create a Department of Agriculture and Commerce; adopt the code of 1906; provide for Jefferson Davis and Forrest Counties; for a memorial to Mississippi Confederate soldiers at the Vicksburg Military Park; and for a geological, economic, and topographical survey of the State.

1908   Importation and sale of alcoholic liquor in Mississippi is prohibited.
County agricultural high schools are established.

1910   Population, 1,797,114.
State Board of Health succeeds Health Department created 50 years before.
County agricultural high schools act is amended to provide equal opportunities for the Negro.

CHRONOLOGY 519

March 30. Mississippi Normal College is created.
April 14. State schools placed in hands of one board of trustees.

1912 River overflows. Delegates to Democratic National Convention at Baltimore instructed for Hon. Oscar Underwood, of Alabama, as required by the people in the first Presidential preference primary held in Mississippi.
Child Labor Law forbidding girls under 14 and boys under 12 to work in industrial establishments is passed, with 8-hour day for older youths.
Bureau of Vital Statistics is inaugurated.

1914 An act guaranteeing bank deposits passed.
State Factory Inspectorship created; State Board of Nurse Examiners authorized.
State Truck Growers (cooperative) Association organized.

1916 Rural schools consolidated by authority of act of 1910.
January 18. T. G. Bilbo inaugurated Governor.
By constitutional amendment Supreme Court increased to six judges, elected for term of eight years.
Public hangings are made illegal.
Law is passed making it a misdemeanor to mutilate or misuse the U. S. flag, the State flag, and Confederate flag.
State Highway, State Tax, and Illiteracy Commissions are created.
March 25. Sanatorium for tubercular patients established at Magee.
March 28. Mississippi Industrial and Training School established at Columbia.

1917 March 27. Mississippi musters its First Regiment and opens State recruiting office.
April 6. Mississippi ratifies Wilson's Declaration of War on Germany.

1918 National Prohibition Act is ratified by State.
Plant Board is created.
Pat Harrison is elected to the U. S. Senate.

1920 Population, 1,790,618.
Two amendments are adopted to State Constitution: 1. A uniform poll tax of $2.00 to be used in aid of common schools in the county. 2. Pensions for Confederate soldiers and sailors, residents of Miss., and their widows.
April 3. Mississippi State School for the feebleminded is established at Ellisville.

1922 March 25. An act is passed permitting women to vote.
A higher gasoline tax secures funds for improvement of highways.
Rehabilitation Act passed.

1923 March 3. John Sharp Williams, distinguished U. S. Senator, having declined renomination, retires to private life.

1924 Inheritance Tax Law passed.
Income Tax Bill of 1912 is modified.

| | Commission of Education is established.
Delta State Teachers College is organized at Cleveland.
Sea Wall Bill is passed; extending along Gulf Coast, wall cost $5,000,000. |
|---|---|
| 1926 | Mississippi Library Commission and Mississippi Forestry Commission are inaugurated.
An act is passed to prohibit teaching in State-supported schools that man evolved from a lower order.
First condensery, or factory for canning milk, in the South is opened at Starkville, Miss.
First gas producing field is opened at Amory. |
| 1927 | April 21. The Mississippi River floods the Mississippi-Yazoo Delta more disastrously than in floods of 1897 and 1903. |
| 1928 | U. S. Flood Control Act passed.
Theodore G. Bilbo becomes Governor.
July 1. First Mississippi Market Bulletin appears.
State Blind Commission and Malaria Control Commission are created.
Sexual sterilization of insane becomes legal, when such action is deemed advisable. |
| 1930 | Population, 2,009,821.
Tobacco and theatre taxes are imposed.
Research Commission is created to study Mississippi local government.
Official Code of 1930, containing in two large volumes the laws of Mississippi, is adopted. |
| 1931 | Jackson Gas Field is opened.
Governor Bilbo reorganizes faculties of all State institutions of higher learning, except Delta State Teachers College. In consequence, these colleges are removed from list of Association of Southern Colleges. |
| 1932 | Game and Fish Commission is established.
Kidnapping is made a capital offense.
Sales Tax is passed.
Mississippi balances its budget.
Governor Conner reorganizes colleges and they are reinstated in Southern Association of Colleges.
November. Relief work organization is set up. |
| 1933 | Twelve Civilian Conservation Corps camps are established in Mississippi. |
| 1934 | State Health Officer made report: "Mississippi's death rate is practically the lowest in U. S."
February 26. An act authorizes sale of light wines and beer.
Reforestation and Conservation Act is passed.
Act exempting small homesteads from State tax is passed. |
| 1936 | January 21. Hugh L. White inaugurated Governor. |

February 21. An act to raise number of trustees of colleges from nine to twelve is passed.

March 23. Old age Pension, Teachers' Pensions, and Unemployment Compensation Acts are passed.

Industrial Act is passed, providing means to "balance agriculture with industry."

Funds are provided for the Mississippi Advertising Commission.

Act is passed to tax retail chain stores.

April 5. Tornado strikes Tupelo; 200 killed, 1,500 injured. 200 homes destroyed; property loss $4,000,000.

1937 Durant is first city to issue bonds under new industrial program.

Industrial Act held valid by court at Winona.

Bibliography

This bibliography is of necessity only a brief selective list. It is not a complete record of sources consulted in the preparation of this book, nor is it restricted to these sources. The Division of Bibliography of the Library of Congress has prepared *A List of References Relating to Mississippi;* many items from the list have been included in this bibliography.

GENERAL INFORMATION

Mississippi. Secretary of State. *Mississippi Blue Book.* Jackson, 1937, 291 p. A biennial report from July 1, 1935 to July 1, 1937.
Wall, E. G. *Handbook of the State of Mississippi.* Jackson, Power and Barksdale, 1882. The author was commissioner of immigration and agriculture.
Whitfield, H. L. *Know Mississippi.* Jackson, Jackson Printing Co., 1926. 112 p.

DESCRIPTION AND TRAVEL

Cobb, Joseph B. *Mississippi Scenes.* Philadelphia, Hart, 1851. 250 p. A word panorama of Mississippi by a traveler in the 1840's.
Hildebrand, T. R. "Machines Come to Mississippi." *National Geographic Magazine,* September 1937, v. 12: 263-318. A more general description of life in Mississippi than the title implies.
Ingraham, J. H. *The Southwest by a Yankee.* New York, Harper, 1835. 570 p. 2 v. The account of a visit during the 1830's to the Southwest, including the Natchez area. Statistics on population and farm production of the time.
―――. *The Sunny South, or The Southerner at Home.* Philadelphia, G. G. Evans, 1860. 526 p. A romantic picture of the Natchez country just prior to the War between the States.
Olmstead, Fred L. *A Journey in the Back Country.* New York, Mason, 1863. 565 p. A critical tourist's observations on the domestic life of Mississippians in the 1850's.

NATURAL SETTING

Bolton, Willa. *Our State; a Geographical Reader of Mississippi.* Richmond, Va. Johnson Pub. Co., 1925. 310 p. il.
Connell, John T. and Wm. T. *Fishing on the Gulf Coast in Mississippi.* Gulfport, Miss., Gulfport Printing Co., 1930. 63 p. il. The what, when, and how of fishing on the Coast by an authority.
Foster, L. E. "Jackson Adds a New Source of Wealth to Resources of Mississippi" [natural gas]. *Manufacturers Record,* July 31, 1930, v. 98; 44-46.
Grim, Ralph E. *The Eocene Sediments of Mississippi.* Jackson, 1936. 240 p.

il., maps, photographs. (Mississippi State Geological Survey. Bulletin 30). Technical but valuable as a reference.

———. *Recent Oil and Gas Prospecting in Mississippi.* With a brief study of subsurface geology. Oxford, University of Mississippi, 1928. 98 p. (Mississippi State Geological Survey. Bulletin 21).

Lowe, Ephraim N. *Mississippi, Its Geology, Geography, Soils, and Mineral Resources.* Jackson, Tucker Printing House, 1915. 335 p. il. (Mississippi State Geological Survey. Bulletin 12.) A non-technical treatment of the physiography of the State designed to meet needs of general public.

———. *Plants of Mississippi: a List of Flowering Plants and Ferns.* Jackson, Hederman Bros., 1921. 292 p. (Mississippi State Geological Survey. Bulletin 17).

Sinclair, J. D. "Studies of Soil Erosion in Mississippi." *Journal of Forestry,* April 1931, v. 29: 533-540.

Stephenson, Lloyd W., and others. *The Ground-water Resources of Mississippi.* With discussions of the chemical character of the waters by C. S. Howard. Prepared in cooperation with the Mississippi State Geological Survey. Washington, Govt. Printing Office, 1928. 515 p. (U. S. Geological Survey. Water-supply paper 576).

Mississippi. State Geological Survey. *Forest Conditions of Mississippi.* Jackson, 1913. 166 p. (Bulletin 11). A reprint with additions of bulletins 5 and 7.

FIRST AMERICANS

ARCHEOLOGY

Brown, Calvin S. *Archeology of Mississippi.* University, Oxford, 1926. 372 p. il., charts. Reconnaissance by an acknowledged authority.

Collins, Henry B. *Archeology of Mississippi.* Birmingham, Dec. 1932: pp. 37-42. Address before Committee of State Archeological Survey. An unpublished survey of archeology in Mississippi, State Dept. of Archives and History. Comprehensive resume of archeological research to date.

INDIANS

Byington, Cyrus. *A Dictionary of the Choctaw Language.* Edited by John R. Swanton and H. S. Halbert. Washington, Govt. Printing Office, 1915. 611 p. (U. S. Bureau of American ethnology. Bulletin 46). An excellent but not exhaustive study.

Cushman, H. B. *History of Choctaw, Chickasaw, and Natchez Indians.* Greenville, Tex., Headlight, 1899. 607 p. Readable story of Mississippi's three most important tribes.

Halbert, H. S. *Choctaw Creative Legends.* In Mississippi Historical Society *Publications,* Oxford, 1901. v. 4, p. 267-270.

———. *Funeral Customs of the Choctaw.* In Mississippi Historical Society *Publications,* Oxford, 1900. v. 3, p. 353-366.

Lincecum, Gideon. *The Choctaw Traditions: about Their Settlements in Mississippi and the Origin of Their Mounds.* In Mississippi Historical Society *Publications,* Oxford, 1904. v. 8, p. 521-542.   Not so readable as Halbert, but authoritative.

Ray, Florence R. *Greenwood Leflore.* Memphis, Davis, 1935. 141 p. il. An idealized account of the Choctaw chief by his granddaughter.

Swanton, John R. *Indian Tribes of the Lower Mississippi Valley and Adjacent Coast of the Gulf of Mexico.* Washington, Govt. Printing Office, 1911. 387 p. il. (U. S. Bureau of American Ethnology. Bulletin 43).

———. *Source Material for the Social and Ceremonial Life of the Choctaw Indians.* Washington, Govt. Printing Office, 1931. 282 p. (U. S. Bureau of American Ethnology. Bulletin 103).

Warren, Harry. *Chickasaw Traditions, Customs,* etc. In Mississippi Historical Society *Publications,* Oxford, 1904. v. 8, p. 543-553.

General History

Claiborne, J. F. H. *Mississippi as a Province, Territory, and State.* Jackson, Power & Barksdale, 1880. 545 p. v. 1. History of the State to the Civil War period, enlivened with brief biographies.

Du Bois, William E. B. *Black Reconstruction.* New York, Harcourt, Brace, 1935. 737 p.

Fant, Mabel, and John C. *History of Mississippi.* Jackson, Mississippi Pub. Co., 1928. 340 p. il., maps. School history.

Galloway, Charles B. *Great Men and Great Movements; a Volume of Addresses.* Nashville, Tennessee; Dallas, Texas; Publishing House Methodist Episcopal Church South, Smith and Lamas agents, 1914. 328 p. Mississippi and Mississippians, p. 119-250.

Guyton, Pearl Vivian. *History of Mississippi.* Syracuse, Iroquois Pub. Co., 1935. 362 p. il., maps. A political and economic history for children.

Lynch, John R. *The Facts of Reconstruction.* New York, Neale Pub. Co., 1913. 325 p. The Negro's side of reconstruction as seen by a Negro reconstruction leader.

Rainwater, Percy Lee. *An Economic Interpretation of Secession. Opinions in Mississippi in 1850's.* Baton Rouge, Franklin Press, 1935. 18 p.

———. *Mississippi: Storm-Center of Secession, 1856–1861.* Unpublished thesis in University of Mississippi library. An almost exhaustive study of the conflicting issues that swept Mississippi and led to secession.

Riley, Franklin L. *School History of Mississippi.* Richmond, Va., Johnson, 1900. 492 p. il., maps.

Rowland, Dunbar. *Mississippi: the Heart of the South.* Chicago, S. J. Clarke, 1925. 1,838 p. 2 v. il., maps.

———. *Mississippi; an Encyclopedic History.* Atlanta, Southern Historic Pub. Assn., 1917. 3000 p. 3 v. Excellent for quick reference.

Sydnor, Charles and Claude Bennett. *Mississippi History.* Chicago, Rand McNally, 1930. 394 p. il., maps. One of the best histories of the State.

Tate, Allen. *Jefferson Davis.* New York, Minton, 1929. 311 p. Excellent study of Davis and picture of ante-bellum agrarian society by a modern agrarian.

Early

Barcia Carballido y Zuniga, Andres Gonzalez de. *Ensayo cronologico para la historia general de la Florida.* Madrid, 1723. 366 p.

BIBLIOGRAPHY

Chambers, Henry E. *Mississippi Valley Beginnings.* New York and London, Putnam, 1922. 389 p. il., maps. An excellent study of early explorations and settlement of the Louisiana Territory.

Claiborne, J. F. H. *Life and Times of Sam Dale, the Mississippi Partisan.* New York, Harper, 1860. 233 p. il. Insight into history as made by "the greatest Indian fighter of them all."

Gayarre, Charles E. A. *History of Louisiana.* New Orleans, Hansell, 1903. v. 1. 558 p. Story of Mississippi as part of Louisiana Territory, too picturesque to be fully accurate, but readable.

Gomara, Francisco Lopez de. *Histoire des generalle des Indes Occidentales and terres neuues.* Paris, Chez Michael Sonnius, 1569. 258 p.

Hakluyt, Richard. *Divers voyages touching the discovery of America and the islands adjacent.* Published by Richard Hakluyt, 1582. Edited by John Winter Jones, printed for the Hakluyt Society, London, 1850.

Hall, James. *A Brief History of the Mississippi Territory.* Oxford, 1906. In Mississippi Historical Society *Publications.* v. 9. A reprint of Hall's 60-page history which appeared in 1801.

Latane, John Holladay. *A History of the United States.* Boston. Allyn and Bacon, 1918. 589 p.

Lewis, G. H. *The Chroniclers of the De Soto Expedition.* In Mississippi Historical Society *Publications,* Oxford, 1903. v. 7, p. 379-387. An adequate study of first exploration records.

Lummis, Charles Fletcher. *The Spanish Pioneers.* Chicago, A. C. McClurg, 1893. 292 p.

Parkman, Francis. *The Works of Francis Parkman.* Boston, Little, Brown and Company, 1903, 491 p.

Riley, Franklin L. *A Contribution to the History of the Colonization Movement in Mississippi.* In Mississippi Historical Society *Publications,* Oxford, 1906. v. 9, p. 313-414.

Romans, Bernard. *Natural History of East and West Florida.* New York, printed for the author, 1775. 342 p., il. A good reference for Mississippi history under British and Spanish rule.

Rowland and Sanders. *Mississippi Provincial Archives. (1729-1740).* Jackson, Press of Mississippi Department of Archives and History, 1927. 488 p., maps.

Smith, Buckingham. *Coleccion de Varios documentos para la historia de la Florida y tierras adyacentes.* Londres, Trubner Z. Compania 1857. Tomo I. (With the exception of five documents all the papers belong to the period 1516-69).

———. *Narrative of Alvar Nunez Cabeca de Vaca.* Translated 1851. San Francisco, Grabhorn Press, 1929.

Ternaux-Compans, Henri. *Recueil de pieces sur la Floride.* Paris, A. Bertrand, 1841. 368 p.

Tschan, Francis J. *The Catholic Contribution in the Colonial Period.* New York, Catholic Book Company, 1935. v. 1, *Catholic Builders of the Nation,* p. 129-147. Reviews the Spanish period in the Mississippi region.

LATER

Bancroft, Frederic. *Slave-trading in the Old South.* Baltimore, J. H. Furst, 1931. 415 p.

Claiborne, J. F. H. *Life and Correspondence of John A. Quitman.* New York, Harper, 1860. 792 p. 2 v. Good picture of Mississippi politics in 1840's and 1850's.

Davis, Reuben. *Recollections of Mississippi and Mississippians.* Boston, Houghton Mifflin, 1891. 446 p. Interesting for its informal style and fund of personal knowledge of the State and its citizens. Written by one of Mississippi's most trenchant political figures of the middle nineteenth century.

Dickson, Harris. *Old-fashioned Senator.* New York, Stokes, 1925. 205 p. A romantic biography of John Sharp Williams.

Foote, Henry S. *Casket of Reminiscences.* Washington, Chronicle Pub. Co., 1874. 498 p. Material, for the most part, deals with State politics from 1840 to 1870.

Garner, James W. *Reconstruction in Mississippi.* New York, Macmillan, 1901. 422 p. An excellent study by a thorough student.

Henry, Robert Selph. *A Story of the Confederacy.* Indianapolis, Bobbs-Merrill, 1931. 514 p. il. The rise and fall of the Confederacy described in popular style.

Sydnor, Charles S. *Slavery in Mississippi.* New York, Appleton-Century, 1933. 270 p. Comprehensive and accurate; excellent for reference and as source material.

GOVERNMENT

Butts, Alfred B. "The Court System of Mississippi." *Mississippi Law Journal,* Nov. 1930, v. 3: 97-125.

Cason, Clarence E. "The Mississippi Imbroglio." *Virginia Quarterly Review,* April 1931, v. 7: 229-240.

Cohn, David Lewis. *Picking America's Pockets.* New York, Harper, 1936. The story of the costs and consequences of our tariff policy.

Ethridge, George H. "Jurisdiction of the Circuit Court." *Mississippi Law Journal,* February, 1934, v. 6: 195-211.

Mississippi. *Statutes of the Mississippi Territory.* Natchez, Samuel Terrell, 1807. 660 p.

———. *Mississippi Constitution.* Jackson, Mississippi, Tucker Printing Co., 1928. 784 p. Contains the act of Congress organizing Mississippi Territory and the act enabling Mississippi to form a State government.

———. *Revised Code of the Laws of Mississippi.* Natchez, Francis Baker, 1824. 743 p. Cited as Poindexter's code.

———. *Revised Code of the Statute Laws of Mississippi.* Jackson, printed by E. Barksdale, 1857. 943 p. 2 v.

Rowland, Dunbar. *Jefferson Davis, Constitutionalist.* Jackson, printed for Mississippi Department of Archives and History, 1923. 6,041 p. 10 v. Excellent source material.

SOCIAL AND ECONOMIC DEVELOPMENT

AGRICULTURE AND INDUSTRY

Baldwin, J. G. *The Flush Times of Alabama and Mississippi.* San Francisco, Bancroft-Whitney, 1899. 330 p. An account of the opening of the newly released Indian lands.

Boeger, Ernest A., and Goldenweiser, E. A. *A Study of the Tenant System of Farming in the Yazoo-Mississippi Delta.* Washington, Govt. Printing Office, 1916. 18 p. (U. S. Dept. of Agriculture. Bulletin 337.)

Cohn, David L. *God Shakes Creation.* New York, Harper, 1935. 448 p. il. A fast moving account of life in the Yazoo-Mississippi Delta, with emphasis on economic conditions.

Dickson, Harris. *Story of King Cotton.* New York, Funk & Wagnalls, 1937. 309 p. il. A popular but authentic review of Mississippi's cotton economy.

Riley, Franklin L., ed. *Diary of a Mississippi Planter.* In Mississippi Historical Society *Publications,* Oxford, 1909. v. 10, p. 311-482. Unvarnished, everyday life on a cotton plantation.

Smedes, Susan Dabney. *Memorials of a Southern Planter.* Baltimore, Cushings and Bailey, 1887. 342 p.

United States Department of Agriculture. *Agricultural Census, 1935.* Washington, Govt. Printing Office, 1936. 27 p. A reprint of the Mississippi section of the National agricultural census.

White, H. "Mississippi Bids for Industry." *Review of Reviews,* December 1936, v. 94: 30-31.

TRANSPORTATION

Coates, Robert M. *The Outlaw Years.* New York, Macaulay, 1930. 308 p. A thrilling story of life and bandits on the old Natchez Trace.

Quick, Edward. *Mississippi Steamboating.* New York, Holt, 1926. 342 p. il.

———. "Mississippi Pioneers in Zoning State Highways." *American City,* October 1930. v. 43, 129.

EDUCATION

Butts, Alfred B. *Public Administration in Mississippi.* In Mississippi Historical Society *Publications,* Centenary Series, Oxford, 1919. v. 3, p. 20-147.

George, Jennings B. *The Influence of Court Decisions in Shaping School Policies in Mississippi.* Nashville, Tenn., George Peabody College for Teachers, 1932. 265 p. An unpublished dissertation.

Jones, Laurence C. *Piney Woods and Its Story.* New York, Fleming H. Revell, 1922. 154 p. An interesting history of the Piney Woods Country Life School.

Mayes, Edward. *History of Education in Mississippi.* Washington, Govt. Printing Office, 1899. 290 p. il. Comprehensive study of the development of education in Mississippi up to the twentieth century.

State Department of Education. *Mississippi Program for the Improvement of Instruction.* Jackson, Better Printing Co., 1934. 123 p. (Bulletin 1). A thought-provoking study program for Mississippi teachers, with a good selected reference list.

Timberlake, Elise. *Did the Reconstruction Regime Give Mississippi Her Public Schools?* In Mississippi Historical Society *Publications,* Oxford, 1912. v. 12, p. 73-93. Excellent source material on the origin of public education in Mississippi.
United States Department of the Interior, Bureau of Education. *Survey of Negro Colleges and Universities.* Washington, Govt. Printing Office, 1928. 964 p. A study of the principal Negro colleges and universities in the United States.
Weathersby, W. H. *History of Educational Legislation in Mississippi from 1798 to 1860.* Chicago, Univ. of Chicago Press, 1921. 203 p.
Woodson, Carter Godwin. *The Education of the Negro Prior to 1861.* New York, Putnam, 1915. 454 p.

RELIGION AND SOCIAL AGENCIES
Robinson, E. "Federal Aid Comes to Mississippi." *Mississippi Library Journal,* February 1, 1935, v. 60: 95-98.
Rossell, B. S. "Book Relief in Mississippi." *Survey,* March 1935, v. 71: 73-74.
Taylor, H. "How Firm a Foundation." *Virginia Quarterly Review,* October 1931, v. 7: 562-572. Of religious institutions and affairs.

ARTS AND LETTERS
LITERATURE
Bradford, Roark. *John Henry.* New York, Harper, 1931. 225 p. il. Tales of a Negro stevedore of heroic strength and ingenuity.
Clemens, Samuel. *Life on the Mississippi.* New York, Harper, 1908. 527 p. Steamboat days on the river.
Cochran, Ed. Louis. *Son of Haman.* Caldwell, Idaho, Caxton Printers, 1937. 330 p. The story of an ambitious boy of the tenant class in the Mississippi Delta.
Deavours, Ernestine C., comp. *The Mississippi Poets.* Memphis, E. H. Clarke, 1922. 204 p.
Dickson, Harris. *Old Reliable.* Indianapolis, Bobbs-Merrill, 1911. 341 p. A fictional Negro character made real.
―――. *Black Wolf's Breed.* Indianapolis, Bobbs-Merrill, 1899. 288 p. "A story of France in the Old World and the new happenings in the reign of Louis XIV."
Faulkner, William. *Sartoris.* New York, Harcourt, Brace, 1929. 380 p.
―――. *Absalom, Absalom!* New York, Random House, 1936. 384 p.
Hudson, A. P. *Humor of the Old Deep South.* New York, Macmillan, 1936. 548 p. Mostly about the folkways of Mississippi preachers, politicians, doctors, farmers, and Negroes.
James, Alice, comp. "Mississippi Poets." *American Mercury,* May 1932, v. 26: 38-40.
―――, ed. *Mississippi Verse.* Chapel Hill, Univ. of N. Carolina Press, 1924. 94 p. With biographical notes on the authors.
McDowell, Mrs. Katherine Sherwood Bonner. *Dialect Tales.* New York, Harper, 1883. 187 p.

Percy, William Alexander. *Sappho in Levkas and Other Poems.* New Haven, Yale Univ. Press, 1915. 78 p.

———. *In April Once.* New Haven, Yale Univ. Press, 1920. 134 p. A collection of poems.

———. *Enzio's Kingdom and Other Poems.* New Haven, Yale Univ. Press, 1924. 140 p.

Russell, Irwin. *Christmas-night in the Quarters, and Other Poems.* With an introduction by Joel Chandler Harris and an historical sketch by Maurice Garland Fulton. New York, Century, 1917. 182 p. il. by E. W. Kemble.

Rylee, Robert. *Deep Dark River.* New York, Farrar & Rinehart, 1935. 308 p. The story of a Southern woman lawyer who defended a Negro.

———. *St. George of Weldon.* New York, Farrar & Rinehart, Inc., 1937. 432 p. A fatalistic story of a decadent family.

Street, James A. *Look Away: A Dixie Note Book.* New York, Viking, 1936. A collection of stories, some from Mississippi.

Sale, John B. *A Tree Named John.* Chapel Hill, Univ. of N. Carolina Press, 1929. 151 p. il. A little boy's life on a plantation, with Negro folklore furnishing the backdrop.

Saxon, Lyle. *Father Mississippi.* New York, Century, 1929. 427 p. il. A readable account of the river and of the people who make up the pattern of river life. There is a good chapter on Negro voodooism, as practiced in the southwestern counties. The 1927 flood is presented in detail.

Talley, Thomas W. *Negro Folk Rhymes.* New York, Macmillan, 1922. 347 p. il. A good collection of Negro folk rhymes, with a better study of the making of these rhymes in slavery days. Many common to Mississippi.

Young, Stark. *So Red the Rose.* New York, Scribner's, 1934. 410 p. An idealization of ante-bellum life in the Natchez area.

———. *Heaven Trees.* New York, Scribner's, 1926. 286 p. Ante-bellum life on a plantation "forty miles from Memphis by the carriage-road."

———. *River House.* New York, Scribner's, 1929. 304 p. The scene is in northwest Mississippi. A conflict of wills between the previous Southern generation and the present.

PAINTING, SCULPTURE, MUSIC

Hare, Maude Cuney. *Negro Musicians and Their Music.* Washington, D. C., Associated Publishers, Inc., 1936. 439 p. Pictures and musical illustrations. African influence on American music; Negro idioms and rhythms; musical pioneers; world musicians of Negro race, including some Mississippians.

Hudson, A. P. *Folk Songs of Mississippi.* Chapel Hill, Univ. of N. Carolina Press, 1936. 321 p. A collection of folksongs indigenous to the State. Without musical notation.

Sutton, C. V., ed. *History of Art in Mississippi.* Gulfport, Dixie Press, 1929. 177 p. il. Material collected by the Art Study Club of Jackson.

Rowland, Dunbar. *Biographical Guide to the Mississippi Hall of Fame.* Jackson, 1935. 36 p. The emphasis is placed upon paintings.

Young, Stark. "Ballads in Mississippi." *New Republic,* September 23-30, 1936, v. 86; 186-229.

Index

Index

Abbay, Dick, 316
Adair (James), 53
Affleck, Thomas, 334
Agriculture
Cotton:
    early varieties of, 94; introduction of Mexican seed, 95, 96; beginning of "Great Cotton Era," 96; land boom of 1830, 98; effect of War between the States, 98, 99; credit tenant system, 99; opening of Delta, 99, 100; selective breeding, 100; fight against weevil, 100; marketing of, 191; effect of erosion, 99, 203; shipping of, 197; financing of, 191; ginning and compressing, 192, 265.
Diversification of crops, 100
Fruit, 419, 420, 423, 430, 459, 470
Hay, 100, 376, 398
Indigo, 94, 95, 239
Legumes, 100, 105
Pecans, 287, 291, 319, 321, 333, 347, 371, 419, 420, 423, 429, 430
Soil Conservation, 105, 203, 378
Tobacco, 94, 239
Trucking, 6, 100, 393, 394, 396, 471
Tung Nut Culture, 111, 420, 431, 432, 470
Airlines (see Transportation)
Alcorn, James L., 74, 138, 317
Allen, Betsy, 487
Allen, Creighton, 161
Allen, Private John M., 138, 265
Amberson, William, 348
American Revolution, 65, 66
Ames, Adelbert, 74, 216
Amos Ogden Mandamus, 65
Annandale (site), 390
Arboretum, 233
Archeology, 45, 46, 47 (see Indians)
Architecture, 143-156
    Black Belt, 144-145, 149; church, 145, 146, 461; commercial, 153; contemporary, 150-156, 165, 166, 182, 189, 190, 195, 209, 228, 261, 262, 267; "dog-trot," 143, 144, 472; English influence on, 143; French influence on, 143, 146; Georgian, 147, 148, 149; Government, 156; Grand Manner, 144; Industrial, 155; Institutional, 155; mill houses, 152, 153; Southern Planter, 144, 148; Spanish Influence, 144, 146, 147, 148; tenant houses, 151; Victorian Gothic, 152.
Archusa Springs, 371

Art, 134-142
    early aspects, 134, 135, 136; Negro, 134, 135; contemporary, 135, 219-220, 281. (See Collections and Museums)
Ashe Pine Tree Nursery, 418
Audubon, John James, 139, 333, 335

Baily, Francis, 139
Ball, J. T., 228
Ball of a Thousand Candles, 341
Bali, Mrs. Harry, 353
Ball's Mill, 479
Ballads (see Folkways, Music)
Bankhead, William B., 368
Barbecue (see Folkways, Customs)
Bartram, William, 139
Bass Pecan Orchard, 430
Battles
    Ackia, 436, 485; Big Black River, 313; Booneville, 363; Brice's Crossroads, 363; Bruinsburg, 330; Chickasaw Bayou, 272, 323; Champion's Hill, 312; Corinth, 362; Grand Gulf, 326; Harrisburg, 263; Iuka, 443; 501; Jackson, 213; Pass Christian, 297, 299; Tallahatchie Bridge, 489; Tupelo, 263. (See Holly Springs, Vicksburg)
Bayous
    Acadian, 298; Cadet, 301; Cassidy, 421; Davis, 291; DeLisle, 298; Graveline, 290; Herring, 291; Hobson, 407; Mulatto, 301; Pierre, 326; Portage, 298; Rotten, 298.
Bays
    Pascagoula, 64, 286; St. Louis, 64, 298.
Beatty, Ellen Adair, 259
Beauregard, P. G. T., 263, 328, 345, 362
Beauvoir, 292-294
Benachi Avenue (Biloxi), 178
Berryhill, S. Newton, 141
Bienville, Jean Baptiste le Moyne, Sieur de, 63, 172, 238, 299, 485
Big Rock, 369
Bilbo, Theodore G., 77, 431
Biloxi Lighthouse, 178
Biloxi Yacht Club, 168
Bird Sanctuary (Jackson), 222; (State Teachers' College), 417
Bishop, Dock, 472
Bisland, Elizabeth, 336
Black Prairie, 7, 33, 34, 361, 373, 374, 377, 397
Blake, Benson, 323
Blanton, Col. W. W., 352
Blennerhassett, Harmon, 240, 246, 327
Blessing of Fleet (Biloxi), 169, 176

INDEX

Bluff Hills, 33
Boating (*see Recreation*)
Bodley, Hugh, 271
Bonner, Sherwood, 140, 206
Bonnie Blue Flag, 216
Borden, Gail, 481
Bowie, James, 328
Bowie knife, 328
Bowling Green (ruins), 345
Bowman Hotel (site), 220
Bragg, Braxton, 362
Brandon, Gerard Chittocque, I, 333, 338
Brandon, Gerard Chittocque, II, 307, 333, 346, 359
Brandon, William L., 359
Bridges
 Bayou Pierre, 326; Big Black, 313; Iberville, 178; Pontchartrain, 434; Railroad (Bucatunna), 373; Reddochs, 450; Rigolets, 434; Russell Memorial, 326; Tallahatchie River, 437; Tibbee Creek, 375; Vicksburg, 314; War Memorial Bridge, 292, 175; Woodrow Wilson, 308.
Brooks, Jonathan, 125
Brown, Albert Gallatin, 120, 138, 392-393, 394
Bull, Ole, 159
Burr, Aaron, 67, 240, 332, 334, 360, 338
Burr Oaks, 334
Burrows, Rube, 373, 385
Bus lines (*see Transportation*)
Buteux, Father Louis Stanislaus Marie, 300
Butler, Benjamin, 304
Butler, Frances Parke Lewis, 297

Caldwell, Isaac, 311
Capitol, new, 75, 152, 217
Capitol, old, 214
Carmer, Carl, 373
Carr, "Turkey Bill," 488
Carroll, Charles, 403
Carter's Point, 351
Carver, Eleazer, 107
Cary, Archibald, 327
Cary, Constance, 327
Casket Girls, 63, 172, 303
Cemeteries
 Aberdeen, 365; Biloxi, 179; Catholic (Port Gibson), 328; Chapel of the Cross, 390; Concordia, 349; Confederate: Beauvoir, 294; Newton, 306; Marion, 370; Okolona, 374; Oxford, 260; Davis Family, 484; Friendship, 187; Gibeon, 400; Greenfield, 357; Greenway, 352; Greenwood, 218; Holmesville, 480; Kingston Public Burying Ground, 343; Krebs, 289; Lakewood, 309; Live Oak, 298; Memorial Park, 249; National (Corinth), 362, 363; National (Vicksburg), 323; Sargent's Private, 340; Paradise Point, 295; Raleigh, 497; Routh, 251; Shady Grove, 442; Southern Memorial Park, 292; St. Peter's, 257.
Central Hills, 7, 34, 401, 434, 463

Chancery Clerk's Office (Holmesville), 480
Chapman, Walter, 161
Chaumont, Duchess de, 64, 286
Chickasaw Indian Agency (site), 462
Chisholm, John, 255
Chisholm Massacre, 378
Chisholm, William, 378
Choctaw Indian Agency, 465 (*see also Indians*)
Choctaw Indian Agency (site), 400
Church Buildings (by denomination)
 Baptist:
  Bethlehem, 502; Big Creek, 450; China Grove, 480; Clear Creek, 333; Gary Springs, 472; Juniper Grove, 431; Mont Zion, 451; New Hope, 371; Primitive Providence, 502; Shiloh, 447; Toxish, 462; Woodville, 344.
 Christian:
  Columbus, 184
 Episcopal:
  Chapel of the Cross, 389; Christ (Vicksburg), 279; Christ (Holly Springs), 204; Christ, 332; St. John's (site), 356; Saint Mark's Chapel, 295; St. Paul's, 344; Trinity (Natchez), 250; Trinity (Pass Christian), 298; Church of the Redeemer, 176.
 Holiness:
  Holiness Tabernacle, 496
 Lutheran:
  Gulfport, 199
 Methodist:
  Holly Springs, 204; Iuka, 443; Kingston, 343; Mount Carmel, 342; Natchez, 237; Old Valley, 502; Washington, 334; Woodville, 344.
 Presbyterian:
  Church with the Iron Hand, 328; Enterprise, 425; First (Natchez), 243; Holly Springs, 206; Laurel, 155; Liberty, 482; Old Bethel, 330; Pine Ridge, 335; Rodney, 330.
 Roman Catholic:
  Our Lady of Good Hope, 298; Our Lady of the Gulf, 300; Paulding, 426; Port Gibson, 328; St. Mary's Cathedral, 249.
Cities (*see Towns*)
Civil War (*see War between the States*)
Claiborne, J. F. H., 49, 131, 139, 301, 453
Claiborne, William Charles Cole, 69, 211
Clark, Charles, 73
Clark, John, 318
Clay, Henry, 211, 336
Climate, 35
Clifton, Chalmers, 160
Cloud, Adams, 66, 113
Coast, 4, 34, 285, 286
Cobb, Joseph B., 137
Cobb, Sam, 495
Cohn, David, 3, 142
Colbert, Pittman, 437, 486

INDEX

Cole's Creek Valley, 332
Collections, private
　Antique furniture, 422, 193; books, 251, 317; china, 317; dolls, 419; heirlooms, 193, 248; Indian relics, 46, 47; paintings, 393; weaving, 417.
Colleges (Negro)
　Alcorn A. & M., 119, 330; Campbell, 124, 221, 222; Jackson, 125; Leflore Teachers Training School, 405; Mary Holmes Seminary, 123, 375; Mississippi Industrial, 124; Natchez, 124; Okolona Institute, 123; Prentiss Normal and Industrial School, 125, 452; Rust, 125, 206; Saints Industrial Institute, 124; Southern Christian Institute, 122, 312; St. Augustine Seminary, 300; Tougaloo, 125, 390; Utica Institute, 125, 392.
Colleges (white)
　All Saints, 122; Belhaven, 219; Blue Mountain, 128, 458; Chickasaw, 460; Clark Memorial Jr., 122, 306; Copiah-Lincoln Jr., 395; East Central Jr., 469; East Mississippi Jr., 370; Delta State Teachers, 127, 320; Grenada, 122, 383; Gulf Park, 296; Harrison-Stone-Jackson Jr., 419; Hillman, 122, 310, 311; Hinds County Jr., 392; Holmes County Jr., 386; Jones County Jr., 428; Millsaps, 128, 219; Mississippi, 119, 310; Mississippi State, 127, 398, 399; Mississippi State College for Women, 127, 186, 187; Mississippi State Teachers, 417; Mississippi Synodical, 205; Mississippi Woman's, 418; Northwest Jr., 380, 381; Southwest Mississippi Jr., 396; Sunflower Jr., 405; University of Mississippi, 125, 126, 127, 259, 260; Whitworth, 454; Wood Jr., 122, 401.
Collins, Ross, 378
Colmer, William, 287
Commercial Bank Building, 243
Community House (Biloxi), 177
Connelly's Tavern, 245, 246
Conner, Martin Sennett, 77
Constitution Fire Company House, 279
Cooper, Preston, 391
Copeland, James, 476
Copeland Clan, 476
Coronado (*see de Coronado*)
Cotton (*see Agriculture*)
Cotton Gin Port, 485
Cotton Textile Road, 351
Courthouses
　Adams County, 241; Amite County, 481; Calhoun, 473; DeSoto County, 380; Franklin County, 455; Hinds County (Jackson), 214; Hinds County (Raymond), 391; Itawamba, 435; Lafayette, 254; Leake County, 495; Leflore County, 192; Madison County, 388; Marshall, 200; Quitman County, 490; Smith County, 497; Warren County, 277.
Covered Bridge, 488
Covington, Leonard, 333
Cox, Lida, 439
Cox, Toby, 439
Cox, William Henry, 439
Craft, Bryant, 498
Craft, Jesse, 497
Craig, John, 255
Creeks
　Big Bear, 502; Chunky, 305; Little, 476; Tishtony, 435; Pottoxchitto, 305; Rahoma, 497; Tallahalla, 449, 450; Tallahoma, 450; Tibbee, 375.
Crismoreland Rose Gardens, 309
Crockett, David, 349
Crosby, L. O., 432
Crowell, Jesse, 357
Crozat, Anthony, 63, 172
Cuming, Fortescue, 139
Curtis, Richard, 66, 113
Customs (*see Folkways*)

Dairying (*see Industry*)
Dale, Sam, 378, 379
Dancing Rabbit Treaty (*see Indians*)
D'Artaguiette, Pierre, 461, 487
Davion, Father Anthony, 113, 170, 359
Davis, Jefferson
　Election to Presidency of Confederacy, 71; memorial to the family of, 176; "Night Shirt Address," 184; inspection of fortifications at Snyder's Bluff, 323; visits to Jackson, 213, 217; homes: Beauvoir, 292, 294; Palmyra Island, 325; Rosemont, 484; *Rise and Fall of the Confederate Government*, 294; last public appearance of, 216; death of, 294.
Davis, Joseph Emory, 320
Davis, J. J., 499
Davis, Lucinda, 484
Davis, Reuben, 139, 365
Davis, Varina Anne, 294
Davis, Varina Howell, 253, 294
Davis Windows, 176
de Coronado, Francisco, 60
DeFrance, Abraham, 211
De Kalb, Baron, 378
De Lisle, Comte, 298
Delta, 3, 4, 31, 32, 99, 315, 406, 407, 411, 420, 421
Delta Cooperative Farm, 348
Delta Experiment Station, 321
Delta and Pine Land Company, 103, 321, 350
Delta Planter's Company Plantation, 349
Delta Staple Cotton Festival, 319
Democratic Party, 74
de Niza, Marcos, 60
Department of Archives and History, 218
De Soto, Hernando, 60, 182, 316, 324, 366, 380
De Tonti, Henri, 170
De Vaudreuil, 485

d'Iberville, Pierre Le Moyne, Sieur, 61, 63, 170, 238, 291, 303
Dickson, Harris, 141, 412
Dix, Dorothy, 298, 433
Dow, Lorenzo, 116, 139
Doxey, Wall, 203
Duels, (Caldwell-Peyton), 311; (Hindman-Falkner), 458
Dunbar, Sir William, 360
Dunn's Falls, 425
Durant, Louis, 386

Eastman, Lauren Chase, 225
Eddy, Sherwood, 348
Education, 118-128
Church schools, 119, 120, 128; development of agricultural high schools, 121, 122; early schools, 118, 119, 120; first free school in State, 182, 183; land-grant schools, 120; Smith-Hughes Act, 122; Negro schools, 120, 121, 122, 124, 125; Chinese, 123; Indian, 123. (See Colleges and Schools.)
Eggleston, B. B. (Buzzard), 213
El Camino Real, 85
Elizabeth Female Academy, 119, 335
Ellicott, Andrew, 66, 139, 246
Eliot, John, 385
Elliott, William St. John, 336
Ellis, Powhatan, 372
Engle, A. Lehman, 161
Epstein, Jacob, 352
Esplanade, 244
Evans, Lewis, 341

Falkner, W. C., 456-459 (see Faulkner)
Farish Street (Jackson), 221
Farm Homestead Project, 470
Farragut, David Glasgow, 272, 290
Farragut Home (site), 290
Farthing, Richard, 416
Faulkner, II, William, 3, 141, 256, 458 (see Falkner)
Fauna, 42
Favre, Simon, 79
Federal Music Project, 161
Federation of Music Clubs, 159
Ferguson, Thomas, 323
Ferries, Mississippi River
Dundee, 316; Friar Point, 317; Greenville, 406; Natchez, 233; Vicksburg, 266.
Field Trials (see Hunting)
Finlay, Mrs. Ann, 353
First Free School, 185
First Memorial Day Service in America, 187, 188
First Railroad Station, 344
Fishing, commercial (see Industry); recreational (see Recreation)
Fisk, Alvarez, 246, 410
Flat Woods, 34
Flood, Dr. William, 287
Flood Control, 76, 382
Flood of 1927, 76, 277
Flora, 40
Foley, Daniel, 328

Folklore
Ghost: 295, 356, 359, 395, 421, 497. Legends, Indian: 176, 200, 287, 288, 375, 464, 494, 498; Miscellaneous: 290, 296. Superstitions: 14, 27, 28, 29, 30.
Folkways
Ballads: 15, 157, 158, 408, 421, 472, 495, 503. Customs: Negro, 22-30; white, 8-21, 433, 472, 473, 492, 495, 503; Indian, 50-58; foreign, 169. Spirituals, Negro, 157.
Folsom, David, 385, 400
Foote, Henry S., 138, 139, 212
Ford, John, 79, 479
Foreign Groups
Acadian French, 175, 298; Austrian, 166; Chinese, 351, 408; Czechs, 166; French, 165, 285, 286; Poles, 166, 175; Slavs, 168.
Forest Reserves
Ashe Nursery, 418; Bienville National, 306; Delta Purchase Unit, 322; De Soto National, 419, 429, 470; Holly Springs National, 438, 446; Homochitto National, 454; Natchez Trace Forestry and Game Preserve, 374; Leaf River, 417; Virgin Pine, 290. (See Parks, State)
Forrest, Nathaniel Bedford, 72, 263, 363, 381, 443, 495
Fortification Street (Jackson), 218
Forts
Adams, site of, 359; Dearborn, site of, 333; Nogales, site of, 282; Massachusetts, 303; Maurepas, site of, 291; McHenry, site of, 282; Old Spanish, 288-289; Patton's, site of, 372; Pemberton, site of, 422; Robinett, site of, 363; Rosalie, site of, 244; St. Peter (Snyder), site of, 322.
Frantz, A. J., 132
"Free State of Jones," 223, 427, 428
French and Indian War, 65, 436, 485
Friendship Oak, 296
Furr, Allison, 487
Furr, Tobias, 487

Gailor, Charlotte, 352
Gaines Trace, 86
Garner, James W., 120
Gas (see Industry)
Gayarré, Charles E. A., 49, 52
Gayoso, Don Manuel, 252
Geodetic Survey, 326
Geography, 31-35
Geology, 35-40
Geology Hill, 463
George, James Z., 74, 403
Gibbs Building, 391
Gibson, Tobias, 113, 280
Gibson, Samuel, 327
Giles, Jacob, 370
Gillam, Alva C., 73
Gillespie, James Alcorn, 342
Gipson, Ambrose, 357
Golf (see Recreation)
Good Springs, 502
Gordon, Robert, 364, 462

INDEX

Gore, T. P., 474
Gore Springs, 474
Governor's Mansion (Jackson), 220
Grandpré, Don Carlos de, 251
Grant, Ulysses S., 72, 201, 255, 272, 309, 317, 326, 327, 330, 361, 362, 443, 444
Grant's Pass, 317
Grave
  Betsy Allen, 487; Gerard Brandon, II, 359; Resin P. Bowie, 328; William Cocke, 188; Sam Dale, 379; Earl Van Dorn, 328; Gentle South Wind, 498; Samuel Gibson, 327; Tobias Gibson, 280; L. P. Gore, 474; Gypsy Queen, 232; Judge Hill, 257; Thomas Isom, 257; Caleb King, 343; Felix La Bauve, 380; L. Q. C. Lamar, 257; A. B. Longstreet, 257; John R. Lynch, 218; Judge Edward McGehee, 345; D. N. McGill, 277; Senator Sullivan, 257; Old Bachelor, 386.
Gravel (see Industry)
Gray and Edward Feud, 401
Green, Benjamin T., 320
Green, Col. Thomas Marsden, 332
Green, W. W., 131
Griffin, John, 100
Guion, Isaac, 246, 338
Gulfport Harbor and Ship Canal, 198
Gully, John, 378
Gum Springs, 496
Gunn, James, 363
Guzman, Nunez Beltran, 60
Gwin, Samuel, 311

Hagen, James, 131
Halleck, Henry W., 361, 362
Hall of Fame, 218
Hamilton, Raymone, 452
Hand Brothers, 295
Handy, W. C., 161
Harding, Lyman G., 252
Hardy, William H., 76, 196, 199, 417
Hare, Joseph Thompson, 84
Harpe (Harp) Brothers, 84, 331
Harris, George, 390
Harris, Wiley Pope, 394
Harris, W. R., 262
Harrison, Byron Patton, 394
Harrison County Courthouse (old), 295
Hays, Peter B., 248
Healy, George, 328
Healy, Thomas, 328
Henderson, John, 248
Henderson Point, 298
Henry, Robert S., 263
Hilgard, Eugene W., 99, 259
Hilgard's Cut, 259
Hill, R. A., 257
Hillman, Mrs. Adelia, 310
Hillman, Walter, 310
Hills, 33, 34
  Blue Mountain, 458; Buffalo, 450; Mount Barton, 228; Pontotoc Ridge, 436; Tennessee Hills, 500; Woodall's Mountain, 501.

Hills, The, site of, 358
Hindman, Thomas, 458
Hinds, Thomas E., 210, 242, 331
History
  Exploration and Settlement: 60-66, 135, 170, 172, 238, 239, 269, 270, 271; West Florida Rebellion, 67, 68. (See French and Indian War.)
  Early Statehood: Pearl River Convention, 479; First Constitutional Convention, 70, 334; War of 1812, 69, 70; selection of capital site, 210, 211; flush times, 89, 99, 136, 201, 240. War between the States (see War between the States). Reconstruction, 73, 74, 132. Since 1900, 74-77.
Hoard, Col. L. M., 345
Hoggatt, James, 455
Holmes, David, 242
Homes
  Airlie, 248; Anderson, 428; *Arcole*, 359; *Arlington*, ' 250; *Ashwood*, 345, 346; *Auburn*, 252; *Banker's*, 243; Bankhead, 368; Barnard, 322; Batson, 430; *Beauvoir*, 292, 293, 294; *Bellevue*, 389; *Belmont* (Neilson), 366; *Belmont* (Worthington), 354; Bilbo, 431; Billups, 186; *Blakely*, 323; Blocker, 441; Boler, 469; Bolton, 460; Bonner-Belk, 206; Borden, 481; Brame, 217; Brent, 480; *Briars*, The, 253; Brinkley, 444; Britton, 243; Brooks, 454; Brown, 392, 393; Buntura, 244; Burrus, 350; Burton, 388; Campbell, 383; *Canemount*, 330; Castle, 474; Castleman, 410; *Cedar Grove*, 412; *Cedars*, 488; Chisholm, 378; *Choctaw*, 246; *Churchhill Downs*, 413; Claiborne, 301; Clapp-Fant, 205; Clark, 460; Cohen, 384; Coker, 312; *Coldspring*, 359; *College Annex* (Hull Home), 205; Collins, 480; Coman, 444; Conti, 242; Cook-Allein, 280; Corey, 343; *Cotesworth*, 403; *Cottage Garden*, 248; Coxe-Dean, 205; Craft-Daniel, 207; Crump, 207; Curl, 447; Curlee, 362; Cutrer, 319; Davis, 365; Deavours, 426; *Desert*, 359; D'Evereux, 336, 337; Dickson, 483; Dix, 298; *Dixie White House*, 297; *Doll's House*, 419; Dubose, 393; *Dunleith*, 251; *Eagle's Nest*, 317; *Edgewood*, 335; *Elgin*, 342; Elgin, 362; Ellzey, 480; *Elms*, The, 250; *Elmscourt*, 341; Episcopal Rectory, 389; *Erwin*, 355; *Everhope*, 356; *Faisonia*, 409; Farrington, 380; Farthing, 417; Faulkner, 256; Featherstone-Buchanan, 207; Fontaine, 460; Ford, 479; Foster, 335; Freeman, 204; *French*, 177; *Galena*, 439; Gant, 393; Gardner, 440; Gary, 232; *Gibeon*, 400; Giles, 370;

INDEX

Homes (*Continued*)
Gillespie, 400; Gillard, 458; *Glenbernie*, 340, 341; *Glenwild*, 384; *Glenwood*, 341; *Gloucester*, 340; Goodman, 440; *Gray Gables*, 204; Green, 279; *Greenleaves*, 250; Griffin, 463; *Hampton Hall*, 345; Hand, 295; Hardy, 454; Harper, 496; Harris, 394; Harvey, 389; *Haunted House*, 295; Heflin, 381; *Hermitage* (Foster), 343; *Hermitage* (Humphreys), 325; *Hermitage* (Poitevent), 432; Hill, 258; *Hil*, The, 328; Hindman, 458; Hinton, 430; *Holliday Haven*, 365; *Hollywood* (Gillespie), 342; *Hollywood*, 409; *Home Hill*, 331; Homewood, 339; *Hopedale*, 319; *Hope Farm*, 251; Horne, 371; Howle, 156; *Ingleside* (Calhoun), 340; *Ingleside*, 389; *Inglewood*, 334; Isom, 257; Ivy, 447; Jayne, 396; Jones, 205; Kearney, 413; Keller, 176; Kennebrew, 186; Klein, 280; Knotts, 410; Knox, 401; 402; Koch, 302; Laird, 382; Lake, 384; *Lakeside*, 357; Lamar, 257; Lang, 371; Lansdowne, 340; Leatherman, 316; Lee, 185; Leigh, 185; Lewis, 461; *Linden* (Hampton), 356; *Linden* (Reed), 339; *Lochinvar*, 462; *Locust*, 353; *Longwood*, 340; *Longwood* (Smith), 354; *Loughborough*, 351; Luckett, 280, 389; *Magnolia Vale*, 247; *Malmaison*, 403; *Mandamus*, 343; Manship, 218; Marshall-Bryan, 279; Mason-Tucker, 207; *Matagorda*, 317; Matthews, 443; McCaskill, 307; McCutcheon, 297; McDonald, 444; *McGehee's Gate*, 381; McGowan-Crawford, 205; McKnight, 443; McLaren, 187; McLaurin, 307; McLemore, 231; McNeese, 503; McNutt, 277; McShann, 364; Mead, 334; Meek, 186; *Melmont* (Sans Souci), 248; *Melrose*, 339; Mercer, 241; Metcalf, 244; Miller, 440; Minor, 252; Monette, 335; *Monmouth*, 338; Montgomery, 400; *Monteigne*, 337, 338; Moore, Austin, 440; Moore, "Hatter," 435; Moore, John Taylor, 325; Mosby, 388; Moss, 311; *Mount Holly*, 356; *Mount Repose*, 336; Murry, 458; Nason, 384; Neilson, 259; Newsome, 384; Nicholson, 480; Nugent-Shands, 220; *Oaks*, The, 437; *Oakland*, 338; Oldest house in Montgomery County, 402; *Ossian Hall*, 297; Outlaw, 400; Pace, 403; Parasott, 410; Parker, 427; *Peachland*, 336; Pearson, 461; Percy, 352; Peyton, 391; Pirate's, 300; *Plain Gables*, 279; Polk, 207; Power, 217; Presbyterian Manse, 335; *Propinquity*, 333; Ralston, 317; Ratliff, 392; *Ravenna*, 250; *Red Brick*, 176; *Red Frame*, 481; Reed, 156; Rice, 400; Richardson, 280; *Richland* (Richardson), 357; *Richland* (Cox), 332; *Richmond*, 253; Robinson, 317; Rogers, 423; Roland, 496; Rollin, 384; *Rosalie*, 244; *Rosedale*, 188; *Rosemont*, 484; Rowan, 395, 152; Rowell, 381; Rucker, 389; Sabine, 481; *Salisbury*, 358; *Selma*, 333; Shannon, 278; Shields, 332; Skinner, 482; Skipwith, 259; Smith, 480; Spanish (Biloxi), 177; Spanish (Natchez), 242; Spanish (Washington), 334; Spencer, 460; *Springfield*, 331, 332; *Stanton Hall*, 246; Staton, 421; *Stony Lonesome*, 461; Street, 483; Strickland, 204; *Summer Trees*, 440; *Swiftwater*, 353; Tabb, 463; Talbert, 483; Terry, 193; Thomason, 460; *Towers*, The, 248; Townes, 421; *Travellers Rest*, 455; Tullos, 497; Valliant, 352; Waite-Bowers, 208; Walker, 486; Wall, 358; *Wallace Park*, 381; Walters, 207; *Walnut Grove*, 358; Walthall, 384; Watson, 204; *Waverly*, 366, 367; Weaver, 362; White, 478; *Wigwam*, 247; *Wildwood*, 353; Williams, 327; Willis-Cowan, 280; Wilson, James, 412; Wilson, 468; *Windy Hill Manor*, 338; Winningham, 380; *Woodstock*, 342; Woodward, 187.

Hoffman, Malvina, 352
Hoggart, Col. James, 455
Homesteads, Tupelo, 364
Honey Island Swamp, 433
Hood, Thomas B., 362
Hospital Hill, 252
Hough Cave, 278
Houston, Sam, 70, 463
Howell, William Burr, 253
Hudson, A. P., 115, 138
Humphreys, Benjamin G., 73, 213, 325, 326
Humphreys, George Wilson, 325
Hunting (*see Recreation*)

Iberville (*see D'Iberville*)
Iberville Cannon, 177, 291
Indian Charlie's Trace, 88
Indian Point, 350
Indians, 47-59, 400, 465
  Customs (*see Folkways*)
  Legends (*see Folklore*)
  Mounds, 45, 48, 463, 464
  Treaties, 59, 70, 71, 369
  Tribes, 47, 49, 58, 59
Industrial Act, 79, 112
Industrial Plants
  Back Bay Boatbuilding Factories, 178; Buckeye Cotton Oil Company, 193; Carnation Milk Plant, 266; Chicago Mill and Lumber Company, 353; Columbia Box Factory, 478; Columbus Marble Plant, 187; Dorgan-

INDEX 539

Industrial Plants (*Continued*)
  McPhillips Vegetable Packing Plant, 478; Durant Silk Mill, 386; Federal Compress and Warehouse, 193; Filtrol Corporation, 392; Hamm Lumber Mill, 232; Knox Glass Company, 308; Luce Products Company, 471, 492; Masonite Plant, 225; Mayhew Canning Plant, 225; McComb Cotton Mill, 396; Meridian Garment Factory, 232; Meridian Grain and Elevator Company, 232; Milam Manufacturing Company, 266; Okolona Cheese Factory and Creamery, 374; Owens Greenhouse and Nursery, 189; Pine Felt Factory, 477; Pioneer Silk Mill, 418; Planters' Oil Mill Gin, 193; Poultry Packing Plant, 375; Reed's Manufacturing Company, 266; Rowlands Tung Oil Mill, 432; Soule Steam Feed Works, 231; Southern Naval Stores Plant, 477; Staple Cooperative Association Warehouse, 193; Stonewall Cotton Mill, 425; Supreme Instruments Corporation, 193; Southern United Ice Company, 396; Sweet Potato Starch Plant, 225; Swift and Company Oil Mill, 232; Tie Plant Creosoting Plant, 384; Tupelo Cotton Mill, 265; Tupelo Garment Company, 265; United States Gypsum, 353.
Industry, 106-111
  Bentonite, 307
  Boatbuilding, 169, 287
  Dairying, 7, 110, 112, 203, 362, 373, 374, 398, 400, 401, 427, 436, 442, 459
  Fishing, 168, 169, 198, 297, 349, 422
  Garment factories, 112
  Gravel, 442
  Lumber:
    Contemporary, 231, 435; development of, 6, 196, 223, 247, 302, 423; peak of, 196, 287, 295, 414, 430; decline of, 224, 302, 414, 423, 469, 470.
  Miscellaneous, 110, 111
  Natural Gas, 214, 308
  Naval Stores, 477, 478
  Seafood Packing, 168, 175
  Shipbuilding, 169
  Turpentine, 432, 470
Ingraham, James, 333
Ingraham, Joseph, 139
Inn-By-the-Sea, 298
Institutions
  East Mississippi Insane Hospital, 233; Ellisville State School, 123, 428; Mississippi Industrial and Training School, 123, 477; Mississippi Insane Hospital, 155, 308; Mississippi Institute for Blind, 123, 219; Mississippi School for Deaf, 123, 222; Protestant Orphanage, 248.

Islands
  Chandeleur, 304; Honey, 433; Palmyra, 325; Ship, 63, 170, 303.
Island Hill, 501
Isom, Sally, 258
Isom, Thomas, 255, 258
Iuka Battlefield, 501
Iuka, Chief, 442
Iuka Mineral Springs, 442

Jackson, Andrew, 69, 211, 216, 241, 301, 326, 332, 333, 334, 367, 369, 391, 479, 494, 502
Jackson City Hall, 214
Jackson Prairie Belt, 34
Jackson's Military Road, 86, 87, 299, 305, 368
Jackson, Rachel Donaldson Robards, 332
Jayne, Samuel, 395, 453
Jenkins, John C., 342
"Jim Crow" Law, 75
Johnston, Joseph, E., 213
Johnston, Oscar, 349, 350
Johnston, J. E., 224
Johnstone, George, 65
Johnstone, Helen, 390
Johnstone, John, 390
Jones Boarding House, 363
Jones, J. T., 196
Jones, Kate, 256
Jones, Reuben, 436
Jones, Thomas Catesby, 299
Joor, John, 358

Kearney, Belle, 413
Kemper Brothers, 67, 359
Ker, David, 342
Key Aviation Field, 425
Kilrain, Jake, 428
King, Benjamin, 395
King, Caleb, 342, 343
King, Joseph, 342
King, Paul, 450
Kingsbury, Cyrus, 375
King's Tavern, 249
Knight, Newt, 223, 428, 448, 450
Knox, Andrew, 356
Kosciusko Mound, 495
Kosciusko, Thaddeus, 494
Kossuth, Louis, 446
Koury, Leon, 135, 352
Ku Klux Klan (*see* History, Reconstruction)

La Bauve, Felix, 380
La Bauve Fellowship, 380
L'Adner, Jacques, 172
L'Adner, Christian, 296
Lakes
  Beulah, 349, 359; Bolivar, 350; Booneville, 363; Chautauqua, 393; Cormorant, 315; Dawson, 410; Deserter's End, 450; Eagle, 323; Farragut, 290; Ferguson, 352; Hazle, 394; Jackson, 354; Lee, 354; Moon, 317; Rosalba, 486; Pickwick, 500; Tchula, 422; Walden,

INDEX

Lakes (*Continued*)
  363; Washington, 354. (*See Fishing.*)
Lamar Life Building, 155
Lamar, L. Q. C., 74, 138, 257, 488
Langdon, Richard C., 130
La Salle, Robert Cavelier, Sieur de, 61
Lattimore, William, 211
Lauderdale Pottery, 370
Laurel Garden Club, 223
Lauren Rogers Library and Art Museum, 225, 226, 450
Law, John, 64, 65, 172, 299
Law Office of William Van Amburg Sullivan, 258
Lawyers' Row, 242
Leaf River Swamp, 471
Leake, Walter, 309
Lee, Stephen D., 72, 185
Le Fleur, Louis, 210, 404
Leflore, Greenwood, 190, 193, 369, 379, 403, 404
Legends (*see Folklore*)
Lemos, Manuel Gayoso de, 249
Levee Street, 281
Lewis, John, 345
Lewis, Henry Clay, 137
Libraries
  Attala County, 495; Carnegie, Clarksdale, 319; Carnegie, Houston, 463; Fiske Memorial, 243; Lauren Rogers, 227; Greenville Public, 352, 353; Historical Reference, 282.
Lighthouses
  Biloxi, 174, 178; Ship Island 304.
Lincecum, Gideon, 182, 183
Lind, Jenny, 159, 341, 482
Lindsay, Vachel, 296
Link, Theodore, 217
Lipton Cup Races, 168
Literature
  early expressions, 136-140; since 1865, 140, 141.
Little, Peter, 244, 247
Little Red School, 386
Longstreet, Augustus Baldwin, 137, 255, 488
Lotterhos, A., 393
Lowrey, M. P., 128
Lowry, Robert, 307
Lynch, Charles, 453
Lynch, John R., 218
Lyons, William, 388

Maffit, John Newland, 344
Magnolia Hotel, 178
Manatchee, Chief, 435
Markers
  Dancing Rabbit Treaty, 369; D'Artaguiette, 461; De Soto Camp, 366; De Soto's March, 266; Confederate, 281, 445; First Constitutional Convention, 334; Fort Rosalie (site), 244; Franklin Academy, 185; Indian Burial Grounds, 375; Indian Camp, 375; Iberville Landing, 178; Natchez Trace, 331, 401, 486, 495, 502; Union, 281, 361.

Marschalk, Andrew, 129, 245, 345
Marschalk's Printing Office, 245
Martin, John D., 255
Martin, William T., 240, 337, 338
Martineau, Harriet, 139
Mashulatubbee's Home, site of, 368
Mason, Samuel, 84, 331
Masonic Halls, (Handsboro), 295; (Meadville), 455
Mayhew Apiary, 375
Mayhew Mission, 375
Mays, James, 331
McCain, William D., 218
McCaleb, Jonathan, 356
McCasky, T. W., 137
McCarthy, Harry, 216
McClung, Alexander, 131, 138, 220
McComb, H. S., 396
McCrady, John, 135, 256
McGehee, Abner, 381
McGehee, Dan, 455
McGehee, Edward, 344, 345, 359
McGruder, Admiral, 412
McIntosh, Sheriff, 492
McLaurin, Anslem, 307
McLemore, Richard, 228, 231
McNutt, Alexander, 220, 277
McRae, John J., Jr. (Governor), 372
McRae, John J., Sr., 372
Mead, Cowles, 70, 332; home, site of, 334
Memorial Hall, 243
Merchants Bank Building (Jackson), 155
Meriwether, Charles, 380
Merrill, Ayres P., 341
Merrill, Jennie, 341
Middlegate Japanese Gardens, 297
Millsaps, Ruben W., 219
Minor, Don Estevan, 252, 338
Miro, Estevan, 252
Mississippi Bubble, 64, 65
Mississippi Centennial Exposition, 199
Mississippi Highway Department, 91
Mississippi Penal Farm, 407
Mississippi State Fairgrounds, 220
Mitchel, Kelly, 232
Mitchell, Emil (Gypsy King), 232
Monette, John W., 139, 335
Money, Hernando De Soto, 403
Money, William F., 403
Monroe Mission, 462
Montgomery, Isaiah T., 320
Montgomery Point, 349
Montigny, Father, 113, 170
Montross Hotel, 173
Monuments
  Alcorn, 317; Bodley, 278; Brice's Cross Roads, 363; Confederate, 216, 281, 482; Colonel Falkner, 458; Davis, Jefferson, 216; Gibson, 280; Hardy, 199; Percy, LeRoy, 352; Poindexter, George, 218; Rogers, Col. William, 363; Tilghman, 312; Union, 281.
Moore, "Hatter," 435
Moore, John Taylor, 325
Mound Bayou Founders' Day, 320

INDEX

Mounds, Indian
  Blanchard, 349; Deer Creek, 322; De Be Vois, 316; Foster's, 335; Leatherman, 316; Mattson, 407; Mound Place, 46; Nanih Waiya, 464; Pocahontas, 413; Prentiss, 410; Selsertown, 45, 332; Winterville, 351.
Municipal Clubhouse and Yacht Club, 199
Murdock, John, 330
Murrell, James, 84, 331
Museums
  Brown Collection, 46; Clark Indian Collection, 46, 319; Delta State Teachers College, Natural History, 320; Department of Archives and History, 218; Starling Collection (Greenville), 352; Hall of Fame, 218; Historical Museum (Vicksburg), 282; Irwin Russell Memorial, 327; Lauren Rogers, Art, 225, 450; Millsaps College, 47; Municipal Art (Jackson), 219.
Music, 157-161 (*see also Folkways, music*)
Nanih Waiya, 464
Natchez District, 5, 66, 94, 145, 324, 325
Natchez Garden Club, 245
Natchez Trace, 84, 85 (*see also Markers*)
Natchez-under-the-Hill, 244
Natural gas, Rankin County field, 308
Neibuhr, Reinhold, 348
Negro
  Contemporary, 166, 167, 182, 190, 195, 196, 200, 201, 209, 221, 224, 230, 237, 255, 262, 268, 269, 320, 359, 421. (*See Art, Education, Folklore, Religion, Folkways, History, Customs, Reconstruction*)
Neilson, William, 366
Neshoba County Fairgrounds, 468
Newspapers
  History of, 128-133, 212; early, 212, 239, 271
Nolan, Philip, 360
Northeast Mississippi Singing Convention, 435

Oak Hill Farm, 453
Oakland College (site), 330
Oak Tree Inn (site), 391
Office of Woodville *Republican*, 345
Ogden, Amos, 342
Old Opera House (Oxford), 258
Old Opera House (Liberty), 482
Olmstead, Frederick L., 139
Osmun, Benijah, 338
Otey, Bishop, 356
Pakenham, Sir Edward, 303
Parish House of San Salvador, 241
Parks
  State: Clarkco, 371; Holmes County, 386; Legion, 464; LeRoy Percy, 321; Percy Quin, 396, 481; Roosevelt, 307; Tishomingo, 502; Tombigbee, 435.
  Other: Battlefield, 221; Confederate, 363; Duncan, 252; Edgewater, 294; Highland, 233; Iuka Mineral Springs, 442; City, Laurel, 227; Livingston, 222; Municipal, Okolona, 374; Naval Reserve, 178; Vicksburg National Military, 281.
Passes, Pass Christian, 296; Menteur, 434
Patrons Union Camp Ground, 306
Patton, James, 211
Paulding Jail, 426
Payne, A. M., 384
Pecans (*see Agriculture*)
Pemberton, John Clifford, 272, 312
Perier, Gov., 65
Percy, LeRoy, 321, 352
Percy, William Alexander, 352
Percy, William Alexander, II, 142, 352
Petrified Forest, 413
Peyton, John R., 309, 311
Piazza, N., 393
Pickwick Dam, 500
Picnics (*see Folkways*)
Piernas, Don Pedro, 250
Piney Woods, 6, 34, 223, 414, 415, 423, 469, 470
Piney Woods Singers, 414
Pinson, Joel, 461, 463
Pirate Pitcher, 296
Pitcher's Point, 296
Pitchlyn, John, 336, 367, 369
Pitchlyn, Peter Perkins, 367
Pitts, S. L., 448
Pitts Cave, 448
Plantations
  Archerleader, 422; Blanchard, 349; Bowling Green, 345; Calverton, 332; Cedar Grove, 412; Churchill Downs, 413; Coldspring, 359; Columbian Springs, 359; Delta Cooperative Farm, 348; Delta Planters' Company, 349; Delta and Pine Land Company, 103, 350; Dunleith, 406; Faisonia, 409; Gayoso Farms, 380; Glenwild, 384; Greengrove, 348; Gritman-Barksdale, 408; Harvey, 389; Hopedale, 357; Moss, 450; Lakeside, 357; Lone Pine, 353; Nita Yuma, 322; Panther Burn, 321; Rainey Estate, 459; Ringolsky, 420; Rosemont, 484; Selma, 333; Sherard, 347; Swan Farm, 422.
Plummer, Franklin, 383, 453
Poindexter, George, 70; 218, 248, 345, 346
Poindexter, Weenonah, 160
Poitevent, Eliza Jane ("Pearl Rivers"), 432
Poitevent, John, 432
Political Rally (*see Folkways*)
Polk, Leonidas, 207, 232, 279, 362
Polk, Thomas, 207
Pollock, Oliver, 359
Pontotoc Ridge, 34, 436, 484
Pope, John, 139
Postlewaite, Ann Dunbar, 248
Powe, William, 372
Prentiss, Seargent S., 138, 340, 391, 410, 453
Price, Madeleine, 338

542 INDEX

Purnell Springs, 308
Purvis, Will, 429
Pushmataha, 69, 138, 305

Quarantine Station (Ship Island), 196, 304
Quin, Percy E., 481
Quitman, John, A., 338

Radio Stations
  WAML (Laurel), 222; WCOC (Meridian), 227; WGAM (Grenada), 383; WGCM (Gulfport), 194; WJDX (Jackson), 208; WTJS (Jackson), 208.
Ragsdale, L. A., 228
Rainey, Paul, 459
Ralston, Blanche, 317, 319
Rameau, Pierre, 432
Randolph, George, 382
Randolph, William, 201
Rankin, John R., 363
Reber, Thomas, 240
Recreation
  Boating: 168, 197, 198, 199, 304, 317, 441
  Fishing:
    Freshwater, XXII, 317, 321, 323, 349, 405, 410, 421, 422, 435, 486.
    Salt water, 198, 287
  Golf: 292, 294, 298, 309, 378, 395, 449
  Hunting: XXII, 290, 298, 354, 369, 409, 418, 433, 438, 439
  Resorts:
    Allison's Wells, 388; Brown's Wells, 395; Castalian Springs, 386; Cooper's Wells, 391; Eagle Lake, 323; Fairley's Camp, 290; Greenwood Springs, 484, 485; Gulf Hills, 292; Lakeview, 315; Maywood Recreational Center, 441; Nelson's Camp, 290; Stafford Springs, 426, 427.
  Swimming: 168, 177, 198, 199, 303, 317, 374, 435, 441
Reed, Thomas, 339
Reforestation Lookout Tower, 497
Religion, 112-118
  Early Catholic missions, 112, 113; First Protestant church, 114; beginnings of Protestantism, 113, 114; spread of Protestantism, 114-116; second Mississippi Methodist conference, 479; Diocese of Natchez, 115; first Negro churches, 116; present day aspects, 117; first Jewish synagogue, 117; church schools (see Education).
Resorts (see Recreation)
Resources, 39, 40
Revival Meetings (see Folkways)
Rich, Charlie, 429
Richard, Father, 113
Richardson, Edmund, 357
Ring in Oak, 176
Rivers
  Amite, 482; Big Black, 35, 84; Big Flower, 35; Bogue Chitto, 35; Chickasawhay, 35, 425, 471, 491; Coldwater, 35, 489; Escatawpa, 35; Homochitto, 35, 343; Leaf, 35, 471; Little Flower, 35; Luxapalia, 182; Mississippi, 35, 79, 82, 247, 275, 276; Noxubee, 368; Pascagoula, 35, 287,*471; Pearl, 35, 79, 211, 302, 452; Singing, 287; Skuna, 35; Strong, 35; Tallahatchie, 34, 381, 489; Tennessee, 35; Tombigbee, 35, 80, 84, 182, 366; Yazoo, 35, 64, 190, 275, 411; Yalobusha, 35; Yocona, 35; Yokahockana, 35.
Rivers, Pearl (see Poitevent, Eliza Jane)
Roach, Spirus, 182
Rogers, William P., 362
Rosalba Mill, 486
Rosecrans, William S., 362, 443, 501
Rosenwald, Julius, 124
Rosenwald Fund, 124
Rowland, Dunbar, 218
Rowlands, Lamont, 432
Runnels, Harmon, 453
Runnels, Hiram, 383, 453
Rushton, B. J., 448
Rushton Pottery Kiln (site), 448
Ruskin Oak, 291
Russell, D. M., 317
Russell, Irwin, 140, 141, 325, 326, 327
Rust, John, 348
Rylee, Robert, 142

Sacred Harp Singings (see Folkways)
Sage, Jerome, 161
Saint Augustine Seminary, 300
St. Cosme, Father, 113
Sales Tax, 77
Sanctuary, 141
San Germaine, Juan, 253
Sardis Dam and Reservoir, 382
Sargent, Winthrop, 128, 340
Saucier, Phillip, 420
Sauvolle, M. de la Villantry, 170
Schools
  Creole:
    Live Oak Pond, 290
  Indian:
    Bogue Homa, 427; Conehatta Day, 306; Pearl River, 496; Tucker, 467, 468.
  Negro:
    Doddsville Experimental, 408; Gulfside, 300; Oak Park Vocational, 224; Piney Woods High, 125, 414; Sacred Heart Academy, 352.
  White:
    Castle Heights Academy, 459; Crystal Springs Consolidated, 394; Gulf Coast Military Academy, 295; Jefferson College, 118, 333, 334; Little Red School, 386; Saint Rose of Lima Academy, 352; Saint Joseph's Academy, 249; St. Mary of the Pines, 397; St. Stanislaus, 300; Tippah Union, 459.
Scott, Abram, 346

INDEX

Scott, Bud, 161
Scott, Charles, 349
Scottish Rite Cathedral, 231
Seashore Camp Grounds, 179
Secession Convention, 71, 216
Shannon, Marmaduke, 278
Sharkey, William L., 73, 138
Shearwater Pottery, 292
Sherman, William Tecumseh, 72, 213, 230, 307, 388, 496
Shegog, Robert, 256
Shipbuilding (see *Industry*)
Ship Island Lighthouse, 304
Shreve, Henry, 81
Shrine of Our Lady of the Woods, 300
Shultz, Christian, 139
Siege of Vicksburg (see *History*)
Slave Barrack (site), 337
Slave Block (site), 337
Small Craft Harbor, 199
Smith, A. J., 256, 323
Smith, Joe, 263
Smith, John, 385
Smith-Hughes Act, 122
Solitude (ruins), 489
So Red The Rose, 141, 248, 259
Southern Planter (see *Architecture*)
Spanish Fort, 288, 289
Sports (see *Recreation*)
Springs (see *Recreation*)
Stanton, Elizabeth Brandon (writer), 338
Stanton, Frederick, 246, 342
Stapps, Emily, 419
Stapps, Marie, 419
Star of West wreck, 422
State Tuberculosis Hospital, 416
State Penal Farm, 407, 408
Steel, John, 247
Stevans, Daisy McLaurin, 497
Stewart, Thomas C., 462
Still, William Grant, 160
Stone, Alfred H., 77
Stone, John M., 74, 444
Stovall, Ralph, 480
Street, James, 142, 497, 499
Stuart, Gilbert, 218
Sturgis, James, 393
Sullivan, John L., 295, 428
Sullivan, William Van Amburg, 258, 259
Sullivan Brothers, 498
Sullivan-Ryan fight, 295; Sullivan-Kilrain fight, 428
Sullivan's Hollow, 498
Sully, Thomas, 340
Surget, Frank, 341
Swanton, John, 49
Swayze, Richard, 343
Swayze, Samuel, 66, 342
Sylvester Treasure, 475

Tallaha Springs, 421
Tecumseh, 305, 368, 494
Tennessee Hills, 6, 361, 397, 398, 442, 500
Tennessee Valley Authority, 77, 264, 500
Tenant System, 99, 101, 103, 104, 105
Terry, Mrs. Cora, 193
Thaylor, Mrs. Caroline V., 335

Theobald, Harriet B., 352
Thompson, C. C., 262
Thompson, Jacob, 256; home, site of, 256
Three Chopped Way, 85
Threefoot Building, 155, 228
Thurmond, R. J., 458
Tichenor, G. H., 482
Tilghman, Lloyd, 312
Tishomingo, Chief, 442
Tocowa Springs, 382
Tolstoy, Leo, II, 199
Toby Tubby, 488
Torlonia, Prince Alex, 249
Tower Building, 155
Towns
Extinct:
Augusta, Old, 476; Belmont, 382; Biloxi, Old, 291; Blythe's Crossing, 442; Brookhaven, Old 395; Bruinsburg Landing, 329; China Grove, 480; Commerce, 316; Cotton Gin Port, 485; Danville, 363; East Port, 442; Gallatin, 394; Greenville, Old, 331; Grand Gulf, 326; Gum Springs, 496; Hamilton, Old, 366; Hopoca, 495; Houlka, Old, 462; Leota Landing, 354; Lizelia, 378; Middleton, Old 402; Mineral Wells, 441; Mount Carmel, 451; Panola, 382; Point Leflore, 190; Prentiss, 350; Plymouth, 367; Princeton, 354; Richland, 386; Richmond, 435; Rodney, 330; Shongalo, 386; Warrenton, 325; Williamsburg, 451; Winchester, Old, 372.
Present Day:
Abbeville, 488; Aberdeen, 364-366; Ackerman, 463; Agricola, 493; Alligator, 319; Amory, 485; Anguilla, 322; Arcola, 320; Artesia, 375; Baldwyn, 363; Basic, 425; Batesville, 382; Bay Springs, 469, 470; Bay St. Louis, 64, 298, 299, 300; Beaumont, 476; Beauregard, 395; Belden, 436; Bellefontaine, 474; Belmont, 503; Belzoni, 410; Benoit, 350; Berclair, 405; Beulah, 349; Big Creek, 474; Biloxi, 62, 63, 165-179; Bissell, 486; Blue Mountain, 458; Blue Springs, 437; Bobo, 319; Bolton, 312; Booneville, 363; Brandon, 307; Brookhaven, 453, 454; Brooklyn, 418; Brookville, 375; Bruce, 473; Bucatunna, 372, 373; Bude, 455; Burnside, 464; Byhalia, 460; Calhoun City, 473, 474; Canaan, 446; Canton, 388, 389; Carthage, 495, 496; Centreville, 483; Chalybeate, 446; Chunky, 305; Clarksdale, 318, 319; Clay, 434; Cleveland, 320; Clinton, 309-311; Coahoma, 317; Cohay, 497; Collins, 417; Columbia, 80, 477; Columbus, 179-189; Como, 381; Conehatta, 306; Corinth, 361-363; Cottondale, 408; Cotton Plant, 459; Courtland, 382;

544 INDEX

Towns, Present Day (*Continued*)
Crystal Springs, 393; Daleville, 378; Decatur, 469; Deeson, 349; De Kalb, 378; Dennis, 502; D'Lo, 416; Doddsville, 409; Dorsey, 435; Drew, 408; Duck Hill, 385; Duncan, 319; Dundee, 316; Durant, 386; East Tupelo, 436; Ecru, 459; Eddiceton, 455; Edwards, 312; Eggville, 435; Egypt, 374; Electric Mills, 370; Elkland, 354; Elliott, 385; Ellisville, 427, 428; Enterprise, 425; Estabutchie, 428; Estill, 321; Eupora, 401; Falkner, 456; Fayette, 331; Flora, 413; Fontainebleau, 290; Forest, 306; Fort Adams, 359, 360; Foxworth, 479; Friar Point, 317; Fruitland Park, 419; Fulton, 434; Gautier, 290; Glen Allan, 356; Gloster, 483; Goodman, 386; Greenville, 351-353; Greenwood, 189-193; Greenwood Springs, 484; Grenada, 383; Gulfport, 194-199; Gunnison, 349; Guntown, 363; Handsboro, 295; Harleston, 493; Harriston, 331; Harperville, 496; Hattiesburg, 417; Hazlehurst, 394; Hebron, 450; Hernando, 380; Hickory, 305; Hickory Flat, 438; Hillhouse, 348; Hillsboro, 496; Hollandale, 321; Holly Springs, 200-208; Holmesville, 480; Hot Coffee, 499, 500; Houston, 463; Hushpuckena, 319; Indianola, 409; Ingomar, 459; Inverness, 409; Isola, 410; Itta Bena, 405; Iuka, 442-445; Jackson, 208-222; Jonestown, 317; Kewanee, 305; Kilmichael, 401; Kiln, 298; Kingston, 343; Kipling, 378; Kokomo, 480; Kosciusko, 494, 495; Kossuth, 445; Kreole, 286; Lake, 306; Lake Cormorant, 315; Lakeview, 315; Langsdale, 371; Lauderdale, 370; Laurel, 222-227; Leakesville, 492; Leland, 320-321; Lexington, 422; Liberty, 481; Lobdell, 350; Logtown, 302; Long Beach, 296; Lorman, 331; Louin, 469; Louisville, 464; Lucedale, 492; Lula, 317; Lumberton, 430; Lyman, 420; Maben, 463; Macon, 368; Madison, 389; Magee, 416; Magnolia, 396; Mantachie, 435; Marion, 370; Marks, 490; Mashulaville, 368, 369; Matherville, 371; Mathiston, 401; Mattson, 407; Mayersville, 357; Mayhew, 375; McComb, 396; McHenry, 419; McLain, 475; Meadville, 455; Mendenhall, 416; Meridian, 227-232; Merigold, 320; Midnight, 411; Minter City, 421; Mississippi City, 295; Mize, 498; Monticello, 452; Montrose, 469; Mooreville, 435; Moorhead, 405; Morton, 307; Moss Point, 286; Mound Bayou, 320; Mt. Olive, 417; Mt. Pleasant, 447; Myrtle, 438; Natchez, 233-253; Nettleton, 364; New Albany, 437; New Augusta, 476; Newton, 306; Nitta Yuma, 322; Norfield, 396; North Carrollton, 403; Noxapater, 464; Ocean Springs, 291; Okolona, 374; Old Carrollton, 403; Olive Branch, 441; Osyka, 397; Oxford, 254-261; Pachuta, 426; Parchman, 407; Pascagoula, 286-289; Pass Christian, 296-298; Paulding, 426; Pearlington, 302; Pelahatchie, 307; Percy, 321; Perkinston, 419; Perthshire, 349; Philadelphia, 464-467; Piave, 492; Picayune, 432; Pickens, 388; Pinckneyville, 359; Pittsboro, 473; Plantersville, 486; Pocahontas, 413; Pontotoc, 460; Poplarville, 430; Port Gibson, 327, 328; Potts Camp, 438; Prentiss, 451, 452; Purvis, 429; Quentin, 455; Quitman, 371; Raleigh, 497; Randolph, 472; Raymond, 391; Red Banks, 440; Renalara, 348; Richton, 470; Ripley, 456; Robinsonville, 316; Rolling Fork, 322; Rome, 407; Rosedale, 349; Ruleville, 408; Sandersville, 427; Sanatorium, 416; Santa Rosa, 433; Sardis, 381, 382; Sarepta, 472; Satartia, 412; Saucier, 420; Scooba, 370; Scott, 350; Senatobia, 380; Shannon, 364; Shaw, 320; Shelby, 319; Shellmound, 422; Sherman, 436; Shubuta, 371; Shuqualak, 369; Silver City, 410, 411; Silver Creek, 452; Slate Springs, 474; Slayden, 446; Smithville, 504, 505; Soso, 450; Springville, 472; Stafford Springs, 426; Star, 414; Starkville, 398; Stoneville, 321; Stonewall, 425; Summit, 396; Sumner, 421; Sunflower, 409; Swan Lake, 421; Taylorsville, 497; Tchula, 422; Terry, 392; Tie Plant, 384; Tilden, 503; Tipple, 442; Tishomingo, 502; Toccopola, 487; Toomsuba, 305; Tucker, 467; Tunica, 316; Tupelo, 261-266; Tutwiler, 407; Tylertown, 480; Union, 469; Utica, 392; Vaiden, 385; Vancleave, 290; Verona, 364; Vicksburg, 267-282; Wallerville, 437; Walls, 315; Walnut, 446; Walnut Grover, 496; Walthall, 474; Washington, 333; Water Valley, 488; Waynesboro, 371; Waveland, 300; Webb, 421; Wesson, 395; West, 386; West Point, 374; Whitney, 408; Whynot, 305; Wiggins, 419; Williamsville, 495; Winborn, 438; Winchester, 372; Winona, 402; Winterville, 351; Woodville, 344; Wyandotte, 320; Yazoo City, 412; Yokena, 325.

Transportation, 79-92
Air, 92; bus, 92; early trails, 84-88; highway, 91; railroads (development of), 88-91, 196, 212, 213,

INDEX

Transportation (*Continued*)
228-230; water, 79-92, 238, 239, 240, 269-271, 276, 277, 281. (*See also Natchez Trace*)
Treaties (*see Indians*)
Trucking Belt, 6, 391
Trucking (*see Agriculture*)
Tucker, Gov., 220
Tupelo Fish Hatchery, 265
Tupelo Homesteads, 364
Tupelo Tornado, 264
Turpentine (*see Industry*)
Twain, Mark, 327
Tyler, William G., 480

United States Agricultural Experiment Station, 432
United States Coast Guard Air Base, 175
United States Dry Docks and Repair Yards, 289
United States Branch Horticultural Experiment Station, 370
United States Soil Conservation Project Branch Station, 203, 378, 381
United States Veterans Facility, 178
United States Veterans Facility No. 74, 199
United States Waterways Experiment Station, 277, 313
Utica Singers, 392

Van Dorn, Earl, 201, 207, 328, 362
Van Dorn, Peter, 211
Vardaman, James K., 75, 138, 402
Ventress, James A., 358
Vick, Henry Crew, 390
Vick, Newitt, 269
Vicksburg National Military Park (*see Parks*)
Vidal, Don Jose, 248

Wagner, Kinnie, 492
Wailes, B. L. C., 334
Wall, Evans, 358
Walker, Robert J., 71, 131, 138
Walthall, Edward Cary, 74, 204, 384
Ward, Junius, 355
War between the States, 71-73. (*See also Battles and Agriculture*)
Warfield Landing, 406
Watermelon Festival (Water Valley), 488
Water Mill, 470
Watson, Anna Robinson, 205
Watson, J. W. C., 205
Weeks, Levi, 243
Wesley House, 176
Wesson, J. M., 395
West, Benjamin, 218
White, Judge Godentia, 208
White, Hugh L., 79, 477, 478
White, T. W., 380
White Harbor, 296
White Horse Tavern (site), 340
Whitaker Negroes, 359
Whitfield, James, 186
Wilkinson, James, 67, 84, 139, 332, 360
Williams, John, 190
Williams, John Sharp, 138, 204, 412
Williams, Robert, 248
Willing, James, 66
Wilson, Alexander, 139
Wilson, James, 468
Wilson, Woodrow, 199, 297
William's Store, 468
Winans, William, 483
Windsor Ruins, 329
Woodward, Ellen Sullivan, 259

Yazoo Canal, 324
Yellin, Samuel, 225
Yellow Fever Epidemic, 203, 230, 383
Young, George, 366
Young, Stark, 3, 141, 248, 259, 381

Zoo (Jackson), 222